The
AMERICAN
HERITAGE®

THESAURUS
for Learners of English

Joyce LeBaron *&* Susannah LeBaron

With the Editors of the
American Heritage® Dictionaries

HOUGHTON MIFFLIN COMPANY
Boston & New York

To our good friend Paul A. Hellweg, for his
constant support and encouragement.

Visit our website: www.houghtonmifflinbooks.com

Library of Congress Cataloging-in-Publication Data

LeBaron, Joyce.
   The American heritage thesaurus for learners of English / Joyce LeBaron & Susannah LeBaron ; with the editors of the American heritage dictionaries.
      p. cm.
   ISBN 0-618-12990-1
      1. English language--Synonyms and antonyms. 2. English language--Texbooks for foreign speakers. I. Title: Thesaurus for learners of English. II. LeBaron, Susannah. III. Title.

PE1591 .L36 2002
428.1--dc21

2002075937

Book design by Catherine Hawkes, Cat & Mouse

Manufactured in the United States of America

TABLE OF CONTENTS

ACKNOWLEDGMENTS

Margery S. Berube, *Vice President and Publisher of Dictionaries,* initiated the project and oversaw its development. She is committed to improving the resources available to ESL students, and her enthusiasm for this project was a great inspiration.

David R. Pritchard, *Editorial Project Director,* helped to get the project started, edited the entire manuscript, and put the book into its final form. His friendly manner and professional expertise make him a pleasure to work with.

Jacquelyn Pope, *Editor,* helped develop the book's format and served as contact person while the book was being written.

Wade A. Ostrowski, *Associate Editor,* and **Uchenna C. Ikonné,** *Assistant Editor,* helped format the electronic manuscript and proof the composed pages.

Kevin McCarthy, *Administrative Assistant,* provided administrative and secretarial support. His courteous and professional handling of bureaucratic details helped keep us rolling.

Joyce LeBaron would like to thank: Dan and Florence Angelelo, Shoneen Bergholdt, Bud and Fern Davis, Faith Fastabend, Carl and Frances Hoffman, Swithin and Berene Lindbeck, Veida and Ray McClain, June Mohler, Dr. Donna Stevens, D.R. Rockhold, and Carol Webb.

Susannah LeBaron would like to thank: Michael Brewer, Anne Fleming, Kimberly Idol, George and Catherine Lindbeck, Swithin and Berene Lindbeck, Michael Steinman, and especially Brendan Steinman.

In addition, we both would like to extend a special thanks to: Dr. Sharon Klein, who gave freely of her time and expertise during the conceptual stage of this project.

Tina Carlisle, Kate Donahue, and all the folks at the Coffee Cantina who kept the caffeine coming during our final edit of the manuscript.

INTRODUCTION

Welcome to *The American Heritage Thesaurus for Learners of English*. This book has been designed with the ESL student in mind. Learning a new language is exciting, but it can also be hard work. If you are a high school, college, or adult learner of English as a second language (or third or fourth language), this book can help you as you grow in your ability to speak and write in English.

What Is a Thesaurus?

A thesaurus is a book of synonyms. Synonyms are words that are very close in meaning. For example, *agreeable, enjoyable, nice, pleasing,* and *pleasurable* are synonyms for the word *pleasant.* Words that do not have synonyms, such as *stapler, nephew,* or *light bulb,* are not listed in a thesaurus.

A thesaurus helps to increase your vocabulary and make your writing more interesting. For instance, if you are describing a person and you keep using the word *beautiful,* you can look in your thesaurus under *beautiful* and find a list of synonyms that include the words *attractive, cute, good-looking, gorgeous, handsome, lovely,* and *pretty.* By using a different word, you make your writing more interesting to read, and you learn more ways to express yourself.

What Is a Thesaurus for Learners of English?

A Thesaurus for Learners of English is different from other thesauruses because it focuses more on helping you build your vocabulary. *The American Heritage Thesaurus for Learners of English* does this by providing each synonym with a brief definition and a sample sentence. The definitions help you see the differences and similarities between the various synonyms. The sample sentences give you an idea of how the word looks and sounds in an everyday sentence.

Always remember that even though synonyms can be very close in meaning, they may not fit into a sentence in the same way. This book's definitions and sample sentences will help you find the word that is best for your needs, and at the same time build and refine your English vocabulary.

A Final Word

The writers, editors, and publishers of *The American Heritage Thesaurus for Learners of English* want this to be a source of help and encouragement to you at this stage of your learning. We would enjoy hearing from students, teachers, and parents. If you have questions or comments, please contact us: Dictionary Department, Houghton Mifflin Company, 222 Berkeley Street, Boston, MA 02116.

HOW TO USE THIS THESAURUS

The Explanatory Diagram on pages *viii–ix* points out the different features of *The American Heritage Thesaurus for Learners of English*. Please refer to this Diagram when reading the following descriptions of these features.

Main Entry

The main entry contains all of the information you need to learn about a particular word and its synonyms. It begins with the **main entry word,** which is printed by itself on a line at the top of the entry. The **part of speech** of the main entry word is printed in italics on the next line, telling you whether the word is a *noun, verb, adjective, adverb, preposition,* or *conjunction.* All of the synonyms of the main entry word have the same part of speech as it does.

Following the part of speech is a brief **definition** that tells you what the word means, and an **example sentence** that shows you how the word is typically used in this meaning.

The rest of the entry is an alphabetical list of the most important **synonyms** of the main entry word. Each synonym is marked with the symbol ▸, and each has its own brief definition and example sentence. By studying each synonym's definition and seeing how it is used in the examples, you can see the differences and similarities that it has with the main entry word. Sometimes the synonyms are very close to each other in meaning, while in other cases there are important distinctions that can be made.

In some cases, a main entry word or one of its synonyms may have two different meanings that are closely related to each other. For example, a *mask* can be an actual covering that disguises a person's face, and it can also be something like an expression that hides a person's true feelings. In such cases, this Thesaurus includes both meanings at the same word separated by the symbol ▷. (See the synonym **mask** at the main entry **disguise** in the Diagram on page *ix.*)

Antonym

At the end of certain main entries you will find an **antonym** of the main entry word along with a brief definition. Antonyms are words that have an opposite meaning to another word. As with the synonyms, the antonym always has the same part of speech as the main entry word.

Cross-Reference Entry

Instead of using an index to find where a particular synonym is explained, you can simply look the synonym up at its alphabetical place in the main body of the Thesaurus. At these entries you will find the appropriate part of speech, a brief definition, and a **cross-reference** to the main entry at which the synonym is listed. For example, if you look up the word *disciple* in the Thesaurus, you can see that it is given as one of the synonyms at the main entry for the noun **follower**. (See the Diagram on page *viii.*)

Entries That Are Spelled the Same

There are three kinds of entries in this Thesaurus that are spelled the same way. The first kind, called homographs, are words that have completely different, unrelated meanings even though they have the same spelling. For example, there are two English words that are spelled *hide*—one means "the skin of an animal" and the other means "to keep or put something out of sight." Homographs included in this Thesaurus are marked with small numbers printed after the entry word. (See **hide**[1] and **hide**[2] on page 136.) Cross-references to these entries include the homograph numbers so that you can easily see which main entry is the correct one.

The second kind are words that have different meanings even though they are the same English word having the same part of speech. For example, the adjective *bad* can mean "being below an acceptable standard," and it can also mean "misbehaved; causing trouble." In these cases, the two meanings are placed in separate entries and are marked with numbers printed in square brackets after the part of speech. (See **bad** *adjective* [1] and **bad** *adjective* [2] on page 22.) Cross-references to these entries include the numbers in brackets so that you can be sure to find the correct one.

Finally, there are entries that are the same English word but that have meanings with different parts of speech. For example, the word *clean* can be a verb meaning "to rid something of dirt, trash, or disorder," and it can also be an adjective meaning "free from dirt, stains, or impurities." Because entries like this have different parts of speech, there is no need to mark them with numbers. (See **clean** *verb* and **clean** *adjective* on page 50.)

Guideword

Guidewords tell you which main entries are the first one on a left-hand page and the last one on a right-hand page. This way you can tell at a glance whether a particular word will be found on those two pages or not. In the Diagram, the guidewords tell you that the entries for **disaster** and **dishonest**, along with all the other entries that are between them in alphabetical order, can be found on these two pages.

EXPLANATORY DIAGRAM

guideword

disaster

main entry

disaster

noun something that causes widespread destruction: *The eruption of the Krakatoa volcano in 1883 was a **disaster** that killed an estimated 36,000 people.*

▸ **calamity** an event that causes great distress and suffering: *The drought was a **calamity** for the farmers and ranchers.*

▸ **catastrophe** a great and sudden disaster from which recovery is difficult or impossible: *It would be an enormous **catastrophe** if the earth were hit by a large meteor.*

▸ **crisis** a situation of great difficulty or danger: *There was a financial **crisis** when the school budget was not approved by the voters.*

▸ **emergency** a serious situation or occurrence that happens suddenly and calls for immediate action: *Where can I reach you in case of an **emergency**?*

▸ **tragedy** a disastrous event involving great loss or suffering: *The sinking of the Titanic was one of the worst **tragedies** of the 20th century.*

cross-references

disburse *verb* to pay money to someone, as from a fund; to expend: *see* **spend**

discard *verb* to throw something away: *see* **abandon**

discharge *verb* to release someone, as from duty or work: *see* **dismiss**

disciple *noun* a person who believes in and often helps to spread the teachings of another: *see* **follower**

discipline *verb* to punish someone in order to correct or train: *see* **punish**

discipline *noun* controlled behavior resulting from training of the mind, body, or character: *see* **will**

discomfort *noun* mental or bodily distress: *see* **embarrassment**

discount

noun an offer to sell something at a reduced price: *I got this washing machine at a **discount** because it was the floor model.*

▸ **deduction** an amount that is subtracted from the selling price: *The salesman offered me an extra **deduction** if I bought the car before the end of the month.*

▸ **markdown** the amount by which a price is reduced: *The **markdown** on last year's model has been increased to 15 percent.*

▸ **rebate** a return of part of the amount paid for an item: *Mail this form to the manufacturer and you will get a **rebate** on your new printer.*

▸ **reduction** the amount by which the price of an item is reduced: *Many people go shopping after Christmas to take advantage of the **reductions** on merchandise.*

discourage

verb to make one less hopeful or confident: *The difficulty of the job did not **discourage** me.*

▸ **disappoint** to fail to satisfy the hope, desire, or expectation of someone: *The movie **disappointed** me, but my friends enjoyed it.*

▸ **dishearten** to cause one to lose courage and hope: *The artist was **disheartened** by the lack of interest in his work.*

▸ **dismay** to fill one with dread, anxiety, or apprehension: *We were **dismayed** when our car broke down on the freeway.*

▸ **dispirit** to lower one's spirit or enthusiasm: *The team was **dispirited** after losing three games in a row.*

ANTONYM **encourage** to give courage, hope, or confidence to someone

discourteous *adjective* not polite: *see* **rude**

discover

verb to be the first to find or learn of something: *Many explorers hoped to **discover** Eldorado, the fabled City of Gold.*

▸ **detect** to become aware of the existence, presence, or fact of something: *An odor is added to natural gas to help people to **detect** leaks.*

80

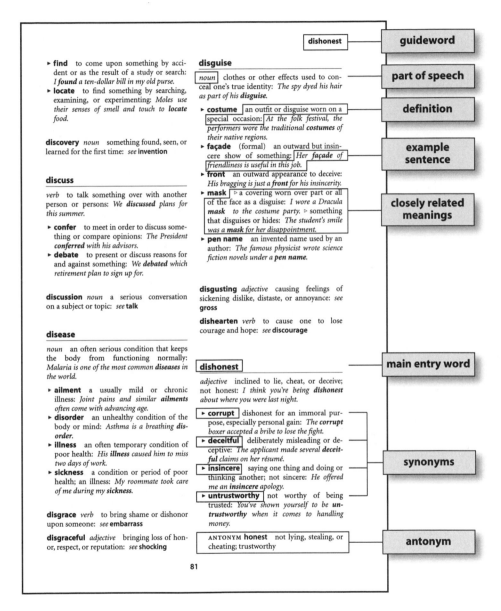

guideword — dishonest

> **find** to come upon something by accident or as the result of a study or search: *I found a ten-dollar bill in my old purse.*
> **locate** to find something by searching, examining, or experimenting: *Moles use their senses of smell and touch to locate food.*

discovery *noun* something found, seen, or learned for the first time: *see* **invention**

discuss

verb to talk something over with another person or persons: *We discussed plans for this summer.*

> **confer** to meet in order to discuss something or compare opinions: *The President conferred with his advisors.*
> **debate** to present or discuss reasons for and against something: *We debated which retirement plan to sign up for.*

discussion *noun* a serious conversation on a subject or topic: *see* **talk**

disease

noun an often serious condition that keeps the body from functioning normally: *Malaria is one of the most common diseases in the world.*

> **ailment** a usually mild or chronic illness: *Joint pains and similar ailments often come with advancing age.*
> **disorder** an unhealthy condition of the body or mind: *Asthma is a breathing disorder.*
> **illness** an often temporary condition of poor health: *His illness caused him to miss two days of work.*
> **sickness** a condition or period of poor health; an illness: *My roommate took care of me during my sickness.*

disgrace *verb* to bring shame or dishonor upon someone: *see* **embarrass**

disgraceful *adjective* bringing loss of honor, respect, or reputation: *see* **shocking**

disguise

noun clothes or other effects used to conceal one's true identity: *The spy dyed his hair as part of his disguise.* — **part of speech**

> **costume** an outfit or disguise worn on a special occasion: *At the folk festival, the performers wore the traditional costumes of their native regions.* — **definition**
> **façade** (formal) an outward but insincere show of something: *Her façade of friendliness is useful in this job.* — **example sentence**
> **front** an outward appearance to deceive: *His bragging is just a front for his insincerity.*
> **mask** ▷ a covering worn over part or all of the face as a disguise: *I wore a Dracula mask to the costume party.* ▷ something that disguises or hides: *The student's smile was a mask for her disappointment.* — **closely related meanings**
> **pen name** an invented name used by an author: *The famous physicist wrote science fiction novels under a pen name.*

disgusting *adjective* causing feelings of sickening dislike, distaste, or annoyance: *see* **gross**

dishearten *verb* to cause one to lose courage and hope: *see* **discourage**

dishonest — **main entry word**

adjective inclined to lie, cheat, or deceive; not honest: *I think you're being dishonest about where you were last night.*

> **corrupt** dishonest for an immoral purpose, especially personal gain: *The corrupt boxer accepted a bribe to lose the fight.*
> **deceitful** deliberately misleading or deceptive: *The applicant made several deceitful claims on her résumé.*
> **insincere** saying one thing and doing or thinking another; not sincere: *He offered me an insincere apology.*
> **untrustworthy** not worthy of being trusted: *You've shown yourself to be untrustworthy when it comes to handling money.* — **synonyms**

ANTONYM **honest** not lying, stealing, or cheating; trustworthy — **antonym**

81

ix

A

abandon

verb to leave something or someone and not come back: *We had to **abandon** our house because it had become infected with deadly mold spores.*

- ▸ **desert** to leave a responsibility or duty: *We **deserted** our chores to go see a movie.*
- ▸ **discard** to throw something away: *When are you going to **discard** that old T-shirt?*
- ▸ **dump** to get rid of something: *I **dumped** the newspapers in the recycling bin.*
- ▸ **forsake** to give up something that one loves or values: *She had to **forsake** her dream of buying a new car.*
- ▸ **relinquish** to let go of something; to give up something of value: *He **relinquished** his claim to the inheritance.*

abbreviate

verb to reduce something to a shorter form by leaving out words or letters: *The word "road" is **abbreviated** as "Rd."*

- ▸ **abridge** to reduce the length of something, especially a piece of writing: *The teacher helped me **abridge** my report from ten pages to seven pages.*
- ▸ **condense** to shorten something so as to make it brief and clear: *The reporter **condensed** the senator's remarks for use in a newspaper article.*
- ▸ **shorten** to make something short or shorter: *I **shortened** my speech by three minutes.*

abdicate *verb* to formally give up power or responsibility: *see* **resign**

abdomen *noun* the front part of the body from the chest to the hips: *see* **stomach**

abhor *verb* to regard someone or something with horror or loathing: *see* **hate**

abide *verb* (formal) to live in a place: *see* **dwell**

ability

noun the power to do something: *I am taking classes to develop my dancing **ability**.*

- ▸ **aptitude** a natural ability or talent: *He has an **aptitude** for math.*
- ▸ **capability** the ability to perform reliably or satisfactorily: *I finally got the chance to prove my **capability** for the job.*
- ▸ **capacity** the ability to perform or to produce something: *My new computer has the **capacity** to send and receive faxes.*
- ▸ **skill** an ability that one gains from training or experience: *The magician's **skill** was amazing.*
- ▸ **talent** an outstanding natural ability: *My cousin has a lot of musical **talent**.*

ANTONYM **inability** the lack of ability to do something

able

adjective having the power, means, or ability to do something: *Are you **able** to give me a ride home after work?*

- ▸ **adept** very skillful and effective at doing something: *She is **adept** at finding bargains.*
- ▸ **capable** having the capacity or ability to do something: *My grandfather is not **capable** of reading without his glasses.*
- ▸ **competent** able to do something with satisfactory skill: *I am a **competent** swimmer, but I'm not fast enough to make the swim team.*
- ▸ **proficient** able to do something well: *He is a **proficient** typist and an excellent proofreader.*
- ▸ **skilled** having or showing specialized ability or training: *She is taking cooking lessons from a **skilled** chef.*

abnormal *adjective* differing from what is considered normal, usual, or expected: *see* **strange**

abode *noun* (formal)   the place where one lives: *see* **home**

abolish *verb*   to put an official end to something: *see* **erase**

abominable *adjective*   causing disgust or hatred: *see* **terrible**

abominate *verb*   to detest something thoroughly: *see* **hate**

about

adverb   close to, but not quite: *The school year is **about** over.*

- ▶ **almost**   slightly short of; nearly: *I am **almost** as tall as my father.*
- ▶ **approximately**   close in number, amount, or degree; almost exactly: *He lives **approximately** five miles from school.*
- ▶ **around**   near the time or place of something: *We left **around** four o'clock.*
- ▶ **nearly**   almost, but not quite: *It is **nearly** lunchtime.*
- ▶ **practically**   very nearly; for all practical purposes: *My printer is **practically** out of ink.*

about

preposition   having to do with: *Do you know much **about** training dogs?*

- ▶ **concerning**   having to do with; dealing with: *I am looking for a book **concerning** the geography of North America.*
- ▶ **regarding**   in reference to; relating to: *I called the phone company **regarding** my bill.*

above

adverb   in or to a higher place: *We hung the picture **above** the fireplace.*

- ▶ **over**   higher than; above: *They put a light **over** the bathroom mirror.*
- ▶ **overhead**   above the level of the head: *An airplane flew high **overhead**.*
- ▶ **up**   from a lower to a higher position: *I raised the blinds **up** to let in the sunlight.*

ANTONYM **below**   in or to a lower place or position

abridge *verb*   to reduce the length of something, especially a piece of writing: *see* **abbreviate**

abrupt *adjective*   sudden and unexpected: *see* **sudden**

absence *noun*   a complete lack: *see* **lack**

absent

adjective   not present in an expected or usual place: *I was **absent** from school because I was sick.*

- ▶ **away**   not at this place; elsewhere: *He is **away** from the office for the rest of the afternoon.*
- ▶ **gone**   away from a place: *We were **gone** on vacation for two weeks.*
- ▶ **missing**   not in the expected place; not to be found: *One of my red shoes is **missing**.*
- ▶ **truant**   absent without permission: *The student was **truant**.*

ANTONYM **present**   being at hand or in attendance; here

absolutely *adverb*   completely and unquestionably: *see* **certainly**

absolve *verb*   to clear someone of blame or guilt: *see* **forgive**

absorbed *adjective*   completely occupied or interested: *see* **busy**

absorbing *adjective*   holding one's complete interest or attention: *see* **interesting**

absurd *adjective*   plainly not true or contrary to common sense: *see* **silly**

absurdity *noun*   something that is too ridiculous to be believed: *see* **nonsense**

abundant

adjective   existing in great supply; more than enough: *We have an **abundant** supply of water in this part of the country.*

- ▶ **ample**   large in size, amount, or capacity: *This car has **ample** room for our whole family.*
- ▶ **copious**   very large in quantity; abundant: *My garden produced a **copious** amount of zucchini this year.*

▸ **generous** given or offered in large amounts: *My friend always has spending money because her parents give her a **generous** allowance.*

▸ **liberal** ▷ large or generous in amount: *My grandmother gave me a **liberal** serving of ice cream.* ▷ tending to give freely or generously: *They have been **liberal** donors to the college library fund.*

▸ **lush** being abundant in growth or comfort; luxurious: *There are **lush** forests in the Pacific Northwest.*

▸ **plentiful** being more than enough; in abundant supply: *The harvest was **plentiful** this year.*

abuse *verb* to hurt or injure someone by physical or psychological maltreatment: *see* **hurt**

academy *noun* a school for a special field of study; a private high school: *see* **school**

accent *verb* to focus attention on something: *see* **emphasize**

accept *verb* to receive something that is offered: *see* **get**

accept *verb* to put up with something patiently: *see* **cope**

acceptable *adjective* not up to a high level, but good enough to be accepted: *see* **satisfactory**

accepted *adjective* regarded as correct or true: *see* **proper**

accessory

noun something that adds to the usefulness or beauty of something else: *The car comes with **accessories** such as a sunroof and a built-in CD player.*

▸ **decoration** something that adorns or beautifies: *We have special **decorations** for every holiday.*

▸ **jewelry** ornaments for the body, often made of precious metals and gems: *She prefers to wear expensive silver **jewelry**.*

▸ **ornament** something that makes a person or thing more attractive or beautiful: *I collect antique hair **ornaments**.*

▸ **trim** something added as a finishing decoration: *Her dress has lace **trim** on the neck and shoulders.*

accident

noun ▷ something that happens without being planned: *It was an **accident** that I called the wrong number.* ▷ something bad that happens unexpectedly: *Traffic was slowed because of an **accident** on the highway.*

▸ **collision** ▷ the act of colliding or crashing: *She was lucky to survive the head-on **collision** of the two cars.* ▷ a conflict of opposing interests or ideas: *There was a **collision** of opinions at the meeting.*

▸ **crash** a violent collision: *Two people were hurt in the car **crash**.*

▸ **mishap** an unfortunate accident: *I had a **mishap** with a knife and cut my finger.*

▸ **wreck** a serious or destructive collision; a crash: *The train **wreck** was caused by a malfunction of the signal.*

accommodate *verb* to do someone a favor: *see* **indulge**

accompany *verb* to go along with someone: *see* **escort**

accomplice *noun* a person who helps another do something wrong or illegal: *see* **partner**

accomplish *verb* to carry out or complete something: *see* **achieve**

accomplishment *noun* something accomplished: *see* **success**

accord *noun* (formal) a state of agreement: *see* **peace**

account *noun* a written or spoken description of events: *see* **report**

accumulate *verb* to mount up or collect in one place, especially over time: *see* **gather**

accurate *adjective* free from errors or mistakes: *see* **true**

accuse *verb* to make a declaration charging someone with wrongdoing: *see* **blame**

ache *noun* a dull, steady pain: *see* **pain**

achieve

verb to accomplish, produce, or gain something by effort: *I achieved all A's last semester.*

- ▸ **accomplish** to carry out or complete something: *I accomplished a major goal when I finished my first marathon.*
- ▸ **attain** to gain something, especially by effort or persistence: *He attained his college diploma after four years of hard work.*
- ▸ **do** to perform a task or goal: *Can you do it by yourself?*
- ▸ **fulfill** to make a dream or goal come true: *She has fulfilled her dream of opening her own business.*
- ▸ **gain** to get or obtain something, especially by effort: *He gained valuable experience from working at his uncle's store last summer.*
- ▸ **reach** to arrive at a place, position, or goal: *The hikers reached the summit in three hours.*

achievement *noun* an outstanding accomplishment: *see* **success**

acknowledge *verb* to declare the existence or truth of something: *see* **admit**

acknowledgment *noun* something done in reply to another's gift, favor, or message: *see* **answer**

acme *noun* (formal) the highest point, as of perfection: *see* **prime**

acquaintance *noun* a person one knows but who is not a close friend: *see* **friend**

acquire *verb* to take possession of something, especially something desirable: *see* **get**

acquit *verb* to free or clear someone from a formal accusation: *see* **forgive**

acreage *noun* land area measured in acres: *see* **field [1]**

across *preposition* on, at, or from the other side of something: *see* **after**

act *noun* something done or performed: *see* **action**

act *verb* to serve or function as something: *see* **behave**

action

noun ▷ something done: *The drowning child was saved by the lifeguard's swift action.* ▷ the process of doing something: *The firefighters sprang into action when the alarm sounded.*

- ▸ **act** something done or performed: *He is known for his acts of kindness.*
- ▸ **deed** an act or action that is meaningful: *Returning the wallet was a good deed.*
- ▸ **feat** an outstanding deed or accomplishment; an exploit that requires much skill or daring: *She's attempting the feat of sailing around the world.*
- ▸ **stunt** an act that shows unusual skill or daring, often done to attract attention: *The motorcycle rider was injured in his attempt to perform the stunt of jumping over sixteen cars.*

activate *verb* to set something in motion: *see* **begin**

active *adjective* engaged in lively or energetic activity: *see* **busy**

activity *noun* a planned or organized thing to do: *see* **recreation**

actual *adjective* existing or happening in fact: *see* **real [2]**

ad *noun* an advertisement: *see* **advertisement**

adapt *verb* to change so as to suit new conditions or circumstances: *see* **change**

add

verb ▷ to combine two or more numbers to form a sum: *I used a calculator to add the long column of numbers.* ▷ to contribute something extra: *She added two new stamps to her collection.*

- ▸ **calculate** to find an answer or a result by using mathematics: *Today we learned how to calculate the circumference of a circle.*
- ▸ **compute** to work out a result, an answer, or a solution by using mathematics: *Would you help me compute the interest on this loan?*

▸ **count**   to find the total number of something by listing items one by one: *Please count the books on this shelf.*

▸ **figure**   to calculate an amount: *She figured how much money to leave for the tip.*

▸ **total**   to find the sum of something; to add something up completely: *I totaled my expenses for the month.*

ANTONYM **subtract**   to take a number or quantity away from another

added *adjective*   in addition: *see* **more**

additional *adjective*   more than what is usual or expected: *see* **more**

address *noun*   the location of a person or organization: *see* **home**

adept *adjective*   very skillful and effective at doing something: *see* **able**

adequate *adjective*   up to a minimum or acceptable standard: *see* **satisfactory**

adequate *adjective*   as much as is needed for a specific purpose: *see* **enough**

adhere *verb*   to stick or hold fast to something: *see* **fasten**

adjust *verb*   to change something so that it works better or is more suitable: *see* **change**

administer *verb*   to direct the affairs of something, such as a government or school: *see* **manage**

administration *noun*   the people who manage the operation of something, such as a school, business, or government: *see* **government**

administrator *noun*   a person who works as a manager, especially in a business, school, or government agency: *see* **boss**

admiration *noun*   a feeling of sincere appreciation of the worth of someone or something: *see* **respect**

admire *verb*   to have a high opinion of someone or something: *see* **respect**

admirer *noun*   someone who deeply admires another person: *see* **follower**

admit

verb   to acknowledge that something is true, especially something embarrassing or dishonest: *I must admit that I have forgotten your name.*

▸ **acknowledge**   to declare the existence or truth of something: *The scientist acknowledged that another theory was possible.*

▸ **concede**   to admit that something is true, often without wanting to: *I had to concede defeat in the chess game.*

▸ **confess**   to admit that one has done something bad, wrong, or illegal: *The suspect confessed that he had robbed the bank.*

ANTONYM **deny**   to say that something is not true

adolescent *noun*   a person in the period of growth and physical development that leads from childhood to adulthood: *see* **teenager**

adorable *adjective*   sweet and lovable: *see* **charming**

adoration *noun*   great and reverent or devoted love: *see* **love**

adore *verb*   to love someone deeply and devotedly: *see* **love**

adorn *verb*   to make something beautiful by adding decorations: *see* **decorate**

adult

adjective   fully grown or developed: *The world's largest animal is an adult blue whale.*

▸ **grown**   having reached full physical growth: *My little sister will probably be taller than I am when she's grown.*

▸ **mature**   ▷ having reached full natural growth or development: *Giant redwoods can grow to over 300 feet when fully mature.* ▷ having the mental and emotional qualities associated with an adult: *My parents think I shouldn't get a credit card until I can show that I'm more mature.*

▸ **ripe**   fully developed; ready to be used or eaten: *We picked the peaches when they were ripe.*

ANTONYM **juvenile**   young; immature

advance

verb to move forward, onward, or ahead: *After the baby turtle hatched, it slowly **advanced** across the beach toward the ocean.*

- ▶ **continue** to keep on doing something: *I must **continue** studying or I won't be ready for the test.*
- ▶ **proceed** to go forward or onward, especially after an interruption: *Now that we've had lunch, let's **proceed** with our shopping.*
- ▶ **progress** to move forward, especially toward a goal: *I've **progressed** from beginning to intermediate in my swimming lessons.*

ANTONYM **recede** to move back or away from something

advantage *noun* a beneficial factor or feature: *see* **privilege**

adventure

noun a bold, dangerous, or exciting undertaking: *He said that his white-water rafting trip was a real **adventure**.*

- ▶ **expedition** an excursion, journey, or voyage made for some specific purpose, as of war or exploration: *Lewis and Clark led the first scientific **expedition** to the Pacific Northwest.*
- ▶ **exploit** a brilliant act or heroic deed: *I like to read about the **exploits** of famous explorers.*
- ▶ **quest** an adventurous expedition undertaken in order to secure or achieve something: *Ponce de León was on a **quest** for the fountain of youth when he discovered Florida.*
- ▶ **venture** an undertaking that is dangerous, daring, or of uncertain outcome: *Starting a new business is an exciting **venture**.*

adventurous *adjective* fond of adventure: *see* **brave**

adversary *noun* an opponent or enemy: *see* **enemy**

advertise *verb* to call public attention to something such as a product or business: *see* **announce**

advertisement

noun a public notice that calls attention to a product, a service, or a coming event: *I saw an **advertisement** for a carpet sale on television.*

- ▶ **ad** an advertisement: *I placed an **ad** for our yard sale in the local newspaper.*
- ▶ **commercial** an advertisement on radio or television: *He got something to drink while the **commercials** were on.*
- ▶ **flyer** a printed sheet or pamphlet; a circular: *The drama club posted **flyers** all over campus to publicize the performance.*
- ▶ **promotion** publicity for a product on sale; advertising: *The car dealership had a special **promotion** in December offering cash back on every purchase.*

advice *noun* an opinion about how to solve a problem or do something unfamiliar: *see* **suggestion**

advise *verb* to give information or advice to someone: *see* **alert**

advisor *noun* a person who offers advice, especially officially or professionally: *see* **teacher**

affair *noun* a social gathering: *see* **party**

affect *verb* (formal) to pretend to have or feel something that isn't true: *see* **pretend**

affection *noun* a fond or tender feeling toward someone: *see* **love**

affectionate

adjective having or showing a strong liking or love for someone: *They are an **affectionate** couple.*

- ▶ **caring** feeling or showing concern for others: *He is a **caring** father.*
- ▶ **fond** having a strong liking or affection for something or someone: *I am very **fond** of chocolate.*
- ▶ **friendly** showing friendship; kind: *Our **friendly** neighbors invited us over for dinner.*
- ▶ **loving** feeling or showing love: *The sisters are very **loving** with each other.*
- ▶ **warm** showing friendliness and enthusiasm: *His parents gave us a **warm** welcome.*

affluence *noun*   a plentiful supply of goods or money: *see* **wealth**

affluent *adjective*   having plenty of money, property, or possessions: *see* **rich**

afraid

adjective   filled with fear: *Many people are **afraid** of heights.*

- ▶ **alarmed**   filled with a sudden fear caused by a sense of danger: *I was **alarmed** when I saw the snake.*
- ▶ **fearful**   feeling fear or worry: *She was **fearful** that the traffic jam would make her late to work.*
- ▶ **frightened**   filled with sudden, intense fear; startled: *My dog was **frightened** by the loud firecrackers.*
- ▶ **scared**   frightened or alarmed: *I don't like horror movies because they make me too **scared**.*
- ▶ **terrified**   filled with terror; overwhelmed with fear and alarm: *We were **terrified** when the bear came into our camp.*

after

conjunction   following the time that: *We went to the restaurant **after** we saw the movie.*

- ▶ **once**   as soon as: *We went into the ballpark **once** we bought our tickets.*
- ▶ **when**   at the time that: *We will leave for the airport **when** we finish packing.*

after

preposition   behind or later than something in place or order: *May I read that magazine **after** you?*

- ▶ **across**   on, at, or from the other side of something: *My friend lives **across** the street from me.*
- ▶ **behind**   at the back or in the rear of something: *We have a swimming pool **behind** our house.*
- ▶ **beyond**   on the far side of something; past: *Her house is just **beyond** the school.*
- ▶ **past**   beyond something in time or place: *I drove **past** the exit where I should have turned off.*

aftertaste *noun*   a taste that remains in the mouth: *see* **flavor**

again

adverb   an additional time; anew: *I would like to visit Washington, D.C. **again**.*

- ▶ **another time**   once more; again: *The movie was so good that I'm going to see it **another time**.*
- ▶ **once again**   for another time; again: *After several years of holding steady, inflation has **once again** started to rise.*
- ▶ **over and over**   again and again; repeatedly: *The radio station plays that song **over and over**.*
- ▶ **repeatedly**   said, done, or occurring again and again: *Our teacher has **repeatedly** reminded us that our papers are due next week.*

against

preposition   in a direction or course opposite to something: *I voted **against** the ballot measure because it was too expensive.*

- ▶ **contrary to**   completely different from something else: *His opinions about politics are **contrary to** mine.*
- ▶ **opposed to**   in opposition or resistance to something: *I prefer ice skating as **opposed to** in-line skating.*
- ▶ **versus**   against someone or something in a contest: *Tonight's basketball game is the L.A. Lakers **versus** the Boston Celtics.*

age

noun   a distinctive period of history: *The space **age** has been marked by great advances in technology.*

- ▶ **era**   a period of time marked from a specific date or event: *The Vietnam War **era** was a time of political and social unrest in the United States.*
- ▶ **generation**   a group of people who grew up at the same time, often having similar social and cultural attitudes: *The new show on cable TV is aimed at the younger **generation**.*

- **heyday** the period of something's greatest popularity, success, or power: *The heyday of the hula hoop was in the 1950s.*
- **period** a span of time, especially during which a culture, technology, or set of beliefs is dominant: *Alcohol was illegal in America during the Prohibition period.*
- **time** a span of years marked by similar events and conditions, or associated with certain historical figures: *Many people moved to California during the time of the 1849 gold rush.*

aged *adjective* having reached old age: *see* **old**

agency

noun a business or service authorized to act for others: *He filed a claim with his insurance agency.*

- **branch** a division of a business or other organization: *I work at the downtown branch of the telephone company.*
- **bureau** an office for a specific kind of business: *I made my vacation plans through a travel bureau.*
- **department** a division of an organization: *I work in the shipping and receiving department.*
- **division** a specific unit of a corporation or a government: *Congress is one division of the U.S. government.*
- **office** a place in which business, clerical, or professional work is done: *I was late getting to the office this morning because of a traffic jam.*

agenda *noun* a list of things to be considered or done: *see* **plan**

agent *noun* a person with the power or authority to act for another: *see* **representative**

aggressive

adjective bold and forceful in pursuing a goal: *Her aggressive plan helped her business succeed in a short time.*

- **assertive** bold and self-confident, especially in putting forward one's opinions: *Our teacher encourages students to be assertive during class discussions.*
- **belligerent** eager to fight; warlike: *His belligerent attitude makes people avoid him.*
- **combative** ready or inclined to fight or argue: *The subject of politics makes many people combative.*
- **hostile** feeling or showing hatred or ill will, as between enemies: *Relations between the two countries are hostile.*
- **pushy** disagreeably aggressive or forward: *The pushy salesperson wouldn't leave us alone.*

agile

adjective able to move quickly and easily: *Nobody could score against the agile goalie.*

- **deft** quick and skilled: *The artist painted with deft strokes.*
- **nimble** quick and light in movement: *I was nimble and caught my pen before it fell to the floor.*
- **spry** active or lively; full of energy: *The spry squirrel raced up the tree.*

ANTONYM **clumsy** lacking grace or skill

agitate *verb* to move something to and fro with strong, jerky movements: *see* **shake**

agony *noun* intense and prolonged pain or suffering: *see* **suffering**

agree

verb to share the same opinion as someone else; to accept someone's idea or intention: *I agree with you that we need to repaint the living room.*

- **concur** (formal) to have the same opinion as someone else: *We concurred that the ending of the movie was dumb.*
- **conform** to follow or be in agreement with a set standard or rule: *That outfit does not conform to the school dress code.*
- **correspond** to have an exact relationship to something else; to be in agreement: *I made sure that the quotations I used in my*

*paper **corresponded** with the sources in my bibliography.*

▸ **harmonize** to be or come into agreement with something; to be harmonious: *Those colors **harmonize** nicely with the wallpaper.*

▸ **match** to be similar to or identical with another: *I can't find the sock that **matches** this one.*

ANTONYM **disagree** to fail to agree with someone; to have a different opinion

agreeable *adjective* suited to one's liking or interest: *see* **pleasant**

agreeable *adjective* willing to agree or say yes: *see* **willing**

agreement

noun an arrangement or understanding between two parties: *We made an **agreement** to share the housework.*

▸ **bargain** an agreement between two parties, often involving payment or trade: *My friend and I have made a **bargain** to share the expenses of the trip.*

▸ **contract** a written agreement that can be enforced by law: *The band just signed a new record **contract**.*

▸ **deal** an agreement, as in business or politics: *The salesman made a **deal** with the customer.*

▸ **treaty** a formal agreement between two or more countries: *The nations' leaders signed the **treaty**.*

ahead *adverb* in advance: *see* **before**

aid *verb* to give help to someone in need: *see* **help**

aide *noun* a person who provides help in carrying out duties or assignments: *see* **assistant**

ailing *adjective* suffering from a minor illness or disease: *see* **sick**

ailment *noun* a usually mild or chronic illness: *see* **disease**

aim *noun* a desired result; a purpose: *see* **goal**

air *verb* to express one's feelings, beliefs, or ideas in public: *see* **express**

aisle *noun* a passageway between two rows of seats: *see* **path**

alarm *verb* to fill someone with sudden fear or anxiety: *see* **scare**

alarmed *adjective* filled with a sudden fear caused by a sense of danger: *see* **afraid**

alert

adjective quick to notice or act: *The **alert** dog barked when the stranger walked up to the house.*

▸ **awake** not sleeping; conscious: *I couldn't stay **awake** through the late movie.*

▸ **aware** informed or mindful of something: *He wasn't **aware** that he had won the lottery.*

▸ **observant** quick to perceive or understand: *The **observant** child quickly learned how to play the game.*

▸ **vigilant** on the alert, especially against danger: *The security guard was **vigilant** for any signs of intruders.*

▸ **watchful** paying close attention to something; vigilant: *The nurse was **watchful** against a return of her patient's fever.*

ANTONYM **unaware** not alert or aware

alert

verb to make someone aware of something; to warn someone of something dangerous: *The smoke alarm **alerted** us that the toast was burning.*

▸ **advise** to give information or advice to someone: *The police officer **advised** the suspect of her rights.*

▸ **caution** to warn someone against possible trouble or danger: *Pregnant women are **cautioned** by their doctors not to drink alcohol or smoke cigarettes.*

▸ **notify** to give notice to someone; to inform someone of something: *The landlord **notified** us that he would be replacing the carpet soon.*

▸ **threaten** to give signs that something troublesome or dangerous is about to happen: *Those dark clouds **threaten** rain.*

▸ **warn** to make someone aware of present or possible danger: *The parents* **warned** *their children to look both ways before crossing the street.*

alibi *noun* a claim made by an accused person of not being present when a crime was committed: see **excuse**

alien *noun* a person who belongs to or comes from another country: *see* **stranger**

alike *adjective* being the same as or similar to one another: *see* **same**

all

adjective being the total number or amount of something: *I have* **all** *the books that this author has written.*

▸ **complete** having all necessary or desired parts: *This is a* **complete** *list of the club members who have paid their dues.*

▸ **entire** all in one piece; having no part missing or left out: *I slept the* **entire** *afternoon.*

▸ **full** containing all that is normal or possible: *We need a* **full** *deck of cards to play that game.*

▸ **total** complete in extent or degree; being an entire amount: *What's the* **total** *amount of the bill?*

▸ **whole** being the entire amount, extent, or duration of something: *We ate the* **whole** *pizza.*

allegiance *noun* loyalty or devotion: *see* **loyalty**

alley *noun* a narrow street or passageway between or behind buildings: *see* **road**

alliance *noun* a close association of nations or other groups that is formed to promote their common interests: *see* **club**

allocate

verb to set something aside for a particular purpose: *These medical supplies are* **allocated** *for emergency relief.*

▸ **appropriate** to officially reserve something for a specific use: *The school district* **appropriates** *a certain amount of money for buying textbooks each year.*

▸ **dedicate** to reserve something for a special or solemn purpose: *I* **dedicate** *an hour every day to practicing the piano.*

▸ **designate** to select someone or something for a particular duty or purpose: *I am* **designating** *you to represent us at the conference.*

▸ **earmark** to identify something as reserved for a particular purpose: *I* **earmark** *ten percent of my paycheck for savings.*

▸ **reserve** to hold or save something for a particular person or use: *That parking place is* **reserved** *for the president of the company.*

allow *verb* to let someone do something: *see* **authorize**

allowable *adjective* permitted or approved: *see* **legal**

allowance *noun* an amount given at regular intervals or for a specific purpose: *see* **income**

all right *adjective* satisfactory, but not excellent: *see* **satisfactory**

allure *noun* a strong attraction or fascination: *see* **attraction**

alluring *adjective* having the power to attract: *see* **interesting**

almost *adverb* slightly short of: *see* **about**

alone

adjective apart from the presence of anyone or anything else: *I spent the afternoon* **alone** *in my room.*

▸ **lone** being the only one of its kind: *There is a* **lone** *pine tree in our yard.*

▸ **single** not accompanied by another or others; lone: *There is a* **single** *piece of pizza left in the box.*

▸ **solitary** existing or living alone; happening with no one else present: *I like to go for long,* **solitary** *walks.*

▸ **solo** made or done by one person: *This art project was a* **solo** *effort.*

▸ **unaccompanied** being without a companion: *She went to the party* **unaccompanied**.

alone

adverb without others; without aid or help: *He built this boat* **alone**.

▸ **by oneself** without the company or help of others: *It is not possible to go water skiing* **by oneself**.
▸ **independently** apart from another; not connected to anyone or anything else: *My brother likes to study* **independently**.
▸ **individually** one at a time; separately: *These candies are* **individually** *wrapped*.

alphabetize *verb* to arrange something in alphabetical order: *see* **sort**

already *adverb* by this time: *see* **before**

also

adverb in addition; besides: *Does that sweater* **also** *come in pink?*

▸ **besides** in addition: *Are we doing anything* **besides** *going shopping?*
▸ **furthermore** in addition; further: *This sweater is my favorite color, and* **furthermore** *I got it on sale.*
▸ **in addition** also; as well as: *Would you like some coffee* **in addition** *to your dessert?*
▸ **likewise** moreover; besides: *I read poetry and* **likewise** *enjoy writing it.*
▸ **too** in addition; also: *Will you be at the meeting* **too?**

alter *verb* to change something for a particular use or purpose: *see* **change**

alternate *verb* to do, perform, or use something in turns: *see* **shift**

alternate *noun* a person or thing available to serve in another's place: *see* **substitute**

alternative *noun* one of two or more possibilities from which to choose: *see* **choice**

although *conjunction* regardless of the fact that: *see* **but**

always

adverb on every occasion; without exception: *She* **always** *takes her briefcase to work.*

▸ **constantly** happening continually or regularly: *He* **constantly** *complains about the neighbor's dog.*
▸ **forever** for everlasting time; eternally: *The train ride seemed to take* **forever**.
▸ **regularly** at a fixed or usual time: *I* **regularly** *brush my teeth before bedtime.*

ANTONYM **never** at no time

amateur *noun* a person who engages in an art, science, or sport for enjoyment rather than money: *see* **beginner**

amaze *verb* to fill someone with great wonder: *see* **surprise**

amazing *adjective* causing great surprise and astonishment: *see* **awesome**

ambassador *noun* an official of the highest rank who represents a government to another country: *see* **representative**

ambition *noun* a strong desire to achieve something: *see* **will**

amble *verb* to walk or move at a slow, leisurely pace: *see* **walk**

ambush *verb* to attack someone from a concealed position: *see* **trap**

amend *verb* to change something so as to make it more accurate or correct: *see* **change**

amount

noun something grouped or gathered to form a quantity: *I added a small* **amount** *of salt to the soup.*

▸ **bulk** the major portion of something; the greatest part: *He makes the* **bulk** *of his money from investments.*
▸ **number** an indefinite quantity: *Any* **number** *of people would be happy to win the lottery.*
▸ **quantity** a specified or indefinite amount or number: *The factory shipped a large* **quantity** *of spare parts to its customers last month.*

▸ **size** the physical dimensions and proportions of an object: *What size pizza do you want to order?*

▸ **sum** the whole amount, quantity, or number: *She spends great sums of money on her clothes.*

▸ **volume** the amount of space something occupies or contains: *The trunk of our car has enough volume to accommodate two large suitcases.*

amphitheater *noun* a round building with tiered seats around a central arena: *see* **theater**

ample *adjective* large in size, amount, or capacity: *see* **abundant**

amuse *verb* to give simple enjoyment to someone: *see* **entertain**

amusement *noun* something that amuses, entertains, or pleases: *see* **fun**

amusing *adjective* pleasantly entertaining: *see* **funny**

analyze *verb* to examine something closely: *see* **examine**

anarchy *noun* disorder and confusion resulting from lack of authority: *see* **confusion**

ancestor *noun* a person from whom one is descended: *see* **parent**

ancient *adjective* from a long time ago: *see* **old**

anecdote *noun* a short account of an interesting or humorous event: *see* **story**

anger

noun a feeling of great displeasure or hostility toward someone or something: *His rudeness filled me with anger.*

▸ **displeasure** the condition of being displeased; dissatisfaction: *The professor showed displeasure when the student left class early.*

▸ **fury** violent anger: *In his fury at losing the race, he pounded the wall with his fists.*

▸ **indignation** anger aroused by something unjust, mean, or unworthy: *Many people felt indignation when the results of the trial were announced.*

▸ **rage** violent anger or a fit of such anger: *The driver was in a rage when someone hit his new car.*

▸ **wrath** (formal) violent, vengeful anger: *The reporter's article provoked the wrath of the officials he criticized.*

anger

verb to make someone angry: *Her sarcastic tone of voice angered me.*

▸ **enrage** to put someone into a rage: *The man was enraged when the store wouldn't take back the faulty product.*

▸ **infuriate** to make someone intensely or violently angry: *The student was infuriated when he failed the class.*

angle *noun* a particular way of looking at something: *see* **opinion**

angry

adjective feeling or showing anger: *Why are you angry with me?*

▸ **furious** full of intense, often violent anger: *I was furious when the gophers dug up my garden.*

▸ **irate** extremely angry or upset: *She was irate when she saw the electric bill.*

▸ **irritated** angry and impatient; annoyed: *I felt irritated that I had to wait in line for so long.*

▸ **mad** very irritated; angry: *I was mad when I found out I'd bought the wrong size screws.*

▸ **sore** (informal) full of resentment; bitter: *I was sore when I wasn't picked for the lead in the school play.*

▸ **upset** full of angry or worried feelings: *He was upset when he didn't get the promotion.*

anguish *noun* unrelieved suffering, especially of the mind: *see* **suffering**

animal

noun a living thing that can move from place to place on its own: *Tigers are beautiful animals.*

▸ **beast** a large, four-footed animal: *Camels are considered beasts of burden.*

▸ **creature** a living being, especially an animal: *Most bats are harmless creatures.*

▸ **critter** (informal) a creature: *I took pictures of the critters at the zoo.*

▸ **organism** a living individual, such as a plant or animal: *In our science class we are studying single-cell organisms.*

▸ **pet** an animal kept for amusement or companionship: *Dogs and cats are the most popular pets.*

▸ **varmint** an animal that is thought of as undesirable, obnoxious, or troublesome: *Most rodents are considered to be varmints.*

announce

verb to bring something to public notice; to give formal notice of something: *Our teacher announced that we were going to have a quiz.*

▸ **advertise** to call public attention to something such as a product or business: *The owners put up a banner to advertise the store's grand opening.*

▸ **broadcast** to make something known over a wide area: *The election results were broadcast over both TV and radio.*

▸ **circulate** to spread widely among people or places: *The rumor circulated around the office.*

▸ **proclaim** to announce something officially and publicly; to declare: *After the hurricane, the governor proclaimed a state of emergency.*

▸ **publicize** to give information to the media as a means of attracting public attention to a person, group, or event: *The clothing store publicized its annual sale by handing out fliers.*

▸ **televise** to broadcast something by television: *The city council plans to televise its meetings.*

announcement

noun a public statement that makes something known in writing or in speech: *The newspaper publishes wedding announcements.*

▸ **bulletin** a short announcement on a matter of public interest: *The TV program was interrupted for an important news bulletin.*

▸ **declaration** an explicit, formal announcement, either oral or written: *The President signed the declaration of war.*

▸ **notice** a published or displayed announcement: *The health department published a notice on the quality of the local drinking water.*

▸ **proclamation** an official public announcement: *The end of the war was announced by proclamation.*

annoy

verb to cause someone to lose patience or become angry, especially by minor disturbances: *The mosquitoes annoyed me all night long.*

▸ **bother** to disturb or irritate someone; to make someone anxious or upset: *It bothers me when I wake up late.*

▸ **bug** (informal) to annoy or pester someone, especially with requests: *My little sister kept bugging me to take her to the mall.*

▸ **harass** to irritate or torment someone persistently: *The flies harassed the horse with their constant biting.*

▸ **irk** to cause someone to be frustrated or angry: *It really irked me when the copier jammed.*

▸ **irritate** to make someone angry or impatient: *He gets irritated when he is stuck in traffic.*

▸ **pester** to harass someone with demands or requests: *The reporters pestered the celebrity for an interview.*

another *adjective* being an additional one: *see* **more**

another time *adverb* once more: *see* **again**

answer

noun a spoken or written reply to a question, request, or letter: *I never got an answer to my question about who was at the party.*

▸ **acknowledgment** something done in reply to another's gift, favor, or message: *She sent a thank-you card as an acknowledgment of the gift.*

▸ **confirmation** something that confirms; proof: *The school sent confirmation of my enrollment.*

▸ **reply** a response to a question, statement, or greeting; an answer: *I told him good morning but he gave me no* **reply**.

▸ **response** a reply or answer: *I wrote a letter to my senator and received a* **response**.

▸ **retort** a quick, witty answer: *His quick* **retort** *made us all laugh*.

ANTONYM **question** something that is asked

answer

verb to respond to someone or something in words or action: *I* **answered** *all the test questions*.

▸ **react** to act in response to a situation, person, or influence: *I didn't know how to* **react** *to his strange behavior*.

▸ **reply** to say or give an answer: *I* **replied** *to the interviewer's questions as best I could*.

▸ **respond** to make a reply: *She* **responded** *by nodding her head*.

antagonist *noun* (formal) one who opposes or seeks to defeat someone or something: *see* **enemy**

anticipate *verb* to foresee or consider something in advance: *see* **expect**

antidote *noun* a substance that works against a poison: *see* **remedy**

antique *adjective* from a previous time or era: *see* **old**

anxiety *noun* a feeling of uneasiness and distress about something in the future: *see* **worry**

anxious *adjective* eagerly or earnestly desiring something: *see* **impatient**

anxious *adjective* nervous or afraid about something uncertain: *see* **nervous**

any *adjective* one, some, or all: *see* **every**

anyway

adverb in any case; at least: *It is no problem to give you a ride because I am driving that direction* **anyway**.

▸ **however** in whatever way; by whatever means: *You can decorate your room* **however** *you want*.

▸ **nevertheless** in spite of that; still: *I was tired, but I kept studying* **nevertheless**.

▸ **nonetheless** even though; nevertheless: *His speech was brief, but it received applause* **nonetheless**.

▸ **regardless** in spite of everything: *We finished the hike* **regardless** *of the rain*.

▸ **yet** at this time; for the present; thus far: *We haven't* **yet** *decided which movie to see*.

apartment *noun* a usually rented room or group of rooms to live in: *see* **house**

apologetic *adjective* expressing or making an apology: *see* **sorry**

apology *noun* a statement expressing regret for an offense or fault: *see* **excuse**

apparel *noun* (formal) the things that are worn by a person: *see* **clothing**

apparent *adjective* readily understood or seen: *see* **clear** [1]

appeal *noun* the power of attracting or of arousing interest: *see* **attraction**

appeal *verb* to make a sincere or earnest request of someone: *see* **beg**

appear

verb [1] to come into view: *Our house* **appeared** *when we turned the corner*.

▸ **arise** to come into being; to come forth: *Problems began to* **arise** *after the manager quit*.

▸ **arrive** to reach a destination; to come to a place: *We* **arrived** *at the concert early*.

▸ **come** to advance toward a person or thing; to approach: *My neighbor* **came** *over when I waved at him*.

▸ **emerge** to come forth into view or notice: *The butterfly* **emerged** *from its cocoon*.

▸ **loom** to come into view, often with a threatening appearance: *Rain clouds* **loomed** *on the horizon*.

▸ **show up** to make an appearance: *She* **showed up** *at the party late*.

appear

verb [2] to give the impression of something without necessarily being so: *We* **appear** *to have lost the game, but there's still a minute left.*

► **look like** to give the impression or appearance of something: *This* **looks like** *a good sturdy table.*
► **resemble** to have a similarity or likeness to someone or something; to be like something: *I* **resemble** *my grandmother, especially around the eyes.*
► **seem** to give the impression of something as far as can be determined: *She* **seems** *interested in applying for the job, though she hasn't actually filled out a form.*

appetite *noun* an instinctive desire for something, especially food and drink: *see* **hunger**

applause

noun praise or approval expressed by the clapping of hands: *There was loud* **applause** *after the concert.*

► **cheering** shouts of happiness, approval, encouragement, or enthusiasm: *We could hear the* **cheering** *of the baseball fans as we walked past the stadium.*
► **clapping** the striking of hands together with a sudden loud sound: *The* **clapping** *stopped when the actors left the stage.*
► **ovation** a loud and enthusiastic display of approval, usually in the form of applause: *The singer received a standing* **ovation.**

appliance *noun* a machine used to perform a household task: *see* **machine**

apply *verb* to put something into action: *see* **use**

appoint *verb* to select or designate someone for an office, position, or duty: *see* **assign**

appointment

noun an arrangement for a meeting at a particular time and place: *I scheduled my doctor's* **appointment** *for the afternoon.*

► **booking** a reservation, as for a room at a hotel: *The travel agent took care of all our* **bookings** *for the whole trip.*
► **date** an agreement to meet someone or to be somewhere at a particular time, especially as a social engagement: *He and I have a* **date** *to go sailing.*
► **engagement** a promise to be at a particular place at a certain time: *We have an* **engagement** *to meet them for dinner on Friday.*
► **rendezvous** a prearranged meeting: *They have a monthly* **rendezvous** *at a nice restaurant.*
► **reservation** an arrangement for securing something in advance, such as a table at a restaurant or a room at a hotel: *That restaurant requires a* **reservation.**

appraise *verb* to judge the equality, importance, or value of something: *see* **judge**

appreciate *verb* to recognize the worth, quality, or importance of something: *see* **enjoy**

appreciation

noun recognition of the worth, quality, or importance of something: *The mayor expressed his* **appreciation** *for the committee's hard work.*

► **gratitude** the state of being grateful; thankfulness: *I'm filled with* **gratitude** *for my blessings.*
► **recognition** acknowledgment or approval, especially for one's accomplishments: *The actress received an award in* **recognition** *of her excellent performance.*
► **thankfulness** a feeling of appreciation for a benefit or favor: *I was full of* **thankfulness** *that the car accident was not serious.*
► **thanks** an acknowledgment of a favor or gift: *The parents gave the babysitter a tip as* **thanks** *for her staying late.*

appreciative *adjective* showing recognition of another's worth or effort: *see* **grateful**

apprehend *verb* to take a person into official custody: *see* **capture**

apprehend *verb* (formal) to have consciousness of something: *see* **understand**

apprentice *noun*   a person who is learning a craft or trade from a skilled worker: *see* **student**

approach *noun*   a way or method of working or dealing with something: *see* **method**

appropriate *verb*   to officially reserve something for a specific use: *see* **allocate**

appropriate *adjective*   suitable for a particular person, condition, occasion, or place: *see* **proper**

approval *noun*   favorable regard: *see* **respect**

approve *verb*   to give one's official permission for something: *see* **authorize**

approximately *adverb*   close in number, amount, or degree: *see* **about**

apt *adjective*   more likely than not: *see* **prone**

aptitude *noun*   a natural ability or talent: *see* **ability**

arbitrate *verb*   to settle a dispute between two sides by acting as an impartial judge: *see* **negotiate**

arbitrator *noun*   a person chosen to settle a dispute or controversy: *see* **judge**

arch *noun*   a curved structure that extends across an opening and serves as a support: *see* **curve**

ardent *adjective*   full of warmth or passion for something: *see* **enthusiastic**

ardor *noun*   intense enthusiasm or devotion: *see* **enthusiasm**

area

noun   a section or region, as of land or space: *We removed all the chairs to make an area for dancing.*

- ▸ **region**   an area of the earth's surface, usually a large one: *The plane went down in a mountainous region of northern Mexico.*
- ▸ **territory**   the land and waters under the authority of a single government: *The territory of the continental United States stretches from the Atlantic to the Pacific Ocean.*
- ▸ **tract**   an expanse of land or water: *This tract of land has been set aside as a wildlife refuge.*

- ▸ **vicinity**   the area near or about a place: *I lost my watch in the vicinity of the library.*
- ▸ **zone**   an area or region set off from another by a special characteristic or use: *The speed limit is slower in a school zone.*

arena *noun*   a large building used especially for the presentation of sports events and spectacles: *see* **theater**

argument *noun*   a heated verbal disagreement: *see* **fight**

arid *adjective*   having little or no rainfall: *see* **dry**

arise *verb*   to come into being: *see* **appear [1]**

arm *verb*   to provide someone with something needed for an action: *see* **equip**

aroma *noun*   a rich, pleasant smell: *see* **smell**

around *adverb*   near the time or place of something: *see* **about**

arouse *verb*   to awaken something: *see* **excite**

arrange *verb*   to plan or prepare for something: *see* **plan**

arrangement *noun*   the manner or style in which something is arranged: *see* **design**

array *noun*   an orderly arrangement of items: *see* **assortment**

arrest *verb*   to seize and hold a person under authority of law: *see* **capture**

arrive *verb*   to reach a destination: *see* **appear [1]**

arrogance *noun*   the quality of being excessively proud: *see* **pride**

arrogant *adjective*   excessively and unpleasantly proud of oneself: *see* **proud**

art

noun   a skill gained through practice, experience, or study: *He is learning the art of cooking at a culinary school.*

- ▸ **craft**   skill in making something, especially with the hands: *This chair was put together with great craft.*

▶ **expertise** skill or knowledge in a particular area: *Brain surgery calls for a tremendous amount of* **expertise**.

▶ **knack** a special talent or ability: *She has a* **knack** *for calling at the wrong time.*

▶ **know-how** the knowledge and skill required to do something correctly: *He has the* **know-how** *to build a house.*

▶ **technique** skill or command in handling the fundamentals of creating an art or sport: *That dancer has great* **technique**.

article *noun* a piece of writing that forms an independent part of a newspaper, magazine, or book: *see* **essay**

articulate *verb* to utter a speech sound clearly and distinctly: *see* **say**

as *conjunction* seeing that; since: *see* **because**

as a result *adverb* consequently: *see* **therefore**

ashen *adjective* having a pale skin color: *see* **pale**

ask

verb to seek an answer to a question: *Feel free to* **ask** *any questions you may have about the company health plan.*

▶ **inquire** to seek information by asking questions: *I called to* **inquire** *about the ad in the paper.*

▶ **invite** to ask someone to come somewhere or do something: *My boss* **invited** *me over for dinner.*

▶ **question** to ask someone directly or closely for information: *The lawyer* **questioned** *the witness about what he had seen the night of the crime.*

▶ **request** to express a desire for something; to ask someone to do something: *She* **requested** *that I finish the report today.*

▶ **solicit** to seek to obtain something from someone: *The Red Cross is* **soliciting** *people to donate blood.*

ANTONYM **answer** to give a reply or response

aspect *noun* a particular way of considering something: *see* **quality**

aspire *verb* to have a great ambition: *see* **hope**

assassinate *verb* to murder a prominent person by surprise attack: *see* **kill**

assault *verb* to attack someone with force or violence: *see* **attack**

assemble *verb* to fit the parts of something together: *see* **build**

assembly *noun* a group of persons gathered together for a common purpose: *see* **meeting**

assert *verb* to claim something strongly and confidently: *see* **claim**

assertive *adjective* bold and self-confident, especially in putting forward one's opinions: *see* **aggressive**

assess *verb* to determine the value, significance, or extent of something: *see* **judge**

assets *noun* all the property owned by a person or business: *see* **property**

assign

verb to select someone for a duty or office: *He was* **assigned** *to the night watch.*

▶ **appoint** to select or designate someone for an office, position, or duty: *I have been* **appointed** *to organize the office party.*

▶ **delegate** to authorize another person to be one's representative; to entrust a task to someone else: *A good manager knows how to* **delegate** *authority to other employees.*

▶ **name** to nominate or appoint someone to a specific office or position: *He was* **named** *employee of the month.*

▶ **nominate** to propose someone as a candidate for an office, responsibility, or honor: *She was* **nominated** *for the promotion by her boss.*

assignment *noun* something assigned, especially a job or task: *see* **chore**

assist *verb* to help someone do or accomplish something: *see* **help**

assistance *noun* help or aid that contributes to another person's effort: *see* **relief**

---

assistant

noun a person who assists someone else, especially with routine tasks: *The manager asked her **assistant** to make the travel reservations.*

▸ **aide** a person who provides help in carrying out duties or assignments: *I work as a teacher's **aide**.*
▸ **helper** a person who helps or assists someone: *The elderly woman hired a **helper** to run errands for her.*

---

associate *noun* a person who regularly spends time with another: *see* **partner**

association *noun* a group of people joined together for a common purpose or interest: *see* **club**

assorted *adjective* consisting of a variety of usually related items: *see* **various**

---

assortment

noun a large collection of different kinds of things: *The gallery sells a wide **assortment** of paintings, sculptures, and posters.*

▸ **array** an orderly arrangement of items: *The table held an **array** of wonderful foods.*
▸ **collection** a group of things brought or kept together for study or enjoyment: *I added a piece of rose quartz to my rock **collection**.*
▸ **medley** a variety or series of selected items: *We danced to a **medley** of waltzes.*
▸ **mixture** a combination of different ingredients, things, or kinds: *This fabric is a **mixture** of cotton and linen.*
▸ **variety** a number of different kinds of things within the same group or category: *This shirt comes in a **variety** of colors.*

assume *verb* to take something for granted without knowing for sure: *see* **guess**

assured *adjective* feeling confident, especially as a result of experience: *see* **confident**

astonish *verb* to overwhelm someone with surprise or disbelief: *see* **surprise**

astound *verb* to greatly astonish someone, as at something previously unimaginable: *see* **surprise**

asylum *noun* a place of safety or refuge: *see* **refuge**

at *preposition* in or near the location of something: *see* **by**

athletic *adjective* having a strong, muscular body: *see* **healthy**

at last *adverb* after a long or difficult time: *see* **eventually**

---

atmosphere

noun a general feeling or mood, often associated with a particular place: *There is a festive **atmosphere** in New Orleans during Mardi Gras.*

▸ **aura** a distinctive but intangible quality that seems to surround a person or thing: *The rock star had an **aura** of success around her.*
▸ **climate** a general condition or set of attitudes in human affairs: *The political **climate** is tense in that part of the world.*
▸ **environment** all of the surroundings and conditions that affect the growth of something: *The library is an excellent **environment** for studying.*
▸ **setting** the surrounding area, especially a spot where something takes place: *The garden was a beautiful **setting** for the wedding.*

at once *adverb* at this very moment: *see* **immediately**

attach *verb* to join or fix something to something else: *see* **fasten**

---

attack

verb to set upon someone or something in an attempt to capture, harm, or defeat it: *The cat **attacked** my wiggling toes.*

▸ **assault** to attack someone with force or violence: *The mugger **assaulted** the woman and stole her purse.*

▸ **invade** to enter a place in great numbers for purposes of attacking or raiding: *The ants invaded the kitchen and went straight for the sugar bowl.*

▸ **raid** to carry out a sudden attack by a small armed force: *They raided the enemy camp in order to rescue the prisoners.*

▸ **strike** to make a military attack against an enemy: *The forces struck the invaders simultaneously by land and sea.*

attain *verb* to gain something, especially by effort or persistence: *see* **achieve**

attempt *verb* to try to do something, especially something difficult: *see* **try**

attend *verb* to take care of someone's needs: *see* **protect**

attention

noun the act of noticing or giving careful thought to something or someone: *We gave the teacher our full attention.*

▸ **consideration** careful thought for the purpose of making a judgment or forming an opinion: *After much consideration I have decided to invest in this stock.*

▸ **focus** a concentration or emphasis: *The focus of the seminar was on developing better communications skills.*

▸ **notice** respectful or critical attention; close observation: *I took notice of the dark clouds and put on a raincoat.*

▸ **regard** careful thought or attention: *She gives little regard to what others think about her.*

attentive *adjective* considerate and polite: *see* **kind**[1]

attire *noun* (formal) clothing, costume, or apparel: *see* **clothing**

attitude *noun* a state of mind, especially one that a person has some control over: *see* **feeling**

attract *verb* to cause someone to draw near or take notice: *see* **interest**

attraction

noun the power to cause something or someone to draw near: *Most tourists feel a strong attraction to visit the Eiffel Tower when they are in Paris.*

▸ **allure** a strong attraction or fascination that leads one on: *The allure of sunken treasure has caused many people to explore the ocean.*

▸ **appeal** the power of attracting or of arousing interest: *The idea of being an exchange student holds a lot of appeal for me.*

▸ **fascination** the condition of having one's whole interest captured and held: *She watched in fascination as the bee gathered pollen from the sunflower.*

▸ **temptation** a strong appeal exerted by something usually regarded as unwise or wrong: *I resisted the temptation of eating a second piece of cake.*

attractive *adjective* pleasing to the eye or mind: *see* **beautiful**

auction *verb* to sell something to the highest bidder: *see* **sell**

audition *noun* a trial performance designed to measure artistic skill: *see* **test**

auditorium *noun* a large room or building used for public meetings or performances: *see* **theater**

aura *noun* a distinctive but intangible quality that seems to surround a person or thing: *see* **atmosphere**

authentic *adjective* not counterfeit or copied: *see* **real** [1]

author *noun* the creator of an original literary work, such as a novel, poem, or essay: *see* **writer**

author *verb* to write something such as a book or play, especially for publication: *see* **write**

authoritarian *adjective* favoring absolute obedience to authority: *see* **strict**

authority *noun* an accepted source of expert information: *see* **expert**

authorize

verb to officially approve or give permission for something: *My boss has **authorized** me to buy all the office supplies.*

▸ **allow** to let someone do something; to let something happen: *She **allows** her dog to sleep on the couch.*

▸ **approve** to give one's official permission for something; to treat someone or something with favor: *My request for a work permit has been **approved**.*

▸ **bless** to call for divine or official favor upon something or someone: *The minister **blessed** the congregation.*

▸ **consent** to agree to someone's wish or request: *Her parents **consented** to let her pierce her navel.*

▸ **let** to grant permission to someone or for something: *I **let** my brother borrow my car.*

▸ **permit** to let someone do something; to allow: ***Permit** me to introduce myself.*

▸ **sanction** to give official approval to something: *The Constitution **sanctions** religious freedom.*

authorized *adjective* approved by an authority: *see* **legal**

autocrat *noun* a person with unlimited power or authority: *see* **tyrant**

autograph *verb* to write one's signature in or on something: *see* **write**

automobile *noun* a car: *see* **car**

autonomy *noun* the condition of not being controlled by others: *see* **freedom**

avenue *noun* a wide street or thoroughfare: *see* **road**

average *adjective* being of a typical kind or a usual level or degree: *see* **normal**

avoid

verb to keep away from something or someone: *I **avoid** that restaurant on the weekends because it is too busy.*

▸ **boycott** to refuse, as part of an organized protest, to buy from or deal with a store, company, person, or nation: *We're boycotting that company because they abuse child labor laws.*

▸ **bypass** to go around something so as to avoid it: *I took another route to **bypass** all the road construction.*

▸ **dodge** to avoid something by moving quickly out of the way: *The referee **dodged** the ball.*

▸ **duck** to lower the head and body quickly so as to get out of something's way: *The tall man **ducked** as he stepped through the doorway.*

▸ **refrain** (formal) to hold oneself back from doing or saying something: *Please **refrain** from applauding in between movements of the symphony.*

▸ **shun** to make every effort to avoid something unpleasant: *The writer **shuns** publicity.*

▸ **sidestep** to avoid an issue or responsibility: *The politician **sidestepped** the reporter's question.*

await *verb* to wait for something: *see* **expect**

awake *adjective* not sleeping: *see* **alert**

award

noun something that is given to someone because of outstanding performance or quality: *He was given a special **award** for his many contributions to the city.*

▸ **medal** a flat piece of metal with a special design that is given as an award: *The soldier was given a **medal** for courage in battle.*

▸ **prize** something offered or won as an award in a competition or contest: *I won the **prize** for Best Costume at the Halloween party.*

▸ **reward** something valuable, especially money offered or given for a special service: *The people who lost their cat are offering a 50-dollar **reward** to anyone who finds it.*

▸ **trophy** a prize or memento received as a symbol of victory, especially in sports: *The tennis player kissed the silver **trophy** that she had just won.*

aware *adjective* informed or mindful of something: *see* **alert**

away *adjective*   not at this place: *see* **absent**

awesome

adjective inspiring a feeling of wonder, fear, and respect: *The cowboy said that riding a bull is an **awesome** experience.*

- ▸ **amazing**   causing great surprise and astonishment: *It was **amazing** to run into my old friend after all these years.*
- ▸ **impressive**   making a strong or vivid impression; commanding attention: *The President gave an **impressive** State of the Union speech.*
- ▸ **miraculous**   so astounding as to suggest a miracle; phenomenal: *His doctors said that his cancer was terminal, but he made a **miraculous** recovery.*
- ▸ **sensational**   arousing great interest or excitement, especially by being extraordinary or shocking: *The football team made a **sensational** comeback in the last quarter and won the game.*
- ▸ **spectacular**   impressive and exciting: *The fireworks over the bay were **spectacular**.*

awful *adjective*   very bad or unpleasant: *see* **terrible**

awkward

adjective not graceful; physically or socially clumsy: *I felt **awkward** the first time I had to use crutches.*

- ▸ **clumsy**   lacking grace or skill in motion or action: *It was **clumsy** of me to trip on the step.*
- ▸ **graceless**   lacking grace, elegance, or charm: *Seals are **graceless** on land, but they are excellent swimmers.*
- ▸ **inept**   lacking skill or competence: *She is **inept** at telling a joke.*
- ▸ **uncoordinated**   having muscles not able to perform complicated movements or tasks: *The puppy was **uncoordinated** at first, but soon it was running up the stairs without tripping.*

ANTONYM **graceful**   showing grace, especially when moving

babble *verb* to talk without pausing about foolish or idle matters: *see* **talk**

baby *noun* a very young child: *see* **child**

baby *verb* to treat someone like a baby; coddle: *see* **indulge**

back *verb* to give approval or support to someone or something: *see* **sponsor**

background *noun* a person's past experience, training, and education: *see* **knowledge**

backpack *noun* a canvas, nylon, or leather bag that is worn on the back to carry items such as books or camping supplies: *see* **bag**

bad

adjective [1] being below an acceptable standard: *My grades have been **bad** this semester.*

- ▸ **defective** having a defect or flaw: *The **defective** chair broke when she sat on it.*
- ▸ **faulty** not in working order; imperfect: *I returned the purse because it had a **faulty** clasp.*
- ▸ **flawed** containing an imperfection or defect: *This **flawed** flowerpot was sold for half price.*
- ▸ **imperfect** flawed, but often still usable; not perfect: *The first sweater I knit was **imperfect**.*
- ▸ **inferior** low in quality or value: *Some people think that generic brands are **inferior** to name brands.*
- ▸ **unsatisfactory** not satisfactory; inadequate: *They thought the service at the restaurant was **unsatisfactory**.*

ANTONYM **good** having positive or desirable qualities

bad

adjective [2] misbehaved; causing trouble: *The teacher had the students stay after school because they had all been **bad**.*

- ▸ **disobedient** refusing to obey: *The **disobedient** child refused to put away his toys.*
- ▸ **mischievous** showing a tendency to play pranks or cause trouble: *It was **mischievous** of you to put a frog in her bed.*
- ▸ **naughty** behaving in a disobedient or mischievous way: *The **naughty** child was sent to her room for drawing on the wall.*
- ▸ **unruly** difficult or impossible to discipline or control: *The **unruly** children were running around the restaurant.*

badger *verb* to trouble someone with many questions: *see* **nag**

bad luck *noun* the chance happening of disagreeable or unpleasant events: *see* **misfortune**

baffle *verb* to frustrate and confuse someone through an inability to understand: *see* **confuse**

bag

noun a container made of flexible material such as paper, cloth, or plastic: *The clerk put my groceries into a plastic **bag**.*

- ▸ **backpack** a canvas, nylon, or leather bag that is worn on the back to carry items such as books or camping supplies: *I put my **backpack** under my chair during the class.*
- ▸ **duffle bag** a large canvas bag that is shaped like a tube and is used to carry personal belongings: *The hockey player put his **duffle bag** in the locker during practice.*
- ▸ **handbag** a woman's purse, often having a handle or carrying strap: *I always carry a pen and a small notebook in my **handbag**.*
- ▸ **knapsack** a backpack, especially one worn by soldiers or hikers: *All the hikers carried **knapsacks** with their lunches in it.*
- ▸ **luggage** bags, such as suitcases and trunks, that a person takes on a trip: *The porter helped me load my **luggage** onto the train.*

▶ **pouch** a bag, often closing with a drawstring, that is used for holding or carrying various things: *The diamonds were stored in a velvet* **pouch**.

▶ **purse** a woman's bag, held in the hand or by a strap or handle, that is used for carrying personal items: *She bought a beaded* **purse** *to wear with her evening gown.*

▶ **sack** a large bag of strong, coarse material used for holding objects in bulk: *He bought a* **sack** *of grain at the feed store.*

▶ **suitcase** a sturdy, often rectangular piece of luggage: *I packed my* **suitcase** *with everything I would need for the cruise.*

baggy *adjective* fitting or hanging loosely: *see* **loose**

bait *verb* to try to provoke someone with repeated insults: *see* **tease**

bake *verb* to cook food in an oven with dry heat: *see* **cook**

balance

noun something left over; a remainder: *When I got out of class, I spent the* **balance** *of the afternoon at the library.*

▶ **leftover** the amount that remains unused or uneaten: *She put the* **leftovers** *in the refrigerator.*

▶ **remainder** the remaining part; the rest: *I did the first part of my homework in study hall and finished the* **remainder** *after dinner.*

▶ **residue** something that remains after a part is used or removed: *The honey left a sticky* **residue** *on the countertop.*

▶ **rest** the part that has not yet been used, consumed, selected, or experienced: *The first part of the movie was boring, but I liked the* **rest**.

bald *adjective* lacking a natural or usual covering, such as hair on the top of the head: *see* **naked**

ball *noun* a formal social dance: *see* **party**

ballad *noun* a poem or song that tells a story, usually about love: *see* **song**

ban *verb* to prohibit something by law: *see* **forbid**

band *noun* a group of people or animals acting together: *see* **group**

bang

noun a loud, sharp, sudden noise: *The door shut with a* **bang**.

▶ **blast** a loud, sudden sound, especially one produced by forced air: *The* **blast** *of the fog horn warned the ship that it was close to land.*

▶ **boom** a deep, hollow sound, as from an explosion: *I could hear the distant* **boom** *of the thunder.*

▶ **explosion** the act of bursting apart suddenly with great force and noise: *There was an* **explosion** *in the garage when the can of gasoline caught fire.*

▶ **thud** a dull, heavy sound: *The book made a* **thud** *when it hit the floor.*

banish *verb* to force someone to leave a country or place by official decree: *see* **throw out**

bank *noun* the sloping ground along the edge of a river or stream: *see* **beach**

bankrupt *adjective* legally declared unable to pay personal or company debts: *see* **poor**

banquet *noun* a large, formal meal for many people: *see* **feast**

baptize *verb* to give a name to a person who is being baptized: *see* **call [1]**

bar *verb* to keep someone from doing something: *see* **block**

bar *verb* to keep someone out or away: *see* **exclude**

bar *noun* a place with a counter at which alcoholic drinks and sometimes food are served: *see* **tavern**

barbeque *noun* a social gathering at which food is cooked over a open fire or hot coals: *see* **feast**

bare *adjective* lacking the usual furnishings, supplies, or decorations: *see* **empty**

bare *adjective* without clothing or covering: *see* **naked**

barely *adverb* by very little: *see* **hardly**

bargain *noun* an agreement between two parties, often involving payment or trade: *see* **agreement**

bargain *noun* something bought or sold at a price that is good for the buyer: *see* **sale**

bargain *verb* to discuss the terms of an agreement, especially of a price to be paid: *see* **sell**

bark

noun the short, gruff sound made by a dog and certain other animals: *The little dog had a high-pitched bark.*

- ▸ **growl** a low, throaty, menacing sound made by an animal: *The wolf's growl was a warning.*
- ▸ **howl** a long, loud, mournful sound made by certain animals: *I heard the howl of the coyotes last night.*
- ▸ **roar** a loud, deep, threatening sound made by a wild animal: *The roar of the lion frightened the antelope.*
- ▸ **snarl** a vicious growl that is made while baring the teeth: *The sudden snarl of the big dog frightened me.*
- ▸ **squeak** a thin, high-pitched cry or sound: *I thought I heard the squeak of a mouse.*
- ▸ **squeal** a loud, shrill cry or sound: *My little brother let out a squeal when I started tickling him.*
- ▸ **yelp** a short, sharp bark or cry: *The puppy gave a yelp when I stepped on its tail.*

barrel

noun a large container with round, flat ends of equal size: *It used to be a popular stunt to ride in a barrel over Niagara Falls.*

- ▸ **cask** a barrel for holding liquids: *Wines are traditionally aged in oak casks.*
- ▸ **drum** a large metal container having a cylindrical or drum-like shape: *The dock workers used a crane to unload the drums of oil.*
- ▸ **keg** a small wooden or metal barrel: *Carpenters used to buy nails by the keg.*

barren *adjective* lacking plants or crops: *see* **empty**

barricade *noun* a quickly built structure set up to block passage or keep back attackers: *see* **obstacle**

barrier *noun* something that blocks movement or passage: *see* **obstacle**

barter *verb* to trade goods or services without using money: *see* **sell**

base *noun* the bottom part on which something rests: *see* **bottom**

base *noun* a supply center for a large force of military personnel: *see* **fort**

bashful *adjective* timid and uncomfortable with other people: *see* **shy**

basic

adjective serving as a starting point or basis: *I can play some basic chords on the guitar.*

- ▸ **elemental** being a primary or essential part of something: *One of the elemental factors in learning to play the piano well is lots of practice.*
- ▸ **elementary** being the simplest or most basic aspect of something: *Addition and subtraction are elementary functions of math.*
- ▸ **fundamental** forming a foundation; essential for further development: *Reading and writing are fundamental skills.*
- ▸ **key** being the most important element: *Flour is the key ingredient in bread.*

basis

noun the part or element on which something rests or depends: *What is the basis for your accusation?*

- ▸ **cause** someone or something that produces a certain feeling, action, or decision: *The cause of his itchy skin was poison ivy.*
- ▸ **foundation** a basis for the development or support of something: *The work of Isaac Newton forms the foundation of early physics.*
- ▸ **origin** the source or beginning of something: *The origin of the universe is a subject of debate among physicists.*

► **root** the point of origin or the cause of something: *The **root** of their problem is a lack of communication.*

► **source** a place or thing from which something comes; a point of origin: *I have found a great **source** for inexpensive furniture.*

bat *verb* to hit something with or as if with a bat: *see* **hit**

bathe *verb* to take a bath or give someone else a bath: *see* **groom**

battle *noun* an encounter between opposing forces: *see* **war**

bawl *verb* to cry or sob loudly: *see* **cry**

bay *noun* a part of the sea that extends into the land: *see* **harbor**

beach

noun the sandy or pebbly shore of a sea or lake: *The children built sand castles at the **beach**.*

► **bank** the sloping ground along the edge of a river or stream: *The fisherman stood on the **bank** of the river.*

► **coast** the edge of the land next to or near the sea: *It is often foggy along the **coast**.*

► **shore** the land along the edge of a body of water: *We walked along the **shore** and looked for shells.*

bead *noun* a small, round object, such as a drop of moisture: *see* **drop**

beaker *noun* a container with a straight side and a lip for pouring, used especially in laboratories: *see* **bottle**

beam *verb* to smile with joy or delight: *see* **smile**

bear *verb* to carry something of value or use: *see* **carry**

bear *verb* to endure something unpleasant or difficult: *see* **cope**

beast *noun* a large, four-footed animal: *see* **animal**

beat *verb* to defeat or overcome an opponent: *see* **defeat**

beat *verb* to stir something rapidly so as to mix it: *see* **mix**

beautiful

adjective very pleasing to the senses or the mind: *I think roses are **beautiful** flowers.*

► **attractive** pleasing to the eye or mind; appealing: *You look very **attractive** in that dress.*

► **cute** very pretty or charming: *That baby is so **cute**!*

► **good-looking** having a pleasing appearance; attractive: *She is a **good-looking** woman.*

► **gorgeous** extremely beautiful or magnificent: *There are many **gorgeous** pieces of art in the museum.*

► **handsome** pleasing and dignified in form and appearance: *He is a **handsome** man.*

► **lovely** having pleasing or attractive qualities of character or appearance: *The sunset was **lovely** tonight.*

► **pretty** pleasing, attractive, or appealing to the eye or ear: *That hairstyle looks very **pretty** on you.*

ANTONYM **ugly** not pleasing to look at

beautify *verb* to make something beautiful: *see* **decorate**

because

conjunction for the reason that: *I went to the dentist **because** I had a toothache.*

► **as** seeing that; since: *I will return your library book **as** I have one of my own to take back.*

► **due to** because of: *The outdoor concert was canceled **due to** rain.*

► **for** being that; considering: *I stopped by to see my friend **for** I knew she was not feeling well.*

► **since** as a result of the fact that: *I overslept **since** I forgot to set my alarm clock.*

beckon *verb* to signal for someone to come, as with a movement of the head or hand: *see* **signal**

bed-and-breakfast *noun* a private residence that offers overnight lodging and breakfast: *see* **hotel**

bedridden *adjective* confined to bed because of sickness or weakness: *see* **sick**

bedspread *noun* a decorative covering for a bed: *see* **cover**

before

adverb earlier in time: *I wish you had told me about this before.*

▸ **ahead** in advance: *He called ahead and made reservations.*

▸ **already** by this time: *I've already made plans for the weekend.*

▸ **earlier** near the beginning of a period of time or course of events: *If you had called earlier I could have gone with you.*

▸ **formerly** at an earlier time; once: *The lecturer was formerly an engineer at NASA.*

▸ **previously** existing or occurring before the present time: *I previously lived in the city, but now I live in the country.*

ANTONYM **after** at a later time

beg

verb to ask someone earnestly, humbly, or urgently for something: *My brother begged our parents to let him go to the party.*

▸ **appeal** to make a sincere or earnest request of someone: *I appealed to my professor to let me hand in my paper a day late.*

▸ **beseech** (formal) to ask someone earnestly for something: *I beseech you to reconsider your decision.*

▸ **entreat** (formal) to urge someone seriously to do something: *The teacher entreated her students to hand in their homework on time.*

▸ **implore** to ask someone urgently or anxiously for something; to beg: *The students implored the teacher to postpone the exam.*

▸ **plead** to make an urgent or insistent appeal to someone: *My sister pleaded with me to let her wear my new earrings.*

beggar

noun a person who begs, especially as a means of living: *The beggar stood on the corner and held out a cup for people to put money into.*

▸ **bum** a person who avoids work: *My sister told me to stop being a bum and do my chores.*

▸ **derelict** a homeless person who is unable to live in society, especially due to mental illness or alcohol abuse: *The derelict got a hot meal at the mission.*

▸ **drifter** a person who moves aimlessly from place to place or from job to job: *Louis L'Amour was a drifter for many years before becoming a famous novelist.*

▸ **homeless person** a person who has no permanent address or home: *The homeless person went to a shelter to get a bed for the night.*

▸ **loafer** a person who spends time aimlessly or idly: *He could usually be found with the group of loafers who hung out in the park after school.*

▸ **tramp** a person who travels and works from place to place: *During the Great Depression, there were many tramps who caught rides in railroad cars.*

▸ **vagrant** a person with no permanent home or way of earning money: *The vagrant slept in the alley.*

begin

verb to take the first step in doing something: *I plan to begin my homework after dinner.*

▸ **activate** to set something in motion: *This code activates the alarm system.*

▸ **commence** (formal) to perform the first part of an action: *Our family commences dinner by saying a prayer.*

▸ **establish** to settle something or someone securely in a position or condition: *It took several years for the business to establish itself in this town.*

▸ **initiate** to take a first step toward something; to begin something: *I have initiated the process of applying for a student loan.*

▸ **introduce** to bring something new into use or practice: *Our office introduced a new dress code.*

▸ **launch** to set a process or event in motion: *Clothing designers* **launch** *new fashion trends in the fall and the spring.*

▸ **start** to begin an action or movement; to set something in operation: *We have to* **start** *making dinner soon.*

beginner

noun a person who is just starting to learn or do something: *When I was a* **beginner** *in swimming, I often got water up my nose.*

▸ **amateur** a person who engages in an art, science, or sport for enjoyment rather than for money: *The members of our choir sing very well for* **amateurs.**

▸ **greenhorn** an inexperienced person, especially one who is easily fooled: *My grandmother is a* **greenhorn** *when it comes to computers.*

▸ **novice** a person who is new to a field or activity: *This acting class is for* **novices.**

beginning

noun the time or point when something begins or is begun: *I like to buy new clothes at the* **beginning** *of the school year.*

▸ **birth** a beginning or origin, as of an idea or process: *The Declaration of Independence marks the* **birth** *of the United States.*

▸ **dawn** the first appearance of something: *The* **dawn** *of the information age changed the way many people work.*

▸ **genesis** (formal) the origin or creation of something: *The* **genesis** *of the inventor's idea was a discovery made while observing how metals behave when heated.*

▸ **onset** a beginning; a start: *When did you notice the* **onset** *of the symptoms?*

beguile *verb* to deceive someone by using charm: *see* **deceive**

behave

verb to act or function in a certain way: *My cat was* **behaving** *strangely, so I took him to the vet.*

▸ **act** to serve or function as something: *I have a radio that also* **acts** *as an alarm clock.*

behavior

noun the way in which someone or something acts or behaves: *Talking during a movie is considered rude* **behavior.**

▸ **conduct** the way a person acts, especially with regard to rules or expectations: *The students'* **conduct** *was excellent during the long assembly.*

▸ **etiquette** the rules of proper behavior: *There are many books on the proper* **etiquette** *for weddings.*

▸ **manners** socially proper behavior: *He has very nice* **manners** *at the dinner table.*

behind *preposition* at the back or in the rear of something: *see* **after**

being *noun* someone or something that exists: *see* **human being**

belated *adjective* being, coming, or happening late: *see* **late**

belfry *noun* a tower in which a bell or bells are hung: *see* **tower**

belief *noun* something accepted as true: *see* **opinion**

believe *verb* to accept the truthfulness of something: *see* **think**

believe in *verb* to have faith or confidence in someone or something even without sure proof: *see* **trust**

believer *noun* one who has faith, confidence, or trust in something or someone: *see* **follower**

belittle *verb* to speak of someone or something as small or unimportant: *see* **scorn**

belligerent *adjective* eager to fight: *see* **aggressive**

bellow *verb* to shout in a deep voice: *see* **shout**

belly *noun*   the front part of the body below the chest: *see* **stomach**

belongings *noun*   personal items that one owns: *see* **property**

beloved *adjective*   very much loved: *see* **dear**

below *preposition*   in or to a lower place: *see* **under**

bend *verb*   to incline the body: *see* **bow**

bend *noun*   a turn, curve, or bent part: *see* **curve**

bender *noun* (slang)   a drinking spree: *see* **spree**

beneath *preposition*   lower than something else: *see* **under**

beneficial *adjective*   producing or promoting a favorable result: *see* **useful**

benefit *noun*   something that is of help: *see* **privilege**

beseech *verb* (formal)   to ask someone earnestly for something: *see* **beg**

beside *preposition*   next to or at the side of something: *see* **by**

besides *adverb*   in addition: *see* **also**

best

adjective   surpassing all others in excellence, quality, or achievement: *I wore my **best** dress to the concert.*

- ► **favorite**   being a person or thing treated with special regard and preferred above all others: *Apple pie is my **favorite** dessert.*
- ► **finest**   of the highest possible quality, skill, or appearance: *This shop sells only the **finest** chocolates.*
- ► **greatest**   the most remarkable or outstanding: *Winning the Super Bowl is the **greatest** achievement for a professional football team.*
- ► **supreme**   greatest in power, authority, or rank: *My sister considers herself the **supreme** authority on fashion.*

bestow *verb*   to give or present something, especially as a gift or honor: *see* **give**

bet *verb*   to make an agreement that one will forfeit something if one's prediction is incorrect: *see* **gamble**

betray *verb*   to be disloyal to someone or something: *see* **deceive**

better

adjective   greater in excellence or higher in quality than another of the same kind: *I think that your blue shirt is the **better** choice to wear to the party.*

- ► **exceptional**   well above average: *The cherry harvest was **exceptional** this year.*
- ► **finer**   of superior quality, skill, or appearance: *This brand of coffee is **finer** quality than any other brand.*
- ► **preferable**   more desirable than others; preferred: *I think natural light is **preferable** to artificial light.*
- ► **superior**   higher in quality or nature than another: *The company's success is due to their **superior** product.*

better

verb   to make something better in quality or nature: *Regularly changing the oil in your car **betters** its performance.*

- ► **enhance**   to make something greater, as in value, beauty, or reputation: *I think that a diffrent frame would **enhance** this painting.*
- ► **improve**   to increase the quality, value, or performance of something: *I added some salt to **improve** the taste of the soup.*
- ► **reform**   to improve something by the correction of error or the removal of defects: *Jane Addams was a key figure in **reforming** America's social problems in the late 19th century.*

bewilder *verb*   to completely confuse someone, especially with conflicting statements, situations, or objects: *see* **confuse**

beyond *preposition*   on the far side of something: *see* **after**

biased *adjective*   showing a preference for or hostile feeling against a person or thing: *see* **unfair**

big

adjective   of great size or number: *Elephants are **big** animals.*

- **enormous**   very large in size, number, or degree: *An Olympic-size swimming pool holds an **enormous** amount of water.*
- **gigantic**   extremely large in size, strength, or power: *A tsunami is a **gigantic** ocean wave caused by an earthquake.*
- **great**   impressively large: *A **great** crowd filled the auditorium for the rock concert.*
- **huge**   extremely or impressively large: *I have a **huge** amount of homework to do.*
- **immense**   of great or immeasurable size, extent, or degree: *I have **immense** faith in her ability to finish the project on time.*
- **jumbo**   extra large; oversized: *We were so hungry we ordered a **jumbo** pizza.*
- **large**   greater than average in size, amount, or degree: *This restaurant serves very **large** portions.*
- **massive**   unusually or impressively large: *The doctor prescribed **massive** doses of antibiotics to stop the infection.*
- **tremendous**   extremely large in amount, extent, or degree: *The engines on the space shuttle need **tremendous** power in order to escape the earth's gravity.*

ANTONYM **small**   little in size, amount, or extent

bill

noun   a statement of charges for goods supplied or work performed: *The gas company sends me a **bill** every month.*

- **check**   a statement showing the amount due, as at a restaurant: *The waitress put our **check** on the table.*
- **invoice**   a bill that lists all goods delivered or services performed: *The clerk checked the shipment against the **invoice** to make sure that everything was there.*
- **statement**   a periodic report sent to a debtor or a bank depositor: *My credit card company sends me a **statement** of my account every month.*
- **tab**   (informal)   a bill or check, especially for a meal in a restaurant: *He picked up the **tab** for everyone's lunch.*

bin   *noun*   an enclosed space for storing food, grain, coal, or other dry substances: *see* **container**

bind   *verb*   to fasten something together by or as if by tying: *see* **join**

binge   *noun*   a period of unrestrained activity, as of drinking, eating, or shopping: *see* **spree**

birth   *noun*   a beginning or origin, as of an idea or process: *see* **beginning**

bit   *noun*   a tiny piece: *see* **scrap**

bite

verb   to cut, grip, or tear something with the teeth: *Guard dogs are trained to **bite** on command.*

- **chew**   to bite and grind something with the teeth: *It is important to **chew** your food thoroughly before you swallow.*
- **chomp**   to chew or bite on something noisily: *The horse **chomped** on the apple I gave her.*
- **gnaw**   to bite, chew, or wear something down with the teeth: *The dog **gnawed** on his bone.*
- **nip**   to seize and pinch something sharply with the teeth: *The goat **nipped** at the farmer's pants.*

bitter   *adjective*   full of deep resentment or angry disappointment: *see* **resentful**

bitter   *adjective*   having a sharply unpleasant taste: *see* **tasty**

bitterness   *noun*   deep resentment or angry disappointment: *see* **resentment**

black   *adjective*   having no light: *see* **dark**

blame

noun   responsibility for a fault or error: *The secretary took the **blame** for the missing fax.*

- **fault**   responsibility for a mistake or offense: *It's my **fault** that we arrived late.*
- **guilt**   the fact of having done wrong: *The prosecutor was unable to prove the suspect's **guilt** in the crime.*

blame

verb   to hold a person or thing responsible or at fault for something: *Don't* **blame** *the computer for your mistake.*

- ▸ **accuse**   to make a declaration charging someone with wrongdoing: *The city* **accused** *the factory of polluting the river.*
- ▸ **charge**   to make a formal claim of wrongdoing against someone: *The suspect was* **charged** *with robbery.*
- ▸ **condemn**   to express a strong feeling or moral opinion against someone or something: *My family* **condemns** *racism.*
- ▸ **criticize**   to judge someone or something, especially negatively: *My parents are always* **criticizing** *my choice of clothing.*
- ▸ **scold**   to criticize someone harshly or angrily; to express severe disapproval of someone: *My boss* **scolded** *me because I was late three days in a row.*

blank *adjective*   free of marks or writing: *see* **empty**

blanket *noun*   a covering used to keep a person warm: *see* **cover**

blaring *adjective*   loud and harsh in sound: *see* **loud**

blast *noun*   a loud, sudden sound, especially one produced by forced air: *see* **bang**

blaze *verb*   to burn or shine brightly: *see* **burn**

blazing *adjective*   (informal) very hot or bright: *see* **hot**

bleak *adjective*   ▷ barren and desolate ▷ not hopeful or promising: *see* **gloomy**

blemish *noun*   a mark on something that makes it less than perfect: *see* **stain**

blend *verb*   to combine different materials thoroughly or completely: *see* **mix**

bless *verb*   to call for divine or official favor upon something or someone: *see* **approve**

blind *noun*   something that shuts out light: *see* **curtain**

blind *adjective*   unable or unwilling to notice or understand: *see* **ignorant**

bliss *noun*   very great happiness or joy: *see* **happiness**

blizzard *noun*   a very long, heavy snowstorm with strong winds: *see* **storm**

block

verb   to stop the movement or action of someone or something: *This password* **blocks** *other people from opening my computer files.*

- ▸ **bar**   to keep someone from doing something: *The police officers* **barred** *people from entering the crime scene.*
- ▸ **clog**   to stop or slow the movement of something through a passage: *Something has* **clogged** *the sink drain.*
- ▸ **dam**   to hold something back: *Dead leaves* **dammed** *the flow of water in the rain gutter.*
- ▸ **impede**   to make it difficult for something to move or advance: *Her negative attitude has* **impeded** *her progress in the company.*
- ▸ **obstruct**   to make it difficult to pass through something: *The trail was* **obstructed** *by the fallen tree.*

blockade *noun*   the closing of an area, such as a city or harbor, so as to prevent the movement of people and supplies: *see* **obstacle**

blockhead *noun*   a person who is considered very stupid: *see* **fool**

blood *noun*   descent from a common ancestor: *see* **family**

bloom *verb*   to grow or flourish: *see* **thrive**

blotch *noun*   a large spot or stain, as of ink: *see* **stain**

blow up *verb*   to destroy something with explosives: *see* **explode**

blueprint *noun*   ▷ a photographic copy of architectural plans appearing as white lines on a blue background ▷ a carefully worked-out plan: *see* **chart**

bluff *noun*   a misleading or deceiving statement or action: *see* **lie**

blunder *noun*   a mistake caused by ignorance or confusion: *see* **mistake**

blunt

adjective   direct and frank in manner; spoken honestly without regard for another person's feelings: *My sister always gives me a blunt answer when I ask her how I look.*

- ► **curt**   rudely brief in speech and manner: *The salesman became curt once he learned that we weren't going to buy a car that day.*
- ► **gruff**   rough or stern in manner or voice: *The substitute teacher was gruff with the rowdy students.*
- ► **terse**   brief and to the point; concise: *He was so busy that all his answers were terse.*

board *noun*   an organized body of administrators or investigators: *see* **committee**

board *noun*   a piece of lumber that has more length and width than thickness: *see* **wood**

boarding house *noun*   a private home that provides meals and lodging for long-term paying guests: *see* **hotel**

boast *verb*   to praise oneself, one's belongings, or one's actions in an excessive manner: *see* **brag**

body

noun   the whole physical structure of a living thing: *Physiology is the study of the systems of the body and how they work.*

- ► **corpse**   a dead body, especially that of a human: *The mortician prepared the corpse for the funeral.*
- ► **figure**   the shape or form of a human body: *Exercise has really improved your figure.*
- ► **frame**   the structure of a human or animal body: *He has the tall, lanky frame of a basketball player.*
- ► **physique**   the body considered in terms of its proportions, muscle development, and appearance: *The artist chose her model based on his physique.*
- ► **skeleton**   the framework of bones that supports the body and protects the inner organs: *Archaeologists have found the fossilized skeletons of many dinosaurs.*

bog *noun*   soft, undrained, water-soaked ground: *see* **swamp**

bogus *adjective*   made up or invented in order to deceive: *see* **fake**

bold *adjective*   having or showing no fear: *see* **brave**

boldness *noun*   lack of fear or caution: *see* **courage**

bolt *verb*   to fasten or lock something with a bolt: *see* **close**

bonnet *noun*   a hat tied with ribbons under the chin and often framing the face: *see* **hat**

book

noun   a set of printed, written, or blank pages fastened together along one edge and enclosed between covers: *I bought a book about gardening.*

- ► **handbook**   a concise manual or reference book, providing specific information or instruction about a subject or place: *He read the handbook that came with his computer.*
- ► **notebook**   a book of blank, often lined pages used for writing notes: *I copied the week's vocabulary words into my notebook.*
- ► **reference book**   a book, such as a dictionary or thesaurus, containing authoritative information: *Translators need good reference books to help them find the exact word in another language.*
- ► **textbook**   a book used for the study of a subject; a book used in education: *I bought my textbooks at the campus bookstore.*
- ► **tome**   a large or scholarly book: *The researcher looked through several tomes to find the right information.*
- ► **volume**   one book in a related set or series of books: *I am reading the first volume of The Lord of the Rings trilogy.*
- ► **workbook**   a booklet containing problems and exercises that a student may do directly on the pages: *The teacher assigns homework out of the workbook twice a week.*

booking *noun*   a reservation, as for a room at a hotel: *see* **appointment**

booklet

noun a small book, usually having a binding: *I bought a **booklet** about flag etiquette.*

- ▸ **brochure** a small pamphlet or leaflet containing information about a product or service: *He picked up a few travel **brochures** to decide where he wanted to take his vacation.*
- ▸ **catalog** a book or pamphlet containing a list of items with a description and sometimes an illustration of each item: *I ordered a lamp from the home furnishings **catalog**.*
- ▸ **circular** a printed advertisement, notice, or other statement intended for public distribution: *In the newspaper was a **circular** with coupons for the local market.*
- ▸ **leaflet** a printed, usually folded sheet intended for free distribution: *We handed out **leaflets** advertising the upcoming fundraiser.*
- ▸ **pamphlet** a short essay or commentary, usually on a current topic, published without a binding: *This **pamphlet** is about the importance of sulfur in one's diet.*
- ▸ **tract** a leaflet or pamphlet containing a declaration, especially of a religious or political nature: *The man handed me a religious **tract** as I came out of the store.*

boom *noun* a deep, hollow sound, as from an explosion: *see* **bang**

booming *adjective* loud, deep, and hollow in sound: *see* **loud**

border *noun* an edge or the area immediately inside it: *see* **edge**

bore *verb* to make a hole by drilling or digging: *see* **dig**

boring

adjective lacking in interest, excitement, or variety: *I watched a long and **boring** movie in which nothing much really happened.*

- ▸ **drab** lacking color or charm; dull or commonplace in character: *The **drab** apartment looked better after we hung some pictures on the wall.*
- ▸ **dull** arousing no interest or curiosity; unexciting: *This is supposed to be an adventure story, but it's very **dull**.*

- ▸ **monotonous** all the same; lacking in variety: *The security guard found it **monotonous** to sit in front of the monitors all night long.*
- ▸ **tedious** long and tiring; boring: *Many people think that housework is **tedious**.*
- ▸ **tiresome** causing a person to be tired, bored, or annoyed: *The children's whining got **tiresome** after a while.*
- ▸ **uninteresting** not interesting; boring: *He thought that the poetry reading would be **uninteresting**, but he enjoyed it.*

ANTONYM **interesting** causing interest or attention

borrow *verb* to get something from someone else with the understanding that it will be returned: *see* **rent**

boss

noun a person who employs or directs workers: *My **boss** gave me a raise in pay.*

- ▸ **administrator** a person who works as a manager, especially in a business, school, or government agency: *I'm an assistant to the **administrator** of the adult education program.*
- ▸ **director** a person who supervises, controls, or manages something: *The **director** of the film received an award.*
- ▸ **employer** a person or business that hires and pays people to perform work: *The company I work for is a good **employer**.*
- ▸ **executive** a person who manages the affairs of an organization, especially a corporation or government: *The President is the chief **executive** of the United States government.*
- ▸ **head** a person who leads, rules, or is in charge of something: *He's the **head** of the sales department.*
- ▸ **manager** a person who directs the operations of a business or organization: *She spoke to the restaurant **manager** about the poorly cooked food.*
- ▸ **superintendent** a person who supervises or is in charge of something: *The **superintendent** asked the construction crew to work through the weekend.*

► **supervisor** a person who oversees or manages someone or something: *A teacher is the supervisor of a classroom.*

bother *verb* to disturb or irritate someone: *see* **annoy**

bottle

noun a container, usually made of glass or plastic, that has a narrow neck and a mouth that can be corked or capped: *I brought a bottle of wine to the party.*

► **beaker** a container with straight sides and a lip for pouring, used especially in laboratories: *The chemist mixed the two liquids in a beaker.*
► **canteen** a sturdy container for drinking water, usually carried on a strap or belt: *The hikers filled their canteens with water before setting out.*
► **flask** a bottle or other container with a narrow neck: *The waitress brought a flask of wine to our table.*
► **jar** a container with a wide mouth and no handles, usually made of glass or plastic: *She opened a jar of peanut butter.*
► **jug** a tall, rounded vessel with a handle and a narrow mouth: *He bought a gallon jug of apple cider at the store.*
► **pitcher** a container for liquids, usually having a handle and a lip or spout for pouring: *I put a pitcher of milk on the breakfast table.*
► **vase** an open container used for holding flowers: *The couple received a crystal vase as a wedding present.*
► **vessel** a hollow container or holder, such as a bowl, pitcher, or jar: *Archaeologists found the remains of ancient clay vessels used to store food and water.*

bottom

noun the deepest or lowest part of something: *I burned the bottom of the cookies.*

► **base** the bottom part on which something rests: *There is a historical plaque on the base of the statue.*
► **floor** the lowermost surface, especially of a room: *I sat on the floor at my friend's new apartment because she doesn't have any furniture yet.*
► **foot** the lowest part of something: *He stood at the foot of the stairs and waited for her to come down.*
► **foundation** the basis on which a thing stands, is founded, or is supported: *The foundation of the building was cracked because of the earthquake.*

ANTONYM **top** the highest or upper part, point, or surface

boulder *noun* a large, rounded rock: *see* **rock**

boulevard *noun* a broad street, often with trees and grass planted in the center or along the sides: *see* **road**

bounce *verb* to come back after hitting a surface: *see* **jump**

bound *verb* to leap forward or upward: *see* **jump**

boundary *noun* a border that serves as a limit: *see* **edge**

boundless *adjective* having no known limits: *see* **infinite**

bountiful *adjective* providing more than enough: *see* **fertile**

bow

verb to bend the body, head, or knee, as in greeting, agreement, or respect: *A student of the martial arts traditionally bows before stepping into the practice area.*

► **bend** to incline the body; to stoop: *I had to bend down to tie my shoes.*
► **curtsy** to make a special bow used by women and girls as a sign of respect: *The ballerina curtsied to the audience.*
► **kneel** to rest or fall on one or both knees: *I knelt on the kitchen floor to scrub it.*

bowl *noun* a stadium or outdoor theater shaped like a bowl: *see* **theater**

box *noun* a stiff container usually having four sides, a bottom, and often a top or lid: *see* **container**

boy *noun*   a male child: *see* **child**

boycott *verb*   to refuse, as part of an organized protest, to buy from or deal with a store, company, person, or nation: *see* **avoid**

brace

verb   to strengthen or give support to something: *I **braced** the bookshelf by screwing it to the wall.*

▸ **prop**   to place an object beneath or against a structure to keep it from falling: *He **propped** the window open with a book.*

▸ **reinforce**   to make something stronger by adding extra support to it: *I stitched over the seam twice to **reinforce** it.*

▸ **strengthen**   to make something strong or stronger: *Weightlifting helps to **strengthen** one's muscles.*

▸ **support**   to bear or carry the weight of a structure or object: *Is this shelf strong enough to **support** those heavy books?*

brag

verb   to speak with too much pride about oneself or something related to oneself: *Many parents **brag** about their children.*

▸ **boast**   to praise oneself, one's belongings, or one's actions in an excessive manner: *The athlete **boasted** about his many trophies.*

▸ **flaunt**   to show something off; to make a display of oneself: *She **flaunted** her expensive jewelry.*

▸ **gloat**   to think or speak about something with selfish or spiteful satisfaction: *I couldn't help **gloating** when my brother got into trouble after trying to blame me.*

▸ **show off**   ▷ to display something in a proud or boastful manner: *He likes to **show off** his skateboarding tricks.* ▷ to behave in a showy way: *She's always **showing off** on the basketball court.*

brainstorm *verb*   to solve specific problems or develop new ideas by group discussion: *see* **think**

brake *verb*   to slow or stop something with a mechanical device: *see* **stop**

branch *noun*   a division of a business or other organization: *see* **agency**

brand *noun*   a name or symbol that identifies a product as coming from a certain company: *see* **label**

brave

adjective   having or showing courage in the face of danger, pain, or adversity: *The **brave** child did not cry when he broke his arm.*

▸ **adventurous**   fond of adventure; seeking new and daring experiences: *The **adventurous** woman is a location scout for a Hollywood movie studio.*

▸ **bold**   having or showing no fear: *Leif Erickson was a **bold** Viking who sailed to America hundreds of years before Columbus.*

▸ **courageous**   able to face danger or hardship with confidence, resolution, and firm control of oneself: *The **courageous** firefighters got the whole family out of the burning house.*

▸ **daring**   willing to take risks; adventurous: *The **daring** boy grew up to be a stuntman.*

▸ **fearless**   having no fear; afraid of nothing: *I am **fearless** when it comes to playing basketball.*

▸ **gallant**   brave and noble: *The **gallant** man rescued the stranded motorist.*

▸ **heroic**   having the qualities of a hero; very brave or daring: *It was **heroic** of you to rescue the drowning child.*

▸ **valiant**   courageous and bold in a difficult situation; brave: *She was **valiant** during her mother's long illness.*

ANTONYM **cowardly**   having no courage

bravery *noun*   the quality of showing courage: *see* **courage**

brawl *noun*   a noisy physical fight: *see* **fight**

brawny *adjective*   having large, strong muscles: *see* **strong**

break

noun   a period of rest, as from work: *The work crew took a **break** in order to eat lunch.*

▶ **breather**   a short period or rest: *I took a breather in the middle of the hike.*

▶ **intermission**   an interruption in activity, as between the acts of a play: *He got something to drink during the intermission.*

▶ **interval**   a period of time between two events or actions: *There is usually a short interval of silence between songs on a CD.*

▶ **lull**   a calm period in the middle of great activity or commotion: *I saw some blue sky during a lull in the storm.*

▶ **pause**   a temporary stop: *There was a brief pause before the speaker continued.*

▶ **recess**   a temporary pause in usual activity: *The planning committee continued their discussion after a short recess.*

▶ **rest**   a period of inactivity, relaxation, or sleep: *I needed a rest after rowing across the lake.*

break

verb   to cause something to separate into two or more pieces as the result of force: *The guitar string broke because it was stretched too tight.*

▶ **chip**   to break off a small piece from something as by hitting, jarring, or scraping: *I chipped my tooth on a hard seed.*

▶ **crack**   to break without completely separating: *My windshield cracked when a rock hit it.*

▶ **crumble**   to break something into small pieces or crumbs: *I crumbled some crackers into my soup.*

▶ **fracture**   to break or crack something hard, such as bone: *She fractured her leg in two places when she fell skiing.*

▶ **shatter**   to break suddenly into many small pieces, as from a violent blow: *The glass bowl shattered when it fell to the floor.*

▶ **snap**   to break suddenly with a sharp sound: *The twig snapped when I stepped on it.*

▶ **splinter**   to split or break into sharp, slender pieces: *The icicle splintered when it fell to the ground.*

breakable *adjective*   capable of being broken with normal use: *see* **delicate**

breakfast *noun*   the first meal of the day: *see* **meal**

breathe

verb   to inhale and exhale air: *I had a hard time breathing at the high altitude.*

▶ **gasp**   to inhale in a sudden, sharp way, as from shock, surprise, or great exertion: *The runners were gasping by the end of the race.*

▶ **pant**   to breathe in short, quick gasps: *On hot afternoons our dog just lays in the grass and pants.*

▶ **wheeze**   to breathe with difficulty, producing a hoarse whistling sound: *A person with asthma will sometimes wheeze.*

▶ **yawn**   to open the mouth wide with a deep inward breath, as when sleepy or bored: *He was so tired that he began to yawn.*

breather *noun*   a short period of rest: *see* **break**

breathy *adjective*   marked by audible or noisy breathing: *see* **hoarse**

breed *noun*   a particular type or variety of animal or plant: *see* **kind**[2]

breed *verb*   to cause animals to reproduce: *see* **raise [1]**

breeze *noun*   a light, gentle wind: *see* **wind**

brief *adjective*   lasting only a short time: *see* **short [2]**

brig *noun*   a prison on a ship: *see* **jail**

bright

adjective   giving off or filled with a lot of light: *We could see every detail of the scene in the bright floodlights.*

▶ **brilliant**   shining very brightly; full of light: *The light from the full moon was brilliant.*

▶ **dazzling**   so bright as to make a person momentarily blind: *The sunlight reflecting off the snow was dazzling.*

▶ **gleaming**   emitting a beam or flash of light; emitting a soft, steady glow: *We could see the gleaming of her car's taillights as we followed her to the party.*

▶ **light**   filled with light; bright: *All these windows make the room very light.*

- **radiant** giving off light or heat; glowing: *The sun is a **radiant** ball of gases.*
- **shiny** bright from reflected light: *A cat's eyes are **shiny** in the dark.*

ANTONYM **dim** giving off little light

brilliant *adjective* shining very brightly: *see* **bright**

brilliant *adjective* extremely intelligent or inventive: *see* **smart**

bring *verb* to take something with oneself to a place: *see* **carry**

brink *noun* the upper edge of a steep or vertical slope: *see* **edge**

brisk *adjective* moving or acting in a lively or energetic manner: *see* **fast**

broad *adjective* ▷ wide from side to side ▷ large in size, extent, or scope: *see* **wide**

broadcast *verb* to make something known over a wide area: *see* **announce**

brochure *noun* a small pamphlet or leaflet containing information about a product or service: *see* **booklet**

broil *verb* to cook food under a flame or direct heat: *see* **cook**

broke *adjective* (informal) having no money at all: *see* **poor**

broker *noun* a person who buys and sells property for other people: *see* **representative**

brood *verb* to think or worry quietly for a long time: *see* **pout**

brook *noun* a small, natural stream: *see* **river**

browse

verb to look at something in a leisurely or casual way: *I **browsed** through the magazine in the bookstore.*

- **scan** to look something over quickly and systematically: *I always **scan** my tests when I finish to make sure that I have answered all the questions.*

- **skim** to read something quickly, skipping over parts: *I **skimmed** through the boring parts of the novel.*
- **survey** to take a general or comprehensive look at something: *She **surveyed** the crowd to see if her friends had arrived.*

brunch *noun* a meal eaten late in the morning that combines breakfast and lunch: *see* **meal**

brush *verb* to clean, polish, sweep, or groom someone or something with a brush: *see* **groom**

brutal *adjective* very cruel and harsh: *see* **mean**[1]

bucket

noun a round, open container with a curved handle, used for carrying liquids or solids: *I filled the **bucket** with soapy water and took it outside to wash the car.*

- **kettle** a metal pot, usually with a lid: *The stew was simmering in the **kettle**.*
- **pail** a cylindrical container, open at the top and fitted with a handle: *The children used a plastic **pail** to make sand castles at the beach.*
- **pan** a wide, shallow, open container used especially for cooking: *She baked the cake in a round **pan**.*
- **pot** any of various deep, rounded containers made of metal, pottery, or glass, used especially for cooking: *He used a large aluminum **pot** to cook the pasta.*
- **tub** an open, flat-bottomed, usually round container: *We shared a **tub** of popcorn at the movie.*

buddy *noun* (informal) a good friend: *see* **friend**

budget *noun* a plan for how money will be spent: *see* **plan**

budget *verb* to plan one's spending in advance: *see* **plan**

bug *verb* (informal) to annoy or pester someone, especially with requests: *see* **annoy**

build

verb to make or form something by putting together materials or parts: *It takes knowledge and skill to **build** a house from the ground up.*

- **assemble** to fit the parts of something together: *He **assembled** the dollhouse for his daughter.*
- **construct** to build or put something together; to engineer something: *The Romans **constructed** a great system of roads and bridges throughout their empire.*
- **erect** to put a structure up; to build something so that it stands on its own: *The campers **erected** their tent for the night.*
- **make** to create something by shaping, modifying, or assembling material: *I am learning how to **make** jams and jellies.*
- **manufacture** to make something, especially by using machinery: *This company **manufactures** phones.*

ANTONYM **demolish** to destroy something by reducing it to ruins

bulb *noun* a rounded, underground plant part, such as a tulip or an onion, from which a new plant can grow: *see* **seed**

bulge *noun* an outward curve or swelling: *see* **bump**

bulk *noun* the major portion of something: *see* **amount**

bulky *adjective* extremely large: *see* **heavy [1]**

bulletin *noun* a short announcement on a matter of pubic interest: *see* **announcement**

bum *noun* a person who avoids work: *see* **beggar**

bump

noun a small swelling, as from a blow or an insect sting: *I have a **bump** where I hit my head.*

- **bulge** an outward curve or swelling; a protruding part: *There was a **bulge** in my coat pocket where I had stuffed an orange.*

- **knob** a rounded lump or mass: *The calf had two bony **knobs** on its head where the horns were growing.*
- **knot** a hard lump or swelling, as from an enlarged gland: *The **knot** on my dog's leg turned out to be a cyst.*
- **lump** a swelling or bump: *The doctors removed the **lump** from the patient's neck.*
- **swelling** a spot that has increased in size or volume as a result of internal pressure, especially through disease or injury: *The bee sting caused a **swelling** on my hand.*

bumpy *adjective* ▷ full of bumps or lumps ▷ moving with jerks or jolts: *see* **rough**

bunch *noun* (informal) a group of people who regularly associate together: *see* **group**

bundle *noun* a number of things bound or wrapped together: *see* **package**

burden

noun something weighty that is carried; a load: *The hikers rested after removing the **burden** of their heavy packs.*

- **load** something that is carried or transported, as by a vehicle, a person, or an animal: *Elephants can carry a heavy **load**.*
- **weight** a load or burden: *The dogsled moved slowly with its **weight** of food and supplies.*

bureau *noun* an office for a specific kind of business: *see* **agency**

bureaucracy *noun* the administration of a government through bureaus and departments with appointed officials: *see* **government**

burglar *noun* a person who breaks into a building in order to steal: *see* **thief**

burglary *noun* the crime of breaking into a building with the intention of stealing: *see* **theft**

burly *adjective* heavy and strong: *see* **strong**

burn

verb to set something on fire; to consume something with fire: *We* **burned** *some wood in the fireplace.*

- **blaze** to burn or shine brightly: *The campfire* **blazed** *cheerfully.*
- **flame** to burn with a bright, moving light: *The torches* **flamed** *high as the procession passed.*
- **flare** to burn suddenly with a brief, intense light: *The fireworks* **flared** *in the sky.*
- **scald** to burn someone or something with hot liquid or steam: *I* **scalded** *my hand when I spilled the hot coffee.*
- **scorch** to burn the surface of something: *I* **scorched** *the toast.*
- **smolder** to burn with little smoke and no flame: *The ruins of the burned building* **smoldered** *for several days.*

burning *adjective* ▷ being on fire ▷ very hot: *see* **hot**

burrow *verb* to make a tunnel, hole, or shelter by digging in the ground: *see* **dig**

burst *verb* to break open suddenly and violently: *see* **explode**

bury *verb* to hide something by placing it in the ground and covering it with earth: *see* **hide²**

bus *noun* a long motor vehicle with rows of seats for carrying passengers: *see* **car**

bushed *adjective* (informal) extremely tired: *see* **tired**

business

noun [1] a commercial establishment, such as a store or factory: *He just opened his own computer repair* **business.**

- **company** a business enterprise; a firm: *The* **company** *I work for is sending me to a conference.*
- **corporation** a group of people who run a business as a unit that is legally separate from the people themselves: *She worked her way up through the ranks of the* **corporation.**
- **firm** a business partnership of two or more people: *My brother went to work for*

a large law **firm** *after he graduated from law school.*

- **shop** a small retail store or a specialty department in a large store: *I stopped at the flower* **shop** *to pick out a bouquet.*
- **stall** a small booth or stand used for selling or displaying goods: *We bought some handmade jewelry from a* **stall** *at the fair.*
- **store** a place where merchandise is offered for sale: *I went to the pet* **store** *to buy an iguana.*

business

noun [2] commercial, financial, or industrial activity: *Real estate is a booming* **business** *right now.*

- **commerce** the exchange and distribution of goods or commodities: **Commerce** *between the two nations has led to peace and stability in the region.*
- **industry** the production and manufacture of goods or commodities on a large scale: *Agriculture is often now an* **industry** *run by large corporations instead of individual farmers.*
- **trade** the business of buying and selling commodities: *My uncle is in the furniture* **trade.**
- **traffic** commercial activity, especially of an illegal or improper nature: *Great measures are being taken to stop the* **traffic** *of illegal drugs.*

bustle *verb* to move around in a busy or excited way: *see* **hurry**

busy

adjective engaged in work or activity: *I had a* **busy** *day at work.*

- **absorbed** completely occupied or interested: *She was* **absorbed** *in the novel she was reading.*
- **active** engaged in lively or energetic activity: *The children kept* **active** *playing hide-and-seek until bedtime.*
- **dynamic** characterized by continuous change, activity, or progress: *A river is a* **dynamic** *ecosystem.*

▸ **hectic** marked by intense activity, confusion, or excitement: *The holidays are a **hectic** time for most people.*

▸ **industrious** working hard as a steady habit: *If I'd been more **industrious** this semester I could have brought my grades up.*

▸ **involved** closely occupied or engaged in something: *They have been very **involved** in making the plans for their wedding.*

▸ **occupied** devoting time to an activity or purpose: *I did not hear the phone ring because I was **occupied** in the garden.*

▸ **preoccupied** excessively concerned with something; distracted: *He is too **preoccupied** with his job to take any time off this week.*

ANTONYM **idle** not working or being used

but

conjunction on the contrary; nevertheless: *I thought I had done badly on the test, **but** I actually did quite well.*

▸ **although** regardless of the fact that; even though: *The weather report predicts rain, **although** the skies are clear now.*

▸ **however** in spite of that; nevertheless: *I would like to go to the movie with you; **however**, I need to study.*

▸ **so** with the result that: *He takes his lunch to work **so** that he doesn't have to eat out.*

▸ **though** despite the fact that: *I believe we should take this exit, **though** I am not certain.*

▸ **yet** nevertheless; despite this: *She is allergic to cats, **yet** she has adopted two.*

buzz *verb* to make a low, droning or vibrating sound like that of a bee: *see* **hum**

buy

verb to get something in exchange for money: *I **buy** groceries once a week.*

▸ **pay** to give an amount of money in return for goods or services: *I **paid** 60 dollars for this week's groceries.*

▸ **purchase** to obtain something in exchange for money; to buy: *She **purchased** her first computer last week.*

ANTONYM **sell** to offer something for sale

by

preposition close to something in space: *Please put that book **by** my backpack.*

▸ **at** in or near the location of something: *I will meet you **at** the library.*

▸ **beside** next to or at the side of something: *Is the seat **beside** you available?*

▸ **near** close to something, as in time, space, or degree: *It is **near** my bedtime.*

by oneself *adverb* without the company or help of others: *see* **alone**

bypass *verb* to go around something so as to avoid it: *see* **avoid**

cabin *noun*   a small, simply built house: *see* **house**

cabinet *noun*   a case or cupboard that has drawers, shelves, or compartments for storing or displaying objects: *see* **shelf**

cable *noun*   a strong, thick rope made of fiber or strands of steel wire: *see* **rope**

cackle *verb*   to laugh or speak in a shrill, noisy way: *see* **laugh**

cad *noun*   an unprincipled, unmannered man: *see* **villain**

café *noun*   a small restaurant or bar: *see* **restaurant**

cafeteria *noun*   a restaurant in which the customers buy their food at a counter and carry it to their tables: *see* **restaurant**

cage

noun   an enclosure for confining birds or other animals that has an opening covered with wire mesh or bars: *I cleaned out our canary's* **cage**.

▸ **coop**   a cage or pen, especially one for poultry: *The farmer built a new* **coop** *for his chickens.*

▸ **corral**   a fenced-in area for cattle or horses: *The horses ran around in their* **corral**.

▸ **kennel**   a small shelter for one or more dogs: *The dog was sleeping in its* **kennel**.

▸ **pen**   a small, fenced-in area where animals are kept: *There were pygmy goats in a* **pen** *at the petting zoo.*

▸ **stall**   a compartment for a single animal in a barn or stable: *Each horse has its own* **stall**.

▸ **sty**   a pen where pigs are kept: *There were five pigs in the* **sty**.

cajole *verb*   to persuade someone by flattery or insincere talk: *see* **persuade**

calamity *noun*   an event that causes great distress and suffering: *see* **disaster**

calculate *verb*   to find an answer or a result by using mathematics: *see* **add**

call

verb [1]   to give a name to someone or something: *What are you going to* **call** *your new kitten?*

▸ **baptize**   to give a name to a person who is being baptized: *The priest* **baptized** *the baby.*

▸ **dub**   to give someone a nickname: *I have* **dubbed** *my brother "The Nuisance."*

▸ **name**   to give a name to someone or something by which that person or thing is known: *My parents* **named** *me George after my uncle.*

▸ **title**   to name a book, painting, musical composition, or other work: *I haven't decided what to* **title** *my painting yet.*

call

verb [2]   to say something in a loud voice so as to get someone's attention: *She* **called** *to her friend across the street.*

▸ **page**   to summon or call someone by name in a public place: *The store clerk* **paged** *the mother of the lost child.*

▸ **summon**   to send for someone; to request someone to appear: *The king* **summoned** *his advisors.*

caller *noun*   a person who makes a short visit to someone: *see* **guest**

call to mind *verb*   to cause one to remember: *see* **remember**

calm

adjective   peacefully quiet; not excited or upset: *I always feel* **calm** *after I exercise.*

▸ **peaceful**   undisturbed by turmoil, strife, or disagreement: *Mahatma Gandhi believed in* **peaceful** *resistance.*

▸ **placid**   pleasantly peaceful or calm: *The lake was very placid after the wind died down.*

▸ **restful**   producing a quiet and peaceful feeling: *The weekend at the spa was restful.*

▸ **sedate**   quiet and dignified: *The swan glided over the water in a sedate manner.*

▹ **serene**   unaffected by disturbances; perfectly quiet: *The sky looked serene in the moonlight.*

▸ **tranquil**   free from commotion or disturbance; peaceful: *Studies have shown that regular meditation helps people become more tranquil.*

calmness *noun*   absence of excitement or disturbance: *see* **patience**

camouflage *verb*   to hide or disguise things, people, or animals by making them look like what is around them: *see* **hide²**

camp *noun*   an outdoor area with temporary shelters such as tents or cabins: *see* **fort**

campaign

noun   an organized activity to attain a political, social, or commercial goal: *He is helping with that senator's campaign for re-election.*

▸ **cause**   an idea or goal to which many people are dedicated: *They give money to environmental causes.*

▸ **crusade**   a campaign or movement for a reform, cause, or ideal: *Prohibition was the result of a crusade against alcohol.*

▸ **movement**   the activities of a large group of people toward a specific goal: *There was a huge civil rights movement in the 1960s.*

▸ **operation**   a coordinated action, especially by an army or government: *Desert Storm was the name of the military operation during the Gulf War.*

can *noun*   an airtight, often cylindrical metal container in which food and beverages are preserved: *see* **container**

cancel *verb*   to end, call off, or invalidate something: *see* **erase**

candid *adjective*   direct and frank; not holding anything back: *see* **honest**

canteen *noun*   a sturdy container for drinking water: *see* **bottle**

canyon *noun*   a deep valley with steep walls on both sides that were formed by running water: *see* **valley**

cap *noun*   a head covering that has no brim but sometimes has a visor: *see* **hat**

capability *noun*   the ability to perform reliably or satisfactorily: *see* **ability**

capable *adjective*   having the capacity or ability to do something: *see* **able**

capacity *noun*   the ability to perform or to produce something: *see* **ability**

capital *noun*   wealth that can be used to produce more wealth: *see* **wealth**

caprice *noun*   an impulsive notion or change of mind: *see* **impulse**

capsule *noun*   a small container, usually made of gelatin, that contains a dose of a medicine to be taken by mouth: *see* **pill**

captain *noun*   the leader of a group or team: *see* **leader**

captive *noun*   a person held prisoner or under the control of another: *see* **prisoner**

capture

verb   to seize and hold a person or animal, as by force or skill: *The animal control officer captured the lost dog.*

▸ **apprehend**   to take a person into official custody: *The police apprehended the suspect at the scene of the crime.*

▸ **arrest**   to seize and hold a person under authority of law: *The stockbroker was arrested on charges of fraud.*

▸ **catch**   to capture a person or animal, especially after a chase: *I finally managed to catch the goldfish and move it to another tank.*

▸ **nab**   (informal) to catch someone in the act of wrongdoing: *He was nabbed for drunk driving.*

▸ **seize**   ▷ to take someone prisoner: *The agents seized three suspected drug traffickers* *at the border.* ▷ to take possession of something legally: *The police **seized** several pounds of cocaine during the raid.*

ANTONYM **release**   to set a person or animal free

car

noun   a vehicle with four wheels and a gasoline engine that is designed to carry passengers: *Now that I have my driver's license, I am going to buy a **car**.*

- ▸ **automobile**   a car: *One of their **automobiles** is a convertible.*
- ▸ **bus**   a long motor vehicle with rows of seats for carrying passengers: *She reads the newspaper when she rides the **bus**.*
- ▸ **taxicab**   an automobile that carries passengers for a fare, usually calculated on a meter; a cab; a taxi: *She had the **taxicab** drop her off at the airport.*
- ▸ **truck**   any of various heavy motor vehicles designed for carrying or pulling loads: *We rented a **truck** when we moved to a new house.*
- ▸ **vehicle**   a device for transporting people or things, especially a motor vehicle: *The police inspected the abandoned **vehicle**.*

caravan *noun*   a group of people or vehicles traveling together: *see* **parade**

care *noun*   worry or stress caused by one's responsibilities: *see* **worry**

career *noun*   a profession or occupation that a person follows as a life's work: *see* **job**

careful

adjective [1]   done with special care and attention to detail: *You did a very **careful** job of hanging that wallpaper.*

- ▸ **comprehensive**   large in scope or content; including many different things: *The doctor gave me a **comprehensive** physical examination.*
- ▸ **mindful**   attentive; heedful: *We were **mindful** that we needed to leave in an hour.*
- ▸ **painstaking**   involving or showing great care or thoroughness: *Weaving that tapestry must have been **painstaking** work.*

- ▸ **thorough**   not overlooking anything; very careful: *Please do a **thorough** job of cleaning the kitchen.*

ANTONYM **careless**   not taking the necessary care; done or made without care

careful

adjective [2]   attentive to possible danger, error, or harm: *Be **careful** of that loose stairstep.*

- ▸ **cautious**   taking care to avoid danger or trouble: *She is always **cautious** around dogs that she doesn't know.*
- ▸ **wary**   on guard against possible danger: *Be **wary** when walking alone at night.*

careless

adjective   done or made without care or attention: *It was **careless** of me to lock my keys in my car.*

- ▸ **heedless**   paying little or no attention; unmindful: *The **heedless** boy was always getting into trouble.*
- ▸ **irresponsible**   lacking a sense of responsibility; unreliable or untrustworthy: *It was **irresponsible** of you to not call home.*
- ▸ **lax**   not careful or strict, especially about enforcing rules: *The teacher grew **lax** about assigning homework as summer vacation drew near.*
- ▸ **negligent**   guilty of neglect; lacking in proper care or concern: *Parents who are **negligent** in caring for their children can be arrested.*
- ▸ **thoughtless**   lacking thought or care; inconsiderate of other people: *It was **thoughtless** of me not to offer him a ride home.*

ANTONYM **careful**   taking the necessary care; done or made with care

caring *adjective*   feeling or showing concern for others: *see* **affectionate**

carnival *noun*   an outdoor show that offers entertainment such as rides and games: *see* **fair²**

carol *noun* a song of joy, especially one that is sung at Christmas: *see* **song**

carouse *verb* to engage in noisy drinking, especially of alcohol: *see* **party**

carpet *noun* a heavy, woven fabric used as a covering for a floor: *see* **pad**

carry

verb to take something from one place to another: *Please help me **carry** this chair into the house.*

▸ **bear** to carry something of value or use: *My uncle always comes back from his travels **bearing** presents for me and my brother.*

▸ **bring** to take something with oneself to a place: *I'll **bring** a salad to the barbecue.*

▸ **haul** to pull or drag something with great effort: *The horse **hauled** the wagon out of the mud.*

▸ **shoulder** to carry something on the shoulders: *He **shouldered** the lumber and carried it across the construction site.*

▸ **take** to carry, transport, or lead someone or something to another place: *I **took** my little sister to her dancing lesson.*

▸ **transport** to carry someone or something, especially in a vehicle: *The injured person was **transported** to the hospital by helicopter.*

carton *noun* a cardboard or plastic box made in various shapes and sizes: *see* **container**

carve

verb to shape or decorate something by cutting: *These wooden buttons have little chickens **carved** in them.*

▸ **chisel** to shape a material with a chisel: *The sculptor **chiseled** the block of marble into a statue.*

▸ **engrave** to carve, cut, or etch writing or a design into a material: *The clerk **engraved** the winner's name on the trophy.*

▸ **etch** to cut a design into metal, glass, or other material by using acid: *The artist **etched** a mountain scene into the glass.*

▸ **whittle** to cut small pieces or shavings from a piece of wood: *The carpenter **whittled** the end of his pencil to a sharp point.*

cascade *verb* to fall in or like a waterfall: *see* **pour**

case *noun* a container, especially one designed to hold a particular item: *see* **container**

case *noun* an individual occurrence of something: *see* **example**

cash *noun* money in the form of bills or coins: *see* **money**

cask *noun* a barrel for holding liquids: *see* **barrel**

castle *noun* a large group of buildings, often the residence of a noble or lord, having high, thick walls, towers, or other defenses against attack: *see* **fort**

casual

adjective not formal; relaxed: *The party is **casual**, and you can wear jeans if you want.*

▸ **easygoing** living without undue worry or concern; carefree: *She is **easygoing** and fun to be with.*

▸ **informal** made or done without following set rules or custom; casual: *We had an **informal** meeting to create ideas for the new project.*

▸ **mellow** relaxed and unhurried: *I felt **mellow** after the stress of finals was over.*

▸ **relaxed** free from tension or anxiety: *He became more **relaxed** as he got to know the other guests.*

casualty *noun* an person who is killed or injured in an accident or a battle: *see* **victim**

catalog *noun* a book or pamphlet containing a list of items with a description and sometimes an illustration of each item: *see* **brochure**

catastrophe *noun* a great and sudden disaster from which recovery is difficult or impossible: *see* **disaster**

catch *verb* to capture a person or animal, especially after a chase: *see* **capture**

catch *verb* to get hold of or grasp something that is moving: *see* **grab**

catch *noun* a device such as a hook or latch used for fastening or closing something: *see* **hook**

categorize *verb* to put something into a specific, defined division: *see* **sort**

category *noun* a division or group within a system: *see* **kind²**

cause *noun* someone or something that produces a certain feeling, action, or desire: *see* **basis**

cause *noun* an idea or goal to which many people are dedicated: *see* **campaign**

caution *verb* to warn someone against possible trouble or danger: *see* **alert**

cautious *adjective* taking care to avoid danger or trouble: *see* **careful [2]**

cavalcade *noun* a ceremonial procession of people on horseback, in carriages, or in automobiles: *see* **parade**

cavity *noun* a hollow place or area: *see* **hole**

cease *verb* to bring something to an end: *see* **stop**

celebrate *verb* to observe a day or event with ceremonies of respect, festivity, or rejoicing: *see* **party**

celebrated *adjective* widely praised, especially for one's achievements: *see* **famous**

celebration *noun* a party or other festive activity to honor a special occasion: *see* **party**

cell *noun* a small room, as in a prison or convent, having little or no furniture: *see* **jail**

cell *noun* the smallest unit of an organized group or movement: *see* **team**

censor *verb* to remove material from or prevent the publication of something: *see* **suppress**

center

noun [1] a person or thing that is the chief object of attention, interest, or emotion: *The rock star was the **center** of attention at the concert.*

► **core** the basic or most important part of something: *The **core** of the problem was a lack of communication.*

► **essence** the most important ingredient; the crucial element: *The **essence** of this perfume is rose oil.*

► **heart** the central or main part: *The Midwest is sometimes called the **heart** of America.*

► **hub** a center of activity or interest; a focal point: *The city hall is the **hub** of the town.*

► **nucleus** a central or essential part around which other parts are grouped: *Gertrude Stein was the **nucleus** of a group of American authors who lived in Paris in the 1920s.*

center

noun [2] a point or place that is equally distant from the sides or outer boundaries of something: *The **center** of the chocolate is filled with caramel.*

► **middle** the area or point equally distant from two points or extremes: *The road crew painted a yellow line down the **middle** of the road.*

► **midpoint** a position midway between two extremes: *Our town is the **midpoint** between two large cities.*

► **midst** a position that is completely surrounded by something: *In the **midst** of the woods is a clearing with a beautiful meadow.*

central *adjective* most basic or important: *see* **main**

ceremony

noun a formal act performed in honor of an event or special occasion: *We attended a wedding **ceremony** last weekend.*

► **rite** the customary form for conducting a religious or other solemn ceremony: *The priest was called to offer last **rites** to the dying man.*

► **ritual** the proper form or order of a religious or other ceremony: *Lighting candles* *for the Sabbath dinner is a **ritual** performed by the woman of a Jewish household.*

▶ **service** a religious ceremony or gathering: *We attended the church **service**.*

certain

adjective sure to come or happen: *According to the weather report, it is **certain** to rain today.*

▶ **definite** beyond doubt; unquestionable: *His answer was a **definite** "no."*
▶ **positive** marked by or expressing certainty, acceptance, or affirmation: *I am **positive** that I will do well on the test.*
▶ **sure** impossible to doubt or dispute; feeling no doubt: *Are you **sure** that you have the plane tickets with you?*

ANTONYM **uncertain** not sure; not definite

certainly

adverb without a doubt; definitely: *There **certainly** are a lot of people at this concert.*

▶ **absolutely** completely and unquestionably; perfectly: *You look **absolutely** gorgeous in that dress!*
▶ **definitely** beyond any doubt; certainly: *I will **definitely** be there tonight.*
▶ **indeed** in fact; actually: *I hoped he would call and **indeed** he did.*
▶ **positively** absolutely; with certainty: *Your idea is **positively** brilliant.*
▶ **really** in actual truth or fact: ***Really**, it's no problem to give you a ride.*
▶ **surely** certainly; without doubt: ***Surely** you can't expect me to believe that crazy story.*
▶ **undoubtedly** without any doubt or question: *He is **undoubtedly** the strangest person I have ever met.*

certificate *noun* a document testifying to the truth of something: *see* **document**

certify *verb* to assure the quality, value, or standard of something: *see* **prove**

chafe *verb* to irritate the skin by rubbing: *see* **scratch**

chagrin *noun* (formal) a strong feeling of unease or annoyance caused by disappoint-ment, embarrassment, or humiliation: *see* **embarrassment**

chain *noun* a row of metal links joined together: *see* **rope**

challenge *noun* a test of one's abilities or resources: *see* **problem**

challenging *adjective* requiring all of a person's efforts and skills: *see* **hard**

chamber *noun* a room in a large house, especially a bedroom: *see* **room**

champion *noun* a defender or supporter of a cause or of another person: *see* **hero**

champion *verb* to fight for a cause or movement: *see* **sponsor**

championship *noun* a contest held to determine a champion: *see* **contest**

chance

noun the happening of things without any apparent cause or intention: *She heard about the job by **chance** from someone she met at a party.*

▶ **coincidence** a combination of events or circumstances that is accidental but seems to have been planned or arranged: *They met by **coincidence** when his car broke down in front of her apartment.*
▶ **luck** the chance happening of good or bad events; fortune: *My brother wished me good **luck** when I went off to my audition.*
▶ **opportunity** a favorable combination of circumstances: *This is a great **opportunity** for you to advance your career.*

change

verb to make something different from how it was before: *I'm thinking about **changing** my hair color.*

▶ **adapt** to change so as to suit new conditions or circumstances: *Humans have **adapted** to all sorts of different climates.*
▶ **adjust** to change something so that it works better or is more suitable: *I **adjusted** my schedule so I didn't have classes on Friday.*

- **alter** to change something for a particular use or purpose: *She had the suit **altered** so that it fit better.*
- **amend** to change something so as to make it more accurate or correct: *I would like to **amend** my previous statement.*
- **convert** ▷ to change something from one form into another: *Plants **convert** sunlight into food.* ▷ to make something suitable for a different use: *We **converted** the spare bedroom into an office.*
- **modify** to change something, especially in a limited way: *Her argument made me **modify** my opinion on several points.*
- **revise** to make changes, especially to something written: *I **revised** the bread recipe after the first loaf turned out too flat.*
- **tailor** to alter or adapt something for a particular situation or purpose: *He **tailored** his remarks to suit the younger audience.*

changeable *adjective* subject to sudden and unpredictable changes: *see* **moody**

channel *noun* a course or passage through which something may move or be directed: *see* **path**

chant *noun* a melody with many words sung on the same pitch: *see* **song**

chaos *noun* a condition or place of great disorder or confusion: *see* **confusion**

chaperon *verb* to attend and supervise a dance or party for young, unmarried people: *see* **escort**

character *noun* the combination of qualities that makes one person different from another; a person's moral character: *see* **personality**

characteristic *noun* a distinguishing feature or quality: *see* **quality**

charge *verb* to make a formal claim of wrongdoing against someone: *see* **blame**

charge *noun* an amount asked or made as payment: *see* **price**

charity *noun* the giving of money or other help to needy people: *see* **relief**

charley horse *noun* (informal) a severe muscle cramp or stiffness in the arm or leg: *see* **cramp**

charm *noun* the power or ability to please or delight: *see* **elegance**

charmed *adjective* very lucky, as if by magic: *see* **lucky**

charming

adjective very pleasing; delightful: *She has a **charming** manner.*

- **adorable** sweet and lovable: *The children were **adorable** as they romped in the snow.*
- **delightful** giving delight; greatly pleasing: *The trip on the sailboat was **delightful**.*
- **enchanting** having the power to enchant; charming: *He is an **enchanting** storyteller.*
- **sweet** easy to love; gentle and kind: *It was very **sweet** of you to remember my birthday.*

ANTONYM **unpleasant** not pleasing; disagreeable

chart

noun something written or drawn that presents information in an organized, easily viewed form: *Mom made a **chart** of all the chores we're supposed to do.*

- **blueprint** ▷ a photographic copy of architectural plans appearing as white lines on a blue background: *The architect sent the **blueprints** to the client.* ▷ a carefully worked-out plan: *This book gives you a **blueprint** for success in starting your own business.*
- **diagram** a plan, drawing, or sketch that shows how something works or how its parts are put together: *This **diagram** shows how to assemble the bookcase.*
- **graph** a drawing or diagram that shows relationships between various quantities: *Here is a **graph** of the company's profits over the past ten years.*
- **map** a drawing or chart of all or part of the earth's surface: *The invitation included a **map** to their house.*
- **table** an orderly presentation of data, usually arranged in columns and rows: *This **table** compares the features of several different computers.*

▶ **visual aid** an instructional aid that presents information visually: *Our professor uses the chalkboard as a **visual aid**.*

charter *verb* to hire or rent something for a limited time: *see* **rent**

chase *verb* to follow someone or something in order to catch it: *see* **follow**

chat *verb* to talk in a relaxed, friendly way: *see* **talk**

chatter *verb* to talk fast without much purpose: *see* **talk**

cheap

adjective very low in price: *This restaurant serves great food at **cheap** prices.*

- ▶ **inexpensive** low to moderate in price: *His first car was an **inexpensive** one.*
- ▶ **low-cost** inexpensive; affordable: *This area has a lot of **low-cost** housing.*

ANTONYM **expensive** having a high price

cheat

verb ▷ to act in a dishonest way: *The teacher caught someone **cheating** on the test.* ▷ to treat someone dishonestly: *The lawyer claimed that his client was **cheated** out of a fair trial.*

- ▶ **chisel** (informal) to cheat someone or obtain something by deception: *That salesman **chiseled** me out of an extra hundred dollars.*
- ▶ **con** (informal) to trick or coax someone into doing something by first winning the person's trust: *She **conned** me into believing her.*
- ▶ **defraud** (formal) to cheat someone by deliberate deception; to swindle: *The law prosecutes people who **defraud** others.*
- ▶ **swindle** to cheat or defraud someone of money or property: *The crooked real estate agent had **swindled** people out of millions of dollars.*

check *noun* a statement showing the amount due, as at a restaurant: *see* **bill**

check *verb* to cause something to stop suddenly: *see* **control**

check *verb* to test or examine something critically: *see* **examine**

check *noun* a written order to pay money from a person's bank account: *see* **money**

cheer *noun* good spirits, especially in a social setting: *see* **happiness**

cheerful *adjective* full of good spirits and happiness: *see* **happy**

cheering *noun* shouts of happiness, approval, encouragement, or enthusiasm: *see* **applause**

cherish *verb* to regard someone or something fondly: *see* **love**

chest *noun* a large, sturdy box with a lid, used especially for holding or storing things: *see* **container**

chew *verb* to bite and grind something with the teeth: *see* **bite**

chief *noun* a person of the highest rank or authority: *see* **leader**

chief *adjective* most important: *see* **main**

child

noun a person between birth and physical maturity: *The **child** is learning how to ride a bicycle.*

- ▶ **baby** a very young child; an infant: *Babies need a lot of care.*
- ▶ **boy** a male child: *The **boys** had a good time at the scout camp.*
- ▶ **girl** a female child: *She has been studying the piano since she was a little **girl**.*
- ▶ **infant** a child in the earliest period of life; a newborn: *Most **infants** sleep a lot.*
- ▶ **kid** (informal) a child or young person: *The teacher had all the **kids** line up to go to the assembly.*
- ▶ **toddler** a young child who is just learning how to walk: *The **toddler** was grabbing everything she could reach.*
- ▶ **youngster** a child or young person: *My grandfather likes to tell stories about when he was a **youngster**.*

ANTONYM **adult**   a person who is fully developed and mature; a grownup

chilly *adjective*   cold enough to cause or feel discomfort: *see* **cold**

chip *verb*   to break off a small piece from something as by hitting, jarring, or scraping: *see* **break**

chisel *verb*   to shape a material by using a chisel: *see* **carve**

chisel *verb* (informal)   to cheat someone or obtain something by deception: *see* **cheat**

choice

noun ▷ the freedom or opportunity to choose from two or more possibilities: *The professor gave the class a **choice** between a final paper or a final exam.* ▷ a variety from which to choose: *There was a wide **choice** of dishes on the menu.*

- ► **alternative**   one of two or more possibilities from which to choose: *My parents said that I don't have to go to college as long as I have a good **alternative**.*
- ► **option**   a choice, especially one that is offered by someone else: *The bank gave us three **options** for repaying the loan.*
- ► **preference**   a choice based on one's values, biases, or tastes: *Which of these videos is your **preference**?*
- ► **selection**   a variety of things or people to choose from: *This store carries a great **selection** of shoes.*

choke

verb   to be unable to breathe, swallow, or speak normally, as when the throat is blocked: *Chew slowly so that you don't **choke** on your food.*

- ► **gag**   to choke and vomit or nearly vomit: *The smell of rotten eggs makes me **gag**.*
- ► **smother**   to die from lack of air: *The doctor told us not to worry about the baby **smothering** under the blanket in its crib.*
- ► **strangle**   to kill a person by choking or suffocating: *The killer **strangled** his victim with a rope.*

- ► **suffocate**   to kill a person or living thing by depriving it of air: *Too much water can **suffocate** the roots of a potted plant.*

chomp *verb*   to chew or bite on something noisily: *see* **bite**

choose

verb   to make a choice, especially on the basis of what one likes best: *Which TV show do you **choose** to watch?*

- ► **decide**   to make up one's mind regarding a question: *I haven't **decided** which college I want to attend.*
- ► **elect**   (formal)   to make a deliberate choice: *He **elected** to stay home and study instead of going out with his friends.*
- ► **opt**   to make a choice or decision: *She **opted** to keep her baby instead of giving it up for adoption.*
- ► **pick**   to choose something with care or forethought: *She **picked** a blue dress to wear on her date.*
- ► **prefer**   to choose something as more desirable; to like something better: *I **prefer** cotton sweaters over wool.*
- ► **select**   to choose something from among several possibilities: *He **selected** a blue tie to wear to his interview.*

chop *verb*   to cut something by striking it with a heavy, sharp tool, such as an ax or cleaver: *see* **cut**

chore

noun   a routine or minor task: *Vacuuming the carpet is one of my household **chores**.*

- ► **assignment**   something assigned, especially a job or task: *The reporter was given her first big **assignment**.*
- ► **errand**   a short trip taken to perform a task: *My **errands** included going to the grocery store and getting the oil changed in the car.*
- ► **task**   a piece of work assigned or done as part of one's duties: *A receptionist usually has the **task** of answering the phones.*

chronic *adjective* lasting a long period of time or recurring frequently: *see* **constant**

chronicle *noun* a record of events arranged in the order that they happened: *see* **report**

chubby *adjective* having plenty of flesh; round and plump: *see* **fat**

chuckle *verb* to laugh quietly or to oneself: *see* **laugh**

chum *noun* an intimate friend or companion: *see* **friend**

chunk

noun a thick piece of something: *I sliced off a* ***chunk*** *of cheese.*

- ▸ **clod** a lump of earth or clay: *We broke up all the* ***clods*** *before planting our garden.*
- ▸ **gob** a small, sticky lump: *My hamburger dripped a* ***gob*** *of ketchup onto my shirt.*
- ▸ **hunk** a large piece: *He tore off a* ***hunk*** *of bread.*
- ▸ **lump** an irregularly shaped mass or piece: *If you don't stir the batter well enough, the cake will have* ***lumps*** *in it.*
- ▸ **wad** a small mass of soft material: *She found a crumpled* ***wad*** *of paper in her coat pocket.*

churn *verb* to move or shake a liquid vigorously: *see* **mix**

circular *noun* a printed advertisement, notice, or other statement intended for public distribution: *see* **booklet**

circulate *verb* to spread widely among people or places: *see* **announce**

circumstance *noun* a condition or fact that decides or influences a course of events: *see* **situation**

citadel *noun* a large, high-walled fortress, usually in or near a city: *see* **fort**

citizen *noun* a legal member of a country, city, or town, especially one entitled to vote and enjoy other privileges: *see* **public**

city *noun* a place where many people live close to one another: *see* **town**

civil *adjective* observing accepted social practices: *see* **polite**

civilization *noun* a human society that has a high level of development in language, science, agriculture, and art: *see* **culture**

claim

verb to state that something is true although it has not yet been proven: *If he's as fast as he* ***claims****, then he'll win the race easily.*

- ▸ **assert** to claim something strongly and confidently: *The scientist* ***asserted*** *that she could prove her theory.*
- ▸ **contend** to argue that something is true, often without proof: *He* ***contends*** *that he's a vegetarian, but I've seen him eat meat recently.*
- ▸ **declare** to state something with force: *My sister* ***declared*** *that no one is allowed in her room without permission.*
- ▸ **maintain** to claim something repeatedly: *The prisoner* ***maintained*** *that he was innocent.*
- ▸ **profess** to declare something openly: *They* ***professed*** *their love for each other.*

clamor *noun* a loud noise, as of a crowd shouting: *see* **noise**

clan *noun* a group of families that claim the same ancestor: *see* **family**

clapping *noun* the striking of hands together with a sudden loud sound: *see* **applause**

clarify *verb* to make something clear or easier to understand: *see* **explain**

clasp *verb* to hold or embrace something tightly: *see* **hold**

clasp *noun* something, such as a hook or buckle, that is used to hold two things together: *see* **hook**

class

noun [1] a group of students who meet regularly to study the same subject: *There's a test today in my history* ***class****.*

► **course** a complete body of studies or a unit of such studies: *I have four more courses to finish before I can graduate from college.*

► **lecture** a prepared talk providing information about a given subject, delivered before an audience or class: *The speaker answered questions from the audience when the lecture was over.*

► **lesson** a period of time devoted to teaching or learning something: *He enjoys his trombone lessons.*

► **subject** a course or area of study: *What is your favorite subject in school?*

class *noun* [2] a kind or category: *see* kind²

classify *verb* to put something into groups or classes: *see* **sort**

clean

verb to rid something of dirt, trash, or disorder: *We cleaned the house before our guests arrived.*

► **dust** to remove dust from something by wiping or brushing: *I dusted the lamp with a soft cloth.*

► **launder** to wash something, especially clothes: *She laundered her sweaters on the delicate cycle.*

► **mop** to clean something with a mop: *He mopped the floor and then waxed it.*

► **polish** to make something smooth and shiny by rubbing: *Orange oil is good for polishing wood.*

► **scour** to clean, polish, or wash something by scrubbing vigorously: *I scoured the frying pan to remove the grease.*

► **scrub** to rub something hard in order to clean it, usually with a brush: *He scrubbed the bathtub.*

► **sweep** to clean or gather something with a broom or brush: *I swept the pieces of the broken jar into the dustpan.*

► **wash** to clean something with soap and water: *She washes her silk shirts by hand.*

► **wipe** to rub something with cloth or paper in order to clean or dry it: *The waiter wiped the table before we sat down.*

clean

adjective free from dirt, stains, or impurities: *I folded the clean laundry and put it away.*

► **neat** orderly and clean; tidy: *He always puts his things away so that his room stays neat.*

► **orderly** arranged or done in a careful or thoughtful way: *She stacked the canned goods in orderly rows in the cupboard.*

► **sanitary** free of germs; hygienic: *The instruments used in surgery are sanitary.*

► **spotless** free from stain or blemish; perfectly clean: *I spent all day cleaning the kitchen and now it is spotless.*

► **sterile** free from live bacteria or other microorganisms: *The woman who pierced my ears used a sterile needle.*

► **tidy** orderly and neat; well cared for: *She weeds her garden every day to keep it tidy.*

ANTONYM **dirty** full of or covered with dirt

clear

adjective [1] easy to see, hear, or understand: *We got lost because the directions were not clear.*

► **apparent** readily understood or seen: *It is apparent from what you say that you don't agree.*

► **explicit** clearly stated so that nothing is misunderstood: *The commanding officer gave his soldiers explicit orders to be ready for inspection at noon.*

► **legible** capable of being read: *Many doctors do not have legible handwriting.*

► **obvious** easily noticed or understood: *The spelling mistake in the very first sentence was obvious.*

► **plain** easy to see or understand; clear: *The sign made it plain that we were not to enter that part of the building.*

clear

adjective [2] free from anything that dims, darkens, or obscures: *The air was so clear after the storm that we could see the distant mountains.*

▸ **see-through** allowing light to pass through; transparent: *This water bottle is made of see-through plastic.*

▸ **sheer** thin, fine, and transparent: *Her wedding veil was made of a sheer fabric.*

▸ **transparent** allowing most or all light to pass through: *Glass is a transparent material.*

clench *verb* to take hold of or hold on to something tightly: *see* **grab**

clever *adjective* able to figure things out quickly; quick-witted: *see* **smart**

client *noun* a person who uses the services of a professional person: *see* **customer**

climate *noun* a general condition or set of attitudes in human affairs: *see* **atmosphere**

climb

verb to move upward by using the feet and sometimes the hands: *I climbed to the top of the stairs.*

▸ **mount** to go up; climb: *The bird mounted higher and higher into the air.*

▸ **scale** to climb up or over something: *The climbers scaled the face of the cliff.*

▸ **scramble** to move or climb hurriedly, especially on the hands and knees: *We scrambled up the rocky slope.*

ANTONYM **descend** to move from a higher to a lower place or position; to go or come down

clip *verb* to cut, cut off, or cut out something with scissors or shears: *see* **cut**

clod *noun* a lump of earth or clay: *see* **chunk**

clog *verb* to stop or slow any movement through a passage: *see* **block**

close

verb to shut something: *Please close the door behind you.*

▸ **bolt** to fasten or lock something with a bolt: *We bolted the front door when we left the house.*

▸ **latch** to close or fasten something with a latch: *She latched the door of the rabbit pen to keep them from getting out.*

▸ **lock** to fasten or secure something with a lock: *She locked her desk drawer.*

▸ **shut** to close something, especially so as to block passage: *He shut the blinds to keep out the afternoon sun.*

closet *noun* a small room in which clothes or household supplies can be kept: *see* **shelf**

cloth *noun* material produced by weaving or knitting natural or synthetic fibers: *see* **fabric**

clothing

noun coverings, such as shirts, pants, or dresses, worn on the human body: *Most of her clothing is black.*

▸ **apparel** (formal) the things that are worn by a person; clothing: *This store sells men's apparel.*

▸ **attire** (formal) clothing worn for a certain purpose: *I prefer cotton sleeping attire.*

▸ **dress** a style of clothing: *Tuxedos are appropriate dress for a formal occasion.*

▸ **garment** an article of clothing: *Some garments need to be dry-cleaned.*

▸ **outfit** a set of clothing and accessories that go together: *She bought the outfit that she saw in the store window.*

▸ **suit** a set of matching outer garments, especially one consisting of a coat and trousers or a skirt: *He wears a suit and tie to work.*

▸ **uniform** a suit of distinctive clothing worn by members of a group, such as the police or the military: *Each branch of the military wears a different uniform.*

cloud *noun* a visible mass of tiny drops of water or particles of ice floating in the air: *see* **mist**

cloudburst *noun* a sudden, heavy rainfall: *see* **rain**

cloudy *adjective* marked by or covered with clouds: *see* **overcast**

club

noun a group of people organized for a common purpose: *The hiking **club** explores a new trail every month.*

▸ **alliance** a close association of nations or other groups that is formed to promote their common interests: *The rebel groups formed an **alliance** to overthrow the government.*

▸ **association** a group of people joined together for a common purpose or interest: *This **association** raises money for cancer research.*

▸ **guild** an association of people who share an occupation, interest, or cause: *The glass blowers' **guild** meets once a month.*

▸ **league** a group of nations, people, or organizations working together for a common goal: *Our softball **league** consists of six teams.*

▸ **organization** a group of people united for some purpose or work: *We donate money to an **organization** that helps plant trees in urban areas.*

▸ **society** an organization or association of people who share common interests or activities: *The bird-watching **society** took a trip to the wildlife preserve.*

▸ **union** an organization of workers formed to protect and promote their interests: *The labor **union** fought for an increase in wages.*

clue

noun something that helps to solve a problem or mystery: *The murder weapon is the only **clue** that the police have.*

▸ **hint** a slight sign or suggestion; a piece of useful information: *I'll give you a **hint** about what you're getting for your birthday.*

▸ **tip** a piece of useful information; a helpful hint: *The accountant gave her client a **tip** on how to save more money.*

clumsy *adjective* lacking grace or skill in motion or action: *see* **awkward**

clutch *verb* to grasp and cling tightly to something: *see* **hold**

clutter *noun* a disordered or confused collection: *see* **mess**

cluttered *adjective* full of a disordered collection of things: *see* **messy**

coach *verb* to teach or train athletes, athletic teams, or performers: *see* **teach**

coarse *adjective* not smooth to the touch: *see* **rough**

coast *noun* the edge of the land next to or near the sea: *see* **beach**

coat *verb* to cover something with a thin layer: *see* **cover**

coat *noun* a natural covering such as the skin, fur, or wool of an animal: *see* **hide**[1]

coating *noun* a layer of a substance spread over a surface: *see* **layer**

coax *verb* to persuade or try to persuade someone by gentle urging and flattery: *see* **persuade**

coddle *verb* to treat someone tenderly: *see* **indulge**

code *noun* a system of rules, regulations, or laws: *see* **philosophy**

coffeehouse *noun* a restaurant where coffee and other refreshments are served: *see* **restaurant**

coil *noun* a series of spirals or rings formed by winding: *see* **curve**

coin *noun* a piece of metal issued by a government for use as money: *see* **money**

coincidence *noun* a combination of events or circumstances that is accidental but seems to have been planned: *see* **chance**

cold

adjective having or being at a low or relatively low temperature: *To keep the ice cream **cold**, I put it in the freezer.*

▸ **chilly** cold enough to cause or feel discomfort: *The weather becomes **chilly** during the fall.*

▸ **cool** neither warm nor very cold: *He put on his sweater when the evening became **cool**.*

► **freezing** cold enough to turn a liquid into a solid; very cold: *It must have been freezing last night because all the puddles have ice on them.*

► **frigid** extremely cold: *The air in Antarctica is frigid.*

► **frosty** so cold as to produce frost; covered with small icy crystals: *My milkshake was served in a frosty mug.*

► **icy** containing or covered with ice; frozen: *I slipped on the icy sidewalk.*

► **raw** unpleasantly damp and chilly: *A raw winter wind blew off the ocean.*

ANTONYM **hot** having or giving off great heat

coliseum *noun* a large amphitheater for public sports events, entertainment, or assemblies: *see* **theater**

collapse *verb* to fall down or inward suddenly: *see* **fall**

colleague *noun* a fellow member of a staff or organization: *see* **partner**

collect *verb* to bring an assortment of items together in a group: *see* **gather**

collection *noun* a group of things brought or kept together for study or enjoyment: *see* **assortment**

college *noun* a school of higher learning that grants a bachelor's degree: *see* **school**

collision *noun* ▷ the act of colliding or crashing ▷ a conflict of opposing interests or ideas: *see* **accident**

color

noun a quality of light that makes things appear as red, blue, yellow, and so forth: *The color blue has been proven to make people feel calm.*

► **hue** the basic color of something: *Orange and yellow are both hues of the rainbow.*

► **shade** a dark or light variety of a color; the degree with which it is mixed with black: *That shade of green looks very nice on you.*

► **tinge** a hint of color: *The yellow rose had a tinge of pink at the center.*

► **tint** a light, pale, or delicate color: *I added a tint of blue to the frosting.*

colorful

adjective ▷ full of color, especially several vivid colors: *The fields of flowers were very colorful.* ▷ full of interest or variety: *He gave a colorful description of his trip to the West Indies.*

► **flamboyant** so richly or brightly colored as to attract attention: *The dancers wore flamboyant red and yellow costumes.*

► **flashy** creating a brief impression of brilliance; eye-catching: *She likes to wear flashy jewelry.*

► **gaudy** too fancy and bright to be in good taste: *The movie star wore a gaudy outfit to the award ceremony.*

► **vivid** bright and strong; brilliant: *The parrot's feathers were vivid green and red.*

colorless *adjective* completely lacking in color: *see* **pale**

column *noun* an upright structure used in a building as a support: *see* **pole**

comb *verb* to smooth or arrange the hair with a comb: *see* **groom**

combat *noun* fighting, especially armed battle: *see* **war**

combative *adjective* ready or inclined to fight or argue: *see* **aggressive**

combine *verb* to join two or more substances into a single substance: *see* **mix**

combined *adjective* joined together: *see* **joint**

come *verb* to advance toward a person or thing; to approach: *see* **appear [1]**

come to pass *verb* to happen, especially as one of a series of events: *see* **happen**

comfort

verb to make someone feel better in a time of pain, loss, or fear: *The mother comforted the crying children her arms.*

▶ **console** to comfort someone in a time of disappointment or sorrow: *The coach consoled the losing team by telling them they had played their best.*

▶ **ease** to free someone from worry, pain, or trouble: *Knowing that you are safe has eased my mind.*

▶ **lull** to cause someone to sleep or rest: *The soft music lulled me to sleep.*

▶ **soothe** to calm or quiet a person or animal: *She soothed the frightened dog by petting it.*

comfortable

adjective providing physical comfort: *This easy chair is very comfortable.*

▶ **cozy** warm and snug: *They live in a cozy little cabin in the woods.*

▶ **snug** giving comfort and protection: *I couldn't wait to get into my nice snug bed.*

ANTONYM **uncomfortable** experiencing or causing physical discomfort

comforter *noun* a thick, warm quilt used as a bed cover: *see* **cover**

comic *adjective* very funny; amusing: *see* **silly**

comical *adjective* causing amusement, especially by being ridiculous or silly: *see* **funny**

commander *noun* a person in charge, especially in the military: *see* **leader**

commence *verb* (formal) to perform the first part of an action: *see* **begin**

commend *verb* to speak highly of someone: *see* **praise**

comment

noun a remark or written note that explains something or gives an opinion: *My teacher always writes comments on our papers.*

▶ **observation** a comment or remark drawn from experience: *Bill Cosby is famous for his funny observations on parenting.*

▶ **remark** a casual statement or comment: *He made a remark about her flashy jewelry.*

▶ **statement** something expressed in words; a declaration: *The lawyer prepared a final statement to present to the jury.*

commerce *noun* the exchange and distribution of goods or commodities: *see* **business [2]**

commercial *noun* an advertisement on radio or television: *see* **advertisement**

commission *noun* money paid to someone for each piece of work done or for each thing sold: *see* **income**

committee

noun a group of people officially chosen to perform a function, such as making decisions or conducting an investigation: *The graduate student presented his thesis to the committee.*

▶ **board** an organized body of administrators or investigators: *The school board discussed giving the teachers a raise.*

▶ **council** a body of people elected or appointed to administrate, legislate, or advise: *Our city is governed by a council and a mayor.*

▶ **panel** a group of people gathered together to plan or discuss an issue, judge a contest, or take part in a game show: *The panel of scientists did not always agree.*

commodity *noun* something that is bought and sold: *see* **merchandise**

common

adjective found or occurring often: *It is common to serve cake and ice cream at a birthday party.*

▶ **everyday** happening often or regularly; not unusual: *Minor scrapes and bruises are an everyday occurrence at a daycare center.*

▶ **familiar** often encountered or seen; well known because of frequent occurrence: *Rain clouds are a familiar sight in the Pacific Northwest.*

▶ **general** not limited or specialized: *This book has general appeal.*

▶ **generic** not distinguished from others of its kind; usual: *We removed the generic* *tub from the bathroom and replaced it with a Victorian clawfoot tub.*

▸ **ordinary** commonly met with; usual: *It is **ordinary** for rock bands to have a lead singer.*

▸ **prevalent** widely or commonly occurring or practiced: *Coyotes are **prevalent** in this area.*

▸ **widespread** existing, happening, or used in many places by many people: *There was **widespread** celebrating when the war was over.*

ANTONYM **unusual** not usual, common, or ordinary

commonly *adverb* ordinarily; usually: *see* **often**

common sense *noun* good judgment gained from everyday experience: *see* **wisdom**

commotion

noun noisy activity; confusion: *There was a **commotion** when the fire alarm went off.*

▸ **fuss** nervous or useless activity or concern: *She made a **fuss** when the sofa wasn't delivered on time.*

▸ **scuffle** a rough, disorderly struggle: *There was a minor **scuffle** when both children wanted to play with the same toy.*

▸ **tumult** noise and commotion; the uproar of a large crowd: *The **tumult** from the stadium could be heard for blocks.*

commune *noun* a small, often rural community, whose members share common interests and often income and property: *see* **town**

communicate *verb* ▷ to make something known ▷ to express oneself in such a way that one is clearly understood: *see* **tell**

community

noun a group of people living in the same area or under the same government: *Our **community** voted to build a new public swimming pool.*

▸ **district** an area or region that has a certain use or characteristic: *We went shopping in Albuquerque's Old Town **district.***

▸ **neighborhood** a particular area or section of a city or town: *There is a grade school in this **neighborhood.***

compact *adjective* occupying little space in comparison to others of its type: *see* **short [1]**

companion *noun* a person who often associates with or accompanies another person: *see* **friend**

company *noun* a business enterprise: *see* **business [1]**

company *noun* a guest or guests: *see* **guest**

compare

verb to examine things to see how they are alike or different: *She **compares** prices when she goes grocery shopping.*

▸ **contrast** to compare things in order to reveal important differences: *The teacher asked us to **contrast** two different systems of government.*

▸ **liken** to describe something as being like something else: *The shadows on the moon have been **likened** to a man's face.*

▸ **parallel** to match something else feature for feature: *The movie **paralleled** the novel in most ways, but it had a different ending.*

compartment *noun* a separate section or room, often set off by walls: *see* **room**

compassion *noun* a feeling of sharing the suffering of someone else, along with a desire to help: *see* **sympathy**

compel *verb* to make someone do something by force or necessity: *see* **demand**

competent *adjective* able to do something with satisfactory skill: *see* **able**

competition *noun* a test to see who has greater skill or ability: *see* **contest**

compile *verb* to put items together in a single list or collection: *see* **gather**

complain

verb to express feelings of pain, dissatisfaction, or resentment: *She* **complained** *to the manager about the rude salesperson.*

- **gripe** (informal) to complain in a nagging or irritating way: *My brother always* **gripes** *when it's his turn to do the dishes.*
- **grumble** to complain in a sullen or discontented way; to mutter: *The staff began to* **grumble** *when they were told that they had to work late again.*
- **object** to express an opposing opinion or argument; to protest: *He* **objected** *to the additional fee.*
- **whine** to complain in a childish, annoying way: *The tired child began to* **whine** *and cry.*

complaint

noun an expression of dissatisfaction, resentment, or pain: *She filed a* **complaint** *about the neighbor's dog.*

- **criticism** an expression of critical or unfavorable opinion: *My main* **criticism** *of your paper is that it's too long.*
- **grievance** a real or imagined wrong regarded as just cause for protest: *A mediator was called in to settle the* **grievances** *of each party.*
- **objection** a statement of an opposing view or argument: *Does anyone have an* **objection** *to going out for pizza tonight?*
- **protest** a formal declaration of disapproval or objection: *The workers held a* **protest** *against the terrible conditions of the factory.*

complete *adjective* having all necessary or desired parts: *see* **all**

complete *verb* to bring something to an end: *see* **finish**

completed *adjective* having come or been brought to an end: *see* **done**

completely

adverb in a manner that includes everything or leaves nothing out: *We have* **completely** *redecorated the living room.*

- **entirely** with no doubt or exception; completely: *I'm not* **entirely** *sure of the address.*
- **fully** to a full extent or degree; completely: *The salesperson said that we could bring the appliance back if we were not* **fully** *satisfied.*
- **perfectly** fully; entirely: *I was* **perfectly** *happy lying in bed and watching a movie.*
- **thoroughly** in a very thorough way; completely: *The police* **thoroughly** *inspected the crime scene.*
- **totally** fully; absolutely: *We were* **totally** *drenched after washing the car.*
- **wholly** entirely; completely: *She is* **wholly** *convinced that her cat understands what she says to it.*

complex *adjective* consisting of many parts or aspects: *see* **fancy**

complicated *adjective* not easy to understand, deal with, or solve: *see* **hard**

compliment *verb* to express praise to someone: *see* **praise**

comply *verb* to follow a request or rule: *see* **obey**

component *noun* one of the parts that make up a whole: *see* **ingredient**

compose *verb* to create a musical or literary work: *see* **write**

composition *noun* an arrangement of parts to form a whole: *see* **design**

composition *noun* a short essay, especially one written as an academic exercise: *see* **essay**

compost *noun* a mixture of decaying organic matter used to enrich the soil: *see* **garbage**

comprehend *verb* to understand something fully: *see* **understand**

comprehensive *adjective* large in scope or content: *see* **careful [1]**

compress

verb to make something more compact by pressing on it: *I **compressed** the down sleeping bag by rolling it up.*

▸ **condense** to reduce the volume of something: *This soup has been **condensed** so you have to add water when you cook it.*

▸ **constrict** to make something smaller or narrower by binding or squeezing: *Some snakes wrap around their prey and **constrict** it so that it can't breathe.*

▸ **contract** to get smaller in size by drawing closer together: *Many materials expand when they are heated and **contract** when they are cooled.*

▸ **shrink** to become smaller in size, amount, or value: *The wool sweater **shrank** when it got washed in hot water.*

compute *verb* to work out a result, an answer, or a solution by using mathematics: *see* **add**

comrade *noun* a companion, especially one who shares one's activities: *see* **friend**

con *verb* (informal) to trick or coax someone into doing something by first winning the person's trust: *see* **cheat**

con artist *noun* a swindler who tricks someone into doing something by first winning the person's confidence: *see* **imposter**

conceal *verb* to keep someone or something from being noticed or known: *see* **hide²**

concede *verb* to admit that something is true, often without wanting to: *see* **admit**

conceit *noun* too high an opinion of oneself: *see* **pride**

conceited *adjective* having an overly high opinion of oneself: *see* **proud**

conceivable *adjective* capable of being thought of: *see* **possible**

conceivably *adverb* possibly; in theory: *see* **maybe**

conceive *verb* to develop something in one's mind: *see* **invent**

concept *noun* a general idea: *see* **idea**

concern *noun* something that causes one to feel troubled or anxious: *see* **worry**

concerning *preposition* having to do with: *see* **about**

concert *noun* a musical performance given by a musician or a number of musicians: *see* **show**

conclude *verb* to bring something to a close, especially formally or ceremoniously: *see* **finish**

conclusion *noun* the end result of a process: *see* **result**

concoct *verb* to devise something using skill and intelligence: *see* **invent**

concoction *noun* something prepared or created, especially a mixture of different ingredients: *see* **invention**

concrete *adjective* existing in reality as something that can be perceived by the senses: *see* **real [2]**

concur *verb* to have the same opinion as someone else: *see* **agree**

condemn *verb* to express a strong feeling or moral opinion against something or someone: *see* **blame**

condense *verb* to shorten something so as to make it brief and clear: *see* **abbreviate**

condense *verb* to reduce the volume of something: *see* **compress**

condition *noun* the way someone or something is: *see* **situation**

condominium *noun* an apartment building in which the individual apartments are owned by the people living in them: *see* **house**

condone *verb* to overlook, forgive, or disregard an offense without protest or disapproval: *see* **forgive**

conduct *noun* the way a person acts: *see* **behavior**

conduct *verb* to lead, guide, or direct someone: *see* **escort**

confer *verb* to meet in order to discuss something or compare options: *see* **discuss**

conference *noun* a meeting to discuss one or more subjects: *see* **meeting**

confess *verb* to admit that one has done something bad, wrong, or illegal: *see* **admit**

confidence *noun* a feeling of certainty that a person or thing will not fail: *see* **trust**

confident

adjective feeling sure of oneself; having no self-doubt: *The skateboarder felt **confident** that he could win the competition.*

▸ **assured** feeling confident, especially as a result of experience: *The popular comedian was **assured** in front of the audience.*

▸ **poised** calm and confident in manner; not nervous: *The speaker was **poised** as she answered questions.*

▸ **secure** feeling safe and sure; not frightened or worried: *My little niece feels more **secure** when she has her blanket with her.*

confirm *verb* to offer sure proof that something is true or correct: *see* **prove**

confirmation *noun* something that confirms: *see* **answer**

conflict *noun* a state of open, often prolonged fighting: *see* **war**

conform *verb* to follow or be in agreement with a set standard or rule: *see* **agree**

confront *verb* to meet or face someone with anger or resolution: *see* **face**

confuse

verb to make someone unable to think clearly: *The complicated directions for installing the new software **confused** me.*

▸ **baffle** to frustrate and confuse someone through an inability to understand: *The disappearance of my other tennis shoe **baffles** me.*

▸ **bewilder** to completely confuse someone, especially with conflicting statements, situations, or objects: *The overwhelming selection of cereal **bewildered** her so much that she ended up not buying any.*

▸ **disorient** to cause a loss of one's sense of direction or position: *The poorly marked street signs **disoriented** him, and he went the wrong way.*

▸ **mystify** to confuse someone beyond any hope of understanding: *Calculus **mystifies** me.*

▸ **perplex** to confuse someone even after much thought: *The strange message that was left on his answering machine **perplexed** him.*

▸ **puzzle** to baffle someone by presenting a seemingly unsolvable problem: *Her miraculous recovery **puzzled** her doctors.*

confusion

noun lack of order or discipline; disorderly action or behavior: *There was **confusion** in the store when the power went out.*

▸ **anarchy** disorder and confusion resulting from lack of authority: *There was **anarchy** when the ruler died without having named a successor.*

▸ **chaos** a condition or place of great disorder or confusion: *The children's birthday party turned to **chaos** when the piñata was broken open.*

▸ **turmoil** a state of extreme confusion, emotional disturbance, or excitement: *I was in **turmoil** after my boyfriend and I broke up.*

▸ **upheaval** a sudden, violent disruption or upset: *The sudden resignation of the CEO caused a lot of **upheaval** in the company.*

congratulate *verb* to give praise or good wishes to someone at a happy event or for something done well: *see* **praise**

congregate *verb* to come together as a crowd: *see* **meet**

connect *verb* to link two or more things together: *see* **join**

connection *noun* the point at which something is joined or fastened together: *see* **joint**

conquer *verb* to overcome an opponent or enemy by force: *see* **defeat**

consent *verb*   to agree to someone's wish or request: *see* **authorize**

consequence *noun*   something that happens as a result of another action or condition: *see* **result**

consequently *adverb*   as a result: *see* **therefore**

conservative

adjective   wanting things to stay as they are or as they used to be; opposed to change: *The **conservative** members of the school board voted against increasing the budget.*

- ▸ **conventional**   following accepted practice, custom, or taste: *They chose a **conventional** color scheme for the outside of the house.*
- ▸ **moderate**   not excessive or extreme; kept within reasonable limits: *This shop has good clothes at **moderate** prices.*
- ▸ **traditional**   passed down by or in agreement with tradition: *My cousin and her fiancé decided to have a **traditional** church wedding.*

conserve *verb*   to use something carefully so as not to waste or harm it: *see* **keep**

consider

verb   to think carefully about something before deciding: *She **considered** her options before choosing which programs to apply to.*

- ▸ **reflect**   to take time to think seriously about something: *It is good to **reflect** on one's blessings.*
- ▸ **weigh**   to think about something in great detail in order to make a decision: *The committee will **weigh** the advantages and disadvantages of each proposal.*

considerate *adjective*   thoughtful of others and their feelings: *see* **kind¹**

consideration *noun*   careful thought for the purpose of making a judgment or forming an opinion: *see* **attention**

consideration *noun*   thoughtful concern for others: *see* **sympathy**

consistent *adjective*   happening or behaving in the same way all the time: *see* **regular**

console *verb*   to comfort someone in a time of disappointment or sorrow: *see* **comfort**

conspire *verb*   to plan together secretly to do something wrong: *see* **plot**

constant

adjective   happening all the time; not changing: *A newborn infant requires almost **constant** attention.*

- ▸ **chronic**   lasting a long period of time or recurring frequently: *His smoking habit has given him a **chronic** cough.*
- ▸ **continual**   repeated regularly and frequently: *It is hard to study with your **continual** interruptions.*
- ▸ **continuous**   continuing without any pause: *The human brain needs a **continuous** supply of oxygen-rich blood.*
- ▸ **persistent**   insistently repetitive or continuous: *I could hear the **persistent** ringing of the telephone in the apartment next door.*
- ▸ **steady**   free or almost free from change; uniform: *He drove at a **steady** speed.*

constantly *adverb*   happening continually: *see* **always**

constrict *verb*   to make something smaller or narrower by binding or squeezing: *see* **compress**

construct *verb*   to build or put something together: *see* **build**

consume *verb*   to eat or drink something completely: *see* **eat**

contact *verb*   to get in touch with someone: *see* **meet**

contain *verb*   to have or hold something within: *see* **include**

container

noun   an object that is used to hold something; a receptacle: *She stores her tea in a colorful tin **container**.*

‣ **bin** an enclosed space for storing food, grain, coal, or other dry substances: *The coal **bin** is almost empty.*

‣ **box** a stiff container usually having four sides, a bottom, and often a top or lid: *We put our winter clothes in a **box** and stored them in the attic.*

‣ **can** an airtight, often cylindrical metal container in which food and beverages are preserved: *I bought three **cans** of soup at the market.*

‣ **carton** a cardboard or plastic box made in various shapes and sizes: *Please buy a **carton** of milk when you go to the store.*

‣ **case** a container, especially one designed to hold a particular item: *The gold necklace came in a velvet **case**.*

‣ **chest** a large, sturdy box with a lid, used especially for holding or storing things: *We have an old **chest** in which we store games and toys.*

‣ **crate** a case that is made for packing and shipping something: *The washing machine was shipped in a wooden **crate**.*

‣ **trunk** a large, sturdy box in which clothes or belongings can be packed for travel or storage: *My father has a **trunk** that he used when he was in the Air Force.*

contaminate *verb* to make something impure or unfit for use: *see* **pollute**

contemporary *adjective* being part of today's world: *see* **modern**

contempt *noun* a feeling of scorn or cold superiority: *see* **hate**

contend *verb* to argue that something is true, often without proof: *see* **claim**

content

adjective happy with what one is or has: *I couldn't go to the ball game, so I had to be **content** to watch it on TV.*

‣ **pleased** filled with pleasure; gratified: *I was **pleased** that my friend came to visit me.*

‣ **satisfied** filled with satisfaction; not wanting anything more: *She was very **satisfied** with all the bargains she found when she went shopping.*

contentment *noun* quiet happiness and satisfaction; peace of mind: *see* **happiness**

contest

noun a struggle for victory or superiority among participants: *His bread won second place in the cooking **contest**.*

‣ **championship** a contest held to determine a champion: *Our school volleyball team won the **championship**.*

‣ **competition** a test to see who has greater skill or ability; a contest: *They won first prize in the salsa-dancing **competition**.*

‣ **lottery** a contest in which tickets are sold and the winner is determined in a random drawing: *We bought two tickets for the **lottery**.*

‣ **tournament** a contest made up of a series of games: *Our team advanced to the second round of the wrestling **tournament**.*

context *noun* the particular circumstances in which something exists or occurs: *see* **situation**

continual *adjective* repeated regularly and frequently: *see* **constant**

continue *verb* to keep on doing something: *see* **advance**

continuous *adjective* continuing without any pause: *see* **constant**

contract *noun* a written agreement that can be enforced by law: *see* **agreement**

contract *verb* to get smaller in size by drawing closer together: *see* **compress**

contraction *noun* the shortening and thickening of a muscle in action: *see* **cramp**

contrary to *preposition* completely different than something else: *see* **against**

contrast *verb* to compare things in order to reveal important differences: *see* **compare**

contribute *verb* to give something in common with others: *see* **give**

contribution *noun* something given toward a goal or purpose: *see* **gift**

control

verb ▷ to hold someone or something back: *I struggled to* **control** *my anger at the speaker's remarks.* ▷ to exercise authority or influence over something: *The finance officer* **controls** *the spending of the company.*

- ► **check** to cause something to stop suddenly: *A sandbag dike* **checked** *the rising flood waters.*
- ► **curb** to check, restrain, or control something: *I am trying to* **curb** *my habit of interrupting people when they are speaking to me.*
- ► **curtail** (formal) to cut something short: *We* **curtailed** *our stay at the beach because the weather was too hot.*
- ► **dominate** to rule, control, or govern something or someone by superior power or authority: *Among many animals, the strongest male* **dominates** *the group.*
- ► **leash** to restrain an animal with a leash: *I* **leashed** *my dog before taking her for walk.*
- ► **restrain** to hold something or someone back by physical force: *The police* **restrained** *the violent man by holding his arms.*

convenient *adjective* ▷ suited to one's comfort or purpose ▷ close at hand; nearby: *see* **useful**

convention *noun* a formal assembly or meeting: *see* **meeting**

convention *noun* a practice or procedure widely observed in a group: *see* **tradition**

conventional *adjective* following accepted practice, custom, or taste: *see* **conservative**

conversation *noun* an exchange of thought or ideas between two or more people: *see* **talk**

converse *verb* (formal) to exchange thoughts or ideas with another person: *see* **talk**

convert *verb* ▷ to change something from one form to another ▷ to make something suitable for a different use: *see* **change**

convey *verb* to communicate something: *see* **mean²**

convict *noun* a person serving a prison sentence: *see* **criminal**

conviction *noun* a strong belief: *see* **opinion**

convince *verb* to persuade someone to do or believe something: *see* **persuade**

convulsion *noun* a violent, involuntary muscular contraction: *see* **cramp**

cook

verb to prepare food for eating by using heat: *I* **cooked** *eggs and toast for breakfast.*

- ► **bake** to cook food in an oven with dry heat: *We* **baked** *potatoes in the oven.*
- ► **broil** to cook food under a flame or direct heat: *He likes to* **broil** *fish until the top is golden brown.*
- ► **fry** to cook food in hot oil or fat: *She* **fried** *the bacon in a skillet.*
- ► **grill** to cook food over a flame or direct heat: *We* **grilled** *hot dogs at the beach.*
- ► **heat** to make food warm or hot: *She* **heated** *the baby's bottle by holding it under hot water.*
- ► **microwave** to cook or heat something in a microwave oven: *He* **microwaved** *his socks in order to dry them.*
- ► **roast** to cook food with dry heat, as in an oven or near hot coals: *We* **roasted** *marshmallows over the campfire.*
- ► **simmer** to be cooked gently or just at the boiling point: *The soup* **simmered** *gently on the stove.*

cool *adjective* neither warm nor very cold: *see* **cold**

coop *noun* a cage or pen, especially one for poultry: *see* **cage**

cooperative *adjective* willing to help or work with others for a common purpose: *see* **willing**

coordinate *verb* to cause two or more things to work together well: *see* **plot**

cope

verb to deal with a problem or difficult situation successfully: *The babysitter had a tough time* **coping** *with five children.*

▶ **accept** to put up with something patiently: *Sometimes it is hard to **accept** not having a car.*

▶ **bear** to endure something unpleasant or difficult: *She cannot **bear** to wear anything made of wool because it makes her skin itch.*

▶ **endure** to bear something with patience or tolerance: *He **endured** the harsh comments of his critics because he knew he was right.*

▶ **handle** to take care of a difficult task or situation: *My boss asked me to **handle** the arrangements for the upcoming conference.*

▶ **put up with** to bear or accept something without complaint: *I'm not going to **put up with** any more of your lies about me.*

▶ **suffer** to endure great pain or distress: *He **suffered** a lot of pain before having back surgery.*

▶ **tolerate** to put up with hardship, annoyance, or bad conditions: *Desert plants can **tolerate** hot, dry weather for long periods of time.*

copious *adjective* very large in quantity: *see* **abundant**

copy

verb to make something that is exactly like the original: *I **copied** the quotation word for word.*

▶ **duplicate** (formal) to copy something exactly, as my photocopying: *She **duplicated** her book report in case something happened to the original.*

▶ **echo** to repeat a sound: *The crowd's cheering **echoed** loudly in the gymnasium.*

▶ **imitate** to follow something as a model or example: *Comedians often **imitate** the mannerisms of famous people.*

▶ **mimic** to imitate something or someone exactly: *My parrot **mimics** a lot of what he hears people say.*

▶ **repeat** to say or do what someone has already said or done: *She **repeated** the good news to everyone she saw.*

▶ **reproduce** to make a copy of something: *I thought the article was interesting so I **reproduced** it to share with my friends.*

cord *noun* a small rope of twisted strands: *see* **rope**

core *noun* the basic or most important part of something: *see* **center** [1]

cork *noun* a bottle stopper that is made out of a light, spongy wood: *see* **lid**

corner *noun* the point or place at which two lines or surfaces meet: *see* **joint**

corporation *noun* a group of people who run a business as a unit that is legally separate from the people themselves: *see* **business** [1]

corpse *noun* a dead body, especially that of a human: *see* **body**

corral *noun* a fenced-in area for cattle or horses: *see* **cage**

correct *adjective* free from error: *see* **true**

correction *noun* (formal) punishment intended to rehabilitate or improve an offender: *see* **penalty**

correspond *verb* to have an exact relationship to something else: *see* **agree**

corridor *noun* a hall or passage, especially in a large building: *see* **hall**

corrupt *noun* dishonest for an immoral purpose: *see* **dishonest**

corrupt *verb* to infect or spoil something: *see* **pollute**

cost *noun* the amount paid or charged for something: *see* **price**

costly *adjective* high-priced: *see* **expensive**

costume *noun* an outfit or disguise worn on a special occasion: *see* **disguise**

cottage *noun* a small house in the country: *see* **house**

council *noun* a body of people elected or appointed to administrate, legislate, or advise: *see* **committee**

counsel *noun* (formal) an opinion about what should be done: *see* **suggestion**

counselor *noun* a person who gives counsel or guidance, as with personal problems: *see* **teacher**

count *verb* to find the total number of something by listing items one by one: *see* **add**

counter *verb* to oppose an idea or action with something different or opposite: *see* **reverse**

counterfeit *adjective* made in imitation of what is genuine with the intent to deceive: *see* **fake**

countless *adjective* too many to count: *see* **many**

count on *verb* to rely on someone or something to perform as expected: *see* **trust**

country

noun a land in which people live under a single government; a nation: *Canada and Mexico are the countries that border the United States.*

- ► **empire** a group of territories or nations headed by a single ruler: *India was once a part of the British empire.*
- ► **homeland** the country in which one was born or has lived for a long time: *My grandparents left their homeland in Asia and settled in America.*
- ► **kingdom** a country that is ruled by a queen or king: *Saudi Arabia is a kingdom that was founded in 1932.*
- ► **nation** a group of people who share the same territory and are organized under a single government; a country: *It was inspiring to watch the athletes march into the Olympic arena behind their nations' flags.*
- ► **state** a political body that makes up a nation: *The state of Israel was created in 1948.*

couple *noun* two people who are closely associated with each other: *see* **pair**

courage

noun the quality that makes a person able to face danger or difficulty with confidence, determination, and firm control of oneself: *The firefighters were praised for their great courage in rescuing people from the burning building.*

- ► **boldness** lack of fear or caution: *Moving to a new city was an act of boldness for her.*
- ► **bravery** the quality of showing courage: *I admire the bravery of the astronauts who flew the first mission to the moon.*
- ► **heroism** courageous action that results in great achievement: *I read an article about the heroism of a boy who saved his mother from drowning.*
- ► **nerve** courage and control under pressure: *I was going to try a backflip from the diving board, but at the last minute I lost my nerve.*
- ► **pluck** courage and daring; spirit: *It took a lot of pluck for me to ask my boss for a raise.*
- ► **valor** courage and boldness in combat: *My uncle received the Silver Star for valor during the Gulf War.*

courageous *adjective* able to face danger or hardship with confidence, resolution, and firm control of oneself: *see* **brave**

course *noun* a complete body of studies or a unit of such studies: *see* **class**

court *verb* to try to win the love of someone in order to marry him or her: *see* **romance**

courteous *adjective* considerate towards others: *see* **polite**

courtesy *noun* a polite gesture or remark: *see* **favor**

courtyard *noun* an open space surrounded by buildings or enclosed by walls: *see* **park**

cove *noun* a small, sheltered bay or inlet: *see* **harbor**

covenant *noun* a formal agreement between people or groups: *see* **promise**

cover

noun something placed on or attached to something else to close, protect, or conceal it: *I need a cover to keep the dust off my computer.*

- ► **bedspread** a decorative covering for a bed: *My great-aunt crocheted a beautiful bedspread for me.*

▸ **blanket** a covering used to keep a person warm: *You'll need an extra* **blanket** *on the bed when the weather gets colder.*

▸ **comforter** a thick, warm quilt used as a bed cover: *My* **comforter** *matches my bedroom curtains.*

▸ **duvet** a quilt, usually with a washable cover, used in place of a bedspread and top sheet: *She bought a new cover for her* **duvet**.

▸ **quilt** a bed covering made of two layers of cloth with a layer of soft cotton or wool in between and held together by decorative stitching: *I bought some fabric to make a* **quilt**.

▸ **sheet** a large piece of thin cloth used as a bed covering, especially in pairs: *The* **sheets** *I bought are too small for our double bed.*

cover

verb to spread out over the surface of something: *The first snow of the season* **covered** *the ground.*

▸ **coat** to cover something with a thin layer: *Dust* **coated** *me as I sanded the walls.*

▸ **glaze** to apply a smooth, shiny coating to something: *She* **glazed** *the cake with a thin frosting.*

▸ **smear** to spread, cover, or stain something with a sticky or greasy substance: *He* **smeared** *sunscreen on his arms.*

covering *noun* something that covers so as to protect or conceal: *see* **layer**

covet *verb* to wish for something that belongs to another: *see* **want**

covetous *adjective* wanting something that belongs to another: *see* **jealous**

coy *adjective* pretending to be shy or bashful, especially in a flirtatious way: *see* **shy**

cozy *adjective* warm and snug: *see* **comfortable**

crack *verb* to break without completely separating: *see* **break**

crack *noun* a narrow opening: *see* **gap**

crackle *noun* a slight, sharp, snapping sound: *see* **rustle**

craft *noun* skill in making something, especially with the hands: *see* **art**

crafty

adjective skilled at deceiving or outwitting others: *Genghis Khan was a* **crafty** *and fearless leader.*

▸ **cunning** clever in deceiving people or in gaining an advantage: *The* **cunning** *spy was able to enter enemy headquarters without being noticed.*

▸ **shrewd** clever, sharp, and practical: *The* **shrewd** *stockbroker has a reputation for knowing when to buy and sell.*

▸ **sly** clever or cunning in a secretive way: *She appeared to be a sweet person but actually was very* **sly**.

▸ **sneaky** skilled at acting without anyone noticing: *The* **sneaky** *dog pulled the ham off the table while no one was looking.*

▸ **wily** full of plans and tricks intended to deceive others; cunning: *The* **wily** *boy was always finding ways to avoid doing his chores.*

cram *verb* to force or squeeze something tightly into a space: *see* **fill**

cramp

noun a sudden, painful contraction of a muscle: *I awoke in the night with a* **cramp** *in my leg.*

▸ **charley horse** (informal) a severe muscle cramp or stiffness in the arm or leg: *The runner had to stop because of a* **charley horse** *in her leg.*

▸ **contraction** the shortening and thickening of a muscle in action: *Hiccups are caused by an involuntary* **contraction** *of the diaphragm.*

▸ **convulsion** a violent, involuntary muscular contraction: *The patient went into* **convulsions** *because of a high fever.*

▸ **crick** a painful cramp or muscular spasm, especially in the back or neck: *He got a* **crick** *in his back from hunching over the computer for so many hours.*

▶ **spasm** a sudden, involuntary contraction of a muscle or group of muscles: *A muscle **spasm** can be very painful.*

▶ **twitch** an involuntary jerk or spasm of a muscle: *I get **twitches** in my eyelid when I'm overtired.*

cranky *adjective* in a bad mood: *see* **irritable**

cranny *noun* a small opening, as in a wall or rock: *see* **gap**

crash *noun* a violent collision: *see* **accident**

crate *noun* a case that is made for packing and shipping something: *see* **container**

crater *noun* a hollow area shaped like a bowl, as at the mouth of a volcano: *see* **hole**

crave *verb* to have an intense desire for something: *see* **want**

crawl

verb to move slowly on the hands and knees: *Babies learn to **crawl** before they walk.*

▶ **creep** to move slowly or cautiously with the body close to the ground: *The lion **crept** toward its prey.*

▶ **slink** to move in a quiet, sneaky way: *I watched the cat **slink** through the grass toward the bird feeder.*

▶ **slither** to move along by sliding or gliding like a snake: *The alligator **slithered** down the muddy bank into the river.*

craze *noun* something that is very popular for a short time: *see* **fashion**

craziness *noun* extreme foolishness: *see* **nonsense**

crazy *adjective* affected with mental illness: *see* **mentally ill**

crease *noun* a mark or line, usually formed by wrinkling or folding: *see* **fold**

create *verb* to bring something into being: *see* **invent**

creation *noun* an original product of human invention or artistic imagination: *see* **invention**

creative

adjective having the ability to create things; having original ideas: *e.e. cummings was an American poet who was very **creative** in how he placed words on the page.*

▶ **imaginative** having a strong, creative imagination: *The **imaginative** child liked to make up new games.*

▶ **ingenious** marked by inventive skill and imagination: *She came up with an **ingenious** solution to the problem.*

▶ **innovative** new and different; unlike anything before: *Our language instructor is trying some **innovative** teaching methods this year.*

▶ **inventive** having the ability to produce something new and creative: *He is an **inventive** cook and is always making variations to his recipes.*

▶ **resourceful** able to act effectively or imaginatively, especially in a difficult situation: *The lost hikers were **resourceful** and were able to build a shelter out of branches and vines.*

creativity *noun* originality and inventiveness: *see* **imagination**

creature *noun* a living being, especially an animal: *see* **animal**

credit card *noun* a card that entitles the holder to buy things and pay for them later: *see* **money**

creed *noun* a system of guiding beliefs or principles: *see* **philosophy**

creek *noun* a small stream of water, often one that flows into a river: *see* **river**

creep *verb* to move slowly or cautiously with the body close to the ground: *see* **crawl**

creepy *adjective* (informal) producing a feeling of uneasiness or fear: *see* **scary**

crest *noun* the highest part of something, especially a mountain or wave: *see* **top**

crevice *noun* a small, narrow, often shallow opening: *see* **gap**

crew *noun* a group of people who work together at a particular task: *see* **team**

crick *noun*   a painful cramp or muscular spasm, especially in the back or neck: *see* cramp

crime

noun   a violation of the law; unlawful activity: *Shoplifting is a crime.*

- **felony**   a serious crime such as murder, rape, or burglary: *He was found guilty of a felony and sent to prison.*
- **misdemeanor**   a crime less serious than a felony: *Driving on private property without the owner's permission is a misdemeanor.*
- **offense**   a violation of a moral, legal, or social code: *Jaywalking is a minor offense.*
- **sin**   the act of breaking a religious or moral law: *Most religions consider lying and stealing to be sins.*
- **trespass** (formal)   a violation of a moral or social law: *Reading someone's email without permission is a trespass against the rules of privacy.*
- **violation**   a breaking of the legal code: *I received a ticket for a parking violation.*

criminal

noun   a person who has committed a crime or been convicted of one: *The criminal violated his parole.*

- **convict**   a person serving a prison sentence: *Three convicts escaped from the state prison.*
- **crook** (informal)   a person who makes a living by dishonest methods: *A crook sold me a fake ticket to the Super Bowl.*
- **culprit**   a person who is guilty of wrongdoing: *Who's the culprit who ate my ice cream?*
- **felon**   a person who has committed a serious crime such as murder, rape, or burglary: *The felon was sentenced to serve twenty years in a state prison.*
- **fugitive**   a person who is running away, especially from the police: *Sheriff deputies caught the three fugitives before they had gone a hundred miles.*
- **gangster**   a member of an organized group of criminals: *The FBI arrested the gangster on charges of illegal drug dealing.*
- **outlaw**   a person who defies the law; a declared criminal: *Billy the Kid was a notorious outlaw of the Old West.*

cringe *verb*   to draw back in fear: *see* wince

crisis *noun*   a situation of great difficulty or danger: *see* disaster

critic *noun*   a person whose job it is to evaluate books, movies, or other artistic efforts: *see* judge

critical *adjective*   being in a state of crisis or emergency: *see* urgent

criticism *verb*   an expression of an unfavorable opinion: *see* complaint

criticize *verb*   to judge someone or something, especially negatively: *see* blame

critter *noun*   (informal)   a creature: *see* animal

crook *noun*   (informal)   a person who makes a living by dishonest methods: *see* criminal

croon *verb*   to hum or sing something softly: *see* hum

cross *adjective*   angry or annoyed: *see* irritable

crowd

noun   a large number of people gathered together: *A crowd of people gathered to watch the parade.*

- **horde**   a large, often active or disorderly crowd; a swarm: *There was a horde of people at the street fair.*
- **mass**   a large gathering of people or things: *A mass of people filled the city plaza to protest the cuts in city services.*
- **mob**   a large, disorderly or threatening crowd: *The soccer fans became an angry mob after their team lost the championship.*
- **multitude**   a very large number of people: *A multitude of tourists visited the city during its annual festival.*
- **swarm**   a large number of people, especially in motion: *A swarm of fans ran onto the field after the game.*

► **throng**   a large group of people crowded closely together: *A **throng** of people always gathers to celebrate New Year's Eve in Times Square in New York City.*

crown *noun*   an ornamental circlet or head covering often made of precious metal, set with jewels, and worn as a symbol of royalty: *see* **hat**

crown *noun*   the top part, especially of the head: *see* **top**

crucial *adjective*   of the utmost importance: *see* **urgent**

cruel *adjective*   liking or intended to cause pain or suffering: *see* **mean**[1]

cruise *verb*   to sail or travel about in an unhurried way: *see* **travel**

crumble *verb*   to break something into small pieces or crumbs: *see* **break**

crusade *noun*   a campaign or movement for a reform, cause, or ideal: *see* **campaign**

crush

verb   to press or squeeze something with enough force to break or injure it: *I always **crush** aluminum cans before recycling them.*

► **grind**   to crush something into small bits or a fine powder: *Millstones were once used to **grind** grain into flour.*

► **mash**   to convert something to a soft, pulpy mixture: *He **mashed** the potatoes before serving them.*

► **pound**   to strike or beat something forcefully and repeatedly: *I **pounded** the pill into a powder before putting it in my cat's food.*

► **press**   to squeeze the juice or other contents from something: *I **pressed** the juice from the lemon.*

► **smash**   to break something into pieces noisily and violently: *The thief **smashed** the window to get inside the car.*

► **squash**   to beat something into a pulp or a flattened mass: *I stepped on my nephew's toy car and **squashed** it.*

► **stamp**   to extinguish or destroy something by trampling it underfoot: *We **stamped** out the campfire before leaving.*

cry

verb   to shed tears, usually because of strong emotion: *Many people **cry** at weddings.*

► **bawl**   to cry or sob loudly: *The little boy **bawled** when he couldn't find his teddy bear.*

► **sob**   to weep aloud with gasps and sniffles; to cry uncontrollably: *I **sobbed** for hours when my cat died.*

► **wail**   to make loud, long crying sounds, especially in grief or protest: *In many cultures, it is traditional to **wail** aloud when mourning.*

► **weep**   to shed tears as an expression of deep emotion: *I began to **weep** as I read the tragic story.*

cuddle

verb   to hold someone tenderly and close to the body: *The little girl **cuddled** her teddy bear when she finally found it.*

► **embrace**   to hold someone close with the arms: *The couple **embraced** each other at the end of their wedding ceremony.*

► **hug**   to embrace someone tightly, especially to show affection: *My dad **hugged** me when I got home from my trip.*

► **nestle**   to settle down snugly and comfortably: *The little boy **nestled** in his grandmother's arms as she read him a story.*

► **nuzzle**   to rub or push against a person or animal gently with the nose or snout: *The kitten **nuzzled** its mother.*

► **snuggle**   to draw something or someone close to the body, as for comfort or in affection: *I **snuggled** into my down coat when the cold wind started to blow.*

cue *noun*   a signal for action, especially in a play: *see* **signal**

culprit *noun*   a person who is guilty of wrongdoing: *see* **criminal**

cultivate *verb*   to improve and prepare land for the raising of crops: *see* **raise [1]**

culture

noun   the beliefs and customs of a group of people: *We are studying the **cultures** of ancient Mexico.*

▸ **civilization** a human society that has a high level of development in language, science, agriculture, and art: *There are still many fascinating mysteries about Egyptian civilization.*

▸ **society** a group of people who share a common culture: *Margaret Mead was an anthropologist who studied the society of American Samoans.*

cumbersome *adjective* awkward to carry, wear, or manage: *see* **heavy [1]**

cunning *adjective* clever in deceiving people or in gaining an advantage: *see* **crafty**

cup *noun* a small open container, usually with a handle: *see* **glass**

curb *verb* to check, restrain, or control something: *see* **control**

cure *noun* a medical treatment or a medicine that makes a sick person get better: *see* **remedy**

curious

adjective eager to learn more: *I am curious about famous people, and so I read biographies.*

▸ **inquiring** moved to find things out, especially by asking questions: *It is easy to think of questions when you have an inquiring mind.*

▸ **inquisitive** habitually curious, especially about other people's lives: *Our neighbor was inquisitive about our new car.*

▸ **prying** excessively curious about things that are not one's business: *I lock my diary in my desk to keep it away from my brother's prying eyes.*

▸ **questioning** asking questions; wondering: *He looked at me in a questioning way.*

ANTONYM **uninterested** not interested; indifferent

currency *noun* the form of money in actual use in a country: *see* **money**

current *adjective* belonging to the present time: *see* **modern**

curse *noun* something that causes great evil or harm: *see* **misfortune**

curt *adjective* rudely brief in speech and manner: *see* **blunt**

curtain

noun cloth or other material hanging in a window or door: *I made new curtains for the kitchen windows.*

▸ **blind** something that shuts out light: *The waiter lowered the blind because the sun was shining in our faces.*

▸ **drape** a long, often heavy curtain that hangs straight in loose folds: *The beautiful mansion had velvet drapes in the bedrooms.*

▸ **screen** a frame covered with wire or plastic mesh, used in a window or door to keep out insects: *Our tent has a small screen that serves as a window.*

▸ **shutter** a hinged screen or cover for a window: *We bought wooden shutters for the windows on our house.*

curtail *verb* (formal) to cut something short: *see* **control**

curtsy *verb* to make a special bow used by women and girls as a sign of respect: *see* **bow**

curve

noun a line or surface that bends smoothly without sharp angles: *There are a lot of dangerous curves in the road.*

▸ **arch** a curved structure that extends across an opening and serves as a support: *There are many arches in the bridge that goes over the river.*

▸ **bend** a turn, curve, or bent part: *I live just around this bend in the road.*

▸ **coil** a series of spirals or rings formed by winding: *The rancher bought a coil of barbed wire to repair his fences.*

cushion *noun* a soft pad or pillow that is used to sit, lie, or rest on: *see* **pad**

custom *noun* something that a person regularly does: *see* **habit**

custom *noun* a practice followed by people of a particular group or region: *see* **tradition**

customary *adjective*   according to custom or habit: *see* **regular**

customer

noun   a person who buys goods or services, especially on a regular basis: *The store always has lots of customers during its annual sale.*

▶ **client**   a person who uses the services of a professional person: *A good accountant is likely to have many clients.*

▶ **patron**   a regular customer of a store, restaurant, or other business: *The barbershop has dozens of patrons from the neighborhood.*

cut

verb   to make an opening in something with a sharp edge or instrument: *Please use this knife to cut the watermelon.*

▶ **chop**   to cut something by striking it with a heavy, sharp tool, such as an ax or cleaver: *I chopped the onions for the meatloaf.*

▶ **clip**   to cut, cut off, or cut out something with scissors or shears: *My sister clipped my bangs for me.*

▶ **mow**   to cut down grass or hay: *The grass is too wet to mow right now.*

▶ **shear**   to remove fleece or hair by clipping it with a sharp instrument: *Sheep are usually sheared at least once a year.*

▶ **slash**   to cut something with forceful, sweeping strokes: *The explorers slashed through the thick undergrowth with their machetes.*

▶ **trim**   to make something neat, even, or tidy by clipping, smoothing, or pruning: *We trimmed the rosebushes and covered them with straw for the winter.*

cute *adjective*   very pretty or charming: *see* **beautiful**

cycle *noun*   a regularly repeated sequence of events: *see* **sequence**

cyclone *noun*   a rotating windstorm: *see* **storm**

cylinder *noun*   a hollow or solid object that is shaped like a tube or pipe: *see* **tube**

dabble

verb to do or work on something casually or without serious intent: *She **dabbles** with watercolors on the weekend.*

- **fiddle** to tinker with something in an attempt to fix or adjust it: *I **fiddled** with the knobs on the TV until the picture was clear.*
- **putter** to keep busy without really accomplishing much: *She likes to **putter** in the garden after work.*
- **tinker** to make minor repairs or adjustments without skilled or certain knowledge: *My brother likes to **tinker** with his car.*
- **toy** to amuse oneself idly: *The bored girl **toyed** with her hair.*
- **trifle** to play or toy with something: *I **trifled** with the pencil as I talked on the phone.*

dainty *adjective* lovely in a fine, delicate way: *see* **delicate**

dale *noun* (formal) a small valley: *see* **valley**

dam *verb* to hold something back: *see* **block**

damp *adjective* slightly wet; moist: *see* **wet**

dance *noun* a gathering at which people dance: *see* **party**

danger

noun the chance or risk of harm or destruction: *A racecar driver's occupation is full of **danger**.*

- **hazard** a possible source of injury or harm: *That large pothole is a **hazard** to cars and bicycles.*
- **jeopardy** danger of dying, being injured, or being lost; peril: *When the computer crashed, it put the whole project in **jeopardy**.*
- **menace** a serious threat or danger: *The criminal was considered a **menace** to society.*
- **peril** the condition of being in danger or at risk of harm or loss: *The sailors were in **peril** during the terrible storm.*
- **risk** the possibility of suffering harm or loss: *War correspondents often take **risks** to get their stories.*
- **threat** an indication of possible danger or harm: *The forecast said there was a **threat** of severe thunderstorms.*

dangerous

adjective filled with danger; able or likely to cause harm: *Most snakes are not **dangerous**, though most people are usually afraid of them anyway.*

- **harmful** capable of causing harm; injurious: *Smoking is **harmful** to your lungs.*
- **hazardous** full of risk or danger: *Fire-fighters have **hazardous** jobs.*
- **perilous** full of grave danger; hazardous: *The westward journey of the pioneers was often **perilous**.*
- **risky** involving risk; dangerous: *Driving when you're tired is **risky**.*
- **treacherous** marked by hidden or unforeseen hazards: *Climbing Mt. Everest is a **treacherous** undertaking.*
- **unsafe** not safe; dangerous: *This toy is considered **unsafe** for children under three years of age.*

ANTONYM **safe** not causing harm; free from danger

dangle *verb* to swing loosely from a fixed point: *see* **hang**

dangling *adjective* hanging or swinging loosely from a single point: *see* **loose**

daring *adjective* willing to take risks: *see* **brave**

dark

adjective   lacking light or having very little light: *It was hard to find a seat in the **dark** theater.*

- ▸ **black**   having no light; completely dark: *When the electricity went out, our whole street was **black**.*
- ▸ **dim**   lacking in brightness; giving off little light: *The light from the flickering candle was **dim**.*
- ▸ **murky**   very dark or gloomy: *It was **murky** in the cave.*
- ▸ **shadowy**   full of or dark with shadows: *The woods turned **shadowy** as the sun went down.*
- ▸ **shady**   full of shade; casting shade: *I like to sit underneath the **shady** oak tree.*

ANTONYM **bright**   giving off or filled with a lot of light

darkness *noun*   partial or total absence of light: *see* **night**

darling *adjective*   regarded with special favor and affection: *see* **dear**

dart *verb*   to move suddenly and swiftly: *see* **zoom**

dash *verb*   to move with sudden speed: *see* **zoom**

data *noun*   facts and figures, especially for use in making decisions: *see* **fact**

date *noun*   an agreement to meet someone or be somewhere at a particular time: *see* **appointment**

dawdle *verb*   to take more time than necessary: *see* **stay**

dawn *noun*   the first appearance of something: *see* **beginning**

dawn *noun*   the time each morning when light first appears: *see* **morning**

daybreak *noun*   the beginning of the day: *see* **morning**

daze *verb*   to stun or confuse someone, as with a blow or shock: *see* **surprise**

dazzle *verb*   to blind someone with too much light: *see* **shine**

dazzling *adjective*   so bright as to make a person momentarily blind: *see* **bright**

dead

adjective   no longer living: *All my grandparents are **dead**.*

- ▸ **deceased**   no longer living, especially recently dead: *Many people attended the funeral of the **deceased** woman.*
- ▸ **departed**   (formal)   having left this life; deceased: *The obituaries list those people who are recently **departed**.*
- ▸ **extinct**   no longer existing anywhere in living form: *Saber-toothed tigers have been **extinct** for thousands of years.*
- ▸ **lifeless**   having no life; dead or inanimate: *I was sad to find the **lifeless** body of my hamster in his nest.*
- ▸ **passed away**   no longer living; dead: *I'm sorry to hear that your mother has **passed away**.*

ANTONYM **alive**   having life; living

deadly *adjective*   capable of killing: *see* **fatal**

deafening *adjective*   so loud as to make one unable to hear: *see* **loud**

deal *noun*   an agreement, as in business or politics: *see* **agreement**

deal *verb*   to distribute in an orderly way: *see* **distribute**

deal *noun*   (informal) a sale that is favorable, especially to the buyer: *see* **sale**

dealer *noun*   a person engaged in selling or distributing something: *see* **merchant**

dear

adjective   loved and cherished: *She has been my **dear** friend since childhood.*

- ▸ **beloved**   very much loved; dear to one's heart: *The dying man paid a last visit to the **beloved** town where he grew up.*
- ▸ **darling**   regarded with special favor and affection: *The **darling** child got many presents for her birthday.*

▸ **precious** highly valued or esteemed; cherished: *The time you spend with loved ones is* **precious**.

debate *verb* to present or discuss reasons for and against something: *see* **discuss**

debris *noun* the scattered remains of something broken or destroyed: *see* **garbage**

decay

verb to cause plant or animal matter to break down as the result of natural processes: *Sugar can* **decay** *your teeth.*

▸ **decompose** to break down into basic elements or components; to decay: *The fallen leaves will* **decompose** *and become part of the soil.*
▸ **deteriorate** to weaken or fall apart gradually: *The old house was* **deteriorating**.
▸ **rot** to spoil or break down from the action of bacteria or fungi: *Those leftovers are beginning to* **rot**.
▸ **rust** to become corroded or oxidized: *The tools are beginning to* **rust** *because they were left out in the rain.*
▸ **spoil** to become unfit for consumption, as from decay; to go bad: *The milk will* **spoil** *if you don't put it back in the refrigerator.*

deceased *adjective* no longer living: *see* **dead**

deceitful *adjective* deliberately misleading or deceptive: *see* **dishonest**

deceive

verb to make someone believe something that is not true: *The company was accused of* **deceiving** *the public about the safety of its product.*

▸ **beguile** to deceive someone by using charm: *The saleswoman* **beguiled** *me into buying more than I needed.*
▸ **betray** to be disloyal to someone or something: *I did not mean to* **betray** *your confidence.*

▸ **dupe** to trick or deceive an unwary or naive person: *The ad* **duped** *us into believing that all of the camping equipment was on sale.*
▸ **mislead** to give the wrong idea to someone: *I didn't mean to* **mislead** *you about the difficulty of this task.*

decent *adjective* conforming to standards of proper social behavior: *see* **moral**

deception *noun* something that deceives, such as a lie or trick: *see* **lie**

decide *verb* to make up one's mind regarding a question: *see* **choose**

decipher *verb* to read or interpret something that is hard to understand: *see* **solve**

decision

noun a conclusion or judgment reached as a result of making up one's mind: *Have you made a* **decision** *about whether or not you're going to the party?*

▸ **judgment** an opinion made after careful consideration: *It is my* **judgment** *that we should go ahead with the project despite all the difficulties.*
▸ **ruling** an official decision: *The court's* **ruling** *will be announced this afternoon.*
▸ **verdict** the decision reached by a jury at the end of a trial: *Has the jury reached a* **verdict**?

deck *verb* to decorate something with festive touches: *see* **decorate**

deck *noun* an outdoor platform attached to a building: *see* **platform**

declaration *noun* an explicit, formal announcement, either oral or written: *see* **announcement**

declare *verb* to state something with force: *see* **claim**

decline *verb* to politely refuse to accept or do something: *see* **reject**

decompose *verb* to break down into basic elements or components: *see* **decay**

decorate

verb to furnish or adorn something with attractive or beautiful items: *The house has been **decorated** with lovely antiques.*

‣ **adorn** to make something beautiful by adding decorations: *Her hair was **adorned** with flowers.*
‣ **beautify** to make something beautiful: *We **beautified** our home by landscaping the yard.*
‣ **deck** decorate something with festive touches: *During the holidays, we **deck** the house with pine boughs.*
‣ **embellish** to enhance the beauty of something: *The book cover has been **embellished** with gold.*
‣ **embroider** to add ornamental beauty to something with needlework: *She **embroidered** flowers on her denim jacket.*
‣ **garnish** to decorate food with something that adds color or flavor: *The plate of food was **garnished** with parsley.*
‣ **ornament** to supply something with beautiful or decorative additions: *Red fringe was used to **ornament** the dress.*

decorated *adjective* furnished with attractive or beautiful things: *see* **fancy**

decoration *noun* something that adorns or beautifies: *see* **accessory**

decoy *verb* to lure another into danger or a trap by using deception: *see* **trap**

decrease

verb to cause something to become gradually less or smaller at a steady rate: *Exercise helps **decrease** the risk of getting heart disease.*

‣ **diminish** to gradually grow smaller by taking something away: *Daylight **diminished** as the sun went down.*
‣ **dwindle** to decrease bit by bit: *Our savings have **dwindled** since I lost my job.*
‣ **prune** to shorten or improve something by removing unnecessary parts: *My essay was better after I **pruned** out some of the repetitive parts.*
‣ **reduce** to bring something down in size, degree, or strength: *Our teacher decided to **reduce** the amount of homework he assigns.*

ANTONYM **increase** to make something greater or larger

decree *verb* to order something in an authoritative or official way: *see* **dictate**

dedicate *verb* to reserve something for a special or solemn purpose: *see* **allocate**

dedicated *adjective* to be fully committed to something: *see* **loyal**

deduct *verb* to take away a quantity from another: *see* **subtract**

deduction *noun* an amount that is subtracted from the selling price: *see* **discount**

deed *noun* an act or action that is meaningful: *see* **action**

deed *noun* a legal document, especially one relating to property: *see* **document**

defeat

verb to win victory over someone or something: *Our soccer team has **defeated** every team we've played this season.*

‣ **beat** to defeat or overcome an opponent, as in a contest: *I can finally **beat** my dad at arm wrestling.*
‣ **conquer** to overcome an opponent or enemy by force, as in a war: *Rome **conquered** England in the first century A.D.*
‣ **overthrow** to bring about the downfall or destruction of an established power: *The rebels were plotting to **overthrow** the government.*
‣ **overwhelm** to defeat someone completely and decisively: *The powerful army **overwhelmed** their enemy.*
‣ **subdue** to bring under control by physical force or persuasion: *The ruler **subdued** the rebellion by promising economic reforms.*
‣ **vanquish** to defeat an opponent in a conflict, contest, or competition: *We **vanquished** the opposing team in the final period.*

defect *noun* a lack of something necessary for proper functioning: *see* **flaw**

defective *adjective* having a defect or flaw: *see* **bad [1]**

defend *verb* to keep someone or something safe from attack or danger: *see* **protect**

defense *noun* the act of defending against attack, danger, or damage: *see* **protection**

defiance *noun* open resistance to authority: *see* **rebellion**

deficiency *noun* a lack of something needed, especially for good health: *see* **lack**

define *verb* to explain or define something in detail: *see* **explain**

definite *adjective* beyond doubt; unquestionable: *see* **certain**

definitely *adverb* beyond any doubt: *see* **certainly**

defraud *verb* (formal) to cheat someone by deliberate deception; to swindle: *see* **cheat**

defrost *verb* to free something of ice or frost: *see* **melt**

deft *adjective* quick and skilled: *see* **agile**

defy *verb* to oppose someone or something boldly: *see* **rebel**

degrade *verb* to lower someone's dignity: *see* **embarrass**

degree

noun the relative amount or extent of something: *That archer has a high **degree** of accuracy.*

- ▸ **extent** the degree or level to which something reaches: *What is the full **extent** of the damage?*
- ▸ **level** a relative position or rank: *The trainer works with athletes who are at many different **levels** of development.*
- ▸ **magnitude** the greatness of something's position, size, or significance: *The hurricane caused destruction of enormous **magnitude** throughout the region.*
- ▸ **measure** the extent, amount, or degree of something: *This recipe calls for equal **measures** of sugar and flour.*
- ▸ **range** the spread or extent of something: *We are looking for applicants with a wide **range** of abilities and interests.*
- ▸ **scale** the relative size or extent of something: *The investigation uncovered*

*corruption taking place on a large **scale** throughout the government.*

- ▸ **stage** a level, degree, or period of time in the course of a process: *When a butterfly emerges from its cocoon, it is in the final **stage** of development.*

dejected *adjective* feeling depressed and gloomy: *see* **sad**

dejection *noun* low spirits: *see* **sadness**

delay

verb to cause something or someone to be later or slower: *We have to **delay** our vacation until next month.*

- ▸ **postpone** to delay something until a later time: *She **postponed** the meeting because she had to go out of town.*
- ▸ **put off** (informal) to delay or postpone something, especially something unpleasant: *I try not to **put off** doing my homework.*

delayed *adjective* prevented from being on time: *see* **late**

delegate *verb* to authorize another person to be one's representative: *see* **assign**

delegate *noun* a person chosen to speak and act for another or others: *see* **representative**

delete *verb* to remove something by striking out or canceling: *see* **erase**

deliberately

adverb with full awareness of one's motives; on purpose: *She **deliberately** moved the knife out of the child's reach.*

- ▸ **intentionally** with conscious intent; deliberately: *He **intentionally** mentioned Tahiti so that he could tell us about his trip.*
- ▸ **knowingly** with full knowledge, information, or understanding: *When I described my symptoms to the doctor, she smiled **knowingly** and told me what to do.*

▶ **purposely** with the purpose of achieving a desired result or effect: *He **purposely** drove home by a different route in order to avoid the traffic.*

▶ **willfully** with stubborn insistence in spite of knowing better: *You are **willfully** misunderstanding what I am saying.*

delicate

adjective easily broken or damaged: *A butterfly's wings are strong but **delicate**.*

▶ **breakable** capable of being broken with normal use: *He prefers plastic dishes to china because the plastic ones are not **breakable**.*

▶ **dainty** lovely in a fine, delicate way: *Her dress is embroidered with **dainty** flowers.*

▶ **flimsy** not solid or strong; likely to fall apart: *The **flimsy** chair broke when I sat in it.*

▶ **fragile** easily damaged, broken, or destroyed; delicate: *Be careful handling the antique lace because it is very **fragile**.*

delicatessen *noun* a store that sells prepared foods such as cheeses, salads, and cooked meats: *see* **restaurant**

delight *noun* great or active pleasure: *see* **happiness**

delight *verb* to please someone greatly: *see* **please**

delighted *adjective* very pleased or happy: *see* **happy**

delightful *adjective* giving delight: *see* **charming**

deliver *verb* to take something to the proper person or place: *see* **send**

delusion *noun* a false belief or opinion: *see* **illusion**

demand

verb to ask for something urgently or insistently: *I **demand** that you tell me the truth.*

▶ **compel** to make someone do something by force or necessity: *The storm **compelled** us to seek shelter.*

▶ **insist** to assert or demand something forcefully and persistently: *Our science teacher **insists** that we wear safety goggles when working in the lab.*

▶ **order** to issue a command or instruction: *He **ordered** the children to clean up their bedrooms.*

▶ **require** to call for something as necessary or essential: *To be on the honor roll **requires** that one earn high grades.*

demanding *adjective* requiring much effort or attention: *see* **hard**

demolish *verb* to destroy something by reducing it to ruins: *see* **destroy**

demonstrate *verb* to present by experiments or examples of how something works or is done: *see* **show**

den *noun* a cozy, private room for personal use, as for study: *see* **room**

denote *verb* to express or indicate something directly: *see* **mean²**

dense *adjective* hard to penetrate: *see* **solid**

deny *verb* to refuse to allow someone to have something: *see* **deprive**

depart *verb* to go away, especially on a journey or trip: *see* **leave**

departed *adjective* having left this life: *see* **dead**

department *noun* a division of an organization: *see* **agency**

dependable

adjective capable of being depended upon; trustworthy: *That news program has the most **dependable** weather reports.*

▶ **reliable** capable of being relied upon; dependable: *This car is old, but it is still **reliable**.*

▶ **responsible** deserving trust or confidence; trustworthy: *She received a raise in pay because she has been so **responsible** in doing her job.*

▶ **stable** firm or steady in purpose or character: *I invested in that company because its performance has been **stable** for many years.*

▸ **trustworthy** able to be trusted; reliable: *People confide in him because he is **trustworthy**.*

depend on *verb* to place trust in someone or something, especially for help or support: *see* **trust**

deplete *verb* to gradually use up a supply of something: *see* **tire**

deposit *verb* to lay or put something down: *see* **place**

depressed *adjective* feeling sad and low in spirits: *see* **sad**

depressing *adjective* causing a feeling of sadness and discouragement: *see* **gloomy**

depression *noun* the condition of being sad and discouraged, especially over a long period of time: *see* **sadness**

deprive

verb to take something valuable away from someone or prevent someone from having something: *Don't let your worries **deprive** you of sleep.*

▸ **deny** to refuse to allow someone to have something: *He **denied** my request for his secret lasagna recipe.*

▸ **withhold** to keep something back; to refrain from giving or permitting something: *My parents **withhold** my allowance until all my chores are done.*

deputy *noun* a person appointed to act for another or to take the place of another: *see* **representative**

deranged *adjective* having serious mental or emotional problems; mentally disturbed: *see* **mentally ill**

derelict *noun* a homeless person who is unable to live in society: *see* **beggar**

deride *verb* to laugh at someone or something with contempt or scorn: *see* **scorn**

descend *verb* to move from a higher to a lower place or position: *see* **fall**

describe *verb* to use words to tell about something: *see* **tell**

description *noun* an account or a statement describing something: *see* **story**

desert *noun* a dry area, often covered with sand, in which few plants or animals live: *see* **wilderness**

desert *verb* to leave a responsibility or duty: *see* **abandon**

deserve *verb* to be worthy of or have a right to something: *see* **earn**

design

noun a plan or drawing showing how something is to be made: *The architect drew up several **designs** for the new school.*

▸ **arrangement** the manner or style in which something is arranged: *I'm not sure if I like this furniture **arrangement**.*

▸ **composition** an arrangement of parts to form a whole: *The **composition** of this painting is pleasing to me.*

▸ **layout** a planned arrangement of parts or areas: *The **layout** of the garden featured gravel paths radiating from a central fountain.*

▸ **motif** a repeated idea, symbol, figure or design: *Their house is decorated in a Southwestern **motif**.*

▸ **pattern** a diagram or model used to make things: *She used a **pattern** to cut out the dress.*

designate *verb* to select someone or something for a particular duty or purpose: *see* **allocate**

desirable *adjective* worth wanting, seeking, or doing: *see* **good**

desire *verb* to want something strongly or passionately: *see* **want**

despair *noun* complete lack of hope: *see* **sadness**

desperate *adjective* reckless or violent because of despair: *see* **wild [2]**

despise *verb* to regard someone or something with scorn or disgust: *see* **hate**

despot *noun* a ruler with absolute power, especially one who rules oppressively: *see* **tyrant**

destiny

noun a future development or course of events, viewed as inevitable or predetermined: *Her destiny was to be a famous opera star.*

▸ **fate** the invisible force or power that is believed to determine future events: *My mom says that fate smiled on her the day she met my dad.*

▸ **fortune** the good or bad luck that comes to a person; chance: *It was good fortune to find a parking space at the crowded mall.*

▸ **karma** the belief that a person's conduct determines his or her destiny in this life or the next: *Kind acts are said to create good karma.*

▸ **lot** one's luck or circumstances in life: *It was his lot to be born into poverty, from which he later escaped.*

destroy

verb to eliminate or do away with something in a violent manner: *The wildfires destroyed many acres of forest.*

▸ **demolish** to destroy something by reducing it to ruins; to tear something down completely: *A tornado demolished the trailer park.*

▸ **devastate** to reduce something to ruins: *The eruption of Mt. Vesuvius in A.D. 79 completely devastated the city of Pompeii.*

▸ **ruin** to damage something beyond repair: *The puppy ruined my leather belt by chewing on it.*

▸ **wreck** to damage something badly or beyond repair, as by physical force: *My brother accidentally wrecked my bike when he backed his car over it.*

ANTONYM **restore** to bring something back into existence or to original condition

detail

noun a small part of a whole; an item: *His model train is accurate in every detail.*

▸ **fine print** the part of a written agreement containing qualifications or restrictions, usually in small type or obscure language: *I took the time to read the fine print in the contract.*

▸ **particular** a single item, fact, or detail: *Did she tell you the particulars of their problem?*

▸ **point** a significant item, especially one of a series: *Our teacher reviewed the main points of the chapter.*

detect *verb* to become aware of the existence, presence, or fact of something: *see* **discover**

deter *verb* to prevent or discourage someone from doing something: *see* **prevent**

deteriorate *verb* to weaken or fall apart gradually: *see* **decay**

determination *noun* firmness of purpose: *see* **will**

determine *verb* to settle or decide something beyond doubt: *see* **shape**

determined *adjective* fixed on a particular course or purpose: *see* **stubborn**

detest *verb* to dislike intensely: *see* **hate**

detonate *verb* to cause a device or substance to explode: *see* **explode**

devastate *verb* to reduce something to ruins: *see* **destroy**

develop *verb* to make something more effective or advanced: *see* **invent**

development *noun* the act of making more effective or advanced: *see* **growth**

device *noun* a piece of equipment that is made for a particular purpose: *see* **tool**

devise *verb* to form something, such as a plan, in one's mind: *see* **invent**

devoted *adjective* feeling or expressing strong affection or attachment: *see* **loyal**

devotion *noun* loyalty and deep affection: *see* **loyalty**

devotion *noun* passionate attachment to a person, cause, or deity: *see* **worship**

devour *verb* to eat something quickly and greedily: *see* **eat**

devout *adjective* having or showing devotion to a religion: *see* **religious**

diagram *noun* a plan, drawing, or sketch that shows how something works or how its parts are put together: *see* **chart**

dialogue *noun* a formal exchange of thoughts on a particular subject: *see* **talk**

diary *noun* a daily written record of a person's thoughts, activities, opinions, and experiences: *see* **report**

dictate

verb to issue an authoritative order or command: *Company policy **dictates** that unused vacation days cannot be carried over to the next year.*

- ▸ **decree** to order something in an authoritative or official way: *The governor **decreed** a pay raise for the state's teachers.*
- ▸ **impose** to establish something as compulsory: *The library **imposed** new fines for overdue books.*
- ▸ **ordain** (formal) to order something by means of superior authority; to decree: *In 1981 President Reagan **ordained** that the air traffic controllers' strike was illegal and ordered them to return to work.*
- ▸ **prescribe** to set something down as a rule or guide: *The government **prescribes** standards for the purity of food.*

dictator *noun* a usually unelected ruler who has great power and often governs a country in a cruel or unfair way: *see* **tyrant**

die

verb to stop living; to become dead: *The flowers **died** after the first severe frost.*

- ▸ **expire** to die, especially while being cared for: *The patient **expired** last night after a long illness.*
- ▸ **perish** to die or be destroyed, especially in a violent manner: *Many people **perished** in the hurricane.*

ANTONYM **live** to be alive; to exist

difference *noun* a usually minor disagreement or quarrel: *see* **disagreement**

different

adjective partly or completely unlike another: *These two authors have very **different** styles of writing.*

- ▸ **dissimilar** having little in common with another: *The two brothers have **dissimilar** tastes in music.*
- ▸ **incompatible** not capable of existing in agreement or harmony with something else: *He is **incompatible** with the rest of my friends.*
- ▸ **unlike** not like something else; different: *Although a whale and a mouse are both mammals, they are **unlike** in size and appearance.*

ANTONYM **same** exactly alike; identical

difficult *adjective* hard to make, do, or understand: *see* **hard**

difficulty *noun* something that causes trouble or gets in the way: *see* **trouble**

dig

verb to make a hole in the ground: *Workers had to **dig** a deep trench for the new water line.*

- ▸ **bore** to make a hole by drilling or digging: *The miners **bored** through the rock to reach the coal.*
- ▸ **burrow** to make a tunnel, hole, or shelter by digging in the ground: *Turtles **burrow** in the sand to lay their eggs.*
- ▸ **excavate** to uncover or expose something by digging: *Archaeologists **excavated** King Tutankhamen's tomb in 1922.*
- ▸ **mine** to extract metals or minerals from the earth by digging or tunneling: *Gold, silver, and other minerals are **mined** in Nevada.*
- ▸ **scoop** to remove loose material with a spoon-like utensil or with cupped hands: *I **scooped** the seeds out of the pumpkin before carving it.*
- ▸ **shovel** to move or remove something with a shovel: *He **shoveled** the ashes from the fireplace.*

digest *noun* a collection of previously published material, usually edited or condensed: *see* **magazine**

dilapidated *adjective* being in poor condition because of neglect: *see* **ragged**

dilemma *noun* a situation that requires a person to choose between options that are equally bad or unfavorable: *see* **trouble**

dim *adjective* lacking in brightness or obscure: *see* **faint**

diminish *verb* to gradually grow smaller by taking something away: *see* **decrease**

diminutive *adjective* (formal) extremely small in size: *see* **short [1]**

din *noun* loud and harsh noise: *see* **noise**

dine *verb* (formal) to eat a meal, especially dinner: *see* **eat**

diner *noun* a restaurant where patrons can eat in booths or at a long counter: *see* **restaurant**

dingy *adjective* darkened with grime or soot: *see* **dirty**

dinner *noun* the main meal of the day, eaten either at midday or in the evening: *see* **meal**

dip

verb to plunge something briefly into a liquid: *I **dipped** my hand into the bathtub to check the water's temperature.*

- ▸ **dunk** to briefly submerge something in a liquid: *Some people like to **dunk** their doughnuts into their coffee.*
- ▸ **immerse** to cover something completely with a liquid: *I **immersed** the dishes in the soapy water.*
- ▸ **rinse** to let water flow over something so as to clean it: *I **rinsed** the dishes in hot water before I dried them.*

direct *verb* to be in charge of something: *see* **manage**

director *noun* a person who supervises, controls, or manages something: *see* **boss**

dirt *noun* earth or soil: *see* **earth [2]**

dirty

adjective covered with dirt, soil, or filth; unclean: *My hands are **dirty** from working in the garden.*

- ▸ **dingy** darkened with grime or soot; dirty or discolored: *The **dingy** room needed to be cleaned and painted.*
- ▸ **filthy** thoroughly or disgustingly dirty: *My friends and I were **filthy** after playing football in the mud.*
- ▸ **grimy** covered with black, greasy dirt or soot: *They were **grimy** after working on the car.*
- ▸ **nasty** offensively dirty; disgusting: *A **nasty** smell came from the garbage can.*
- ▸ **soiled** dirty, especially from use or wear: *I put the **soiled** sheets in the laundry.*

ANTONYM **clean** free from dirt, stains, or clutter

disagreeable *adjective* not to one's liking: *see* **unpleasant**

disagreement

noun a failure or refusal to agree; a difference of opinion: *The peace talks were delayed by a **disagreement** between the two nations.*

- ▸ **difference** a usually minor disagreement or quarrel: *My brother and I had an argument but soon settled our **differences**.*
- ▸ **dissent** a disagreement on a matter of policy or belief: *There was **dissent** in the senate about the proposed tax cut.*
- ▸ **opposition** resistance to something that one disagrees with: *The managers tried to overcome their employees' **opposition** to the proposed change in health benefits.*

disallow *verb* to refuse to allow something as a matter of policy: *see* **forbid**

disappear *verb* to pass out of sight: *see* **fade**

disappoint *verb* to fail to satisfy the hope, desire, or expectation of someone: *see* **discourage**

disaster

noun something that causes widespread destruction: *The eruption of the Krakatoa volcano in 1883 was a* **disaster** *that killed an estimated 36,000 people.*

- ▸ **calamity** an event that causes great distress and suffering: *The drought was a* **calamity** *for the farmers and ranchers.*
- ▸ **catastrophe** a great and sudden disaster from which recovery is difficult or impossible: *It would be an enormous* **catastrophe** *if the earth were hit by a large meteor.*
- ▸ **crisis** a situation of great difficulty or danger: *There was a financial* **crisis** *when the school budget was not approved by the voters.*
- ▸ **emergency** a serious situation or occurrence that happens suddenly and calls for immediate action: *Where can I reach you in case of an* **emergency***?*
- ▸ **tragedy** a disastrous event involving great loss or suffering: *The sinking of the Titanic was one of the worst* **tragedies** *of the 20th century.*

disburse *verb* to pay money to someone, as from a fund; to expend: *see* **spend**

discard *verb* to throw something away: *see* **abandon**

discharge *verb* to release someone, as from duty or work: *see* **dismiss**

disciple *noun* a person who believes in and often helps to spread the teachings of another: *see* **follower**

discipline *verb* to punish someone in order to correct or train: *see* **punish**

discipline *noun* controlled behavior resulting from training of the mind, body, or character: *see* **will**

discomfort *noun* mental or bodily distress: *see* **embarrassment**

discount

noun an offer to sell something at a reduced price: *I got this washing machine at a* **discount** *because it was the floor model.*

- ▸ **deduction** an amount that is subtracted from the selling price: *The salesman offered me an extra* **deduction** *if I bought the car before the end of the month.*
- ▸ **markdown** the amount by which a price is reduced: *The* **markdown** *on last year's model has been increased to 15 percent.*
- ▸ **rebate** a return of part of the amount paid for an item: *Mail this form to the manufacturer and you will get a* **rebate** *on your new printer.*
- ▸ **reduction** the amount by which the price of an item is reduced: *Many people go shopping after Christmas to take advantage of the* **reductions** *on merchandise.*

discourage

verb to make one less hopeful or confident: *The difficulty of the job did not* **discourage** *me.*

- ▸ **disappoint** to fail to satisfy the hope, desire, or expectation of someone: *The movie* **disappointed** *me, but my friends enjoyed it.*
- ▸ **dishearten** to cause one to lose courage and hope: *The artist was* **disheartened** *by the lack of interest in his work.*
- ▸ **dismay** to fill one with dread, anxiety, or apprehension: *We were* **dismayed** *when our car broke down on the freeway.*
- ▸ **dispirit** to lower one's spirit or enthusiasm: *The team was* **dispirited** *after losing three games in a row.*

ANTONYM **encourage** to give courage, hope, or confidence to someone

discourteous *adjective* not polite: *see* **rude**

discover

verb to be the first to find or learn of something: *Many explorers hoped to* **discover** *Eldorado, the fabled City of Gold.*

- ▸ **detect** to become aware of the existence, presence, or fact of something: *An odor is added to natural gas to help people to* **detect** *leaks.*

▸ **find**   to come upon something by accident or as the result of a study or search: *I **found** a ten-dollar bill in my old purse.*

▸ **locate**   to find something by searching, examining, or experimenting: *Moles use their senses of smell and touch to **locate** food.*

discovery *noun*   something found, seen, or learned for the first time: *see* **invention**

discuss

verb   to talk something over with another person or persons: *We **discussed** plans for this summer.*

▸ **confer**   to meet in order to discuss something or compare opinions: *The President **conferred** with his advisors.*

▸ **debate**   to present or discuss reasons for and against something: *We **debated** which retirement plan to sign up for.*

discussion *noun*   a serious conversation on a subject or topic: *see* **talk**

disease

noun   an often serious condition that keeps the body from functioning normally: *Malaria is one of the most common **diseases** in the world.*

▸ **ailment**   a usually mild or chronic illness: *Joint pains and similar **ailments** often come with advancing age.*

▸ **disorder**   an unhealthy condition of the body or mind: *Asthma is a breathing **disorder**.*

▸ **illness**   an often temporary condition of poor health: *His **illness** caused him to miss two days of work.*

▸ **sickness**   a condition or period of poor health; an illness: *My roommate took care of me during my **sickness**.*

disgrace *verb*   to bring shame or dishonor upon someone: *see* **embarrass**

disgraceful *adjective*   bringing loss of honor, respect, or reputation: *see* **shocking**

disguise

noun   clothes or other effects used to conceal one's true identity: *The spy dyed his hair as part of his **disguise**.*

▸ **costume**   an outfit or disguise worn on a special occasion: *At the folk festival, the performers wore the traditional **costumes** of their native regions.*

▸ **façade**   (formal)   an outward but insincere show of something: *Her **façade** of friendliness is useful in this job.*

▸ **front**   an outward appearance to deceive: *His bragging is just a **front** for his insincerity.*

▸ **mask**   ▷ a covering worn over part or all of the face as a disguise: *I wore a Dracula **mask** to the costume party.* ▷ something that disguises or hides: *The student's smile was a **mask** for her disappointment.*

▸ **pen name**   an invented name used by an author: *The famous physicist wrote science fiction novels under a **pen name**.*

disgusting *adjective*   causing feelings of sickening dislike, distaste, or annoyance: *see* **gross**

dishearten *verb*   to cause one to lose courage and hope: *see* **discourage**

dishonest

adjective   inclined to lie, cheat, or deceive; not honest: *I think you're being **dishonest** about where you were last night.*

▸ **corrupt**   dishonest for an immoral purpose, especially personal gain: *The **corrupt** boxer accepted a bribe to lose the fight.*

▸ **deceitful**   deliberately misleading or deceptive: *The applicant made several **deceitful** claims on her résumé.*

▸ **insincere**   saying one thing and doing or thinking another; not sincere: *He offered me an **insincere** apology.*

▸ **untrustworthy**   not worthy of being trusted: *You've shown yourself to be **untrustworthy** when it comes to handling money.*

ANTONYM **honest**   not lying, stealing, or cheating; trustworthy

dishonor *verb* to damage or destroy someone's honor or reputation: *see* **embarrass**

dislike *verb* to feel displeasure or aversion toward someone or something: *see* **hate**

dismal *adjective* causing low spirits: *see* **gloomy**

dismay *verb* to fill one with dread, anxiety, or apprehension: *see* **discourage**

dismiss

verb to end the employment or service of someone: *Sales were slow, and the company had to **dismiss** several employees.*

▶ **discharge** to release someone, as from duty or work: *The soldier was honorably **discharged** from the Army.*

▶ **fire** (informal) to dismiss someone from a job, usually for poor performance: *The man was **fired** because he missed too many days of work.*

▶ **lay off** to dismiss or suspend an employee because there is not enough work to be done: *Thousands of workers were **laid off** during the recession.*

▶ **sack** (slang) to fire someone from a job: *My boss was going to **sack** me, but I talked her out of it.*

▶ **terminate** to discontinue the employment of someone: *The temporary employees were **terminated** at the end of the holiday season.*

disobedience *noun* a refusal or failure to obey: *see* **rebellion**

disobedient *adjective* refusing to obey: *see* **bad [2]**

disobey *verb* to refuse to obey someone or something: *see* **rebel**

disorder *noun* an unhealthy condition of the body or mind: *see* **disease**

disorder *noun* a lack of order: *see* **mess**

disorganized *adjective* not organized; full of confusion or disorder: *see* **messy**

disorient *verb* to cause a loss of one's sense of direction or position: *see* **confuse**

disparage *verb* to speak of someone or something as unimportant: *see* **scorn**

dispatch *verb* to send something off quickly to a certain place or person: *see* **send**

dispense *verb* to distribute portions from a central location: *see* **distribute**

disperse *verb* (formal) to move or send something in different directions: *see* **spread**

dispirit *verb* to lower one's spirit or enthusiasm: *see* **discourage**

display *verb* to put something on view: *see* **show**

displeasure *noun* the condition of being displeased: *see* **anger**

disposed *adjective* willing or ready: *see* **prone**

disposition *noun* a person's usual mood or attitude: *see* **personality**

disregard *verb* to pay little or no attention to something: *see* **forget**

disrespectful *adjective* having a lack of respect for others: *see* **rude**

disrupt *verb* to throw something into confusion or disorder: *see* **disturb**

dissent *noun* a disagreement on a matter of policy or belief: *see* **disagreement**

dissertation *noun* a lengthy formal treatise: *see* **essay**

dissimilar *adjective* having little in common with another: *see* **different**

dissolve *verb* to change something from a solid to a liquid: *see* **melt**

distance

noun ▷ the extent of space between two places, things, or points: *The shortest **distance** between two points is a straight line.* ▷ a faraway point or region: *We could see snowcapped mountains in the **distance**.*

▶ **expanse** a wide and open area of land, sea, or sky: *The bird flew across the **expanse** of the sky.*

▸ **length** the distance of something from end to end: *We traveled the entire **length** of the Mississippi River.*

▸ **space** the open area between or within objects; a blank or empty area: *How much **space** will we need for the entertainment center?*

▸ **span** the horizontal distance between two points or ends: *The Brooklyn Bridge has a **span** of 1600 feet.*

distant *adjective* far away in space or time: *see* **far**

distinguish *verb* to perceive someone or something as being different or distinct: *see* **recognize**

distinguished *adjective* well known or highly regarded: *see* **famous**

distract *verb* to draw someone's attention away from something: *see* **disturb**

distress *noun* physical or mental discomfort, especially a state of anxious unrest: *see* **suffering**

distribute

verb to give out individual portions or shares: *The manager **distributed** our weekly paychecks.*

▸ **deal** to distribute in an orderly way: *It's your turn to **deal** the cards.*

▸ **dispense** to distribute portions from a central location: *The charity **dispenses** food and clothing to needy families.*

▸ **divide** to separate something into parts or portions for distribution: *We **divided** the pizza among the four of us.*

▸ **hand out** to give something directly, as to those in need: *Our local fire department **hands out** toys and food at Christmas.*

▸ **ration** to give something out in fixed, limited amounts, especially so as to conserve it: *The shipwrecked sailors **rationed** the remaining food and water.*

▸ **share** to allow another or others to have part of something: *The managers **shared** the company's profits with their employees.*

ANTONYM **collect** to bring things together in a group

district *noun* an area or region that has a certain use or characteristic: *see* **community**

distrust *verb* to lack confidence or trust in someone or something: *see* **doubt**

distrustful *adjective* feeling or showing doubt: *see* **jealous**

disturb

verb to annoy or upset someone, as with interruptions or distractions: *Please don't **disturb** me while I am doing my homework.*

▸ **disrupt** to throw something into confusion or disorder: *He burst through the door and **disrupted** our meeting.*

▸ **distract** to draw someone's attention away from something: *My sister **distracted** me just as I was telling a joke.*

▸ **fluster** to make someone nervous or upset: *Shouts from the protesters **flustered** the speaker.*

▸ **interrupt** to stop the action of someone or something; to break in on someone or something: *The TV program was **interrupted** for an important news bulletin.*

▸ **intrude** to break or come in without being wanted or asked: *The noise from our neighbor's party **intruded** on our quiet evening.*

▸ **ruffle** to momentarily upset someone or something: *It **ruffled** my composure when I realized that my zipper was down.*

dive *verb* to drop or descend, especially into or through water: *see* **fall**

diverse *adjective* differing from others in a general group: *see* **various**

diversion *noun* something that distracts the mind and relaxes or entertains: *see* **fun**

divert *verb* to entertain someone by turning their attention away from something else: *see* **entertain**

divide *verb* to separate something into parts or portions for distribution: *see* **distribute**

divide *verb* to separate into two or more parts or groups: *see* **separate**

divine *adjective* relating to God or a god: *see* **holy**

division *noun*   a specific unit of a corporation or a government: *see* **agency**

divorce *verb*   to separate closely connected things: *see* **separate**

dizzy *adjective*   having a sensation of whirling or being about to fall: *see* **sick**

do *verb*   to perform a task or goal: *see* **achieve**

dock

noun   a structure, often supported on posts, that extends into the water: *We tied our boat to the end of the dock.*

▸ **pier**   a platform that extends from a shore out over the water and serves for loading and unloading ships and boats: *Several gift shops and a seafood restaurant are located on the fish pier.*

▸ **wharf**   a landing facility built along a shore where ships can load or unload: *Fisherman's Wharf, in Monterey, California, was built in 1846 for trading vessels that brought goods from around Cape Horn.*

doctor

noun   a person who is trained and licensed to practice any of the healing arts, such as medicine or dentistry: *I have an appointment for a checkup with my doctor tomorrow.*

▸ **midwife**   a woman who is trained to assist women in childbirth: *Many women use a midwife when they give birth at home.*

▸ **nurse**   a person who is trained to care for sick and disabled people: *Several wonderful nurses took care of me when I was in the hospital.*

▸ **paramedic**   a person who is trained to give emergency treatment or to assist medical professionals: *Paramedics rushed to the scene of the accident.*

▸ **physician**   a person licensed to practice medicine; a medical doctor: *You should see a physician if you don't feel better soon.*

▸ **surgeon**   a doctor who specializes in surgery: *The surgeon told me that she would have to operate on my knee.*

document

noun   a written or printed paper that can be used to give official or legal evidence or information: *A driver's license is an important personal document.*

▸ **certificate**   a document testifying to the truth of something, such as ownership or the completion of a course of study: *You need a birth certificate in order to get a passport.*

▸ **deed**   a legal document, especially one relating to property: *We keep the deed to our house in a safe place.*

▸ **paper**   an official document, especially one that establishes the identity of the bearer: *The immigrants made sure that their papers were in order.*

dodge *verb*   to avoid something by moving quickly out of the way: *see* **avoid**

dogma *noun*   a doctrine or system of doctrines proclaimed by a religion to be true: *see* **philosophy**

dolt *noun*   a person regarded as stupid: *see* **fool**

domain *noun* (formal)   an area of special interest or expertise: *see* **field [2]**

dominant *adjective*   having the most influence or control: *see* **main**

dominate *verb*   to rule, control, or govern something or someone by superior power or authority: *see* **control**

donate *verb*   to give something to a fund or cause: *see* **give**

donation *noun*   something given to a fund or cause: *see* **gift**

done

adjective   carried out or accomplished; finished: *I will be glad when exam week is done.*

▸ **completed**   having come or been brought to an end: *I turned in my completed art project.*

▸ **finished**   having been brought to a desired or required state: *The finished quilt was different than I had imagined it would be.*

▸ **over** completely finished: *The party was over by midnight.*

▸ **through** having finished; at a point of completion: *Are you through with your homework yet?*

ANTONYM **unfinished** not finished; incomplete

door *noun* a movable panel that is used to open or close an entrance to a room, building, or vehicle: *see* **entrance**

dose *noun* the amount of medicine or other treatment given or taken at one time: *see* **pill**

doubt

verb ▷ to question or distrust someone or something: *I doubt that he is telling the truth.* ▷ to be uncertain or unsure about something: *I doubt if we'll get home before midnight.*

▸ **distrust** to lack confidence or trust in someone or something: *I distrust TV commercials that make products seem too good.*

▸ **query** to express doubt or uncertainty about something; to question something: *The scientist queried the accuracy of the new study.*

▸ **question** to have or express doubt, especially about the truth or validity of something: *He questioned the total of his hotel bill.*

▸ **suspect** to have doubts about something; to have a reason to distrust someone or something: *I suspect his motives for offering to help me, since he's never paid any attention to me before.*

ANTONYM **trust** to have or put confidence in someone or something

doubtful *adjective* open to doubt or suspicion: *see* **incredible**

downfall *noun* a sudden loss of wealth, reputation, happiness, or status: *see* **misfortune**

downhearted *adjective* in low spirits; discouraged: *see* **sad**

downpour *noun* a heavy fall of rain: *see* **rain**

doze *verb* to sleep lightly: *see* **sleep**

drab *adjective* lacking color or charm: *see* **boring**

draft *noun* a current of air: *see* **wind**

drag *verb* to pull something with great effort: *see* **pull**

drain *verb* to use up all of a person's energy, attention, or emotion: *see* **tire**

drama *noun* a written story meant to be acted out on stage: *see* **show**

drape *noun* a long, often heavy curtain that hangs straight in loose folds: *see* **curtain**

drastic *adjective* so great as to have serious or dangerous effects: *see* **extreme**

draw

verb to make a picture of something, using mostly lines: *I like to draw scenes from nature with colored pencils.*

▸ **outline** to draw only the outer edge of something: *Police used chalk to outline the body of the corpse.*

▸ **portray** to show something by means of a picture: *Our manager used graphs to portray the earnings of the company.*

▸ **sketch** to make a rough or quick drawing of something: *The cartoonist sketched a caricature of us.*

▸ **trace** to copy something exactly by following lines seen through a sheet of transparent paper: *I traced the picture.*

drawing *noun* a picture made by making lines on a surface to represent forms and figures: *see* **picture**

dread *noun* fearful or unpleasant anticipation: *see* **fear**

dreadful *adjective* causing dread or alarm: *see* **terrible**

dream *verb* to think or believe something is possible in the future: *see* **hope**

dreary *adjective* boring or dull: *see* **gloomy**

drench *verb* to wet something through and through: *see* **flood**

drenched *adjective* wet through and through: *see* **wet**

dress *noun* a style of clothing: *see* **clothing**

dribble *verb* to flow slowly in an unsteady stream: *see* **leak**

drift *verb* to be carried along slowly by a current of water or air: *see* **float**

drifter *noun* a person who moves aimlessly from place to place or from job to job: *see* **beggar**

drill *verb* to give instruction in a subject by having students repeat something again and again: *see* **teach**

drink

verb to take a liquid into the mouth and swallow it: *I drink a glass of carrot juice every morning.*

- ▶ **gulp** to swallow something rapidly in large amounts: *I was so thirsty that I gulped down the glass of water.*
- ▶ **guzzle** to drink something greedily: *I felt a little sick after guzzling all that soda.*
- ▶ **sip** to drink in something in small amounts: *We slowly sipped coffee and enjoyed our visit.*
- ▶ **swallow** to cause food or drink to pass from the mouth through the throat and into the stomach: *I'm so full I can't swallow another bite.*
- ▶ **swig** to take large swallows of a liquid: *He swigged the iced tea to relieve his thirst.*

drip *noun* liquid or moisture that falls in drops: *see* **drop**

drip *verb* to fall in drops: *see* **leak**

drippings *noun* the fat and juices from roasting meat, often used to make gravy: *see* **fat**

drive *noun* a strong motivation that prompts activity: *see* **will**

drizzle *noun* a fine, misty rain: *see* **rain**

drone *verb* to make a continuous, dull humming sound: *see* **hum**

droop

verb to bend or hang downward; sag: *The flag drooped because there was no wind.*

- ▶ **sag** to sink, droop, or settle from pressure or weight: *The clothesline sagged when we hung up our wet beach towels.*
- ▶ **sink** to move to a lower level, especially slowly or in stages: *The sun finally sank below the horizon.*
- ▶ **wilt** to become limp; to loose stiffness: *The flowers wilted from lack of water.*

drop

noun a small mass of liquid in a rounded shape: *Drops of rain splashed into the puddle.*

- ▶ **bead** a small round object, such as a drop of moisture: *A bead of water ran down the cold glass.*
- ▶ **drip** liquid or moisture that falls in drops: *Drips of paint were spattered on the floor.*
- ▶ **droplet** a tiny drop: *The lawn sprinkler threw droplets of water through the air.*
- ▶ **glob** a rounded mass or lump of thick liquid: *I dropped a glob of mustard on my pants.*

droplet *noun* a tiny drop: *see* **drop**

drown *verb* to cover something thoroughly or excessively with a liquid: *see* **flood**

drowse *verb* to be half asleep: *see* **sleep**

drowsy *adjective* half-asleep; dull with sleepiness: *see* **tired**

drudgery *noun* hard, boring, or unpleasant work: *see* **work**

drum *noun* a large metal container having a cylindrical or drum-like shape: *see* **barrel**

dry

adjective free from liquid or moisture: *Deserts can be hot or cold but they are always dry.*

- ▶ **arid** having little or no rainfall; dry: *My grandparents moved to Arizona because the arid climate is good for their health.*

▸ **parched** very dry, as from intense heat: *The long drought has left the cornfields parched and brown.*

▸ **thirsty** ▷ wanting or needing to drink: *Working in this heat has made me thirsty.* ▷ needing rain or watering: *The houseplants were thirsty after a week without watering.*

ANTONYM **wet** being covered, moistened, or soaked with a liquid, especially water

dub *verb* to give someone a nickname: *see* **call [1]**

duck *verb* to lower the head and body quickly so as to get out of something's way: *see* **avoid**

due process *noun* an established process that is designed to protect the legal rights of an individual: *see* **justice**

due to *conjunction* because of: *see* **because**

duel *noun* a fight between two people that is arranged in advance and witnessed by two other people, and in which weapons are used: *see* **fight**

duffle bag *noun* a large canvas bag that is shaped like a tube and is used to carry personal belongings: *see* **bag**

dull *adjective* arousing no interest or curiosity: *see* **boring**

dumb *adjective* foolish or stupid: *see* **stupid**

dummy *noun* a stupid or foolish person: *see* **fool**

dump *verb* to get rid of something: *see* **abandon**

dunce *noun* a stupid or ignorant person: *see* **fool**

dune *noun* a hill or ridge of windblown sand: *see* **hill**

dungeon *noun* a dark, underground prison: *see* **jail**

dunk *verb* to briefly submerge something in a liquid: *see* **dip**

duo *noun* two performers working together: *see* **pair**

dupe *verb* to trick or deceive an unwary or naive person: *see* **deceive**

duplicate *verb* (formal) to copy something exactly, as by photocopying: *see* **copy**

durable *adjective* capable of standing hard wear or long use: *see* **tough**

dusk *noun* the time of evening just before dark: *see* **sunset**

dust *noun* fine, dry particles of soil or other matter: *see* **earth [2]**

dust *verb* to remove dust from something by wiping or brushing: *see* **clean**

duty

noun something that a person should or must do: *In a democracy, one duty of a citizen is to vote.*

▸ **mission** an important assignment that a person or group is sent to carry out: *The ambassador was sent on a mission to negotiate a peace settlement.*

▸ **obligation** a legal, social, or moral requirement: *Police officers have an obligation to uphold the law.*

▸ **responsibility** something that one is responsible for; a duty or task: *It is my responsibility to clean the bathroom this week.*

duvet *noun* a quilt, usually with a washable cover, used in place of a bedspread and top sheet: *see* **cover**

dwell

verb to live in a place as a resident: *People have dwelled in cities for thousands of years.*

▸ **abide** (formal) to live in a place: *My family abides in an apartment downtown.*

▸ **inhabit** to live or reside in a place, as people or animals do: *Many rare species of insects inhabit the rain forests of South America.*

▸ **live** to reside or dwell in a place: *How long have you lived in your house?*

▸ **lodge** to live in a place temporarily: *I lodged in my professor's house while he was in Europe.*

▸ **reside** to live in a place permanently or for an extended time: *I reside on the west side of town.*

dwelling *noun* a place to live in: *see* **home**

dwindle *verb* to decrease bit by bit: *see* **decrease**

dynamic *adjective* characterized by continuous change, activity, or progress: *see* **busy**

each *adjective* considered individually: *see* **every**

eager *adjective* wishing immediate action: *see* **impatient**

eagerness *noun* keen interest or desire: *see* **enthusiasm**

earlier *adverb* near the beginning of a period of time or a course of events: *see* **before**

earliest *adjective* happening near the beginning of a time period, series, or course of events: *see* **original [2]**

earmark *verb* to identify something as reserved for a particular purpose: *see* **allocate**

earn

verb to receive something as a result of one's efforts or behavior: *I earned a lot of respect in my family when I graduated with honors.*

- ► **deserve** to be worthy of or have a right to something: *He deserves recognition for his years of volunteer work.*
- ► **merit** to deserve something, especially as a result of superior performance: *My boss said that my good work merits a raise.*
- ► **rate** (informal) to merit or deserve something: *The excellent performance rated a standing ovation.*
- ► **warrant** to provide good reason for something; to be justified in claiming something: *Your suggestion warrants further consideration.*

earnest *adjective* showing great sincerity or seriousness: *see* **serious [1]**

earth

noun [1] the planet on which human beings live: *The earth is the third planet from the sun.*

- ► **globe** ▷ the planet earth: *Magellan's expedition of 1519–1522 was the first to completely circle the globe.* ▷ a ball-shaped map of the earth: *I used a globe to show my friend the country where I was born.*
- ► **planet** a celestial body that does not produce light and that revolves around a star: *My friends and I sometimes debate whether or not there is life on other planets.*
- ► **world** the earth and all its people: *There are many different cultures in the world.*

earth

noun [2] the loose top layer of the earth's surface; soil: *A bulldozer is designed to move large amounts of earth.*

- ► **dirt** earth or soil, especially when considered to be unclean: *I got dirt under my fingernails while working in the garden.*
- ► **dust** fine, dry particles of soil or other matter: *I wiped the dust off the top of the refrigerator.*
- ► **ground** the solid surface of the earth: *I found a twenty-dollar bill lying on the ground.*
- ► **land** the part of the earth's surface not covered by water: *Only one third of the earth's surface is land.*
- ► **loam** soil composed of sand, clay, silt, and decayed plant matter: *The rich loam produced abundant crops.*
- ► **mud** wet, sticky, soft dirt: *I left my boots outside because they were covered with mud.*
- ► **soil** earth or dirt, especially when considered as a material for plants to grow in: *The soil became dry and cracked during the drought.*

ease *verb* to free someone from worry, pain, or trouble: *see* **comfort**

easy

adjective requiring little or no effort or trouble; not hard: *Some people think that math is an easy subject.*

- **effortless** requiring or showing little or no effort: *The dancer was so good that her performance seemed **effortless**.*
- **no problem** (informal) easy: *It was **no problem** to hem your pants.*
- **simple** not involved or complicated; easy because it is not complex: *The recipe is so **simple** that even a beginner can follow it.*
- **smooth** free from difficulties or obstacles: *Good planning ensured that the wedding was a **smooth** operation.*
- **straightforward** simple and clear; easy to understand: *A smile is a **straightforward** expression of happiness.*
- **uncomplicated** not complex or involved; easy to understand or solve: *This **uncomplicated** dress pattern is good for someone just learning to sew.*

easygoing *adjective* living without undue worry or concern: *see* **casual**

easygoing *adjective* not strict or demanding: *see* **indulgent**

eat

verb to take solid food into the body through the mouth: *My family **eats** dinner together every night.*

- **consume** to eat or drink something completely: *I **consumed** a pint of ice cream.*
- **devour** to eat something quickly and greedily: *The stray cat **devoured** the food I gave it.*
- **dine** (formal) to eat a meal, especially dinner: *We **dined** at a fancy restaurant.*
- **gobble** to devour food in big, greedy gulps: *We **gobbled** up the last of the brownies.*
- **munch** to chew food in a noisy, steady manner: *I **munched** on popcorn while I watched the movie.*
- **nibble** to eat something with small, quick bites: *The rabbit **nibbled** the carrot.*
- **peck** to eat small amounts of what one is served: *I **pecked** at my food because I wasn't very hungry.*
- **wolf** to eat something quickly, hungrily, or greedily: *I was in a hurry so I **wolfed** down my breakfast.*

eccentric *adjective* odd or unusual in appearance: *see* **strange**

echo *verb* to repeat a sound: *see* **copy**

economical *adjective* making the most of one's money: *see* **thrifty**

ecstasy *noun* intense joy or delight: *see* **happiness**

edge

noun the area or part of something that is farthest from the middle: *We planted flowers around the **edge** of our garden.*

- **border** an edge or the area immediately inside it: *The **border** of the quilt is made from purple fabric.*
- **boundary** a border that serves as a limit: *That line of trees marks the **boundary** of our property.*
- **brink** the upper edge of a steep or vertical slope: *I stood at the **brink** of the cliff and looked down.*
- **fringe** an outer part or area, especially one of secondary importance: *She grew up in a poor neighborhood on the **fringe** of town.*
- **hem** a usually stitched edge of a garment or piece of cloth: *The **hem** on my favorite pair of jeans is becoming frayed.*
- **margin** an outer area, especially the blank space bordering a printed page: *I write in the **margin** of the paper when I take notes in class.*
- **rim** the edge of something that is circular or curved: *The **rim** of this coffee cup is chipped.*

edgy *adjective* nervous or irritable: *see* **nervous**

educate *verb* to provide someone with fundamental or thorough knowledge: *see* **teach**

education

noun ▷ the process of giving or receiving formal instruction: *I plan to continue my **education** by going to graduate school after college.* ▷ the knowledge or skill obtained by such a process: ***Education** is highly valued in my family.*

▸ **instruction** something that is taught; a lesson or series of lessons: *I gave my mother some **instruction** on how to use her computer.*

▸ **learning** knowledge gotten from study or instruction: *My professors are people of great **learning**.*

▸ **schooling** instruction or training given at school; formal education: *I plan to continue my **schooling** after I graduate from high school.*

eerie *adjective* inspiring fear without a clear reason: *see* **scary**

effect *noun* something brought about by a cause: *see* **result**

effective *adjective* producing a strong impression or response: *see* **powerful**

effort *noun* the use of physical or mental energy to do something: *see* **work**

effortless *adjective* requiring or showing little or no effort: *see* **easy**

eject *verb* to throw or drive someone out: *see* **throw out**

elaborate *adjective* planned or made with careful attention or with much detail: *see* **fancy**

elastic *adjective* easily resuming its original shape after being stretched or expanded: *see* **flexible**

elbow *noun* something having a bend or an angle similar to an elbow in a human being: *see* **joint**

elbow *verb* to push or shove someone with the elbows: *see* **push**

elderly *adjective* approaching old age: *see* **old**

elect *verb* (formal) to make a deliberate choice: *see* **choose**

elegance

noun refinement, grace, and beauty in appearance or behavior: *The beautiful hotel is known for its **elegance**.*

▸ **charm** the power or ability to please or delight: *The cottage was small but full of **charm**.*

▸ **grace** ease and beauty of movement, form, or manner: *The ballerina danced with **grace**.*

▸ **polish** a refined style or manner achieved through careful preparation: *He delivered his speech with **polish**.*

▸ **politeness** good or courteous manners: *The headwaiter treated everyone with **politeness**.*

▸ **refinement** polite and cultured manners or behavior: *People of **refinement** treat others with courtesy.*

elegant

adjective marked by refinement, grace, and beauty in appearance or behavior: *She dresses in an **elegant** style.*

▸ **exquisite** highly pleasing because of its beauty or excellence: *Their **exquisite** home had been professionally decorated.*

▸ **refined** polite or cultivated: *You look very **refined** in that tuxedo.*

▸ **sophisticated** having acquired worldly knowledge or refinement: *Traveling abroad has made her more **sophisticated**.*

▸ **stylish** conforming to the current style; fashionable: *That **stylish** haircut looks good on you.*

▸ **tasteful** having, showing, or being in keeping with good taste: *It was **tasteful** of you to bring a small gift for the hostess of the party.*

element *noun* a basic or essential part of a whole: *see* **ingredient**

elemental *adjective* being a primary or essential part of something: *see* **basic**

elementary *adjective* being the simplest or most basic aspect of something: *see* **basic**

elevate *verb* to raise something to a higher position: *see* **raise [2]**

elevated *adjective* raised or placed above a given level: *see* **tall**

eliminate *verb* to get rid of something completely: *see* **erase**

eliminate *verb* to remove someone or something from consideration: *see* **exclude**

elongated *adjective* having grown or been made longer: *see* **long**

else *adjective* in addition: *see* **more**

elude *verb* to avoid someone by skill, cunning, or daring: *see* **escape**

e-mail *verb* to send a message by electronic mail: *see* **send**

embarrass

verb to cause someone to feel nervous, self-conscious, or ill at ease: *I embarrassed myself when I spilled my drink.*

► **degrade** to lower someone's dignity; to make someone feel low or mean: *You degraded me by yelling at me in public.*
► **disgrace** to bring shame or dishonor upon someone: *He disgraced himself by lying.*
► **dishonor** to damage or destroy someone's honor or reputation: *The gambler dishonored his family by bringing them to financial ruin.*
► **humiliate** to deeply hurt someone's self-respect or pride: *The author was publicly humiliated by the revelation that she plagiarized large parts of her book.*
► **shame** to cause someone to feel a strong, often painful sense of guilt, embarrassment, unworthiness, or disgrace: *The teacher shamed me when he made me read the note I was passing in class.*

embarrassment

noun the feeling of being ill at ease or self-conscious: *I felt embarrassment when I introduced him by the wrong name.*

► **chagrin** (formal) a strong feeling of unease or annoyance caused by disappointment, embarrassment, or humiliation: *Much to my chagrin, my credit card was declined.*
► **discomfort** mental or bodily distress; uneasiness: *I was in a lot of discomfort when my parents said we should have a talk about sex.*

► **humiliation** the state of feeling humiliated or disgraced; a lowering of pride, dignity, or self-respect: *He felt humiliation when he was caught cheating on the final exam.*
► **uneasiness** a feeling of awkwardness or of being unsure: *He felt some uneasiness the first time he asked her out on a date.*

embellish *verb* to enhance the beauty of something: *see* **decorate**

embezzle *verb* to take money or property that has been left in one's care for one's own use: *see* **steal**

embrace *verb* to hold someone close with the arms: *see* **cuddle**

embroider *verb* to add ornamental beauty to something with needlework: *see* **decorate**

emerge *verb* to come forth into view or notice: *see* **appear** [1]

emergency *noun* a serious situation or occurrence that happens suddenly and calls for immediate action: *see* **disaster**

emit

verb to give off or send forth something: *Automobiles emit carbon monoxide in their exhaust.*

► **exude** to discharge or emit something gradually; to ooze something: *The pine tree exuded sap where it had been cut.*
► **radiate** to give something off in rays or waves: *Our wood-burning stove radiates lots of heat.*

emotion *noun* a deep or strong feeling: *see* **feeling**

emperor *noun* a man who is the ruler of an empire: *see* **ruler**

emphasize

verb to give special weight or importance to something: *Our teacher emphasizes the importance of getting our homework done on time.*

- **accent** to focus attention on something; to make something stand out: *That scarf accents your outfit.*
- **highlight** to give prominence to something, especially a significant or interesting detail or event: *I use a yellow marker to highlight important parts of my class notes.*
- **note** to show or indicate something: *The recipe noted the amount of time needed to bake the casserole.*
- **stress** to place special significance or emphasis on something: *My parents stress the importance of honesty.*

empire *noun* a group of territories or nations headed by a single ruler: *see* **country**

employ *verb* (formal) to make use of something: *see* **use**

employee

noun a person who works for another in return for financial or other compensation: *I work at a small store that has five employees.*

- **hired hand** a paid employee, especially on a farm or ranch: *My friend spent last summer working as a hired hand on a ranch.*
- **laborer** a person engaged in physical work, especially work that requires little skill: *The laborers worked all day repairing the road.*
- **worker** one who does manual or industrial labor: *The local factory is hiring workers for the night shift.*

employer *noun* a person or business that hires and pays people to perform work: *see* **boss**

employment *noun* the work in which one is engaged or the activity to which one devotes time: *see* **job**

empress *noun* a woman who is the ruler of an empire: *see* **ruler**

empty

adjective holding or containing nothing: *The waitress refilled my empty water glass.*

- **bare** lacking the usual furnishings, supplies, or decorations: *I covered the bare walls of my dorm room with posters.*
- **barren** lacking plants or crops: *The Sahara Desert is a barren wasteland except for scattered oases.*
- **blank** free of marks or writing: *She has three blank pages left in her sketchbook.*
- **hollow** having an empty space or opening inside: *The bear made its den in a hollow log.*
- **vacant** not currently used, filled, or occupied: *There are two vacant apartments in the building where I live.*
- **void** containing no matter; empty: *Outer space is mostly void of matter.*

ANTONYM **full** holding as much as possible

encase *verb* to enclose something in or as if in a case: *see* **wrap**

enchanting *adjective* having the power to enchant: *see* **charming**

encounter *verb* to experience something directly: *see* **face**

encourage

verb to give hope, courage, or confidence to someone; to stimulate someone to do something: *My parents have been encouraging me to attend college.*

- **hearten** to give strength or courage to someone; to cheer someone up: *The coach's words heartened the team.*
- **inspire** to stimulate someone to creativity or action: *The paintings of Gustav Klimt inspire me to continue with my art classes.*
- **motivate** to provide someone with an incentive; to move someone to action: *The manager motivated her employees to work better by offering them a bonus program.*
- **urge** to encourage or inspire someone to take action or make an effort: *The jockey urged his horse to run faster.*

end *noun* something toward which one strives: *see* **goal**

end *verb* to come to a conclusion: *see* **finish**

endeavor *verb* to make a serious or sustained effort: *see* **try**

endless *adjective* being or seeming to be without an end: *see* **permanent**

endorse *verb* to give official approval of something: *see* **sponsor**

endurance

noun the ability to withstand strain, pain, hardship, or use: *A marathon tests a runner's* ***endurance***.

▶ **fortitude** strength of mind that allows one to endure pain or adversity with courage: *He faced his problems with* ***fortitude***.

▶ **perseverance** the act or quality of holding to a course of action, a belief, or a purpose despite obstacles or difficulties: *It takes a lot of* ***perseverance*** *to get a college degree.*

▶ **stamina** the power to resist fatigue or illness while working hard: *The sport of outdoor adventure racing calls for lots of* ***stamina***.

▶ **staying power** the ability to endure or last: *The long-distance swimmer had incredible* ***staying power***.

endure *verb* to bear something with patience or tolerance: *see* **cope**

endure *verb* to continue in existence in spite of difficulties: *see* **last²**

enduring *adjective* continuing to exist for a long time: *see* **permanent**

enemy

noun one who feels hatred toward or intends injury to another: *The North and the South were* ***enemies*** *during the American Civil War.*

▶ **adversary** an opponent or enemy: *Russia and Germany were allies at the beginning of World War II, but they later became* ***adversaries***.

▶ **antagonist** (formal) one who opposes or seeks to defeat someone or something: *The senator was known as an* ***antagonist*** *to campaign finance reform.*

▶ **foe** a personal enemy: *Brutus pretended to be a friend of Julius Caesar, but he was actually a* ***foe***.

▶ **nemesis** an opponent that cannot be beaten or overcome: *She lost every tennis match to her* ***nemesis***.

▶ **opponent** a person or group that opposes another in a battle, contest, controversy, or debate: *He defeated two other* ***opponents*** *to win the gold medal.*

▶ **rival** a person who attempts to equal or outdo another: *They are* ***rivals*** *for the promotion.*

ANTONYM **friend** a person one knows, likes, and trusts

energize *verb* to give someone or something new or extra energy: *see* **refresh**

energy

noun the capacity for work or vigorous activity: *I've had more* ***energy*** *since I started exercising.*

▶ **pep** high spirits or energy: *The volunteers worked with a lot of* ***pep***.

▶ **verve** energy and enthusiasm in the expression of ideas: *The professor lectured with* ***verve***.

▶ **vigor** physical or mental energy or strength: *He argued his point with great* ***vigor***.

▶ **vim** liveliness and energy; enthusiasm: *My grandmother is still full of* ***vim***.

▶ **vitality** physical or intellectual vigor; energy: *She is regaining her* ***vitality*** *after a long illness.*

▶ **zip** high energy; spirit: *The comedian added some different jokes to give his routine more* ***zip***.

enfold *verb* to enclose something with or as if with folds of material: *see* **wrap**

engage *verb* to hold someone's attention closely: *see* **interest**

engagement *noun* a promise to be at a particular place at a certain time: *see* **appointment**

engine *noun* a machine that makes something run or move by using energy, such as that produced by oil or steam: *see* **machine**

engrave *verb* to carve, cut, or etch writing or a design into a material: *see* **carve**

enhance *verb* to make something greater, as in value, beauty, or reputation: *see* **better**

enjoy

verb to receive pleasure or satisfaction from something: *I enjoy reading science-fiction novels.*

- ▸ **appreciate** to recognize the worth, quality, or importance of something: *I appreciate all your help.*
- ▸ **relish** to have a keen appetite or liking for something: *She is a strong athlete who relishes all kinds of outdoor sports.*
- ▸ **savor** to taste or enjoy fully; relish: *We savored every moment of our vacation.*

ANTONYM **dislike** to regard someone or something with distaste or aversion

enjoyable *adjective* giving joy or happiness: *see* **pleasant**

enjoyment *noun* a form or source of pleasure: *see* **fun**

enlarge *verb* to make something larger: *see* **increase**

enlist *verb* to enter the armed forces: *see* **enroll**

enormous *adjective* very large in size, number, or degree: *see* **big**

enough

adjective sufficient to meet a need or satisfy a desire: *It is important to get enough sleep at night.*

- ▸ **adequate** as much as is needed for a particular purpose: *There was adequate food for everybody at the reception.*

- ▸ **plenty of** completely adequate in amount or supply; ample: *We have plenty of time to clean the house before our guests arrive.*
- ▸ **sufficient** as much as is needed or wanted: *We bought a sufficient amount of wood to last all winter.*

ANTONYM **insufficient** not enough; inadequate

enrage *verb* to put someone into a rage: *see* **anger**

enroll

verb to place one's name on a list in order to enter or participate in something: *I plan to enroll at the university next fall.*

- ▸ **enlist** to enter the armed forces: *She enlisted in the Air Force after she graduated from high school.*
- ▸ **register** to enroll officially or formally, especially in order to vote or attend classes: *I registered to vote as soon as I became a citizen.*
- ▸ **sign up** to agree to be a participant or recipient by signing one's name: *He signed up for a rock-climbing class.*

enterprise *noun* an important undertaking or project, especially one that is complicated and sometimes risky: *see* **project**

entertain

verb to hold the attention of someone with something amusing or diverting: *He entertained us with stories about the movie industry.*

- ▸ **amuse** to give simple enjoyment to someone; to occupy someone pleasantly: *The kitten amused itself by attacking a ball of yarn.*
- ▸ **divert** to entertain someone by turning the attention away from something else: *The street musicians diverted us while we waited in line.*

entertaining *adjective* amusing: *see* **interesting**

entertainment *noun* something that amuses or diverts, especially a performance or show: *see* **fun**

enthusiasm

noun great interest in or excitement for a subject or cause: *His **enthusiasm** for science makes him a great teacher.*

- ▸ **ardor** intense enthusiasm or devotion: *He spoke with **ardor** about his bowling league.*
- ▸ **eagerness** keen interest or desire: *The children expressed their **eagerness** to bake some cookies.*
- ▸ **excitement** great activity or high emotion; agitation: *There was a lot of **excitement** when the circus came to town.*
- ▸ **fervor** powerful or intense emotion: *The actor brought great **fervor** to his performance.*
- ▸ **fire** burning intensity of feeling; ardor: *There was **fire** in her eyes when she spoke about her desire to travel around the world.*
- ▸ **passion** overwhelming enthusiasm for a certain activity or subject: *She has a **passion** for snowboarding.*
- ▸ **zeal** enthusiastic devotion to a cause, ideal, or goal: *He pursues his medical studies with **zeal**.*

enthusiastic

adjective having great enthusiasm or excitement: *I was not **enthusiastic** about doing the dishes.*

- ▸ **ardent** full of warmth or passion for something: *She is an **ardent** fan of that football team.*
- ▸ **keen** full of eager enthusiasm: *Our whole family is **keen** about moving to a larger apartment.*
- ▸ **passionate** full of strong or overwhelming feeling: *He is **passionate** about gardening.*

ANTONYM **indifferent** having or showing no interest

entice *verb* to attract someone by arousing hope or desire: *see* **tempt**

entire *adjective* all in one piece: *see* **all**

entirely *adverb* with no doubt or exception: *see* **completely**

entitlement *noun* a right or privilege granted by an authority: *see* **privilege**

entrance

noun a means or point by which to enter something: *The fancy hotel had a beautiful entrance.*

- ▸ **door** a movable panel that is used to open or close an entrance to a room, building, or vehicle: *Please close the **door** behind you.*
- ▸ **entryway** a passage or an opening by which to enter: *The old house has a narrow **entryway** leading to the front hall.*
- ▸ **gate** an opening in a wall or fence: *We keep the **gate** closed so that our dog can't get out of the yard.*
- ▸ **hatch** an opening in the deck of a ship: *The **hatches** on a submarine make a watertight seal.*
- ▸ **threshold** the piece of wood or stone put beneath a door; an entrance or doorway: *It is an old custom for the groom to carry his bride over the **threshold** of their new home.*

entreat *verb* (formal) to urge someone seriously to do something: *see* **beg**

entryway *noun* a passage or an opening by which to enter: *see* **entrance**

envelop *verb* to enclose or surround something completely with or as if with a covering: *see* **wrap**

envious *adjective* resenting the advantages or success of another person and wanting them for oneself: *see* **jealous**

environment *noun* all of the surroundings and conditions that affect the growth and development of living things: *see* **atmosphere**

envy *noun* a feeling of resentment at the advantages or success of another person: *see* **resentment**

epic *noun* a long poem about the achievements and adventures of a hero or heroes: *see* **story**

episode *noun* an event that forms a distinct part of a story: *see* **event**

equal *adjective* being exactly the same in amount, extent, or other measured quality: *see* **same**

equip

verb to supply something or someone with needed items or gear: *They have* **equipped** *their kitchen with high-tech appliances.*

- ▸ **arm** to provide someone with something needed for an action or operation: *She* **armed** *herself with a flashlight before going out to investigate the strange noise.*
- ▸ **furnish** to provide the items or equipment needed for a purpose or activity: *We have to* **furnish** *our own supplies for the painting class.*
- ▸ **outfit** to furnish someone with the necessary equipment or clothing for a specific activity: *We had to* **outfit** *ourselves with sleeping bags and a tent before going camping.*
- ▸ **prepare** to make something ready beforehand for some purpose, task, or event: *It took us two days to* **prepare** *our Thanksgiving feast.*
- ▸ **supply** to make something available for use: *I volunteered to* **supply** *the food for our next meeting.*

equipment

noun the things needed or used for a particular purpose: *The ambulance is supplied with the latest lifesaving* **equipment**.

- ▸ **gear** equipment, such as tools or clothing, needed for a particular activity: *The climber's* **gear** *was covered in red dust after climbing in Red Rocks Canyon.*
- ▸ **kit** a set of articles or tools for a certain purpose: *I keep a first-aid* **kit** *in the trunk of my car.*
- ▸ **supplies** materials or provisions stored and dispensed when needed: *That cabinet contains all the office* **supplies**.

equity *noun* the state of being just and impartial: *see* **justice**

equivalent *adjective* equal to something else: *see* **same**

era *noun* a period of time marked from a specific date or event: *see* **age**

erase

verb ▷ to remove something written or drawn by rubbing, scraping, or wiping: *The teacher* **erased** *the blackboard when class was over.* ▷ to eliminate something completely: *The government announced a plan to* **erase** *the budget deficit in three years.*

- ▸ **abolish** to put an official end to something: *The Thirteenth Amendment to the Constitution* **abolished** *slavery in the United States.*
- ▸ **cancel** to end, call off, or invalidate something: *He* **canceled** *his subscription to the magazine.*
- ▸ **delete** to remove something by striking out or canceling: *I* **deleted** *the last paragraph of my essay.*
- ▸ **eliminate** to get rid of something completely: *She has been working on* **eliminating** *sugar from her diet.*

erect *verb* to put a structure up: *see* **build**

ergo *adverb* consequently; hence: *see* **therefore**

erode *verb* to wear something away or make something gradually disappear: *see* **undermine**

errand *noun* a short trip taken to perform a task: *see* **chore**

erroneous *adjective* containing error or developed from error: *see* **wrong**

error *noun* something that is incorrect or wrong: *see* **mistake**

erupt *verb* to burst out suddenly and violently: *see* **explode**

escape

verb ▷ to break free of confinement: *I can't figure out how my dog is* **escaping** *from the yard.* ▷ to avoid capture, danger, or harm: *I barely* **escaped** *injury when the ladder fell.*

- ▸ **elude** to avoid someone by skill, cunning, or daring: *The criminals **eluded** the police for two days before being caught.*
- ▸ **evade** to escape or avoid something, as by cleverness or deceit: *They were charged with conspiracy to **evade** taxes.*
- ▸ **flee** to run away, as from trouble or danger: *The deer **fled** when it saw a mountain lion.*

escort

verb to accompany someone so as to give protection, guidance, or honor: *Her father **escorted** the bride down the aisle.*

- ▸ **accompany** to go along with someone: *I **accompanied** my little brother to the movies.*
- ▸ **chaperon** to attend and supervise a dance or party for young, unmarried people: *Teachers and parents **chaperoned** the school dance.*
- ▸ **conduct** to lead, guide, or direct someone to a place: *A bellhop **conducted** us to our room.*
- ▸ **usher** to show people to their seats, as in a theater: *The restaurant hostess **ushered** us to our table.*

essay

noun a short piece of writing that gives the author's opinions on a certain subject: *I have to write an **essay** about these two poems.*

- ▸ **article** a piece of writing that forms an independent part of a newspaper, magazine, or book: *He writes **articles** for many different magazines.*
- ▸ **composition** a short essay, especially one written as an academic exercise: *She has to write a two-page **composition** every week for her college English class.*
- ▸ **dissertation** a lengthy formal treatise, especially one written by a candidate for a PhD: *She will receive her doctorate as soon as she finishes her **dissertation**.*
- ▸ **paper** a written work assigned in school: *The teacher said that our research **papers** are due in three weeks.*
- ▸ **thesis** a dissertation that advances an original point of view, especially as

required for an academic degree: *The student had to submit a **thesis** in order to earn his master's degree.*
- ▸ **treatise** a piece of formal writing that deals with a certain topic and is usually longer and more detailed than an essay: *The scientist published a **treatise** on the effects of space radiation on astronauts.*

essence *noun* the most important ingredient: *see* **center [1]**

essential *adjective* of the greatest importance: *see* **necessary**

establish *verb* to settle something or someone securely in a position or condition: *see* **begin**

establish *verb* to show clearly that something is true: *see* **prove**

esteem *noun* recognition of superior worth or achievement: *see* **respect**

estimate *verb* to calculate something roughly: *see* **guess**

etch *verb* to cut a design into metal, glass, or other material by using acid: *see* **carve**

eternal *adjective* having no beginning and no end: *see* **permanent**

ethical *adjective* conforming to accepted standards of right behavior or conduct: *see* **moral**

etiquette *noun* the rules of proper behavior: *see* **behavior**

evade *verb* to escape or avoid something: *see* **escape**

evaluate *verb* to find out, judge, or estimate the value of something: *see* **judge**

evaporate *verb* ▷ to disappear by changing into a vapor ▷ to vanish or go away: *see* **fade**

even *adjective* being at the same height or level: *see* **flat**

evenhanded *adjective* dealing fairly with all: *see* **fair¹**

evening *noun* the time between sunset and the time to go to bed: *see* **night**

event

noun an occurrence or experience, especially one of significance: *Getting married is a significant **event** in a person's life.*

- ▶ **episode** an event that forms a distinct part of a story or experience: *The year I spent studying abroad was an important **episode** in my life.*
- ▶ **happening** something that takes place; an event or occurrence: *The fall of the Berlin Wall in 1989 was a **happening** of great historical significance.*
- ▶ **incident** a particular occurrence, especially one of minor importance: *Getting lost on the freeway was an unpleasant **incident**.*
- ▶ **occasion** an important or festive event: *We save our best dishes for special **occasions**.*
- ▶ **occurrence** something that happens or takes place: *With the new security regulations, flight delays have become a common **occurrence**.*

eventually

adverb in due time; in the course of events: *This traffic is terrible, but we'll get there **eventually**.*

- ▶ **at last** after a long or difficult time; finally: *I finished my homework **at last**.*
- ▶ **finally** at the end of a certain period; at last: *After two years of trying, I **finally** got my student visa.*
- ▶ **ultimately** after all is done; in the end: *I have a good job now, but **ultimately** I want to own my own business.*

everglade *noun* a large area of marshland covered in places with tall grass: *see* **swamp**

every

adjective each and all without exception: *Every employee gets a review once a year.*

- ▶ **any** one, some, or all: *Any person over seventeen may attend this movie.*
- ▶ **each** considered individually; every: *The teacher met with **each** student regarding his or her progress.*

everyday *adjective* happening often or regularly: *see* **common**

evict *verb* to make a tenant leave by a legal process: *see* **throw out**

evidence *noun* facts that help one find out the truth or come to a decision: *see* **fact**

evil

adjective morally bad or wrong, especially to a profound degree: *The theme of many stories is that of good versus **evil**.*

- ▶ **hateful** arousing or deserving hatred or revulsion: *The **hateful** crime shocked the whole city.*
- ▶ **immoral** going against what is considered fair, right, or good: *Most people believe that cheating is **immoral**.*
- ▶ **sinister** suggesting or threatening evil: *I think that moray eels have a **sinister** appearance.*
- ▶ **vile** hateful and disgusting: *This medicine tastes **vile**.*
- ▶ **wicked** morally bad; evil: *To enjoy other people's suffering is **wicked**.*

exact

adjective accurate in every detail: *Be sure to use the **exact** amount of each ingredient.*

- ▶ **literal** word for word; avoiding exaggeration or embellishment: *The paper published a **literal** translation of the ambassador's speech.*
- ▶ **precise** very accurate; clearly expressed: *The carpenter took **precise** measurements before sawing the boards.*
- ▶ **specific** stated clearly and in detail: *The teacher gave us **specific** directions for our book reports.*

exaggerate *verb* to claim that something is greater or larger than it actually is: *see* **increase**

exam *noun* an examination: *see* **test**

examination *noun* a set of questions or exercises that measure one's ability: *see* **test**

examine

verb to observe something carefully and in detail: *He **examined** the document before signing it.*

- **analyze** to examine something closely for the purpose of drawing conclusions: *The scientist carefully **analyzed** the results of her experiment.*
- **check** to test or examine something critically to make sure it is correct or satisfactory: *She **checked** all her answers before turning in her test.*
- **inspect** to examine something carefully, especially for flaws: *Every automobile is carefully **inspected** before it leaves the factory.*
- **interrogate** to seek information from someone by close questioning: *The police are **interrogating** their prime suspect.*
- **investigate** to research something carefully for facts, knowledge, or information: *A reporter has been assigned to **investigate** the story.*

example

noun a person or thing that is typical of a whole class or group: *This antique chair is an **example** of Victorian furniture.*

- **case** an individual occurrence of something, whether or not it is considered typical: *The police are investigating two **cases** of arson.*
- **instance** a particular occurrence; a case: *They waived the usual requirements in this **instance**.*
- **sample** a part or amount that is considered representative of the whole: *The nurse took a blood **sample** to send to the laboratory.*
- **specimen** something that is chosen to represent the group, especially a sample taken for scientific analysis: *These dinosaur bones are considered to be the finest **specimens** ever found.*

excavate *verb* to uncover or expose something by digging: *see* **dig**

excellent

adjective of the highest or finest quality: *This restaurant is famous for its **excellent** food.*

- **first-rate** foremost in quality, rank, or importance: *The company pays for him to stay in **first-rate** hotels.*
- **outstanding** noticeably superior to others of its kind: *She won an award for her **outstanding** performance.*
- **super** (informal) first-rate; excellent: *You did a **super** job of decorating this cake.*
- **superb** of unusually high quality; excellent: *My friend has a **superb** collection of arrowheads.*
- **terrific** very good or fine; splendid: *I had a **terrific** time at your party.*

ANTONYM **inferior** low in quality or ability

excellently *adverb* in a manner that is excellent: *see* **well**

exceptional *adjective* well above average: *see* **better**

excess *adjective* greater than what is used or needed: *see* **extra**

excessive *adjective* greater than is normal, desirable, or necessary: *see* **extreme**

exchange *verb* to give one thing in return for another: *see* **substitute**

excite

verb to stir something or someone to activity: *Studying fashion design has **excited** my interest in designing clothes.*

- **arouse** to awaken something, as from inactivity: *The magazine article **aroused** my curiosity.*
- **ignite** to start something suddenly; to touch something off: *The movie star's comments **ignited** a controversy.*
- **inflame** to stir up anger or other strong emotion in someone: *The angry speaker **inflamed** the mob.*
- **kindle** to bring something to life; to arouse something: *Her exciting stories have **kindled** my imagination.*
- **spark** to set something in motion; to ignite something: *News of the arrests **sparked** angry protests in the nation's capital.*
- **stimulate** to excite something or someone to an active state: *Adrenaline is a hormone that **stimulates** the nervous system.*

excited *adjective*   emotionally stirred up or stimulated: *see* **impatient**

excitement *noun*   great activity or high emotion: *see* **enthusiasm**

exciting

adjective   creating or producing excitement: *Downhill skiing is an **exciting** sport.*

▸ **inspiring**   arousing great emotion that moves a person to action: *The history professor's **inspiring** lecture made me want to study the Revolutionary War.*
▸ **rousing**   exciting the emotions; inspiring: *The **rousing** speech made the audience cheer.*
▸ **stimulating**   stirring the mind or body to greater activity: *We had a **stimulating** conversation about our hopes for the future.*
▸ **thrilling**   causing a sudden, intense sensation, as of joy, fear, or excitement: *The roller coaster ride was a **thrilling** experience.*

exclude

verb   to prevent someone or something from being included, considered, or accepted: *It is illegal to **exclude** any job applicant on the basis of race, creed, or color.*

▸ **bar**   to keep someone out or away, as by force: *The police **barred** reporters from the crime scene.*
▸ **eliminate**   to remove someone or something from consideration: *The gymnast was **eliminated** from the competition when she failed to complete her routine.*
▸ **pass over**   to leave someone out; to disregard or ignore someone: *He was upset at being **passed over** for a promotion.*
▸ **shut out**   (informal)   to leave someone out of a process or activity: *All but the most essential personnel were **shut out** of the negotiations.*

excursion *noun*   a short pleasure trip: *see* **journey**

excuse

noun   an explanation offered to justify oneself or to obtain forgiveness: *The teacher accepted my **excuse** for being absent.*

▸ **alibi**   a claim made by an accused person of not being present when a crime was committed: *The suspect came up with three witnesses who supported her **alibi**.*
▸ **apology**   a statement expressing regret for an offense or fault: *I offered an **apology** when I realized that I had hurt his feelings.*
▸ **explanation**   something that makes something plain or that gives an interpretation of something: *The police looked for an **explanation** for the crime.*
▸ **reason**   a statement or fact that justifies or explains an action: *She had a good **reason** for being late to work.*

excuse *verb*   to forgive someone by agreeing to overlook a mistake or fault: *see* **forgive**

execute *verb*   to put to death, especially as legal punishment for a crime: *see* **kill**

executive *noun*   a person who manages the affairs of an organization, especially a corporation: *see* **boss**

exercise *verb*   to do physical activity in order to develop or maintain fitness: *see* **practice**

exertion *noun*   the act of making a great effort to do something: *see* **work**

exhaust *verb*   to use up all of a person's strength or energy: *see* **tire**

exhausted *adjective*   completely tired or worn out: *see* **tired**

exhibit *verb*   to present something for the public to view: *see* **show**

exhibition *noun*   a large-scale public showing or display, as of art: *see* **fair**[2]

exile *verb*   to force a person to leave his or her country: *see* **throw out**

exit *verb*   to go out of a place: *see* **leave**

exonerate *verb*   to free someone from blame: *see* **forgive**

exotic *adjective*   from another part of the world: *see* **strange**

expand *verb*   to increase in size, number, volume, or scope: *see* **increase**

expanse *noun*   a wide and open area of land, sea, or sky: *see* **distance**

expansion *noun* the act of making something larger in size, volume, or amount: *see* **growth**

expect

verb to look for something as being likely to happen or appear: *The forecaster said that we could* **expect** *rain tonight.*

▸ **anticipate** to foresee or consider something in advance: *She* **anticipated** *what I was going to say.*
▸ **await** to wait for something: *He is* **awaiting** *his friend's phone call.*
▸ **look forward to** to anticipate something with pleasure: *I* **look forward to** *hearing from you soon.*

expectant *adjective* looking forward to the probable occurrence or appearance of: *see* **optimistic**

expedition *noun* an excursion, journey, or voyage made for some specific purpose, as of war or exploration: *see* **adventure**

expel *verb* to force someone to leave a group or organization: *see* **throw out**

expend *verb* (informal) to spend money: *see* **spend**

expense *noun* something spent to attain a goal or accomplish a purpose: *see* **price**

expensive *adjective* requiring a large amount of money to buy: *My friend drives an* **expensive** *car.*

▸ **costly** high-priced; expensive: *Diamonds are* **costly**.
▸ **extravagant** costing far too much; excessively expensive: *The price of this emerald necklace is* **extravagant**.
▸ **overpriced** costing more than is reasonable: *These computers are* **overpriced** *for what you get.*

Antonym **cheap** low in price; inexpensive

experience *noun* knowledge or skill gotten through practice: *see* **knowledge**

expert

noun a person with great knowledge of or skill in a particular field: *We went to an* **expert** *to get our antique clock appraised.*

▸ **authority** an accepted source of expert information: *He is a well-known* **authority** *on modern art.*
▸ **master** a person of great learning, skill, or ability: *Salvador Dali is considered a* **master** *of surrealistic painting.*
▸ **professional** a person whose occupation requires special training and study: *The members of this dance troupe are all* **professionals**.
▸ **specialist** a person whose work is restricted to a particular activity or to a particular branch of study or research: *My doctor referred me to a* **specialist** *in sports medicine.*

expertise *noun* skill or knowledge in a particular area: *see* **art**

expire *verb* to die, especially while being cared for: *see* **die**

explain

verb to make something plain or understandable: *Our biology teacher* **explained** *the difference between a frog and a toad.*

▸ **clarify** to make something clear or easier to understand: *The coach* **clarified** *his instructions after seeing our looks of confusion.*
▸ **define** to explain or describe something in precise detail: *The Constitution* **defines** *the powers of Congress.*
▸ **illustrate** to explain or clarify something by using pictures or examples: *The teacher* **illustrated** *her point by drawing a diagram on the chalkboard.*
▸ **interpret** to explain the meaning or importance of something obscure or complicated: *I have a book about how to* **interpret** *dreams.*

explanation *noun* something that defines, interprets, or makes something plain: *see* **excuse**

explicit *adjective* clearly stated so that nothing is misunderstood: *see* **clear** [1]

explode

verb to burst with a loud noise: *Fireworks exploded in the sky.*

- ▸ **blow up** to destroy something with explosives: *The terrorists used a bomb to blow up the bridge.*
- ▸ **burst** to break open suddenly and violently: *The building was flooded when the water pipes burst.*
- ▸ **detonate** to cause a device or substance to explode: *The engineers detonated the explosives to make a tunnel through the mountain.*
- ▸ **erupt** to burst out suddenly and violently: *Mount Saint Helens erupted in May 1980.*
- ▸ **pop** to burst open with a sharp explosive sound: *My balloon popped when it touched the hot radiator.*

exploit *noun* a brilliant act or heroic deed: *see* **adventure**

explore *verb* to travel in or search through an unfamiliar area for the purpose of discovery: *see* **search**

explosion *noun* the act of bursting apart suddenly with great force and noise: *see* **bang**

exposed *adjective* made visible; revealed: *see* **naked**

express

verb to make one's opinions or feelings known, as by statement or act: *Everyone expressed a preference for multiple-choice rather than essay questions.*

- ▸ **air** to express one's feelings, beliefs, or ideas in public: *The employees aired their grievances at the meeting with the managers.*
- ▸ **vent** to give forceful expression to a strong, pent-up emotion: *I felt better once I vented my anger.*
- ▸ **voice** to make one's outlook or viewpoint known by speaking or writing: *She called the talk show to voice her opinion.*

expression *noun* a particular way of saying something: *see* **term**

exquisite *adjective* highly pleasing because of its beauty or excellence: *see* **elegant**

extend *verb* to stretch something to a greater or fuller length: *see* **stretch**

extended *adjective* lengthened in space or time: *see* **long**

extensive *adjective* large in quantity, area, or range: *see* **wide**

extent *noun* the degree or level to which something reaches: *see* **degree**

exterior *adjective* outer or outside: *see* **outside**

exterminate *verb* to get rid of living things by destroying them completely; wipe out: *see* **kill**

external *adjective* on the outside or outer surface of something: *see* **outside**

extinct *adjective* no longer existing anywhere in living form: *see* **dead**

extortion *noun* the act of obtaining something from another by threats or force: *see* **theft**

extra

adjective more than what is normal, expected, or required: *I have a flashlight and extra batteries for emergencies.*

- ▸ **excess** greater than what is used or needed: *We froze the excess spaghetti sauce.*
- ▸ **spare** beyond what is usually needed; extra: *We have a spare bedroom that we use when we have guests.*
- ▸ **surplus** left over after normal or actual use: *We gave the surplus vegetables from our garden to the senior center.*

extract *verb* to remove one thing from another: *see* **subtract**

extraordinary *adjective* beyond what is ordinary: *see* **wonderful**

extravagance *noun* excessive expense or display: *see* **luxury**

extravagant *adjective* costing far too much: *see* **expensive**

extreme

adjective very great in degree or intensity: *Use **extreme** caution when operating a chain saw.*

- ▸ **drastic** so great as to have serious or dangerous effects: *Having your jaw wired shut would be a **drastic** way to lose weight.*
- ▸ **excessive** greater than is normal, desirable, or necessary: *The **excessive** rains caused widespread flooding.*
- ▸ **radical** favoring extreme or rapid changes, especially in politics, law, or government: *The early American patriots were considered **radical** by those who supported the British monarchy.*
- ▸ **severe** great enough to cause damage, harm, or suffering: *The refugees suffered **severe** difficulties before reaching safety.*

ANTONYM **moderate** not too much or too little

extremely *adverb* to an exceptionally high degree: *see* **very**

exude *verb* to discharge or emit something gradually: *see* **emit**

eye *verb* to look at something closely: *see* **look**

fable *noun* a story that is meant to teach a useful lesson: *see* **story**

fabric

noun a material that is produced by joining fibers together, as by weaving: *I think that knit **fabrics** are comfortable to wear because they stretch.*

- ▸ **cloth** material produced by weaving or knitting natural or synthetic fibers: *We used a soft **cloth** to polish the silverware.*
- ▸ **material** cloth or fabric: *I went to the fabric store to pick the **material** for my curtains.*
- ▸ **textile** woven or knit fabric: *She went to school to learn how to design **textiles**.*

façade *noun* (formal) an outward but insincere show of something: *see* **disguise**

face

verb to deal with something or someone boldly, firmly, or bravely: *Sometimes you must **face** your fears in order to overcome them.*

- ▸ **confront** to meet or face someone with anger or resolution: *If you don't **confront** that bully he will continue to pick on you.*
- ▸ **encounter** to experience something directly: *They **encountered** difficulties when they tried to sell their home.*

fact

noun something that has really happened or that really exists: *It is a **fact** that the sun rises in the east and sets in the west.*

- ▸ **data** facts and figures, especially for use in making decisions: *The scientist has been collecting **data** on the healing properties of certain plants.*
- ▸ **evidence** facts that help one find out the truth or come to a decision: *The lawyer presented **evidence** that proved her client's innocence.*

- ▸ **information** knowledge and understanding derived from study, experience, or instruction: *I found a lot of **information** for my report at the library.*
- ▸ **truth** something that is true or that accurately describes reality: *The **truth** is that I never really liked your friend very much.*

factor *noun* something that helps bring about a certain result: *see* **ingredient**

factory

noun a building in which goods are manufactured or assembled: *This automobile **factory** stopped producing station wagons last year.*

- ▸ **mill** a building equipped with machinery used for processing something such as grain, paper, or steel: *He works at a steel **mill** that makes giant girders for use in high-rise buildings.*
- ▸ **plant** the buildings and equipment used in making a product; a factory: *That **plant** produces millions of light bulbs each year.*
- ▸ **workshop** a place where manual or light industrial work is done: *My uncle has opened a **workshop** that produces custom cabinets.*

fad *noun* a fashion taken up enthusiastically for a brief period of time: *see* **fashion**

fade

verb to gradually lose brightness, freshness, or loudness: *My blue T-shirt **faded** after I washed it several times.*

- ▸ **disappear** to pass out of sight; to vanish: *The magician made the rabbit **disappear** into the hat.*
- ▸ **evaporate** ▷ to disappear by changing into a vapor: *If you boil water long enough, it will completely **evaporate** from the pot.* ▷ to vanish or go away: *My fear of dogs **evaporated** once we got one as a pet.*

▶ **vanish**   to disappear without a trace: *My keys seem to have **vanished**.*

▶ **wither**   to dry up or shrivel from loss of moisture: *The flowers began to **wither** in the hot sun.*

faded *adjective*   having lost brightness or freshness: *see* **faint**

fail

verb   to be unsuccessful; to fall short of what is expected of one: *I **failed** to get the house clean before the guests arrived for the party.*

▶ **fizzle**   to fail or end weakly, especially after a hopeful beginning: *His enthusiasm for Rugby **fizzled** after he broke his arm during a game.*

▶ **flop**   (informal)   to fail utterly: *The comedian's first two jokes **flopped**.*

▶ **flunk**   (informal)   to fail a test or subject in school: *I was very upset that I **flunked** the test.*

▶ **lose**   to fail to win or keep something: *Our team **lost** the game by one point.*

ANTONYM **succeed**   to carry out something desired or attempted

faint

adjective   not distinct or clear; difficult to see or hear: *The music became **faint** when I turned down the volume on the stereo.*

▶ **dim**   somewhat dark or obscure; giving off little light: *It was hard to read in the **dim** light.*

▶ **faded**   having lost brightness or freshness: *The back of the couch has become **faded** where the sun shines on it.*

▶ **indistinct**   not clearly heard, seen, or understood: *The little boy's words were **indistinct** because he was crying and hiccuping.*

fair¹

adjective   done or made according to the rules or without cheating: *I don't think that the referee's call was **fair**.*

▶ **evenhanded**   dealing fairly with all; impartial: *Our teacher is **evenhanded** when grading our papers.*

▶ **impartial**   not favoring either side: *My parents try to be **impartial** when dealing with my brothers and me.*

▶ **just**   following what is right and fair: *The actor felt that the bad review of his performance was not **just**.*

▶ **neutral**   not taking sides in a war, quarrel, or contest: *Switzerland remained **neutral** during World War II.*

▶ **objective**   not influenced by personal feelings or prejudice: *He gave me some **objective** advice.*

▶ **unbiased**   without strong feelings for or against something; without bias or prejudice: *She gave me her **unbiased** opinion.*

ANTONYM **unfair**   not just or evenhanded; biased

fair²

noun   an exhibition, as of farm products, usually accompanied by various competitions and entertainments: *I won a prize for my raspberry jam at the county **fair**.*

▶ **carnival**   an outdoor show that offers entertainment such as rides and games: *I liked the Ferris wheel at the **carnival**.*

▶ **exhibition**   a large-scale public showing or display, as of art: *This **exhibition** of her sculptures will help her career as an artist.*

▶ **festival**   a series of special cultural events, such as films, concerts, or exhibitions: *I want to go to the Sundance Film **Festival**.*

▶ **jubilee**   a special anniversary, such as the 25th or 50th: *Queen Victoria's Diamond **Jubilee** was celebrated on June 22, 1897.*

fairness *noun*   the state of being free from favoritism or bias: *see* **justice**

faith *noun*   strong belief or confidence in a person or thing, even without conclusive proof: *see* **trust**

faithful *adjective*   firm in allegiance or support: *see* **loyal**

fake

adjective   having a false or misleading appearance; not genuine: *I got a **fake** tattoo before committing to a real one.*

▶ **bogus**   made up or invented in order to deceive; counterfeit or fake: *Her resumé was full of **bogus** information about schools she never actually attended.*
▶ **counterfeit**   made in imitation of what is genuine with the intent to deceive: *He was arrested for making **counterfeit** money.*
▶ **imitation**   made to resemble another, usually superior item or material: *This purse is less expensive because it's made of **imitation** leather.*
▶ **phony**   not genuine or real; fake: *He tried to use a **phony** I.D. to get into the bar.*

ANTONYM **real**   not artificial; genuine

fall

verb   to drop or come down freely under the influence of weight or gravity: *The book **fell** off my desk and onto the floor.*

▶ **collapse**   to fall down or inward suddenly; cave in: *The roof **collapsed** under the weight of the heavy snow.*
▶ **descend**   to move from a higher to a lower place or position: *She **descended** the staircase.*
▶ **dive**   to drop or descend, especially into or through water: *Pelicans **dive** into the water to catch fish.*
▶ **plummet**   to drop straight down rapidly: *The heavy branch broke off and **plummeted** to the ground.*
▶ **plunge**   to descend sharply and rapidly, especially into water: *The children **plunged** into the lake to go swimming.*
▶ **slip**   to slide involuntarily and lose one's balance or foothold: *I **slipped** on the wet floor.*
▶ **topple**   to totter and fall, especially from being too heavy on top: *The stack of magazines **toppled** when it got too high.*
▶ **trip**   to strike the foot against something and almost fall: *He **tripped** over the tree root.*
▶ **tumble**   to fall suddenly: *The value of the company's stock **tumbled** after the national crisis.*

false *adjective*   contrary to fact or truth: *see* **wrong**

falsehood *noun*   a statement that is not true: *see* **lie**

falter *verb*   to lose confidence or purpose: *see* **hesitate**

familiar *adjective*   often encountered or seen: *see* **common**

family

noun   a group consisting of closely related people, especially parents and their children: *My **family** gathers together during the holidays.*

▶ **blood**   descent from a common ancestor; biological relationship: *People related by **blood** share many of the same genes.*
▶ **clan**   a group of families that claim the same ancestor: *The Stuart **clan** are all descendants of Angus Stewart.*
▶ **folk**   ▷ the people who make up a national, regional, or other broad group: *This area was settled mainly by **folk** from Virginia and the Carolinas.* ▷ (informal) a person's family or relatives: *All her **folk** live nearby.*
▶ **kin**   all of a person's relatives: *We rarely see my father's **kin** because they live so far away.*
▶ **relatives**   people related to one another by descent, marriage, or adoption: *Our **relatives** are coming for a visit this summer.*
▶ **tribe**   (informal)   a large family: *The whole **tribe** gathered together to celebrate Grandma's 90th birthday.*

famine *noun*   an extreme and widespread lack of food: *see* **hunger**

famous

adjective   very well known: *Albert Einstein was a **famous** scientist.*

▶ **celebrated**   widely praised, especially for one's achievements: *She is a **celebrated** actress.*

▸ **distinguished** well known or highly regarded: *We had a distinguished speaker at our graduation.*

▸ **notorious** well known for something bad or unpleasant: *Al Capone was a notorious gangster.*

▸ **popular** having many friends or admirers: *He is a popular teacher.*

▸ **prominent** widely known for one's achievement or success: *Bill Gates is a prominent businessman.*

▸ **renowned** having widespread honor and fame: *Dr. Martin Luther King, Jr., was a renowned civil rights leader.*

▸ **well-known** known to many people: *Mark Twain is a well-known American writer.*

fan *noun* a person with enthusiastic interest in or admiration for someone or something: *see* **follower**

fancy

adjective not plain or simple; elaborate: *She wore a fancy dress to the big party.*

▸ **complex** consisting of many parts or aspects: *I've been working on this complex puzzle for weeks.*

▸ **decorated** furnished with attractive or beautiful things: *The owners transformed their poorly decorated house into a beautiful home.*

▸ **elaborate** planned or made with careful attention or with much detail: *They had an elaborate wedding.*

▸ **intricate** complicated or complex: *We admired the intricate ribbon embroidery on the sweater.*

▸ **ornate** having lavish or elaborate decorations: *She wore an ornate necklace with her plain black dress.*

ANTONYM **plain** not elaborate or complicated; simple

fantastic *adjective* excellent; superb: *see* **wonderful**

fantasy *noun* an imaginary event or situation: *see* **imagination**

far

adjective being at a great distance: *The market isn't far from our house.*

▸ **distant** far away in space or time: *Most of my relatives live in a distant state.*

▸ **faraway** so distant as to be unfamiliar or unknown: *He has traveled to many faraway places.*

▸ **remote** far from settled areas; isolated or secluded: *He built a cabin in a remote part of the forest.*

ANTONYM **near** close in distance or time

faraway *adjective* so distant as to be unfamiliar or unknown: *see* **far**

fare *noun* the money a person must pay to travel, as on a plane, train, or bus: *see* **price**

far-fetched *adjective* hard to believe: *see* **incredible**

farm *verb* to grow crops or raise livestock: *see* **raise [1]**

fascinate *verb* to attract and hold someone's attention: *see* **interest**

fascinating *adjective* absorbing one's interest and attention: *see* **interesting**

fascination *noun* the condition of having one's whole interest captured and held: *see* **attraction**

fashion

noun a style, as of dressing or behaving, that is popular at a certain time: *This magazine has pictures of the latest women's fashions.*

▸ **craze** something that is very popular for a short time; a fad: *Marathon dance contests were a craze during the 1930s.*

▸ **fad** a fashion taken up enthusiastically for a brief period of time: *My parents don't approve of the current fads for tattoos and body piercing.*

▸ **style** a particular way of dressing or acting: *That style of suit looks good on you.*

▸ **trend** a new or developing fashion or style: *The trend in home entertainment is toward widescreen TVs.*

fast

adjective moving, acting, or done with great speed: *Race cars are designed to be as **fast** as possible.*

- ▸ **brisk** moving or acting in a lively or energetic manner: *I had to hurry to keep up with her **brisk** pace.*
- ▸ **hasty** done too quickly to be accurate or wise: *I made a **hasty** decision and bought the wrong size shirt as a result.*
- ▸ **prompt** ▷ being right on time: *He is usually **prompt** about meeting his deadlines.* ▷ done without delay; immediate: *This matter needs your **prompt** attention.*
- ▸ **quick** done or occurring in a short amount of time: *She made a **quick** stop at the grocery store.*
- ▸ **rapid** marked by great speed; fast: *The jet made a **rapid** climb at takeoff.*
- ▸ **speedy** taking very little time; quick: *I received a **speedy** reply to my e-mail.*
- ▸ **swift** moving or able to move very fast: *He is the **swiftest** runner on the track team.*

ANTONYM **slow** moving or going at a low speed

fasten

verb to join something firmly to something else: *I **fastened** the bookcase to the wall.*

- ▸ **adhere** to stick or hold fast to something: *The burnt food **adhered** to the bottom of the pan.*
- ▸ **attach** to join or fix something to something else; fasten: *We **attached** the fabric to the wall by using liquid starch.*
- ▸ **glue** to stick things together with glue: *She **glued** the broken cup back together.*
- ▸ **nail** to fasten things together with nails: *He **nailed** a board over the hole in the fence.*
- ▸ **pin** to fasten or secure something with a pin: *I **pinned** my nametag to my shirt.*
- ▸ **staple** to fasten or hold something by means of a staple: *He **stapled** the papers together.*

fat

adjective having much or too much body fat: *I decided I was too **fat** and so started taking a walk every day.*

- ▸ **chubby** having plenty of flesh; round and plump: *He was **chubby** as a child.*
- ▸ **heavy** above average in body weight; fat: *The men in my family are mostly tall and **heavy**.*
- ▸ **obese** very fat; extremely overweight: *The vet said that my cat is **obese** and needs to go on a special diet.*
- ▸ **overweight** weighing more than is normal or healthy: *My doctor said I was 20 pounds **overweight** for my age and height.*
- ▸ **plump** rounded and full in shape: ***Plump** figures on women are out of fashion today.*

ANTONYM **thin** having little fat on the body; slender

fat

noun an oily substance found in plant and animal tissues: *He cut the **fat** off the steak.*

- ▸ **drippings** the fat and juices from roasting meat, often used to make gravy: *She used the **drippings** from the turkey to make gravy.*
- ▸ **grease** soft or melted animal fat: *Don't pour that bacon **grease** down the sink.*
- ▸ **lard** a white, greasy substance made from the melted-down fat of a pig: *I mix **lard**, peanut butter, birdseed, and raisins together to make treats for the wild birds.*
- ▸ **oil** any of a large group of slippery, usually liquid substances that burn easily and do not mix with water: *Cooking **oil** comes from many different sources, such as olives, corn, and sunflower seeds.*

fatal

adjective causing or capable of causing death: *My uncle has a **fatal** heart disease.*

- ▸ **deadly** capable of killing: *The suspect was arrested for assault with a **deadly** weapon.*
- ▸ **lethal** causing or intended to cause death: *The prisoner was executed by injection with a **lethal** drug.*
- ▸ **malignant** threatening to one's life and health: *The surgeon removed a **malignant** tumor from the patient.*
- ▸ **poisonous** capable of harming or killing by means of poison: *The Mojave green is a **poisonous** snake of the southwestern U.S.*

▸ **toxic** capable of causing injury or death, especially by chemical means: *The wood pulp mill was fined for emitting toxic wastes into the air.*

▸ **venomous** containing or producing poison; poisonous: *The black widow and brown recluse are both venomous spiders.*

fate *noun* the invisible force or power that is believed to determine future events: *see* **destiny**

fatigue *verb* to tire someone out after long effort: *see* **tire**

fault *noun* responsibility for a mistake or offense: *see* **blame**

fault *noun* something that keeps something else from being as good as it could be: *see* **flaw**

faultless *adjective* being without fault or flaw: *see* **perfect**

faulty *adjective* not in working order: *see* **bad [1]**

favor

noun a kind or helpful act: *My friend did me a favor by letting me use her computer to write my paper.*

▸ **courtesy** a polite gesture or remark: *We treat all our customers with courtesy.*

▸ **good deed** a kind act done for someone: *She did a good deed for her neighbors by watering their plants while they were on vacation.*

▸ **kindness** a helpful or considerate act: *I appreciate your kindness to me when I was feeling sad.*

favorite *adjective* being a person or thing treated with special regard and preferred above all others: *see* **best**

fear

noun a feeling caused by a sense of danger or the expectation that something harmful or evil may happen: *She felt her fear increase as the sound grew louder.*

▸ **dread** fearful or unpleasant anticipation: *He faced the long drive home with dread.*

▸ **fright** a sudden, strong fear: *Fright caused the flock of birds to fly away.*

▸ **horror** great fear, terror, or shock: *They felt horror when they drove up to their house and saw that it was on fire.*

▸ **panic** a sudden feeling of great fear, especially without a clear cause: *She was in a panic before the test.*

▸ **terror** an intense, overpowering fear: *The rabbit froze in terror when it saw the coyote.*

fearful *adjective* feeling fear or worry: *see* **afraid**

fearless *adjective* having no fear: *see* **brave**

feast

noun a large elaborate meal, especially one prepared for a special occasion: *We were invited to their wedding feast.*

▸ **banquet** a large, formal meal for many people: *The youth organization held a Valentine's Day banquet.*

▸ **barbeque** a social gathering at which food is cooked over an open fire or hot coals: *Our neighbors invited us to a barbecue in their backyard.*

▸ **picnic** a party in which people carry their food with them and then eat it outdoors: *My boyfriend and I had a picnic in the park.*

▸ **potluck** a meal at which each guest brings food to be shared by all: *I took a shrimp dish to the club's potluck, and my friend took strawberry shortcake.*

feat *noun* an outstanding deed or accomplishment; an exploit that requires much skill or daring: *see* **action**

feature *noun* a special or noticeable part, characteristic, or quality: *see* **quality**

fee *noun* a fixed cost, especially one charged by a school or government: *see* **price**

feeble *adjective* woefully lacking in strength, as from old age or illness: *see* **weak**

feed

verb to give food to a person or animal: *There are signs at the zoo saying Don't* **Feed** *the Animals.*

▶ **fuel** to provide something with a material that produces heat or energy: *He* **fueled** *the motor home before going on vacation.*

▶ **nourish** to provide someone or something with what is needed for growth and development: *The rainfall* **nourished** *the fields of wheat.*

▶ **nurture** to feed and protect a person or animal: *I* **nurtured** *the injured possum until it was ready to be released back to the wild.*

▶ **sustain** to supply someone or something with necessities; nourish: *The brain is* **sustained** *by a constant supply of blood that carries oxygen and nutrients.*

feel *verb* to be or become aware of something through the sense of touch: *see* **touch**

feeling

noun a mental state such as sorrow, anger, love, or joy: *Going biking gives me a* **feeling** *of excitement.*

▶ **attitude** a state of mind, especially one that a person has some control over: *He brings a positive* **attitude** *to his work.*

▶ **emotion** a deep or strong feeling: *Music has the power to stir people's* **emotions**.

▶ **mood** a temporary state of mind: *She has been in a bad* **mood** *all day.*

▶ **passion** a powerful or intense feeling: *He has a* **passion** *for rock climbing.*

▶ **sentiment** a thought or attitude based on emotion: *I was full of nostalgic* **sentiment** *when I went back to my old neighborhood.*

feign *verb* (formal) to give a false appearance of something: *see* **pretend**

felon *noun* a person who has committed a serious crime such as murder, rape, or burglary: *see* **criminal**

felony *noun* a serous crime such as murder, rape, or burglary: *see* **crime**

fellow *noun* a man or a boy: *see* **man**

female *noun* a female person, animal, plant, or plant part: *see* **woman**

fence *noun* a structure set up to prevent entry into an area or to mark it off: *see* **wall**

ferocious *adjective* full of savage fury: *see* **fierce**

fertile

adjective capable of producing or sustaining life: *The Midwest is called "the breadbasket of the nation" because its soil is* **fertile**.

▶ **bountiful** providing more than enough; plentiful: *The apple harvest was* **bountiful** *this year.*

▶ **fruitful** ▷ producing or bearing fruit in abundance: *This variety of tomato plant is especially* **fruitful**. ▷ producing good results: *The company's advertising campaign has been very* **fruitful**.

▶ **productive** producing steadily and abundantly: *The milk cows became more* **productive** *after their feed was changed.*

▶ **prolific** producing something in great numbers: *Stephen King is a* **prolific** *writer.*

ANTONYM **barren** not able to produce plants, crops, or offspring

fervor *noun* powerful or intense emotion: *see* **enthusiasm**

festival *noun* a series of special cultural events, such as films, concerts, or exhibitions: *see* **fair²**

feud *noun* a long, bitter quarrel between two people, families, or groups: *see* **fight**

few

adjective amounting to a small number; not many: *Only a* **few** *people came to the play.*

▶ **limited** confined or restricted within certain limits: *The small market had a* **limited** *selection of cereal.*

▶ **meager** lacking in quantity or richness; scanty: *We should not waste our* **meager** *resources on things that we don't really need.*

▶ **not many** just a few: *There are* **not many** *students in my drama class.*

▸ **scanty** so little as to be barely sufficient: *There is a* **scanty** *amount of peanut butter left in the jar.*

▸ **skimpy** inadequate in size or amount; very small: *She wore a* **skimpy** *swimsuit to the beach.*

fewer *adjective* smaller in number: *see* **less**

fewest *adjective* smallest in number: *see* least

fib *noun* an insignificant or childish lie: *see* lie

fiddle *verb* to tinker with something in an attempt to fix or adjust it: *see* **dabble**

fidelity *noun* faithfulness to an obligation or duty: *see* **loyalty**

field

noun [1] a broad area of open or cleared land, as for growing crops or playing games: *We practiced on the soccer* **field**.

▸ **acreage** land area measured in acres: *The farmer leases some of his* **acreage** *to a neighbor.*

▸ **lot** a piece of land having specific boundaries, especially one that is a part of a city or town: *Somebody is building a house on that* **lot**.

▸ **meadow** an area of grassy ground: *The mountain* **meadow** *was dotted with wildflowers.*

▸ **pasture** ground where animals are put to graze: *The sheep were herded into the* **pasture**.

field

noun [2] an area of interest or activity: *She works in the medical* **field**.

▸ **domain** (formal) an area of special interest or expertise: *The librarian's* **domain** *is children's literature.*

▸ **line** one's trade, occupation, or field of interest: *What* **line** *of work are you in?*

▸ **province** (formal) an area of knowledge, authority, or responsibility: *Repairing old cars is his* **province**.

▸ **specialty** a special study, profession, or skill: *Her* **specialty** *is public relations.*

fierce

adjective having a hostile or menacing nature; unyielding in battle: *The Caribs were said to be* **fierce** *warriors.*

▸ **ferocious** full of savage fury: *The treasure was guarded by a* **ferocious** *dragon.*

▸ **savage** unrestrained in violence or cruelty: *He barely survived the* **savage** *attack by the mountain lion.*

▸ **vicious** cruel and mean; malicious: *I'm tired of your* **vicious** *remarks about other people's looks.*

▸ **violent** physically forceful: *The* **violent** *storm blew down the power lines.*

ANTONYM **gentle** easily managed; tame

fiery *adjective* full of fire; burning fiercely: *see* hot

fight

noun an angry physical or verbal dispute: *They got into a terrible* **fight** *that ended their friendship.*

▸ **argument** a heated verbal disagreement: *They got into an* **argument** *about politics.*

▸ **brawl** a noisy physical fight: *There was a* **brawl** *outside the tavern.*

▸ **duel** a fight between two people that is arranged in advance and witnessed by two other people, and in which weapons are used: *Aaron Burr killed Alexander Hamilton in a* **duel** *in 1804.*

▸ **feud** a long, bitter quarrel between two people, families, or groups: *The neighbors'* **feud** *over the property line lasted for years.*

▸ **quarrel** an angry, usually verbal dispute: *The couple had a loud* **quarrel** *in the restaurant.*

▸ **row** a loud quarrel; a brawl: *I could hear the* **row** *in the next apartment.*

figure *verb* to calculate an amount: *see* add

figure *noun* the shape or form of a human body: *see* **body**

figure out *verb* to solve, decipher, or discover something: *see* **solve**

file *verb* to arrange a collection of papers, cards, records, or other information in a certain order: *see* **sort**

fill

verb to make something full: *I filled my glass with water.*

- ▸ **cram** to force or squeeze something tightly into a space: *She can't cram anymore clothes into her closet.*
- ▸ **jam** to force something roughly or hurriedly into a space: *He jammed his books into his backpack and ran off.*
- ▸ **load** to fill or partly fill something with items: *They loaded their car with camping equipment and drove to the beach.*
- ▸ **pack** to fill a container neatly with items, as for storage or travel: *She packed her suitcase for a business trip.*
- ▸ **stuff** to put something carelessly into a space: *The little boy stuffed his toy cars into his pockets.*
- ▸ **squeeze** to press something tightly into a small space: *I squeezed the folded towels into the cupboard.*

ANTONYM **empty** to make something empty

film *noun* a thin layer or coating: *see* **layer**

filthy *adjective* thoroughly or disgustingly dirty: *see* **dirty**

final *adjective* being or occurring at the end: *see* **last¹**

final *noun* the last examination of an academic course: *see* **test**

finally *adverb* at the end of a certain period: *see* **eventually**

finance *verb* to provide money for someone or something: *see* **sponsor**

find *verb* to come upon something by accident or as the result of a study or search: *see* **discover**

fine *noun* a sum of money that has to be paid as a penalty for breaking a law or rule: *see* **penalty**

fine *adverb* very well: *see* **well**

fine print *noun* the part of a written agreement containing qualifications or restrictions, usually in small type or obscure language: *see* **detail**

finer *adjective* of superior quality, skill, or appearance: *see* **better**

finest *adjective* of the highest possible quality, skill, or appearance: *see* **best**

finish

verb to bring something to an end: *I have finished writing my paper.*

- ▸ **complete** to bring something to an end; finish: *The roofers are coming back tomorrow to complete the job.*
- ▸ **conclude** to bring something to a close, especially formally or ceremoniously: *We concluded our New Year's party by singing "Auld Lang Syne."*
- ▸ **end** to come to a conclusion: *After the movie ended, we left the theater.*
- ▸ **wrap up** to settle something finally or successfully: *They wrapped up the negotiations in time for the holidays.*

ANTONYM **start** to begin an activity or movement

finished *adjective* having been brought to a desired or required state: *see* **done**

fire *verb* (informal) to dismiss someone from a job: *see* **dismiss**

fire *noun* burning intensity of feeling: *see* **enthusiasm**

firm *noun* a business partnership of two or more people: *see* **business [1]**

first *adjective* coming before all others: *see* **original [2]**

first-rate *adjective* foremost in quality, rank, or importance: *see* **excellent**

fit *adjective* in good physical condition: *see* **healthy**

fitting *adjective*   appropriate for or suitable to an occasion: *see* **proper**

fix

verb   to restore something to its proper condition or working order: *We called a plumber to fix the leaky faucet.*

- ▸ **heal**   to make or become healthy again: *His broken arm healed quickly.*
- ▸ **mend**   to make minor repairs to something: *I mended the tear in the curtain.*
- ▸ **patch**   to cover or mend something with a patch: *The mechanic patched the hole in the tire.*
- ▸ **repair**   to return something to proper or useful condition after being damaged: *The shoemaker repaired my boots.*
- ▸ **restore**   to bring something back to an original condition: *I restored the old table by cleaning and waxing it.*

fizzle *verb*   to fail or end weakly, especially after a hopeful beginning: *see* **fail**

flag *verb*   to signal someone with or as if with a flag: *see* **signal**

flamboyant *adjective*   so richly or brightly colored as to attract attention: *see* **colorful**

flame *verb*   to burn with a bright, moving light: *see* **burn**

flap *verb*   to move or swing sharply while fixed at one edge or corner: *see* **wave**

flare *verb*   to burn suddenly with a brief, intense light: *see* **burn**

flash *noun*   an extremely short time: *see* **moment**

flash *verb*   to give out a sudden bright light: *see* **shine**

flashy *adjective*   creating a brief impression of brilliance: *see* **colorful**

flask *noun*   a bottle or other container with a narrow neck: *see* **bottle**

flat

adjective   having a smooth, even surface: *They skated on the flat sidewalk.*

- ▸ **even**   being at the same height or level: *The mother and daughter are even in height.*
- ▸ **horizontal**   parallel to the horizon; level or straight across: *My T-shirt has horizontal stripes.*
- ▸ **level**   having a flat, even surface: *The carpenter made sure that the countertop was level.*

ANTONYM **uneven**   not level, smooth, or straight

flatter *verb*   to praise someone in a way that is not sincere, especially in order to get something in return: *see* **praise**

flaunt *verb*   to show something off: *see* **brag**

flavor

noun   the quality that causes something to have a distinctive taste: *What flavor of ice cream would you like?*

- ▸ **aftertaste**   a taste that remains in the mouth: *Coffee has a somewhat bitter aftertaste.*
- ▸ **tang**   a sharp, strong flavor or taste: *I like the tang of lemon.*
- ▸ **taste**   the sensation of sweet, sour, salty, or bitter flavors produced by a substance placed in the mouth: *Do you like the taste of onions?*
- ▸ **zest**   added flavor or interest: *She gives zest to her cooking by adding herbs and spices.*

flaw

noun   something that takes away from the value or usefulness of something else: *Flaws in a diamond will reduce its price.*

- ▸ **defect**   a lack of something necessary for proper functioning: *I took the coffeemaker back because it had a defect.*
- ▸ **fault**   something that keeps something else from being as good as it could be: *My teacher said the main fault in my essay was incorrect punctuation.*
- ▸ **imperfection**   a usually minor flaw in something: *The dress was sold at a discount because it had an imperfection.*

flawed *adjective* containing an imperfection or defect: *see* **bad [1]**

flee *verb* to run away, as from trouble or danger: *see* **escape**

fleeting *adjective* passing quickly: *see* **short [2]**

flexible

adjective capable of bending or being bent: *They served the Italian soda with a* **flexible** *straw.*

▸ **elastic** easily resuming its original shape after being stretched or expanded: *These pants have an* **elastic** *waistband.*

▸ **limber** bending or moving easily; flexible: *The yoga instructor is very* **limber**.

▸ **pliable** easily bent or shaped: *The sculptor worked with the* **pliable** *clay.*

▸ **supple** moving and bending with grace and agility: *The dancers moved with* **supple** *grace.*

ANTONYM **rigid** not bending; stiff

flighty *adjective* given to unsteady or changeable behavior: *see* **moody**

flimsy *adjective* not solid or strong: *see* **delicate**

flinch *verb* to shrink or jerk back suddenly, as from surprise or pain: *see* **wince**

fling *noun* a brief period of doing whatever one wants: *see* **spree**

fling *verb* to throw something with force or violence: *see* **throw**

flirt *verb* to act romantically, especially in a playful or teasing way: *see* **romance**

float

verb to remain suspended in air or on the surface of a liquid: *The red autumn leaves* **floated** *down the stream.*

▸ **drift** to be carried along slowly as if by a current of water or air: *We* **drifted** *down the river on inner tubes.*

▸ **glide** to move smoothly, quietly, and with ease: *The ice skater* **glided** *across the ice.*

▸ **waft** to move gently through the air: *The smell of baking bread* **wafted** *through the house.*

flood

verb to cover dry land with a large flow of water: *Every spring when the snows melt, the stream* **floods** *the meadow.*

▸ **drench** to wet something through and through: *The sudden rainstorm* **drenched** *the laundry that was hanging on the clothesline.*

▸ **drown** to cover something thoroughly or excessively with a liquid: *I* **drowned** *my salad in dressing.*

▸ **saturate** to wet something until it cannot absorb any more liquid: *The French fries* **saturated** *the paper bag with grease.*

▸ **soak** to make something completely wet: *She* **soaked** *the stained shirt in detergent.*

▸ **steep** to immerse something in a liquid: *I* **steeped** *the tea bag in hot water.*

▸ **submerge** to place or plunge something into a liquid: *He* **submerged** *the dirty dishes in soapy water.*

floor *noun* the lowermost surface, especially of a room: *see* **bottom**

flop *verb* (informal) to fail utterly: *see* **fail**

floppy *adjective* loose and flexible: *see* **loose**

flourish *verb* to grow or develop very well: *see* **thrive**

flow *verb* to move in a steady and smooth way, like a stream: *see* **pour**

flower *noun* (formal) the best example of something: *see* **prime**

flower *verb* to develop fully: *see* **thrive**

flowing *adjective* hanging loosely and gracefully: *see* **loose**

fluctuate *verb* to change or vary irregularly: *see* **shift**

fluffy *adjective* having hair, feathers, or fibers that stand out in a soft, full mass: *see* **soft [1]**

fluid *noun* a substance that flows easily and takes the shape of its container: *see* **juice**

flunk *verb* (informal)   to fail a test or subject in school: *see* **fail**

fluster *verb*   to make someone nervous or upset: *see* **disturb**

flutter *noun*   a light sound of quick flapping or beating: *see* **rustle**

fly

verb   to move through the air with the aid of wings: *Many birds* ***fly*** *south in the winter.*

- ▶ **hover**   to stay in one place in the air: *The butterfly* ***hovered*** *over the flower.*
- ▶ **sail**   to move smoothly and effortlessly: *Big clouds* ***sailed*** *slowly across the sky.*
- ▶ **soar**   to rise or glide high in the air: *The hot-air balloon* ***soared*** *over the hills.*

flyer *noun*   a printed sheet or pamphlet: *see* **advertisement**

focus *noun*   a concentration or emphasis: *see* **attention**

foe *noun*   a personal enemy: *see* **enemy**

fog *noun*   a mass of water droplets floating near the surface of the ground or water: *see* **mist**

foggy *adjective*   full of or covered by fog: *see* **overcast**

fold

noun   a line formed by bending something so that one part lies over another: *She tore the paper along the* ***fold***.

- ▶ **crease**   a mark or line, usually formed by wrinkling or folding: *There was a* ***crease*** *in her brow as she concentrated.*
- ▶ **pleat**   a flat fold that is made by doubling fabric on itself: *A kilt has many* ***pleats***.
- ▶ **wrinkle**   a small fold or crease on a normally smooth surface: *I ironed the* ***wrinkles*** *out of the shirt.*

folk *noun*   ▷ the people who make up a national, regional, or other broad group ▷ (informal)   a person's family or relatives: *see* **family**

follow

verb   to go or come after someone or something: *We* ***followed*** *the usher to our seats.*

- ▶ **chase**   to follow someone or something in order to catch it: *The children* ***chased*** *each other around the playground.*
- ▶ **pursue**   to chase someone closely or persistently: *The highway patrol* ***pursued*** *the speeding driver.*
- ▶ **shadow**   to follow someone closely, especially in secret: *The police detective* ***shadowed*** *the suspect.*
- ▶ **stalk**   to move in a stealthy way toward something, especially so as to capture it: *The cat* ***stalked*** *the bird.*
- ▶ **tail** (informal)   to follow someone closely in order to watch: *The spy* ***tailed*** *the diplomat for two days in order to learn her routine.*
- ▶ **track**   to follow the footprints or trail of someone or something: *The hunters* ***tracked*** *the deer through the snow.*
- ▶ **trail**   to follow the traces or scent of someone or something: *The hound dog* ***trailed*** *the bear to its cave.*

follower

noun   one who believes in the teachings or methods of another: *He is a* ***follower*** *of Gandhi.*

- ▶ **admirer**   someone who deeply admires another person: *I am an* ***admirer*** *of people who start their own businesses.*
- ▶ **believer**   one who has faith, confidence, or trust in something or someone: *She's a firm* ***believer*** *in the health benefits of wheatgrass juice.*
- ▶ **disciple**   a person who believes in and often helps to spread the teachings of another: *Joseph Pilates attracted many* ***disciples*** *to his methods of physical fitness.*
- ▶ **fan**   a person with enthusiastic interest in or admiration for someone or something: *Elvis Presley still has many* ***fans***.
- ▶ **supporter**   a person who promotes or aids someone or something: *They are enthusiastic* ***supporters*** *of the high-school marching band.*

folly *noun*   something lacking in good sense or foresight: *see* **nonsense**

fond *adjective* having a strong liking or affection for something or someone: *see* **affectionate**

fondness *noun* warm affection: *see* **love**

fool

noun a person who lacks judgment or good sense: *He was a **fool** to mistake her friendship for love.*

▸ **blockhead** a person who is considered very stupid: *That **blockhead** burned my pizza.*

▸ **dolt** a person regarded as stupid: *My sister begged me not to act like a **dolt** around her friends.*

▸ **dummy** a stupid or foolish person: *Sometimes I am such a **dummy**!*

▸ **dunce** a stupid or ignorant person: *He felt like a **dunce** when he didn't know the name of the President.*

▸ **idiot** a stupid or bungling person: *I felt like an **idiot** when I couldn't remember my own phone number.*

▸ **imbecile** a stupid or silly person: *She was so nervous that she acted like an **imbecile**.*

▸ **simpleton** a person who lacks common sense or intelligence: *I am a **simpleton** when it comes to balancing my checkbook.*

foolish *adjective* causing amusement, especially by being or seeming to be stupid: *see* **silly**

foolishness *noun* something that shows a lack of good sense, judgment, or wisdom: *see* **nonsense**

foot *noun* the lowest part of something: *see* **bottom**

for *conjunction* being that; considering: *see* **because**

forage *verb* to hunt through an area, especially for food: *see* **search**

forbearance *noun* the act of exercising tolerance and restraint in the face of provocation: *see* **patience**

forbid

verb to refuse to allow something: *Both Jewish and Muslim dietary laws **forbid** the eating of pork.*

▸ **ban** to forbid something by law; to make something illegal: *The county **bans** the burning of trash during certain times of the year.*

▸ **disallow** to refuse to allow something as a matter of policy: *The restaurant **disallows** bare feet.*

▸ **outlaw** to declare something illegal: *The state **outlawed** the sale of fireworks.*

▸ **prohibit** to forbid something by law or authority: *It is **prohibited** to fire a gun within city limits.*

▸ **veto** to prevent or reject something, especially by executive authority: *The governor **vetoed** the new bill.*

ANTONYM **allow** to let something happen; to permit something

force *noun* the application of strength or power, as to do work or cause physical change: *see* **strength**

forceful *adjective* full of strength, power, and energy: *see* **strong**

forebear *noun* (formal) an ancestor: *see* **parent**

forecast *verb* to indicate in advance what might or will happen: *see* **predict**

foreigner *noun* a person from a foreign country or place: *see* **stranger**

foremost *adjective* first in rank, position, or importance: *see* **main**

foresee *verb* to see or know something in advance: *see* **predict**

forest *noun* a dense growth of trees covering a large area: *see* **wilderness**

foretell *verb* (formal) to tell of something in advance: *see* **predict**

forever *adverb* for everlasting time: *see* **always**

forget

verb to be unable to bring something to mind; to fail to remember something: *Don't **forget** to mail the bills.*

▸ **disregard** to pay little or no attention to something: *I **disregarded** his rude comment.*

- **ignore** to completely and deliberately disregard someone or something: *Stop ignoring me—I'm talking to you!*
- **miss** to let go by: *She missed the deadline to submit her application.*
- **neglect** to fail to give proper care and attention to something: *He neglected to file his tax return on time.*
- **omit** to leave something out; to not include something: *Our teacher omitted our lowest test score when computing our grades.*
- **overlook** to intentionally or unintentionally fail to notice something: *The boss overlooked the new employee's mistakes.*

forgive

verb to stop blaming or being angry at someone: *Please forgive me for being late.*

- **absolve** to clear someone of blame or guilt: *The investigation absolved them of any wrongdoing.*
- **acquit** to free or clear someone from a formal accusation: *The jury acquitted the defendant on both charges.*
- **condone** to overlook, forgive, or disregard an offense without protest or disapproval: *She can't condone his abuse of prescription drugs.*
- **excuse** to forgive someone by agreeing to overlook a mistake or fault: *I hope you will excuse me for asking about your personal life.*
- **exonerate** to free someone from blame: *New evidence exonerated him of any connection to the crime.*
- **pardon** ▷ to release someone from punishment: *The governor pardoned the prisoner who was on death row.* ▷ to excuse an offense or inconvenience: *Please pardon my messy room.*

forlorn *adjective* appearing sad or lonely because of being abandoned: *see* **lonely**

form *verb* to give a definite shape or appearance to something: *see* **shape**

formal *adjective* following the usual forms, customs, or rules: *see* **grand**

former *adjective* from or belonging to an earlier time: *see* **previous**

formerly *adverb* at an earlier time: *see* **before**

forsake *verb* to give up something that one loves or values: *see* **abandon**

fort

noun a fortified area or building: *The first fighting of the Civil War took place at Fort Sumter.*

- **base** a supply center for a large force of military personnel: *Edwards Air Force Base is located in the Mojave Desert.*
- **camp** an outdoor area with temporary shelters such as tents or cabins: *We set up our camp along the tree line.*
- **castle** a large building, often the residence of noble or lord, having high, thick walls, towers, and other defenses against attack: *We explored the ruins of the 16th-century Scottish castle.*
- **citadel** a large, high-walled fortress, usually in or near a city: *The soldiers fired at the enemy from the walls of the citadel.*
- **fortress** a large fortified place, especially a permanent military stronghold: *The Bastille was a fortress and prison in Paris that was destroyed during the French Revolution.*
- **garrison** a military post or the troops stationed at such a post: *The garrison was transferred to the war zone.*
- **stockade** a defensive barrier made of strong, upright posts driven into the ground: *The pioneers commonly built stockades for protection.*
- **stronghold** a place where one is safe from invasion or attack: *My brother treats his bedroom as a stronghold.*

forthright *adjective* direct and without evasion: *see* **honest**

fortitude *noun* strength of mind that allows one to endure pain or adversity with courage: *see* **endurance**

fortress *noun* a large fortified place, especially a permanent military stronghold: *see* **fort**

fortunate *adjective* having good fortune: *see* **lucky**

fortune *noun*   the good or bad luck that comes to a person: *see* **destiny**

fortune *noun*   a large amount of money or property: *see* **wealth**

forward *adjective*   going beyond what is right and proper: *see* **rude**

foster parent *noun*   a person who provides parental care to a child who is not legally or biologically related: *see* **parent**

foul *adjective*   sickening in taste, smell, or appearance: *see* **rotten**

foundation *noun*   a basis for the development or support of something: *see* **basis**

foundation *noun*   the basis on which a thing stands, is founded, or is supported: *see* **bottom**

fraction *noun*   a usually small part of a whole: *see* **piece**

fracture *verb*   to break or crack something hard: *see* **break**

fragile *adjective*   easily damaged, broken, or destroyed: *see* **delicate**

fragment *noun*   a piece or part broken off from a whole: *see* **scrap**

fragrance *noun*   a sweet or pleasant odor: *see* **smell**

frail *adjective*   lacking physical strength or endurance: *see* **weak**

frame *noun*   the structure of a human or animal body: *see* **body**

frank *adjective*   free and open in expressing one's thoughts and feelings: *see* **honest**

frantic

adjective   very excited with fear or anxiety: *I was frantic when I couldn't find my car keys and I was already late to work.*

▶ **frenzied**   in a state of wild excitement: *The frenzied fans tried to rush the stage where the band was playing.*

▶ **hysterical**   so excited or upset that one laughs and cries uncontrollably: *He became hysterical when he found out that he'd won the lottery.*

▶ **panic-stricken**   overcome by sudden fear or panic; terrified: *The mother became*

panic-stricken when she couldn't find her child.

ANTONYM **calm**   not excited or upset

fraud *noun*   one who assumes a false pose: *see* **imposter**

frayed *adjective*   worn away, especially along an edge, so that loose threads show: *see* **ragged**

free *adjective*   not controlled by another or others: *see* **independent**

free *verb*   to give someone or something freedom: *see* **release**

freedom

noun   the condition of being free: *The Constitution guarantees freedom of religion.*

▶ **autonomy**   the condition of not being controlled by others; self-reliance: *His new job as a sales representative allows him more autonomy.*

▶ **independence**   the condition of being independent; self-government: *Vietnam achieved independence from France in 1954.*

▶ **liberty**   freedom to act, believe, or express oneself as one wishes: *In 1775, U.S. patriot Patrick Henry said, "Give me liberty or give me death."*

▶ **license**   official permission to do or own something: *He has license to sign legal documents for his mother.*

freeway *noun*   a wide highway on which vehicles may travel without paying tolls: *see* **road**

freezing *adjective*   cold enough to turn a liquid into a solid: *see* **cold**

freight *noun*   goods carried by train, ship, truck, or other vehicle: *see* **merchandise**

frenzied *adjective*   in a state of wild excitement: *see* **frantic**

frequently *adverb*   often; many times: *see* **often**

fresh *adjective*   new and unusual: *see* **original [1]**

friend

noun   a person one knows, likes, and enjoys being with: *I'm so glad you are my new friend.*

- ▸ **acquaintance**   a person one knows but who is not a close friend: *She is only an **acquaintance**, but I hope to get to know her better.*
- ▸ **buddy** (informal)   a good friend; a pal: *He and his **buddies** went dirt bike riding.*
- ▸ **chum**   an intimate friend or companion: *They have been **chums** since grade school.*
- ▸ **companion**   a person who often associates with or accompanies another person: *The elderly woman hired a **companion** to travel with her.*
- ▸ **comrade**   a companion, especially one who shares one's activities: *My dad has stayed in touch with many of his army **comrades**.*
- ▸ **pal** (informal)   a close friend; a chum: *I went to a movie with my **pals**.*
- ▸ **peer**   a person of the same age, rank, or standing as another; an equal: *Her dedication to her duties has won her the respect of her **peers**.*

ANTONYM **enemy**   a person, animal, or group that hates or wishes harm to another

friendless *adjective*   without friends: *see* **lonely**

friendly *adjective*   showing friendship: *see* **affectionate**

fright *noun*   a sudden, strong fear: *see* **fear**

frighten *verb*   to make someone afraid or alarmed: *see* **scare**

frightening *adjective*   causing fright or anxiety: *see* **scary**

frightened *adjective*   filled with sudden, intense fear: *see* **afraid**

frigid *adjective*   extremely cold: *see* **cold**

fringe *noun*   an outer part or area, especially one of secondary importance: *see* **edge**

frolic *verb*   to behave playfully: *see* **play**

front *noun*   an outward appearance intended to deceive: *see* **disguise**

frosty *adjective*   so cold as to produce frost: *see* **cold**

frown

verb   to wrinkle the forehead when puzzled, unhappy, or thinking: *I **frowned** as I considered which video to rent.*

- ▸ **glare**   to stare in an angry way: *My brother **glared** at me when I refused to give him the remote control.*
- ▸ **grimace**   to tighten and twist the face muscles, as in pain or disgust: *She **grimaced** when she saw her test score.*
- ▸ **pucker**   to contract the lips into wrinkles or folds: *He **puckered** his lips in anger.*
- ▸ **purse**   to tighten one's lips, as in disapproval: *My grandmother **pursed** her lips when I showed her my tattoo.*
- ▸ **scowl**   to lower the eyebrows in anger or strong disapproval: *The angry customer **scowled** at the clerk.*

ANTONYM **smile**   to have a pleased or happy expression on the face

frugal *adjective*   spending only what is needed for necessities: *see* **thrifty**

fruitful *adjective*   ▷ producing or bearing fruit in abundance. ▷ producing good results: *see* **fertile**

frustrate *verb*   to prevent someone from accomplishing something: *see* **prevent**

fry *verb*   to cook food in hot oil or fat: *see* **cook**

fuel *verb*   to provide something with a material that produces heat or energy: *see* **feed**

fugitive *noun*   a person who is running away, especially from the police: *see* **criminal**

fulfill *verb*   to make a dream or goal come true: *see* **achieve**

full *adjective*   containing all that is normal or possible: *see* **all**

fully *adverb*   to a full extent or degree: *see* **completely**

fume

noun   an irritating or strong-smelling smoke, vapor, or gas: *The chlorine **fumes** from the pool gave me a headache.*

- ▸ **gas**   a substance that is neither solid nor liquid and can expand to fill a container: *The balloons were filled with helium **gas.***
- ▸ **pollution**   something that contaminates the air, water, or earth: ***Pollution** from factories can cause acid rain.*
- ▸ **smog**   air pollution caused mainly by substances in automobile exhaust: *Strict legislation has resulted in a dramatic reduction of **smog** in many cities.*
- ▸ **smoke**   the mixture of gases and particles that rises from burning material: *The **smoke** from the campfire stung my eyes.*

fun

noun   a good time; pleasure: *We had a lot of **fun** at the beach.*

- ▸ **amusement**   something that amuses, entertains, or pleases: *The school carnival provided **amusement** for the community.*
- ▸ **diversion**   something that distracts the mind and relaxes or entertains: *She plays the guitar as a **diversion**.*
- ▸ **enjoyment**   a form or source of pleasure: *What do you like to do for **enjoyment**?*
- ▸ **entertainment**   something that amuses or diverts, especially a performance or show: *Movies are my favorite form of **entertainment**.*
- ▸ **pleasure**   something that pleases or delights: *It was a **pleasure** to meet you.*
- ▸ **treat**   a source of special enjoyment or pleasure: *Seeing my favorite band in a live concert was a real **treat**.*

function *verb*   to perform in the normal or proper way: *see* **behave**

fund *verb*   to provide money for something: *see* **sponsor**

fund *noun*   a sum of money or other resources set aside for a specific purpose: *see* **supply**

funds *noun*   available money: *see* **money**

fundamental *adjective*   forming a foundation: *see* **basic**

funny

adjective   causing amusement or laughter: *He told us a **funny** story.*

- ▸ **amusing**   pleasantly entertaining: *I taught my bird an **amusing** trick.*
- ▸ **comical**   causing amusement, especially by being ridiculous or silly: *He looked **comical** in his Halloween costume.*
- ▸ **humorous**   funny, especially in the manner of a joke or amusing story: *She laughed at the **humorous** cartoon in the morning newspaper.*
- ▸ **witty**   expressing amusing insights; original and clever: *Dorothy Parker was a very **witty** writer.*

ANTONYM **sad**   showing or filled with sorrow or unhappiness

fur *noun*   the thick, soft hair that covers the body of certain animals: *see* **hide**[1]

furious *adjective*   full of intense, often violent anger: *see* **angry**

furlough *noun*   a vacation or leave of absence from a duty, especially one given to soldiers or sailors: *see* **vacation**

furnish *verb*   to provide the items needed for a purpose: *see* **equip**

furthermore *adverb*   in addition: *see* **also**

fury *noun*   violent anger: *see* **anger**

fuse *verb*   to unite two or more substances into a strong union, as by melting: *see* **mix**

fuss *noun*   nervous or useless activity or concern: *see* **commotion**

fussy *adjective*   easily upset, especially over small matters: *see* **irritable**

futile *adjective*   having no useful results: *see* **useless**

fuzzy *adjective*   covered with soft, short fibers or hairs: *see* **soft [1]**

G

gadget *noun* a small mechanical or electronic device: *see* **tool**

gag *verb* to choke and vomit or nearly vomit: *see* **choke**

gag *noun* a playful joke or trick: *see* **joke**

gain *verb* to get or obtain something, especially by effort: *see* **achieve**

gallant *adjective* brave and noble: *see* **brave**

gallivant *verb* to roam about in search of pleasure or amusement: *see* **wander**

gallop *verb* ▷ to move at the fastest pace of a horse ▷ to move swiftly: *see* **run**

gamble

verb ▷ to bet on an uncertain outcome, as of a contest: *They lost money **gambling** at the casino.* ▷ to take a risk in hopes of gaining an advantage or a benefit: *The doctor said I was **gambling** with my health by continuing to smoke.*

- ▶ **bet** to make an agreement that one will forfeit something if one's prediction is incorrect: *I'll **bet** you five dollars that he forgets to return the movies.*
- ▶ **stake** to gamble or risk one's money or property: *He **staked** his entire paycheck on the horse race.*
- ▶ **wager** to risk an amount or possession on an uncertain outcome: *I'll **wager** twenty dollars that you're wrong.*

game *noun* a sport or other form of play carried on according to a special set of rules: *see* **recreation**

gang *noun* a group of people who gather together regularly on a social basis: *see* **group**

gangster *noun* a member of an organized group of criminals: *see* **criminal**

gap

noun an opening or break; a blank or empty space: *She has a **gap** between her two front teeth.*

- ▶ **crack** a narrow opening: *The mouse slipped in and out of a **crack** in the wall.*
- ▶ **cranny** a small opening, as in a wall or rock: *A pink wildflower was growing out of the **cranny** in the cliff.*
- ▶ **crevice** a small, narrow, often shallow opening: *A weed grew in the **crevice** of the sidewalk.*
- ▶ **opening** an open space or clearing: *We made an **opening** in the wall to put in a window.*

garbage

noun food and trash to be thrown away, as from a kitchen: *It is my job to take out the **garbage**.*

- ▶ **compost** a mixture of decaying organic matter used to enrich the soil: *We added **compost** and fertilizer to the soil in our garden.*
- ▶ **debris** the scattered remains of something broken or destroyed: *The investigators searched through the **debris** of the accident.*
- ▶ **junk** unwanted or discarded materials that can often be used again in some way: *We sold a lot of **junk** at the yard sale.*
- ▶ **litter** empty cans and bottles, pieces of paper, and other waste material left lying around: *They picked up all their **litter** after the picnic.*
- ▶ **refuse** something to be thrown away: *The garbage truck picked up the **refuse**.*
- ▶ **rubbish** discarded or worthless material; trash: *We loaded the **rubbish** into the back of the truck and drove to the dump.*
- ▶ **trash** objects to be thrown away, usually not including food: *Please separate the **trash** from the recycling.*

► **waste**   worthless or useless material, often left over from a process: *The city is developing a new plan for disposing of industrial waste.*

garden *noun*   a piece of land where flowers, vegetables, and fruit are grown: *see* **park**

garment *noun*   an article of clothing: *see* **clothing**

garnish *verb*   to decorate food with something that adds color or flavor: *see* **decorate**

garrison *noun*   a military post or the troops stationed at such a post: *see* **fort**

gas *noun*   a substance that is neither solid nor liquid and can expand to fill a container: *see* **fume**

gasp *verb*   to inhale in a sudden, sharp way, as from shock, surprise, or great exertion: *see* **breathe**

gate *noun*   an opening in a wall or fence: *see* **entrance**

gather

verb   to bring things together in one place: *We gathered up the toys and put them away.*

► **accumulate**   to mount up or collect in one place, especially over time: *A lot of dust has accumulated on the chandelier.*
► **collect**   to bring an assortment of items together in a group: *I collect shells every time I go to the beach.*
► **compile**   to put items together in a single list or collection: *She compiled all her notes before writing the paper.*
► **glean**   ▷ to gather loose grain left by reapers: *The peasants were allowed to glean the landowner's fields after the harvest.* ▷ to gather something, such as information, little by little: *After weeks of investigation, the reporter gleaned enough information for the article.*
► **harvest**   to gather a crop: *He harvested the apples when they were ripe.*
► **reap**   to cut grain or gather a crop by hand or machine: *The farmer hired extra help when it was time to reap the corn.*

ANTONYM **scatter**   to separate and go in many directions

gaudy *adjective*   too fancy and bright to be in good taste: *see* **colorful**

gauge *verb*   to evaluate or judge something in advance: *see* **guess**

gaunt *adjective*   very thin and bony, as from starvation or disease: *see* **thin**

gay *adjective*   merry and carefree: *see* **happy**

gaze *verb*   to look at something intently, as with strong emotion: *see* **look**

gear *noun*   equipment, such as tools or clothing, needed for a particular activity: *see* **equipment**

general *adjective*   not limited or specialized: *see* **common**

generally *adverb*   as a rule; usually: *see* **often**

generation *noun*   a group of people who grew up at the same time, often having similar social and cultural attitudes: *see* **age**

generic *adjective*   not distinguished from others of its kind; usual: *see* **common**

generous *adjective*   given or offered in large amounts: *see* **abundant**

generous *adjective*   willing to give or share: *see* **kind¹**

genesis *noun* (formal)   the origin or creation of something: *see* **beginning**

genre *noun*   a particular type of literary, musical, or artistic composition: *see* **kind²**

gentle

adjective   easily managed or controlled; not unruly or wild: *They gave me a gentle horse to ride at the dude ranch.*

► **meek**   showing patience and humility: *The defendant's meek behavior pleased the judge.*
► **mild**   gentle or kind in disposition or behavior: *His mild personality makes him easy to get along with.*

▶ **tame** not afraid of people; easily handled or taught: *My cockatiel is **tame** and will sit on my finger.*

▶ **tender** considerate and protective; loving: *The father put his arm around his son's shoulders in a **tender** gesture.*

gentleman *noun* a man or boy, especially one who is polite: *see* **man**

genuine *adjective* being exactly what is claimed: *see* **real [1]**

gesture *noun* a motion of the hands, arms, head, or body that expresses a feeling or idea: *see* **signal**

get

verb to come into possession of something: *We **got** a new rug for the living room.*

▶ **accept** to receive something that is offered: *She was happy to **accept** the flowers that he brought to her.*

▶ **acquire** to take possession of something, especially something desirable: *I **acquired** some valuable antiques when my grandfather died.*

▶ **obtain** to gain or get something, especially by means of planning or effort: *She worked hard to **obtain** her college degree.*

▶ **procure** to obtain by special effort: *We **procured** seats at the last minute.*

▶ **receive** to take or acquire something given, offered, or sent: *He **received** the award for best athlete.*

get-together *noun* (informal) a small party or gathering: *see* **party**

get together *verb* to meet or assemble in an informal way: *see* **meet**

giant *noun* a huge, very strong, imaginary creature resembling a human being: *see* **monster**

gift

noun something given voluntarily and with no payment in return: *I received a lot of **gifts** for my birthday.*

▶ **contribution** something given toward a goal or purpose: *He has made large **contributions** to his old school.*

▶ **donation** something given to a fund or cause: *We made a **donation** to the library building fund.*

▶ **grant** a gift of funds for a specific purpose: *The artist received a **grant** to design a monument.*

▶ **offering** something given as an act of worship or tribute: *She put flowers on the altar as an **offering**.*

▶ **present** something presented; a gift: *All the **presents** were stacked under the Christmas tree.*

gift-wrap *verb* to wrap something as a gift with fancy paper, ribbon, or other trimmings: *see* **wrap**

gigantic *adjective* extremely large in size, strength, or power: *see* **big**

giggle *verb* to laugh in a silly or nervous way: *see* **laugh**

girl *noun* a female child: *see* **child**

give

verb to make a gift of something; to put something in another's possession: *I **gave** my sister a couple of my old sweaters.*

▶ **bestow** to give or present something, especially as a gift or honor: *She **bestowed** a kiss on his cheek.*

▶ **contribute** to give something in common with others: *Everybody in the office **contributed** money to buy her a birthday present.*

▶ **donate** to give something to a fund or cause: *We **donate** money to our synagogue every month.*

▶ **offer** to present something for acceptance or rejection: *He **offered** to help her move into her new apartment.*

▶ **provide** to give something that is needed or useful: *This company **provides** daycare for its employees' children.*

▶ **volunteer** to offer help or a service of one's own free will: *They **volunteered** to deliver meals to senior citizens.*

ANTONYM **take** to get possession or use of something

give up *verb* to abandon something that one possesses: *see* **resign**

glad *adjective* pleased: *see* **happy**

gladden *verb* to make someone glad: *see* **please**

gladness *noun* happiness or pleasure: *see* **happiness**

glamorous *adjective* having or showing romantic charm or excitement: *see* **interesting**

glance *verb* to take a quick look at something: *see* **look**

glare *verb* to stare in an angry way: *see* **frown**

glass

noun a container typically made of glass and used for drinking: *He drank a **glass** of water.*

- ▸ **cup** a small open container, usually with a handle: *Would you like another **cup** of coffee?*
- ▸ **goblet** a fancy drinking glass with a stem and a base: *We bought crystal **goblets** for the dinner party.*
- ▸ **tumbler** a drinking glass having no handle or stem: *The little girl had a plastic **tumbler** full of juice.*

glaze *verb* to apply a smooth, shiny coating to something: *see* **cover**

gleam *noun* a beam or flash of bright light: *see* **shine**

gleaming *adjective* emitting a beam or flash of light: *see* **bright**

glean *verb* ▹ to gather loose grain left by reapers ▹ to gather something, such as information, little by little: *see* **gather**

glee *noun* excited delight: *see* **happiness**

glide *verb* to move smoothly, quietly, and with ease: *see* **float**

glimpse *verb* to get a brief view of something: *see* **look**

glisten *verb* to shine with reflected light: *see* **shine**

glitter *verb* to sparkle brilliantly: *see* **shine**

gloat *verb* to think or speak about something with selfish or spiteful satisfaction: *see* **brag**

glob *noun* a rounded mass or lump of thick liquid: *see* **drop**

global *adjective* relating to the entire earth: *see* **international**

globe *noun* ▹ the planet earth ▹ a ball-shaped map of the earth: *see* **earth [1]**

gloom *noun* lowness of spirit: *see* **sadness**

gloomy

adjective ▹ partially or totally dark: *The abandoned warehouse looked **gloomy**.* ▹ having low spirits; glum: *We went home feeling **gloomy** after losing the math competition.*

- ▸ **bleak** ▹ barren and desolate: *The Arctic landscape is cold and **bleak**.* ▹ not hopeful or promising; dismal: *My chances of getting a scholarship look **bleak**.*
- ▸ **depressing** causing a feeling of sadness and discouragement: *The rapid extinction of so many species of animals is **depressing**.*
- ▸ **dismal** causing low spirits; gloomy: *My bank account looks **dismal** these days.*
- ▸ **dreary** boring or dull; tiresome: *I listened to her **dreary** talk about her many illnesses.*
- ▸ **glum** moody and melancholy; dejected: *I felt **glum** when no one at the party talked to me.*

ANTONYM **cheerful** being in good spirits; merry

glorious *adjective* ▹ deserving great honor, praise, and fame ▹ having great beauty: *see* **wonderful**

glorify *verb* to give high praise or honor to someone: *see* **praise**

gloss *noun* a bright shine on a smooth surface: *see* **shine**

glow *noun* a soft, steady light, like that produced by something hot but not flaming: *see* **shine**

glue *verb* to stick things together with glue: *see* **fasten**

glum *adjective* moody and melancholy: *see* **gloomy**

gnaw *verb* to bite, chew, or wear something down with the teeth: *see* **bite**

go

verb to pass from one place to another; to move along: *Do you want to go to the game with us?*

► **head** to proceed or go in a certain direction: *The elk headed north.*
► **move** to change from one place or position to another: *The cat moved from the sofa to the chair.*
► **pass** to go across, over, or through something; to move past: *They passed through a series of small towns.*

goal

noun something wanted or worked for: *It is my goal to lose ten pounds this year.*

► **aim** a desired result; a purpose: *His only aim in life is to go surfing.*
► **end** something toward which one strives; a goal: *Financial stability is her ultimate end.*
► **intent** something done or attempted on purpose: *I had no intent to offend you with that joke.*
► **intention** a goal that guides one's actions: *It is my intention to graduate from college in four years.*
► **object** the purpose or goal of a specific action or effort: *The object of this homework assignment is to develop your research skills.*
► **objective** something that one tries to achieve or reach: *One of the park department's objectives is to plant more trees in our town.*
► **purpose** an intended or desired result: *What is the purpose of this meeting?*

gob *noun* a small, sticky lump: *see* **chunk**

gobble *verb* to devour food in big greedy gulps: *see* **eat**

goblet *noun* a fancy drinking glass with a stem and a base: *see* **glass**

gone *adjective* away from a place: *see* **absent**

good

adjective having positive or desirable qualities: *This is a good, reliable car.*

► **desirable** worth wanting, seeking, or doing: *Many people feel that it is desirable to own a home.*
► **satisfying** fulfilling or gratifying: *That was a satisfying meal.*
► **worthwhile** worth the time, effort, or cost involved: *Attending the music festival was a worthwhile experience.*

ANTONYM **bad** not good; inferior

good deed *noun* a kind act done for someone: *see* **favor**

good-looking *adjective* having a pleasing appearance: *see* **beautiful**

goods *noun* things that can be bought and sold: *see* **merchandise**

goods *noun* personal belongings: *see* **property**

goodwill *noun* a kindly or friendly attitude: *see* **sympathy**

gore *verb* to pierce or stab someone with a horn or tusk: *see* **stab**

gorge *noun* a deep, narrow passage, as between mountains: *see* **valley**

gorgeous *adjective* extremely beautiful or magnificent: *see* **beautiful**

gossip *verb* to talk and spread rumors about other people: *see* **talk**

gouge *verb* to cut or scoop something out, as with a sharp utensil: *see* **stab**

govern *verb* to direct the public affairs of a country or state: *see* **manage**

governess *noun* a woman employed to teach and train the children of a household: *see* **teacher**

government

noun a system by which a political unit, such as a country or city, is governed: *He works as a tax accountant for the government.*

▸ **administration** the people who manage the operation of something, such as a school, business, or government: *It is usual for the administration to change when a new leader is elected.*

▸ **bureaucracy** the administration of a government through bureaus and departments with appointed officials: *The state bureaucracy seems to get larger every year.*

▸ **ministry** a department of government under the charge of a minister: *The officials of the foreign ministry met to discuss the budget.*

▸ **regime** a government in power, especially in a nondemocratic country: *The dictator's regime ended when he died.*

▸ **reign** the period during which a monarch rules: *England prospered greatly during the reign of Queen Elizabeth the First.*

grab

verb to take hold of something suddenly and roughly: *The monkey grabbed the peanut out of my hand.*

▸ **catch** to get hold of or grasp something that is moving: *The outfielder ran to catch the ball.*

▸ **clench** to take hold of or hold onto something tightly: *She clenched her purse when the mugger tried to take it from her.*

▸ **seize** to take hold of something suddenly: *The little boy seized the cookies from the plate and ran outside with them*

▸ **snatch** to grab something quickly or eagerly: *The frog snatched the fly out of the air.*

grace *noun* ease and beauty of movement, form, or manner: *see* **elegance**

graceless *adjective* lacking grace, elegance, or charm: *see* **awkward**

gracious *adjective* courteous and kind, especially in social situations: *see* **polite**

grade *verb* to give a mark or grade to something: *see* **judge**

gradual *adjective* advancing by regular or continuous degrees: *see* **slow**

grain *noun* the small, hard, edible seed of cereal plants: *see* **seed**

grand

adjective large and very fine in appearance: *New York City's Metropolitan Opera House is a grand building.*

▸ **formal** following the usual forms, customs, or rules; stiffly ceremonious: *The embassy reception was a formal affair.*

▸ **luxurious** very splendid and comfortable: *We stayed at a luxurious resort in Mexico.*

▸ **magnificent** full of splendor or majesty; very impressive: *There is a magnificent view from the balcony of our apartment.*

grandeur *noun* the quality or condition of being grand: *see* **luxury**

grant *noun* a gift of funds for a specific purpose: *see* **gift**

graph *noun* a drawing or diagram that shows relationships between various quantities: *see* **chart**

grasp *verb* to seize and hold something firmly: *see* **hold**

grasp *verb* to take something into the mind: *see* **understand**

grate *verb* to break something into fragments or shreds by rubbing it against a rough surface: *see* **scratch**

grateful

adjective feeling or showing gratitude or thankfulness: *We are grateful for all the help you've given us.*

▸ **appreciative** showing recognition of another's worth or effort: *I am appreciative of your hard work on this project.*

▸ **indebted** morally, socially, or legally obligated to another: *She was indebted to him for saving her life.*

▸ **thankful** aware and appreciative of a benefit; grateful: *I am thankful for my good health.*

ANTONYM **ungrateful** not feeling or expressing thanks

gratify *verb* to please or satisfy someone: *see* **please**

grating *adjective* displeasing in sound; harsh-sounding: *see* **hoarse**

gratitude *noun* the state of being grateful: *see* **appreciation**

grave *adjective* having a serious manner appropriate to weighty matters: *see* **serious [1]**

gravel *noun* a loose mixture of pebbles or small pieces of rock: *see* **rock**

graze *verb* to touch or scrape something lightly in passing: *see* **scratch**

grease *noun* soft or melted animal fat: *see* **fat**

great *adjective* impressively large: *see* **big**

greatest *adjective* being the most remarkable or outstanding: *see* **best**

greedy

adjective filled with a selfish desire for more than one needs or deserves: *It was* **greedy** *of you to take a second dessert when some people didn't get any.*

- ▸ **selfish** concerned mainly with oneself without thinking of others: *She broke up with her boyfriend because he was* **selfish**.
- ▸ **stingy** giving or spending reluctantly; not generous: *My boss is too* **stingy** *to replace the broken chairs in the office.*
- ▸ **ungenerous** not willing to give or share: *The* **ungenerous** *child would not let anyone else play with her toys.*

green *adjective* (informal) lacking training or experience: *see* **inexperienced**

greenhorn *noun* an inexperienced person, especially one who is easily fooled: *see* **beginner**

greet

verb to welcome or speak to someone in a friendly or polite way: *My mother* **greeted** *me with a hug.*

- ▸ **hail** to greet or welcome someone by calling out: *My friend* **hailed** *me from across the street.*

- ▸ **receive** to welcome someone, especially to one's home: *Her family* **received** *me warmly during my visit.*
- ▸ **salute** to show respect to someone by raising the right hand stiffly to the forehead or by firing guns: *The soldier* **saluted** *his officer.*
- ▸ **welcome** to greet someone with pleasure, hospitality, or special ceremony: *The teacher* **welcomed** *the exchange student to our class.*

grief *noun* great sadness; deep sorrow: *see* **suffering**

grievance *noun* a real or imagined wrong regarded as just cause for protest: *see* **complaint**

grieve *verb* to feel very sad over a loss or death: *see* **mourn**

grill *verb* to cook food over a flame or direct heat: *see* **cook**

grimace *verb* to tighten and twist the face muscles, as in pain or disgust: *see* **frown**

grimy *adjective* covered with black, greasy dirt or soot: *see* **dirty**

grin *verb* to smile with pleasure: *see* **smile**

grind *verb* to crush something into small bits or a fine powder: *see* **crush**

grip *verb* to grasp and hold on to something with steady pressure: *see* **hold**

gripe *verb* (informal) to complain in a nagging or irritating way: *see* **complain**

groan *verb* to make a deep sound low in the throat that expresses pain, annoyance, or good-natured disapproval: *see* **moan**

groom

verb to make an animal or person neat and attractive in appearance, as by brushing or combing: *She* **grooms** *her horse after every ride.*

- ▸ **bathe** to take a bath or give someone else a bath: *The mother* **bathed** *the baby in the kitchen sink.*
- ▸ **brush** to clean, polish, sweep, or groom someone or something with a brush: *I* **brush** *my hair one hundred strokes every night.*

▸ **comb** to smooth or arrange the hair with a comb: *He combed his hair before going to work.*

gross

adjective extremely unpleasant, especially to the senses: *An onion milkshake would be gross.*

▸ **disgusting** causing feelings of sickening dislike, distaste, or annoyance: *My sister says that my messy room is disgusting.*
▸ **nauseating** causing a feeling of sickness in the stomach characterized by the need to vomit; disgusting: *The smell of certain foods was nauseating to her while she was pregnant.*
▸ **repulsive** causing extreme dislike or aversion: *The rotting seal on the beach was repulsive.*
▸ **revolting** causing great disgust; offensive: *His table manners are revolting.*
▸ **sickening** so disgusting as to make one feel sick: *Where is that sickening smell coming from?*

grouchy *adjective* cross, grumbling, or complaining: *see* **irritable**

ground *noun* the solid surface of the earth: *see* **earth [2]**

group

noun a number of people that share the same interests or activities: *He belongs to a men's study group.*

▸ **band** a group of people or animals acting together: *Early humans probably lived in small bands that hunted and gathered food cooperatively.*
▸ **bunch** (informal) a group of people who regularly associate together: *I have some friends in the drama bunch at school.*
▸ **gang** a group of people who gather together regularly on a social basis: *I have had the same gang of friends since high school.*
▸ **herd** a group of animals of one kind, such as cattle, that stay together or are kept together: *My aunt and uncle have a herd of llamas.*

▸ **pack** a group of animals that run and hunt together: *Wolf packs are fascinating to study.*

grow *verb* to plant and tend a crop: *see* **raise [1]**

grow *verb* to increase and spread; to gain size or strength: *see* **thrive**

growl *noun* a low, throaty, menacing sound made by an animal: *see* **bark**

grown *adjective* having reached full physical growth: *see* **adult**

growth

noun an increase, as in size or strength: *The city has experienced a great deal of growth in the past decade.*

▸ **development** the act of making something more effective or advanced: *The development of the computer has resulted in smaller and faster machines.*
▸ **expansion** the act of making something larger in size, volume, or amount: *The expansion of the railroads in the mid-19th century contributed to the industrial revolution.*
▸ **progress** steady improvement or advancement: *I have been making progress in my math class now that I have a tutor.*
▸ **rise** an increase in status, prosperity, or importance: *The polls show that the candidate is experiencing a rise in popularity.*

gruff *adjective* rough or stern in manner or appearance: *see* **blunt**

grumble *verb* to complain in a sullen or discontented way: *see* **complain**

grumpy *adjective* easily angered or upset: *see* **irritable**

guarantee *noun* something that gives assurance, especially a promise that a product will be fixed if anything goes wrong with it: *see* **promise**

guard *verb* to watch over someone or something so as to provide protection: *see* **protect**

guardian *noun* a person who is legally responsible for the care of a child: *see* **parent**

guess

verb to form an opinion about something without enough information to be sure: *I had to guess at a couple answers on the test.*

- **assume** to take something for granted without knowing for sure: *I assume that you got my message.*
- **estimate** to calculate something roughly: *The mechanic estimated the cost of the repairs.*
- **gauge** to evaluate or judge something in advance: *The pole-vaulter gauged the height of the crossbar he had to jump over.*
- **presume** to assume something on the basis of likelihood or reason: *I presume that you two know each other, since you live on the same street.*
- **speculate** to think or ponder about something without having adequate information: *William James, the American philosopher, speculated that the state of the body determines one's emotions.*
- **suppose** to be inclined to think or conclude something: *Do you suppose that anyone would notice if we left early?*

guest

noun one to whom entertainment or hospitality has been extended by another, as at a party: *They greeted their dinner guests at the door.*

- **caller** a person who makes a short visit to someone: *You have a caller waiting downstairs.*
- **company** a guest or guests: *We're having company over for dinner.*
- **visitor** someone who visits a person or place: *Sometimes I think that my brother is a visitor from outer space.*

guffaw *verb* to laugh heartily or in an unrestrained way: *see* **laugh**

guide

verb to serve as one who directs, leads, or shows the way: *The seeing-eye dog guided the blind woman across the street.*

- **lead** to direct someone along the way, as by going in front: *The guide led us on a tour through the museum.*
- **navigate** to direct or follow a planned course, as in a ship or other vehicle: *We navigated our way across the U.S. during our road trip.*
- **pilot** to lead, guide, or conduct a vehicle, especially a ship or aircraft: *He piloted the boat out of harbor.*
- **shepherd** to herd, guard, or guide someone closely: *The crossing guard shepherded the children across the street.*
- **steer** to direct the course of something or someone: *He steered the car into the driveway.*

guideline *noun* a statement, policy, or procedure intended to give practical guidance: *see* **rule**

guild *noun* an association of people who share an occupation, interest, or cause: *see* **club**

gulf *noun* a large area of a sea or ocean that is partly enclosed by land: *see* **harbor**

guilt *noun* the fact of having done wrong: *see* **blame**

guilt *noun* a bad feeling about having done wrong: *see* **sorrow**

guilty *adjective* feeling very bad about an immoral action or thought: *see* **sorry**

gulp *verb* to swallow something rapidly in large amounts: *see* **drink**

guru *noun* a Hindu spiritual teacher: *see* **minister**

gush *verb* to flow forth suddenly and in a great amount: *see* **pour**

gust *noun* a sudden, strong rush of wind: *see* **wind**

gut *noun* the digestive tract: *see* **stomach**

guy *noun* (informal) a man; a fellow: *see* **man**

guzzle *verb* to drink something greedily: *see* **drink**

H

habit

noun an activity or action done so often that one does it without thinking: *She has the **habit** of locking the house when she leaves.*

▸ **custom** something that a person regularly does: *It is his **custom** to go for a run every morning.*

▸ **pattern** actions or events that are repeated in a recognizable arrangement: *She left her marriage to break the **pattern** of abuse.*

▸ **routine** a series of regular or usual activities; standard procedure: *It is his evening **routine** to eat dinner while he watches the news.*

▸ **practice** a customary action or way of doing something: *Their **practice** of saving money regularly has made it possible for them to buy their first home.*

habitat *noun* the place in which a person, plant, or animal is most likely to be found: *see* **home**

habitual *adjective* established by long use or habit: *see* **regular**

hail *verb* to greet or welcome someone by calling out: *see* **greet**

hale *adjective* strong and healthy: *see* **healthy**

hall

noun a usually long, narrow passage between rooms in a house or building: *The bathroom is down the **hall** and to the left.*

▸ **corridor** a hall or passage, especially in a large building: *The carpet in the hotel **corridor** had a wild pattern.*

▸ **lobby** an entrance hall or a waiting area in a hotel, apartment house, or theater: *He waited for her by the elevators in the **lobby**.*

▸ **passageway** a narrow way or path leading from one place to another: *There is an enclosed **passageway** on the third floor that connects the two buildings.*

▸ **tunnel** an underground or underwater passage: *The train went through the harbor **tunnel**.*

hallowed *adjective* set apart as holy: *see* **holy**

hallucination *noun* an illusion of being aware of something that does not exist: *see* **illusion**

halt *verb* to stop or come to an end, often temporarily: *see* **stop**

hammer *verb* to strike or pound something with heavy, loud blows: *see* **hit**

hamper *verb* to make it difficult for someone to do something: *see* **prevent**

hand out *verb* to give something directly, as to those in need: *see* **distribute**

handbag *noun* a woman's purse, often having a handle or carrying strap: *see* **bag**

handbook *noun* a concise manual or reference book, providing specific information or instruction about a subject or place: *see* **book**

handle *verb* to take care of a difficult task or situation: *see* **cope**

handle *verb* to touch, hold, or manipulate something with the hands: *see* **touch**

handsome *adjective* pleasing and dignified in form and appearance: *see* **beautiful**

handy *adjective* readily accessible: *see* **useful**

hang

verb to fasten something at the upper end only: *Where shall we **hang** this picture?*

▸ **dangle** to swing loosely from a fixed point: *She likes long earrings that **dangle**.*

▸ **suspend** to attach something from above, especially so as to hang freely in midair: *The chandelier is **suspended** from the ceiling above the dining table.*

hanger *noun* a frame of wire, wood, or plastic used for hanging clothes: *see* **hook**

happen

verb to take place by chance or in the course of events: *What happened to you last night?*

- **come to pass** to happen, especially as one of a series of events: *The psychic said that strange things would come to pass after I left home.*
- **occur** to happen or come about: *The witness saw the accident occur.*
- **take place** to happen, especially as an event: *Where will the wedding take place?*
- **transpire** (formal) to happen: *Strange events transpired in the old mansion many years ago.*

happening *noun* something that takes place: *see* **event**

happiness

noun the condition of feeling pleasure, satisfaction, or joy: *Her idea of happiness was a night out with her friends.*

- **bliss** very great happiness or joy: *The couple lives in married bliss.*
- **cheer** good spirits, especially in a social setting: *Everyone at the party was full of holiday cheer.*
- **contentment** quiet happiness and satisfaction; peace of mind: *The man sighed with contentment after he finished dessert.*
- **delight** great or active pleasure: *It gives me great delight to introduce our next speaker.*
- **ecstasy** intense joy or delight: *The skater was in ecstasy when he won an Olympic gold medal.*
- **gladness** happiness or pleasure: *I was filled with gladness to see my friend.*
- **glee** excited delight: *The little children were full of glee as they played in the first snowfall.*
- **joy** unrestrained happiness or delight: *He laughed with joy to see his grandchild's first steps.*
- **mirth** fun and laughter: *Our family reunion was filled with happiness and mirth.*

happy

adjective showing or feeling pleasure or joy: *It would make me happy to live in Jackson Hole, Wyoming.*

- **cheerful** full of good spirits and happiness: *I am cheerful in the morning.*
- **delighted** very pleased or happy: *I'm delighted to meet you.*
- **gay** merry and carefree: *Everyone was in a gay mood at the Halloween party.*
- **glad** pleased; happy: *I'm glad I could be of help.*
- **jolly** full of good spirits and fun: *We had a jolly time on the hayride.*
- **joyful** feeling or showing joy: *His bar mitzvah was a joyful celebration.*
- **merry** full of good humor and gaiety: *The little town's holiday fair was a merry and festive occasion.*
- **thrilled** filled with a sudden sensation of joy, delight, or excitement: *He was thrilled to meet the pitcher of his favorite baseball team.*

ANTONYM **sad** showing, filled with, or causing sorrow or unhappiness

harass *verb* to irritate or torment someone persistently: *see* **annoy**

harbor

noun a sheltered place along a coast where ships can safely anchor or dock: *We anchored our boat in the harbor.*

- **bay** a part of the sea that extends into the land: *There was a white, sandy beach along the bay.*
- **cove** a small, sheltered bay or inlet: *We rowed across the cove.*
- **gulf** a large area of a sea or ocean that is partly enclosed by land: *The Gulf of Mexico is bordered by the United States, Mexico, and Cuba.*
- **inlet** a small or narrow body of water, as a bay or cove, along a coast: *We explored the inlets of Puget Sound.*
- **port** a town or city that has a harbor; a place along a body of water where ships can dock or anchor: *Two tugboats guided the ocean liner into port.*

hard

adjective difficult to solve, understand, or express: *My math homework is usually hard.*

▸ **challenging** requiring all of a person's efforts and skills: *A marathon is a challenging athletic event.*

▸ **complicated** not easy to understand, deal with, or solve; complex: *I need help filling out this complicated tax form.*

▸ **demanding** requiring much effort or attention: *She is a demanding child.*

▸ **difficult** hard to make, do, or understand: *English is a difficult language to learn.*

▸ **strenuous** requiring great effort, energy, or exertion: *The bodybuilder has a strenuous exercise routine.*

▸ **trying** causing strain, hardship, or distress: *The trying experience brought them closer together.*

ANTONYM **easy** needing very little effort

hardly

adverb to almost no degree; almost not: *I can hardly hear you when you whisper like that.*

▸ **barely** by very little; only just: *She barely passed the class.*

▸ **scarcely** by a small margin; barely: *We had scarcely sat down to dinner when the phone rang.*

▸ **slightly** to a small degree or extent: *The toast was slightly burnt.*

▸ **somewhat** to some extent or degree; rather: *He resembles his brother somewhat.*

hardship *noun* something that causes suffering or difficulty: *see* **misfortune**

hardy *adjective* strong and healthy: *see* **tough**

harm *verb* to do injury or damage to someone: *see* **hurt**

harmful *adjective* capable of causing harm: *see* **dangerous**

harmonize *verb* to be or come into agreement with something: *see* **agree**

harmony *noun* agreement in feeling or opinion: *see* **peace**

harsh *adjective* very severe or cruel: *see* **mean**[1]

harvest *verb* to gather a crop: *see* **gather**

haste *noun* swiftness in moving or acting: *see* **speed**

hasty *adjective* done too quickly to be accurate or wise: *see* **fast**

hat

noun a covering for the head, especially one with a crown and a brim: *She wears a large straw hat at the beach.*

▸ **bonnet** a hat tied with ribbons under the chin and often framing the entire face, worn formerly by women but now usually by very young children: *Pioneer women wore bonnets to protect their faces from the sun.*

▸ **cap** a covering for the head that has no brim but sometimes has a visor: *His girlfriend made him a knitted cap to wear skiing.*

▸ **crown** an ornamental circlet or head covering, often made of precious metal, set with jewels, and worn as a symbol of royalty: *The queen wore a crown of diamonds and rubies.*

▸ **helmet** a protective head covering made of a hard material such as metal or plastic: *He always wears a helmet when he rides his motorcycle.*

hatch *noun* an opening in the deck of a ship: *see* **entrance**

hatch *verb* to think something up, especially in secret: *see* **plot**

hate

noun strong or passionate dislike; hatred: *Hate is a destructive emotion.*

▸ **contempt** a feeling of scorn or cold superiority: *My professor has contempt for spelling errors.*

▸ **hostility** angry resistance or opposition to something or someone: *There is a longtime hostility between the two countries.*

▸ **ill will** unfriendly feelings; hostility: *I could sense her ill will toward me.*

- **malice** a desire to hurt others or to see others suffer: *Abraham Lincoln said, "With **malice** toward none, with charity for all" in a speech just one month before he was assassinated.*
- **spite** a mean desire to hurt or humiliate another person: *He ignored her out of **spite**.*

ANTONYM **love** strong affection and warm feeling for another

hate

verb to feel a strong or passionate dislike for someone or something: *She **hates** to see people make fun of others.*

- **abhor** to regard someone or something with horror or loathing: *Radical vegetarians **abhor** the very thought of eating meat.*
- **abominate** to detest something thoroughly; abhor: *They **abominate** cruelty to animals.*
- **despise** to regard someone or something with scorn or disgust: *I **despise** self-righteous people.*
- **detest** to dislike intensely: *He **detests** doing dishes.*
- **dislike** to feel displeasure or aversion toward someone or something: *I **dislike** beets.*
- **loathe** to feel deep dislike or disgust for someone or something; to hate: *He **loathes** the long commute to work.*

hateful *adjective* arousing or serving hatred: *see* **evil**

haughty *adjective* proud about oneself and looking down on others: *see* **proud**

haul *verb* to pull or drag something with great effort: *see* **carry**

have

verb to be in temporary or permanent possession of something: *Do you **have** a pen I could borrow?*

- **own** to have as something belonging to oneself: *I **own** too many books.*
- **possess** to have as a property or as a quality: *He **possesses** great self-confidence.*

hazard *noun* a possible source of injury or harm: *see* **danger**

hazardous *adjective* full of risk or danger: *see* **dangerous**

haze *noun* fine dust, smoke, or water vapor floating in the air: *see* **mist**

hazy *adjective* full of or covered with haze: *see* **overcast**

head *noun* a person who leads, rules, or is in charge of something: *see* **boss**

head *verb* to proceed or go in a certain direction: *see* **go**

headstrong *adjective* insisting on having one's own way: *see* **stubborn**

heal *verb* to make or become healthy again: *see* **fix**

healthy

adjective in good health; free from disease or injury: *The vet said that my guinea pig is **healthy**.*

- **athletic** having a strong, muscular body: *The young man had an **athletic** build.*
- **fit** in good physical condition: *She works out at the gym to stay **fit**.*
- **hale** strong and healthy: *The farmer and his sons were **hale** men.*
- **robust** full of health and energy: *My **robust** grandfather goes dancing once a week.*
- **vigorous** strong, energetic, and active in mind or body: *Susan B. Anthony was a **vigorous** crusader for women's rights.*

heap *noun* a pile of things thrown on top of each other: *see* **pile**

hear *verb* to take in sounds through the ear: *see* **listen**

heart *noun* the central or main part: *see* **center [1]**

hearten *verb* to give strength or courage to someone: *see* **encourage**

hearty *adjective* strong and healthy: *see* **strong**

heat *verb* to make food warm or hot: *see* **cook**

heave *verb* to throw something with effort or force: *see* **throw**

heaven *noun* a condition or place of great happiness, delight, or pleasure: *see* **paradise**

heavy

adjective [1] weighing a lot: *All these books make my backpack* **heavy***.*

- ▸ **bulky** extremely large; massive: *The* **bulky** *couch wouldn't fit through the doorway.*
- ▸ **cumbersome** awkward to carry, wear, or manage: *My bike is* **cumbersome** *to get up the stairs.*
- ▸ **unwieldy** difficult to carry or handle because of shape or size: *The huge potted plant was so* **unwieldy** *that we just left it where it was.*
- ▸ **weighty** having great weight; heavy: *The statue has a* **weighty** *base.*

heavy *adjective* [2] above average in body weight: *see* **fat**

hectic *adjective* marked by intense activity, confusion, or excitement: *see* **busy**

hedge *noun* a row of shrubs or small trees that are planted closely together to form a fence or boundary: *see* **wall**

heed *verb* to pay close attention to something or someone: *see* **listen**

heedless *adjective* paying little or no attention: *see* **careless**

heel *noun* (informal) a dishonest person: *see* **villain**

height *noun* the highest point or most advanced degree of something: *see* **prime**

helmet *noun* a protective head covering made of a hard material such as metal or plastic: *see* **hat**

help

verb to do what is needed or useful: *May I* **help** *you get dinner ready?*

- ▸ **aid** to give help to someone in need: *We stopped to* **aid** *the stranded motorist.*

- ▸ **assist** to help someone do or accomplish something: *She* **assisted** *the old woman up the stairs.*
- ▸ **relieve** ▷ to give someone aid or assistance: *We collected food and clothing to* **relieve** *the victims of the earthquake.* ▷ to lessen or reduce pain, discomfort, or anxiety; ease: *The aspirin* **relieved** *my headache.*
- ▸ **serve** to be of assistance to or promote the interests of someone: *Members of Congress are elected to* **serve** *the people of the United States.*
- ▸ **support** to supply someone with things needed to live or survive: *My parents are helping to* **support** *me while I'm in school.*

ANTONYM **hinder** to get in someone's way; to make something more difficult to do

helper *noun* a person who helps or assists someone: *see* **assistant**

helpful *adjective* providing assistance: *see* **useful**

helpless

adjective not able to take care of or defend oneself: *Newborn babies are* **helpless***.*

- ▸ **incapable** lacking the ability to do something: *My mother is* **incapable** *of seeing very well without her glasses.*
- ▸ **incompetent** not capable of doing a good job: *The woman was fired from her job because she was* **incompetent***.*
- ▸ **powerless** lacking the force, strength, or ability to do or accomplish something: *We are* **powerless** *to change the past.*
- ▸ **unable** lacking the necessary power, authority, or means to do something: *He is* **unable** *to help us move on Saturday.*

helpmate *noun* a helper or helpful companion, especially a husband or wife: *see* **spouse**

hem *noun* a usually stitched edge of a garment or piece of cloth: *see* **edge**

hence *adverb* for this reason: *see* **therefore**

herald *noun* a person or thing that gives a sign of something to come: *see* **sign**

herd *noun* a group of animals of one kind, such as cattle, that stay together or are kept together: *see* **group**

hero

noun a person who is admired for great courage, special achievements, or noble character: *My older brother is my* **hero**.

- ▸ **champion** a defender or supporter of a cause or of another person: *Dian Fosse was a* **champion** *of preservation of gorillas and their habitat.*
- ▸ **heroine** a woman or girl admired for her great courage, special achievements, or noble character: *Amelia Earhart was a national* **heroine** *who flew an airplane across the Atlantic Ocean by herself in 1932.*
- ▸ **idol** a person who is admired or loved very much: *Ella Fitzgerald, the singer, is my* **idol**.
- ▸ **role model** a person who serves as an example for another person to imitate: *Teachers sometimes serve as* **role models** *for their students.*

heroic *adjective* having qualities of a hero: *see* **brave**

heroine *noun* a woman or girl admired for her great courage, special achievements, or noble character: *see* **hero**

heroism *noun* courageous action that results in great achievement: *see* **courage**

hesitant

adjective pausing because of doubt or uncertainty; wavering: *I was* **hesitant** *to ask for a job.*

- ▸ **reluctant** lacking an inclination to do something; unwilling: *He was* **reluctant** *to read his poem in front of the class.*
- ▸ **tentative** not definite or positive; not fully worked out: *We made* **tentative** *plans for Friday night.*
- ▸ **uncertain** not certain; doubtful: *The results of the experiment were* **uncertain**.
- ▸ **undecided** not yet settled or decided; having reached no decision: *I am* **undecided** *as to what to wear on my date.*
- ▸ **unsure** not sure; uncertain: *She was* **unsure** *about which street to turn onto.*

- ▸ **unwilling** not willing or inclined to do something: *The police were* **unwilling** *to give any further details about the incident.*

hesitate

verb to pause or hold back because of feeling unsure: *She* **hesitated** *before jumping into the pool.*

- ▸ **falter** to lose confidence or purpose: *Our determination* **faltered** *when we realized how difficult the work would be.*
- ▸ **waver** to be uncertain or indecisive: *I am* **wavering** *about which job offer to accept.*

heyday *noun* the period of something's greatest popularity, success, or power: *see* **age**

hibernate *verb* to spend the winter sleeping, as some animals do: *see* **sleep**

hide[1]

noun the skin of an animal: *The* **hide** *of the cow was black and white.*

- ▸ **coat** a natural covering such as the skin, fur, or wool of an animal: *The fox had a thick winter* **coat**.
- ▸ **fur** the thick, soft hair that covers the body of certain animals: *Rabbits have soft* **fur**.
- ▸ **pelt** an animal skin, especially with the hair or fur still on it: *The beaver* **pelts** *were sewn into a coat.*
- ▸ **skin** the hide or pelt that has been removed from the body of an animal: *Kangaroo* **skin** *is much more durable than cow leather.*

hide[2]

verb to keep or put something out of sight: *She* **hid** *his present at the back of the closet.*

- ▸ **bury** to hide something by placing in the ground and covering it with earth: *The squirrel* **buried** *the nuts in the ground.*
- ▸ **camouflage** to hide or disguise things, people, or animals by making them look like what is around them: *Zebras are* **camouflaged** *by their stripes.*
- ▸ **conceal** to keep someone or something from being noticed or known: *She used*

makeup to **conceal** the dark circles under her eyes.

▶ **shroud** to conceal or hide something by surrounding or enveloping it: *The trees* **shroud** *the house.*

▶ **veil** to conceal or disguise something behind something else: *Clouds* **veiled** *the moon.*

ANTONYM **reveal** to make something known; to disclose something

hideous *adjective* very ugly and disgusting: *see* **ugly**

high *adjective* having relatively great height: *see* **tall**

highlight *verb* to give prominence to something, especially a significant detail: *see* **emphasize**

highly *adverb* to a high degree: *see* **very**

high school *noun* a secondary school that usually includes grades 9 through 12: *see* **school**

highway *noun* a main public road: *see* **road**

hijack *verb* to seize control of a vehicle by force: *see* **steal**

hike *verb* to go on a long walk for pleasure or exercise: *see* **walk**

hill

noun a raised, usually rounded part of the earth's surface: *We rode our bikes down the* **hill**.

▶ **dune** a hill or ridge of windblown sand: *They got lost among the* **dunes** *at the beach.*

▶ **knoll** a small, round hill: *We picnicked on a* **knoll** *in the park.*

▶ **mountain** an area of land that rises to a great height: *There is a ski lodge on the* **mountain**.

▶ **rise** a gently sloping hill: *We walked to the top of the* **rise**.

▶ **slope** a stretch of ground that forms an incline: *The children rolled down the grassy* **slope**.

hinder *verb* to get in the way of someone or something: *see* **prevent**

hinge *noun* a device with joints on which something turns: *see* **joint**

hint *noun* a slight sign or suggestion: *see* **clue**

hire *verb* to pay for using something temporarily: *see* **rent**

hired hand *noun* a paid employee, especially on a farm or ranch: *see* **employee**

historic *adjective* important or famous in history: *see* **memorable**

history *noun* a written record of past events: *see* **report**

hit

verb to give a punch, slap, or blow to someone or something: *He* **hit** *the tennis ball with the racket.*

▶ **bat** to hit something with or as if with a bat: *The cat* **batted** *at the toy mouse with its paw.*

▶ **hammer** to strike or pound something with heavy, loud blows: *I* **hammered** *a nail into the wall.*

▶ **kick** to strike out at someone or something with the foot or feet: *The football player* **kicked** *the ball between the goal posts.*

▶ **knock** to hit something with a sharp blow or blows: *The delivery man* **knocked** *on our door.*

▶ **punch** to hit someone or something with the fist: *The boxer* **punched** *his opponent in the jaw.*

▶ **rap** to strike a surface quickly and sharply: *He* **rapped** *out a rhythm on the drum.*

▶ **slap** to strike sharply with or as if with the palm of the hand: *The boss* **slapped** *my shoulder in congratulation.*

▶ **spank** to slap a person or animal with the open hand or with a flat object: *The farmer* **spanked** *the cow on the side to get her moving.*

▶ **strike** to hit something or someone with or as if with the hand: *They gave each child several chances to* **strike** *the piñata with the stick.*

▶ **swat** to deliver a sudden, sharp blow to something: *He* **swatted** *the fly with a rolled up newspaper.*

▸ **whack** to strike something with a hard blow: *She broke the chocolate orange into segments by whacking it against the table.*

hoard *noun* a supply that is hidden away: *see* **supply**

hoarse

adjective low, rough, or harsh in sound; raspy in voice: *She has a hoarse voice because she yelled so loud at the football game.*

▸ **breathy** marked by audible or noisy breathing; having a weak or whispery voice: *The actress has a breathy voice that many people find attractive.*
▸ **grating** displeasing in sound; harsh-sounding: *We heard the grating sound of the neighbor dragging his garbage can to the sidewalk.*
▸ **husky** deep or rough in sound or voice: *The radio announcer has a low, husky voice.*
▸ **raspy** harsh and grating in voice: *My voice is raspy because I have a cold.*
▸ **scratchy** making a harsh, scraping sound: *The bushes made a scratchy sound against the window.*

hoax *verb* a trick or an act intended to deceive others: *see* **joke**

hobble *verb* to walk with a slow, awkward motion: *see* **stagger**

hobby *noun* an activity done for pleasure in one's spare time: *see* **recreation**

hoist *verb* to lift or haul something up, often with a mechanical device: *see* **raise [2]**

hold

verb to have or keep something in the arms or hands: *Would you please hold this for me while I unlock the door?*

▸ **clasp** to hold or embrace something tightly: *I clasped my first paycheck to my chest happily.*
▸ **clutch** to grasp and cling tightly to something: *The baby clutched her father's beard.*

▸ **grasp** to seize and hold something firmly: *He grasped the electric drill tightly in his hand.*
▸ **grip** to grasp and hold on to something with steady pressure: *She gripped my hand in silent sympathy.*

hole

noun an opening into or through something: *I dug a hole in the yard to plant the maple tree.*

▸ **cavity** a hollow place or area: *The squirrels nest in a cavity in that old tree.*
▸ **crater** a hollow area shaped like a bowl, as at the mouth of a volcano: *The meteorite left a huge crater in the desert.*
▸ **mine** an underground hole or tunnel from which minerals such as coal, iron, salt, or gold can be taken: *We bought stock in a Nevada gold mine.*
▸ **pit** a hole in the ground: *Rainwater filled the pit.*
▸ **quarry** an open pit from which stone, especially for building, is gotten by digging, cutting, or blasting: *The blasts at the rock quarry produced a lot of dust.*

holiday *noun* a day on which general business activity halts in order to celebrate a particular event: *see* **vacation**

holler *verb* (informal) to yell or shout: *see* **shout**

hollow *adjective* having an empty space or opening inside: *see* **empty**

holy

adjective associated with a divine power; worthy of worship or veneration: *The Torah, the Bible, and the Qur'an are all holy books.*

▸ **divine** relating to God or a god: *She prayed for divine guidance.*
▸ **hallowed** set apart as holy; regarded with reverence or respect: *Some people feel that battlefields are hallowed ground.*
▸ **sacred** worthy of religious veneration; holy: *Jerusalem is a sacred city to Christians, Jews, and Muslims.*

home

noun the place in which one lives: *Our home has three bedrooms.*

- ▸ **address** the location of a person or organization: *What is your address?*
- ▸ **abode** (formal) the place where one lives: *Welcome to my humble abode.*
- ▸ **dwelling** a place to live in; a residence: *The city plans to build more low-income dwellings in several neighborhoods.*
- ▸ **habitat** the place in which a person, plant, or animal is most likely to be found: *Forests provide good habitats for a variety of plants and animals.*
- ▸ **residence** the house or other building that a person lives in: *This suburban street is restricted to private residences.*

homeland *noun* the country in which one was born or has lived for a long time: *see* **country**

homeless person *noun* a person who has no permanent address or home: *see* **beggar**

homely *adjective* not pretty or attractive: *see* **ugly**

honest

adjective telling the truth; not lying, stealing, or cheating: *Were you being honest when you said you like my new haircut?*

- ▸ **candid** direct and frank; not holding anything back: *Please give me your candid opinion about my painting.*
- ▸ **forthright** direct and without evasion; straightforward: *She gave a forthright answer to my question.*
- ▸ **frank** free and open in expressing one's thoughts and feelings: *It took me a little while to get used to his frank manner.*
- ▸ **sincere** not lying or pretending; genuine: *She gave me a sincere apology for her rudeness.*
- ▸ **truthful** telling the truth; honest: *They were not completely truthful about the reasons for their visit.*

honor *verb* to show special respect for someone or something: *see* **praise**

honorable *adjective* conforming to a code of right or just behavior: *see* **moral**

hook

noun a curved or bent object that is used to catch, hold, fasten, or pull something: *He hung his hat on a hook on the door.*

- ▸ **clasp** something, such as a hook or buckle, that is used to hold two things together: *She fastened the clasp of her necklace.*
- ▸ **catch** a device such as a hook or latch used for fastening or closing something. *He fixed the catch on the cupboard so that it would close properly.*
- ▸ **hanger** a frame of wire, wood, or plastic used for hanging clothes: *She bought several new shirt hangers at the store.*
- ▸ **peg** a pin, often of wood, used to fasten or hang things: *He hung the damp towel on a peg in the bathroom.*
- ▸ **pin** a short, sharp-pointed piece of wire, used for fastening: *He fixed the flower to his lapel with a pin.*

hop *verb* to move with light, quick leaps: *see* **jump**

hope

verb to wish for something with the expectation that it will be fulfilled: *She hopes to go to Thailand on her next vacation.*

- ▸ **aspire** to have a great ambition; to desire something strongly: *He aspires to be well known as a science-fiction writer.*
- ▸ **dream** to think or believe that something is possible in the future: *They dream of buying land and building their own home.*
- ▸ **wish** to have or feel a desire for something: *I wish you would hurry.*

hopeful *adjective* feeling or showing hope: *see* **optimistic**

hopeless *adjective* offering no hope of success: *see* **useless**

horde *noun* a large, often active or disorderly crowd: *see* **crowd**

horizontal *adjective* parallel to the horizon: *see* **flat**

horrible *adjective* causing great fear, shock, or disgust: *see* **terrible**

horrid *adjective* causing horror: *see* **terrible**

horror *noun* great fear, terror, or shock: *see* **fear**

horse around *verb* (informal) to indulge in silly or rowdy play: *see* **play**

hose *noun* a long flexible tube used for carrying fluid or air: *see* **tube**

hostage *noun* a person held by an enemy to be used in exchange for the fulfillment of certain demands: *see* **prisoner**

hostel *noun* an inexpensive lodging house for travelers and tourists: *see* **hotel**

hostile *adjective* feeling or showing hatred or ill will, as between enemies: *see* **aggressive**

hostility *noun* angry resistance or opposition to something or someone: *see* **hate**

hot

adjective having or giving off great heat: *The sidewalk is so **hot** that you could fry an egg on it!*

- ► **blazing** (informal) very hot or bright: *I shaded my eyes from the **blazing** desert sun.*
- ► **burning** ▷ being on fire: *Everyone got out safely from the **burning** building.* ▷ very hot: *I ran barefoot over the **burning** sand at the beach.*
- ► **fiery** full of fire; burning fiercely: *We took a helicopter tour over the **fiery** crater of the volcano.*
- ► **tepid** moderately warm; lukewarm: *I let my tea cool until it was **tepid**.*
- ► **warm** somewhat hot; pleasantly heated: *She took a **warm** bath.*

ANTONYM **cold** being at a low temperature

hotel

noun a house or building that provides lodging and often meals to travelers for pay: *That **hotel** is getting a new phone system.*

- ► **bed-and-breakfast** a private residence that offers overnight lodging and break-

fast: *I received a gift certificate to stay at a charming **bed-and-breakfast**.*
- ► **boarding house** a private home that provides meals and lodging for long-term paying guests: *The widow earns money by running a **boarding house**.*
- ► **hostel** an inexpensive lodging house for travelers and tourists: *When I backpacked around Europe, I stayed in **hostels** to keep my expenses down.*
- ► **inn** a place that offers meals and lodging for travelers: *The small seaside town has several **inns**.*
- ► **lodge** a cottage or cabin, especially one used as a temporary place to stay: *My family gathered at our mountain **lodge** for the holidays.*
- ► **lodging** a place to live or stay: *He looked for temporary **lodging** until he had enough money for an apartment.*
- ► **lodgings** a rented room or rooms: *She has **lodgings** in a boarding house for theater students.*
- ► **motel** a hotel for motorists with parking spaces near the rooms: *The businessman stayed in a **motel** near the airport.*

hound *verb* to urge or ask someone over and over: *see* **nag**

house

noun a building serving as a residence for a person or persons, especially a family: *The real estate agent took the couple to look at several **houses**.*

- ► **apartment** a usually rented room or group of rooms to live in: *We live in a small **apartment** that has a balcony.*
- ► **cabin** a small, simply built house: *The family rented a small **cabin** by the lake.*
- ► **condominium** an apartment building in which the individual apartments are owned by the people living in them: *The retired man moved to a **condominium** in Florida.*
- ► **cottage** a small house in the country: *She dreams of living in a small white **cottage** in the English countryside.*
- ► **hut** a small, simple house or shelter: *They took shelter in a **hut** during the storm.*
- ► **palace** a ruler's official residence: *There are guards in front of the queen's **palace**.*

▸ **shack** a small, crudely built cabin: *The rancher stored miscellaneous equipment in the shack behind the barn.*

hover *verb* to stay in one place in the air: *see* **fly**

however *adverb* in whatever way: *see* **anyway**

however *conjunction* in spite of that: *see* **but**

howl *noun* a long, loud, mournful sound made by certain animals: *see* **bark**

hub *noun* a center of activity or interest: *see* **center** [1]

hubbub *noun* noisy confusion; uproar: *see* **noise**

hue *noun* the basic color of something: *see* **color**

hug *verb* to embrace someone tightly, especially to show affection: *see* **cuddle**

huge *adjective* extremely or impressively large: *see* **big**

hum

verb to make a low, droning sound; to sing something without opening the lips or forming words: *I hummed four notes of the song so she could get the melody.*

▸ **buzz** to make a low, droning or vibrating sound like that of a bee: *It was pleasant to listen to the insects buzz among the flowers.*
▸ **croon** to hum or sing something softly: *The father crooned a lullaby to his baby.*
▸ **drone** to make a continuous, dull humming sound: *The small airplane droned as it flew across the sky.*
▸ **purr** to make a soft, low, vibrant sound in the throat: *My cat purred when I petted it.*
▸ **whir** to make an airy buzzing or vibrating sound: *The fan whirred noisily overhead.*

human being *noun* a member of the human species; a man, woman, or child: *Human beings are now thought to have evolved in Africa over a period of several million years.*

▸ **being** someone or something that exists: *Science fiction is full of imaginary beings from other planets.*
▸ **individual** a single person or animal considered separately from a group: *There was a gift for each individual at the party.*
▸ **mortal** a human being, especially as distinct from a divine or mythological figure: *We are all mortals here on earth.*
▸ **person** a human being; an individual: *What is a person supposed to do in a situation like this?*
▸ **soul** the animating and vital force of human beings; a human being: *Not a soul was in sight.*

humane *adjective* showing kindness and thoughtful concern for people or animals: *see* **kind¹**

humiliate *verb* to deeply hurt someone's self-respect or pride: *see* **embarrass**

humiliation *noun* the state of feeling humiliated or disgraced: *see* **embarrassment**

humor *verb* to go along with the wishes or whims of someone: *see* **indulge**

humorous *adjective* funny, especially in the manner of a joke or amusing story: *see* **funny**

hunch *noun* a feeling or belief that one has without knowing for certain: *see* **intuition**

hunger

noun a strong desire for food: *Hunger drove the bears to come into camp and raid for food.*

▸ **appetite** an instinctive desire for something, especially food and drink: *I lost my appetite when I was sick.*
▸ **famine** an extreme and widespread lack of food: *The long drought resulted in a terrible famine.*
▸ **munchies** (informal) a craving for snack food: *I get the munchies when I watch TV.*
▸ **starvation** the condition or process of suffering from prolonged lack of food: *With the advances in modern agriculture, there is no reason for people to die of starvation.*

hunk *noun*   a large piece: *see* **chunk**

hunt *verb*   to make a careful search: *see* **search**

hurdle *noun*   an obstacle or difficulty to be overcome: *see* **obstacle**

hurl *verb*   to throw something with great force: *see* **throw**

hurricane *noun*   a very powerful tropical storm with extremely strong winds over 75 miles per hour: *see* **storm**

hurry

verb   to act or move quickly: *She **hurried** home from work.*

- ▸ **bustle**   to move around in a busy or excited way: *I **bustled** through the house as I got ready for my friend's visit.*
- ▸ **hustle**   to work or move energetically: *The mechanics **hustled** to change the tires when the racecar entered the pit.*
- ▸ **rush**   to move or act with great speed or eagerness: *They **rushed** to catch the train.*
- ▸ **scurry**   to move lightly or quickly: *The little girl **scurried** up the ladder into her tree house.*

hurt

verb   to cause pain or injury to a living thing: *I **hurt** myself when I fell down.*

- ▸ **abuse**   to hurt or injure someone by physical or psychological maltreatment: *People who **abuse** animals can be arrested.*
- ▸ **harm**   to do injury or damage to someone: *To my surprise, the cat didn't **harm** the bird.*
- ▸ **injure**   to cause physical harm to someone: *Were they **injured** when they fell from the wall?*
- ▸ **maim**   to disable someone badly: *He was **maimed** in the car accident.*
- ▸ **wound**   to hurt a person or animal by cutting or breaking the body: *The elk was **wounded** when it was hit by a speeding car.*

husband *noun*   a man who is married: *see* **spouse**

hushed *adjective*   free of most or all sound: *see* **quiet**

husky *adjective*   deep or rough in sound or voice: *see* **hoarse**

hustle *verb*   to work or move energetically: *see* **hurry**

hut *noun*   a small, simple house or shelter: *see* **house**

hymn *noun*   a song of joy, praise, or thanksgiving, especially one the that is sung to God: *see* **song**

hysterical *adjective*   so excited or upset that one laughs and cries uncontrollably: *see* **frantic**

icy *adjective* containing or covered with ice: *see* **cold**

idea

noun a thought or plan carefully formed in the mind: *Everyone had a different **idea** about where we should hold the family reunion.*

▸ **concept** a general idea: *Jules Verne wrote about the **concept** of space flight long before it was a reality.*

▸ **notion** a sudden inclination, impulse, or idea: *She had the **notion** to turn the garage into a greenhouse.*

▸ **thought** a result of thinking; an idea or group of ideas: *What are your **thoughts** on the project?*

ideal *adjective* meeting the highest standard of perfection or excellence: *see* **perfect**

idealistic *adjective* having the ability to envision things in their ideal form: *see* **optimistic**

ideology *noun* a set of doctrines or beliefs that is shared by members of a group: *see* **philosophy**

identical *adjective* being exactly alike: *see* **same**

identify *verb* to establish the identity of someone or something: *see* **recognize**

identity *noun* who a particular person is: *see* **personality**

idiot *noun* a stupid or bungling person: *see* **fool**

idiotic *adjective* showing great stupidity or foolishness: *see* **stupid**

idle *adjective* not working or being used: *see* **lazy**

idol *noun* a person who is admired or loved very much: *see* **hero**

idolize *verb* to regard someone with blind admiration: *see* **love**

ignite *verb* to start something suddenly: *see* **excite**

ignorant

adjective lacking education or knowledge: *I am **ignorant** of Chinese history.*

▸ **blind** unable or unwilling to notice or understand: *Many people are **blind** to the dangers of secondhand smoke.*

▸ **innocent** unaware of wrongdoing or evil: *The scientist was **innocent** of his partner's plans to steal credit for their research.*

▸ **naive** showing a lack of experience or judgment: *He felt **naive** when he started bargaining with the car salesman.*

▸ **oblivious** completely unaware, as from failure or inability to pay attention: *I was concentrating so hard on my work that I was **oblivious** to the conversations around me.*

▸ **unaware** not aware; not conscious: *She was **unaware** of how long she had talked on the phone.*

▸ **unsophisticated** inexperienced or naive; not worldly: *Most **unsophisticated** investors lose money in the stock market.*

ignore *verb* to completely and deliberately disregard someone or something: *see* **forget**

ill *adjective* not healthy: *see* **sick**

illness *noun* an often temporary condition of poor health: *see* **disease**

illusion

noun an unreal or misleading appearance or image: *The mural gave the **illusion** that there was really a door in the wall.*

▸ **delusion** a false belief or opinion: *We were under the **delusion** that we were going to get a tax refund this year.*

▸ **hallucination** an illusion of seeing, hearing, or otherwise being aware of something that does not really exist: *Some drugs cause **hallucinations**.*

▸ **image** a mental picture of something that is not real or present: *I have an **image** of what I want my bedroom to look like when I'm finished decorating it.*

▸ **mirage** an optical illusion in which something that is not really there appears to be seen in the distance: *The most common **mirage** is to see nonexistent water on a road.*

illustrate *verb* to explain or clarify something by using pictures or examples: *see* **explain**

illustration *noun* a picture, diagram, or map that explains or decorates something: *see* **picture**

ill will *noun* unfriendly feelings: *see* **hate**

image *noun* a mental picture of something that is not real or present: *see* **illusion**

image *noun* a reproduction of a person or object: *see* **picture**

imagination

noun the ability of the mind to form pictures of things that are not present or real; creative power: *The novelist created a whole town and its inhabitants from his **imagination**.*

▸ **creativity** the quality of being creative; originality and inventiveness: *The screenwriter was known for her **creativity** in writing witty dialogue.*

▸ **fantasy** an imaginary event or situation, especially one that fulfills a wish: *My **fantasy** is to become a famous dancer.*

▸ **inspiration** the power of exciting the mind or emotions: *The coach's speech to her team was full of **inspiration**.*

▸ **originality** the capability to think up new ideas: *Walt Disney showed great **originality** in creating some of the first animated cartoons.*

▸ **whimsy** creativity that is marked by playfulness and humor: *Alice in Wonderland is a book that is full of **whimsy**.*

imaginative *adjective* having a strong, creative imagination: *see* **creative**

imagine *verb* to form a mental picture or idea of something: *see* **think**

imbecile *noun* a stupid or silly person: *see* **fool**

imitate *verb* to follow something as a model or example: *see* **copy**

imitation *adjective* made to resemble another, usually superior item or material: *see* **fake**

immediate *adjective* taking place at once or very soon: *see* **sudden**

immediately

adverb without any time passing; without delay: *I returned her call **immediately**.*

▸ **at once** at this very moment; immediately: *I need to leave **at once** if I am going to catch the bus.*

▸ **instantly** in an instant; at once: *He picked up the burrito but set it down **instantly** because it was too hot.*

▸ **promptly** in a timely manner; without being late: *I like to arrive **promptly** at appointments.*

▸ **quickly** without wasting any time; with great speed: *I **quickly** washed the dishes so I wouldn't miss my favorite TV show.*

▸ **right away** without undue delay; soon: *I'll be with you **right away**.*

▸ **soon** within a short time; before long: *Will you be ready **soon**?*

▸ **suddenly** quickly, without warning; unexpectedly: *The car in front of us stopped **suddenly**.*

immense *adjective* of great or immeasurable size, extent, or degree: *see* **big**

immerse *verb* to cover something completely with a liquid: *see* **dip**

immigrant *noun* a person who leaves one country to settle permanently in another: *see* **stranger**

immobile *adjective* not capable of moving: *see* **stationary**

immoral *adjective* going against what is considered fair, right, or good: *see* **evil**

impact *noun*   the effect of something on an observer, reader, or listener: *see* **result**

impartial *adjective*   not favoring either side: *see* **fair¹**

impatient

adjective   not able or willing to wait calmly: *He became* **impatient** *with the slow service at the restaurant.*

- ▸ **anxious**   eagerly or earnestly desiring something: *I am* **anxious** *for you to meet my cousin.*
- ▸ **eager**   full of impatient desire; wishing immediate action: *I am* **eager** *to start my art class.*
- ▸ **excited**   emotionally stirred up or stimulated; active: *The fans became* **excited** *when the team scored a touchdown.*
- ▸ **restless**   unable to rest, relax, or be still: *The* **restless** *tiger paced back and forth in its cage.*

ANTONYM **patient**   able to put up with trouble, hardship, annoyance, or delay without complaining

impede *verb*   to make it difficult for something to move or advance: *see* **block**

imperfect *adjective*   flawed, but often still usable: *see* **bad [1]**

imperfection *noun*   a usually minor flaw in something: *see* **flaw**

implement *noun*   a specially made object used in doing a task or a kind of work: *see* **tool**

implore *verb*   to ask someone urgently or anxiously for something: *see* **beg**

imply *verb*   to say or mean something without expressing it directly: *see* **mean²**

impolite *adjective*   discourteous: *see* **rude**

important *adjective*   strongly affecting the course of events: *see* **serious [2]**

impose *verb*   to establish something as compulsory: *see* **dictate**

impossible *adjective*   not capable of happening or existing: *see* **incredible**

imposter

noun   a person who tries to fool people by pretending to be someone else: *The man claimed to be a movie director, but he was an* **imposter.**

- ▸ **con artist**   a swindler who tricks someone into doing something by first winning the person's confidence: *The* **con artist** *convinced her clients to buy stock in a company that didn't exist.*
- ▸ **fraud**   one who assumes a false pose; an imposter: *The professor was a* **fraud** *who presented his students' work as his own.*
- ▸ **liar**   a person who says things that are not true: *Don't believe him, he's a* **liar.**
- ▸ **swindler**   a person who cheats someone out of money or property: *The man was a* **swindler** *who overcharged his customers.*

impressive *adjective*   making a strong or vivid impression: *see* **awesome**

imprison *verb*   to put someone in prison: *see* **punish**

impromptu *adjective*   spoken or done with little or no preparation: *see* **spontaneous**

improve *verb*   to increase the quality, value, or performance of something: *see* **better**

impulse

noun   a sudden wish or urge to do something: *We had a sudden* **impulse** *to go visit the neighborhood where I grew up.*

- ▸ **caprice**   (formal) an impulsive notion or change of mind; a whim: *She went shopping for school clothes, but on a* **caprice**, *she bought a pair of fancy boots instead.*
- ▸ **spur**   something that urges one to action; a stimulus: *His good example served as a* **spur** *for me to start exercising.*
- ▸ **whim**   a sudden wish, desire, or idea: *I don't read much, but I bought this book on a* **whim.**

impulsive *adjective*   acting on impulse rather than by thinking things through or planning carefully: *see* **spontaneous**

in

preposition within the bounds or area of something: *I put the dishes in the cupboard after I finished drying them.*

▸ **inside** within the inner part, side, or surface of something: *The air conditioner kept it nice and cool inside the car.*

▸ **into** to the inside of something: *She lost her keys and got into the house through a window.*

▸ **within** inside the limits or extent of something: *We are within ten miles of home.*

inactive *adjective* not active or functioning: *see* **lazy**

in addition *adverb* also; as well as: *see* **also**

incalculable *adjective* too large in number to be calculated: *see* **infinite**

incapable *adjective* lacking the ability to do something: *see* **helpless**

incentive *noun* something that urges a person to do something or make a special effort: *see* **motive**

incident *noun* a particular occurrence, especially one of minor importance: *see* **event**

inclination *noun* a tendency based on personal preference: *see* **tendency**

inclined *adjective* having a preference or tendency: *see* **prone**

include

verb to be made up of something, at least in part: *The price of the meal includes a drink and French fries.*

▸ **contain** to have or hold something within: *This folder contains all the reports I wrote this year.*

▸ **incorporate** to put something into a single larger thing; to include: *The new version of the computer program incorporates all the best features of the old one.*

▸ **integrate** to combine an item or group of items into a whole; to unite: *The teacher integrated math, history, art, and geography in the unit on Africa.*

▸ **involve** to include something as a necessary part or feature: *His job involves a great deal or traveling.*

ANTONYM **exclude** to leave someone or something out; to omit something

income

noun the amount of money that a person or business receives during a certain time: *My sister's after-school job is her only source of income.*

▸ **allowance** an amount, as of money or food, given at regular intervals or for a specific purpose: *My company gives a travel allowance to its salespeople.*

▸ **commission** money paid to someone for each piece of work done or for each thing sold: *A real estate agent gets a commission on each house he or she sells.*

▸ **pay** money given in exchange for goods or services: *I got a new job with good pay.*

▸ **pension** a sum of money paid regularly to people who are retired: *She will be eligible for a full pension after the age of 65.*

▸ **revenue** money that a government collects, as through taxes: *School districts are supported by bonds and tax revenues.*

▸ **royalty** a fixed percentage of money paid to a writer or a composer resulting from the sale or performance of his or her work: *The author's royalties were enough to buy a new car.*

▸ **salary** a fixed sum of money that is paid to a person on a regular basis for doing a job: *The salaries of government workers are public information.*

▸ **wage** payment for work or services: *It is hard to save any money when you work for the minimum wage.*

incompatible *adjective* not capable of existing in agreement or harmony with something else: *see* **different**

incompetent *adjective* not capable of doing a good job: *see* **helpless**

inconsiderate *adjective* not considerate of others: *see* **rude**

incorporate *verb* to put something into a single larger thing: *see* **include**

incorrect *adjective* not correct: *see* **wrong**

increase

verb to become larger in size, number, or power: *The world's population is increasing by an estimated 80 to 90 million people a year.*

- ▸ **enlarge** to make something larger: *The city is planning to enlarge the airport by building two new runways.*
- ▸ **exaggerate** to claim that something is greater or larger than it actually is: *He exaggerated the amount of time he spent studying for the test.*
- ▸ **expand** to increase in size, volume, amount, or scope: *A balloon expands when you blow air into it.*
- ▸ **inflate** to fill something with gas and expand it: *He can inflate a balloon with just one breath.*
- ▸ **magnify** to enlarge the appearance of something: *I used a microscope to magnify the cells so that I could study them.*
- ▸ **swell** to increase in size or volume as a result of pressure from the inside: *My finger swelled from the bee sting.*

ANTONYM **decrease** to become less or smaller in size, number, or power

incredible

adjective too unlikely to be believed: *Your excuse about aliens stealing your homework is incredible.*

- ▸ **doubtful** open to doubt or suspicion; not reliable: *That businessman has a doubtful reputation.*
- ▸ **far-fetched** hard to believe: *He told us a far-fetched story about meeting Bigfoot in the forest.*
- ▸ **impossible** not capable of happening or existing: *It is impossible to be at two places at the same time.*
- ▸ **unbelievable** not to be believed in; incredible: *People often tell stories that seem unbelievable but later are proved to be true.*
- ▸ **unlikely** not having a strong chance of happening; not likely to be true: *She thought it unlikely that what she saw in the sky was a UFO.*

indignation *noun* anger aroused by something unjust, mean, or unworthy: *see* **anger**

indebted *adjective* morally, socially, or legally obligated to another: *see* **grateful**

indeed *adverb* in fact; actually: *see* **certainly**

indefinite *adjective* not clearly defined: *see* **vague**

independence *noun* the condition of being independent: *see* **freedom**

independent

adjective free from the influence, guidance, or control of another or others: *My brother feels very independent now that he has his own apartment.*

- ▸ **free** not controlled by another or others; able to do, act, or think as one wishes: *The prisoner was free after serving a five-year sentence.*
- ▸ **self-sufficient** able to provide for oneself without help; independent: *Parents are responsible for teaching their children how to be self-sufficient.*
- ▸ **sovereign** self-governing; independent: *The United States became a sovereign nation on September 3, 1783.*

ANTONYM **dependent** relying on someone else for help or support

independently *adverb* apart from another: *see* **alone**

indicate *verb* to show or point something out: *see* **signal**

indication *noun* something that shows or points something out: *see* **sign**

indistinct *adjective* not clearly heard, seen, or understood: *see* **faint**

individual *noun* a single person or animal considered separately from a group: *see* **human being**

individually *adverb* one at a time: *see* **alone**

induce *verb* to persuade or influence someone: *see* **persuade**

indulge

verb to yield too easily to the desires of one-self or another: *I* **indulged** *my craving for something sweet and bought an ice-cream cone.*

- ▶ **accommodate** to do someone a favor or satisfy someone's request: *She* **accommodated** *the patient by finding him a room with a television.*
- ▶ **baby** to treat someone like a baby, as by giving constant attention: *I* **babied** *my roommate when she was sick.*
- ▶ **coddle** to treat someone tenderly or overprotectively: *My grandmother* **coddled** *my grandfather when he came home from the hospital.*
- ▶ **humor** to go along with the wishes or whims of someone: *I* **humor** *my little brother by playing board games with him.*
- ▶ **oblige** to do a service or favor for someone: *My friend* **obliged** *me by giving me a ride home.*
- ▶ **pamper** to treat someone with extreme indulgence, especially in an attempt to satisfy luxurious desires: *I decided to* **pamper** *myself by getting a professional manicure.*
- ▶ **spoil** to do harm to someone's character by overindulgence or by praising too much: *They* **spoil** *their children by buying them everything they want.*

indulgent

adjective yielding too often or too easily to someone's desires of someone: *My grandparents are* **indulgent** *toward their grandchildren.*

- ▶ **easygoing** not strict or demanding; relaxed: *The man next door lives an* **easygoing** *life since he retired.*
- ▶ **lenient** inclined not to be harsh or strict; generous or tolerant: *My father was* **lenient** *the first time I arrived home late after being out with my friends.*
- ▶ **permissive** allowing much freedom; tolerant or lenient: *Our manager is* **permissive** *about the hours we work as long as we get our work done.*

industrious *adjective* working hard as a steady habit: *see* **busy**

industry *noun* the production and manufacture of goods or commodities on a large scale: *see* **business [2]**

inept *adjective* lacking skill or competence: *see* **awkward**

inexpensive *adjective* low to moderate in price: *see* **cheap**

inexperienced

adjective lacking experience or the knowledge gained from experience: *They hired me even though I was* **inexperienced** *at working the cash register.*

- ▶ **green** (informal) lacking training or experience: *The other workers teased me at first because I was so* **green**.
- ▶ **new** inexperienced or untrained: *The* **new** *recruits soon learned the importance of keeping their equipment in good order.*
- ▶ **raw** untrained and inexperienced: *The coach transformed the* **raw** *players into a skilled team.*
- ▶ **unskilled** lacking skill or technical training: **Unskilled** *workers usually make less money than those with special training.*

infant *noun* a child in the earliest period of life: *see* **child**

inferior *adjective* low in quality or value: *see* **bad [1]**

infinite

adjective having or seeming to have no limits; endless: *The number of stars in the sky seems* **infinite**.

- ▶ **boundless** having no known limits; infinite: *His enthusiasm for fishing is* **boundless**.
- ▶ **incalculable** too great or too large in number to be calculated: *There was* **incalculable** *damage from the earthquake.*
- ▶ **limitless** having no limit or boundary; unrestricted or infinite: *The open ocean seems* **limitless**.
- ▶ **unlimited** having no limits or bounds: *The doctor's discovery has* **unlimited** *possibilities.*

inflame *verb* to stir up anger or other strong emotion in someone: *see* **excite**

inflate *verb* to fill something with gas and expand it: *see* **increase**

inflexible *adjective* not bending at all: *see* **stiff**

influence *verb* to cause changes or have an effect on someone or something without using direct force: *see* **shape**

influential *adjective* having the power to cause changes or produce an effect: *see* **powerful**

inform *verb* to tell someone about something specific: *see* **tell**

informal *adjective* made or done without following set rules or custom; casual: *see* **casual**

information *noun* knowledge and understanding derived from study, experience, or instruction: *see* **fact**

infrequently *adverb* not very often and not on a regular basis: *see* **rarely**

infuriate *verb* to make someone intensely or violently angry: *see* **anger**

ingenious *adjective* marked by inventive skill and imagination: *see* **creative**

ingredient

noun one of the parts that make up a mixture or combination: *Milk and ice cream are the main **ingredients** of a milk shake.*

- ▶ **component** one of the parts that make up a whole: *A modem and a sound card are **components** of a home computer.*
- ▶ **element** a basic or essential part of a whole: *The **elements** of a successful movie include an interesting story and good acting.*
- ▶ **factor** something that helps bring about a certain result: *Age is a **factor** that is considered when movies are assigned ratings.*

inhabit *verb* to live or reside in a place: *see* **dwell**

inhabitant *noun* a resident of a place, such as a neighborhood, city, or region: *see* **occupant**

inhibit *verb* to restrain or hold someone back: *see* **suppress**

initial *adjective* of or happening at the very beginning: *see* **original [2]**

initiate *verb* to take a first step toward something: *see* **begin**

initiative *noun* the ability to begin or carry out a task or plan: *see* **will**

injure *verb* to cause physical harm to someone: *see* **hurt**

inlet *noun* a small or narrow body of water, as a bay or cove, along a coast: *see* **harbor**

inn *noun* a place that offers meals and lodging for travelers: *see* **hotel**

innocent *adjective* unaware of wrongdoing or evil: *see* **ignorant**

innovative *adjective* new and different: *see* **creative**

inquire *verb* to seek information by asking questions: *see* **ask**

inquiring *adjective* moved to find things out, especially by asking questions: *see* **curious**

inquisitive *adjective* habitually curious, especially about other people's lives: *see* **curious**

insane *adjective* affected with mental illness: *see* **mentally ill**

inscribe *verb* to write, print, carve, or engrave something: *see* **write**

insecure *adjective* lacking self-confidence: *see* **shy**

insecure *adjective* not sure or certain: *see* **unstable**

inside *preposition* within the inner part of something: *see* **in**

insignificant *adjective* of little importance: *see* **unimportant**

insincere *adjective* saying one thing and doing or thinking another: *see* **dishonest**

insist *verb* to assert or demand something forcefully and persistently: *see* **demand**

inspect *verb* to examine something carefully: *see* **examine**

inspiration *noun* the power of exciting the mind or emotions: *see* **imagination**

inspire *verb* to stimulate someone to creativity or action: *see* **encourage**

inspiring *adjective* arousing great emotion that moves a person to action: *see* **exciting**

instance *noun* a particular occurrence: *see* **example**

instant *noun* a very brief period of time: *see* **moment**

instantly *adverb* at once: *see* **immediately**

instinct *noun* an inner feeling or way of behaving that is automatic rather than learned: *see* **intuition**

institute *noun* a place for specialized study: *see* **school**

institution *noun* an established custom, practice, or pattern of behavior: *see* **tradition**

instruct *verb* to teach someone in an organized way: *see* **teach**

instruction *noun* something that is taught: *see* **education**

instructor *noun* a person who instructs: *see* **teacher**

instrument *noun* a tool used for a special purpose: *see* **tool**

insult *verb* to treat someone rudely or disrespectfully, especially on purpose: *see* **offend**

integrate *verb* to combine an item or group of items into a whole: *see* **include**

intelligence *noun* the ability to learn, think, and understand: *see* **wisdom**

intelligent *adjective* able to learn, think, understand, and know: *see* **smart**

intent *noun* something done or attempted on purpose: *see* **goal**

intention *noun* a goal that guides one's actions: *see* **goal**

intentionally *adverb* with conscious intent: *see* **deliberately**

interest

verb to arouse someone's curiosity or hold someone's attention: *Everything about airplanes **interests** me.*

- ▶ **attract** to cause someone to draw near or take notice: *The sound of the can opener always **attracts** my cat to the kitchen.*
- ▶ **engage** to hold someone's attention closely: *My uncle and I were totally **engaged** in my new computer game and lost track of time.*
- ▶ **fascinate** to attract and hold someone's attention as if unable to turn away: *We were **fascinated** by the glass blowers.*
- ▶ **intrigue** to arouse someone's curiosity or wonder: *Many people are **intrigued** by the pyramids and how they were built.*

interesting

adjective arousing or holding interest or attention: *She told us an **interesting** story about communicating with dolphins.*

- ▶ **alluring** having the power to attract, especially by arousing desire; tempting: *Her perfume was **alluring**.*
- ▶ **absorbing** holding one's complete interest or attention: *The novel was so **absorbing** that I didn't want to stop reading.*
- ▶ **entertaining** causing time to pass pleasantly; amusing; agreeably diverting: *The **entertaining** movie made us all laugh.*
- ▶ **fascinating** absorbing one's interest and attention; captivating: *Our teacher has the ability to make learning **fascinating**.*
- ▶ **glamorous** having or showing romantic charm or excitement: *The fashion model leads a **glamorous** life.*

ANTONYM **boring** not interesting; dull

interfere

verb to get in the way of something so as to hinder or stop it: *The rain **interfered** with our plans to go on a picnic.*

▶ **intervene** to come between people or events, especially in order to stop or change something: *My mother intervened when my brother and I were arguing.*

▶ **meddle** to interfere in other people's business: *I told my friend to stop meddling in my love life.*

▶ **pry** to inquire inappropriately into private matters: *It's not polite to pry into other people's affairs.*

▶ **tamper** to interfere in a harmful manner: *They were caught tampering with the telephone in an effort to get free calls.*

▶ **snoop** to pry into the private affairs of others, especially by prowling about: *Her brother snooped in her diary.*

intermission *noun* an interruption in activity, as between the acts of a play: *see* **break**

intermittent *adjective* stopping and starting at intervals: *see* **irregular**

international

adjective relating to or carried on between two or more countries or peoples: *The first international conference on environmental pollution was held in 1972.*

▶ **global** relating to the entire earth; worldwide: *What is the global population?*

▶ **universal** relating to or affecting the whole world: *Esperanto was developed in hopes that it would become a universal language.*

▶ **worldwide** involving or extending throughout the entire world: *The famous music group has a worldwide following.*

interpret *verb* to explain the meaning or importance of something complicated: *see* **explain**

interrogate *verb* to seek information from someone by close questioning: *see* **examine**

interrupt *verb* to stop the action of someone or something: *see* **disturb**

interval *noun* a period of time between two events or actions: *see* **break**

intervene *verb* to come between people or events, especially in order to stop or change something: *see* **interfere**

interview *noun* a formal conversation between two people during which one person asks for facts or information from the other: *see* **talk**

intimate *adjective* marked by familiarity or close association: *see* **personal**

intimidate *verb* to frighten or discourage someone, as with threats or superior force: *see* **scare**

into *preposition* to the inside of something: *see* **in**

intricate *adjective* complicated or complex: *see* **fancy**

intrigue *verb* to arouse someone's curiosity or wonder: *see* **interest**

introduce *verb* to bring something new into use or practice: *see* **begin**

introduce *verb* to provide someone with a first experience or a beginning knowledge of something: *see* **teach**

intrude *verb* to break or come in without being wanted or asked: *see* **disturb**

intuition

noun the power of knowing or understanding something without reasoning or proof: *My intuition told me not to trust him.*

▶ **hunch** a feeling or belief that one has without knowing for certain: *He had a hunch that there would be a quiz in English class today.*

▶ **instinct** an inner feeling or way of behaving that is automatic rather that learned: *Spiders spin their webs by instinct.*

▶ **sense** an intuitive or acquired feeling about something: *The singer's sense of timing was very good.*

▶ **suspicion** a feeling or belief, especially that something is wrong or bad, but with little evidence to support it: *She had a suspicion that the weather would delay their trip.*

invade *verb* to enter a place in great numbers for purposes of attacking or raiding: *see* **attack**

invent

verb to produce or create something new by using the imagination: *Alexander Graham Bell invented the telephone in 1876.*

▸ **conceive** to develop something in one's mind; to think something up: *Isaac Newton is said to have conceived the idea of gravity when he saw an apple fall from a tree.*

▸ **concoct** to devise something using skill and intelligence: *She concocted a delicious soup with leftover meat and vegetables.*

▸ **create** to bring something into being: *The new factory is expected to create many new jobs.*

▸ **develop** to make something more effective or advanced: *Education and experience develop a person's mind.*

▸ **devise** to form something, such as a plan or invention, in one's mind: *He devised a simple way to keep the window open by using a stick.*

▸ **pioneer** to initiate or participate in the development of something new: *Nicholas Tesla pioneered several applications of high-voltage electricity.*

invention

noun an original device, system, or process: *Thomas Edison created many well-known inventions, including the microphone and the first practical light bulb.*

▸ **concoction** something prepared or created, especially a mixture of different ingredients: *Her story was a concoction of truth and fiction.*

▸ **creation** an original product of human invention or artistic imagination: *The seven-layer wedding cake was a wonderful creation that took several hours to make.*

▸ **discovery** something found, seen, or learned for the first time: *The structure of DNA is one of the great discoveries of modern science.*

▸ **opus** a creative work, especially a musical piece: *Brandenburg Concerto #1 is an opus by J.S. Bach.*

inventive *adjective* having the ability to produce something new and creative: *see* **creative**

inventory *noun* the supply of goods on hand, as in a store or school: *see* **supply**

investigate *verb* to research something carefully: *see* **examine**

invite *verb* to ask someone to come somewhere or do something: *see* **ask**

invoice *noun* a bill that lists all goods delivered or services performed: *see* **bill**

involve *verb* to include something as a necessary part or feature: *see* **include**

involved *adjective* closely occupied or engaged in something: *see* **busy**

irate *adjective* extremely angry or upset: *see* **angry**

irk *verb* to cause someone to be frustrated or angry: *see* **annoy**

irregular

adjective uneven in occurrence or rate: *The patient had an irregular heartbeat.*

▸ **intermittent** stopping and starting at intervals: *The beacon sent out intermittent flashes of light.*

▸ **occasional** occurring from time to time: *The weather has been fine except for an occasional afternoon rain shower.*

▸ **periodic** happening or repeating at regular intervals: *Victims of malaria have periodic bouts of fever.*

irresponsible *adjective* lacking a sense of responsibility: *see* **careless**

irritable

adjective easily annoyed or angered: *Lack of sleep can make a person irritable.*

▸ **cranky** in a bad mood; irritable: *Little children often get cranky if they stay up too late.*

▸ **cross** angry or annoyed: *My father was cross with me because I left his tools outside.*

▸ **fussy** easily upset, especially over small matters: *She becomes fussy if her food is not prepared right.*

▸ **grouchy** cross, grumbling, or complaining: *We can't do anything about the weather so why be grouchy about it?*

▸ **grumpy** easily angered or upset: *My brother is grumpy when he first gets up.*

▸ **peevish** ill-humored and easily annoyed: *Some people become peevish when they are sick.*

▸ **testy** irritable, impatient, or exasperated: *The man was testy because the traffic was moving slowly.*

ANTONYM **pleasant** pleasing in manner; friendly

irritate *verb* to make someone angry or impatient: *see* **annoy**

irritated *adjective* angry and impatient: *see* **angry**

issue *noun* something that is being discussed or argued about: *see* **topic**

J

jab *verb* to poke or pierce someone or something with something pointed: *see* **poke**

jagged *adjective* having sharp notches or indentations: *see* **rough**

jail

noun a place for keeping people who are waiting for trial or are serving sentences for crimes: *The drunk driver was sentenced to spend time in jail.*

> ► **brig** a prison on a ship: *The unruly sailor was put in the brig.*
>
> ► **cell** a small room, as in a prison or convent, having little or no furniture: *The monks live in small individual cells in the monastery.*
>
> ► **dungeon** a dark, underground prison: *We toured the dungeons that were below the castle.*
>
> ► **prison** a place where people convicted or accused of crimes are confined: *The robbers were caught and sent to prison.*

jam *verb* to squeeze or wedge something roughly into a space: *see* **fill**

jar *noun* a container with a wide mouth and no handles, usually made of glass or plastic: *see* **bottle**

jaunt *noun* a short trip taken for fun: *see* **journey**

jealous

adjective fearful of losing one's position or someone's affection to another person: *He was jealous when his parents praised his sister for her good grades.*

> ► **covetous** wanting something that belongs to another: *I am covetous of the beautiful clothes the girl next door is always wearing.*
>
> ► **distrustful** feeling or showing doubt; suspicious: *I am distrustful of telephone solicitors who tell me how much money I can save with their plan.*
>
> ► **envious** resenting the advantages or success of another person and wanting them for oneself: *I am envious of my friend's new apartment.*
>
> ► **possessive** having a desire to dominate or control: *He is very possessive of his car and doesn't let anyone else drive it.*
>
> ► **suspicious** tending to have doubts about something or someone; distrustful: *He was suspicious that the mechanic was charging him for repairs that weren't needed.*

jealousy *noun* a feeling of concern that one will lose one's position or someone's affection to another person: *see* **resentment**

jeer *verb* to speak or shout in a mocking or scornful way: *see* **scorn**

jeopardy *noun* danger of dying, being injured, or being lost: *see* **danger**

jerk *verb* to make something move with sudden, sharp motions: *see* **pull**

jest *noun* something said or done for fun or amusement: *see* **joke**

jewelry *noun* ornaments for the body, often made of precious metals and gems: *see* **accessory**

jiffy *noun* (informal) a moment: *see* **moment**

jingle *noun* a simple, catchy verse or song, often used in radio or television commercials: *see* **song**

job

noun a regular activity performed in exchange for payment: *She has a new job as a restaurant cook.*

> ► **career** a profession or occupation that a person follows as a life's work: *He is planning a career in law enforcement.*
>
> ► **employment** the work in which one is engaged or the activity to which one

devotes time: *He is looking for employment in the aerospace industry.*

▸ **occupation**   a profession, business, or job: *What is your occupation?*

▸ **profession**   an occupation, such as law or medicine, that requires training and special study: *Teaching is an honorable profession.*

▸ **trade**   an occupation, especially one that requires skilled labor; a craft: *I plan to learn a trade after graduating from high school.*

▸ **vocation**   a profession or occupation, especially one for which a person is particularly suited or qualified: *Dr. Albert Schweitzer's vocation led him to set up a medical clinic in Africa.*

jog *verb*   to run at a slow, steady pace: *see* run

join

verb   to bring two or more things together, as by fastening: *A special mechanism is used to join railroad cars together.*

▸ **bind**   to fasten something together by or as if by tying: *I used a rubber band to bind my hair in a pony tail.*

▸ **connect**   to link two or more things together; to join: *The chunnel is an underground rail tunnel that connects Great Britain and France.*

▸ **link**   to join or connect with or as if with a chain: *Railroads were built to link cities together.*

▸ **merge**   to bring two things together so as to form a single unit; to unite: *The two departments were merged to form a large corporation.*

▸ **tie**   to fasten or secure something with a cord or rope: *I tied a tarp over the stack of firewood to keep it dry.*

▸ **unite**   to bring two or more things together so as to form a whole: *Chief Tecumseh's dream was to unite all North American tribes into one Indian nation.*

ANTONYM **separate**   to divide something into parts or sections

joint

adjective   done or shared by two or more people or groups: *My mother and father have a joint checking account.*

▸ **combined**   joined together; united: *We were able to move the heavy log with our combined strength.*

▸ **mutual**   shared in common between two people or groups: *My friend and I have a mutual love of dancing.*

▸ **shared**   used or experienced in common with another or others: *Our shared experiences have strengthened our friendship.*

▸ **united**   combined into one: *The neighborhoods made a united effort to eliminate gang activity.*

joint

noun   a place where two or more things come to together: *I assembled the model spaceship by snapping the joints together.*

▸ **connection**   the point at which something is joined or fastened together: *My car wouldn't start because the battery connections were loose.*

▸ **corner**   the point or place at which two lines or surfaces meet: *He lives on the corner of Cedar Street and Lakeview Drive.*

▸ **elbow**   something having a bend or an angle similar to an elbow in a human being: *The plumber used an elbow to run the pipe around the corner.*

▸ **hinge**   a device with joints on which something turns: *I put some oil on the squeaky hinge.*

▸ **seam**   a line, fold, or groove formed by joining two pieces together at their edges: *The seam of his pants ripped.*

joke

noun   something, such as a trick or short story, that is meant to be funny: *I forgot the punch line to the joke I was telling.*

▸ **gag**   a playful joke or trick: *My brother's favorite gag is to put ketchup on his shirt and say that it's blood.*

▶ **hoax**   a trick or an act intended to deceive others: *The letter that said I was the winner of a new car turned out to be a **hoax**.*

▶ **jest**   something said or done for fun or amusement: *The President made a **jest** that caused the reporters to laugh.*

▶ **practical joke**   a mischievous trick, especially one that causes embarrassment or discomfort: *He put salt in the sugar bowl as a **practical joke**.*

▶ **prank**   a mischievous trick or practical joke: *I played a **prank** on my brother by hiding his keys.*

▶ **trick**   a mischievous action; a prank: *I set her alarm clock ahead an hour as a **trick**.*

jolly *adjective*   full of good spirits and fun: *see* **happy**

jostle *verb*   to shove and push against one another, as in a crowd: *see* **push**

jot *verb*   to write something down quickly or in a short form: *see* **write**

journal *noun*   a periodical presenting articles on a particular subject: *see* **magazine**

journal *noun*   a record that is kept on a regular basis: *see* **report**

journalist *noun*   one who writes for a newspaper or magazine: *see* **writer**

journey

noun   travel from one place to another: *Marco Polo's famous **journey** to China lasted 24 years.*

▶ **excursion**   a short pleasure trip: *My friends and I took an **excursion** to Coney Island during the summer.*

▶ **jaunt**   a short trip taken for fun: *We were restless and decided to go on a weekend **jaunt** to the lake.*

▶ **pilgrimage**   a journey to a sacred place or shrine: *Millions of Muslims make the **pilgrimage** to Mecca every year.*

▶ **tour**   a trip during which many interesting places are visited: *We took a **tour** of the historic sites of Florence, Italy.*

▶ **trek**   a journey or trip, especially one involving difficulty or hardship: *My aunt and uncle are planning a **trek** through the Himalayas.*

▶ **trip**   a going from one place to another; a journey: *We made a **trip** to Mexico to visit our relatives.*

▶ **voyage**   a long journey to a distant place, made on a ship or airplane: *Captain James Cook discovered the Sandwich Islands on his third **voyage** to the South Pacific.*

journey *verb*   to travel, especially over a great distance: *see* **travel**

joy *noun*   unrestrained happiness or delight: *see* **happiness**

joyful *adjective*   feeling or showing joy: *see* **happy**

jubilee *noun*   a special anniversary, such as a 25th or 50th: *see* **fair²**

judge

noun   a public official who makes decisions about cases in a court of law: *The **judge** finalized my family's adoption of my little sister.*

▶ **arbitrator**   a person chosen to settle a dispute or controversy: *Management and labor agreed to have an **arbitrator** settle their dispute.*

▶ **critic**   a person whose job it is to analyze and evaluate books, movies, or other artistic efforts: *The movie **critic** has a popular television program.*

▶ **mediator**   a person or agency that works with all sides in order to bring about agreement in a dispute: *My mother often acts as a **mediator** in arguments between my sisters.*

▶ **referee**   an official who enforces the rules in a sporting event: *The **referee** called a time-out.*

▶ **umpire**   a person who rules on plays in sports, such as baseball: *The third-base **umpire** declared the runner safe.*

judge

verb   to form an opinion about something or someone: *One way to **judge** the quality of a garment is to examine the seams.*

▸ **appraise** to judge the quality, importance, or value of something: *The jeweler **appraised** the customer's ring at $250.*

▸ **assess** to determine the value, significance, or extent of something: *The insurance company is sending an agent to **assess** the damage from the storm.*

▸ **evaluate** to find out, judge, or estimate the value of something: *I **evaluated** my wardrobe to see what clothes I needed to buy for my new job.*

▸ **grade** to give a mark or grade to something: *Lumber is **graded** according to its quality.*

▸ **rank** to assign something to a position on a scale or in a group: *I **ranked** my CDs on the shelf in the order that I like to listen to them.*

▸ **score** to evaluate and assign a grade to something: *The teacher **scored** our tests and gave them back to us.*

judgment *noun* an opinion made after careful consideration: *see* **decision**

jug *noun* a tall, rounded vessel with a handle and a narrow mouth: *see* **bottle**

juice

noun a liquid contained in meats or in the fruit, stem, or roots of plants: *I like orange **juice** for breakfast.*

▸ **fluid** a substance, such as air or water, that flows easily and takes the shape of its container: *All liquids and gases are **fluids**.*

▸ **liquid** a substance that flows easily and is hard to compress: *Water, oil, and milk are all **liquids**.*

▸ **nectar** a sweet liquid found in many flowers: *The hummingbird sipped the **nectar** of the hibiscus.*

▸ **sap** the liquid that flows through plant tissues, carrying water and food: *Maple syrup is made from the **sap** of the sugar maple tree.*

▸ **syrup** a thick, sweet liquid, as that made by boiling sugar and water: *One of the ingredients of pecan pie is corn **syrup**.*

jumble *noun* a group of things that is mixed or thrown together without any order: *see* **mess**

jumbo *adjective* extra large; oversized: *see* **big**

jump

verb to rise up or move through the air by using the leg muscles: *Our dog **jumped** onto the couch as soon as we left the house.*

▸ **bounce** to come back or up after hitting a surface: *I **bounced** up and down on the trampoline.*

▸ **bound** to leap forward or upward in long strides: *The deer **bounded** away.*

▸ **hop** to move with light, quick leaps or jumps: *A rabbit **hopped** across the golf course.*

▸ **leap** to jump quickly or suddenly, especially over a long distance: *A kangaroo can **leap** more than 25 feet in a single bound.*

▸ **lunge** to make a sudden, forceful movement forward: *When I dangled a toy mouse in front of my kitten, she **lunged** for it.*

▸ **skip** to move forward by stepping and hopping lightly: *The little girl **skipped** down the sidewalk.*

▸ **vault** to jump or leap over something, especially with the help of one's hands or a pole: *I **vaulted** over the fence in an attempt to catch the bus.*

jumpy *adjective* easily upset or startled: *see* **nervous**

jungle *noun* a very heavy growth of trees covering a large area: *see* **wilderness**

junk *noun* unwanted or discarded materials that can often be used again in some way: *see* **garbage**

just *adjective* following what is right and fair: *see* **fair**[1]

just *adverb* merely: *see* **only**

justice

noun the quality of being just or fair: *The reporter investigated both sides of the story due to his sense of **justice**.*

► **due process** an established process that is designed to protect the legal rights of an individual: *Every U.S. citizen is entitled to due process of law.*

► **equity** the state of being just and impartial; fairness: *The agency prides itself on treating all its clients with equity and respect.*

► **fairness** the state of being free from favoritism or bias; the act of being fair to all parties: *The instructor is known for her fairness to students.*

juvenile *noun* a young person, especially in a legal context: *see* **teenager**

K

karma *noun*   the belief that a person's conduct determines his or her destiny: *see* **destiny**

keen *adjective*   full of eager enthusiasm: *see* **enthusiastic**

keep

verb   to hold something in one's possession; to have something and not give it up: *Can I keep the book I borrowed for another week?*

- ► **conserve**   to use something carefully, so as not to waste or harm it: *We were asked to conserve water during the drought.*
- ► **maintain**   to keep something in a desirable condition: *I watch my diet in order to maintain my weight.*
- ► **preserve**   to protect something, as from injury or destruction: *Everyone should help to preserve our natural resources.*
- ► **retain**   to continue to keep something, especially when it might be easily lost: *A thick layer of blubber helps whales to retain body heat, even in arctic waters.*

ANTONYM **discard**   to throw away or get rid of something

keepsake *noun*   something that is kept in memory of a person or an occasion: *see* **souvenir**

keg *noun*   a small wooden or metal barrel: *see* **barrel**

kennel *noun*   a small shelter for one or more dogs: *see* **cage**

kernel *noun*   a grain or seed, especially of a cereal plant: *see* **seed**

kettle *noun*   a metal pot, usually with a lid: *see* **bucket**

key *noun*   being the most important element: *see* **basic**

kick *verb*   to strike out at someone or something with the foot or feet: *see* **hit**

kick out *verb*   (slang)   to throw someone out: *see* **throw out**

kid *noun*   (informal)   a child or young person: *see* **child**

kid *verb*   to make fun of someone in a friendly or affectionate manner: *see* **tease**

kidnap *verb*   to carry off and hold someone by force, usually for a ransom: *see* **steal**

kill

verb   to cause the death of someone or something: *I don't kill spiders because they eat flies.*

- ► **assassinate**   to murder a prominent person by surprise attack: *President Lincoln was assassinated five days after the Civil War ended.*
- ► **execute**   to put a person to death, especially as legal punishment for a crime: *The traitor was executed by a firing squad.*
- ► **exterminate**   to get rid of living things by destroying them completely: *We had to exterminate a colony of termites that were damaging our home.*
- ► **massacre**   to kill a large number of human beings or animals in a cruel and indiscriminate way: *The troops massacred the villagers.*
- ► **murder**   to unlawfully and deliberately kill a human being: *He was accused of murdering the bank teller during the robbery.*
- ► **slaughter**   ▷ to kill domestic animals for food: *The rancher sold some of his cows to be slaughtered.* ▷ to kill large numbers of people or animals indiscriminately: *The soldiers were slaughtered by machine-gun fire as they tried to storm the enemy position.*
- ► **slay**   to kill someone or something violently: *This movie is about a knight who slays a dragon.*

kin *noun*   all of a person's relatives: *see* **family**

kind¹

adjective   helpful, considerate, and gentle: *A **kind** woman helped me pick up the books I had dropped.*

▸ **attentive**   considerate and polite: *Her fiancé is very **attentive** to her.*
▸ **considerate**   thoughtful of others and their feelings: *It was very **considerate** of you to bring me flowers and vegetables from your garden.*
▸ **generous**   willing to give or share; unselfish: *I appreciate your **generous** offer to give me a ride home.*
▸ **humane**   showing kindness and thoughtful concern for people or animals: *It is important to be **humane** to your pets.*
▸ **thoughtful**   aware of other people's needs and feelings; considerate: *Bringing flowers to your hostess is a **thoughtful** gesture.*

ANTONYM **mean**   not kind or good; cruel

kind²

noun   a group of the same or similar things: *The red panda and the giant panda are two **kinds** of pandas.*

▸ **breed**   a particular type or variety of animal or plant: *The Scottish terrier is my favorite **breed** of dog.*
▸ **category**   a division or group within a system; a class: *Our video store displays movies by **category**.*
▸ **class**   a kind or category: *He is so unusual that he's in a **class** by himself.*
▸ **genre**   a particular type of literary, musical, or artistic composition: *I enjoy reading books in many different **genres**.*
▸ **type**   a group or class sharing common traits or characteristics: *All **types** of people enjoy watching TV.*
▸ **variety**   a group that differs in a certain way from other similar groups: *Though it doesn't look like it, broccoli is actually a **variety** of cabbage.*

kindle *verb*   to bring something to life: *see* **excite**

kindness *noun*   a helpful or considerate act: *see* **favor**

kindness *noun*   kind treatment or a kind act: *see* **sympathy**

king *noun*   a male sovereign: *see* **ruler**

kingdom *noun*   a country that is ruled by a queen or king: *see* **country**

kit *noun*   a set of articles or tools for a certain purpose: *see* **equipment**

knack *noun*   a special talent or ability: *see* **art**

knapsack *noun*   a backpack, especially one worn by soldiers or hikers: *see* **bag**

kneel *verb*   to rest or fall on one or both knees: *see* **bow**

knife *verb*   to stab someone with a knife: *see* **stab**

knob *noun*   a rounded lump or mass: *see* **bump**

knock *verb*   to hit something with a sharp blow or blows: *see* **hit**

knoll *noun*   a small, round hill: *see* **hill**

knot *noun*   a hard lump or swelling, as from an enlarged gland: *see* **bump**

know *verb*   to have a practical understanding of something: *see* **understand**

know-how *noun*   the knowledge and skill required to do something correctly: *see* **art**

knowingly *adverb*   with full knowledge, information, or understanding: *see* **deliberately**

knowledge

noun   awareness or understanding gained through experience or study; facts and ideas: *Our algebra teacher tested our **knowledge** of quadratic equations.*

▸ **background**   a person's past experience, training, and education: *Our music teacher has a strong **background** in jazz.*
▸ **experience**   knowledge or skill gotten through practice: *My father has a lot of **experience** as a carpenter.*
▸ **training**   knowledge or skill gotten through instruction: *My company is sending me for advanced **training** on the computer.*

L

label

noun a tag or sticker attached to something that tells what it is or what it contains: *I read the **label** on the jar of salsa to find out the nutritional information.*

- ▸ **brand** a name or symbol that identifies a product as coming from a certain company: *What's your favorite **brand** of cereal?*
- ▸ **sticker** an adhesive label: *The price was on a **sticker** on the bottom of the vase.*
- ▸ **tag** a strip of paper, metal, or leather attached to something for the purpose of identifying or labeling it: *All items with red **tags** are on sale.*
- ▸ **ticket** a price tag or label attached to something being sold: *According to the **ticket**, this shirt costs 32 dollars.*
- ▸ **trademark** a name or symbol that legally identifies a product: *They had several meetings to decide on a **trademark** for their new product line.*

labor *noun* hard work: *see* **work**

laborer *noun* a person engaged in physical work: *see* **employee**

lack

noun a deficiency or absence of something needed or wanted: *Few plants grow in the desert due to **lack** of water.*

- ▸ **absence** a complete lack: *A prolonged **absence** of vitamin C will cause scurvy.*
- ▸ **deficiency** a lack of something needed, especially for good health: *The nurse told me that my blood test shows an iron **deficiency**.*
- ▸ **scarcity** an insufficient amount or supply of something; a shortage: *Many countries suffer from a **scarcity** of clean drinking water.*
- ▸ **shortage** an amount of something that is not enough; a lack: *There was a water **shortage** in our area last summer.*

lady *noun* a girl or woman, especially one who has polite manners: *see* **woman**

lagoon *noun* a shallow body of water that is separated from the sea by sandbars or reefs: *see* **pool**

lake *noun* a body of fresh or salt water that is surrounded by land: *see* **pool**

lament *verb* to express sorrow or regret over something: *see* **mourn**

lance *verb* to pierce or cut something open with a sharp blade: *see* **stab**

land *noun* the part of the earth's surface not covered by water: *see* **earth [2]**

landing *noun* a level area at the top or bottom of a flight of stairs: *see* **platform**

landscape *noun* an expanse of scenery that can be seen from one place: *see* **view**

lane *noun* a narrow path or road between fences, hedges, or walls: *see* **path**

larceny *noun* the crime of taking another's property without right or permission: *see* **theft**

lard *noun* a white, greasy substance made from the melted-down fat of a pig: *see* **fat**

large *adjective* greater than average in size, amount, or degree: *see* **big**

last[1]

adjective coming, being, or placed after all others; being the only one left: *I was the **last** student to finish the test.*

- ▸ **final** being or occurring at the end: *This is your **final** warning.*
- ▸ **terminal** marking the end of a section or series: *The negotiations are in the **terminal** phase.*

ANTONYM **beginning** being the first or earliest

last²

verb ▷ to continue or go on for a period of time: *This rainy weather is supposed to **last** all week.* ▷ to remain in good condition: *My watch only **lasted** a year before it stopped working.*

- ▸ **endure** to continue in existence in spite of difficulties; to live on: *The ancient Greeks died out but many of their ideas **endure** in our culture today.*
- ▸ **persevere** to continue to try to do something in spite of obstacles: *He **persevered** in his efforts to learn the difficult piano sonata.*
- ▸ **persist** to hold firmly to a purpose; to not give up: *She **persisted** in her search for a job until she finally found one.*
- ▸ **survive** to continue to live or exist through difficult circumstances: *People can only **survive** for a few days without water.*

lasting *adjective* continuing or remaining for a long time: *see* **permanent**

latch *verb* to close or fasten something with a latch: *see* **close**

late

adjective coming after the expected, usual, or proper time: *She was **late** for her appointment.*

- ▸ **belated** being, coming, or happening late; delayed: *I sent a **belated** birthday card.*
- ▸ **delayed** prevented from being on time: *The flight was **delayed** because of a heavy snowstorm.*
- ▸ **overdue** not paid on time: *He paid his **overdue** electricity bill.*
- ▸ **tardy** arriving, coming, or happening after the event has started: *I overslept and was **tardy** to class.*

laugh

verb to smile and make sounds in the throat to express amusement or scorn: *That TV show makes me **laugh**.*

- ▸ **cackle** to laugh or speak in a shrill, noisy way: *My friends **cackled** at the funny joke I told.*
- ▸ **chuckle** to laugh quietly or to oneself: *The newspaper cartoon made me **chuckle**.*
- ▸ **giggle** to laugh in a silly or nervous way: *The girls **giggled** when they met their favorite movie star.*
- ▸ **guffaw** to laugh heartily or in an unrestrained way: *He **guffawed** at my ridiculous story.*
- ▸ **snicker** to laugh in a sly or mean way: *My sister **snickered** at my art project.*

launch *verb* to set a process or event in motion: *see* **begin**

launder *verb* to wash something, especially clothes: *see* **clean**

law *noun* a rule that regulates people's behavior or activities: *see* **rule**

lawful *adjective* allowed or recognized by law: *see* **legal**

lawless *adjective* disregarding or violating the law: *see* **wild [2]**

lawn *noun* a piece of ground planted with grass: *see* **park**

lax *adjective* not careful or strict, especially about enforcing rules: *see* **careless**

lay *verb* to put or set something down: *see* **place**

layer

noun a single thickness or coating of a material that covers a surface: *The chocolate cake had a thick **layer** of frosting.*

- ▸ **coating** a layer of a substance spread over a surface: *There was a thin **coating** of ice on the streets this morning.*
- ▸ **covering** something that covers so as to protect or conceal: *She puts a **covering** over her motorcycle every night.*
- ▸ **film** a thin layer or coating: *I cleaned the **film** of dust off my computer screen.*

lay off *verb* to dismiss or suspend an employee because there is not enough work to be done: *see* **dismiss**

layout *noun* a planned arrangement of parts or areas: *see* **design**

laze *verb* to relax lazily: *see* **relax**

lazy

adjective not willing to work or be active: *I am feeling **lazy** today and probably won't do much.*

▸ **idle** not working or being used: *The town's snowplow stood **idle** until the January snowstorm.*

▸ **inactive** not active or functioning: *Snakes become **inactive** during cold weather.*

▸ **listless** too tired or weak to want to do anything: *She was **listless** after her illness.*

▸ **sluggish** moving or acting in a slow way; lacking energy: *Our neighbor's potbellied pig became **sluggish** in the afternoon heat.*

ANTONYM **active** full of energy; busy

lead *verb* to direct someone along the way, as by going in front: *see* **guide**

leader

noun a person who leads, guides, or has authority over others: *The President is the **leader** of our nation.*

▸ **captain** the leader of a group or team: *She is the **captain** of the basketball team.*

▸ **chief** a person of the highest rank or authority: *The **chief** of our local police force gave a talk at our community center.*

▸ **commander** a person in charge, especially in the military: *The **commander** gave orders to his troops.*

leaflet *noun* a printed, usually folded sheet intended for free distribution: *see* **booklet**

league *noun* a group of nations, people, or organizations working together for a common goal: *see* **club**

leak

verb to flow in or out of a crack or hole: *Oil **leaked** slowly from the car's engine.*

▸ **dribble** to flow slowly in an unsteady stream; to trickle: *I let the honey **dribble** onto my cereal.*

▸ **drip** to fall in drops: *I listened to the rain **drip** from the trees outside my window.*

▸ **ooze** to flow or leak out slowly: *Blood **oozed** from the small cut on his finger.*

▸ **seep** to pass slowly through small openings; to ooze: *Cold air **seeped** in through the gap under the door.*

▸ **trickle** to flow or fall in drops or in a thin stream: *Sand **trickled** through the child's hands.*

lean *adjective* not fleshy or fat: *see* **thin**

lean *verb* to place something so that it angles away from an upright position: *see* **tilt**

leaning *noun* a usually moderate tendency: *see* **tendency**

leap *verb* to jump quickly or suddenly: *see* **jump**

learn

verb to gain knowledge, comprehension, or command of something through experience or study: *She **learned** how to knit from her mother.*

▸ **memorize** to fix something in the mind or memory; to learn something by heart: *I **memorized** my friend's phone number.*

▸ **read** to understand the meaning of written or printed words: *Our literature class has to **read** five books this semester.*

▸ **research** to study a subject or problem closely and carefully: *I'm **researching** the role sharks play in the ocean's ecosystem.*

▸ **review** to study or examine something again so as to learn it better: *She **reviewed** her lines for the school play.*

▸ **study** to apply oneself to learning something, especially by reading: *He **studies** philosophy at the university.*

learner *noun* a person who acquires skill or knowledge: *see* **student**

learning *noun* knowledge gotten from study or instruction: *see* **education**

lease *verb* to obtain the use of property by a contract for a certain time: *see* **rent**

leash *verb* to restrain an animal with a leash: *see* **control**

least

adjective smallest in degree, size, amount, or number: *My physical education class has the **least** amount of homework.*

- ▸ **fewest** smallest in number: *In the card game of hearts, whoever ends with the **fewest** points is the winner.*
- ▸ **littlest** least big; smallest: *My sister's baby was the **littlest** person at the family reunion.*
- ▸ **lowest** least high; closest to the bottom: *She put the pots and pans on the **lowest** shelf in the cupboard.*
- ▸ **smallest** least in size, number, amount, or degree: *The beginning skiers practiced on the **smallest** hill.*
- ▸ **slightest** smallest in amount or degree: *This paint color has just the **slightest** tint of green in it.*

ANTONYM **most** greatest in number, size, or degree

leave

verb to go away from a place or person: *I plan to **leave** the house early in the morning.*

- ▸ **depart** to go away, especially on a journey or trip: *What time does the train **depart**?*
- ▸ **exit** to go out of a place: *We **exited** the theater after the performance was over.*
- ▸ **retire** (formal) to withdraw from the company of others, as for rest or seclusion: *I **retired** to my bedroom early because I was tired.*
- ▸ **retreat** to move back the way one came, especially to escape danger: *The army **retreated** across the river after losing the battle.*
- ▸ **vacate** to go away from a place and no longer occupy it: *They plan to **vacate** the house by the end of the month.*
- ▸ **withdraw** to move to another, usually quieter or more private place: *The captain **withdrew** to his quarters after dinner.*

ANTONYM **arrive** to reach a place

lecture *noun* a prepared talk providing information about a given subject: *see* **class**

leftover *noun* the amount that remains unused or uneaten: *see* **balance**

legal

adjective based on or authorized by law: *The **legal** voting age in America is 18 years old.*

- ▸ **allowable** permitted or approved: *What is the highest **allowable** deduction on my income tax?*
- ▸ **authorized** approved by an authority: *I have an **authorized** vacation day coming soon.*
- ▸ **lawful** allowed or recognized by law: *It is **lawful** to carry a gun in the United States if you have a permit.*
- ▸ **permissible** permitted; allowable: *Is it **permissible** to park here?*
- ▸ **permitted** allowed by rule, regulation, or custom: *Smoking is not **permitted** in many restaurants.*

ANTONYM **illegal** against the law or rules

legend *noun* a story handed down from earlier times: *see* **story**

legible *adjective* capable of being read: *see* **clear [1]**

leisure *noun* free time in which one can do as one pleases: *see* **vacation**

lend *verb* to give or allow the use of something with the understanding that it is to be returned: *see* **rent**

length *noun* the distance of something from end to end: *see* **distance**

lengthen *verb* to make something longer: *see* **stretch**

lengthy *adjective* long, especially too long: *see* **long**

lenient *adjective* inclined not to be harsh or strict: *see* **indulgent**

less

adjective not as great in degree, size, amount, or number: *I will have **less** time for going out with my friends once school starts again.*

- ▸ **fewer** smaller in number: *Fewer people attended the party than we expected.*

▸ **reduced** smaller or lower than before: *I bought this sweater at a reduced price.*

▸ **shorter** smaller in height than someone or something else: *My friend is shorter than I am.*

▸ **smaller** less in size, number, amount, or degree: *I am looking for the same shirt in a smaller size.*

ANTONYM **more** greater, as in number, size, amount, or degree

lesson *noun* a period of time devoted to teaching or learning something: *see* **class**

let *verb* to grant permission to someone or for something: *see* **authorize**

lethal *adjective* causing or intended to cause death: *see* **fatal**

letter

noun a written message to someone that is usually sent by mail in an envelope: *I write a letter to my pen pal once a month.*

▸ **memo** an informal letter or note sent between members or departments of an organization: *Did you get the memo about the new policy?*

▸ **message** a short communication that is sent from one person or group to another: *I left a message on her answering machine.*

▸ **note** a short written message: *I left my roommate a note reminding him that our rent was due.*

level *adjective* having a flat, even surface: *see* **flat**

level *noun* a relative position or rank: *see* **degree**

liable *adjective* very likely: *see* **prone**

liar *noun* a person who says things that are not true: *see* **imposter**

libel *noun* a written or printed statement that unjustly damages a person's reputation: *see* **lie**

liberal *adjective* ▷ large or generous in amount ▷ tending to give freely or generously: *see* **abundant**

liberate *verb* to set someone or something free: *see* **release**

liberty *noun* freedom to act, believe, or express oneself as one wishes: *see* **freedom**

license *noun* official permission to do or own something: *see* **freedom**

lid

noun a removable cover, as of a jar, box, or pot: *I used a screwdriver to pry the lid off the can of paint.*

▸ **cork** a bottle stopper that is made out of light, spongy wood: *He pulled the cork from the wine bottle.*

▸ **plug** a piece of rubber, plastic, or other material that is used to stop up a hole or leak: *We need a new plug for the drain in the bathtub.*

▸ **seal** a substance or device that closes an opening and prevents seepage of moisture or air: *I broke the plastic seal on my bottle of vitamins.*

▸ **stopper** a device, such as a cork, that is put into an opening to close it: *A bottle stopper is used to keep the contents of a bottle from going flat.*

lie

noun an untrue statement made on purpose: *I had to tell him a lie or he would have guessed that we were planning a surprise birthday party for him.*

▸ **bluff** a misleading or deceiving statement or action: *I tried to get into the concert with the bluff that I was the rock star's sister.*

▸ **deception** something that deceives, such as a lie or trick: *The Trojan Horse is one of the most famous deceptions in history.*

▸ **falsehood** a statement that is not true; a lie: *He was fired from his job when his employer discovered that his resume was full of falsehoods.*

▸ **fib** an insignificant or childish lie: *That was a fib when I said I had something else to do the night of your party.*

▸ **libel** a written or printed statement that unjustly damages a person's reputation: *The newspaper was sued for **libel** by the famous talk-show host.*

▸ **perjury** deliberately false, misleading, or incomplete testimony while under oath: *The witness was found guilty of **perjury**.*

▸ **slander** a false statement reported or said maliciously in order to damage someone's reputation: *The candidate was accused of using **slander** against her opponent during the political campaign.*

lifeless *adjective* having no life: *see* **dead**

lift *verb* to raise something or someone from a lower to a higher position: *see* **raise [2]**

light *adjective* filled with light: *see* **bright**

light *adjective* of a shade of color closer to white than black: *see* **pale**

like *verb* to find someone or something pleasant or enjoyable: *see* **love**

likely *adjective* showing a strong tendency or probability: *see* **possible**

liken *verb* to describe something as being like something else: *see* **compare**

likewise *adverb* moreover; besides: *see* **also**

limber *adjective* bending or moving easily: *see* **flexible**

limit

noun a point beyond which someone or something cannot go: *This credit card has a **limit** of 2,000 dollars.*

▸ **limitation** something that limits; a restriction: *There is a **limitation** on the number of passengers this elevator can hold.*

▸ **maximum** the greatest or highest possible quantity, degree, or number: *What is the **maximum** amount of time that you can hold your breath?*

▸ **minimum** the smallest possible quantity, degree, or number: *She did the **minimum** amount of work necessary to pass the class.*

▸ **quota** an amount of something assigned to be done, made, or sold; the smallest amount allowable: *I received a bonus for selling more than my **quota** of magazine subscriptions.*

▸ **restriction** something that keeps or confines something else within certain limits: *There are **restrictions** on the use of the activity center at our apartment complex.*

limitation *noun* something that limits: *see* **limit**

limited *adjective* confined or restricted within certain limits: *see* **few**

limitless *adjective* having no limit or boundary: *see* **infinite**

limp *verb* to walk in an uneven or painful way: *see* **stagger**

line *noun* one's trade, occupation, or field of interest: *see* **field [2]**

linger *verb* to stay in a place longer than usual: *see* **stay**

link *verb* to join or connect things with or as if with a ring or loop: *see* **join**

liquefy *verb* to become liquid, as by melting: *see* **melt**

liquid *noun* a substance that flows easily and is hard to compress: *see* **juice**

list *noun* a series of names or items written one after the other: *see* **plan**

listen

verb to try to hear something; to pay attention to a voice or sound: *We **listened** to the instructor as she gave us directions for the project.*

▸ **hear** to take in sounds through the ear: *I could **hear** the conversation in the next room.*

▸ **heed** to pay close attention to something or someone: *I **heeded** his good advice.*

▸ **pay attention** to take careful notice; to concentrate: *I have to **pay attention** in class so I can take good notes.*

listless *adjective* too tired or weak to want to do anything: *see* **lazy**

literal *adjective* word for word; avoiding exaggeration or embellishment: *see* **exact**

litter *noun* empty cans and bottles, pieces of paper, and other waste material left lying around: *see* **garbage**

little *adjective* small in size or quantity: *see* **small**

littlest *adjective* least big; smallest: *see* **least**

live *verb* to reside or dwell in a place: *see* **dwell**

load *noun* something that is carried or transported, as by a vehicle, person, or animal: *see* **burden**

load *verb* to fill or partly fill something with items: *see* **fill**

loaf *verb* to spend time lazily or aimlessly: *see* **relax**

loafer *noun* a person who spends time aimlessly or idly: *see* **bum**

loam *noun* soil composed of sand, clay, silt, and decayed plant matter: *see* **earth [2]**

loan *verb* to lend something to someone, such as money: *see* **rent**

loathe *verb* to feel deep dislike or disgust for someone or something: *see* **hate**

lobby *noun* an entrance hall or a waiting area in a hotel, apartment house, or theater: *see* **hall**

locate *verb* to find something by searching, examining, or experimenting: *see* **discover**

location *noun* a place where something can be found: *see* **place**

lock *verb* to fasten or secure something with a lock: *see* **close**

lodge *noun* a cottage or cabin, especially one used as a temporary place to stay: *see* **hotel**

lodge *verb* to live in a place temporarily: *see* **dwell**

lodger *noun* a person who rents a room in another person's house: *see* **occupant**

lodging *noun* a place to live or stay: *see* **hotel**

lodgings *noun* a rented room or rooms: *see* **hotel**

lofty *adjective* (formal) very high or tall: *see* **tall**

log *noun* an official record of speed, progress, and important events that is kept for a ship or aircraft: *see* **report**

logical *adjective* able to reason clearly and rationally: *see* **wise**

loiter *verb* to stand around doing nothing: *see* **stay**

lone *adjective* being the only one of its kind: *see* **alone**

lone *adjective* by oneself with no others around: *see* **lonely**

lonely

adjective sad at being alone or without companionship: *I was **lonely** when my friend went away for the summer.*

▸ **forlorn** appearing sad or lonely because of being abandoned: *I could not resist taking the **forlorn** dog home with me.*

▸ **friendless** without friends: *She is so outgoing that she will never be **friendless**.*

▸ **lone** by oneself with no others around; alone: *A **lone** apple tree stood in the middle of the field.*

▸ **lonesome** sad because of a lack of companionship; lonely: *I was **lonesome** while you were gone.*

lonesome *adjective* sad because of a lack of companionship: *see* **lonely**

long

adjective measuring a large amount from end to end; having great length: *Florida has a very **long** coastline.*

▸ **elongated** having grown or been made longer: *The mirror in the fun house made us look **elongated**.*

▸ **extended** lengthened in space or time: *We took an **extended** vacation last summer.*

▸ **lengthy** long, especially too long: *The visiting politician made a **lengthy** speech.*

▸ **prolonged** longer in time than expected or required; drawn out: *We had a **prolonged** conversation.*

long-lived *adjective* functioning or living for a long time: *see* **tough**

look

verb to use the eyes to see: *I looked out the window to see who was arriving.*

▸ **eye** to look at something closely: *She eyed the expensive dress longingly.*

▸ **gaze** to look at something intently, as with strong emotion: *We gazed in awe as the full moon rose over the peaks.*

▸ **glance** to take a quick look at something: *I glanced at my homework before dinner.*

▸ **glimpse** to get a brief view of something: *I glimpsed a red-tailed hawk while I was out hiking.*

▸ **observe** to see and pay attention to something: *He called the fire department because he observed smoke coming from his neighbor's garage.*

▸ **peek** to glance or look at something quickly or secretly: *I peeked into the oven to see if the cookies were done baking.*

▸ **see** to take in something with the eyes: *Did you see the beautiful sunset last night?*

▸ **stare** to look with a steady, often wide-eyed gaze: *I stared at her in amazement when she told me the news.*

▸ **watch** to look at something closely for a period of time: *We sat on a bench and watched the people walk by.*

▸ **witness** to see or have personal knowledge of something: *Did you witness the accident?*

look forward to *verb* to anticipate something with pleasure: *see* **expect**

look like *verb* to give the impression or appearance of something: *see* **appear [2]**

loom *verb* to come into view; often with a threatening appearance: *see* **appear [1]**

loose

adjective ▷ not fastened tightly: *I tightened the screws to fix the loose door handle.* ▷ not fitting tightly: *My clothes have become loose since I lost weight.*

▸ **baggy** fitting or hanging loosely: *He likes to wear baggy pants.*

▸ **dangling** hanging or swinging loosely from a single point: *I trimmed the dangling thread.*

▸ **floppy** loose and flexible; moving loosely or limply: *My dog has long, floppy ears.*

▸ **flowing** hanging loosely and gracefully: *She wore a long, flowing gown to the ball.*

▸ **sagging** sinking, drooping, or settling from pressure or weight: *The card table was sagging under the weight of all my computer equipment.*

▸ **slack** not firm or tight; loose: *The rope was slack, so I pulled it tight.*

▸ **untied** having been loosened or come undone: *She saw that her shoelace was untied and bent down to tie it.*

loot *verb* to take things of value, especially during a time of war or social disturbance: *see* **steal**

lope *verb* to run with long, smooth strides: *see* **run**

lose *verb* to fail to win or keep something: *see* **fail**

lot *noun* one's luck or circumstances in life: *see* **destiny**

lot *noun* a piece of land having specific boundaries, especially one that is part of a city or town: *see* **field [1]**

lottery *noun* a contest in which tickets are sold and the winner is determined in a random drawing: *see* **contest**

loud

adjective having a high volume of sound: *The concert was so loud that my friends and I could hardly hear each other speak.*

▸ **blaring** loud and harsh in sound: *The blaring car horn startled me.*

▸ **booming** loud, deep, and hollow in sound: *We could hear the booming sound of the waterfall in the distance.*

▸ **deafening** so loud as to make one unable to hear: *The sound of the jackhammer was deafening.*

▸ **noisy** making a lot of noise: *The classroom was noisy until the teacher walked in.*

▸ **roaring** loud and deep in sound: *We listened to the roaring wind as the storm grew stronger.*

▸ **shrill** high-pitched and piercing: *We stopped playing when we heard the referee's shrill whistle.*

ANTONYM **soft** not loud or harsh; quiet

lounge *verb* to stand, sit, or lie in a lazy or relaxed way: *see* **relax**

love

noun strong, often romantic affection and warm feeling for another: *The couple pledged their love during the wedding ceremony.*

▸ **adoration** great and reverent or devoted love: *Mother Teresa inspired adoration in millions of people.*

▸ **affection** a fond or tender feeling toward someone: *My friends and I have great affection for one another.*

▸ **fondness** warm affection: *She has much fondness for her old cat, even though he's grumpy.*

▸ **tenderness** gentle affection: *Babies bring out a feeling of tenderness in many people.*

love

verb to feel love or strong affection for someone or something: *I love my sister very much.*

▸ **adore** to love someone deeply and devotedly: *They adore their children.*

▸ **cherish** to regard someone or something fondly; to value something highly: *I cherish the necklace that my grandmother gave me.*

▸ **idolize** to regard someone with blind admiration: *Many people idolize their favorite celebrities.*

▸ **like** to find someone or something pleasant or enjoyable: *I like cinnamon rolls.*

▸ **treasure** to value something very highly; to cherish: *My father treasures the portrait that has been in his family for generations.*

ANTONYM **hate** to feel a strong dislike for someone or something

lovely *adjective* having pleasing or attractive qualities of character or appearance: *see* **beautiful**

loving *adjective* feeling or showing love: *see* **affectionate**

low *adjective* not high off the ground: *see* **short [1]**

low-cost *adjective* inexpensive; affordable: *see* **cheap**

lowest *adjective* least high; closest to the bottom: *see* **least**

loyal

adjective firm in supporting a person, country, or cause; faithful: *A loyal friend will stand by you even if you have troubles.*

▸ **dedicated** being fully committed to something: *The dedicated teacher was appreciated by his students and their parents.*

▸ **devoted** feeling or expressing strong affection or attachment: *They are devoted friends.*

▸ **faithful** firm in allegiance or support; loyal: *My dog is my faithful companion.*

▸ **steadfast** firmly loyal or faithful: *He has been a steadfast friend through all my troubles.*

ANTONYM **disloyal** lacking loyalty; unfaithful

loyalty

noun firm, faithful support: *The loyalty of my friend really showed when he let me stay at his house for a year while I started my own company.*

▸ **allegiance** loyalty or devotion: *The class pledged allegiance to the United States.*

▸ **devotion** loyalty and deep affection: *The bride and groom exchanged rings as a sign of devotion.*

▸ **fidelity** faithfulness to an obligation or duty: *The employee's fidelity to the company was rewarded with a large promotion.*

lozenge *noun* a small, sweet tablet that contains medicine or is used as a candy: *see* **pill**

luck *noun* the chance happening of good or bad events: *see* **chance**

lucky

adjective having good luck: *I made a **lucky** guess on the quiz and chose the right answer.*

- ▸ **charmed** very lucky, as if by magic: *He leads a **charmed** life and never seems to have any worries.*
- ▸ **fortunate** having good fortune; lucky: *I feel very **fortunate** in being able to get an education.*
- ▸ **successful** having obtained something desired or intended; ending in success: *That seminar really helped me develop **successful** study habits.*

ANTONYM **unlucky** marked by or having bad luck

lug *verb* to carry something with great difficulty: *see* **pull**

luggage *noun* bags, such as suitcases and trunks, that a person takes on a trip: *see* **bag**

lull *noun* a calm period in the middle of great activity or commotion: *see* **break**

lull *verb* to cause someone to sleep or rest: *see* **comfort**

lullaby *noun* a soothing song meant to lull a child to sleep: *see* **song**

lumber *noun* timber that has been sawed into boards and planks: *see* **wood**

lump *noun* a swelling or bump: *see* **bump**

lump *noun* an irregularly shaped mass or piece: *see* **chunk**

lunch *noun* a meal eaten at midday: *see* **meal**

lunge *verb* to make a sudden, forceful movement forward: *see* **jump**

lurch *verb* to make a sudden, unsteady movement forward or to one side: *see* **stagger**

lure *verb* to attract someone by offering something tempting: *see* **tempt**

lush *adjective* being abundant in growth or comfort: *see* **abundant**

luster *noun* a shine or glow of soft, reflected light: *see* **shine**

luxurious *adjective* very splendid and comfortable: *see* **grand**

luxury

noun something that is not really needed but that gives one great pleasure, enjoyment, or comfort: *Dining at expensive restaurants is a **luxury** for us.*

- ▸ **extravagance** excessive expense or display; the wasteful spending of money: *It was an **extravagance** to buy three sweaters when I only needed one.*
- ▸ **grandeur** the quality or condition of being grand; magnificence: *We admired the **grandeur** of the Lincoln Memorial.*
- ▸ **splendor** a magnificent or beautiful appearance: *She enjoyed the **splendor** of the autumn day.*

M

machine

noun   a mechanical device that performs a certain task: *I got a new sewing machine.*

- ▶ **appliance**   a machine used to perform a household task: *Kitchen appliances range in size from can openers to refrigerators.*
- ▶ **engine**   a machine that makes something run or move by using energy, such as that produced by oil or steam; a motor: *We replaced the engine in our old car.*
- ▶ **mechanism**   a mechanical device; a machine: *The mechanism in this antique clock still works.*
- ▶ **motor**   a device that provides the power to make something move or run; engine: *I left the car motor running while I ran back into the house for my grocery list.*

mad *adjective*   very irritated: *see* **angry**

mad *adjective*   affected with mental illness: *see* **mentally ill**

magazine

noun   a publication, often issued weekly or monthly, that contains articles or stories, and usually pictures and advertising: *I subscribe to two magazines about cars and trucks.*

- ▶ **digest**   a collection of previously published material, usually edited or condensed: *He read a scientific digest to gather information for his report.*
- ▶ **journal**   a periodical presenting articles on a particular subject: *She read an article about the Tang dynasty in a history journal.*
- ▶ **newsletter**   a printed report giving news or information of interest to a special group: *Our company newsletter had an article about changes in health benefits.*
- ▶ **newspaper**   a publication, usually issued daily or weekly, containing current news, editorials, articles, and advertisements: *We have a subscription to the local newspaper.*

- ▶ **paper**   a newspaper: *I picked up a copy of today's paper.*
- ▶ **periodical**   a publication, especially a magazine, that appears at regular intervals: *This room in the library is reserved for periodicals.*
- ▶ **publication**   something that is published and offered for sale, such as a book or magazine: *His list of publications includes three books on rock climbing.*

magnificent *adjective*   full of splendor or majesty: *see* **grand**

magnify *verb*   to enlarge the appearance of something: *see* **increase**

magnitude *noun*   the greatness of something's position, size, or significance: *see* **degree**

maiden *noun*   an unmarried girl or young woman: *see* **woman**

mail *verb*   to send something by the postal system: *see* **send**

maim *verb*   to disable someone badly: *see* **hurt**

main

adjective   most important; chief: *This is the main road through town.*

- ▶ **central**   most basic or important; essential: *A central principal of American government is the system of checks and balances.*
- ▶ **chief**   most important; main: *My father says that his chief concern is the welfare of our family.*
- ▶ **dominant**   having the most influence or control: *The young wolf did not dare challenge the dominant member of the pack.*
- ▶ **foremost**   first in rank, position, or importance: *That physicist is the foremost authority on string theory.*
- ▶ **major**   greater than others in importance or rank: *My major focus this semester is to improve my math grade.*

▸ **primary** first in importance, degree, or quality: *My primary interests are computers, music, and soccer.*
▸ **principal** first or foremost in importance; chief: *Idaho's principal crop is potatoes.*

maintain *verb* to claim something repeatedly: *see* **claim**

maintain *verb* to keep something in a desirable condition: *see* **keep**

majestic *adjective* grand or magnificent: *see* **noble**

major *adjective* greater than others in importance or rank: *see* **main**

make *verb* to create something by shaping, modifying, or assembling material: *see* **build**

make believe *verb* to act as if something imaginary is true: *see* **pretend**

male *noun* a male person, animal, plant, or plant part: *see* **man**

malice *noun* a desire to hurt others or to see others suffer: *see* **hate**

malicious *adjective* feeling or showing a desire to hurt others: *see* **resentful**

malignant *adjective* threatening to one's life and health: *see* **fatal**

man

noun an adult male human being: *A kind man helped us fix our flat tire.*

▸ **fellow** a man or boy: *I met an interesting fellow at the party.*
▸ **gentleman** a man or boy, especially one who is polite: *The gentleman opened the door for us.*
▸ **guy** (informal) a man; a fellow: *I work with a guy from Arkansas.*
▸ **male** a male person, animal, plant, or plant part: *After seahorses mate, the male carries the fertilized eggs for two to three weeks until they hatch into baby seahorses.*

manage

verb to have control over something, such as a business or project: *My aunt owns and manages a flower store.*

▸ **administer** to direct the affairs of something, such as a government or school: *The mayor administers the city government.*
▸ **direct** to be in charge of something: *A police detective directed the investigation.*
▸ **govern** to direct the public affairs of a country or state; rule: *Elections determine who will govern the country.*
▸ **oversee** to watch over the operation of something; to supervise: *He was hired to oversee the work crew.*
▸ **regulate** to control or direct something according to rules: *The veterinarian told me to regulate my cat's diet.*
▸ **supervise** to oversee the work or performance of someone or something: *My friend and I supervised the bake sale.*

manager *noun* a person who directs the operations of a business or organization: *see* **boss**

mandatory *adjective* required or commanded by authority: *see* **necessary**

mangy *adjective* having many bare spots: *see* **ragged**

manners *noun* socially proper behavior: *see* **behavior**

manufacture *verb* to make something, especially by using machinery: *see* **build**

many

adjective being a large but unspecified number: *There are many beautiful roses in her garden.*

▸ **countless** too many to count: *There are countless stars in the sky.*
▸ **multiple** having more than one individual part or component: *Your plan has multiple advantages.*
▸ **numerous** amounting to a large number; many: *There are numerous varieties of wild birds near my home.*

► **several** more than two but not many: *I bought **several** books when I went shopping.*

► **some** being an unspecified, relatively small number or quantity: *We are having **some** people over for dinner this Saturday.*

► **uncounted** ▷ not counted: *The **uncounted** ballots were locked in a safe.* ▷ not capable of being counted: ***Uncounted** millions of plants and animals inhabit the rain forest.*

ANTONYM **few** being small in number; not many

map *noun* a drawing or chart of all or part of the earth's surface: *see* **chart**

march *verb* to walk with regular and measured steps: *see* **walk**

margin *noun* an outer area: *see* **edge**

mark *noun* a visible trace on a surface, such as a scratch, dent, or stain: *see* **stain**

markdown *noun* the amount by which a price is reduced: *see* **discount**

market *verb* to sell or offer items for sale: *see* **sell**

marsh *noun* low, wet land typically filled with grasses, reeds, and bushes: *see* **swamp**

marvel *noun* someone or something that causes surprise, astonishment, or wonder: *see* **wonder**

marvelous *adjective* of the highest or best kind or quality: *see* **wonderful**

mash *verb* to convert something to a soft, pulpy mixture: *see* **crush**

mask *noun* ▷ a covering worn over part or all of the face as a disguise ▷ something that disguises or hides: *see* **disguise**

masquerade *noun* a dance or party at which masks and fancy costumes are worn: *see* **party**

mass *noun* a large gathering of people or things: *see* **crowd**

massacre *verb* to kill a large number of human beings or animals in a cruel and indiscriminate way: *see* **kill**

masses *noun* the common people: *see* **public**

massive *adjective* unusually or impressively large: *see* **big**

mast *noun* an upright pole that supports the sails and rigging of a ship or boat: *see* **pole**

master *noun* a person of great learning, skill, or ability: *see* **expert**

mat *noun* a flat piece of material used as a floor or seat covering: *see* **pad**

match *verb* to be similar to or identical with another: *see* **agree**

mate *noun* ▷ a husband or wife ▷ the male or female of a pair of animals or birds: *see* **spouse**

material *noun* cloth or fabric: *see* **fabric**

matter *noun* a subject of thought, concern, feeling, or action: *see* **topic**

mattress *noun* a pad of heavy cloth filled with soft material that is used on or as a bed: *see* **pad**

mature *adjective* ▷ having reached full natural growth or development ▷ having the mental and emotional qualities associated with an adult: *see* **adult**

maximum *noun* the greatest or highest possible quantity, degree, or number: *see* **limit**

maybe

adverb possibly; perhaps: ***Maybe** we can go hiking tomorrow if it doesn't rain.*

► **conceivably** possibly; in theory: *Life **conceivably** exists on other planets.*

► **perhaps** maybe, but not likely: ***Perhaps** he'll go with us, though I wouldn't count on it.*

► **possibly** perhaps; maybe: *We should be finished soon, **possibly** tomorrow.*

meadow *noun* an area of grassy ground: *see* **field [1]**

meager *adjective* lacking in quantity or richness: *see* **few**

173

meal

noun   the food that is served and eaten at one time: *Our family prepares a large* **meal** *every Thanksgiving.*

- ▸ **breakfast**   the first meal of the day: *I got up late and had to skip* **breakfast**.
- ▸ **brunch**   a meal eaten late in the morning that combines breakfast and lunch: *We have* **brunch** *at a restaurant every Sunday.*
- ▸ **dinner**   the main meal of the day, eaten either at midday or in the evening: *I am responsible for cooking* **dinner** *two nights a week.*
- ▸ **lunch**   a meal eaten at midday: *I usually take a sandwich to work to eat at* **lunch**.
- ▸ **snack**   a light meal: *Let's stop and get a* **snack** *before we go home.*
- ▸ **supper**   the evening meal or the last meal of the day: *We usually eat* **supper** *at seven o'clock.*

mean¹

adjective   not kind or good; intended to make someone feel bad: *I made a* **mean** *remark because I was angry.*

- ▸ **brutal**   very cruel and harsh; ruthless: *War can bring out* **brutal** *behavior in people.*
- ▸ **cruel**   liking or intended to cause pain or suffering: *People who are* **cruel** *to animals can be arrested.*
- ▸ **harsh**   very severe or cruel; extreme: *Many people think that the death penalty is too* **harsh** *a punishment.*
- ▸ **ruthless**   having or showing no pity; cruel: *The* **ruthless** *general took no prisoners.*
- ▸ **unfriendly**   not friendly; unpleasant or hostile: *Our cat is usually* **unfriendly** *to strangers.*
- ▸ **unkind**   not kind or generous; mean: *She apologized for having made an* **unkind** *remark about her friend's appearance.*

ANTONYM   **kind**   helpful, considerate, and gentle

mean²

verb   ▷ to have something as its meaning: *Aloha* **means** *both hello and goodbye in Hawaiian.* ▷ to intend to do, say, or communicate something: *I didn't* **mean** *to hurt your feelings.*

- ▸ **convey**   to communicate something; to make something known: *The dog's wagging tail* **conveyed** *its happiness.*
- ▸ **denote**   to express or indicate something directly: *A skull and crossbones usually* **denotes** *danger.*
- ▸ **imply**   to say or mean something without expressing it directly; to suggest: *His expression* **implied** *that he disagreed with me.*
- ▸ **signify**   to be a sign or indication of something: *Those dark clouds* **signify** *rain.*

meander   *verb*   to move aimlessly and idly without a fixed direction: *see* **wander**

means   *noun*   something, such as a method or course of action, by which an act or end is achieved: *see* **method**

measure   *noun*   the extent, amount, or degree of something: *see* **degree**

mechanism   *noun*   a mechanical device: *see* **machine**

medal   *noun*   a flat piece of metal with a special design that is given as an award: *see* **award**

meddle   *verb*   to interfere in other people's business: *see* **interfere**

mediate   *verb*   to settle differences by working with all sides of a dispute: *see* **negotiate**

mediator   *noun*   a person or agency that works with all sides in order to bring about agreement in a dispute: *see* **judge**

medicine   *noun*   a substance used to treat a disease or to relieve pain: *see* **remedy**

meditate   *verb*   to think quietly; to reflect: *see* **think**

medium   *noun*   a means by which something is done: *see* **method**

medium   *adjective*   being between two extremes: *see* **normal**

medley   *noun*   a variety or series of selected items: *see* **assortment**

meek *adjective* showing patience and humility: *see* **gentle**

meet

verb ▷ to come together by chance or arrangement: *Let's* **meet** *at the bookstore before class.* ▷ to be introduced to someone: *I'd like you to* **meet** *my husband.*

- ▸ **congregate** to come together as a crowd; to assemble: *The entire school* **congregated** *in the gymnasium to hear the guest speaker.*
- ▸ **contact** to get in touch with someone; to communicate with someone: *I* **contacted** *my cousin to let her know I would like to visit her this summer.*
- ▸ **get together** to meet or assemble in an informal way: *We often* **get together** *at my house to study.*
- ▸ **muster** to gather people together for inspection, roll call, or service: *The troops were* **mustered** *for the general's inspection.*
- ▸ **run into** to meet someone by chance: *I* **ran into** *my friend at the grocery store.*

meeting

noun a gathering of people held at a fixed time and place: *The school board* **meeting** *started right on time.*

- ▸ **assembly** a group of people gathered together for a common purpose: *We had a school* **assembly** *to honor our retiring principal.*
- ▸ **conference** a meeting to discuss one or more subjects: *The scientists organized a* **conference** *dedicated to the topic of AIDS prevention.*
- ▸ **convention** a formal assembly or meeting: *He attended a sales* **convention**.
- ▸ **rally** a large meeting held to support a cause or to inspire enthusiasm: *It was exciting to attend the political* **rally**.
- ▸ **trade show** a large meeting focused on the needs and developments of a certain profession: *Every week there is a different* **trade show** *at the convention center.*

melancholy *adjective* feeling a lingering sadness or depression: *see* **sad**

mellow *adjective* relaxed and unhurried: *see* **casual**

melody *noun* a pleasing series of musical tones: *see* **song**

melt

verb to change from a solid to a liquid by heating: *The snow began to* **melt** *as soon as the sun came out.*

- ▸ **defrost** to free something of ice or frost: *We need to* **defrost** *the freezer.*
- ▸ **dissolve** to change something from a solid to a liquid: *The directions say to* **dissolve** *the powder in hot water.*
- ▸ **liquefy** to become liquid, as by melting: *Butter* **liquefies** *at a low temperature.*
- ▸ **soften** to become soft, as by thawing: *We took the ice cream out of the freezer to let it* **soften** *a little before serving it.*
- ▸ **thaw** to change from a solid to a liquid by gradual warming: *The ice on the lake had* **thawed** *too much to be safe for skating.*

memento *noun* something that causes one to remember the past: *see* **souvenir**

memo *noun* an informal letter or note sent between members or departments of an organization: *see* **letter**

memorable

adjective worthy of being remembered; remarkable: *One's graduation is a* **memorable** *event.*

- ▸ **historic** important or famous in history: *We visited the* **historic** *city of Williamsburg, Virginia.*
- ▸ **noteworthy** worthy of notice or attention; significant: *The President's speech was* **noteworthy** *for its mention of new policies.*
- ▸ **unforgettable** not likely to be forgotten; memorable: *seeing the Grand Canyon for the first time was an* **unforgettable** *experience.*

memorize *verb* to fix something in the mind or memory: *see* **learn**

menace *noun* a serious threat or danger: *see* **danger**

mend *verb* to make minor repairs to something: *see* **fix**

mentally ill

adjective having a serious disorder of the mind: *The woman was mentally ill and suffered from paranoid fantasies.*

- ▸ **crazy** affected with mental illness; insane: *A crazy man stood on a street corner shouting at people passing by.*
- ▸ **deranged** mentally disturbed, especially having serious mental or emotional problems: *The long-term use of drugs has made her deranged.*
- ▸ **insane** mentally ill: *The court determined that the defendant was legally insane.*
- ▸ **mad** affected with mental illness; insane: *The movie was about a mad scientist who believed he had invented a time machine.*

  ANTONYM **sane** having a sound, healthy mind

mention *verb* to speak about something briefly or in passing: *see* **tell**

mentor *noun* someone who takes a personal interest in developing another person's skills: *see* **teacher**

merchandise

noun things that are bought and sold; goods: *The new merchandise was displayed in the store window.*

- ▸ **commodity** something that is bought and sold: *Wheat, oil, and aluminum are commodities traded on the international market.*
- ▸ **freight** goods carried by train, ship, truck, or other vehicle: *My uncle owns a big truck and hauls freight all over the United States.*
- ▸ **goods** things that can be bought and sold: *This store sell goods imported from England.*

- ▸ **product** something produced, as by manufacture: *This store carries TVs, stereos, and other electronic products.*
- ▸ **wares** items for sale; goods: *We enjoyed looking at the wares at the swap meet.*

merchant

noun a person who buys and sells goods for profit; a person who runs a retail business: *All the merchants at the mall are having big holiday sales.*

- ▸ **dealer** a person engaged in selling or distributing something: *She is an art dealer.*
- ▸ **seller** a person who sells something; a vendor: *How much is the seller asking for that used truck?*
- ▸ **shopkeeper** a person who owns or manages a shop: *I asked the shopkeeper where the shampoo was located.*
- ▸ **trader** a person who sells or exchanges goods or commodities: *He's a trader in stocks and bonds.*
- ▸ **vendor** a person who sells something, especially on a small scale: *On the weekends I am a vendor at the local farmer's market.*

merge *verb* to bring two things together so as to form a single unit; unite: *see* **join**

merit *verb* to deserve something: *see* **earn**

merry *adjective* full of good humor and gaiety: *see* **happy**

mess

noun a cluttered, untidy, usually dirty condition: *I cleaned up the mess in the kitchen.*

- ▸ **clutter** a disordered or confused collection; a jumble: *There is a lot of clutter on his desk.*
- ▸ **disorder** a lack of order; confusion: *My room was in a state of disorder after I searched through it for my favorite shoes.*

▸ **jumble** a group of things that is mixed or thrown together without any order: *That drawer holds a **jumble** of lids.*

▸ **tangle** a confused state or condition: *Their front yard is a **tangle** of overgrown weeds.*

message *noun* a short communication that is sent from one person or group to another: *see* **letter**

messy

adjective dirty and untidy: *I enjoyed putting the **messy** house back in order.*

▸ **cluttered** full of a disordered collection of things: *We decided to clean out our **cluttered** garage.*

▸ **disorganized** not organized; full of confusion or disorder: *This workshop is so **disorganized** I don't see how you can find anything.*

▸ **sloppy** lacking neatness or order; untidy: *I couldn't read his **sloppy** handwriting.*

▸ **tangled** mixed together in a confused mass; snarled: *The spools of thread in this box have become **tangled**.*

▸ **unkempt** not neat or tidy; messy: *Sometimes our lawn looks **unkempt** because no one has time to mow it.*

▸ **untidy** not tidy and neat; sloppy: *My room gets pretty **untidy** when I don't put my CDs and magazines away.*

ANTONYM **neat** clean and tidy

method

noun a regular or deliberate way of doing something: *My **method** of cooking green beans is to steam them first and then simmer in tomato sauce.*

▸ **approach** a way or method of working or dealing with something: *We need to try a new **approach** to the problem.*

▸ **means** something, such as a method or course of action, by which an act or end is achieved: *Windmills are an alternative **means** of generating electricity.*

▸ **medium** a means by which something is done: *The telephone is a **medium** of communication.*

▸ **mode** a way or style of doing something: *She changed her **mode** of living when she moved to a small apartment in the city.*

▸ **procedure** a way of doing something, often by a series of steps: *Chemotherapy is a medical **procedure** used to treat patients with cancer.*

▸ **process** a series of steps, actions, motions, or operations that lead to a result: *The film showed the complicated manufacturing **process** of making a piano.*

▸ **system** an orderly way of doing something: *The sales department set up a new **system** for processing their orders.*

▸ **vehicle** a medium through which something is transmitted, expressed, or accomplished: *Music often serves as a **vehicle** of relaxation.*

▸ **way** a method, means, or technique: *I am experimenting with different **ways** of wearing my hair.*

metropolis *noun* a large city: *see* **town**

microwave *verb* to cook or heat something in a microwave oven: *see* **cook**

microscopic *adjective* ▷ too small to be seen without magnification ▷ extremely small: *see* **small**

middle *noun* the area or point equally distant from two points or extremes: *see* **center** [2]

midnight *noun* the middle of the night; twelve o'clock at night: *see* **night**

midpoint *noun* a position midway between two extremes: *see* **center** [2]

midst *noun* a position that is completely surrounded by something: *see* **center** [2]

midterm *noun* an examination given at the middle of a school term: *see* **test**

midwife *noun* a woman who is trained to assist women in childbirth: *see* **doctor**

might *noun* great strength or power: *see* **strength**

mighty *adjective* having or showing great power, strength, or force: *see* **powerful**

migrate *verb* to move regularly from one region to another, especially at a particular time of the year: *see* **travel**

mild *adjective* gentle or kind in disposition or behavior: *see* **gentle**

mill *noun* a building equipped with machinery used for processing something such as grain, paper, or steel: *see* **factory**

mimic *verb* to imitate someone or something exactly: *see* **copy**

minaret *noun* a tower on a mosque from which the people are called to prayer: *see* **tower**

mind *verb* to pay attention in order to obey someone: *see* **obey**

mindful *adjective* attentive; heedful: *see* **careful [1]**

mine *verb* to extract metals or minerals from the earth: *see* **dig**

mine *noun* an underground hole or tunnel from which minerals such as coal, iron, salt, or gold can be taken: *see* **hole**

mingle *verb* to bring different or unlike things together: *see* **mix**

miniature *adjective* much smaller than the usual size: *see* **small**

minimum *noun* the smallest possible quantity, degree, or number: *see* **limit**

minister

noun one who is authorized to perform religious functions in a Christian church, especially a Protestant church: *They were married by a Lutheran* **minister**.

‣ **guru** a Hindu spiritual teacher: *Many people traveled to India to visit the famous guru.*

‣ **monk** a man who belongs to a religious order and promises to observe its rules and practices: *One of the rituals of Tibetan Gyuto* **monks** *is harmonic chanting.*

‣ **mullah** a religious teacher or leader of the Islamic faith: *Our* **mullah** *discussed a passage in the Qur'an.*

‣ **nun** a woman who is a member of a religious community: *My aunt is a Catholic* **nun**.

‣ **parson** a minister, especially in the Anglican Church: *Her great-grandfather was a* **parson** *in a little country church.*

‣ **pastor** a Christian minister or priest having spiritual charge over a congregation or other group: *The* **pastor** *led the congregation in a prayer.*

‣ **preacher** a person who preaches, especially a minister: *My grandfather listens to the* **preachers** *on television.*

‣ **priest** a member of the clergy who has the authority to perform religious services or ceremonies: *Shinto* **priests** *wear white robes when performing ceremonies.*

ministry *noun* a department of government under the charge of a minister: *see* **government**

minute *noun* ▷ a unit of time equal to 60 seconds ▷ a short time: *see* **moment**

minutes *noun* an official record of the discussion or events that take place at a meeting: *see* **report**

miraculous *adjective* so astounding as to suggest a miracle: *see* **awesome**

miracle *noun* an event that seems impossible because it cannot be explained by the laws of nature: *see* **wonder**

mirage *noun* an optical illusion in which something that is not really there appears to be seen in the distance: *see* **illusion**

mirth *noun* fun and laughter: *see* **happiness**

miscellaneous *adjective* made up of different things mixed together: *see* **various**

mischievous *adjective* showing a tendency to play pranks or cause trouble: *see* **bad [2]**

misdemeanor *noun* a crime less serious than a felony: *see* **crime**

miserable *adjective* extremely or painfully unhappy: *see* **sad**

misery *noun* prolonged unhappiness due to great pain or distress: *see* **suffering**

misfortune

noun bad luck: *We had the* **misfortune** *to get a flat tire just as we set out on our trip.*

- **bad luck** the chance happening of disagreeable or unpleasant events: *It's an old superstition that breaking a mirror causes a person seven years of **bad luck**.*
- **curse** something that causes great evil or harm: *Greed is a **curse** on the human race.*
- **downfall** a sudden loss of wealth, reputation, happiness, or status: *An investigation resulted in the **downfall** of the dishonest banker.*
- **hardship** something that causes suffering or difficulty: *Every immigrant group has suffered **hardships** adjusting to life in a new country.*
- **plight** a situation of difficulty or peril: *Many animal species are suffering the **plight** of near extinction as their habitat is destroyed.*
- **setback** a sudden reverse in progress; a change from better to worse: *The patient has suffered a **setback** and is not expected to live.*

mishap *noun* an unfortunate accident: *see* **accident**

mislead *verb* to give the wrong idea to someone: *see* **deceive**

miss *verb* to let go by: *see* **forget**

missing *adjective* not in the expected place: *see* **absent**

mission *noun* an important assignment that a person or group is sent to carry out: *see* **duty**

mist

noun a mass of tiny drops of water suspended in the air: *There was a **mist** rising off the lake early in the morning.*

- **cloud** a visible mass of tiny drops of water or particles of ice floating in the air: *The blue October sky didn't have a **cloud** in it.*
- **fog** a mass of water droplets floating near the surface of the ground or water: *The airplane didn't take off until the **fog** cleared.*
- **haze** fine dust, smoke, or water vapor floating in the air: *The early morning **haze** disappeared in the heat of the sun.*

- **steam** the mist that forms when hot water vapor cools and condenses into tiny drops: *The geyser erupted with a huge cloud of **steam**.*
- **vapor** fine particles of matter in the air, such as mist, steam, smoke, or smog: *High-flying jets leave visible trails of water **vapor**.*

mistake

noun an error or a fault resulting from poor judgment, lack of knowledge, or carelessness: *I made a **mistake** and put salt instead of sugar into the cake batter.*

- **blunder** a mistake caused by ignorance or confusion: *Taking the wrong medicine was a serious **blunder**.*
- **error** something that is incorrect or wrong: *There is an **error** on this bill.*
- **misunderstanding** a failure to understand or interpret something correctly: *There was a **misunderstanding** about the time that we were supposed to meet.*
- **oversight** a careless mistake: *It was an **oversight** not to bring the stove on our camping trip.*

mistaken *adjective* wrong or incorrect in opinion, understanding, or perception: *see* **wrong**

misty *adjective* full of or covered by mist: *see* **overcast**

misunderstanding *noun* a failure to understand or interpret something correctly: *see* **mistake**

mix

verb to blend or combine materials into a single mass or substance: *Cement is **mixed** with sand and gravel to make concrete.*

- **beat** to stir something rapidly so as to mix it: *He **beat** the eggs to make an omelet.*
- **blend** to combine different materials thoroughly or completely: *To make a sauce, first **blend** flour and butter and then add milk.*
- **churn** to move or shake a liquid vigorously: *I learned how to **churn** butter when we studied pioneer life.*

▶ **combine** to join two or more substances into a single substance: *If you* **combine** *blue and yellow paint, you'll get green paint.*

▶ **fuse** to unite two or more substances into a strong union, as by melting: *Bronze is made by* **fusing** *copper and tin.*

▶ **mingle** to bring different or unlike things together: *My excitement was* **mingled** *with fear the first time I went skydiving.*

▶ **stir** to mix something by using repeated circular motions: *I* **stirred** *the cake batter until it was smooth.*

▶ **whip** to beat something, such as cream, into a foam: *She* **whipped** *the egg whites until they formed peaks.*

ANTONYM **separate** to divide something into parts or sections

mixed *adjective* made up of a combination of different things or kinds: *see* **various**

mixture *noun* a combination of different things, ingredients, or kinds: *see* **assortment**

moan

verb to make a long, low sound, as of sorrow: *The wind* **moaned** *through the trees.*

▶ **groan** to make a deep sound low in the throat that expresses pain, annoyance, or good-natured disapproval: *The class* **groaned** *as the teacher handed out the tests.*

▶ **sigh** to exhale a long, deep breath while making a sound, as of weariness, sorrow, or relief: *The traveler* **sighed** *as he set down his heavy suitcase.*

▶ **whimper** to cry with weak, broken, whining sounds: *My dog* **whimpered** *to be let out.*

▶ **whine** to make a sad, high-pitched sound, as in pain or complaint: *Little children often* **whine** *when they get tired.*

mob *noun* a large, disorderly or threatening crowd: *see* **crowd**

mock *verb* to imitate someone, especially in a way that insults: *see* **tease**

mode *noun* a way or style of doing something: *see* **method**

model *adjective* worthy of imitation: *see* **perfect**

moderate *adjective* not excessive or extreme: *see* **conservative**

modern

adjective advanced, as in style; up-to-date: *High-rise office buildings are a* **modern** *form of architecture.*

▶ **contemporary** being part of today's world; current: *It's hard to keep up with* **contemporary** *fashions in art.*

▶ **current** belonging to the present times; latest or most recent: *She bought the* **current** *issue of her favorite magazine.*

▶ **new** different from the former or the old: *My grandfather says that every time they pass a* **new** *law they should get rid of an old one.*

▶ **recent** new or fairly new; belonging to the time immediately before the present time: *I went to the bookstore to find a* **recent** *edition of a world atlas.*

ANTONYM **old-fashioned** belonging to or typical of an earlier time and no longer in style

modest *adjective* not thinking too highly of one's own talents, abilities, or accomplishments: *see* **shy**

modify *verb* to change something, especially in a limited way: *see* **change**

moist *adjective* slightly wet; damp: *see* **wet**

mold *verb* to determine the growth or development of someone or something: *see* **shape**

moldy *adjective* being covered with mold: *see* **rotten**

moment

noun a short period of time; a minute: *The doctor will be with you in just a* **moment**.

▶ **flash** an extremely short time: *The accident happened in a* **flash**.

▶ **instant** a very brief period of time; a second: *The nurse gave me a shot, and it was over in an* **instant**.

▶ **jiffy** (informal) a moment: *I'll have this fixed for you in a* **jiffy**.

▸ **minute** ▷ a unit of time equal to 60 seconds: *Microwave these burritos on high for three minutes.* ▷ a short time: *Give me a minute to get my coat.*

▸ **second** ▷ a unit of time equal to 1/60 of a minute: *Wait 30 seconds before restarting the computer.* ▷ a very short period of time: *I'll be with you in a couple of seconds.*

momentary *adjective* lasting only an instant or a moment: *see* **short [2]**

momentum *noun* the force that something has when it moves: *see* **speed**

monarch *noun* one who rules over a state or territory, usually for life and by hereditary right: *see* **ruler**

money

noun a medium of exchange that is issued by a government for use in buying or paying for goods and services: *I am saving money to buy an electric guitar.*

▸ **cash** money in the form of bills or coins: *The little gift shop accepts only cash or personal checks.*

▸ **check** a written order to pay money from a person's bank account: *She wrote a check to pay her water bill.*

▸ **coin** a piece of metal issued by a government for use as money: *I put a coin in the parking meter.*

▸ **credit card** a card that entitles the holder to buy things and pay for them later: *My credit card has a spending limit of a thousand dollars.*

▸ **currency** the form of money in actual use in a country: *We changed our American dollars into Mexican currency before crossing the border.*

▸ **funds** available money; cash: *I am low on funds at the present, so I won't be able to go to the movie with you.*

monk *noun* a man who belongs to a religious order and promises to observe its rules and practices: see **minister**

monotonous *adjective* all the same; lacking in variety: *see* **boring**

monsoon *noun* a wind in southern Asia that changes direction with the seasons and brings heavy rainfall: *see* **storm**

monster

noun an imaginary creature that is huge and frightening: *My favorite monster is a giant lizard that destroys Tokyo.*

▸ **giant** a huge, very strong, imaginary creature resembling a human being: *This book of fairy tales has a story about a giant.*

▸ **ogre** a giant or monster in folklore and fairy tales that eats human beings: *In "Jack and the Beanstalk," Jack plays a trick on the ogre to keep from being eaten.*

monstrous *adjective* very evil, cruel, or wrong: *see* **terrible**

mood *noun* a temporary state of mind: *see* **feeling**

moody

adjective apt to change moods often, especially having spells of anger or gloom: *The moody man was happy one day and sad the next.*

▸ **changeable** subject to sudden and unpredictable changes: *The changeable woman was always dyeing her hair a different color.*

▸ **flighty** given to unsteady or changeable behavior: *Flighty people cannot be depended upon.*

▸ **sensitive** quick to take offense; easily irritated: *She is very sensitive about having lost the promotion.*

▸ **temperamental** excessively sensitive, irritable, or moody: *The artist is known for being temperamental.*

mop *verb* to clean something with a mop: *see* **clean**

mope *verb* to be gloomy and often silent: *see* **pout**

moral

adjective conforming to standards of what is good and just: *A moral person does not cheat or steal.*

▶ **decent** conforming to standards of proper social behavior; honest and considerate: *The decent thing to do is apologize to your friend for missing her party.*

▶ **ethical** conforming to accepted standards of right behavior or conduct: *It is not considered ethical for a doctor to withhold treatment from a patient who can't pay.*

▶ **honorable** conforming to a code of right or just behavior: *The honorable boxer refused to purposely lose the fight.*

▶ **upright** morally respectable; honorable: *The upright citizen was asked to run for mayor.*

▶ **virtuous** having or showing virtue, especially moral excellence: *The official was praised for his virtuous conduct in the midst of the scandal.*

more

adjective additional; extra: *Do you need more time to finish getting ready?*

▶ **added** in addition: *Better health coverage is an added benefit of his new job.*

▶ **additional** more than what is usual or expected; extra: *There was an additional fee for delivering the mattress.*

▶ **another** being an additional one: *I would like another pair of pants in the same size.*

▶ **else** in addition; more: *She looked through the rack to see what else was on sale.*

▶ **other** different: *Do you have this sweatshirt in any other color?*

morn *noun* (formal) morning: *see* **morning**

morning

noun the early part of the day: *I like to sleep in on Saturday mornings.*

▶ **dawn** the time each morning when light first appears: *He has to get up before dawn to go to swim practice.*

▶ **daybreak** the beginning of the day; dawn: *We left at daybreak to go bird watching.*

▶ **morn** (formal) morning: *We rose early to greet the morn.*

▶ **sunrise** the time when the sun rises: *The birds started chirping at sunrise.*

moronic *adjective* stupid: *see* **stupid**

morsel *noun* a small piece of food: *see* **scrap**

mortal *noun* a human being, especially as distinct from a divine or mythological figure: *see* **human being**

motel *noun* a hotel for motorists with parking spaces near the rooms: *see* **hotel**

motif *noun* a repeated idea, symbol, figure, or design: *see* **design**

motion *verb* to signal or direct someone by a motion, such as a wave of the hand: *see* **signal**

motionless *adjective* temporarily without motion: *see* **stationary**

motivate *verb* to provide someone with an incentive: *see* **encourage**

motive

noun a reason that causes a person to act: *My motive for doing extra work is to get a better grade.*

▶ **incentive** something that urges a person to do something or make a special effort: *The magazine offered two years for the price of one as an incentive to new subscribers.*

▶ **reason** a cause for acting, thinking, or feeling in a certain way: *I hope he had a good reason for missing soccer practice.*

▶ **stimulus** something that causes a response or increases activity: *Many people hope that the new sports stadium will be a stimulus to the city's economy.*

motor *noun* a device that provides the power to make something move or run: *see* **machine**

motorcade *noun* a procession of motor vehicles: *see* **parade**

mound *noun* a rounded pile of material such as dirt, sand, or rocks: *see* **pile**

mount *verb* to go up: *see* **climb**

mountain *noun* an area of land that rises to a great height: *see* **hill**

mourn

verb to express or feel sorrow, especially for a death; to grieve: *It is natural to **mourn** when someone we care about dies.*

▸ **grieve** to feel very sad over a loss or death; to mourn: *I **grieved** that I did not get to see her again before she died.*

▸ **lament** to express sorrow or regret over something: *He **lamented** his decision to quit his job when he realized how hard it was to find a new one.*

▸ **pine** (formal) to feel a lingering, often nostalgic desire: *I **pined** after the beautiful necklace I saw at the Renaissance Faire.*

▸ **regret** to feel a sense of sorrow or distress over a past event or act: *Do you **regret** passing up that scholarship?*

▸ **sorrow** to feel grief or sadness because of a loss or injury: *When one of my dogs died, the other one **sorrowed**.*

move *verb* to change from one place or position to another: *see* **go**

movement *noun* the activities of a large group of people toward a specific goal: *see* **campaign**

mow *verb* to cut down grass or hay: *see* **cut**

much *adverb* to a great degree or extent: *see* **very**

mud *noun* wet, sticky, soft dirt: *see* **earth [2]**

muffled *adjective* not loud or distinct: *see* **quiet**

mullah *noun* a religious teacher or leader of the Islamic faith: *see* **minister**

multiple *adjective* having more than one individual part: *see* **many**

multitude *noun* a very large number of people: *see* **crowd**

mumble *verb* to speak in an unclear way, as with the lips partially closed: *see* **whisper**

munch *verb* to chew food in a noisy, steady manner: *see* **eat**

munchies *noun* (informal) a craving for snack food: *see* **hunger**

murder *verb* to unlawfully and deliberately kill a human being: *see* **kill**

murky *adjective* very dark or gloomy: *see* **dark**

murmur *verb* to speak in a low, quiet voice: *see* **whisper**

muscle *noun* muscular strength: *see* **strength**

muscular *adjective* having large, strong muscles: *see* **strong**

muse *verb* to be absorbed in one's thoughts: *see* **think**

mushy *adjective* resembling mush; soft and pulpy: *see* **soft [2]**

muster *verb* to gather people together for inspection, roll call, or service: *see* **meet**

mute *adjective* not speaking; silent: *see* **quiet**

mutiny *noun* open rebellion against authority, especially of soldiers or sailors against their officers: *see* **rebellion**

mutter *verb* to speak in a low voice while barely moving one's lips: *see* **whisper**

mutual *adjective* shared in common between two people or groups: *see* **joint**

mysterious *adjective* impossible to understand or explain: *see* **scary**

mystery *noun* something that is not fully understood or is kept secret: *see* **problem**

mystify *verb* to confuse someone beyond any hope of understanding: *see* **confuse**

myth *noun* a story that gives the reason for the beliefs and practices of a group of people: *see* **story**

N

nab *verb* (informal)   to catch someone in the act of wrongdoing: *see* **capture**

nag

verb   to pester or annoy someone by complaining, scolding, or criticizing all the time: *I **nagged** my mother to go to the doctor for a checkup.*

▸ **badger**   to trouble someone with many questions: *The reporters **badgered** the rock star with questions about his latest romance.*

▸ **hound**   to urge or ask someone over and over; to pester: *She's been **hounding** me for that recipe.*

▸ **pester**   to annoy someone repeatedly: *Please don't **pester** me while I am doing my homework.*

nail *verb*   to fasten things together with nails: *see* **fasten**

naïve *adjective*   showing a lack of experience or judgment: *see* **ignorant**

naked

adjective   wearing no clothing: *My little nephew ran **naked** through the house after his bath.*

▸ **bald**   lacking a natural or usual covering, such as hair on the top of the head: *Many men go **bald** as they get older.*

▸ **bare**   without clothing or covering; naked: *Don't touch the hot pan with your **bare** hands.*

▸ **exposed**   made visible; revealed: *I like the **exposed** beams in that house.*

▸ **nude**   being without clothing; naked: *You can go **nude** at this beach.*

▸ **uncovered**   having the cover removed; revealed: *The **uncovered** bread became stale.*

ANTONYM **covered**   having something on or over that protects or hides something else

name *verb*   to nominate or appoint someone to a specific office or position: *see* **assign**

name *verb*   to give a name to someone or something by which that person or thing is known: *see* **call [1]**

nap *verb*   to sleep lightly and for a short period of time, usually during the night: *see* **sleep**

narrate *verb*   to tell a story in speech or writing: *see* **tell**

narrative *noun*   a usually factual story or description of how something happened: *see* **story**

nasty *adjective*   offensively dirty: *see* **dirty**

nation *noun*   a group of people who share the same territory and are organized under one government: *see* **country**

native *adjective*   originating, growing, or produced in a certain place or region: *see* **wild [1]**

natural *adjective*   found in or produced by nature: *see* **wild [1]**

nature *noun*   the basic character or quality of a person or thing: *see* **personality**

naughty *adjective*   behaving in a disobedient or mischievous way: *see* **bad [2]**

nauseated *adjective*   feeling sick in one's stomach and having a need to vomit: *see* **sick**

nauseating *adjective*   causing a feeling of sickness in the stomach characterized by the need to vomit: *see* **gross**

navigate *verb*   to direct or follow a planned course, as in a ship or other vehicle: *see* **guide**

near *preposition*   close to something, as in time, space, or degree: *see* **by**

nearly *adverb*   almost, but not quite: *see* **about**

neat *adjective*   orderly and clean; tidy: *see* **clean**

necessary

adjective ▷ important to have or do: *Getting adequate sleep is **necessary** for good health.* ▷ needed for a particular result or effect; required: *I filled out all the **necessary** forms.*

- ▸ **essential** of the greatest importance; absolutely necessary: *It is **essential** that you call me as soon as you arrive.*
- ▸ **mandatory** required or commanded by authority: *It is **mandatory** to pay taxes on earned income.*
- ▸ **needed** required or desirable for a purpose: *How much money is **needed** to send you to art school?*
- ▸ **obligatory** legally or morally binding; required or compulsory: *Attendance at the meeting is **obligatory**.*
- ▸ **required** needed to satisfy a condition; obligatory: *I have taken all the **required** courses for my veterinary degree.*

ANTONYM **unnecessary** not necessary; needless

nectar *noun* a sweet liquid found in many flowers: *see* **juice**

needed *adjective* required or desirable for a purpose: *see* **necessary**

needle *verb* to provoke or tease someone in a persistent manner: *see* **tease**

needy *adjective* in need of assistance: *see* **poor**

neglect *verb* to fail to give proper care and attention to something: *see* **forget**

negligent *adjective* guilty of neglect: *see* **careless**

negotiate

verb to settle or arrange something by discussion: *The agent **negotiated** a new contract for her client.*

- ▸ **arbitrate** to settle a dispute between two sides by acting as an impartial judge: *The workers and the management agreed to have an outside party **arbitrate** a settlement.*
- ▸ **mediate** to settle differences by working with all sides of a dispute: *The judge was asked to **mediate** the custody case.*
- ▸ **settle** to arrange or decide something by agreement: *We **settled** the dispute quickly.*
- ▸ **umpire** to act as an impartial judge, especially in a sport: *I often **umpire** baseball games for Little League.*

neighborhood *noun* a particular area or section of a city or town: *see* **community**

nemesis *noun* an opponent that cannot be beaten or overcome: *see* **enemy**

nerve *noun* courage and control under pressure: *see* **courage**

nervous

adjective easily excited or upset; fearful: *Elevators make lots of people **nervous**.*

- ▸ **anxious** nervous or afraid about something uncertain: *Waiting to hear the results of my blood tests made me **anxious**.*
- ▸ **edgy** nervous or irritable: *Coffee makes many people **edgy**.*
- ▸ **jumpy** easily upset or startled; on edge: *That scary movie made me **jumpy** for the rest of the day.*
- ▸ **tense** full of anxiety or nervous tension: *The upcoming test has made me **tense**.*
- ▸ **uneasy** worried or nervous about something that might happen: *I get **uneasy** when the power goes out.*
- ▸ **worried** uneasy or concerned about something; troubled: *I am **worried** because he is so late and hasn't called.*

ANTONYM **calm** not excited or upset

nestle *verb* to settle down snugly and comfortably: *see* **cuddle**

net *verb* to catch something in a net: *see* **trap**

neutral *adjective* not taking sides in a war, quarrel, or contest: *see* **fair¹**

nevertheless *adverb* in spite of that: *see* **anyway**

new *adjective* inexperienced or untrained: *see* **inexperienced**

new *adjective* different from the former or the old: *see* **modern**

new *adjective* existing or appearing for the first time: *see* **original [1]**

newsletter *noun* a printed report giving news or information of interest to a special group: *see* **magazine**

newspaper *noun* a publication, usually issued daily or weekly, containing current news, editorials, articles, and advertisements: *see* **magazine**

nibble *verb* to eat something with small, quick bites: *see* **eat**

nice *adjective* ▷ pleasing and agreeable ▷ thoughtful and well-mannered: *see* **pleasant**

nicely *adverb* in a good, pleasant, or agreeably way: *see* **well**

niche *noun* a hollow place in a wall, as for holding a statue: *see* **shelf**

night

noun the period of time between sunset and sunrise, especially the hours of darkness: *I like to see the fireflies come out at **night**.*

- ▶ **darkness** partial or total absence of light: *I couldn't see anything in the **darkness** of the cave.*
- ▶ **evening** the time between sunset and the time to go to bed; early night: *I watch the news in the **evening**.*
- ▶ **midnight** the middle of the night; twelve o'clock at night: *The party lasted until **midnight**.*

nightfall *noun* the coming of darkness at the end of the day: *see* **sunset**

nimble *adjective* quick and light in movement: *see* **agile**

nip *verb* to seize and pinch something sharply with the teeth: *see* **bite**

noble

adjective having or showing high moral character, courage, generosity, or self-sacrifice: *Helping people learn to read is a **noble** cause.*

- ▶ **majestic** grand or magnificent: *Redwoods are **majestic** trees that can grow to be more than 300 feet tall.*
- ▶ **regal** like a king or queen: *She looked **regal** in her evening dress.*
- ▶ **royal** fit for a monarch; splendid: *The troops received a **royal** welcome when they returned home.*
- ▶ **stately** marked by great dignity or formality: *The presidential inauguration is a **stately** occasion.*

nod *noun* an up-and-down motion of the head, especially to indicate agreement: *see* **signal**

noise

noun a loud, usually unpleasant or unexpected sound: *The **noise** from the barking dogs woke me.*

- ▶ **clamor** a loud noise, as of a crowd shouting: *We could hear the **clamor** from the party next door.*
- ▶ **din** loud and harsh noise: *I rolled up my car window to block out the **din** of the road work.*
- ▶ **hubbub** noisy confusion; uproar: *I lost my friend in the **hubbub** of the crowded mall.*
- ▶ **racket** a loud, annoying noise: *All the pots and pans spilled out of the cupboard and made a terrible **racket**.*
- ▶ **uproar** a condition of noisy excitement and confusion: *The crowd was in an **uproar** when the score became tied.*

ANTONYM **silence** little or no noise

noisy *adjective* making a lot of noise: *see* **loud**

nominate *verb* to propose someone as a candidate for an office, responsibility, or honor: *see* **assign**

nonetheless *adverb* even though: *see* **anyway**

nonsense

noun foolish or ridiculous talk or behavior: *He made up a funny story that was pure **nonsense**.*

▸ **absurdity** something that is too ridiculous to be believed: *The children laughed at the **absurdities** in the cartoon.*

▸ **craziness** extreme foolishness; something completely lacking in reason: *My friends think that it is **craziness** to get a tattoo.*

▸ **folly** something lacking in good sense or foresight; foolishness: *Sometimes an important invention is treated as a **folly** at first.*

▸ **foolishness** something that shows a lack of good sense, judgment, or wisdom: *It was **foolishness** to pay so much money for a dress that I hardly ever wear.*

▸ **silliness** a lack of good sense or reason; frivolous or ridiculous behavior: *We enjoyed the **silliness** of playing children's games at the party.*

▸ **stupidity** the quality of being pointless, worthless, or unintelligent: *It was **stupidity** to go to the airport without our airline tickets.*

nook *noun* a small corner or recess, especially one in a large room: *see* **shelf**

no problem *adjective* (informal) easy: *see* **easy**

normal

adjective ▷ of the usual or regular kind: *The river returned to its **normal** level one week after the flood.* ▷ functioning in a natural, healthy way: *This drug can interfere with **normal** digestion.*

▸ **average** being of a typical kind or a usual level or degree: *He is an **average** student in math but he's excellent in Spanish.*

▸ **medium** being between two extremes: *These T-shirts come in small, **medium**, and large sizes.*

▸ **ordinary** of no exceptional ability, degree, or quality; average: *I had an **ordinary** day at school.*

▸ **standard** of the usual or familiar kind: *The politician gave her **standard** speech.*

▸ **typical** showing the common characteristics that identify a group, kind, or class: *The **typical** American household has at least one TV set.*

▸ **usual** commonly encountered, experienced, or observed; ordinary: *Our **usual** bus driver was absent today.*

ANTONYM **abnormal** not usual or normal; unusual

normally *adverb* usually; customarily: *see* **often**

note *verb* to show or indicate something: *see* **emphasize**

note *noun* a short written message: *see* **letter**

notebook *noun* a book of blank, often lined pages used for writing notes: *see* **book**

noteworthy *adjective* worthy of notice or attention: *see* **memorable**

notice *noun* a published or displayed announcement: *see* **announcement**

notice *noun* respectful or critical attention: *see* **attention**

notify *verb* to give notice to someone: *see* **alert**

notion *noun* a sudden inclination, impulse, or idea: *see* **idea**

not many *adjective* just a few: *see* **few**

notorious *adjective* well known for something bad or unpleasant: *see* **famous**

nourish *verb* to provide someone or something with what is needed for growth and development: *see* **feed**

novel *adjective* very new, unusual, or different: *see* **original [1]**

novelist *noun* one who writes lengthy works of fiction: *see* **writer**

novice *noun* a person who is new to a field or activity: *see* **beginner**

nucleus *noun* a central or essential part around which other parts are grouped: *see* **center [1]**

nude *adjective* being without clothing: *see* **naked**

nudge *verb* to push someone or something in a gentle way, especially in order to attract attention: *see* **poke**

number *noun* an indefinite quantity: *see* **amount**

numerous *adjective* amounting to a large number: *see* **many**

nun *noun* a woman who is a member of a religious community: *see* **minister**

nurse *noun* a person who is trained to care for sick and disabled people: *see* **doctor**

nurture *verb* to feed and protect a person or animal: *see* **feed**

nuzzle *verb* to rub or push against a person or animal gently with the nose or snout: *see* **cuddle**

O

oath *noun* a statement or promise that what one says is true: *see* **promise**

obese *adjective* very fat; extremely overweight: *see* **fat**

obey

verb to do what is commanded or requested: *Soldiers are expected to* **obey** *the orders given by an officer.*

▸ **comply** to follow a request or rule: *Our school* **complies** *with all the fire safety rules.*
▸ **mind** to pay attention in order to obey someone: *The parents told their children to* **mind** *the babysitter.*
▸ **observe** to follow or respect a rule or tradition: *Jews traditionally* **observe** *Passover with a feast known as a Seder.*

ANTONYM **disobey** to refuse or fail to obey a person or rule

object *verb* to express an opposing opinion or argument: *see* **complain**

object *noun* the purpose or goal of a specific action or effort: *see* **goal**

objection *noun* a statement of an opposing view or argument: *see* **complaint**

objectionable *adjective* causing offense or disapproval: *see* **unpleasant**

objective *adjective* not influenced by personal feelings or prejudice: *see* **fair**[1]

objective *noun* something that one tries to achieve or reach: *see* **goal**

obligation *noun* a legal, social, or moral requirement: *see* **duty**

obligatory *adjective* legally or morally binding; required or compulsory: *see* **necessary**

oblige *verb* to do a service or favor for someone: *see* **indulge**

oblivious *adjective* completely unaware: *see* **ignorant**

obscure *adjective* hard to understand: *see* **vague**

observant *adjective* quick to perceive or understand: *see* **alert**

observation *noun* a comment or remark drawn from experience: *see* **comment**

observe *verb* to see and pay attention to something: *see* **look**

observe *verb* to follow or respect a rule or tradition: *see* **obey**

obstacle

noun something that blocks or stands in the way: *The fallen rocks were an* **obstacle** *to the cars on the road.*

▸ **barricade** a quickly built structure set up to block passage or keep back attackers: *Road workers set up* **barricades** *to detour traffic.*
▸ **barrier** something that blocks movement or passage: *The river was a* **barrier** *that the forest fire was unable to cross.*
▸ **blockade** the closing of an area, such as a city or harbor, so as to prevent the movement of people and supplies: *During the Civil War, the North set up a naval* **blockade** *to prevent the South from getting supplies.*
▸ **hurdle** an obstacle or difficulty to be overcome: *Helen Keller overcame the* **hurdles** *of being deaf and blind to become an inspiring speaker.*
▸ **obstruction** something that blocks movement or gets in the way of something: *My dog lies in the hallway and is an* **obstruction** *to vacuuming the carpet.*
▸ **snag** a sudden or unexpected difficulty: *We ran into a* **snag** *and had to change our plans.*

obstinate *adjective* stubbornly holding to an attitude, opinion, or course of action: *see* **stubborn**

obstruct *verb* to make it difficult to pass through something: *see* **block**

obstruction *noun* something that blocks movement or gets in the way of something: *see* **obstacle**

obtain *verb* to gain or get something, especially by means of planning or effort: *see* **get**

obvious *adjective* easily noticed or understood: *see* **clear [1]**

occasion *noun* an important or festive event: *see* **event**

occasional *adjective* occurring from time to time: *see* **irregular**

occasionally *adverb* from time to time but not often or regularly: *see* **rarely**

occupant

noun someone who lives in a place, especially on a temporary basis: *The former occupants of the apartment left it very clean.*

- ▸ **inhabitant** a resident of a place, such as a neighborhood, city, or region: *How many inhabitants are there on this island?*
- ▸ **lodger** a person who rents a room in another person's house: *We decided to take a college student as a lodger.*
- ▸ **resident** a person who lives in a particular place, especially on a permanent basis: *My grandmother has been a resident of Wisconsin all her life.*
- ▸ **tenant** a person who pays rent to use or live on property that is owned by another person: *My parents have found a tenant for their rental home.*

occupation *noun* a profession, business, or job: *see* **job**

occupied *adjective* devoting time to an activity or purpose: *see* **busy**

occur *verb* to happen or come about: *see* **happen**

occurrence *noun* something that happens or takes place: *see* **event**

odd *adjective* not ordinary or usual: *see* **strange**

odor *noun* a smell or scent: *see* **smell**

offend

verb to cause hurt feelings, anger, or annoyance in someone: *My friend was **offended** when I forgot to meet her.*

- ▸ **insult** to treat someone rudely and disrespectfully, especially on purpose: *The man **insulted** his coworker's new haircut.*
- ▸ **outrage** to produce extreme anger or resentment in someone: *She was **outraged** by the rude remark.*
- ▸ **provoke** to incite a person to anger or resentment, often deliberately: *The children sat in the car and made faces to **provoke** one another.*
- ▸ **vex** to irritate or annoy someone: *It **vexed** me when I couldn't find the overdue library book.*

offense *noun* a violation of a moral, legal, or social code: *see* **crime**

offensive *adjective* causing anger, displeasure, or resentment: *see* **unpleasant**

offer *verb* to present something for acceptance or rejection: *see* **give**

offering *noun* something given as an act of worship or tribute: *see* **gift**

office *noun* a place in which business, clerical, or professional work is done: *see* **agency**

often

adverb many times; frequently: *I like to play hockey as **often** as I can.*

- ▸ **commonly** ordinarily; usually: *We **commonly** go to the beach every weekend in the summertime.*
- ▸ **frequently** often; many times: *She **frequently** travels by airplane.*
- ▸ **generally** as a rule; usually: *I **generally** get up at seven a.m.*
- ▸ **normally** usually; customarily: *When do you **normally** go to bed?*
- ▸ **ordinarily** as a regular thing; commonly: *He **ordinarily** takes the bus to work.*
- ▸ **typically** as a usual routine; usually: *I **typically** go to the laundromat on Saturday.*
- ▸ **usually** ordinarily; in the normal course of events: *They **usually** go to the movies twice a month.*

ogre *noun* a giant or monster in folklore and fairy tales that eats human beings: *see* **monster**

oil *noun* any of a large group of slippery, usually liquid substances that burn easily and do not mix with water: *see* **fat**

old

adjective having lived or been in existence for a long time: *Social Security was created to help **old** people after they retire.*

- ▸ **aged** having reached old age: *My **aged** aunt still takes a long walk every day.*
- ▸ **ancient** from a long time ago; very old: *We visited the **ancient** Mayan ruins on our vacation to Central America.*
- ▸ **antique** from a previous time or era; very old: *My stepmother restores **antique** furniture.*
- ▸ **elderly** approaching old age; old: *Our **elderly** neighbor stays active by working in his garden.*

ANTONYM **young** being in an early stage of life or growth; not fully developed

omen *noun* something that is thought to be a sign of a good or bad event to come: *see* **sign**

omit *verb* to leave something out: *see* **forget**

once *conjunction* as soon as: *see* **after**

once again *adverb* for another time: *see* **again**

one-sided *adjective* limited to one side or group: *see* **unfair**

only

adverb exclusively; solely: *That perfume is sold **only** at fine department stores.*

- ▸ **just** merely; only: *I **just** have enough money to buy a small present.*
- ▸ **simply** just; only: *I **simply** called to let you know that I'm on my way home.*
- ▸ **solely** entirely; exclusively: *My decision was based **solely** on the information I had at the time.*

onset *noun* a beginning; a start: *see* **beginning**

ooze *verb* to flow or leak out slowly: *see* **leak**

open

verb to release something from a closed, fastened, or sealed position: *I **opened** the window to let in some fresh air.*

- ▸ **uncover** to remove the cover from something: *The cook **uncovered** the pot roast to let it brown in the oven.*
- ▸ **unearth** to bring up something out of the earth; to dig something up: *The squirrel **unearthed** the nuts she had buried last summer.*
- ▸ **unfasten** to open something, as by disconnecting it or untying it: *I **unfastened** the stall door and let my horse out.*
- ▸ **unlock** to open something by undoing a lock: *She **unlocked** her car.*
- ▸ **unwrap** to remove the wrapping from something: *He **unwrapped** his birthday presents.*

ANTONYM **close** to shut something

opening *noun* an open space or clearing: *see* **gap**

operate *verb* to work or run something: *see* **use**

operation *noun* a coordinated action, especially by an army or government: *see* **campaign**

opinion

noun a belief based on what one thinks or feels, but not on positive knowledge or proof: *It is my **opinion** that we'll have a cold winter.*

- ▸ **angle** a particular way of looking at something: *He considered the job offer from every **angle**.*
- ▸ **belief** something accepted as true: *It's my **belief** that honesty is the best policy.*
- ▸ **conviction** a strong belief: *She has strong **convictions** regarding freedom of the press.*
- ▸ **outlook** a way of looking at things; an attitude: *A positive **outlook** can help you get through a bad day.*

▸ **perspective** a mental view or outlook: *From my* **perspective**, *the problem doesn't look too difficult.*

▸ **viewpoint** a way of thinking about something: *We should consider the situation from his* **viewpoint**.

opponent *noun* a person or group that opposes another in a battle, contest, controversy, or debate: *see* **enemy**

opportunity *noun* a favorable combination of circumstances: *see* **chance**

oppose *verb* to be in conflict with someone or something: *see* **rebel**

opposed to *preposition* in opposition or resistance to something: *see* **against**

opposition *noun* resistance to something that one disagrees with: *see* **disagreement**

opt *verb* to make a choice or decision: *see* **choose**

optimistic

adjective taking a hopeful or cheerful view of things: *Our drama teacher is* **optimistic** *that the school play will be a success.*

▸ **expectant** looking forward to the probable occurrence or appearance of something: *The* **expectant** *audience looked forward to the performance.*

▸ **hopeful** feeling or showing hope: *I am* **hopeful** *that I did better on this test than I did on the last one.*

▸ **idealistic** having the ability to envision things in their ideal form: *He is* **idealistic** *about parenthood.*

ANTONYM **pessimistic** tending to take the gloomiest and least hopeful view of a situation

option *noun* a choice, especially one that is offered by someone else: *see* **choice**

opus *noun* a creative work, especially a musical piece: *see* **invention**

ordain *verb* (formal) to order something by means of superior authority: *see* **dictate**

order *verb* to issue a command or instruction: *see* **demand**

order *verb* to put items into a methodical, systematic arrangement: *see* **sort**

orderly *adjective* arranged or done in a careful or thoughtful way: *see* **clean**

ordinarily *adverb* as a regular thing: *see* **often**

ordinary *adjective* commonly met with: *see* **common**

ordinary *adjective* of no exceptional ability, degree, or quality: *see* **normal**

organism *noun* a living individual, such as a plant or animal: *see* **animal**

organization *noun* a group of people united for some purpose or work: *see* **club**

organize *verb* to arrange things in an orderly way: *see* **plan**

origin *noun* the source or beginning of something: *see* **basis**

original

adjective [1] fresh and newly created; not based on something else: *The idea for your story has to be* **original**, *not copied from something you've read.*

▸ **fresh** new and unusual; different: *She tried a* **fresh** *approach to solving the problem.*

▸ **new** existing or appearing for the first time: *This computer uses* **new** *technology.*

▸ **novel** very new, unusual, or different: *My art teacher said that I have a* **novel** *style of painting.*

▸ **unused** never having been used: *I bought an* **unused** *toaster at a garage sale.*

original

adjective [2] preceding all others in time; first: *Our car still has its* **original** *coat of paint.*

▸ **earliest** happening near the beginning of a time period, series, or course of events: *My* **earliest** *memory is that of my mother singing to me.*

▸ **first** coming before all others: *The* **first** *song on this CD is my favorite.*

▸ **initial** happening at the very beginning; first: *My initial opinion of him has changed since getting to know him better.*

▸ **premier** first to occur or exist; earliest: *We attended the premier performance of the new orchestra.*

originality *noun* the capability to think up new ideas: *see* **imagination**

ornament *noun* something that makes a person or thing more attractive or beautiful: *see* **accessory**

ornament *verb* to supply something with beautiful or decorative additions: *see* **decorate**

ornate *adjective* having lavish or elaborate decorations: *see* **fancy**

ornery *adjective* mean and stubborn: *see* **stubborn**

orthodox *adjective* following accepted or established beliefs or doctrines: *see* **religious**

other *adjective* different: *see* **more**

outcome *noun* something that happens as a result of a process or action: *see* **result**

outer *adjective* located on the outside: *see* **outside**

outermost *adjective* farthest from the center: *see* **outside**

outfit *noun* a set of clothing and accessories that go together: *see* **clothing**

outfit *verb* to furnish someone with equipment or clothing for a specific activity: *see* **equip**

outlaw *noun* a person who defies the law: *see* **criminal**

outlaw *verb* to declare something illegal: *see* **forbid**

outline *verb* to draw only the outer edge of something: *see* **draw**

outlook *noun* a way of looking at things: *see* **opinion**

outrage *verb* to produce extreme anger or resentment in someone: *see* **offend**

outrageous *adjective* exceeding what is right or proper: *see* **shocking**

outside

adjective on or near to the outer surface, side, or part of something: *The outside walls of our building need a new coat of paint.*

▸ **exterior** outer or outside; external: *The exterior surface of the space shuttle has to withstand extremely high temperatures.*

▸ **external** on the outside or outer surface of something: *All insects have six legs and an external skeleton.*

▸ **outer** located on the outside; external: *Crabs and lobsters both have hard outer shells.*

▸ **outermost** farthest from the center: *Pluto is the outermost planet in our solar system.*

outsider *noun* a person who is not part of a certain group or activity: *see* **stranger**

outstanding *adjective* noticeably superior to others of its kind: *see* **excellent**

ovation *noun* a loud and enthusiastic display of approval, usually in the form of applause: *see* **applause**

over *adverb* higher than: *see* **above**

over and over *adverb* again and again: *see* **again**

over *adjective* completely finished: *see* **done**

overcast

adjective covered over with clouds or haze: *The sky was overcast all day, but it never rained.*

▸ **cloudy** marked by or covered with clouds: *It was cloudy in the morning, but the sun came out in the afternoon.*

▸ **foggy** full of or covered by fog: *The airport was closed because of the foggy weather.*

▸ **hazy** full of or covered with haze: *The atmosphere was hazy because of the smoke from the forest fire.*

▸ **misty** full of or covered by mist: *The steam from my shower made the mirror misty.*

ANTONYM **clear** free from clouds, mist, haze, or dust

overdue *adjective* not paid on time: *see* **late**

overhead *adverb* above the level of the head: *see* **above**

overlook *verb* to intentionally or unintentionally fail to notice something: *see* **forget**

overlord *noun* a ruler having power or supremacy over other rulers: *see* **tyrant**

overpriced *adjective* costing more than is reasonable: *see* **expensive**

overripe *adjective* too ripe to be eaten fresh: *see* **rotten**

overrule *verb* to decide against something by virtue of higher authority: *see* **reverse**

oversee *verb* to watch over the operation of something: *see* **manage**

oversight *noun* a careless mistake: *see* **mistake**

overthrow *verb* to bring about the downfall or destruction of an established power: *see* **defeat**

overturn *verb* to invalidate or reverse a decision by legal means: *see* **reverse**

overweight *adjective* weighing more than is normal or healthy: *see* **fat**

overwhelm *verb* to defeat someone completely and decisively: *see* **defeat**

own *verb* to have as something belonging to oneself: *see* **have**

pace *noun* the rate of speed at which a person or animal walks or runs: *see* **speed**

pack *verb* to fill a container neatly with items, as for storage or travel: *see* **fill**

pack *noun* a group of animals that run and hunt together: *see* **group**

package

noun a wrapped or boxed object or group of objects: *The mail carrier left a package on our front porch.*

▸ **bundle** a number of things bound or wrapped together: *I carried a bundle of firewood into the house.*
▸ **packet** a small package or bundle: *In the old trunk was a packet of letters tied with a blue ribbon.*
▸ **parcel** something wrapped up in a bundle; a package: *The post office delivers millions of parcels every year.*

packet *noun* a small package or bundle: *see* **package**

pad

noun a usually flat mass of soft material used to provide comfort or protection: *We used a blanket and a foam pad to make a bed for our dog.*

▸ **carpet** a heavy woven fabric used as a covering for a floor: *We had new carpet installed in our living room.*
▸ **cushion** a soft pad or pillow that is used to sit, lie, or rest on: *Our couch needs new cushions.*
▸ **mat** a flat piece of material used as a floor or seat covering: *She bought a new mat to put in front of the kitchen sink.*
▸ **mattress** a pad of heavy cloth filled with soft material that is used on or as a bed: *I like to sleep on a firm mattress.*
▸ **pillow** a case filled with soft material, typically used to cushion a person's head during sleep: *I bought new pillows because the old ones had become lumpy.*

page *verb* to summon or call someone by name in a public place: *see* **call [2]**

pageant *noun* a play or dramatic spectacle that is often based on an event in history: *see* **show**

pail *noun* a cylindrical container, open at the top and fitted with a handle: *see* **bucket**

pain

noun ▷ physical suffering caused by injury or sickness: *I was surprised that I didn't feel much pain when I broke my arm.* ▷ mental or emotional suffering: *The counselor helped the family deal with the pain of divorce.*

▸ **ache** a dull, steady pain: *I have an ache in my legs from walking so much at the mall.*
▸ **pang** a sudden, sharp feeling, as of pain or strong emotion: *I felt a pang of sadness when I realized that my vacation would end in two days.*
▸ **sting** a sharp, burning pain: *I felt the sting of the cold wind on my ears.*
▸ **stitch** a sudden, sharp pain, especially in the side: *He had to stop running when he got a stitch in his side.*
▸ **twinge** ▷ a sudden but temporary physical pain: *Her old knee injury gives her a twinge every now and then.* ▷ a brief, sharp feeling of something unpleasant: *He felt a twinge of guilt over his mean remark.*

painstaking *adjective* involving or showing great care or thoroughness: *see* **careful [1]**

painting *noun* a picture or design made with paints: *see* **picture**

pair

noun two objects, people, or animals considered together: *We keep a pair of rabbits as pets.*

▸ **couple** two people who are closely associated with each other, as in marriage or a romantic relationship: *My boyfriend and I went dancing with several other couples.*

▸ **duo** two performers working together; two people in close association: *Batman and Robin are a famous duo in the comic books.*

▸ **twosome** two people associated with each other, as in friendship or romance; a couple: *My friend and I are beginning to be known as a twosome.*

pal *noun* (informal) a close friend: *see* **friend**

palace *noun* a ruler's official residence: *see* **house**

pale

adjective containing a large amount of white; light in color: *Her dress is a pale shade of pink.*

▸ **ashen** having a pale skin color, especially due to illness or emotion: *My friend was so ashen that I asked him if he felt sick.*

▸ **colorless** completely lacking in color: *Carbon monoxide is a poisonous gas that is both colorless and odorless.*

▸ **light** of a shade of color closer to white than black: *I painted my bedroom a light yellow.*

▸ **pallid** lacking healthy color; pale: *Her complexion was pallid after being ill for so long.*

▸ **whitish** somewhat white: *Cream is a whitish color.*

ANTONYM **bright** strong or clear in color; vivid

pallid *adjective* lacking healthy color: *see* **pale**

pamper *verb* to treat someone with extreme indulgence: *see* **indulge**

pamphlet *noun* a short essay or commentary, usually on a current topic, published without a binding: *see* **booklet**

pan *noun* a wide, shallow, open container used especially for cooking: *see* **bucket**

panel *noun* a group of people gathered together to plan or discuss an issue, judge a contest, or otherwise act as a team: *see* **committee**

pang *noun* a sudden, sharp feeling, as of pain or strong emotion: *see* **pain**

panic *noun* a sudden feeling of great fear, especially without a clear cause: *see* **fear**

panic-stricken *adjective* overcome by sudden fear or panic: *see* **frantic**

panorama *noun* a view or picture of everything that can be seen over a wide area: *see* **view**

pant *verb* to breathe in short, quick gasps: *see* **breathe**

paper *noun* an official document, especially one that establishes the identity of the bearer: *see* **document**

paper *noun* a written work assigned in school: *see* **essay**

paper *noun* a newspaper: *see* **magazine**

parade

noun an organized public procession on a festive or ceremonial occasion, often with music, costumes, and colorful display: *I like to watch the flower-covered floats in the annual Rose Parade on TV.*

▸ **caravan** a group of people or vehicles traveling together: *My friends and I drove our cars in a caravan to the concert.*

▸ **cavalcade** a ceremonial procession of people on horseback, in carriages, or in automobiles: *The queen's cavalcade included a mounted guard and dozens of fancy carriages.*

▸ **motorcade** a procession of motor vehicles: *The President's motorcade drove through the city to the governor's mansion.*

▸ **procession** a group of people, vehicles, or objects moving along in orderly succession: *A police car was at the head of the funeral procession.*

paradise

noun a place of ideal beauty or loveliness: *Many people consider Hawaii a tropical paradise.*

▸ **heaven** a condition or place of great happiness, delight, or pleasure: *She was in* **heaven** *when she won a full scholarship to the college of her choice.*

▸ **utopia** an ideally perfect place, especially in its social, political, or moral aspects: *In a* **utopia***, there would be no conflict between the personal good and the common good.*

paradox *noun* something that is apparently contradictory: *see* **problem**

parallel *verb* to match something else feature for feature: *see* **compare**

paramedic *noun* a person who is trained to give emergency treatment or to assist medical professionals: *see* **doctor**

parcel *noun* something wrapped up in a bundle: *see* **package**

parched *adjective* very dry, as from intense heat: *see* **dry**

pardon *verb* ▹ to release someone from punishment ▹ to excuse an offense or inconvenience: *see* **forgive**

pare *verb* to remove the skin or rind from something with a knife: *see* **peel**

parent

noun a father or mother: *My* **parents** *are saving money for my college education.*

▸ **ancestor** a person from whom one is descended: *One of my* **ancestors** *fought in the Revolutionary War.*

▸ **forebear** (formal) an ancestor: *Our* **forebears** *came to this country seeking freedom and opportunity.*

▸ **foster parent** a person who provides parental care to a child who is not legally or biologically related: *He lives independently now but is still in touch with his* **foster parents***.*

▸ **guardian** a person who is legally responsible for the care of a child: *She has been named the* **guardian** *of the orphaned child.*

▸ **stepparent** a parent who is related by marriage to one's biological parent: *He is the parent of two children and the* **stepparent** *to another by his second marriage.*

park

noun an area of land used for recreation: *My friends and I like to play softball in the city* **park***.*

▸ **courtyard** an open space surrounded by buildings or enclosed by walls: *The* **courtyard** *behind the church was quiet and shady.*

▸ **garden** a piece of land where flowers, vegetables, or fruit are grown: *The vegetable* **garden** *had a border of flowers around it.*

▸ **lawn** a piece of ground planted with grass: *I mowed the* **lawn** *when I came home from work.*

▸ **playground** an outdoor area for play, sports, and games: *The* **playground** *in our apartment complex has swings and a slide.*

▸ **yard** a piece of ground associated with a building: *We bought this house because we liked the big* **yard***.*

parson *noun* a minister, especially in the Anglican Church: *see* **minister**

part *noun* a portion or division of a whole: *see* **piece**

part *verb* to divide or break something into separate parts: *see* **separate**

partial *adjective* especially attracted or inclined: *see* **prone**

partial *adjective* favoring one person or side over another: *see* **unfair**

particle *noun* a very small piece or amount: *see* **piece**

particular *noun* a single item, fact, or detail: *see* **detail**

partition *noun* something, such as a partial wall, that divides up a room: *see* **wall**

partner

noun one of two or more people associated in a business: *My dad and my uncle are business* **partners***.*

▸ **accomplice** a person who helps another do something wrong or illegal: *The bank robber's* **accomplice** *drove the get-away car.*

▶ **associate** a person who regularly spends time with another: *I went to lunch with some of my work associates.*

▶ **colleague** a fellow member of a staff or organization: *The professor was applauded by her colleagues when she finished her speech.*

party

noun a gathering of people for pleasure or entertainment: *My sisters and I are going to throw a party for our parents' 25th anniversary.*

▶ **affair** a social gathering: *The opening of the new art exhibit was a crowded affair.*

▶ **ball** a formal social dance: *I was asked to attend the Winter Ball.*

▶ **celebration** a party or other festive activity to honor a special occasion: *There was a big celebration when our team won the championship.*

▶ **dance** a gathering at which people dance: *Are you going to the senior class dance?*

▶ **get-together** (informal) a small party or gathering: *We're going to have pizza and watch a movie at the get-together this Friday.*

▶ **masquerade** a dance or party at which masks and fancy costumes are worn: *He went to the masquerade dressed as George Washington.*

▶ **social** an informal social gathering: *Our church group is having a social this Sunday evening.*

party

verb to celebrate by having a party: *We partied all night long after graduation.*

▶ **carouse** to engage in noisy drinking, especially of alcohol: *He used to carouse with his friends but he's settled down now that he's married and has a family.*

▶ **celebrate** to observe a day or event with ceremonies of respect, festivity, or rejoicing: *Our town has a parade and a picnic to celebrate Independence Day.*

▶ **revel** to engage in uproarious festivities; to make merry: *We spent the evening singing and reveling in celebration of Cinco de Mayo.*

pass *verb* to go across, over, or through something: *see* **go**

passageway *noun* a narrow way or path leading from one place to another: *see* **hall**

passed away *adjective* no longer living: *see* **dead**

passion *noun* overwhelming enthusiasm for a certain activity or subject: *see* **enthusiasm**

passion *noun* a powerful or intense feeling: *see* **feeling**

passionate *adjective* full of strong or overwhelming feeling: *see* **enthusiastic**

pass over *verb* to leave someone out: *see* **exclude**

past *preposition* beyond something in time or place: *see* **after**

pastime *noun* an activity that occupies one's time pleasurably: *see* **recreation**

pastor *noun* a Christian minister or priest having spiritual charge over a congregation or other group: *see* **minister**

pasture *noun* ground where animals are put to graze: *see* **field [1]**

pat *verb* to stroke or tap something gently with the open hand: *see* **touch**

patch *verb* to cover or mend something with a patch: *see* **fix**

path

noun a track made for walking: *This gravel path goes all the way around the lake.*

▶ **aisle** a passageway between two rows of seats or shelves: *The little boy got lost in the aisles of the grocery store.*

▶ **channel** a course or passage through which something may move or be directed: *The deep-water channel through the harbor is marked by buoys.*

▶ **lane** a narrow path or road between fences, hedges, or walls: *I live on a country lane that is lined with maple trees.*

► **sidewalk** a paved walkway on the side of a road: *The city is putting in new sidewalks by my apartment building.*

► **track** a path, route, or course: *There is a paved track along the river for bicyclists and skaters.*

► **trail** a path or track, especially through woods: *The park ranger led the children along a trail and told them about the local wildlife.*

patience

noun the quality of being able to put up with trouble, hardship, annoyance, or delay without complaining: *The audience waited with patience for the concert to begin.*

► **calmness** absence of excitement or disturbance; a quiet or peaceful state: *The nurse's calmness was soothing to her patient.*

► **forbearance** the act of exercising tolerance and restraint in the face of provocation: *It takes great forbearance to be a good parent.*

► **restraint** the act of controlling one's emotions or impulses: *It took some restraint to keep from telling my sister what her birthday present was going to be.*

► **tolerance** the capacity for recognizing and respecting the beliefs or practices of others: *Tolerance among nations is vital for world peace.*

patient

adjective able to put up with trouble, hardship, annoyance, or delay without complaining: *She is a popular babysitter because she is so patient.*

► **tolerant** showing willingness to let other people hold opinions or follow practices that are different from one's own: *I try to be tolerant of people's opinions that are different from my own.*

► **understanding** showing or having kind, tolerant, or sympathetic feelings: *Thank you for being so understanding of my situation.*

ANTONYM **impatient** not having the ability to wait patiently

patrol *verb* to move about an area for the purpose of observation, inspection, and security: *see* **protect**

patron *noun* a regular customer of a store, restaurant, or other business: *see* **customer**

pattern *noun* a diagram or model used to make things: *see* **design**

pattern *noun* actions or events that are repeated in a recognizable arrangement: *see* **habit**

pause *noun* a temporary stop: *see* **break**

pause *verb* to stop briefly: *see* **stop**

pay *verb* to give an amount of money in return for goods or services: *see* **buy**

pay *noun* money given in exchange for goods or services: *see* **income**

pay *verb* to give money in exchange for goods or for work done: *see* **spend**

pay attention *verb* to take careful notice: *see* **hear**

payment *noun* an amount of money paid toward the price of something: *see* **price**

peace

noun ▷ the absence of war or fighting: *There has always been peace between the United States and Canada.* ▷ freedom from mental or emotional upset: *I feel more at peace now that I know you're safe.*

► **accord** (formal) a state of agreement: *Many students and teachers are in accord that summer vacation is too short.*

► **harmony** agreement in feeling or opinion; friendly relations: *The committee worked together in harmony.*

► **truce** a temporary stop in fighting: *The generals of the opposing armies called a truce.*

peaceful *adjective* undisturbed by turmoil, strife, or disagreement: *see* **calm**

peak *noun* the point of greatest development or intensity: *see* **prime**

peak *noun* ▷ a tapering point that projects upwards ▷ the pointed top of a mountain: *see* **top**

pebble *noun* a small round stone: *see* **rock**

peck *verb* to eat small amounts of what is served: *see* **eat**

peculiar *adjective* not usual: *see* **strange**

peddle *verb* to travel about while selling something: *see* **sell**

peek *verb* to glance or look at something quickly or secretly: *see* **look**

peel

verb to remove the skin or rind from something: *I was curious to see how the monkey would **peel** its banana.*

- ▸ **pare** to remove the skin or rind from something with a knife: *I **pared** several cups of apples to make a pie.*
- ▸ **shed** to lose something naturally: *I watched our pet snake **shed** its skin.*
- ▸ **shell** to remove the hard outer covering from something: *He **shelled** the peanuts and ate them.*
- ▸ **shuck** to remove the husk or shell from something: *She **shucked** the corn before boiling it.*
- ▸ **strip** to remove the covering or outer layer from something: *We **stripped** all the paint off the cabinet.*

peer *noun* a person of the same age, rank, or standing as another: *see* **friend**

peevish *adjective* ill-humored and easily annoyed: *see* **irritable**

peg *noun* a pin, often of wood, used to fasten or hang things: *see* **hook**

pelt *noun* an animal skin, especially with the hair or fur still on it: *see* **hide**[1]

pen *noun* a small, fenced-in area where animals are kept: *see* **cage**

pen *verb* to write or compose something with or as if with a pen: *see* **write**

penalize *verb* to give a penalty or disadvantage to someone, as for breaking a rule: *see* **punish**

penalty

noun punishment for a crime or offense: *The **penalty** for drunk driving often includes the loss of one's driver's license.*

- ▸ **correction** (formal) punishment intended to rehabilitate or improve an offender: *A prison for persons who have committed minor offenses is often called a house of **correction**.*
- ▸ **fine** a sum of money that has to be paid as a penalty for breaking a law or rule: *I had to pay a **fine** to the city for littering.*
- ▸ **punishment** a penalty for a crime or wrongdoing: *It is a principle of justice that the **punishment** should fit the crime.*
- ▸ **ticket** a legal summons given to a person accused of breaking a traffic law: *We got a parking **ticket** for not putting money in the meter.*

penchant *noun* (formal) a strong inclination: *see* **tendency**

penetrate *verb* to pass into or through something: *see* **stab**

pen name *noun* an invented name used by an author: *see* **disguise**

penniless *adjective* having no money: *see* **poor**

penny-pinching *adjective* giving or spending money very reluctantly: *see* **thrifty**

pension *noun* a sum of money paid regularly to people who are retired: *see* **income**

people *noun* a group of persons living in the same country under one national government: *see* **public**

pep *noun* high spirits or energy: *see* **energy**

perceive *verb* to become aware of something through the senses, especially the senses of sight or hearing: *see* **understand**

perfect

adjective excellent in every way; lacking nothing: *My uncle speaks **perfect** Arabic.*

▶ **faultless** being without fault or flaw: *Her manners are always* **faultless**.

▶ **ideal** meeting the highest standard of perfection or excellence: *He thinks that sushi is the* **ideal** *food*.

▶ **model** worthy of imitation: *She is a* **model** *athlete who plays hard but always shows good sportsmanship*.

perfectly *adverb* fully; entirely: *see* **completely**

perform *noun* to act or function in a specific way: *see* **behave**

performance *noun* a public presentation of something, such as a work of art or entertainment: *see* **show**

perfume *noun* a pleasant-smelling liquid made especially from flowers: *see* **smell**

perhaps *adverb* maybe, but not likely: *see* **maybe**

peril *noun* the condition of being in danger or at risk of harm or loss: *see* **danger**

perilous *adjective* full of grave danger: *see* **dangerous**

period *noun* a span of time, especially one during which a culture, technology, or set of beliefs is dominant: *see* **age**

periodic *adjective* happening or repeating at regular intervals: *see* **irregular**

periodical *noun* a publication, especially a magazine, that appears at regular intervals: *see* **magazine**

perish *verb* to die or be destroyed, especially in a violent manner: *see* **die**

perjury *noun* deliberately false, misleading, or incomplete testimony given while under oath: *see* **lie**

permanent

adjective lasting or meant to last for a long time: *I have a* **permanent** *scar on my arm*.

▶ **endless** being or seeming to be without an end: *We walked for miles along the* **endless** *beach*.

▶ **enduring** continuing to exist for a long time; lasting: *The novels of Edith Wharton have an* **enduring** *place in American literature*.

▶ **eternal** having no beginning and no end; lasting forever: *This poem is about the* **eternal** *rhythm of the seasons*.

▶ **lasting** continuing or remaining for a long time: *My mother and her college roommate have a* **lasting** *friendship*.

▶ **unending** never coming to an end: *His complaints about his job are* **unending**.

ANTONYM **temporary** lasting, used, or working only for a short time; not permanent

permissible *adjective* permitted; allowable: *see* **legal**

permissive *adjective* allowing much freedom: *see* **indulgent**

permit *verb* to let someone do something: *see* **authorize**

permitted *adjective* allowed by rule, regulation, or custom: *see* **legal**

perplex *verb* to confuse someone even after much thought: *see* **confuse**

persevere *verb* to continue to try to do something in spite of obstacles: *see* **last²**

perseverence *noun* the act or quality of holding to a course of action, a belief, or a purpose despite obstacles or difficulties: *see* **endurance**

persist *verb* to hold firmly to a purpose: *see* **last²**

persistence *noun* the quality of refusing to give up or let go: *see* **will**

persistent *adjective* insistently repetitive or continuous: *see* **constant**

persistent *adjective* refusing to give up or let go: *see* **stubborn**

person *noun* a human being: *see* **human being**

personal

adjective concerning a person's private business, interests, or activities: *I keep my* **personal** *thoughts in a daily journal*.

▸ **intimate**   marked by familiarity or close association; very personal: *Only family and intimate friends were invited to the wedding.*

▸ **private**   ▷ not intended for public view or knowledge: *The senator criticized the press for invading her private life.* ▷ reserved for one's exclusive use: *The executive flew to the conference in his private jet.*

▸ **secret**   hidden from general knowledge or view; concealed: *I use a secret password to access my e-mail account.*

personality

noun   all the qualities and character traits that distinguish one person from all others: *The brothers may look alike, but they have very different personalities.*

▸ **character**   a person's moral nature: *We are looking for someone of honest and upright character to manage our finances.*

▸ **disposition**   a person's usual mood or attitude: *My brother has an easygoing disposition.*

▸ **identity**   who a particular person is: *Technology has made it possible to confirm a person's identity through a voiceprint or by scanning the iris of the eye.*

▸ **nature**   the basic character or quality of a person or thing: *It's in his nature to be helpful and friendly.*

▸ **temper**   a person's usual state of mind or emotions; disposition: *My grandfather has a very even temper.*

▸ **temperament**   the manner of thinking, behaving, or reacting that is characteristic to a specific person: *That singer is known for his moody temperament.*

perspective *noun*   a mental view or outlook: *see* **opinion**

persuade

verb   to cause someone to do or believe something, especially by reason or argument: *I'm trying to persuade my cousin to form a rap group with me.*

▸ **cajole**   to persuade someone by flattery or insincere talk: *He cajoled me into lending him my car for the weekend.*

▸ **coax**   to persuade or try to persuade someone by gentle urging or flattery: *My friends coaxed me into driving them to the beach.*

▸ **convince**   to persuade someone to do or believe something: *Your story has convinced me that you are telling the truth.*

▸ **induce**   to persuade or influence someone; to lead someone on: *Nothing can induce me to eat snails.*

▸ **wheedle**   to persuade someone or get something by using flattery or deceit: *My brother wheedled me into helping him with his homework by telling me how smart I am.*

pester *verb*   to harass someone with demands or requests: *see* **annoy**

pester *verb*   to annoy someone repeatedly: *see* **nag**

pet *noun*   an animal kept for amusement or companionship: *see* **animal**

pet *verb*   to stroke or pat a person or animal in a gentle manner: *see* **touch**

petite *adjective*   small and slender: *see* **short [1]**

petty *adjective*   small and unimportant: *see* **unimportant**

phenomenon *noun*   a person or thing that is remarkable or outstanding: *see* **wonder**

philosophy

noun   a formal system of ideas intended to explain life, nature, and human existence: *The ancient Greeks believed that philosophy should guide human conduct.*

▸ **code**   a system of rules, regulations, or laws: *The county fire codes forbid the burning of trash outdoors.*

▸ **creed**   a system of guiding beliefs or principles, especially a formal statement of the beliefs of a religious faith: *It is illegal for employers to discriminate on the basis of a person's race, gender, or creed.*

▸ **dogma**   a doctrine or system of doctrines proclaimed by a religion to be true: *Every religion has dogma that is accepted by its members.*

▸ **ideology** a set of doctrines or beliefs that is shared by members of a group: *Capitalism, communism, and socialism each have a distinctive* **ideology**.

▸ **theory** a statement designed to explain an event or group of events: *The Gaia* **theory** *proposes that the planet earth is a self-regulating system.*

phony *adjective* not genuine or real: *see* **fake**

photograph *noun* an image formed on film by a camera and developed with chemicals to produce a print: *see* **picture**

phrase *noun* a brief expression: *see* **term**

physician *noun* a person licensed to practice medicine: *see* **doctor**

physique *noun* the body considered in terms of its proportions, muscle development, and appearance: *see* **body**

pick *verb* to choose something with care or forethought: *see* **choose**

pickpocket *noun* a thief who steals from someone's pockets: *see* **thief**

pick up *verb* to take hold of and lift someone or something higher: *see* **raise [2]**

picnic *noun* a party in which people carry their food with them and then eat it outdoors: *see* **feast**

picture

noun a painting, drawing, or photograph of a person or thing: *They hired a photographer to take* **pictures** *at the wedding.*

▸ **drawing** a picture made by making lines on a surface, such as paper, to represent forms and figures: *I have to make a series of charcoal* **drawings** *for my art class.*

▸ **illustration** a picture, diagram, or map that explains or decorates something: *The* **illustrations** *of birds in this book were done by a famous artist.*

▸ **image** a reproduction of a person or object: *My friend sent me an e-mail with a digital* **image** *of her new baby.*

▸ **painting** a picture or design made with paints: *We went to see the Impressionist* **paintings** *in the museum.*

▸ **photograph** an image formed on film by a camera and developed with chemicals to produce a print: *I'm learning to develop my own* **photographs** *in the darkroom.*

▸ **poster** a large sheet with a picture or printing on it that is put up as an advertisement, notice, or decoration: *We made* **posters** *to advertise the concert.*

piece

noun a portion of something larger; a part that has been broken, torn, or cut from a whole: *I cut the cake into eight* **pieces**.

▸ **fraction** a usually small part of a whole: *I got only a* **fraction** *of my homework done before the library closed.*

▸ **part** a portion or division of a whole: *Some* **parts** *of the movie were better than others.*

▸ **particle** a very small piece or amount: *The dog ate every* **particle** *of food in her dish.*

▸ **portion** a part of the whole: *I put a* **portion** *of my weekly paycheck into a savings account.*

▸ **section** one of several parts that make up something: *I like to read the sports* **section** *of the newspaper.*

▸ **segment** any of the parts into which something is divided: *I gave several* **segments** *of my orange to my friend.*

▸ **share** a part owned by or distributed to a person or group: *Each employee received a* **share** *of the profits.*

▸ **speck** a small bit; a particle: *The wind blew a* **speck** *of dirt into my eye.*

pier *noun* a platform that extends from a shore out over the water: *see* **dock**

pierce *verb* to pass into or through something, as with a sharp instrument: *see* **stab**

piety *noun* religious devotion and reverence to God: *see* **worship**

pile

noun a mass of objects gathered together: *We raked the leaves into a big* **pile**.

▶ **heap** a pile of things thrown on top of each other: *I changed my clothes in a hurry and left them in a **heap** on the floor.*

▶ **mound** a rounded pile of material such as dirt, sand, or rocks: *Some species of ants form huge **mounds** of soil when they make their nests.*

▶ **stack** an orderly pile, especially one arranged in layers: *There's a **stack** of old magazines in the basement.*

pilfer *verb* to steal things of little value: *see* **steal**

pilgrimage *noun* a journey to a sacred place or shrine: *see* **journey**

pill

noun a small ball or tablet of medicine that is taken by mouth: *I take a vitamin **pill** every morning.*

▶ **capsule** a small container, usually made of gelatin, that contains medicine to be taken by mouth: *I hid the **capsule** of my dog's medicine in a piece of cheese before giving it to her.*

▶ **dose** the amount of medicine or other treatment given or taken at one time: *He has to take a **dose** of the medicine every four hours.*

▶ **lozenge** a small, sweet tablet that contains medicine or is used as a candy: *I've been sucking on **lozenges** to ease my sore throat.*

▶ **tablet** a small, often disk-shaped piece of medicine: *She bought some **tablets** for headache pain.*

pillar *noun* a vertical structure used as a support for a building: *see* **pole**

pillow *noun* a case filled with soft material, typically used to cushion a person's head during sleep: *see* **pad**

pilot *verb* to lead, guide, or conduct a vehicle, especially a ship or aircraft: *see* **guide**

pin *verb* to fasten or secure something with a pin: *see* **fasten**

pin *noun* a short, sharp-pointed piece of wire, used for fastening: *see* **hook**

pine *verb* (formal) to feel a lingering, often nostalgic desire: *see* **mourn**

pinnacle *noun* the highest point of an extraordinary accomplishment: *see* **prime**

pioneer *verb* to initiate or participate in the development of something new: *see* **invent**

pious *adjective* having or showing religious respect or reverence: *see* **religious**

pipe *noun* a usually rigid tube that a liquid or gas can flow through: *see* **tube**

pit *noun* a hole in the ground: *see* **hole**

pitch *verb* to throw an object with careful aim, as in a sport: *see* **throw**

pitch *verb* to cause a boat to alternately dip its bow and stern: *see* **tilt**

pitcher *noun* a container for liquids, usually having a handle and a lip or spout for pouring: *see* **bottle**

pity *noun* a feeling of sorrow or sympathy for the suffering of another: *see* **sympathy**

place

noun a particular location; an area or space: *This is a good **place** to plant the peach tree.*

▶ **location** a place where something can be found: *That store is moving to a new **location** next month.*

▶ **point** a certain place or position: *There are many **points** of interest in Yellowstone National Park.*

▶ **position** the place where someone or something is located or stationed: *The parade will start as soon as all the floats are in their proper **position**.*

▶ **scene** the place where an action or event occurs: *The police marked off the crime **scene** with yellow tape.*

▶ **site** the place where something is or will be located: *We picked a level **site** on which to set up the tent.*

▶ **spot** a place or position: *This fountain is my favorite **spot** in the park.*

place

verb to put something in a particular place or order: *Please **place** a chair at each end of the table.*

▸ **deposit** to lay or put something down: *The wind **deposited** a pile of leaves on our doorstep.*

▸ **lay** to put or set something down: *My cat **laid** a dead mouse at my feet.*

▸ **put** to cause something to be in a particular position or condition: *I need to **put** the flowers in some water.*

▸ **set** to put something in a particular place: *Please **set** the groceries on top of the counter.*

▸ **sit** to be located: *Our house **sits** at the end of the street.*

placid *adjective* pleasantly peaceful or calm: *see* **calm**

plain *adjective* easy to see or understand: *see* **clear [1]**

plain *adjective* lacking beauty or distinction: *see* **ugly**

plan

noun a method of doing something that has been thought out ahead of time: *My brother's **plan** is to attend community college after high school.*

▸ **agenda** a list of things to be considered or done: *The club secretary handed out the **agenda** for the meeting.*

▸ **budget** a plan for how money will be spent: *We increased our food **budget** during the holidays.*

▸ **list** a series of names or items, written one after the other: *I made a **list** of DVDs that I want to buy.*

▸ **program** a list of information, such as the order of events and the names of those taking part in a public performance: *We were handed a **program** when we entered the car show.*

▸ **schedule** a program of appointments, classes, or upcoming events: *The coach gave each player a copy of the year's game **schedule**.*

plan

verb to form a scheme or program for the accomplishment of a goal: *Everyone in the club helped to **plan** the party.*

▸ **arrange** to plan or prepare for something: *The travel agency **arranged** my airline tickets and hotel reservations.*

▸ **budget** to plan one's spending in advance: *I didn't **budget** enough money for gas and car repairs this month.*

▸ **coordinate** to cause two or more things to work together well: *Good swimmers **coordinate** their breathing with their strokes.*

▸ **organize** to arrange things in an orderly way: *I need to **organize** my photos.*

planet *noun* a celestial body that does not produce light and that revolves around a star: *see* **earth [1]**

plank *noun* a long board: *see* **wood**

plant *noun* the building and equipment used in making a product: *see* **factory**

platform

noun a raised floor or surface, as for a speaker or performer: *The speaker glanced at her notes as she approached the **platform**.*

▸ **deck** an outdoor platform attached to a building: *We're building a new **deck** on the west side of our house.*

▸ **landing** a level area at the top or bottom of a flight of stairs: *Our cat likes to sleep on the stair **landing**.*

▸ **podium** an elevated platform, as for an orchestra conductor or someone giving a speech: *The orchestra conductor stepped up to the **podium**.*

▸ **scaffold** a temporary platform used for supporting workers and their materials: *The painters set up a **scaffold** to work on while painting the building.*

▸ **stage** the raised platform in a theater on which entertainers perform: *The theater department raised money to buy new curtains for the **stage**.*

platoon *noun* a group of people working or traveling together: *see* **team**

plausible *adjective* seeming true or reasonable: *see* **possible**

play

verb to occupy oneself in amusement, sport, or recreation: *The children went outside to **play**.*

- ▸ **frolic** to behave playfully: *The lambs frolicked in the field.*
- ▸ **horse around** (informal) to indulge in silly or rowdy play: *The lifeguard told my friends and me to stop **horsing around** in the pool.*
- ▸ **romp** to play in a lively or excited manner: *Just watching the children **romp** on the playground made me feel tired.*

playground *noun* an outdoor area for play, sports, and games: *see* **park**

plead *verb* to make an urgent or insistent appeal to someone: *see* **beg**

pleasant

adjective giving pleasure or enjoyment: *The days in late spring are warm and **pleasant**.*

- ▸ **agreeable** suited to one's liking or interest: *Many people find reading to be an **agreeable** activity.*
- ▸ **enjoyable** giving joy or happiness: *I had an **enjoyable** time at the basketball game.*
- ▸ **nice** ▷ pleasing and agreeable: *We had nice weather for our trip.* ▷ thoughtful and well-mannered: *It was **nice** of you to give me a birthday present.*
- ▸ **pleasing** giving pleasure; agreeable: *That singer has a **pleasing** voice.*
- ▸ **pleasurable** full of pleasure; enjoyable: *Relaxing in the hot tub was a **pleasurable** experience.*

ANTONYM **unpleasant** not pleasing; disagreeable

please

verb to give pleasure or enjoyment to someone: *It **pleased** me when my poem was published in the school magazine.*

- ▸ **delight** to please someone greatly: *I was delighted to hear your voice on the phone.*

- ▸ **gladden** to make someone glad: *My grandmother was **gladdened** that everyone in the family came home to celebrate her birthday.*
- ▸ **gratify** to please or satisfy someone: *The librarian was **gratified** by the success of the children's reading program.*
- ▸ **satisfy** to fulfill or gratify someone's need, desire, or expectation: *The bowl of soup **satisfied** my need for something warm and filling.*
- ▸ **thrill** to give someone a sudden sensation of joy, fear, or excitement: *He was **thrilled** to find out he'd gotten a part in the play.*

pleased *adjective* filled with pleasure: *see* **content**

pleasing *adjective* giving pleasure; agreeable: *see* **pleasant**

pleasurable *adjective* full of pleasure; enjoyable: *see* **pleasant**

pleasure *noun* something that pleases or delights: *see* **fun**

pleat *noun* a flat fold that is made by doubling fabric on itself: *see* **fold**

pledge *noun* a formal promise that one will do something at a later time: *see* **promise**

plentiful *adjective* being more than enough: *see* **abundant**

plenty of *adjective* adequate in amount or supply: *see* **enough**

pliable *adjective* easily bent or shaped: *see* **flexible**

plight *noun* a situation of difficulty or peril: *see* **misfortune**

plodding *adjective* moving in a slow and heavy manner: *see* **slow**

plot

verb to plan something secretly, especially something illegal or deceptive: *The inmates **plotted** their escape from prison.*

- ▸ **conspire** to plan together secretly to do something wrong: *The criminals **conspired** to rob the liquor store.*

▸ **hatch** to think something up, especially in secret: *We **hatched** a plan to throw a surprise birthday party for our friend.*

▸ **scheme** to make up a plan, especially a dishonest or clever one: *The con artist was always **scheming** new ways to cheat people out of their money.*

pluck *noun* courage and daring: *see* **courage**

plug *noun* a piece of rubber, plastic, or other material that is used to fill a hole or stop a leak: *see* **lid**

plummet *verb* to drop straight down rapidly: *see* **fall**

plump *adjective* rounded and full in shape: *see* **fat**

plunder *verb* to rob valuables by force from a city or territory: *see* **steal**

plunge *verb* to descend sharply and rapidly, especially into water: *see* **fall**

pocket-sized *adjective* small enough to be carried in a pocket: *see* **small**

podium *noun* an elevated platform, as for an orchestra conductor or someone giving a speech: *see* **platform**

poem *noun* a piece of writing, often in rhyme, in which words are chosen for their sound and beauty as well as their meaning: *see* **story**

poet *noun* one who writes poems: *see* **writer**

point *noun* a significant item, especially one of a series: *see* **detail**

point *noun* a certain place or position: *see* **place**

pointless *adjective* having no purpose, sense, or meaning: *see* **useless**

poised *adjective* calm and confident in manner: *see* **confident**

poison *verb* to make something toxic or poisonous: *see* **pollute**

poisonous *adjective* capable of harming or killing by means of poison: *see* **fatal**

poke

verb to give someone or something a sudden sharp jab: *I **poked** my friend when I caught a glimpse of the movie star.*

▸ **jab** to poke or pierce someone or something with something pointed: *He **jabbed** me in the ribs with his finger.*

▸ **nudge** to push someone or something in a gentle way, especially in order to attract attention: *I gently **nudged** the lizard to see if it was alive.*

▸ **prod** to stir someone to action, as by poking or nudging: *She **prodded** me in the back to get me to move forward.*

pole

noun ▷ a long, slender rod: *He used a **pole** with a net at the end to clean the swimming pool.* ▷ an upright post: *The bean plants grew up the **pole**.*

▸ **column** an upright structure used in a building as a support; a pillar: *In classical Greek architecture there are three styles of **columns**.*

▸ **mast** an upright pole that supports the sails and rigging of a ship or boat: *They have a small sailboat with a 14-foot **mast**.*

▸ **pillar** a vertical structure used as a support for a building; a column: *Many Southern mansions have **pillars** on the veranda.*

▸ **post** an upright piece of wood or metal that serves as a support or marker: *We spent the weekend putting in fence **posts**.*

▸ **rod** a thin, straight length of wood, metal, or other material: *He has a collection of fishing **rods**.*

▸ **staff** a long stick used as a support, weapon, or symbol of authority: *A **staff** is used as a weapon in many forms of martial arts.*

▸ **stick** a long, slender piece of wood, such as a branch from a tree: *I wrote my name in the sand with a **stick**.*

policy *noun* a general plan or principle that is chosen to help people make decisions: *see* **rule**

polish *verb* to make something smooth and shiny by rubbing: *see* **clean**

polish *noun* a refined style or manner: *see* **elegance**

polite

adjective having or showing good manners; courteous: *A **polite** person treats others with respect.*

▸ **civil** observing accepted social practices; not rude: *He gave a **civil** response to the rude question.*

▸ **courteous** considerate towards others: *The **courteous** driver let me pull into the lane.*

▸ **gracious** courteous and kind, especially in social situations: *They are always **gracious** hosts at their annual holiday party.*

▸ **respectful** showing the proper consideration toward someone or something: *Our team kept a **respectful** silence during the national anthem.*

▸ **tactful** having the ability to speak or act without offending others; considerate and discreet: *The flight attendant was **tactful** when the passenger became airsick.*

▸ **well-mannered** having or showing good social behavior; polite: *They have **well-mannered** children.*

ANTONYM **rude** not considerate of others; impolite

politeness *noun* good or courteous manners: *see* **elegance**

pollute

verb to make something unfit for or harmful to living organisms: *The exhaust from cars and trucks **pollutes** the air.*

▸ **contaminate** to make something impure or unfit for use: *The oil spill **contaminated** several miles of the shoreline.*

▸ **corrupt** to infect or spoil something: *The laboratory samples had been **corrupted** by bacteria.*

▸ **poison** to make something toxic or poisonous: *The chemical spill **poisoned** the water supply.*

▸ **spoil** to damage something and make it less valuable or useful: *The early frosts **spoiled** the fruit on the trees.*

▸ **taint** to spoil something, as with disease or decay: *We threw out the egg salad sandwiches that got **tainted** when we left them too long in the sun.*

pollution *noun* something that contaminates the air, water, or earth: *see* **fume**

pompous *adjective* marked by excessive self-esteem or exaggerated dignity: *see* **proud**

pond *noun* a body of water that is smaller than a lake: *see* **pool**

ponder *verb* to think about something carefully and at length: *see* **think**

pool

noun a small, still body of water: *there was a deep **pool** at the base of the waterfall.*

▸ **lagoon** a shallow body of water that is separated from the sea by sandbars or reefs: *We went swimming in a tropical **lagoon**.*

▸ **lake** a body of fresh or salt water that is surrounded by land: *Many of Minnesota's **lakes** were formed when the glaciers melted at the end of the Ice Age.*

▸ **pond** a body of water that is smaller than a lake: *I like to go rowing on the **pond**.*

▸ **puddle** a small pool of water, especially rainwater: *The little boys were splashing in the **puddles**.*

▸ **reservoir** a place where a large amount of water has been collected and stored for use: *Boating and fishing are allowed on some of the larger **reservoirs**.*

poor

adjective having little or no money or possessions: *I do not mind being **poor** while I am still in college.*

▸ **bankrupt** legally declared unable to pay personal or company debts: *Many people lost their jobs when the company went **bankrupt**.*

▸ **broke** (informal) having no money at all: *She was **broke** until the next payday.*

- **needy** in need of assistance; very poor: *Our synagogue collects canned food to distribute to **needy** families.*
- **penniless** having no money; completely impoverished: *His family was almost **penniless** after the war.*

ANTONYM **rich** having much money or property

pop *verb* to make a sudden, sharp sound: *see* **explode**

popular *adjective* having many friends or admirers: *see* **famous**

populace *noun* the general public; the masses: *see* **public**

population *noun* all of the people who live in a specified area: *see* **public**

port *noun* a town or city that has a harbor; a place along a body of water where ships can dock or anchor: *see* **harbor**

portable *adjective* carried or moved with ease: *see* **useful**

portion *noun* a part that has been separated from the whole: *see* **piece**

portray *verb* to show something by means of a picture: *see* **draw**

pose *verb* to pretend to be someone or something that one is not: *see* **pretend**

position *noun* the place where someone or something is located or stationed: *see* **place**

position *noun* a post of employment or service within an organization: *see* **status**

positive *adjective* marked by or expressing certainty, acceptance, or affirmation: *see* **certain**

positively *adverb* absolutely; with certainty: *see* **certainly**

possess *verb* to have as property or as a quality: *see* **have**

possessions *noun* the things one owns; one's personal property: *see* **property**

possessive *adjective* having a desire to dominate or control: *see* **jealous**

possible

adjective capable of happening or being done: *We worked out a few **possible** solutions to the problem.*

- **conceivable** capable of being thought of; imaginable: *It is **conceivable** that life exists on other planets, though there is no proof.*
- **likely** showing a strong tendency or probability; probable: *The storm is **likely** to hit during the night.*
- **plausible** seeming true or reasonable: *She gave a **plausible** explanation for being late.*
- **potential** capable of being but not yet in existence: *The **potential** winners were called to the stage for the final drawing.*
- **probable** likely to happen or be true: *Investigators are trying to determine the **probable** cause of the fire.*
- **workable** capable of being put into operation: *My sister and I came to a **workable** arrangement for keeping our room clean.*

ANTONYM **impossible** not capable of happening or existing

possibly *adverb* perhaps: *see* **maybe**

post *noun* an upright piece of wood or metal that serves as a support or marker: *see* **pole**

post *verb* to mail a letter or package: *see* **send**

poster *noun* a large sheet with a picture or printing on it that is put up as an advertisement, notice, or decoration: *see* **picture**

postpone *verb* to delay something until a later time: *see* **delay**

pot *noun* any of various deep, rounded containers made of metal, pottery, or glass, used especially for cooking: *see* **bucket**

potent *adjective* possessing great strength or influence: *see* **powerful**

potential *adjective* capable of being but not yet in existence: *see* **possible**

potluck *noun* a meal at which each guest brings food to be shared by all: *see* **feast**

pouch *noun* a bag, often closing with a drawstring: *see* **bag**

pound *verb* to strike or beat something forcefully and repeatedly: *see* **crush**

pour

verb to flow in a steady stream: *Water poured over the dam after the heavy rainfall.*

- ▸ **cascade** to fall in or like a waterfall: *The stack of papers on the desk cascaded to the floor.*
- ▸ **flow** to move in a steady and smooth way, like a stream: *Air flowed in through the window.*
- ▸ **gush** to flow forth suddenly and in a great amount: *The pipe broke open and water gushed everywhere.*
- ▸ **shower** to pour something down in abundance: *The wind caused the cherry tree to shower petals on us.*
- ▸ **spill** to run or flow out of a container, especially by accident: *My drink spilled all over the floor when I dropped my glass.*
- ▸ **splash** to scatter a liquid, such as water, all around: *The bus splashed muddy water all over us.*

pout

verb to show childish displeasure or disappointment: *I pouted when my friend said he couldn't go to the movie with me.*

- ▸ **brood** to think or worry quietly for a long time: *When you make a mistake, don't brood about it.*
- ▸ **mope** to be gloomy and often silent: *She moped all day after she failed the quiz.*
- ▸ **sulk** to be sullenly quiet or angry: *My younger brother sulked because I wouldn't let him play my new guitar.*

power *noun* the ability to do something, especially to produce an effect: *see* **strength**

powerful

adjective having power, authority, or influence: *The speaker presented a powerful argument to support his idea.*

- ▸ **effective** producing a strong impression or response: *The agency produced a highly effective campaign aimed at reducing teenage drug use.*
- ▸ **influential** having the power to cause changes or produce an effect: *The Internet has become very influential in many people's lives.*
- ▸ **mighty** having or showing great power, strength, or force: *Crocodiles have mighty jaws for crushing their prey.*
- ▸ **potent** possessing great strength or influence; powerful: *The new drug is a potent remedy for muscular pain.*

powerless *adjective* lacking the force, strength, or ability to do or accomplish something: *see* **helpless**

practical *adjective* capable of being used or put into effect: *see* **useful**

practical joke *noun* a mischievous trick, especially one that causes embarrassment or discomfort: *see* **joke**

practically *adverb* very nearly: *see* **about**

practice

verb to do something over and over in order to acquire skill: *The marching band practices its program every day before school.*

- ▸ **exercise** to do physical activity in order to develop or maintain fitness: *I exercise by doing yoga and going for walks.*
- ▸ **prepare** to make something ready before it is needed: *My teacher prepares his lesson plans a week in advance.*
- ▸ **rehearse** to practice something in preparation for a public performance: *I rehearsed my oral report in front of my roommates.*
- ▸ **work out** to engage in strenuous exercise so as to prepare for an athletic competition or to improve one's physical fitness: *The soccer team meets twice a week to work out with weights.*

practice *noun* a customary action or way of doing something: *see* **habit**

praise

verb to express approval or admiration for someone or something: *The student was praised for her outstanding science project.*

▸ **commend** to speak highly of someone: *The professor commended me on my research.*

▸ **compliment** to express praise to someone: *He was pleased when I complimented his artwork.*

▸ **congratulate** to give praise or good wishes to someone at a happy event or for something done well: *We all congratulated her when she won the poetry contest.*

▸ **flatter** to praise someone in a way that is not sincere, especially in order to get something in return: *The saleswoman flattered me about how I looked in the jeans.*

▸ **glorify** to give high praise or honor to someone: *The Romans glorified the Caesars by ranking them with the gods.*

▸ **honor** to show special respect for someone or something: *We honor the United States by displaying the Stars and Stripes.*

▸ **recommend** to praise someone as being worthy or desirable: *My boss has recommended me for a promotion.*

prank *noun* a mischievous trick or practical joke: *see* **joke**

preacher *noun* a person who preaches, especially a minister: *see* **minister**

precarious *adjective* dangerously lacking in security or stability: *see* **unstable**

preceding *adjective* coming before another in time, place, rank, or sequence: *see* **previous**

precious *noun* highly valued or esteemed: *see* **dear**

precious *noun* having very great value: *see* **valuable**

precise *adjective* very accurate: *see* **exact**

predicament *noun* a difficult or embarrassing situation: *see* **trouble**

predict

verb to tell or indicate something in advance, especially by reasoning from known facts: *The pollsters predicted that the election would be decided by a runoff.*

▸ **forecast** to indicate in advance what might or will happen; to predict: *The weather channel is forecasting rain showers for tomorrow.*

▸ **foresee** to see or know something in advance: *From the first day I could foresee that this class would be difficult.*

▸ **foretell** (formal) to tell of something in advance: *Do you believe that some people can foretell the future?*

▸ **prophesy** to predict with strong belief what is going to happen in the future: *Those who prophesied that the war would be lost were soon proven wrong.*

prefer *verb* to choose something as more desirable: *see* **choose**

preferable *adjective* more desirable than others: *see* **better**

preference *noun* a choice based on one's values, biases, or tastes: *see* **choice**

preference *noun* a liking of one person or thing over another: *see* **tendency**

prejudiced *adjective* biased for or against someone: *see* **unfair**

premier *adjective* first to occur or exist: *see* **original [2]**

preoccupied *adjective* excessively concerned with something: *see* **busy**

prepare *verb* to make something ready beforehand for some purpose, task, or event: *see* **equip**

prepare *verb* to make something ready before it is needed: *see* **practice**

prescribe *verb* to set something down as a rule or guide: *see* **dictate**

present *noun* something presented: *see* **gift**

present *verb* to offer something for examination or consideration: *see* **show**

present *verb* to recommend something for observation, examination, or consideration: *see* **suggest**

preserve *verb* to protect something, as from injury or destruction: *see* **keep**

preserve *verb* to maintain something in safety or good condition: *see* **protect**

preserve *noun* an area maintained for the protection of wildlife or natural resources: *see* **refuge**

press *verb* to squeeze the juice or other contents from something: *see* **crush**

pressing *adjective* demanding immediate attention: *see* **urgent**

pressure *noun* a burden that causes distress: *see* **worry**

presume *verb* to assume something on the basis of likelihood or reason: *see* **guess**

pretend

verb to put on a false show, as in play or in order to deceive someone: *I **pretended** to be asleep so that my nephew wouldn't bother me.*

- ▶ **affect** (formal) to pretend to have or feel something that isn't true: *She **affected** a British accent for the play.*
- ▶ **feign** (formal) to give a false appearance of something; to pretend: *An opossum will **feign** being dead in order to avoid being attacked.*
- ▶ **make believe** to act is if something imaginary is true: *Let's **make believe** that you're a princess and I'm a dragon.*
- ▶ **pose** to pretend to be someone or something that one is not: *The man **posed** as a reporter to get into the sold-out concert.*
- ▶ **simulate** to take on the appearance, form, or sound of something; to imitate: *I have a computer game that **simulates** driving a racecar.*

pretty *adjective* pleasing, attractive, or appealing to the eye or ear: *see* **beautiful**

prevalent *adjective* widely or commonly occurring or practiced: *see* **common**

prevent

verb to keep something from happening: *A low-fat diet helps **prevent** heart disease.*

- ▶ **deter** to prevent or discourage someone from doing something: *Car alarms are intended to **deter** thieves.*
- ▶ **frustrate** to prevent a person from accomplishing something: *Bad weather **frustrated** our plans to paint the house.*
- ▶ **hamper** to make it difficult for someone to do something: *The wind **hampered** our attempts to start a campfire.*
- ▶ **hinder** to get in the way of someone or something; to make something difficult: *The heavy traffic **hindered** us from getting there on time.*
- ▶ **thwart** to prevent someone from accomplishing a purpose or goal: *I **thwarted** my cat's attempt to catch the bird.*

ANTONYM **allow** to let something happen; to permit something

previous

adjective existing or taking place earlier: *Only people with **previous** experience should apply for this job.*

- ▶ **former** from or belonging to an earlier time: *My **former** boss is now the general manager.*
- ▶ **preceding** coming before another in time, place, rank, or sequence: *The ground was still wet from the **preceding** day's rain.*
- ▶ **prior** existing before the present time; earlier: *Did you have any **prior** knowledge of this problem?*

previously *adverb* before the present time: *see* **before**

prey *noun* an animal hunted or caught by another for food: *see* **victim**

price

noun the amount of money needed to buy something: *The **price** of fresh vegetables varies from season to season.*

- ▶ **charge** an amount asked or made as payment; cost: *What would be the **charge** to have this dress shortened?*
- ▶ **cost** the amount paid or charged for something: *The **cost** of going to college seems to go up every year.*

▶ **expense** something spent to attain a goal or accomplish a purpose: *We kept a list of all the* ***expenses*** *for remodeling the kitchen.*

▶ **fare** the money a person must pay to travel, as on a plane, train, or bus: *I paid my* ***fare*** *as I boarded the bus.*

▶ **fee** a fixed cost, especially one charged by a school or government: *My financial aid covers my tuition* ***fees***.

▶ **payment** an amount of money paid toward the price of something: *I make monthly* ***payments*** *on my car.*

▶ **toll** a fixed charge for a privilege or service: *The* ***toll*** *for using the bridge is two dollars.*

priceless *adjective* of great or inestimable value: *see* **valuable**

prick *verb* to make a small hole or mark in something with a pointed object: *see* **stab**

pride

noun a sense of one's own dignity or worth; self-respect: *He was filled with* ***pride*** *when he finished building the fence.*

▶ **arrogance** the quality of being excessively proud: *The movie star was known for his* ***arrogance***.

▶ **conceit** too high an opinion of oneself: *He's a good athlete, but his* ***conceit*** *makes him difficult to be around.*

▶ **self-importance** an excessively high opinion of one's own importance or position: *Our company's president is full of* ***self-importance***.

▶ **vanity** too much pride in one's looks, ability, or appearance: *She has so much* ***vanity*** *that she looks in every mirror that she passes.*

priest *noun* a member of the clergy who has the authority to perform religious services or ceremonies: *see* **minister**

primary *adjective* first in importance, degree, or quality: *see* **main**

prime

noun the stage of ideal physical perfection and intellectual vigor in a person's life: *The runner is not as fast now as he was in his* ***prime***.

▶ **acme** (formal) the highest point, as of perfection: *Sylvia Plath committed suicide at the* ***acme*** *of her career.*

▶ **flower** (formal) the best example of something: *Picasso was considered the* ***flower*** *of his artistic generation.*

▶ **height** the highest point or most advanced degree of something: *The* ***height*** *of her success was winning two gold medals at the Olympics.*

▶ **peak** the point of greatest development or intensity: *Musicians and mathematicians often reach the* ***peak*** *of their abilities while they are still young.*

▶ **pinnacle** the highest point of an extraordinary accomplishment: *Winston Churchill achieved the* ***pinnacle*** *of his fame as Britain's prime minister during World War II.*

▶ **zenith** the highest point of development or achievement: *The 1950s are considered by many to be the* ***zenith*** *of Hollywood westerns.*

primitive *adjective* ▷ relating to forces of nature ▷ simple and crude: *see* **wild [1]**

principal *adjective* first or foremost in importance: *see* **main**

principle *noun* a rule or standard of behavior: *see* **rule**

prior *adjective* existing before the present time: *see* **previous**

prison *noun* a place where people convicted or accused of crimes are confined: *see* **jail**

prisoner

noun a person who is held by force, especially in a prison: *The guards brought the* ***prisoner*** *into the courtroom.*

▶ **captive** a person held prisoner or under the control of another: *The soldiers who surrendered were held as* ***captives*** *until the end of the war.*

▶ **hostage** a person held by an enemy to be used in exchange for the fulfillment of certain demands: *The nation was relieved when the* ***hostages*** *were released.*

▸ **slave** a person owned by and considered to be the property of someone else: *I feel like I am a slave to my job.*

private *adjective* ▷ not intended for public view or knowledge ▷ reserved for one's exclusive use: *see* **personal**

privilege

noun a special right or benefit that is enjoyed by some people and not by others: *He was given the privilege of using the family car.*

▸ **advantage** a beneficial factor or feature: *The well-equipped engineering department is an advantage to our company.*
▸ **benefit** something that is of help; an advantage: *The new library will be a great benefit to the community.*
▸ **entitlement** a right or privilege granted by an authority: *Public education is one of the entitlements of a U.S. citizen.*
▸ **right** something that one has a moral or legal claim to: *Under U.S. law, a defendant in a criminal case has a right to a trial by jury.*

prize *noun* something offered or won as an award in a competition or contest: *see* **award**

prized *adjective* highly valued, esteemed, or treasured: *see* **valuable**

probable *adjective* likely to happen or be true: *see* **possible**

probe *verb* to explore or examine something carefully: *see* **search**

problem

noun a question that must be solved or thought about: *My sister helped me with the difficult math problem.*

▸ **challenge** a test of one's abilities or resources; something that requires all of a person's efforts and skills: *A triathlon is a challenge to most people's physical abilities.*
▸ **mystery** something that is not fully understood or is kept secret: *It is a mystery how the squirrel got into the house.*

▸ **paradox** something that is apparently contradictory: *The fact that light consists of both waves and particles is a paradox that can be scientifically demonstrated.*
▸ **puzzle** something that is hard to understand; a problem that makes one think and that tests one's skill: *The man's unusual symptoms were a puzzle to the doctor.*
▸ **question** a difficult matter; a problem: *The meeting dealt with the question of gang violence.*
▸ **riddle** a question or statement that is worded in a deliberately puzzling way so that it requires thought to figure out the answer: *In many myths, the hero has to solve a riddle before continuing his journey.*

procedure *noun* a way of doing something, often by a series of steps: *see* **method**

proceed *verb* to go forward or onward, especially after an interruption: *see* **advance**

process *noun* a series of steps, actions, motions, or operations that lead to a result: *see* **method**

procession *noun* a group of people, vehicles, or objects moving along in orderly succession: *see* **parade**

proclaim *verb* to announce something officially and publicly: *see* **announce**

proclamation *noun* an official public announcement: *see* **announcement**

procure *verb* to obtain by special effort: *see* **get**

prod *verb* to stir someone to action, as by poking or prodding: *see* **poke**

product *noun* something produced, as by manufacture: *see* **merchandise**

production *noun* something prepared and presented to the public: *see* **show**

productive *adjective* producing steadily and abundantly: *see* **fertile**

profess *verb* to declare something openly: *see* **claim**

profession *noun* an occupation, such as law or medicine, that requires training and special study: *see* **occupation**

professional *noun* a person whose occupation requires special training and study: *see* **expert**

professor *noun* a teacher at a college or university: *see* **teacher**

proficient *adjective* able to do something well: *see* **able**

profound *adjective* coming from the depth of one's being: *see* **serious [2]**

program *noun* a list of information, such as the order of events and the names of those taking part in a public performance: *see* **plan**

progress *verb* to move forward, especially toward a goal: *see* **advance**

progress *noun* steady improvement or advancement: *see* **growth**

prohibit *verb* to forbid something by law or authority: *see* **forbid**

project

noun an undertaking requiring systematic planning and work: *My latest **project** is to build an outdoor barbecue.*

▸ **enterprise** an important undertaking or project, especially one that is complicated and sometimes risky: *Amundsen's 1911 journey to the South Pole by dogsled was a daring **enterprise**.*
▸ **pursuit** an activity that a person engages in; an occupation: *Photography is my favorite **pursuit**.*
▸ **task** an often difficult or tedious undertaking: *The Greek hero Hercules was assigned twelve **tasks** by the Oracle at Delphi.*
▸ **undertaking** something one decides or agrees to do, especially something difficult or demanding: *Building a space station is a difficult **undertaking**.*

prolific *adjective* producing something in great numbers: *see* **fertile**

prolong *verb* to lengthen the amount of time that something takes: *see* **stretch**

prolonged *adjective* longer in time than expected or required: *see* **long**

prominent *adjective* widely known for one's achievements or success: *see* **famous**

promise

noun a statement that one will do something: *People trust her because she keeps her **promises**.*

▸ **covenant** a formal agreement between people or groups: *The two nations signed a **covenant** to preserve the peace.*
▸ **guarantee** something that gives assurance, especially a promise that a product will be fixed if anything goes wrong with it: *This machine comes with a three-year **guarantee**.*
▸ **oath** a statement or promise that what one says is true: *The witness took an **oath** to tell the truth.*
▸ **pledge** a formal promise that one will do something at a later time: *We made a **pledge** to contribute money to the National Trail System.*
▸ **vow** a solemn promise or oath: *They made a **vow** to love each other forever.*
▸ **word** a spoken assurance or promise: *My friend gave me her **word** that she would return the money I loaned her.*

promote *verb* to aid the progress or growth of something: *see* **sponsor**

promotion *noun* publicity for a product on sale: *see* **advertisement**

prompt *adjective* ▷ being on time ▷ done without delay: *see* **fast**

promptly *adverb* in a timely manner: *see* **immediately**

prone

adjective having a certain tendency: *My friends tease me because I am **prone** to talk too much.*

▸ **apt** more likely than not: *Most people are **apt** to accept the advice of an expert.*
▸ **disposed** willing or ready; inclined: *His story made me **disposed** to believe him.*
▸ **inclined** having a preference or tendency; leaning toward something: *I am **inclined** to follow your suggestion.*

▸ **liable**   very likely; apt: *You're **liable** to get wet if you don't take your umbrella.*

▸ **partial**   especially attracted or inclined: *I am **partial** to Vietnamese food.*

pronounce *verb*   to produce the sounds of a word: *see* **say**

prop *verb*   to place an object beneath or against a structure to keep it from falling: *see* **brace**

proper

adjective   conforming to established standards of behavior or manners: ***Proper** table manners vary from country to country.*

▸ **accepted**   regarded as correct or true: *It is **accepted** that the world is round.*

▸ **appropriate**   suitable for a particular person, condition, occasion, or place; proper: *What would be **appropriate** to wear to that party?*

▸ **fitting**   appropriate for or suitable to an occasion: *It is **fitting** to send a card for someone's birthday.*

▸ **suitable**   right for a certain purpose or occasion; appropriate: *That low-cut dress is not **suitable** for work.*

ANTONYM **improper**   not proper; incorrect

property

noun   something, such as land, that is owned: *My grandparents bought some **property** in the country.*

▸ **assets**   all the property owned by a person or business: *My **assets** include two cars and a house.*

▸ **belongings**   personal items that one owns; possessions: *We packed all our **belongings** into boxes when we moved.*

▸ **goods**   personal belongings: *We loaded all our household **goods** into the moving van.*

▸ **possessions**   the things one owns; one's personal property: *I keep all my **possessions** in good repair.*

▸ **things**   personal belongings: *Where shall I put my **things**?*

prophesy *verb*   to predict with strong belief what is going to happen: *see* **predict**

proposal *noun*   a plan or scheme that is offered for others to consider: *see* **suggestion**

propose *verb*   to put something forward for consideration: *see* **suggest**

prospect *noun* (formal)   something presented to the eye; a scene: *see* **view**

prosper *verb*   to be fortunate or successful: *see* **thrive**

prosperous *adjective*   having much wealth or financial success: *see* **rich**

protect

verb   to keep someone or something safe from harm, attack, or injury: *The Secret Service **protects** the President.*

▸ **attend**   to take care of someone's needs: *The nurse **attended** his patients.*

▸ **defend**   to keep someone or something safe from attack or danger: *The soldiers **defended** the fort.*

▸ **guard**   to watch over someone or something so as to provide protection: *Two big dogs **guard** the junkyard.*

▸ **patrol**   to move about an area for the purpose of observation, inspection, or security: *The security officers **patrolled** the university campus.*

▸ **preserve**   to maintain something in safety or good condition: *Everyone should help to **preserve** our nation's resources.*

▸ **safeguard**   to ensure the safety of someone or something; to protect: *Helmets help to **safeguard** bicyclists.*

▸ **shield**   to protect someone or something, especially by providing cover: *I used a newspaper to **shield** myself from the hot sun.*

protected *adjective*   kept from harm, attack, or injury: *see* **safe**

protection

noun   the condition of being kept safe from harm, attack, or injury: *The thin jacket was his only **protection** against the harsh weather.*

▸ **defense**   the act of defending against attack, danger, or damage: *The best **defense*** against cavities is to brush and floss your teeth regularly.

▸ **safety** freedom from danger or harm: *Rescue workers escorted the accident victims to safety.*

▸ **security** freedom from risk or danger: *Wearing my seat belt gives me a sense of security.*

protest *noun* a formal declaration of disapproval or objection: *see* **complaint**

proud

adjective feeling pleased and satisfied over something one owns, makes, does, or is a part of: *I am proud of my baseball trophies.*

▸ **arrogant** excessively and unpleasantly proud of oneself: *The movie actor became arrogant after winning his second Oscar.*

▸ **conceited** having an overly high opinion of oneself: *The conceited lawyer said that she could win any case.*

▸ **haughty** proud about oneself and looking down on others: *The haughty salesperson offended me.*

▸ **pompous** marked by excessive self-esteem or exaggerated dignity: *We tease our father when he starts sounding pompous.*

▸ **self-important** having an excessively high opinion of one's own importance or position: *He's been acting self-important ever since he was put in charge of the new project.*

▸ **smug** satisfied with oneself in comparison to others: *She was smug when she received A's in all her classes.*

▸ **vain** thinking too highly of one's own appearance, qualities, or achievements: *He is vain about his gourmet cooking.*

prove

verb to show something to be true by producing evidence or using convincing arguments: *I had to prove that I had a driver's license before I was hired as a chauffeur.*

▸ **certify** to assure the quality, value, or standard of something: *This document certifies that you have completed all the training to be a lifeguard.*

▸ **confirm** to offer sure proof that something is true or correct: *The results of the experiment confirmed the theory.*

▸ **establish** to show clearly that something is true: *The witness's statement established the suspect's innocence.*

▸ **uphold** to give support to something: *I used quotes from different sources to uphold my argument in the essay.*

▸ **validate** to declare something to be legally true or binding: *The clerk validated my gift certificate.*

▸ **verify** to prove the truth of something by presenting evidence or testimony: *The lab tests verified the doctor's diagnosis.*

provide *verb* to give something that is needed or useful: *see* **give**

province *noun* (formal) an area of knowledge, authority, or responsibility: *see* **field [2]**

provisions *noun* a stock of necessary supplies, especially food: *see* **supply**

provoke *verb* to incite a person to anger or resentment, often deliberately: *see* **offend**

prudent *adjective* having or showing caution and good sense: *see* **wise**

prune *verb* to improve something by removing unnecessary parts: *see* **decrease**

pry *verb* to inquire inappropriately into private matters: *see* **interfere**

prying *adjective* excessively curious about things that are not one's business: *see* **curious**

pub *noun* a restaurant and bar where food and alcoholic beverages are sold and drunk: *see* **tavern**

public

noun a community or the people as a whole: *The university art museum is open to the public.*

▸ **citizen** a legal member of a country, city, or town, especially one entitled to vote and enjoy other privileges: *Are you a citizen of the United States?*

▸ **masses** the common people: *That candidate has a growing support among the masses.*

▸ **people** a group of persons living in the same country under one national government: *The people of the United States are very diverse.*

▶ **populace** the general public; the masses: *The populace of the United States elects a new president every four years.*

▶ **population** all of the people who live in a specified area: *What is the population of your city?*

publication *noun* something that is published and offered for sale, such as a book or magazine: *see* **magazine**

publicize *verb* to give information to the media as a means of attracting public attention to a person, a group, or an event: *see* **announce**

pucker *verb* to contract the lips into wrinkles or folds: *see* **frown**

puddle *noun* a small pool of water, especially rainwater: *see* **pool**

pull

verb to apply force to something in order to move it toward that force: *Our pickup truck can pull a horse trailer.*

▶ **drag** to pull something with great effort: *I dragged the full garbage can to the curb.*

▶ **jerk** to make something move with sudden, sharp motions: *My dog jerked the leash out of my hands and ran after the cat.*

▶ **lug** to carry something with great difficulty: *I lugged the heavy groceries up two flights of stairs.*

▶ **tow** to pull something along behind with a chain, rope, or cable: *He used his truck to tow our car out of the mud.*

▶ **tug** to pull at something strongly or move something by pulling strongly: *She tugged on my hand to get my attention.*

▶ **yank** to pull something with a sudden, sharp movement: *The baby yanked my glasses off of my face.*

ANTONYM **push** to press against something so as to move it away

punch *verb* to hit someone or something with the fist: *see* **hit**

puncture *verb* to pierce an object or material with something sharp: *see* **stab**

pungent *adjective* biting or sharp to one's sense of taste or smell: *see* **tasty**

punish

verb to cause someone to suffer for a crime, fault, or misbehavior: *Every society punishes those who break its laws.*

▶ **discipline** to punish someone in order to correct or train: *The teacher disciplined the rowdy students by making them stay after school.*

▶ **imprison** to put someone in prison: *He was imprisoned for car theft.*

▶ **penalize** to give a penalty or disadvantage to someone, as for breaking a rule: *Our soccer team was penalized for rough play.*

▶ **sentence** to give someone a legal punishment for a crime: *The judge sentenced the drug dealer to twenty years in prison.*

punishment *noun* a penalty for a crime or wrongdoing: *see* **penalty**

pupil *noun* a person who is being taught in a school or by a private teacher: *see* **student**

purchase *verb* to obtain something in exchange for money: *see* **buy**

purchase *noun* something that has been bought: *see* **sale**

pure *adjective* not mixed with anything else: *see* **real [1]**

purpose *noun* an intended or desired result: *see* **goal**

purposely *adverb* with the purpose of achieving a desired result or effect: *see* **deliberately**

purr *verb* to make a soft, low, vibrant sound in the throat: *see* **hum**

purse *noun* a woman's bag used for carrying personal items: *see* **bag**

purse *verb* to tighten one's lips, as in disapproval: *see* **frown**

pursue *verb*   to chase someone closely or persistently: *see* **follow**

pursuit *noun*   an activity that a person engages in: *see* **project**

push

verb   to press against something so as to move it away: *I pushed the door open and walked into the store.*

- ▶ **elbow**   to push or shove someone with the elbows: *The man elbowed me rudely to one side so he could get to the front of the line.*
- ▶ **jostle**   to shove and push against one another, as in a crowd: *The pigs jostled each other on their way to the feeding trough.*
- ▶ **scoot**   to move someone or something aside in order to make room: *I scooted my backpack off the couch and sat down to watch TV.*
- ▶ **shove**   to push someone or something forcefully or roughly: *She shoved the heavy bed against the wall.*

▶ **thrust**   to push someone or something with sudden force: *I thrust open the door and ran to answer the ringing phone.*

ANTONYM **pull**   to apply force in order to draw something toward the force

pushy *adjective*   disagreeably aggressive or forward: *see* **aggressive**

put *verb*   to cause something to be in a particular position or condition: *see* **place**

put off *verb*   to delay or postpone something: *see* **delay**

putter *verb*   to keep busy without really accomplishing much: *see* **dabble**

put up with *verb*   to bear or accept something without complaint: *see* **cope**

puzzle *verb*   to baffle someone by presenting a seemingly unsolvable problem: *see* **confuse**

puzzle *noun*   something that is hard to understand: *see* **problem**

Q

quake *verb* to shake without being able to stop: *see* **tremble**

quality

noun a property that makes someone or something what it is: *One of the **qualities** of a gas is that it will spread out to fill a container of any size.*

▸ **aspect** a particular way of considering something: *My favorite **aspect** of my job is that I work with nice people.*

▸ **characteristic** a distinguishing feature or quality: *Short legs and floppy ears are two **characteristics** of beagles.*

▸ **feature** a special or noticeable part, characteristic, or quality: *The best **feature** on our new refrigerator is the ice-maker.*

▸ **trait** a typical and clearly defined characteristic: *Generosity and a sense of humor are the **traits** I like best in a person.*

quandary *noun* a condition of uncertainty or doubt: *see* **trouble**

quantity *noun* a specified or indefinite amount or number: *see* **amount**

quarrel *noun* an angry, usually verbal dispute: *see* **fight**

quarry *noun* an open pit from which stone, especially stone for building, is gotten by digging, cutting, or blasting: *see* **hole**

queasy *adjective* somewhat sick to one's stomach: *see* **sick**

queen *noun* a female sovereign: *see* **ruler**

queer *adjective* different in a strange way from what is usual or expected: *see* **strange**

query *verb* to express doubt or uncertainty about something: *see* **doubt**

quest *noun* an adventurous expedition undertaken in order to secure or achieve something: *see* **adventure**

question *verb* to ask someone directly or closely for information: *see* **ask**

question *verb* to have or express doubt: *see* **doubt**

question *noun* a difficult matter: *see* **problem**

questioning *adjective* asking questions; wondering: *see* **curious**

questionnaire *noun* a printed form with a series of questions: *see* **test**

quick *adjective* done or occurring in a short amount of time: *see* **fast**

quickly *adverb* with great speed: *see* **immediately**

quiet

adjective making little or no noise; silent or nearly silent: *Our new air conditioner is very **quiet**.*

▸ **hushed** free of most or all sound; quiet: *The whole neighborhood was **hushed** after the snowfall.*

▸ **muffled** not loud or distinct; deadened: *I could hear the **muffled** conversation of my parents in the kitchen.*

▸ **mute** not speaking; silent: *The shy student was usually **mute** during class discussions.*

▸ **silent** making or having no sound: *The coyotes howled for awhile and then were **silent**.*

▸ **still** no longer making any sound; hushed or subdued: *The wind died down and the night became **still**.*

ANTONYM **noisy** making a lot of noise

quilt *noun* a bed covering made of two layers of cloth with a layer of soft cotton or wool in between: *see* **cover**

quit *verb* to leave or give up something: *see* **resign**

quit *verb* to stop doing something: *see* **stop**

quite *adverb* to the fullest extent: *see* **very**

quiver *verb* to shake with a slight vibrating motion: *see* **tremble**

quiz *verb* a short test that can be either written or oral: *see* **test**

quota *noun* an amount of something assigned to be done, made, or sold: *see* **limit**

R

racket *noun*   a loud, annoying noise: *see* **noise**

radiance *noun*   bright light or intense heat that is given off by a source: *see* **shine**

radiant *adjective*   giving off light or heat: *see* **bright**

radiate *verb*   to give something off in rays or waves: *see* **emit**

radical *adjective*   favoring extreme or rapid changes: *see* **extreme**

rag *noun*   a scrap of torn, frayed, or left-over cloth: *see* **scrap**

rage *noun*   violent anger or a fit of such anger: *see* **anger**

ragged

adjective   worn to rags; tattered: *The old blanket was* ***ragged*** *from so much use.*

- ▸ **dilapidated**   being in poor condition because of neglect; needing repair: *Nobody lives in that* ***dilapidated*** *shack.*
- ▸ **frayed**   worn away, especially along an edge, so that loose threads show: *The cuffs of my jacket are* ***frayed***.
- ▸ **mangy**   having many bare spots; thread-bare: *The old carpeting had become so* ***mangy*** *that we had to replace it.*
- ▸ **shabby**   showing signs of wear or ill-use, worn-out and faded: *I have worn my favorite shirt so much that it has become* ***shabby***.
- ▸ **tattered**   torn into shreds; ragged: *The* ***tattered*** *newspapers blew across the parking lot.*
- ▸ **threadbare**   worn so much that the surface of the fabric is gone and the threads show through: *We put a slipcover over the* ***threadbare*** *couch.*
- ▸ **worn-out**   no longer usable or in good condition: *After backpacking all summer, my hiking boots are* ***worn-out***.

raid *verb*   to carry out a sudden attack by a small armed force: *see* **attack**

rain

noun   water that falls in drops from clouds to the earth: *The weatherman said to expect* ***rain*** *today.*

- ▸ **cloudburst**   a sudden, heavy rainfall: *The* ***cloudburst*** *caught me by surprise as I walked across campus.*
- ▸ **downpour**   a heavy fall of rain: *The* ***downpour*** *caused the gutters to overflow.*
- ▸ **drizzle**   a fine, misty rain: *My clothes were damp from standing in the* ***drizzle*** *waiting for the bus.*
- ▸ **shower**   a brief fall of rain: *The* ***shower*** *of rain was good for the flowers.*
- ▸ **sprinkle**   a light rain: *The passing* ***sprinkle*** *barely wet the ground.*

raise

verb [1]   to grow crops or breed animals, especially in quantity: *That farmer* ***raises*** *organic wheat.*

- ▸ **breed**   to cause animals to reproduce, especially by controlled mating: *My aunt* ***breeds*** *Arabian horses.*
- ▸ **cultivate**   to improve and prepare land for the raising of crops: *The farmer* ***cultivated*** *his fields.*
- ▸ **farm**   to grow crops or raise livestock: *People started* ***farming*** *more than 10,000 years ago.*
- ▸ **grow**   to plant and tend crops: *I always* ***grow*** *corn, tomatoes, and beans in my garden.*
- ▸ **rear**   to care for a child or children during the early years of growth and learning: *She helped* ***rear*** *her brothers and sisters after her mother died.*

raise

verb [2]   to move something to a higher position: *We* ***raised*** *our glasses in a toast.*

- ▸ **elevate**   to raise something to a higher place, position, or level: *The nurse* ***elevated*** *the patient's leg.*

▸ **hoist** to lift or haul something up, often with a mechanical device: *The crane hoisted cargo onto the ship.*

▸ **lift** to raise something or someone from a lower to a higher position or condition: *The father lifted his little daughter onto his shoulders.*

▸ **pick up** to take hold of and lift something or someone higher: *I picked up my cat to give it a hug.*

ANTONYM **lower** to move something down to a level beneath the previous level

rally *noun* a large meeting held to support a cause or to inspire enthusiasm: *see* **meeting**

ramble *verb* to walk about casually or for pleasure: *see* **wander**

rancid *adjective* having the unpleasant smell or taste of decomposed oils or fats: *see* **rotten**

range *noun* the spread or extent of something: *see* **degree**

range *verb* to wander freely over a wide area: *see* **wander**

rank *verb* to assign something to a position on a scale or in a group: *see* **judge**

rank *noun* one's position or standing on a scale or in a group: *see* **status**

rap *verb* to strike a surface quickly and sharply: *see* **hit**

rapid *adjective* marked by great speed: *see* **fast**

rare

adjective not often found, seen, or happening: *He collects rare coins.*

▸ **scarce** in short or inadequate supply; rarely found: *Some people think that honest politicians are scarce.*

▸ **special** different from what is common or usual: *Baptisms are special occasions.*

▸ **uncommon** not common; rare or unusual: *It is uncommon for us to have snow this time of year.*

▸ **unique** being the only one of its kind: *Rhode Island is unique in that it's the smallest state in the United States.*

▸ **unusual** not usual, common, or ordinary: *Her clothes are unusual because she designs them all herself.*

ANTONYM **common** found or occurring often; widespread

rarely

adverb in rare cases; not very often: *It rarely rains in the desert.*

▸ **infrequently** not very often and not on a regular basis: *Comets are of interest because they appear so infrequently.*

▸ **occasionally** from time to time, but not often or regularly: *She occasionally babysits her neighbor's children when their regular sitter can't come.*

▸ **seldom** not often; rarely: *I seldom have time to go dancing now that I work the night shift.*

▸ **sometimes** now and then; at times: *Sometimes my friends and I go bowling.*

rascal *noun* a person who is playfully mischievous: *see* **villain**

rash *adjective* said or done with too little thought: *see* **wild [2]**

raspy *adjective* harsh and grating in voice: *see* **hoarse**

rat *noun* (informal) a hateful, sneaky person, especially one who gives out information about the wrongs of friends or associates: *see* **villain**

rate *verb* (informal) to merit or deserve something: *see* **earn**

rate *noun* an amount of one thing measured against another thing, such as miles per hour: *see* **speed**

ration *verb* to give something out in fixed, limited amounts: *see* **distribute**

rational *adjective* having the ability to think things through: *see* **wise**

rattle *verb* to shake something noisily so that it makes short, sharp sounds: *see* **shake**

ravine *noun*   a narrow, steep-sided valley typically smaller than a gorge: *see* **valley**

raw *adjective*   unpleasantly damp and chilly: *see* **cold**

raw *adjective*   untrained and inexperienced: *see* **inexperienced**

reach *verb*   to arrive at a place, position, or goal: *see* **achieve**

react *verb*   to act in response to a situation, person, or influence: *see* **answer**

read *verb*   to understand the meaning of written or printed words: *see* **learn**

ready *adjective*   feeling in the mood to do something: *see* **willing**

real

adjective [1]   authentic and genuine; not artificial: *This is a **real** diamond.*

- ▶ **authentic**   not counterfeit or copied; having an origin or authorship that can be proven: *The signature on the letter was **authentic**.*
- ▶ **genuine**   being exactly what is claimed; not fake or false; real or pure: *He believes the photograph is of a **genuine** UFO.*
- ▶ **pure**   not mixed with anything else: *This blouse is made of **pure** silk.*

ANTONYM **fake**   not genuine; counterfeit

real

adjective [2]   existing regardless of individual perception or opinion; not imaginary: *Some people think that vampires and werewolves are **real**.*

- ▶ **actual**   existing or happening in fact: *The **actual** cost of the car is more than the advertised price once you add in the extras.*
- ▶ **concrete**   existing in reality as something that can be perceived by the senses: *Trees and rocks are **concrete** objects.*
- ▶ **tangible**   ▷ possible to touch: *The artist delighted in the color and shape of **tangible** objects.* ▷ able to be treated as a fact: *The fingerprints at the crime scene were the only **tangible** evidence linking the defendant to the murder.*

realize *verb*   to become fully aware of something: *see* **understand**

really *adverb*   in actual truth or fact: *see* **certainly**

reap *verb*   to cut grain or gather a crop by hand or machine: *see* **gather**

rear *verb*   to care for a child or children during the early years of growth and learning: *see* **raise [1]**

reason *noun*   a statement or fact that justifies or explains an action: *see* **excuse**

reason *noun*   a cause for acting, thinking, or feeling in a certain way: *see* **motive**

reason *verb*   to use one's ability to think clearly and sensibly: *see* **think**

reasonable *adjective*   showing good judgment or common sense: *see* **wise**

rebate *noun*   a return of part of the amount paid for an item: *see* **discount**

rebel

verb   to resist or defy an authority or generally accepted convention: *The workers **rebelled** against the low wages by going on strike.*

- ▶ **defy**   to oppose someone or something boldly: *The little girl **defied** her parents by refusing to eat her dinner.*
- ▶ **disobey**   to refuse to obey someone or something: *She got a ticket for **disobeying** the speed limit.*
- ▶ **oppose**   to be in conflict with someone or something; to fight against something: *Many people **oppose** the use of pesticides in agriculture.*
- ▶ **resist**   to stand or work against something, such as a force, authority, or influence: *During the Vietnam War, a number of people were imprisoned for **resisting** the draft.*

ANTONYM **obey**   to do what is commanded or requested

rebellion

noun   open, organized, and armed opposition toward a government: *The American Revolution was a **rebellion** against British control.*

▸ **defiance** open resistance to authority: *The students read the banned book as an act of defiance.*

▸ **disobedience** a refusal or failure to obey: *The soldier was punished for his disobedience.*

▸ **mutiny** open rebellion against authority, especially of soldiers or sailors against their officers: *The mutiny on the HMS Bounty in 1789 is one of the most famous in history.*

▸ **resistance** a firm refusal to give into the actions, effects, or force of something; opposition: *I met with resistance when I suggested we clean the house.*

▸ **revolt** an uprising, especially against state authority: *In 1789 the people of France staged a revolt against the nobility.*

▸ **revolution** the overthrow of one government and its replacement with another: *The Russian Revolution in 1917 created the world's first Communist state.*

▸ **riot** a violent disturbance created by a large number of people: *Many windows were broken during the riot over reports of police brutality.*

▸ **uprising** a popular revolt against a government or its policies: *The uprising was stopped by government troops.*

recall *verb* to summon a memory: *see* **remember**

receive *verb* to take or acquire something given, offered, or sent: *see* **get**

receive *verb* to welcome someone, especially to one's home: *see* **greet**

recent *adjective* new or fairly new: *see* **modern**

recess *noun* a temporary pause in usual activity: *see* **break**

recess *noun* a short period for rest or play, as during school: *see* **vacation**

recital *noun* a public performance, as of poetry or music: *see* **show**

recite *verb* to repeat something from memory, or say aloud: *see* **tell**

reckless *adjective* not careful or cautious: *see* **wild [2]**

recline *verb* to lie back or lie down: *see* **relax**

recognition *noun* acknowledgment or approval, especially for one's accomplishments: *see* **appreciation**

recognize

verb to know or identify someone or something from past experience or knowledge: *I recognized my friend's handwriting on the note.*

▸ **distinguish** to perceive someone or something as being different or distinct: *People have trouble distinguishing me from my identical twin.*

▸ **identify** to establish the identity of someone or something: *He can identify several varieties of hummingbirds from the markings on their chest and throat.*

recoil *verb* to draw back in fear or disgust: *see* **wince**

recollect *verb* to recall or remember something: *see* **remember**

recommend *verb* to praise someone as being worthy or desirable: *see* **praise**

recommendation *noun* something that is advised: *see* **suggestion**

record *noun* something written down in order to preserve facts or information: *see* **report**

recount *verb* (formal) to tell about something in detail: *see* **tell**

recover *verb* to get something back: *see* **save**

recreation

noun the refreshment of one's mind or body through some activity such as a sport or game that amuses or excites: *Mountain biking is my favorite form of recreation.*

▸ **activity** a planned or organized thing to do: *My summer camp has lots of outdoor activities like hiking, canoeing, and horseback riding.*

- ▸ **game**   a sport or other form of play carried on according to a special set of rules: *I like to play card **games** such as poker and gin rummy.*
- ▸ **hobby**   an activity done for pleasure in one's spare time: *My father's **hobby** is restoring old cars.*
- ▸ **pastime**   an activity that occupies one's time pleasurably: *One of my favorite **pastimes** is playing computer games.*
- ▸ **sport**   a usually competitive activity involving physical exercise and skill: *I'm better at individual **sports** like swimming and running than at team sports like baseball or football.*

redeem *verb*   to recover ownership of something by paying a specified sum: *see* **save**

reduce *verb*   to bring something down in size, degree, or strength: *see* **decrease**

reduced *adjective*   smaller or lower than before: *see* **less**

reduction *noun*   the amount by which the price of an item is reduced: *see* **discount**

reek *noun*   a strong or unpleasant odor: *see* **smell**

referee *noun*   an official who enforces the rules in a sporting event: *see* **judge**

reference book *noun*   a book, such as a dictionary or thesaurus, containing authoritative information: *see* **book**

refined *adjective*   polite or cultivated: *see* **elegant**

refinement *noun*   polite and cultured manners or behavior: *see* **elegance**

reflect *verb*   to take time to think seriously about something: *see* **consider**

reform *verb*   to improve something by the correction of error or the removal of defects: *see* **better**

refrain *verb* (formal)   to hold oneself back from doing or saying something: *see* **avoid**

refresh

verb   to revive a person with food, drink, or rest: *The short nap **refreshed** me.*

- ▸ **energize**   to give someone new or extra energy: *She was **energized** after the aerobics class.*
- ▸ **renew**   to make something new or as if new again: *Fresh paint **renewed** the look of the old house.*
- ▸ **replenish**   to fill or complete something again: *I need to **replenish** my supply of pens and pencils.*
- ▸ **revive**   to give new health, strength, or spirit to someone: *I was tired, but the cup of coffee **revived** me.*

refuge

noun   a place providing protection or shelter: *Our biology class visited a wildlife **refuge**.*

- ▸ **asylum**   a place of safety or refuge, especially from political persecution: *The refugees sought **asylum** in a neutral country.*
- ▸ **preserve**   an area maintained for the protection of wildlife or natural resources: *Many countries have forest **preserves**.*
- ▸ **reservation**   a tract of land set apart by the federal government, especially for use by a Native American people: *We went camping on the Apache **Reservation** in the White Mountains of Arizona.*
- ▸ **sanctuary**   a place of refuge or protection: *No bikes, skateboards, or boom boxes are allowed in our local wild bird **sanctuary**.*
- ▸ **shelter**   a protected area, especially a place for homeless people or animals to stay temporarily: *We adopted a puppy and two kittens from the animal **shelter**.*

refuse *noun*   something to be thrown away: *see* **garbage**

refuse *verb*   to be unwilling to do, accept, or allow something: *see* **reject**

regal *adjective*   like a king or queen: *see* **noble**

regard *noun*   careful thought or attention: *see* **attention**

regard *noun*   recognition of superior worth or achievement: *see* **respect**

regarding *preposition*   in reference to: *see* **about**

regardless *adverb* in spite of everything: *see* **anyway**

regent *noun* one who acts as a ruler during the absence of a monarch: *see* **ruler**

regime *noun* a government in power, especially in a nondemocratic country: *see* **government**

region *noun* an area of the earth's surface, usually a large one: *see* **area**

register *verb* to enroll officially or formally: *see* **enroll**

regret *verb* to feel a sense of sorrow or distress over a past event or act: *see* **mourn**

regret *noun* sorrow or distress over a past event or act: *see* **sorrow**

regular

adjective happening or behaving according to a pattern; usual: *School did not start at the **regular** time because of the snowstorm.*

- ► **consistent** happening or behaving in the same way all the time; steady: *People bet on that horse because it is a **consistent** winner.*
- ► **customary** according to custom or habit; usual: *It is **customary** to leave a tip for the waiter when dining at a restaurant.*
- ► **habitual** established by long use or habit: *I took my **habitual** morning walk around the park.*
- ► **usual** in accordance with customary or normal practice: *I took my **usual** seat near the front of the classroom.*

regularly *adverb* at a fixed or usual time: *see* **always**

regulate *verb* to control or direct something according to rules: *see* **manage**

regulation *noun* an official rule, as of an organization: *see* **rule**

rehearse *verb* to practice something in preparation for a public performance: *see* **practice**

reign *noun* the period during which a monarch rules: *see* **government**

reinforce *verb* to make something stronger by adding extra support to it: *see* **brace**

reject

verb to be unwilling to accept or consider something: *The city council **rejected** the proposal to build a new mall.*

- ► **decline** to politely refuse to accept or do something: *She **declined** my invitation to go to the movies.*
- ► **refuse** to be unwilling to do, accept, or allow something: *My brother **refused** to loan me his car.*
- ► **snub** to treat someone with scorn or coldness: *The tennis player **snubbed** his rival by refusing to shake hands at the end of the game.*
- ► **turn down** to refuse to accept: *I **turned down** my friend's offer to dye my hair.*

ANTONYM **accept** to receive something offered, especially with gladness

relate *verb* to tell or narrate something: *see* **tell**

relatives *noun* people related to one another by descent, marriage, or adoption: *see* **family**

relax

verb to become less tense or anxious: *I **relaxed** by taking a long, hot bath.*

- ► **laze** to relax lazily; to loaf: *I **lazed** around the house all weekend.*
- ► **loaf** to spend time lazily or aimlessly: *We **loafed** all day watching videos.*
- ► **lounge** to stand, sit, or lie in a lazy or relaxed way: *My dad likes to **lounge** in a hammock on summer afternoons.*
- ► **recline** to lie back or lie down: *I **reclined** on the couch and read a book.*
- ► **rest** to stop doing something, especially so as to recover one's energy: *The soccer player **rested** on the sidelines before being put back in the game.*

▸ **unwind** to become free of anxiety, worry, or tension: *She **unwinds** by working out at the gym.*

relaxed *adjective* free from tension or anxiety: *see* **casual**

release

verb ▷ to set someone or something free from confinement: *He was **released** from prison early for good behavior.* ▷ to let someone or something loose: *The little girl **released** her balloon and watched it float to the ceiling.*

▸ **free** to give someone or something freedom: *The divers **freed** the gray whale from the fishing net.*
▸ **liberate** to set someone or something free, as from oppression, confinement, or foreign control: *The city of Paris was **liberated** from German occupation on August 25th, 1944.*
▸ **unfasten** to open, unlock, or untie something: *I **unfastened** the necklace and put it in the jewelry box.*
▸ **untie** to free an object or person from something that binds or restrains: *He **untied** the boat and rowed away from the dock.*

ANTONYM **hold** to have or keep someone or something in the arms or hands

relentless *adjective* steady and persistent: *see* **stubborn**

reliable *adjective* capable of being relied upon: *see* **dependable**

relief

noun ▷ the easing of a burden, such as pain or anxiety: *This medicine can give you **relief** from a sore throat.* ▷ aid or assistance to someone in need *We donated money to the disaster **relief** fund.*

▸ **assistance** help or aid that contributes to another person's effort: *He gave his mother **assistance** in unloading the groceries.*

▸ **charity** the giving of money or other help to needy people: *That family's **charity** is well known throughout the community.*
▸ **welfare** help, such as money, that is given to those who are in need: *The government provides **welfare** to families in poverty.*

relieve *verb* ▷ to give someone aid or assistance. ▷ to lessen or reduce pain, discomfort, or anxiety: *see* **help**

religious

adjective following the beliefs of a religion: *He was raised in a **religious** family.*

▸ **devout** having or showing devotion to a religion: ***Devout** Muslims are expected to pray five times a day.*
▸ **orthodox** following accepted or established beliefs or doctrines: *In some religions it is not considered **orthodox** to eat pork.*
▸ **pious** having or showing religious respect or reverence: *Many **pious** Mormons make a journey to the Temple in Salt Lake City, Utah.*
▸ **reverent** feeling or showing profound awe, respect, and often love: *I was **reverent** as I entered the great cathedral.*
▸ **spiritual** relating to the soul or to religious experience: *She is studying the **spiritual** teachings of Buddhism.*

relinquish *verb* to let go of something: *see* **abandon**

relish *verb* have a keen appetite or liking for something: *see* **enjoy**

reluctant *adjective* lacking an inclination to do something: *see* **hesitant**

rely on *verb* to have complete confidence in someone or something: *see* **trust**

remain *verb* to stay in the same place or condition: *see* **stay**

remainder *noun* the remaining part: *see* **balance**

remark *noun*   a casual statement or comment: *see* **comment**

remarkable *adjective*   attracting notice as being unusual or extraordinary: *see* **wonderful**

remedy

noun   something used to relieve pain, cure a disease, or correct a disorder: *The best remedy for the common cold is to get plenty of rest.*

▸ **antidote**   a substance that works against a poison: *A paste of baking soda and water is an old-fashioned* **antidote** *for the treatment of bee stings.*
▸ **cure**   a medical treatment or a medicine that makes a sick person get better: *Antibiotics are a widely used* **cure** *for bacterial infections.*
▸ **medicine**   a substance used to treat a disease or to relieve pain: *The doctor gave me some* **medicine** *for my sore throat.*
▸ **therapy**   the treatment of illnesses or disabilities: *I needed a lot of physical* **therapy** *after I broke my leg.*
▸ **tonic**   something, such as a medicine or a healing influence, that restores a person's strength or energy: *The week at the spa was a wonderful* **tonic.**
▸ **treatment**   the use of something to relieve or cure a disease or injury: *Draining small amounts of a person's blood was a common medical* **treatment** *in the Middle Ages.*

remember

verb   to bring something back to the mind; to think of something again: *I can't* **remember** *the name of that actor with the bald head.*

▸ **call to mind**   to cause one to remember: *Seeing her* **called to mind** *the fun day we had together at the beach.*
▸ **recall**   to summon a memory; to remember something: *Do you* **recall** *what time he said to pick him up?*
▸ **recollect**   to recall or remember something: *I seem to* **recollect** *that he said to pick him up at 5:30.*

reminder *noun*   something that makes one remember to do something: *see* **souvenir**

remnant *noun*   a portion or quantity left over: *see* **scrap**

remorse *noun*   bitter regret for having done something wrong: *see* **sorrow**

remorseful *adjective*   filled with bitter regret for having done something wrong: *see* **sorry**

remote *adjective*   far from settled areas: *see* **far**

remove *verb*   to move or take something away from a position or place: *see* **subtract**

rend *verb*   to tear, pull, or wrench something apart violently: *see* **rip**

rendezvous *noun*   a prearranged meeting: *see* **appointment**

renew *verb*   to make something new or as if new again: *see* **refresh**

renounce *verb*   to give up something, especially by formal announcement: *see* **resign**

renowned *adjective*   having widespread honor and fame: *see* **famous**

rent

verb   to make a payment or regular ongoing payments for the use of something: *We rented a houseboat for our vacation.*

▸ **borrow**   to get something from someone else with the understanding that it will be returned: *Can I* **borrow** *your car while mine is being repaired?*
▸ **charter**   to hire or rent something for a limited time: *The company I work for* **chartered** *a river boat for the holiday party.*
▸ **hire**   to pay for using something temporarily; to rent something: *We* **hired** *bicycles for the day.*
▸ **lease**   to obtain the use of property for a certain time by a contract: *He* **leased** *an apartment for the next year.*
▸ **lend**   to give or allow the use of something with the understanding that it is to be returned: *Will you* **lend** *me that book when you're done with it?*

▶ **loan** to lend something to someone, such as money: *She loaned her sister ten dollars.*

repair *verb* to return something to proper or useful condition after being damaged: *see* **fix**

repeat *verb* to say or do what someone has already said or done: *see* **copy**

repeatedly *adverb* said, done, or occurring again and again: *see* **again**

replace *verb* to take or fill the place of another: *see* **substitute**

replacement *noun* a person or thing that replaces another person or thing: *see* **substitute**

replenish *verb* to fill or complete something again: *see* **refresh**

reply *noun* a response to a question, statement, or greeting; an answer: *see* **answer**

reply *verb* to say or give an answer: *see* **answer**

report

noun a spoken or written description of something: *I wrote a report about Neptune for my astronomy class.*

▶ **account** a written or spoken description of events: *She gave a vivid account of her trip to Bermuda.*
▶ **chronicle** a record of events arranged in the order that they happened: *This book is a chronicle of the events that led up to World War I.*
▶ **diary** a daily written record of a person's thoughts, activities, opinions, and experiences: *I have kept a diary since I was fourteen years old.*
▶ **history** a written record of past events: *I am reading a history of opera.*
▶ **journal** a record that is kept on a regular basis: *My mother keeps a gardening journal during the growing season.*
▶ **log** an official record of speed, progress, and important events that is kept for a ship

or aircraft: *The oil tanker's captain made an entry in his log.*
▶ **minutes** an official record of the discussion or events that take place at a meeting: *The secretary read the minutes of the last meeting.*
▶ **record** something written down in order to preserve facts or information: *The hotel keeps a record of its guests.*

representative

noun a person who is chosen or elected to represent others: *In 1917, Jeanette Rankin became the first woman elected as a representative to the U.S. Congress.*

▶ **ambassador** an official of the highest rank who represents his or her government to another country: *I met the Peruvian ambassador to the United States at a reception.*
▶ **agent** a person with the power or authority to act for another: *The talented high-school athlete was recruited by a sports agent.*
▶ **broker** a person who buys and sells property for other people: *My aunt is a real estate broker.*
▶ **delegate** a person chosen to speak and act for another or others; a representative: *I was elected as a delegate to the student council.*
▶ **deputy** a person appointed to act for another or take the place of another: *He is in training to become a sheriff's deputy.*

repress *verb* to hold something down by force or effort: *see* **suppress**

reproduce *verb* to make a copy of something: *see* **copy**

repulsive *adjective* causing extreme dislike or aversion: *see* **gross**

request *verb* to express a desire for something: *see* **ask**

require *verb* to call for something as necessary or essential: *see* **demand**

required *adjective* needed to satisfy a condition: *see* **necessary**

rescue *verb* to save something from danger or harm: *see* **save**

resentful

adjective full of anger as a result of something considered mean, unjust, or hurtful: *I felt resentful when I wasn't invited to the party.*

► **bitter** full of deep resentment or angry disappointment: *He felt bitter when he found out that his friend had lied to him.*

► **malicious** feeling or showing a desire to hurt others: *He spread malicious rumors about her.*

► **spiteful** so full of ill will that one wants to hurt or humiliate another: *Her spiteful remark hurt my feelings.*

► **sullen** showing bad humor or resentment: *The little girl became sullen when she didn't get her way.*

resentment

noun anger caused by a mean, unjust, or hurtful act: *I felt some resentment when my friend took credit for my idea.*

► **bitterness** deep resentment or angry disappointment: *He was full of bitterness after his wife divorced him.*

► **envy** a feeling of discontent at the advantages or success enjoyed by another combined with a strong desire to have them for oneself: *I was filled with envy when I saw my friend's new car.*

► **jealousy** a feeling of concern that one will lose one's position or someone's affection to another person: *She is filled with jealousy when her boyfriend flirts with other girls.*

research *verb* to study a subject or problem closely and carefully: *see* **learn**

resemble *verb* to have a similarity or likeness to someone or something: *see* **appear** [2]

reservation *noun* an arrangement for securing something in advance: *see* **appointment**

reservation *noun* a tract of land set apart by the federal government, especially for use by a Native American people: *see* **refuge**

reserve *verb* to hold or save something for a particular person or use: *see* **allocate**

reserved *adjective* marked by self-restraint and a tendency not to speak out: *see* **shy**

reservoir *noun* a place where a large amount of water has been collected and stored for use: *see* **pool**

reside *verb* to live in a place permanently or for an extended time: *see* **dwell**

residence *noun* the house or other building that a person lives in: *see* **home**

resident *noun* a person who lives in a particular place, especially on a permanent basis: *see* **occupant**

residue *noun* something that remains after a part is used or removed: *see* **balance**

resign

verb to leave or give up a position before filling out one's expected term: *Richard Nixon is the only person to have resigned the presidency of the United States.*

► **abdicate** to formally give up power or responsibility: *In 1936, King Edward VIII abdicated the throne of England in order to marry Wallis Simpson, an American divorcée.*

► **give up** to abandon something that one possesses: *She gave up her right to sue the company in return for a cash payment.*

► **quit** to leave or give up something; to stop doing something: *He quit his job to travel around the world.*

► **renounce** to give up something, especially by formal announcement: *She renounced her fortune when she became a nun and took a vow of poverty.*

► **surrender** to give up something to another, especially under force or in response to a demand: *I had to surrender my passport to the border guards.*

► **yield** to give up or surrender something to another, as by right or authority:

*Drivers coming onto the highway must **yield** the right of way to those already on it.*

resist *verb* to stand or work against something: *see* **rebel**

resistance *noun* a firm refusal to give into the actions, effects, or force of something: *see* **rebellion**

resolute *adjective* firm or determined: *see* **stubborn**

resolve *verb* to find a solution to a conflict or disagreement: *see* **solve**

resolve *noun* firmness or purpose: *see* **will**

resourceful *adjective* able to act effectively or imaginatively, especially in a difficult situation: *see* **creative**

respect

noun a feeling of honor or esteem: *It is important to have **respect** for yourself.*

- ▸ **admiration** a feeling of sincere appreciation of the worth of someone or something: *I have great **admiration** for my mother's paintings.*
- ▸ **approval** favorable regard: *Our swim coach gives his **approval** to team members who work hard at improving their technique.*
- ▸ **esteem** recognition of superior worth or achievement: *Max Planck is held in high **esteem** among physicists for his theory of quantum physics.*
- ▸ **regard** esteem or affection: *We have great **regard** for the firefighters who saved our home.*

respect

verb to have high regard for someone or something: *I **respect** her opinion.*

- ▸ **admire** to have a high opinion of someone or something: *I **admire** his ability to learn languages.*
- ▸ **revere** to regard someone or something with awe, deference, and devotion: *The guru's followers **revered** him.*

▸ **value** to believe something to be of great worth or importance: *I **value** her friendship.*

respectful *adjective* showing the proper consideration toward someone or something: *see* **polite**

respond *verb* to make a reply: *see* **answer**

response *noun* a reply or answer: *see* **answer**

responsibility *noun* something that one is responsible for: *see* **duty**

responsible *adjective* deserving trust or confidence: *see* **dependable**

rest *noun* the part that has not yet been used, consumed, selected, or experienced: *see* **balance**

rest *noun* a period of inactivity, relaxation, or sleep: *see* **break**

rest *verb* to stop doing something, especially so as to recover one's energy: *see* **relax**

restaurant

noun a place where meals are served to the public: *My friend and I ate at our favorite Mexican **restaurant** last night.*

- ▸ **café** a small restaurant or bar: *We can get a quick meal at the **café** across the street.*
- ▸ **cafeteria** a restaurant in which the customers buy their food at a counter and carry it to their tables: *We ate lunch in the hospital **cafeteria** after visiting my cousin and her new baby.*
- ▸ **coffeehouse** a restaurant where coffee and other refreshments are served: *The **coffeehouse** has live music on Saturday nights.*
- ▸ **delicatessen** a store that sells prepared foods such as cheeses, salads, and cooked meats: *I bought a roast beef sandwich at the **delicatessen**.*
- ▸ **diner** a restaurant where patrons can in eat booths or at a long counter: *I like to eat at this **diner** because the food is good but inexpensive.*

restful *adjective* producing a quiet and peaceful feeling: *see* **calm**

restless *adjective* unable to rest, relax, or be still: *see* **impatient**

restore *verb* to bring something back to an original condition: *see* **fix**

restrain *verb* to hold something or someone back by physical force: *see* **control**

restraint *noun* the act of controlling one's emotions or impulses: *see* **patience**

restriction *noun* something that keeps or confines something else within certain limits: *see* **limit**

result

noun something that happens because of something else: *The flood is the **result** of unusually heavy rains.*

▶ **conclusion** the end result of a process, especially of thinking or reasoning: *I reached the **conclusion** that I was wasting my time in trying to win his approval.*

▶ **consequence** something that happens as a result of another action or condition; a result: *I overslept and as a **consequence** missed the bus.*

▶ **effect** something brought about by a cause: *For many people, too much caffeine has the **effect** of making them feel nervous or jittery.*

▶ **impact** the effect of something on an observer, reader, or listener: *This book has had a big **impact** on my life.*

▶ **outcome** something that happens as a result of a process or action: *What was the **outcome** of the ball game?*

retain *verb* to continue to keep something: *see* **keep**

retire *verb* (formal) to withdraw from the company of others, as for rest or seclusion: *see* **leave**

retort *noun* a quick, witty answer: *see* **answer**

retreat *verb* to move back the way one came, especially to escape danger: *see* **leave**

revel *verb* to engage in uproarious festivities: *see* **party**

revenue *noun* money that a government collects, as through taxes: *see* **income**

revere *verb* to regard someone or something with awe, deference, and devotion: *see* **respect**

reverence *noun* a feeling of awe and respect mixed with love: *see* **worship**

reverent *adjective* feeling or showing profound awe, respect, and often love: *see* **religious**

reverse

verb to change something to its opposite: *The Supreme Court can **reverse** the decision of any other U.S. court.*

▶ **counter** to oppose an action with something different or opposite: *He **countered** my suggestion that we order a pizza by proposing that we cook dinner at home.*

▶ **overrule** to decide against something by virtue of a higher authority: *My parents **overruled** my decision to attend an out-of-state college.*

▶ **overturn** to invalidate or reverse a decision by legal means: *New evidence caused the judge to **overturn** the defendant's conviction on charges of drug possession.*

▶ **undo** to reverse the result or effect of something: *I hope I can **undo** the harm caused by my earlier mistakes.*

review *verb* to study or examine something again so as to learn it better: *see* **learn**

revise *verb* to make changes, especially to something written: *see* **change**

revive *verb* to give new health, strength, or spirit to someone: *see* **refresh**

revolt *verb* an uprising, especially against state authority: *see* **rebellion**

revolting *adjective* causing great disgust: *see* **gross**

revolution *noun* the overthrow of one government and its replacement with another: *see* **rebellion**

revolve *verb* to orbit around a central point: *see* **spin**

reward *noun* something valuable, especially money offered or given for a special service: *see* **award**

ribbon *noun* a narrow strip of fabric that is used for decorating or trimming: *see* **string**

rich

adjective having much money or property: *Whoever owns that yacht must be very* **rich**.

▸ **affluent** having plenty of money, property, or possessions: *My* **affluent** *uncle is helping fund my college education.*

▸ **prosperous** having much wealth or financial success: *He owns a* **prosperous** *business.*

▸ **wealthy** having considerable wealth; rich: *Our youth center has a* **wealthy** *benefactor.*

▸ **well-fixed** (informal) financially secure; well-to-do: *My family is* **well-fixed** *now that oil has been discovered on our farm.*

▸ **well-heeled** having plenty of money; prosperous: *The* **well-heeled** *man throws lavish parties at his summer home.*

▸ **well-off** having enough money to live comfortably; affluent: *My grandparents are* **well-off** *and very generous with me.*

▸ **well-to-do** prosperous; affluent: *The popular movie star is* **well-to-do**.

ANTONYM **poor** having little or no money or possessions

riches *noun* great wealth in the form of money, land, or valuable possessions: *see* **wealth**

riddle *noun* a question or statement that is worded in a deliberately puzzling way so that it requires thought to figure out the answer: *see* **problem**

ridge *noun* a long, narrow crest, as of high ground: *see* **top**

ridicule *verb* to make fun of someone or something: *see* **scorn**

ridiculous *adjective* highly absurd or laughable: *see* **silly**

right *noun* something that one has a moral or legal claim to: *see* **privilege**

right *adjective* in accordance with fact, reason, or truth: *see* **true**

right away *adverb* immediately; soon: *see* **immediately**

rigid *adjective* not bending: *see* **stiff**

rigid *adjective* marked by a lack of flexibility, especially regarding rules: *see* **strict**

rim *noun* the edge of something that is circular or curved: *see* **edge**

rinse *verb* to let water flow over something so as to clean it: *see* **dip**

riot *noun* a violent disturbance created by a large number of people: *see* **rebellion**

rip

verb to tear something roughly or forcibly: *I* **ripped** *my jeans on a barbed wire fence.*

▸ **rend** to tear, pull, or wrench something apart violently: *Civil war can* **rend** *a country.*

▸ **shred** to cut or tear something into small strips: *He* **shredded** *the secret documents.*

▸ **slit** to cut something lengthwise into strips: *The stock clerk* **slit** *open the boxes.*

▸ **tear** to pull something apart or into pieces by force: *My gerbils like to* **tear** *apart pieces of paper for nesting material.*

ripe *adjective* fully developed: *see* **adult**

ripple *noun* a sound like that of small waves of water: *see* **rustle**

rise *noun* an increase in status, prosperity, or importance: *see* **growth**

rise *noun* a gently sloping hill: *see* **hill**

risk *noun* the possibility of suffering harm or loss: *see* **danger**

risky *adjective* involving risk: *see* **dangerous**

rite *noun* the customary form for conducting a religious or other solemn ceremony: *see* **ceremony**

ritual *noun* the proper form or order of a religious or other ceremony: *see* **ceremony**

rival *noun*   a person who attempts to equal or outdo another: *see* **enemy**

river

noun   a large, natural stream of water that empties into an ocean, a lake, or another river: *The Mississippi River is often called the Nile of North America.*

- **brook**   a small, natural stream: *The little boys were catching tadpoles down at the brook.*
- **creek**   a small stream of water, often one that flows into a river: *The little creek dries up in the summer.*
- **spring**   a natural fountain or flow of water: *Animals come to the spring to drink.*
- **stream**   a body of water, such as a brook, that flows in a bed or channel: *Hot Creek is a famous trout stream.*

road

noun   an open way for vehicles, people, or animals to pass along or through: *The county is repairing the roads in our town.*

- **alley**   a narrow street or passageway between or behind buildings: *We put our trash cans in the back alley.*
- **avenue**   a wide street or thoroughfare: *New York's avenues are usually busy with traffic and pedestrians.*
- **boulevard**   a broad street, often with trees and grass planted in the center or along the sides: *The beautiful boulevard is lined with palm trees.*
- **freeway**   a wide highway on which vehicles may travel without paying tolls: *The freeways of the United States make it easy to travel throughout the country.*
- **highway**   a main public road: *Will this highway take us to Indianapolis, Indiana?*
- **street**   a public road in a city or town: *We drove down the street and looked at the beautiful houses.*

roam *verb*   to move about freely or restlessly: *see* **wander**

roar *noun*   a loud, deep, threatening sound made by a wild animal: *see* **bark**

roaring *adjective*   loud and deep in sound: *see* **loud**

roast *verb*   to cook food with dry heat, as in an oven or near hot coals: *see* **cook**

rob *verb*   to take property or valuables from a person or place unlawfully, especially by force: *see* **steal**

robber *noun*   a person who takes property from a person or place unlawfully, usually with the threat or use of force: *see* **thief**

robbery *noun*   the act of unlawfully taking property or valuables from a person or place, especially by force: *see* **theft**

robust *adjective*   full of health and energy: *see* **healthy**

rock

noun   ▷ a hard, naturally formed deposit of mineral: *They had to drill through solid rock to find water.* ▷ a piece or mass of stone: *The cabin's fireplace is made out of big, flat rocks.*

- **boulder**   a large, rounded rock: *The landslide scattered many large boulders across the valley floor.*
- **gravel**   a loose mixture of pebbles or small pieces of rock: *We mixed sand, gravel, and cement to make our new driveway.*
- **pebble**   a small, round stone: *I stopped to take the pebble out of my shoe.*
- **stone**   ▷ a naturally hardened mineral material; rock: *The great medieval cathedrals were built mainly of stone.* ▷ a piece of stone; a rock: *I skipped a small stone across the pond.*

rod *noun*   a thin, straight length of wood, metal, or other material: *see* **pole**

rogue *noun*   a person who tricks or cheats others: *see* **villain**

role model *noun*   a person who serves as an example for another person to imitate: *see* **hero**

romance

verb (informal)   to carry on a love affair or courtship with someone: *He romanced her with flowers and presents.*

▸ **court** to try to win the love of someone in order to marry him or her: *My dad did some crazy things when he courted my mom.*

▸ **flirt** to act romantically, especially in a playful or teasing way: *They like to flirt with one another even though they're just friends.*

▸ **woo** to seek someone's affection, especially with the intent of romantic involvement: *My brother sent flowers to his ex-girlfriend in an attempt to woo her back.*

romp *verb* to play or frolic in a lively or excited manner: *see* **play**

roof *noun* the top covering of something, such as a building or vehicle: *see* **top**

room

noun an area of a building that is divided off by walls or partitions: *I am glad I have my own room.*

▸ **chamber** a room in a large house, especially a bedroom: *We toured the chambers of the magnificent Victorian mansion.*

▸ **compartment** a separate section or room, often set off by walls: *I keep my suitcase in a storage compartment in the attic.*

▸ **den** a cozy, private room for personal use, as for study: *Our house has three bedrooms and a den with a fireplace.*

▸ **suite** a series of connected rooms used together: *We stayed in a three-room suite at the hotel.*

root *noun* the point of origin or the cause of something: *see* **basis**

rope

noun a strong, thick cord made of braided or twisted strands, as of hemp or wire: *The cowboy used his rope to lasso the pony.*

▸ **cable** a strong, thick rope make of fiber or strands of steel wire: *The bridge was supported by huge cables that were suspended from towers.*

▸ **chain** a row of metal links joined together: *My brother gave me a gold chain for Christmas.*

▸ **cord** a small rope of twisted strands: *He used a cord to tie up the old newspapers.*

▸ **wire** a thin, flexible metal strand: *The rancher used a roll of wire to repair his fences.*

rot *verb* to break down from the action of bacteria or fungi: *see* **decay**

rotate *verb* to repeat in sequence: *see* **shift**

rotate *verb* to turn on an axis: *see* **spin**

rotten

adjective in a condition of decomposition or decay: *I put the rotten apples in the compost bin.*

▸ **foul** sickening in taste, smell, or appearance: *Spoiled milk has a foul odor.*

▸ **moldy** being covered with mold: *She threw the moldy bread away.*

▸ **overripe** too ripe to be eaten fresh: *Mom made jam out of the overripe peaches.*

▸ **rancid** having the unpleasant smell or taste of decomposed oils or fats: *The butter was rancid after sitting out too long.*

▸ **spoiled** unfit for eating or drinking: *Put the fish in the refrigerator before it gets spoiled.*

▸ **stale** having lost freshness: *The cookies were a little stale, but I ate them anyway.*

rough

adjective having an irregular surface; not even or smooth: *Sand paper has a rough texture.*

▸ **bumpy** ▷ full of bumps or lumps: *The campground was at the end of a bumpy dirt road.* ▷ moving with jerks and jolts: *We had a bumpy flight because of bad weather.*

▸ **coarse** not smooth to the touch; rough: *Some dogs have silky coats, but a wirehaired terrier's coat is coarse.*

▸ **jagged** having sharp notches or indentations; irregular: *She cut her finger on the jagged piece of glass.*

▸ **rugged** having a rough, broken surface, ridged or hilly: *Much of the terrain in the Western United States is rugged.*

▸ **uneven** not level or smooth: *He had difficulty walking over the uneven field.*

ANTONYM **smooth** having a surface that is not rough or uneven

round *noun* a series of similar events or repeated acts: *see* **sequence**

rousing *adjective* exciting the emotions: *see* **exciting**

routine *noun* a series of regular or usual activities: *see* **habit**

rove *verb* to roam or explore at random, especially over a wide area: *see* **wander**

row *noun* a loud quarrel: *see* **fight**

royal *adjective* fit for a monarch; splendid: *see* **noble**

royalty *noun* a fixed percentage of money paid to a writer or a composer resulting from the sale or performance of his or her work: *see* **income**

rub *verb* to move something back and forth against a surface: *see* **touch**

rubbish *noun* discarded or worthless material: *see* **garbage**

rude

adjective not considerate of others; impolite: *It is **rude** to stare at other people.*

- ▸ **discourteous** lacking courtesy; not polite: *Talking during a movie is considered **discourteous**.*
- ▸ **disrespectful** having a lack of respect for others; rude: *The **disrespectful** child was scolded by his parents.*
- ▸ **forward** going beyond what is right and proper; bold: *It was **forward** of him to propose marriage on the first date.*
- ▸ **impolite** not polite; discourteous: *It is **impolite** to chew with your mouth open.*
- ▸ **inconsiderate** not considerate of others; thoughtless: *It was **inconsiderate** of me to call them so late at night.*
- ▸ **uncivil** not using polite manners; intentionally discourteous: *The customer was impatient and **uncivil** to the salesperson.*
- ▸ **unmannerly** having bad manners; impolite: *It was **unmannerly** of them to crowd in front of us.*

ANTONYM **polite** having or showing good manners; courteous

ruffle *verb* to momentarily upset someone or something: *see* **disturb**

rugged *adjective* having a rough, broken surface: *see* **rough**

rugged *adjective* very strong or durable: *see* **tough**

ruin *verb* to damage something beyond repair: *see* **destroy**

rule

noun a statement or principle that is intended to control behavior or action: *The lifeguard enforces the safety **rules** at the swimming pool.*

- ▸ **guideline** a statement, policy, or procedure intended to give practical guidance: *My boss gave my a few **guidelines** and told me to start on the project.*
- ▸ **law** a rule that regulates people's behavior or activities, especially one made by an authority: *If you break a traffic **law**, you usually have to pay a fine.*
- ▸ **policy** a general plan or principle that is chosen to help people make decisions: *According to school **policy**, students may not smoke on campus.*
- ▸ **principle** a rule or standard of behavior: *He is a man of high **principles**.*
- ▸ **regulation** an official rule, as of an organization or government agency: *The employee handbook states the company's **regulations**.*

ruler

noun one who rules or governs: *The pharaohs were the **rulers** of ancient Egypt.*

- ▸ **emperor** a man who is the ruler of an empire: *The **emperor** Kublai Khan was the founder of the Mongol dynasty in China.*
- ▸ **empress** a woman who is the ruler of an empire: *Catherine the Great was **empress** of Russia from 1762 to 1796.*
- ▸ **king** a male sovereign: *France's Louis Philippe was known as the Citizen **King**.*
- ▸ **monarch** one who reigns over a state or territory, usually for life and by hereditary right: *Queen Anne of Great Britain and Ireland was the last **monarch** of the Stuart line.*

▸ **queen**   a female sovereign: *Mary **Queen** of Scots was forced to give up her throne in 1567.*

▸ **regent**   one who acts as a ruler during the absence or disability of a monarch: *King John served as **regent** of England while his brother, King Richard, was fighting in the Crusades.*

▸ **sovereign**   a person with supreme authority over a state; a monarch: *Elizabeth I of England was one of the most powerful **sovereigns** in history.*

ruling *noun*   an official decision: *see* **decision**

run

verb   to move on foot at a pace faster than a walk: *The team **ran** out onto the field.*

▸ **gallop**   ▷ to move at the fastest pace of a horse: *The mustangs **galloped** across the prairie.* ▷ to move swiftly: *Summer is **galloping** by.*

▸ **jog**   to run at a slow, steady speed: *We **jogged** along the trail through the park.*

▸ **lope**   to run with long, smooth strides: *The dog **loped** happily across the beach.*

▸ **sprint**   to run at top speed for a short distance: *I **sprinted** into the house when I heard the phone ring.*

▸ **trot**   to run with slow, short strides: *I **trotted** across the street when the light changed.*

run into *verb*   to meet someone by chance: *see* **meet**

rush *verb*   to move or act with great speed or eagerness: *see* **hurry**

rust *verb*   to become corroded or oxidized: *see* **decay**

rustle

noun   a soft, fluttering sound: *I like the **rustle** of leaves in the wind.*

▸ **flutter**   a light sound of quick flapping or beating: *The **flutter** of the moth against the window caught my attention.*

▸ **crackle**   a slight, sharp, snapping sound: *The **crackle** of the fire was a cheerful sound.*

▸ **ripple**   a sound like that of small waves of water: *We listened to the **ripple** of the waves as we floated in the rowboat.*

▸ **swish**   a hissing or rustling sound: *She enjoyed hearing the **swish** of her silky dress.*

▸ **swoosh**   a rushing or swirling sound: *I was startled by the **swoosh** of a bird flying near my head.*

ruthless *adjective*   having or showing no pity: *see* **mean**[1]

S

sabbatical *noun* an academic leave of absence, often with pay, given every seven years: *see* **vacation**

sabotage *verb* to commit destructive acts in an effort to defeat an enemy or hinder a plan: *see* **undermine**

sack *noun* a large bag of strong, coarse material used for holding objects in bulk: *see* **bag**

sack *verb* (slang) to fire someone from a job: *see* **dismiss**

sacred *adjective* worthy of religious veneration: *see* **holy**

sad

adjective filled with sorrow or unhappiness: *She was **sad** when her boyfriend broke up with her.*

- ▸ **dejected** feeling depressed and gloomy: *We felt **dejected** when our project was canceled for lack of money.*
- ▸ **depressed** feeling sad and in low spirits: *He was **depressed** because he didn't do as well on the exam as he had hoped.*
- ▸ **downhearted** in low spirits; discouraged: *The team became **downhearted** when they realized they couldn't possibly win the game.*
- ▸ **melancholy** feeling a lingering sadness or depression: *I was **melancholy** when I found out that my friend was going to move to another state.*
- ▸ **miserable** extremely or painfully unhappy: *This term paper is making me **miserable**.*
- ▸ **unhappy** not happy; sad: *She was **unhappy** when her parents wouldn't let her go to the concert.*
- ▸ **wistful** full of wishful yearning: *He gave his computer game a **wistful** glance but started his homework anyway.*
- ▸ **wretched** very unhappy or distressed; miserable: *I felt **wretched** when I found out my friend was using drugs.*

ANTONYM **happy** showing or feeling pleasure or joy

sadness

noun sorrow and unhappiness: *Funerals are usually a time of **sadness**.*

- ▸ **dejection** low spirits; gloomy disappointment: *He was filled with **dejection** when he didn't get a part in the play.*
- ▸ **depression** the condition of being sad and discouraged, especially over a period of time: *Helping others is a good way to fight **depression**.*
- ▸ **despair** complete lack of hope: *We looked at each other with **despair** when the car wouldn't start.*
- ▸ **gloom** lowness of spirit; dejection: *There was a feeling of **gloom** in the locker room after we lost the game.*
- ▸ **unhappiness** lack of happiness or joy; sadness: *Poverty and oppression are the source of much **unhappiness** in the world.*

safe

adjective secure or free from danger or harm: *The rabbit felt **safe** in its burrow.*

- ▸ **protected** kept from harm, attack, or injury; guarded: *The President is one of the most **protected** people in America.*
- ▸ **secure** ▷ safe from danger: *She feels more **secure** when she takes her dog hiking with her.* ▷ safe from the risk of loss: *We keep our valuables in a **secure** location.*
- ▸ **unhurt** not hurt or injured; safe: *The rock climber was **unhurt** by the fall.*

safeguard *verb* to ensure the safety of someone or something: *see* **protect**

safety *noun* freedom from danger or harm: *see* **protection**

sag *verb* to bend or droop from pressure or weight: *see* **droop**

sagging *adjective* sinking, drooping, or settling from pressure or weight: *see* **loose**

sail *verb* to move smoothly and effortlessly: *see* **fly**

salary *noun* a fixed sum of money that is paid to a person on a regular basis for doing a job: *see* **income**

sale

noun the exchange of goods or services for an amount of money: *The sale of their house went smoothly.*

- ▸ **bargain** something bought or sold at a price that is good for the buyer: *Many stores offer great bargains after the holidays.*
- ▸ **deal** (informal) a sale that is favorable, especially to the buyer; a bargain: *He got a good deal on his new car.*
- ▸ **purchase** something that has been bought: *She carried her purchases to her car.*
- ▸ **trade** an exchange of one thing for another; a transaction: *I made a trade of my purple sweater for her green one.*

saloon *noun* a room with a bar where alcoholic drinks are sold and drunk: *see* **tavern**

salute *verb* to show respect by raising the right hand stiffly to the forehead or by firing guns: *see* **greet**

salvage *verb* to save or rescue something that would otherwise be lost or destroyed: *see* **save**

same

adjective exactly alike; identical: *My sister and I have eyes of the same color.*

- ▸ **alike** being the same as or similar to another: *No two snowflakes are alike.*
- ▸ **equal** being exactly the same in amount, extent, or other measured quality: *I dealt an equal number of cards to each player.*
- ▸ **equivalent** equal to something else: *The G.E.D. is equivalent to a high-school diploma.*
- ▸ **identical** being exactly alike: *Her computer is identical to mine.*

▸ **similar** alike, but not exactly the same: *We have similar taste in clothes.*

sample *noun* a part or amount that is considered representative of the whole: *see* **example**

sanction *verb* to give official approval to something: *see* **authorize**

sanctuary *noun* a place of refuge or protection: *see* **refuge**

sane *adjective* having or showing good judgment: *see* **wise**

sanitary *adjective* free of germs; hygienic: *see* **clean**

sap *noun* the liquid that flows through plant tissues, carrying water and food: *see* **juice**

satisfactorily *adverb* well enough; adequately: *see* **well**

satisfactory

adjective good enough, but not the best; adequate: *The professor said that the first draft of my paper was satisfactory.*

- ▸ **acceptable** not up to a high level, but good enough to be accepted: *My teacher said that I was making acceptable progress.*
- ▸ **adequate** up to a minimum or acceptable standard: *It was hard to do an adequate job in so little time.*
- ▸ **all right** satisfactory, but not excellent; good enough: *My car is all right, but I'm saving for a new one.*

satisfied *adjective* filled with satisfaction: *see* **content**

satisfy *verb* to fulfill or gratify someone's need, desire, or expectation: *see* **please**

satisfying *adjective* fulfilling or gratifying: *see* **good**

saturate *verb* to wet something until it cannot absorb any more liquid: *see* **flood**

savage *adjective* unrestrained in violence or cruelty: *see* **fierce**

save

verb to rescue someone or something from danger or loss: *Many people worked together to save the birds that had been caught in the oil spill.*

▸ **recover** to get something back; to regain something: *I was happy to recover the book that I thought I had lost.*
▸ **redeem** to recover ownership of something by paying a specified sum: *My uncle redeemed his camera from the pawn shop.*
▸ **rescue** to save something from danger or harm: *My brother helped me rescue my computer files from a virus.*
▸ **salvage** to save or rescue something that would otherwise be lost or destroyed: *I salvaged the old tarp and used it to cover my bicycle.*

savor verb to taste or enjoy something fully: *see* **enjoy**

savory *adjective* highly appealing to one's sense of taste or smell: *see* **tasty**

say

verb to utter a word, phrase, or thought aloud: *Can you say "the frog flopped" ten times in a row?*

▸ **articulate** to utter a speech sound clearly and distinctly: *I had trouble articulating the "r" sound when I first learned English.*
▸ **pronounce** to produce the sounds of a word: *I was embarrassed when I didn't pronounce his name correctly.*
▸ **speak** to utter words; to talk: *Children usually learn to speak around two years old.*
▸ **state** to express something in words: *The witness was asked to state his name for the record.*
▸ **utter** to produce a sound or sounds with the voice: *Nobody uttered a word after the coach ordered us to be quiet.*

scaffold *noun* a temporary platform used for supporting workers and their materials: *see* **platform**

scald verb to burn someone or something with hot liquid or steam: *see* **burn**

scale verb to climb up or over something: *see* **climb**

scale *noun* the relative size or extent of something: *see* **degree**

scamper verb to run or go quickly or lightly: *see* **zoom**

scan verb to look something over quickly and systematically: *see* **browse**

scandalous *adjective* causing scandal or public disgrace: *see* **shocking**

scanty *adjective* so little as to be barely sufficient: *see* **few**

scar *noun* a mark or sign of damage, especially a mark left on the skin by a healed wound: *see* **stain**

scarce *adjective* in short or inadequate supply: *see* **rare**

scarcely *adverb* by a small margin: *see* **hardly**

scarcity *noun* an insufficient amount or supply of something: *see* **lack**

scare

verb to fill someone with fear: *I had a bad dream that scared me.*

▸ **alarm** to fill someone with sudden fear or anxiety: *I was alarmed when the car next to me swerved into my lane.*
▸ **frighten** to make someone afraid or alarmed: *Flying in an airplane frightens me.*
▸ **intimidate** to frighten or discourage someone, as with threats or superior force: *The kitten arched its back and hissed in order to intimidate our dog.*
▸ **terrify** to fill someone with intense fear or terror: *Horror movies terrify me.*

ANTONYM **soothe** to make someone calm or quiet

scared *adjective* frightened or alarmed: *see* **afraid**

scary

adjective   causing fear or alarm: *I was afraid to go upstairs along after watching the **scary** movie.*

- ▶ **creepy** (informal)   producing a feeling of uneasiness or fear: *My brother dared me to sleep in the **creepy** basement overnight.*
- ▶ **eerie**   inspiring fear without a clear reason; strange and frightening: *The **eerie** old house made us feel uneasy.*
- ▶ **frightening**   causing fright or anxiety; scary: *It was **frightening** to be in a car accident.*
- ▶ **mysterious**   impossible to understand or explain: *Many **mysterious** things are said to happen in the Bermuda Triangle.*
- ▶ **spooky** (informal)   ghostly; eerie: *He told the children a **spooky** ghost story.*

scatter *verb*   to throw something here and there in no particular pattern: *see* **spread**

scene *noun*   the place where an action or event occurs: *see* **place**

scene *noun*   a view, especially when thought of as forming a whole: *see* **view**

scent *noun*   a distinctive, often pleasing odor: *see* **smell**

schedule *noun*   a program of appointments, classes, or upcoming events: *see* **plan**

scheme *verb*   to make up a plan, especially a dishonest or clever one: *see* **plot**

school

noun   a place for teaching and learning: *I live across the street from an elementary school.*

- ▶ **academy**   a school for a special field of study; a private high school: *My father thinks that I would do better in a military **academy** than in public high school.*
- ▶ **college**   a school of higher learning that grants a bachelor's degree: *I plan to attend a liberal arts **college** after high school.*
- ▶ **high school**   a secondary school that usually includes grades 9 through 12: *I worked hard in **high school** so I could get into a good college.*
- ▶ **institute**   a place for specialized study: *She attends an **institute** of fine arts.*
- ▶ **seminary**   a school for training priests, ministers, or rabbis: *He attends a Catholic **seminary**.*
- ▶ **university**   a school of higher learning that offers advanced degrees as well as regular undergraduate degrees: *I applied to graduate school at our state **university**.*

schooling *noun*   instruction or training given at school: *see* **education**

scholar *noun*   a person who has gotten a great deal of knowledge from studying: *see* **student**

scoff *verb*   to express mocking contempt or disbelief: *see* **scorn**

scold *verb*   to criticize someone harshly or angrily: *see* **blame**

scoop *verb*   to remove loose material with a spoon-like utensil or with cupped hands: *see* **dig**

scoot *verb*   to move someone or something aside in order to make room: *see* **push**

scorch *verb*   to burn the surface of something: *see* **burn**

score *verb*   to evaluate and assign a grade to something: *see* **judge**

scorn

verb   to consider someone or something as inferior or unworthy: *She was sorry later on that she had **scorned** his advice.*

- ▶ **belittle**   to speak of someone or something as small or unimportant: *He **belittled** her plans to go back to school.*
- ▶ **deride**   to laugh at someone or something with contempt or scorn: *Stravinsky's ballet* The Rite of Spring *was **derided** when it was first performed in 1913.*
- ▶ **disparage**   to speak of someone or something as unimportant or inferior; belittle: *Many people **disparage** cultures that they don't understand.*
- ▶ **jeer**   to speak or shout in a mocking or scornful way: *The audience **jeered** at the comedian's dumb jokes.*

▸ **ridicule** to make fun of someone or something; to laugh at someone: *We **ridicule** our friend because he's such a pack rat.*

▸ **scoff** to express mocking contempt or disbelief: *I **scoffed** at his theory that aliens live among us.*

▸ **sneer** to show contempt or scorn, as with a mocking expression: *He **sneered** at her offer to help him.*

scoundrel *noun* a wicked or dishonorable person: *see* **villain**

scour *verb* to clean, polish, or wash something by scrubbing vigorously: *see* **clean**

scout *verb* to observe or explore carefully in order to obtain information: *see* **search**

scowl *verb* to lower the eyebrows in anger or strong disapproval: *see* **frown**

scramble *verb* to move or climb hurriedly, especially on the hands and knees: *see* **climb**

scrap

noun a small piece or fragment: *I am collecting **scraps** of fabric to make a quilt.*

▸ **bit** a tiny piece: *Bits of confetti floated through the air during the parade.*

▸ **fragment** a piece or part broken off from a whole: *I broke off a **fragment** of my tooth when I bit down too hard on the kernel of popcorn.*

▸ **morsel** a small piece of food: *We fed **morsels** of bread to the ducks at the lake.*

▸ **rag** a scrap of torn, frayed, or leftover cloth: *I used a **rag** to polish the car.*

▸ **remnant** a portion or quantity left over; a remainder: *She used the **remnants** of last night's dinner to make a soup.*

▸ **shard** a fragment of a brittle substance, as of glass or pottery: *Don't step on those **shards** of broken glass.*

▸ **shred** a narrow strip that is cut or torn off of something: *We tore the newspaper into **shreds** for our papier-mâché project.*

scrape *verb* to damage or injure something by rubbing it against something sharp or rough: *see* **scratch**

scratch

verb to make a thin, shallow cut or mark on something: *The thorns on the bush **scratched** my arms while I was picking blackberries.*

▸ **chafe** to irritate the skin by rubbing: *The label on the inside of this shirt is **chafing** my neck.*

▸ **grate** to break something into fragments or shreds by rubbing it against a rough surface: *I **grated** the carrots to put into the salad.*

▸ **graze** to touch or scrape something lightly in passing: *His suitcase **grazed** my leg as he walked past.*

▸ **scrape** to damage or injure something by rubbing it against something sharp or rough: *She **scraped** her knee on the sidewalk when she fell down.*

▸ **scuff** to damage the surface of something by scraping: *He **scuffed** his shoes while working in the yard.*

▸ **shave** to cut something into small pieces with a sharp instrument: *He **shaved** the cheese into thin slices.*

scratchy *adjective* making a harsh, scraping sound: *see* **hoarse**

scrawl *verb* to write something quickly or in a messy way: *see* **write**

scream *verb* to make a long, loud, piercing cry: *see* **shout**

screech *verb* to make a high, harsh cry: *see* **shout**

screen *noun* a frame covered with wire or plastic mesh, used in a window or door to keep out insects: *see* **curtain**

screen *verb* to examine something systematically in order to determine its suitability: *see* **sort**

screen *noun* a light, movable frame used to divide, hide, or protect: *see* **wall**

scribble *verb* to write or draw something quickly or carelessly: *see* **write**

scrub *verb* to rub something hard in order to clean it: *see* **clean**

scuff *verb* to damage the surface of something by scraping: *see* **scratch**

scuffle *noun* a rough, disorderly struggle: *see* **commotion**

sculpt *verb* to shape, mold, or fashion something, especially artistically: *see* **shape**

scurry *verb* to move lightly or quickly: *see* **hurry**

seal *noun* a substance or device that closes an opening and prevents passage of moisture or air: *see* **lid**

seam *noun* a line, fold, or groove formed by joining two pieces together at their edges: *see* **joint**

secure *adjective* ▷ safe from danger. ▷ safe from the risk of loss: *see* **safe**

security *noun* freedom from risk or danger: *see* **protection**

sedate *adjective* quiet and dignified: *see* **calm**

seduce *verb* to persuade someone to engage in wrongful or immoral behavior: *see* **tempt**

see *verb* to take in something with the eyes: *see* **look**

---

search

verb to look thoroughly and carefully: *She likes to **search** through antique stores for old quilts.*

▶ **explore** to travel in or search through an unfamiliar area for the purpose of discovery: *He likes to **explore** old battlegrounds in hopes of finding artifacts.*

▶ **forage** to hunt through an area, especially for food: *The squirrel **foraged** for buried nuts.*

▶ **hunt** to make a careful search: *I had to **hunt** all over the house for my keys.*

▶ **probe** to explore or examine something carefully: *The dentist **probed** my teeth to check for cavities.*

▶ **scout** to observe or explore carefully in order to obtain information: *A father quail **scouts** for danger before letting his chicks come out to eat.*

▶ **seek** to try to find or get something: *I went to the library to **seek** information for my term paper.*

second *noun* ▷ a unit of time equal to 1/60 of a minute ▷ a very short period of time: *see* **moment**

secret *adjective* hidden from general knowledge or view: *see* **personal**

section *noun* one of several parts that make up something: *see* **piece**

secure *adjective* feeling safe and sure: *see* **confident**

---

seed

noun the part of a flowering plant that contains the embryo from which a new plant can grow: *I planted wildflower **seeds** in the garden.*

▶ **bulb** a rounded, underground plant part, such as a tulip or an onion, from which a new plant can grow: *They planted a hundred tulip **bulbs**.*

▶ **grain** the small, hard, edible seed of cereal plants: *Cereals and **grains** are a main part of the diet in every culture.*

▶ **kernel** a grain or seed, especially of a cereal plant: *We took the popcorn off the heat when we heard the last **kernel** pop.*

seek *verb* to try to find or get something: *see* **search**

seem *verb* to give the impression of something as far as can be determined: *see* **appear [2]**

seep *verb* to pass slowly through small openings: *see* **leak**

see-through *adjective* allowing light to pass through: *see* **clear [2]**

segment *noun* any of the parts into which something is divided: *see* **piece**

segregate *verb* to set one group apart from others: *see* **separate**

seize *verb* ▷ to take someone prisoner ▷ to take possession of something legally: *see* **capture**

seize *verb* to take hold of something suddenly: *see* **grab**

seldom *adverb* not often: *see* **rarely**

select *verb* to choose something from among several possibilities: *see* **choose**

selection *noun* a variety of things or people to choose from: *see* **choice**

self-conscious *adjective* overly conscious of one's own appearance or behavior: *see* **shy**

self-importance *noun* an excessively high opinion of one's own importance or position: *see* **pride**

self-important *adjective* having an excessively high opinion of one's own importance or position: *see* **proud**

selfish *adjective* concerned mainly with oneself without thinking of others: *see* **greedy**

self-sufficient *adjective* able to provide for oneself without help: *see* **independent**

sell

verb to give something in exchange for money: *That bookstore **sells** both new and used books.*

- ▶ **auction** to sell something to the highest bidder: *I **auctioned** my old CDs on the Internet.*
- ▶ **bargain** to discuss the terms of an agreement, especially of a price to be paid: *They **bargained** with the car salesman in order to get a better price.*
- ▶ **barter** to trade goods or services without using money: *She **bartered** a haircut in exchange for a manicure.*
- ▶ **market** to sell or offer items for sale: *That store **markets** sporting goods.*
- ▶ **peddle** to travel about while selling something: *My grandfather **peddled** encyclopedia sets to earn money for college.*

ANTONYM **buy** to get something in exchange for money

seller *noun* a person who sells something: *see* **merchant**

seminary *noun* a school for training priests, ministers, or rabbis: *see* **school**

send

verb to transmit by mail: *I'll **send** you an invitation for the party.*

- ▶ **deliver** to take something to the proper person or place: *The florist **delivered** the bouquet of flowers to the address on the card.*
- ▶ **dispatch** to send something off quickly to a certain place or person: *The reporter **dispatched** the story to her editor.*
- ▶ **e-mail** to send a message by electronic mail: *I **e-mailed** the pictures from our trip to my friends.*
- ▶ **mail** to send something through the postal system: *I **mail** a letter to my elderly friend once a week.*
- ▶ **post** to mail a letter or package: *Will you **post** these letters for me when you go to town?*
- ▶ **ship** to send something by a carrier, usually to a distant place: *I paid extra to have my package **shipped** overnight.*
- ▶ **transmit** to send something from one person or place to another: *I **transmitted** my letter by fax.*

ANTONYM **receive** to take or acquire something given, offered, or sent

sensational *adjective* arousing great interest or excitement, especially by being extraordinary or shocking: *see* **awesome**

sense *noun* an intuitive or acquired feeling about something: *see* **instinct**

sensible *adjective* showing good judgment: *see* **wise**

sensitive *adjective* quick to take offense: *see* **moody**

sentence *verb* to give someone a legal punishment for a crime: *see* **punish**

sentiment *noun* a thought or attitude based on emotion: *see* **feeling**

separate

verb to cut, pull, or sort something into parts or sections: *To make vanilla pudding, you must **separate** the egg whites from the egg yolks.*

▶ **divide** to separate into two or more parts or groups: *He divided the pie into six pieces.*

▶ **divorce** to separate closely connected things: *Doctors must sometimes divorce their emotions from the technical skills needed to perform well in their work.*

▶ **part** to divide or break something into separate parts: *I parted my hair before braiding it.*

▶ **segregate** to set one group apart from others: *We segregated the healthy fish from the diseased ones for their protection.*

▶ **sever** to divide or separate one thing from another: *The butcher severed the meat from the bone.*

▶ **split** to divide something into distinct parts: *He split the cards into two stacks before shuffling them.*

ANTONYM **join** to bring parts or sections together, as by fastening

sequence

noun the following of one thing after another in a regular or fixed way: *You have to assemble that bookcase in a specific sequence.*

▶ **cycle** a regularly repeated sequence of events: *The moon's cycle has four main phases.*

▶ **round** a series of similar events or repeated acts: *We attended a round of parties during the holidays.*

▶ **series** a number of similar things in a row or following one another: *The test was a series of multiple-choice questions.*

serene *adjective* unaffected by disturbances: *see* **calm**

series *noun* a number of similar things in a row or following one another: *see* **sequence**

serious

adjective [1] thoughtful or sincere: *I gave his offer serious thought.*

▶ **earnest** showing great sincerity or seriousness; deeply felt: *I made an earnest apology.*

▶ **grave** having a serious manner appropriate to weighty matters: *The newscaster was grave as she reported the tragedy.*

▶ **sober** serious and restrained; solemn: *We were in a sober mood after we heard the bad news.*

▶ **solemn** very serious and dignified; grave: *Everyone at the funeral wore a solemn expression on their faces.*

serious

adjective [2] having great importance or significance; not trivial: *Leaving a disease untreated can have serious consequences.*

▶ **important** strongly affecting the course of events; significant: *I have an important interview today.*

▶ **profound** coming from the depths of one's being; deep and intense: *He has a profound love of music.*

▶ **significant** having an important meaning; notable: *Graduation is a significant event.*

ANTONYM **unimportant** not important; petty

serve *verb* to be of assistance to or promote the interests of someone: *see* **help**

service *noun* a religious ceremony: *see* **ceremony**

set *verb* to put something in a particular place: *see* **place**

setback *noun* a sudden reverse in progress: *see* **misfortune**

setting *noun* the surrounding area, especially a spot where something takes place: *see* **atmosphere**

settle *verb* to arrange or decide something by agreement: *see* **negotiate**

settlement *noun* a small community established by settlers: *see* **town**

sever *verb* to divide or separate one thing from another: *see* **separate**

several *adjective* more than two but not many: *see* **many**

severe *adjective* great enough to cause damage, harm, or suffering: *see* **extreme**

shabby *adjective* showing signs of wear or ill-use: *see* **ragged**

shack *noun* a small, crudely built cabin: *see* **house**

shade *noun* a dark or light variety of a color: *see* **color**

shadow *verb* to follow someone closely, especially in secret: *see* **follow**

shadowy *adjective* full of or dark with shadows: *see* **dark**

shady *adjective* full of or casting shade: *see* **dark**

shaft *noun* a long, narrow, vertical passage or opening, as one that goes into a mine: *see* **tube**

shake

verb to move something back and forth or up and down with short, quick movements: *You play a tambourine by **shaking** it.*

- ▶ **agitate** to move something to and fro with strong, jerky movements: *The storm **agitated** the surface of the sea.*
- ▶ **rattle** to shake something noisily so that it makes short, sharp sounds: *I **rattled** a toy to amuse the baby.*
- ▶ **vibrate** to move back and forth very rapidly: *A tuning fork **vibrates** when you strike it.*
- ▶ **wobble** to move unsteadily from side to side: *The washing machine **wobbled** when the load became off balance.*

shaky *adjective* unsteady and unsound: *see* **weak**

shame *verb* to cause someone to feel a strong, often painful sense of guilt, embarrassment, unworthiness, or disgrace: *see* **embarrass**

shameful *adjective* causing shame; disgraceful: *see* **shocking**

shape

verb to give a certain shape or form to something: *He **shaped** the bread dough into a loaf.*

- ▶ **determine** to settle or decide something beyond doubt: *The result of this field goal will **determine** the winner of the game.*
- ▶ **form** to give a definite shape or appearance to something: *The marching band **formed** a circle in the middle of the football field.*
- ▶ **influence** to cause changes or have an effect on someone or something without using direct force: *The school librarian has **influenced** many of my book choices.*
- ▶ **mold** to determine the growth or development of someone or something; to influence someone: *The behavior of parents **molds** that of their children.*
- ▶ **sculpt** to shape, mold, or fashion something, especially artistically: *I **sculpted** the clay into the shape of a rooster.*

shard *noun* a fragment of a brittle substance, as of glass or pottery: *see* **scrap**

share *verb* to allow another or others to have part of something: *see* **distribute**

share *noun* a part owned by or distributed to a person or group: *see* **piece**

shared *adjective* used or experienced in common with another or others: *see* **joint**

sharp *adjective* alert in noticing or thinking: *see* **smart**

shatter *verb* to break suddenly into many small pieces, as from a violent blow: *see* **break**

shave *verb* to cut something into small pieces with a sharp instrument: *see* **scratch**

shear *verb* to remove fleece or hair by clipping it with a sharp instrument: *see* **cut**

sheathe *verb* to provide something with a protective covering: *see* **wrap**

shed *verb* to lose something naturally: *see* **peel**

sheen *noun* glistening brightness: *see* **shine**

sheer *adjective* thin, fine, and transparent: *see* **clear [2]**

sheet *noun* a large piece of thin cloth used as a bed covering, especially in pairs: *see* **cover**

shelf

noun a flat piece of material, such as wood, metal, or glass, that is attached to a wall or fastened into a frame: *I have a set of* **shelves** *for my books.*

- ▸ **cabinet** a case or cupboard that has drawers, shelves, or compartments for storing or displaying objects: *We keep our important papers in a metal filing* **cabinet**.
- ▸ **closet** a small room in which clothes or household supplies can be kept: *Hang your coat in the* **closet** *under the stairs.*
- ▸ **niche** a hollow place in a wall, as for holding a statue: *She put a large vase of flowers in the* **niche** *in the front hall.*
- ▸ **nook** a small corner or recess, especially one in a large room: *The master bedroom has a reading* **nook** *with a comfortable window seat.*

shell *verb* to remove the hard outer covering from something: *see* **peel**

shelter *noun* a protected area, especially a place for homeless people or animals to stay temporarily: *see* **refuge**

shield *verb* to protect someone or something, especially by providing cover: *see* **protect**

shepherd *verb* to herd, guard, or guide someone closely: *see* **guide**

shift

verb to change the position, direction, or place of something: *She* **shifted** *her purse from one shoulder to the other.*

- ▸ **alternate** to do, perform, or use something in turns: *My brother and I* **alternate** *picking which TV show to watch.*
- ▸ **fluctuate** to change or vary irregularly; to go up and down or back and forth: *His temperature* **fluctuated** *when he was sick.*
- ▸ **rotate** to repeat in sequence; to take turns or alternate: *The order of classes* **rotates** *every week.*

shimmer *verb* to shine with a wavering or flickering light: *see* **shine**

shine

noun brightness that is given off or reflected: *My brother polished his car until it had a bright* **shine**.

- ▸ **gleam** a beam or flash of bright light: *We saw the* **gleam** *of a distant campfire.*
- ▸ **gloss** a bright shine on a smooth surface: *This paint has a high* **gloss**.
- ▸ **glow** a soft, steady light, like that produced by something hot but not flaming: *I could see the* **glow** *of my alarm clock in the dark.*
- ▸ **luster** a shine or glow of soft, reflected light: *The gold necklace had a beautiful* **luster**.
- ▸ **radiance** bright light or intense heat that is given off by a source: *The* **radiance** *of the sun was welcome after the rain.*
- ▸ **sheen** glistening brightness; luster: *The newly polished floor had a soft* **sheen**.

shine

verb to give off or reflect light: *A candle was* **shining** *brightly in the window.*

- ▸ **dazzle** to blind someone with too much light: *I was* **dazzled** *by the daylight when I came out of the movie theater.*
- ▸ **flash** to give out a sudden bright light: *Lightning* **flashed** *across the sky.*
- ▸ **glisten** to shine with reflected light: *The sequins on her dress* **glistened** *in the lamplight.*
- ▸ **glitter** to sparkle brilliantly: *The city lights* **glitter** *at night.*
- ▸ **shimmer** to shine with a wavering or flickering light: *The lights from the cruise ship* **shimmered** *on the dark water.*
- ▸ **sparkle** to give off sparks of light; to glitter: *The newly fallen snow* **sparkled** *in the moonlight.*
- ▸ **twinkle** to shine with slight, quick flashes of light: *The stars* **twinkled** *brightly in the night sky.*

shiny *adjective* bright from reflected light: *see* **bright**

ship *verb*   to send something by a carrier, usually to a distant place: *see* **send**

shiver *verb*   to undergo shaking that cannot be controlled: *see* **tremble**

shock *verb*   to surprise and upset someone greatly: *see* **surprise**

shocking

adjective   very disturbing to the emotions; causing great surprise or distress: *The documentary about the children injured by land mines was **shocking**.*

- ▶ **disgraceful**   bringing loss of honor, respect, or reputation; shameful: *Cheating on tests is **disgraceful**.*
- ▶ **outrageous**   exceeding what is right or proper: *That is an **outrageous** price for a bar of soap.*
- ▶ **scandalous**   causing scandal or public disgrace; offensive to the morality of the community: *The politician's behavior with the young intern was **scandalous**.*
- ▶ **shameful**   causing shame; disgraceful: *Their house is in **shameful** condition of neglect.*

shop *noun*   a small retail store or a specialty department in a large store: *see* **business [1]**

shopkeeper *noun*   a person who owns or manages a shop: *see* **merchant**

shoplifter *noun*   a person who steals merchandise from a store: *see* **thief**

shoplifting *noun*   the act of stealing displayed merchandise from a store: *see* **theft**

shore *noun*   the land along the edge of a body of water: *see* **beach**

short

adjective [1]   not long or tall: *My little niece is too **short** to reach the kitchen counter.*

- ▶ **compact**   occupying little space in comparison to others of its type: *I gave up my SUV for a **compact** car.*
- ▶ **diminutive**   (formal)   extremely small in size: *The hummingbird is a **diminutive** bird.*

- ▶ **low**   not high off the ground; not tall: *We put a **low** fence around the garden.*
- ▶ **petite**   small and slender: *My mother is so **petite** that she can wear some children's clothes.*
- ▶ **slight**   small and thin; delicate: *The young ballerina had a **slight** build.*

short

adjective [2]   lasting or taking a small amount of time: *We had a **short** quiz in our math class today.*

- ▶ **brief**   lasting only a short time; quick: *My neighbor came over for a **brief** visit.*
- ▶ **fleeting**   passing quickly; very brief: *I had a **fleeting** desire to go bungee jumping.*
- ▶ **momentary**   lasting only an instant or a moment: *He felt only **momentary** pain from the injection.*
- ▶ **temporary**   lasting, used, or enjoyed for a limited time only; not permanent: *I am looking for a **temporary** job this summer.*

ANTONYM **long**   lasting for a large amount of time

shortage *noun*   an amount of something that is not enough: *see* **lack**

shorten *verb*   to make something short or shorter: *see* **abbreviate**

shorter *adjective*   smaller in height than someone or something else: *see* **less**

shoulder *verb*   to carry something on the shoulders: *see* **carry**

shout

verb   to cry out loudly, as to get someone's attention: *The fans **shouted** encouragement to the team.*

- ▶ **bellow**   to shout in a deep voice: *The man **bellowed** in pain when he hit his thumb with a hammer.*
- ▶ **holler**   (informal)   to yell or shout: *I **hollered** at my brother to hurry up.*
- ▶ **scream**   to make a long, loud, piercing cry: *Everybody **screamed** as the roller coaster rushed around the track.*

▸ **screech** to make a high, harsh cry: *The blue jays were **screeching** outside my window.*

▸ **shriek** to utter a shrill, frantic cry: *I **shrieked** when I realized I was forty miles past the exit I was supposed to take.*

▸ **thunder** to roar in strong emotion: *The angry men **thundered** at one another.*

▸ **yell** to shout or cry out very loudly: *We had to **yell** to hear each other during the rock concert.*

shove *verb* to push someone or something forcefully or roughly: *see* **push**

shovel *verb* to move or remove something with a shovel: *see* **dig**

show

noun a public exhibition or entertainment: *We entered our collie in the local dog **show**.*

▸ **concert** a musical performance given by a musician or a number of musicians: *We went to hear her sing in the choir **concert**.*

▸ **drama** a written story meant to be acted out on a stage: *Eugene O'Neill's **dramas** are considered among some of the most important in American theater.*

▸ **pageant** a play or dramatic spectacle that is often based on an event in history: *The Ramona **Pageant** portrays the conflict between Native Americans and white settlers in 19th-century California.*

▸ **performance** a public presentation of something, such as work of art or entertainment: *The child enjoyed the silly **performance** of the circus clowns.*

▸ **production** something prepared and presented to the public: *Our school put on a **production** of* Arsenic and Old Lace.

▸ **recital** a public performance, as of poetry or music: *I went to my brother's trombone **recital**.*

▸ **spectacle** an unusual or impressive public show, as of fireworks: *The laser light show was a great **spectacle**.*

show

verb to cause or allow something to be seen: *The geologist **showed** us a fossil and told us how it was formed.*

▸ **demonstrate** to present by experiments or examples how something works or is done: *My teacher **demonstrated** the proper way to use a microscope.*

▸ **display** to put something on view; to exhibit: *Some of my artwork is being **displayed** at the local coffee shop.*

▸ **exhibit** to present something for the public to view: *He **exhibited** his cows at the county fair.*

▸ **present** to offer something for examination or consideration; to bring something before an audience: *The lawyer **presented** evidence that proved her client's innocence.*

shower *verb* to pour something down in abundance: *see* **pour**

shower *noun* a brief fall of rain: *see* **rain**

show off *verb* ▷ to display something in a proud or boastful manner. ▷ to behave in a showy way: *see* **brag**

show up *verb* to make an appearance: *see* **appear [1]**

shred *verb* to cut or tear something into small strips: *see* **rip**

shred *noun* a narrow strip that is cut or torn off of something: *see* **scrap**

shrewd *adjective* clever, sharp, and practical: *see* **crafty**

shriek *verb* to utter a shrill, frantic cry: *see* **shout**

shrill *adjective* high-pitched and piercing: *see* **loud**

shrink *verb* to become smaller in size, amount, or value: *see* **compress**

shroud *verb* to conceal or hide something by surrounding or enveloping it: *see* **hide²**

shuck *verb* to remove the husk or shell from something: *see* **peel**

shudder *verb* to tremble or shiver, especially from fear: *see* **tremble**

shuffle *verb* to walk slowly while dragging one's feet: *see* **stagger**

shun *verb* to make every effort to avoid something unpleasant: *see* **avoid**

shut *verb* to close something, especially so as to block passage: *see* **close**

shut out *verb* (informal) to leave someone out of a process or activity: *see* **exclude**

shutter *noun* a hinged screen or cover for a window: *see* **curtain**

shy

adjective feeling uneasy around people or with strangers: *I was too **shy** to go to the dance without my good friend.*

- ▸ **bashful** timid and uncomfortable with other people: *My younger brother is **bashful** around strangers.*
- ▸ **coy** pretending to be shy or bashful, especially in a flirtatious way: *Her **coy** manner can be irritating.*
- ▸ **insecure** lacking self-confidence: *I felt **insecure** about my new job when I first started it.*
- ▸ **modest** not thinking too highly of one's own talents, abilities, or accomplishments: *The research scientist was **modest** about his discoveries.*
- ▸ **reserved** marked by self-restraint and a tendency not to speak out: *He is **reserved** about his personal life.*
- ▸ **self-conscious** overly conscious of one's own appearance or behavior: *She was **self-conscious** when she got up to give her oral report.*
- ▸ **timid** easily frightened; shy: *The **timid** deer ran into the forest when they saw us.*

sick

adjective suffering from an illness: *I was **sick** with the flu for three whole days.*

- ▸ **ailing** suffering from a minor illness or disease: *My iguana seemed to be **ailing**, so we took her to the vet.*
- ▸ **bedridden** confined to bed because of sickness or weakness: *My aunt was **bedridden** the last month of her pregnancy.*
- ▸ **dizzy** having a sensation of whirling or being about to fall: *The carnival ride made me **dizzy**.*
- ▸ **ill** not healthy; sick: *Our neighbor has been **ill** with cancer for several years now.*

- ▸ **nauseated** feeling sick in one's stomach and having a need to vomit: *The smell of her perfume was so strong that I felt **nauseated**.*
- ▸ **queasy** somewhat sick to one's stomach: *Eating all those greasy onion rings made me feel a bit **queasy**.*
- ▸ **unwell** being in poor health; ill: *I canceled my plans because I was feeling **unwell**.*

sickening *adjective* so revolting as to make one feel sick: *see* **gross**

sickly *adjective* tending to become sick easily: *see* **weak**

sickness *noun* a condition or period of poor health: *see* **disease**

sidestep *verb* to avoid an issue or responsibility: *see* **avoid**

sidewalk *noun* a paved walkway on the side of a road: *see* **path**

sigh *verb* to exhale a long, deep breath while making a sound, as of weariness, sorrow, or relief: *see* **moan**

sight *noun* something seen or worth seeing: *see* **view**

sightsee *verb* to tour sights of interest: *see* **travel**

sign

noun something that indicates a fact, quality, or condition: *Smoke is a **sign** that something is burning.*

- ▸ **herald** a person or thing that gives a sign of something to come: *Robins are considered a **herald** of spring in many parts of the country.*
- ▸ **indication** something that shows or points something out; a sign: *Those dark clouds are an **indication** of rain.*
- ▸ **omen** something that is thought to be a sign of a good or bad event to come: *Some people think that finding a four-leafed clover is an **omen** of good luck.*
- ▸ **symbol** something that stands for or represents something else: *The dove and the olive branch are **symbols** of peace.*
- ▸ **symptom** a sign or indication, especially of illness: *Fever is one **symptom** of the flu.*

signal

noun   a sign, gesture, or device that gives a command, a warning, or other information: *The teacher raised her hand as a **signal** for the class to be quiet.*

▸ **cue**   a signal for action, especially in a play: *The last line of his speech is my **cue** to go on stage.*

▸ **gesture**   a motion of the hands, arms, head, or body that expresses a feeling or idea: *The police officer used hand and arm **gestures** to direct the traffic.*

▸ **nod**   an up-and-down motion of the head, especially to indicate agreement: *I gave her a **nod** when she asked me if I wanted another bowl of soup.*

▸ **wink**   a quick opening and closing of one eye, especially to indicate approval: *My coach gave me a **wink** to let me know I was doing fine.*

signal

verb   to make a sign or gesture to someone: *I **signaled** my friend that I would be off the phone quickly.*

▸ **beckon**   to signal for someone to come, as with a movement of the head or hand: *The bank teller **beckoned** me to come to the counter.*

▸ **flag**   to signal someone with or as if with a flag: *The stranded motorist **flagged** down a passing car.*

▸ **indicate**   to show or point something out: *The usher **indicated** that these were our seats.*

▸ **motion**   to signal or direct someone by a motion, such as a wave of the hand: *He **motioned** for the waitress to bring him coffee.*

significant *adjective*   having an important meaning: *see* **serious [2]**

signify *verb*   to be a sign or indication of something: *see* **mean²**

sign up *verb*   to agree to be a participant or recipient by signing one's name: *see* **enroll**

silent *adjective*   making or having no sound: *see* **quiet**

silky *adjective*   soft, smooth, and glossy like silk: *see* **soft [1]**

silliness *noun*   a lack of good sense or reason: *see* **nonsense**

silly

adjective   not serious; frivolous or ridiculous: *Your suggestion that we just wear our pajamas to the grocery store is **silly**.*

▸ **absurd**   plainly not true or contrary to common sense: *It is **absurd** to say that the moon is made of cheese.*

▸ **comic**   very funny; amusing: *We laughed at the **comic** behavior of the puppy.*

▸ **foolish**   causing amusement, especially by being or seeming to be stupid: *I felt **foolish** when I realized I had my sweater on backwards.*

▸ **ridiculous**   highly absurd or laughable: *My dad has a **ridiculous** tie that lights up like a Christmas tree.*

▸ **zany**   comical in an exaggerated or ridiculous way: *The audience laughed at the clown's **zany** stunts.*

ANTONYM **sensible**   showing good judgment; reasonable

similar *adjective*   alike, but not exactly the same: *see* **same**

simmer *verb*   to be cooked gently or just at the boiling point: *see* **cook**

simper *verb*   to smile in a silly or self-conscious manner: *see* **smile**

simple *adjective*   not involved or complicated: *see* **easy**

simpleton *noun*   a person who lacks common sense or intelligence: *see* **fool**

simply *adverb*   merely: *see* **only**

simulate *verb*   to take on the appearance, form, or sound of something: *see* **pretend**

sin *noun*   the act of breaking a religious or moral law: *see* **crime**

since *conjunction*   as a result of the fact that: *see* **because**

sincere *adjective* not lying or pretending: *see* **honest**

single *adjective* not accompanied by another or others: *see* **alone**

sinister *adjective* suggesting or threatening evil: *see* **evil**

sink *verb* to move to a lower level, especially slowly or in stages: *see* **droop**

sip *verb* to drink something in small amounts: *see* **drink**

sit *verb* to be located: *see* **place**

site *noun* the place where something is or will be located: *see* **place**

situation

noun a particular set of circumstances: *I am in a fortunate financial **situation** at present.*

▸ **circumstance** a condition or fact that decides or influences a course of events: *My mother and father met under dramatic wartime **circumstances**.*
▸ **condition** the way someone or something is; a state of affairs: *The heavy snowfall has created hazardous road **conditions**.*
▸ **context** the particular circumstances in which something exists or occurs: *Horses are out of **context** in modern city life.*

size *noun* the physical dimensions and proportions of an object: *see* **amount**

skeleton *noun* the framework of bones that supports the body and protects the inner organs: *see* **body**

sketch *verb* to make a rough or quick drawing of something: *see* **draw**

skill *noun* an ability that one gains from training or experience: *see* **ability**

skilled *adjective* having or showing specialized ability or training: *see* **able**

skim *verb* to read something quickly, skipping over parts: *see* **browse**

skimpy *adjective* inadequate in size or amount: *see* **few**

skin *noun* the hide or pelt that has been removed from the body of an animal: *see* **hide**[1]

skinny *adjective* very thin: *see* **thin**

skip *verb* to move forward by stepping and hopping lightly: *see* **jump**

skirmish *noun* a minor battle between small forces: *see* **war**

slab *noun* a broad, flat, thick piece of something, as of meat, cheese, or stone: *see* **slice**

slack *adjective* not firm or tight: *see* **loose**

slander *noun* a false statement reported or said maliciously in order to damage someone's reputation: *see* **lie**

slant *verb* to have a direction that is neither horizontal nor vertical: *see* **tilt**

slap *verb* to strike sharply with or as if with the palm of the hand: *see* **hit**

slash *verb* to cut something with forceful, sweeping strokes: *see* **cut**

slat *noun* a narrow strip of metal, plastic, or wood: *see* **wood**

slaughter *verb* ▷ to kill domestic animals for food ▷ to kill large numbers of people or animals indiscriminately: *see* **kill**

slave *noun* a person owned by and considered to be the property of someone else: *see* **prisoner**

slay *verb* to kill someone or something violently: *see* **kill**

sleep

verb to be in the natural condition of rest that occurs regularly and is marked by inactivity and unconsciousness: *Human beings spend about one third of their lives **sleeping**.*

▸ **doze** to sleep lightly; to nap: *He likes to **doze** on the couch after lunch.*
▸ **drowse** to be half asleep; to doze: *The cat was **drowsing** in the sunshine.*
▸ **hibernate** to spend the winter sleeping, as some animals do: *Bears **hibernate** all winter.*

▶ **nap** to sleep lightly and for a short period of time, usually during the day: *Please be quiet, as the baby is **napping**.*

▶ **snooze** (informal) to take a light nap: *I was so tired that I began to **snooze** in class.*

sleepy *adjective* ready for or needing sleep: *see* **tired**

slender *adjective* thin and delicate in build: *see* **thin**

slice

noun a thin, flat piece cut from something, such as a vegetable or loaf of bread: *Our toaster can hold four **slices** of bread at one time.*

▶ **slab** a broad, flat, thick piece of something, as of meat, cheese, or stone: *The lobby of the building was laid with **slabs** of polished granite.*

▶ **sliver** a slender piece of something that has been cut, split, or broken off of a larger piece: *I swept up the **slivers** of glass around the broken window.*

▶ **splinter** a sharp, slender piece broken off from something, such as wood or glass: *The nurse pulled the **splinter** of wood out of my finger with the tweezers.*

▶ **wedge** a block of material, such as wood or cheese, that is wide at one end and tapers to a point at the other: *He used a small **wedge** of wood to hold the door open.*

slick *adjective* having a smooth or slippery surface: *see* **slippery**

slight *adjective* small and thin; delicate: *see* **short [1]**

slightest *adjective* smallest in amount or degree: *see* **least**

slightly *adverb* to a small degree or extent: *see* **hardly**

slim *adjective* attractively thin: *see* **thin**

slimy *adjective* covered with a thick, slippery substance: *see* **slippery**

sling *verb* to hurl or fling something: *see* **throw**

slink *verb* to move in a quiet, sneaky way: *see* **crawl**

slip *verb* to slide involuntarily and lose one's balance or foothold: *see* **fall**

slippery

adjective causing or tending to cause slipping: *I dropped the piece of **slippery** soap in the shower.*

▶ **slick** having a smooth or slippery surface: *The ice on the sidewalk is very **slick**.*

▶ **slimy** covered with a thick, slippery substance: *The rocks in the stream were a bit **slimy** with algae.*

▶ **soapy** covered or filled with soap: *I washed the dishes in **soapy** water.*

slit *verb* to cut something lengthwise into strips: *see* **rip**

slither *verb* to move along by sliding or gliding like a snake: *see* **crawl**

sliver *noun* a slender piece of something that has been cut, split, or broken off of a larger piece: *see* **slice**

slope *noun* a stretch of ground that forms an incline: *see* **hill**

sloppy *adjective* lacking neatness or order: *see* **messy**

slow

adjective not moving, acting, or developing quickly; taking a long time: *The tortoise made **slow** progress across the sand.*

▶ **gradual** advancing by regular or continuous degrees: *There was a **gradual** increase in light as the sun rose.*

▶ **plodding** moving in a slow and heavy manner: *The exhausted players walked off the field with **plodding** steps.*

▶ **unhurried** without hurry; slow and relaxed: *We enjoyed an **unhurried** lunch.*

ANTONYM **fast** moving, acting, or done quickly

sluggish *adjective* moving or acting in a slow way: *see* **lazy**

sly *adjective* clever or cunning in a secretive way: *see* **crafty**

small

adjective little in size, amount, or extent: *There were **small** dinosaurs that were no bigger than a chicken.*

- ► **little** small in size or quantity: *There was **little** milk left in the carton.*
- ► **microscopic** ▷ too small to be seen without magnification: *There are thousands of **microscopic** organisms in a drop of pond water.* ▷ extremely small: *The teacher criticized my report in **microscopic** detail.*
- ► **miniature** much smaller than the usual size: *He has a collection of **miniature** cars.*
- ► **pocket-sized** small enough to be carried in a pocket: *I have a **pocket-sized** flashlight.*
- ► **tiny** extremely small: *The **tiny** flea bit me.*
- ► **wee** (informal) very little; tiny: *I'll have a **wee** bit of sugar in my coffee.*

ANTONYM **big** of great size; large

smaller *adjective* less in size, number, amount, or degree: *see* **less**

smallest *adjective* least in size, number, amount, or degree: *see* **least**

smart

adjective able to learn quickly and easily: *My friend is so **smart** that she can do calculus in her head.*

- ► **brilliant** extremely intelligent or inventive: *Leonardo da Vinci was a **brilliant** artist, scientist, and inventor.*
- ► **clever** able to figure things out quickly; quick-witted: *I like to read novels about **clever** detectives.*
- ► **intelligent** able to learn, think, understand, and know: *My boss is very **intelligent** about which way the market for our products is likely to go.*

sharp alert in noticing or thinking; keen: *It takes a **sharp** mind to complete the New York Times crossword puzzle.*

ANTONYM **stupid** slow to understand; dull

smash *verb* to break something into pieces noisily and violently: *see* **crush**

smear *verb* to spread, cover, or stain with a sticky or greasy substance: *see* **cover**

smell

noun a quality that is perceived by the nose; an odor: *I enjoy the **smell** of cookies baking in the oven.*

- ► **aroma** a rich, pleasant smell: *I like the **aroma** of fresh-brewed coffee.*
- ► **fragrance** a sweet or pleasant odor: *I enjoy the **fragrance** of roses.*
- ► **odor** a smell or scent: *Garlic has a strong **odor**.*
- ► **perfume** a pleasant-smelling liquid made especially from flowers: *The saleswoman gave me a sample of a new **perfume**.*
- ► **reek** a strong or unpleasant odor: *The raccoon was attracted by the **reek** of the garbage.*
- ► **scent** a distinctive, often pleasing odor: *I raise gardenias because I like their **scent**.*
- ► **stench** a strong, unpleasant smell; a stink: *The kitchen was filled with the **stench** of burnt toast.*
- ► **stink** a strong, foul odor: *We could smell the **stink** of rotting fish as we walked along the beach.*
- ► **whiff** a brief, passing odor carried in the air: *I caught a **whiff** of baking bread as I walked past the bakery.*

smile

verb to have a pleased or happy expression on the face: *The photographer told us to **smile**.*

- ► **beam** to smile with joy or delight: *The little girl **beamed** as her family sang "Happy Birthday" to her.*

▶ **grin** to smile with pleasure: *My little brother **grinned** when I said he could come to the movie with me and my friends.*

▶ **simper** to smile in a silly or self-conscious manner: *I **simpered** at myself in the mirror.*

▶ **smirk** to smile in an annoying manner that expresses too much satisfaction in oneself: *He **smirked** when he won the tennis game.*

ANTONYM **frown** to wrinkle the forehead when puzzled, unhappy, or thinking

smirk *verb* to smile in an annoying manner that expresses too much satisfaction in oneself: *see* **smile**

smog *noun* air pollution caused mainly by substances in automobile exhaust: *see* **fume**

smoke *noun* the mixture of gases and particles that rises from burning material: *see* **fume**

smolder *verb* to burn with little smoke and no flame: *see* **burn**

smooth *adjective* free from difficulties or obstacles: *see* **easy**

smooth *adjective* having a surface free from irregularities: *see* **soft** [1]

smother *verb* to cause to die from lack of air: *see* **choke**

smudge *noun* a blurred spot or smear: *see* **stain**

smug *adjective* satisfied with oneself in comparison to others: *see* **proud**

snack *noun* a light meal: *see* **meal**

snag *noun* a sudden or unexpected difficulty: *see* **obstacle**

snap *verb* to break suddenly with a sharp sound: *see* **break**

snare *verb* to trap something in a device such as a noose: *see* **trap**

snarl *noun* a vicious growl that is made while baring the teeth: *see* **bark**

snatch *verb* to grab something quickly or eagerly: *see* **grab**

sneak *verb* to bring, take, or put something secretly: *see* **steal**

sneaky *adjective* skilled at acting without anyone noticing: *see* **crafty**

sneer *verb* to show contempt or scorn, as with a mocking expression: *see* **scorn**

snicker *verb* to laugh in a sly or mean way: *see* **laugh**

snoop *verb* to pry into the private affairs of others, especially by prowling about: *see* **interfere**

snooze *verb* (informal) to take a light nap: *see* **sleep**

snub *verb* to treat someone with scorn or coldness: *see* **reject**

snug *adjective* giving comfort and protection: *see* **comfortable**

snuggle *verb* to draw something or someone close to the body, as for comfort or in affection: *see* **cuddle**

so *conjunction* with the result that: *see* **but**

so *adverb* because of the reason given; consequently: *see* **therefore**

soak *verb* to make something completely wet: *see* **flood**

soaked *adjective* completely wet: *see* **wet**

soapy *adjective* covered or filled with soap: *see* **slippery**

soar *verb* to rise or glide high in the air: *see* **fly**

sob *verb* to weep aloud with gasps and sniffles: *see* **cry**

sober *adjective* serious and restrained: *see* **serious** [1]

social *noun* an informal social gathering: *see* **party**

society *noun* an organization or association of people who share common interests or activities: *see* **club**

society *noun* a group of people who share a common culture: *see* **culture**

soft

adjective [1] smooth or fine to the touch: *My pet hamster has **soft** fur.*

▸ **fluffy** having hair, feathers, or fibers that stand out in a soft, full mass: *The yellow chicks were soft and **fluffy**.*

▸ **fuzzy** covered with soft, short fibers or hairs: *I wore my **fuzzy** angora sweater to the party.*

▸ **silky** soft, smooth, and glossy like silk: *The evening gown was made of **silky** fabric.*

▸ **smooth** having a surface free from irregularities; not rough: *Babies have very **smooth** skin.*

▸ **velvety** having the soft, smooth texture of velvet: *I petted the **velvety** cheek of the horse.*

soft

adjective [2] not hard or firm; easily molded or cut: *She molded the **soft** clay into a ball.*

▸ **mushy** resembling mush; soft and pulpy: *We can use those old, **mushy** bananas to make banana bread.*

▸ **spongy** resembling a sponge; soft, porous, and elastic: *The lawn was **spongy** after the rain.*

▸ **squishy** soft and wet, like mud: *The muddy ground felt **squishy** beneath my bare toes.*

ANTONYM **hard** not bending or yielding when pushed; firm

soften *verb* to become soft, as by thawing: *see* **melt**

soggy *adjective* soaked or heavy with moisture: *see* **wet**

soil *noun* earth or dirt: *see* **earth [2]**

soiled *adjective* dirty, especially from use or wear: *see* **dirty**

solely *adverb* entirely; exclusively: *see* **only**

solemn *adjective* very serious and dignified: *see* **serious [1]**

solicit *verb* to seek to obtain something from someone: *see* **ask**

solid

adjective firm and compact in substance: *We could dig no further once we hit **solid** rock.*

▸ **dense** hard to penetrate; compact: *The possum hid in the **dense** ivy.*

▸ **thick** tightly packed together; impenetrable: *It was impossible to hike through the **thick** undergrowth.*

solitary *adjective* existing or living alone: *see* **alone**

solo *adjective* made or done by one person: *see* **alone**

solve

verb to find an answer or solution to a problem: *I **solved** all the math problems I had been assigned.*

▸ **decipher** to read or interpret something that is hard to understand: *Sometimes it's hard to **decipher** my professor's handwriting.*

▸ **figure out** to solve, decipher, or discover something: *I tried to **figure out** where we were by looking at the map.*

▸ **resolve** to find a solution to a conflict or disagreement: *We **resolved** our debate about which movie to rent by flipping a coin.*

▸ **unravel** to separate the elements of a mystery or problem: *The detective worked hard to **unravel** the clues surrounding the murder.*

some *adjective* being an unspecified, relatively small number or quantity: *see* **many**

sometimes *adverb* now and then: *see* **rarely**

somewhat *adverb* to some extent or degree: *see* **hardly**

song

noun a usually short musical piece that is meant to be sung: *We sang cowboy **songs** around the campfire.*

▸ **ballad** a poem or song that tells a story, usually about love: *The **ballad** "Barbara Allen" is a story of tragic love.*

▶ **carol** a song of joy, especially one that is sung at Christmas: *The* **carol** *"Silent Night" was first performed on December 24, 1818.*

▶ **chant** a melody with many words sung on the same pitch: *I like listening to Gregorian* **chant**.

▶ **hymn** a song of joy, praise, or thanksgiving, especially one that is sung to God: *The composer of the* **hymn** *"Amazing Grace" was once a slave trader.*

▶ **jingle** a simple, catchy verse or song, often used in radio or television commercials: *That toothpaste* **jingle** *keeps running through my head.*

▶ **lullaby** a soothing song meant to lull a child to sleep: *He sang the baby a* **lullaby** *to help it fall asleep.*

▶ **melody** a pleasing series of musical tones; a tune: *The* **melody** *to that Broadway song is stuck in my head.*

▶ **tune** a melody, especially one that is simple and easy to remember: *I can remember the* **tune**, *but not all the words.*

soon *adverb* within a short time: *see* **immediately**

soothe *verb* to calm or quiet a person or animal: *see* **comfort**

sophisticated *adjective* having acquired worldly knowledge or refinement: *see* **elegant**

sore *adjective* (informal) full of resentment: *see* **angry**

sorrow

noun grief or sadness because of a loss or injury: *He felt a deep* **sorrow** *over the death of his friend.*

▶ **guilt** a bad feeling about having done wrong: *He felt a lot of* **guilt** *about not visiting his friend in the hospital.*

▶ **regret** sorrow or distress over a past event or act: *I felt some* **regret** *that I didn't offer to help with our class reunion.*

▶ **remorse** bitter regret for having done something wrong: *She was full of* **remorse** *over the rumor she started about her schoolmate.*

sorrow *verb* to feel grief or sadness because of a loss or injury: *see* **mourn**

sorry

adjective feeling or expressing sympathy or regret: *I am* **sorry** *I forgot your birthday.*

▶ **apologetic** expressing or making an apology: *He was* **apologetic** *for having arrived late.*

▶ **guilty** feeling very bad about an immoral action or thought: *I feel* **guilty** *about cheating on the test.*

▶ **remorseful** filled with bitter regret for having done something wrong: *I was* **remorseful** *for having said those mean things to my sister.*

sort

verb to arrange items according to class, kind, or size: *We* **sorted** *the laundry by color.*

▶ **alphabetize** to arrange something in alphabetical order: *I* **alphabetized** *my CDs by the artist's last name.*

▶ **categorize** to put something into a specific, defined division: *The librarian* **categorized** *the books by the Dewey decimal system.*

▶ **classify** to put something into groups or classes; to sort: *Diamonds are* **classified** *according to their quality.*

▶ **file** to arrange a collection of papers, cards, records, or other information in a certain order: *The salesman* **filed** *his sales orders according to the date of the sale.*

▶ **order** to put items into a methodical, systematic arrangement: *The quilter* **ordered** *her fabric according to color.*

▶ **screen** to examine something systematically in order to determine its suitability: *I* **screened** *the mail for any unsolicited advertisements.*

soul *noun* the animating and vital force of human beings: *see* **human being**

sour *adjective* having a strongly acid taste: *see* **tasty**

source *noun* a place or thing from which something comes: *see* **basis**

souvenir

noun something kept as a reminder of a place or occasion: *My friend brought me a* **souvenir** *from his trip to South Carolina.*

▶ **keepsake** something that is kept in memory of a person or an occasion: *She gave him a lock of her hair as a* **keepsake**.

▶ **memento** something that causes one to remember the past; a keepsake: *I bought a sweatshirt as a* **memento** *of my trip to Mt. Rushmore.*

▶ **reminder** something that makes one remember to do something: *I set my library books by the door as a* **reminder** *to return them.*

▶ **token** something that serves as evidence or proof of something: *Please accept these flowers as a* **token** *of our appreciation.*

sovereign *adjective* self-governing: *see* **independent**

sovereign *noun* a person with supreme authority over a state: *see* **ruler**

space *noun* the open area between or within objects: *see* **distance**

spacious *adjective* having much space: *see* **wide**

span *noun* the horizontal distance between two points: *see* **distance**

spank *verb* to slap a person or animal with the open hand or with a flat object: *see* **hit**

spare *adjective* beyond what is usually needed: *see* **extra**

spark *verb* to set something in motion: *see* **excite**

sparkle *verb* to give off sparks of light: *see* **shine**

spasm *noun* a sudden, involuntary contraction of a muscle or a group of muscles: *see* **cramp**

speak *verb* to utter words: *see* **say**

spear *verb* to pierce or stab something with or as if with a spear: *see* **stab**

special *adjective* different from what is common or usual: *see* **rare**

specialist *noun* a person whose work is restricted to a particular activity or to a particular branch of study or research: *see* **expert**

specialty *noun* a special study, profession, or skill: *see* **field [2]**

specific *adjective* stated clearly and in detail: *see* **exact**

specimen *noun* something that is chosen to represent the group: *see* **example**

speck *noun* a small bit: *see* **piece**

spectacle *noun* an unusual or impressive public show, as of fireworks: *see* **show**

spectacular *adjective* impressive and exciting: *see* **awesome**

speculate *verb* to think or ponder about something without having adequate information: *see* **guess**

speed

noun a measure of how fast something is moving: *The cheetah can run at a* **speed** *of about 60 miles per hour.*

▶ **haste** swiftness in moving or acting: *Since I overslept, I had to dress with* **haste**.

▶ **momentum** the force that something has when it moves: *The bicyclist gained* **momentum** *when she went downhill.*

▶ **pace** the rate of speed at which a person or animal walks or runs: *The marathon runner worked on keeping a steady* **pace**.

▶ **rate** an amount of one thing measured against another thing, such as miles per hour: *If we continue to work at this* **rate**, *we'll have the whole house clean in another half hour.*

speedy *adjective* taking very little time: *see* **fast**

spend

verb to pay out money: *How much did you* **spend** *on your new cell phone?*

▶ **disburse** to pay money to someone, as from a fund: *The financial aid office* **disbursed** *my scholarship money at the beginning of the semester.*

▸ **expend** (formal)   to spend money: *I had to **expend** all my savings to make the down payment on my new condominium.*

▸ **pay**   to give money in exchange for goods or for work done: *How much did you **pay** for your car?*

▸ **squander**   to spend money lavishly or wastefully: *He **squandered** his lunch money on junk food.*

spicy *adjective*   having the flavor, smell, or quality of spice: *see* **tasty**

spill *verb*   to run or flow out of a container, especially by accident: *see* **pour**

spin

verb   to turn about an axis at high speed: *The carousel **spun** around and around.*

▸ **revolve**   to orbit around a central point: *It takes a year for the earth to **revolve** around the sun.*

▸ **rotate**   to turn on an axis: *The earth **rotates** one full turn every 24 hours.*

▸ **turn**   to move or cause something to move around a center: *I **turned** the steering wheel sharply to avoid the pothole.*

▸ **twirl**   to rotate or spin something quickly: *The drum major **twirled** his baton and threw it in the air.*

▸ **whirl**   to turn or cause something to turn quickly: *I **whirled** around when I heard a noise behind me.*

spire *noun*   a structure, such as a steeple, that becomes narrow at the top: *see* **tower**

spiritual *adjective*   relating to the soul or to religious experience: *see* **religious**

spite *noun*   a mean desire to hurt or humiliate another person: *see* **hate**

spiteful *adjective*   so full of ill will that one wants to hurt or humiliate another: *see* **resentful**

splash *verb*   to scatter a liquid, such as water, all around: *see* **pour**

splendid *adjective*   of great beauty or quality: *see* **wonderful**

splendidly *adverb*   very well; magnificently: *see* **well**

splendor *noun*   a magnificent or beautiful appearance: *see* **luxury**

splinter *verb*   to split or break into sharp, slender pieces: *see* **break**

splinter *noun*   a sharp, slender piece broken off from something: *see* **slice**

split *verb*   to divide something into distinct parts: *see* **separate**

spoil *verb*   to become unfit for consumption, as from decay: *see* **decay**

spoil *verb*   to do harm to someone's character by overindulgence or by praising too much: *see* **indulge**

spoil *verb*   to damage something and make it less valuable or useful: *see* **pollute**

spoiled *adjective*   unfit for eating or drinking: *see* **rotten**

spongy *adjective*   resembling a sponge; soft, porous, and elastic: *see* **soft [2]**

sponsor

verb   to be officially responsible for someone or something, as by providing financial support: *Our company **sponsors** a roller hockey team.*

▸ **back**   to give approval or support to someone or something: *My parents **backed** my decision to go to medical school.*

▸ **champion**   to fight for a cause or movement: *Martin Luther King, Jr., **championed** civil rights.*

▸ **endorse**   to give official approval of something: *The school board **endorsed** the teachers' request for a pay raise.*

▸ **finance**   to provide money for someone or something: *I **financed** my brother's trip to Washington D.C.*

▸ **fund**   to provide money for something; to finance: *The Women's Club **funds** a $1,000 scholarship every year.*

▸ **promote**   to aid the progress or growth of something: *The Chamber of Commerce **promotes** local tourism.*

spontaneous

adjective   arising from a natural inclination or impulse; not planned in advance: *Our* teacher set aside her lesson plans and gave us a **spontaneous** talk.

▸ **impromptu** spoken or done with little or no preparation: *We went on an **impromptu** picnic because the day was so beautiful.*

▸ **impulsive** acting on impulse rather than by thinking things through or planning carefully: *This hat was an **impulsive** purchase, but it has actually been quite useful.*

spooky *adjective* (informal) ghostly; eerie: *see* **scary**

sport *noun* a usually competitive activity involving physical exercise and skill: *see* **recreation**

spot *noun* a place or position: *see* **place**

spot *noun* a small mark or stain: *see* **stain**

spotless *adjective* free from stain or blemish: *see* **clean**

spouse

noun a husband or wife: *Have you met his **spouse**?*

▸ **helpmate** a helper or helpful companion, especially a husband or wife: *They have been true **helpmates** all of their married life.*

▸ **husband** a man who is married: *She misses her **husband** when he is away on business trips.*

▸ **mate** ▷ a husband or wife: *The program offers help for people seeking to leave an abusive **mate**.* ▷ the male or female of a pair of animals or birds: *The panda at the zoo has a new **mate**.*

▸ **wife** a woman who is married: *My father says that my mother is the best **wife** in the world.*

sprawl *verb* to spread out in a disorderly way: *see* **spread**

spread

verb to distribute a layer of something over a surface: *I **spread** cream cheese on my bagel.*

▸ **disperse** (formal) to move or send something in different directions: *The winds dis-*

persed the clouds and left the sky sunny and clear.

▸ **scatter** to throw something here and there in no particular pattern: *I **scattered** corn for the chickens.*

▸ **sprawl** to spread out in a disorderly way: *The audience for the outdoor concert **sprawled** across the lawn.*

▸ **sprinkle** to scatter something in drops or particles: *I **sprinkled** flakes of dried coconut on the cake.*

spree

noun overindulgence in an activity: *She is still broke from her last shopping **spree**.*

▸ **bender** (slang) a drinking spree: *He went on a **bender** this weekend.*

▸ **binge** a period of unrestrained activity, as of drinking, eating, or shopping: *I read fifty books during my reading **binge**.*

▸ **fling** a brief period of doing whatever one wants; a spree or a binge: *My friends and I went on one last **fling** before school started.*

spring *noun* a natural fountain or flow of water: *see* **river**

sprinkle *noun* a light rain: *see* **rain**

sprinkle *verb* to scatter something in drops or particles: *see* **spread**

sprint *verb* to run at top speed for a short distance: *see* **run**

spry *adjective* active or lively: *see* **agile**

spur *noun* something that urges one to action: *see* **impulse**

squad *noun* a small, organized group of people who work for a common goal or cause: *see* **team**

squall *noun* a brief, sudden windstorm, often with rain or snow: *see* **storm**

squander *verb* to spend money lavishly or wastefully: *see* **spend**

squash *verb* to beat something into a pulp or a flattened mass: *see* **crush**

squeak *noun* a thin, high-pitched cry or sound: *see* **bark**

squeal *noun* a loud, shrill cry or sound: *see* **bark**

squeeze *verb* to press something tightly into a small space: *see* **fill**

squishy *adjective* soft and wet, like mud: *see* **soft [2]**

staff *noun* a long stick used as a support, weapon, or symbol of authority: *see* **pole**

stage *noun* a level, degree, or period of time in the course of a process: *see* **degree**

stage *noun* the raised platform in a theater on which entertainers perform: *see* **platform**

stab

verb to pierce a person or animal with a pointed weapon or instrument: *The zoo's veterinarian* **stabbed** *the elephant's thick skin with a large needle.*

- ▸ **gore** to pierce or stab someone with a horn or tusk: *Even a good matador is at risk of being* **gored** *by a bull.*
- ▸ **gouge** to cut or scoop something out, as with a sharp utensil: *I* **gouged** *out the center of the watermelon and filled it with grapes.*
- ▸ **knife** to stab someone with a knife: *The mugger tried to* **knife** *his victim when she resisted.*
- ▸ **lance** to pierce or cut something open with a sharp blade: *He* **lanced** *his blister with a needle.*
- ▸ **penetrate** to pass into or through something; to pierce: *An arrow can* **penetrate** *several inches of wood.*
- ▸ **pierce** to pass into or through something, as with a sharp instrument: *A nail* **pierced** *my tire and caused it to go flat.*
- ▸ **prick** to make a small hole or mark in something with a pointed object: *The nurse* **pricked** *my finger with a needle to get a blood sample.*
- ▸ **puncture** to pierce an object or material with something sharp: *The instructions said to* **puncture** *the plastic covering on my microwave dinner.*
- ▸ **spear** to pierce or stab something with or as if with a spear: *She* **speared** *a piece of chicken with her fork.*

stable *adjective* firm or steady in purpose or character: *see* **dependable**

stack *noun* an orderly pile, especially one arranged in layers: *see* **pile**

stadium *noun* a large, usually open structure that is used for sports events with tiered seating for spectators: *see* **theater**

stagger

verb to move unsteadily: *The kids whirled around and around until they* **staggered** *from dizziness.*

- ▸ **hobble** to walk with a slow, awkward motion; to limp: *The injured football player* **hobbled** *off the field.*
- ▸ **limp** to walk in an uneven or painful way: *I* **limped** *for a couple of days after I sprained my ankle.*
- ▸ **lurch** to make a sudden, unsteady movement forward or to one side: *When the elevator stopped suddenly, all the passengers* **lurched** *against each other.*
- ▸ **shuffle** to walk slowly while dragging one's feet: *The weary passengers* **shuffled** *off the plane after the long flight.*
- ▸ **stumble** to trip and almost fall: *I* **stumbled** *when my foot caught the edge of the curb.*
- ▸ **totter** to sway as if about to fall: *The child made a tall stack of blocks that* **tottered** *and finally fell.*

stain

noun a discolored or soiled spot or smudge: *The little boy had grass* **stains** *on his jeans.*

- ▸ **blemish** a mark on something that makes it less than perfect; a flaw: *There was a* **blemish** *on the surface of the antique table.*
- ▸ **blotch** a large spot or stain, as of ink: *My pen leaked and made a* **blotch** *on my backpack.*
- ▸ **mark** a visible trace on a surface, such as a scratch, dent, or stain: *The cup of tea left a wet* **mark** *on my desk.*
- ▸ **scar** a mark or sign of damage, especially a mark left on the skin by a healed wound: *I have a* **scar** *on my knee from an operation.*

▶ **smudge** a blurred spot or smear: *She left a **smudge** of lipstick on my cheek when she kissed me.*

▶ **spot** a small mark or stain: *There are **spots** on the rug where I dripped coffee.*

stake *verb* to gamble or risk one's money or property: *see* **gamble**

stale *adjective* having lost freshness: *see* **rotten**

stalk *verb* to move in a stealthy way toward something, especially so as to capture it: *see* **follow**

stall *noun* a small booth or stand used for selling or displaying goods: *see* **business [1]**

stall *noun* a compartment for a single animal in a barn or stable: *see* **cage**

stamina *noun* the power to resist fatigue or illness while working hard: *see* **endurance**

stamp *verb* to extinguish or destroy something by trampling it underfoot: *see* **crush**

standard *adjective* of the usual or familiar kind: *see* **normal**

stand-in *noun* a temporary substitute, especially an actor who takes another's place while a scene is being set up: *see* **substitute**

standing *noun* the position that a person has relative to others, as in society or an organized group: *see* **status**

staple *verb* to fasten or hold something by means of a staple: *see* **fasten**

stare *verb* to look at with a steady, often wide-eyed gaze: *see* **look**

start *verb* to begin an action or movement: *see* **begin**

startle *verb* to fill someone with sudden alarm: *see* **surprise**

starvation *noun* the condition or process of suffering from prolonged lack of food: *see* **hunger**

state *noun* a political body that makes up a nation: *see* **country**

state *verb* to express something in words: *see* **say**

stately *adjective* marked by great dignity or formality: *see* **noble**

statement *noun* a periodic report sent to a debtor or a bank depositor: *see* **bill**

statement *noun* something expressed in words: *see* **comment**

stationary

adjective fixed in one place; not intended to move: *I like to read while riding my **stationary** bike.*

▶ **immobile** not capable of moving; fixed: *The explorers' ship was caught in the ice and remained **immobile** for the rest of the winter.*

▶ **motionless** temporarily without motion: *The flag was **motionless** because there was no wind.*

▶ **still** not moving or in motion; quiet or at rest: *The children were **still** as their mother read them a story.*

ANTONYM **moveable** capable of being pushed

status

noun a person's place within a group or society, especially as it affects power or prestige: *The **status** of a bank president is higher than that of a teller.*

▶ **position** a post of employment or service within an organization; a job: *My uncle holds a high **position** in the State Department.*

▶ **rank** one's position or standing on a scale or in a group: *Scientists of the highest **rank** were called to an international meeting on cloning.*

▶ **standing** the position that a person has relative to others, as in society or an organized group: *His academic **standing** is in the top 10 percent of his class.*

stay

verb to remain in one place or condition: *We **stayed** in the movie theater until all the credits were done.*

▸ **dawdle** to take more time than necessary; to waste time: *If you* **dawdle** *any longer, we won't make it to the library before it closes.*

▸ **linger** to stay in a place longer than usual: *I* **lingered** *after school to talk to my friends.*

▸ **loiter** to stand around doing nothing: *My friends and I* **loitered** *all afternoon in the video arcade.*

▸ **remain** to stay in the same place or condition: *Beavers can* **remain** *underwater for up to 15 minutes.*

▸ **wait** to stay in a place in expectation of something: *I* **waited** *ten minutes for the bus to come.*

ANTONYM **leave** to go away from a place; to depart

staying power *noun* the ability to endure or last: *see* **endurance**

steadfast *adjective* firmly loyal or faithful: *see* **loyal**

steady *adjective* free or almost free from change: *see* **constant**

steal

verb to take someone's property without right or permission: *Either I lost my purse or somebody* **stole** *it.*

▸ **embezzle** to take money or property that has been left in one's care for one's own use: *The accounting clerk was fired for* **embezzling** *funds.*

▸ **hijack** to seize control of a vehicle by force: *Two men tried to* **hijack** *the airplane but were subdued by the crew.*

▸ **kidnap** to carry off and hold someone by force, usually for ransom: *The rebels* **kidnapped** *the governor of the province and held him in a secret location.*

▸ **loot** to take things of value, especially during a time of war or social disturbance: *The rioters* **looted** *the stores.*

▸ **pilfer** to steal things of little value: *I* **pilfered** *some of my roommate's laundry soap.*

▸ **plunder** to rob valuables by force from a city or territory: *Vikings* **plundered** *Europe's coastal villages about 1,000 years ago.*

▸ **rob** to take property or valuables from a person or place unlawfully, especially by force: *The man who* **robbed** *the convenience store was recently caught by the police.*

▸ **sneak** to bring, take, or put something secretly: *They got caught trying to* **sneak** *firecrackers into the stadium.*

steam *noun* the mist that forms when vapor from hot water cools and condenses into tiny drops: *see* **mist**

steep *verb* to immerse something in a liquid: *see* **flood**

steeple *noun* a tall tower that rises from the roof of a building, especially one on a church or courthouse: *see* **tower**

steer *verb* to direct the course of something or someone: *see* **guide**

stem *verb* to stop the advance or flow of something: *see* **stop**

stench *noun* a strong, unpleasant smell: *see* **smell**

stepparent *noun* a parent who is related by marriage to one's biological parent: *see* **parent**

sterile *adjective* free from live bacteria or other microorganisms: *see* **clean**

stern *adjective* firm and severe in manner or character: *see* **strict**

stick *noun* a long, slender piece of wood, such as a branch from a tree: *see* **pole**

sticker *noun* an adhesive label: *see* **label**

stiff

adjective not easily bent: *Coat hangers are often made from* **stiff** *wire.*

▸ **inflexible** not bending at all; rigid: *The steel bar was* **inflexible**.

▸ **rigid** not bending; hard and stiff: *The frozen fish were* **rigid** *until they thawed.*

▸ **taut** pulled or drawn tight: *Please hold the measuring tape* **taut**.

▸ **unyielding** not bending or flexible; not giving way to pressure: *My feet ached after* *standing all day on the **unyielding** concrete floor.*

ANTONYM **flexible** able to bend or be bent

stifle *verb* to keep something in or hold something back: *see* **suppress**

still *adjective* no longer making any sound: *see* **quiet**

still *adjective* not moving or in motion: *see* **stationary**

stimulate *verb* to excite something or someone to an active state: *see* **excite**

stimulating *adjective* stirring the mind or body to greater activity: *see* **exciting**

stimulus *noun* something that causes a response or increases activity: *see* **motive**

sting *noun* a sharp, burning pain: *see* **pain**

stingy *adjective* giving or spending reluctantly: *see* **greedy**

stink *noun* a strong, foul odor: *see* **smell**

stir *verb* to mix something by using repeated circular motions: *see* **mix**

stitch *noun* a sudden, sharp pain, especially in the side: *see* **pain**

stock *noun* a supply for future use: *see* **supply**

stockade *noun* a defensive barrier made of strong, upright posts driven into the ground: *see* **fort**

stomach

noun ▷ one of the main organs of digestion: *My **stomach** was very full after the Thanksgiving dinner.* ▷ the front part of the body; the belly: *I like to sleep on my **stomach**.*

▸ **abdomen** the front part of the body from the chest to the hips: *I've been doing exercises to strengthen the muscles in my **abdomen**.*

▸ **belly** the front part of the body below the chest: *The cat crouched on its **belly** as it stalked the gopher.*

▸ **gut** the digestive tract; the stomach and intestines: *I removed the **guts** of the fish before cutting it into fillets.*

▸ **tummy** (informal) the human stomach or belly: *After eating all his Halloween candy, my nephew said that his **tummy** hurt.*

stone *noun* ▷ a naturally hardened mass of mineral material ▷ a piece of stone: *see* **rock**

stop

verb to cause someone or something to cease moving, acting, or functioning: *The manager **stopped** the young boys from entering the pool hall.*

▸ **brake** to slow or stop something with a mechanical device: *When riding your bicycle downhill, don't **brake** the front tire or you could flip over your handlebars.*

▸ **cease** to bring something to an end; to stop: *The officer ordered his men to **cease** firing.*

▸ **halt** to stop or come to an end, often temporarily: *Conversation **halted** when the professor entered the classroom.*

▸ **pause** to stop briefly: *The speaker **paused** for a moment to look at his notes.*

▸ **quit** to stop doing something; to cease: *My aunt **quit** smoking a year ago.*

▸ **stem** to stop the advance or flow of something: *She **stemmed** the flow of blood by pressing on the wound with a bandage.*

▸ **suspend** to stop something for a time; to interrupt: *We **suspended** our conversation to answer the door.*

ANTONYM **start** to begin to move, go, or act

stopper *noun* a device, such as a cork, that is put into an opening to close it: *see* **lid**

store *noun* a place where merchandise is offered for sale: *see* **business** [1]

store *noun* a stock or supply: *see* **supply**

storm

noun a strong wind with rain, hail, sleet, or snow: *The summer **storm** was accompanied by thunder and lightning.*

▸ **blizzard** a very long, heavy snowstorm with strong winds: *The blizzard left huge snowdrifts in the streets.*

▸ **cyclone** a rotating windstorm: *Hurricanes are large tropical cyclones.*

▸ **hurricane** a powerful tropical storm with winds over 75 miles per hour: *Hurricanes form over water and lose strength once they pass over land.*

▸ **monsoon** a wind in southern Asia that changes direction with the seasons and brings heavy rainfall: *The monsoons bring heavy rains and flooding every year.*

▸ **squall** a brief, sudden windstorm, often with rain or snow: *The small boat was damaged in the squall.*

▸ **tornado** a violent, whirling wind: *Tornados can spin at speeds of up to 500 miles per hour.*

▸ **typhoon** a tropical hurricane occurring in the western Pacific Ocean: *A large typhoon struck the coast of southern China.*

story

noun an account of something, either made up or true, told to entertain people: *My grandmother told me the story of how she met my grandfather.*

▸ **anecdote** a short account of an interesting or humorous event: *My brother told me an anecdote about a man who sold Cornish game hens as "miniature turkeys."*

▸ **description** an account or statement describing something: *Francis Parkman's description of the Oregon Trail was written in 1849.*

▸ **epic** a long poem about the achievements and adventures of a hero or heroes: *The Tale of Kieu is Vietnam's national epic.*

▸ **fable** a story that is meant to teach a useful lesson: *The most famous fables are those written by Aesop, such as "The Tortoise and the Hare."*

▸ **legend** a story handed down from earlier times: *According to legend, Robin Hood robbed from the rich to give to the poor.*

▸ **myth** a story that gives the reason for the beliefs and practices of a group of people: *There are myths from many cultures describing how the world was made.*

▸ **narrative** a usually factual story or description of how something happened: *I wrote a narrative of my grandmother's life.*

▸ **poem** a piece of writing, often in rhyme, in which words are chosen for their sound and beauty as well as their meaning: *I memorized Tennyson's poem "The Lady of Shallot."*

▸ **tale** a story, often an imaginary or made-up one: *I read a book of Italian folk tales.*

stout *adjective* strong and sturdy: *see* **strong**

straightforward *adjective* simple and clear: *see* **easy**

strain *noun* a severe demand on one's body, mind, or resources: *see* **worry**

strange

adjective out of the ordinary; unusual or striking: *I saw a strange pulsing light in the sky.*

▸ **abnormal** differing from what is considered normal, usual, or expected: *Flooding is caused by an abnormal amount of rain.*

▸ **eccentric** odd or unusual in appearance: *My grandfather says that he's entitled to be a little bit eccentric at his age.*

▸ **exotic** from another part of the world; foreign: *I like to try exotic foods.*

▸ **odd** not ordinary or usual; peculiar: *I took my car to the mechanic because it was making an odd noise.*

▸ **peculiar** not usual; strange or odd: *The duck-billed platypus is a peculiar-looking animal.*

▸ **queer** different in a strange way from what is usual or expected: *She had a queer look on her face when I asked her what she'd been doing.*

▸ **weird** strikingly odd or unusual: *He has the weird habit of closing his eyes when he talks to people.*

ANTONYM **ordinary** commonly met with; usual

stranger

noun a person one has not known or met before: *I asked the stranger what time it was.*

- **alien** a person who belongs to or comes from another country: *To work legally in the United States, an **alien** must obtain a green card from the government.*
- **foreigner** a person from a foreign country or place: *I felt like a **foreigner** when I moved from the city to a small town.*
- **immigrant** a person who leaves one country to settle permanently in another: *I am a recent **immigrant** to the United States.*
- **outsider** a person who is not part of a certain group or activity: *My friend is an athlete who feels like an **outsider** in his family of musicians.*

strangle *verb* to kill a person by choking or suffocating: *see* **choke**

straw *noun* a thin tube made of paper or plastic through which a person can drink a liquid: *see* **tube**

stray *verb* to wander beyond an established limit: *see* **wander**

stream *noun* a body of water that flows in a bed or a channel: *see* **river**

street *noun* a public road in a city or town: *see* **road**

strength

noun the state, quality, or property of being strong: *Weightlifters work hard to develop their **strength**.*

- **force** the application of strength or power, as to do work or cause physical damage: *The **force** of the explosion blew out the windows of the building.*
- **might** great strength or power: *It took all my **might** to move the boulder.*
- **muscle** muscular strength; brawn: *It took a lot of **muscle** to push the broken-down car off to the side of the road.*
- **power** the ability to do something, especially to produce an effect: *This engine has enough **power** to accelerate even on steep hills.*
- **violence** physical force exerted for the purpose of causing damage or injury: *Professional wrestling is full of **violence**.*

ANTONYM **weakness** the condition of feeling or being weak

strengthen *verb* to make something strong or stronger: *see* **brace**

strenuous *adjective* requiring great effort, energy, or exertion: *see* **hard**

stress *verb* to place special significance or emphasis on: *see* **emphasize**

stress *noun* physical or mental pressure: *see* **worry**

stretch

verb to draw something out to a greater length or width: *I had to **stretch** my whole body to get the pot off the top shelf.*

- **extend** to stretch something to a greater or fuller length: *Modern medicine has **extended** the average life span.*
- **lengthen** to make something longer: *She **lengthened** the skirt by letting out the hem.*
- **prolong** to lengthen the amount of time that something takes: *We **prolonged** our visit for another day.*
- **widen** to make something wide or wider: *He **widened** the walkway up to the house.*

strict

adjective demanding or imposing severe discipline: *Most schools and businesses have a **strict** policy against the use of illegal drugs.*

- **authoritarian** favoring absolute obedience to authority: *The **authoritarian** government suppressed the newspapers.*
- **rigid** marked by a lack of flexibility, especially regarding rules: *The military academy is known for its **rigid** discipline.*
- **stern** firm and severe in manner or character: *I received a **stern** look when I slammed the door.*

stride *verb* to walk with long steps: *see* **walk**

267

strike *verb* to make a military attack against an enemy: *see* **attack**

strike *verb* to hit something or someone hard with or as if with the hand: *see* **hit**

string

noun a cord of twisted fibers used for fastening or tying: *I tied the package with a piece of brown* **string**.

▸ **ribbon** a narrow strip of fabric that is used for decorating or trimming: *The little girl had a pretty red* **ribbon** *in her hair.*

▸ **thread** a fine, thin cord made of twisted fibers, used especially in sewing: *I need some black* **thread** *to mend a hole in my shirt.*

▸ **twine** a strong cord or string, as of cotton or hemp: *I used* **twine** *to tie the climbing rose to the trellis.*

▸ **yarn** soft fibers, as of wool or nylon, twisted into long strands for use in weaving or knitting: *I bought some* **yarn** *to knit a hat for my brother.*

strip *verb* to remove the covering or outer layer from something: *see* **peel**

strive *verb* to try hard to achieve something: *see* **try**

stroke *verb* to gently move the hand over something: *see* **touch**

stroll *verb* to walk in a slow, relaxed way: *see* **walk**

strong

adjective having much power, energy, or strength: *Elephants are* **strong** *enough to carry big logs in their trunks.*

▸ **brawny** having large, strong muscles: *The wrestler had big shoulders and a* **brawny** *chest.*

▸ **burly** heavy and strong; muscular: *The movie star traveled with two* **burly** *bodyguards.*

▸ **forceful** full of strength, power, and energy: *Winston Churchill was a* **forceful** *speaker.*

▸ **hearty** strong and healthy: *My great-aunt is still* **hearty** *despite her age.*

▸ **muscular** having large, strong muscles: *I am lifting weights in an effort to become more* **muscular**.

▸ **stout** strong and sturdy: *Saint Bernards are big,* **stout** *dogs.*

ANTONYM **weak** lacking strength, power, or energy; feeble

stronghold *noun* a place where one is safe from invasion or attack: *see* **fort**

struggle *noun* a great or difficult effort to achieve a goal: *see* **war**

strut *verb* to walk with pompous and self-important bearing: *see* **walk**

stubborn

adjective doing only what one wants and not what someone else wants: *The* **stubborn** *child would not put away his toys.*

▸ **determined** fixed on a particular course or purpose; firmly decided: *I made a* **determined** *effort to finish my report by nine o'clock.*

▸ **headstrong** insisting on having one's own way: *My coworker is* **headstrong** *and doesn't like asking the rest of us for our opinions.*

▸ **obstinate** stubbornly holding to an attitude, opinion, or course of action: *The* **obstinate** *mule refused to budge no matter how we tried to coax it.*

▸ **ornery** mean and stubborn: *The* **ornery** *camel spit at me.*

▸ **persistent** refusing to give up or let go: *The* **persistent** *lawyer cross-examined the witness from several angles until he finally admitted he was lying.*

▸ **relentless** steady and persistent; never stopping or resting: *The research scientist was* **relentless** *in her pursuit of a cure to the disease.*

▸ **resolute** firm or determined; unwavering: *The senator was* **resolute** *in his support of stronger environmental controls.*

▸ **unbending** not flexible or yielding; uncompromising: *Our teacher is* **unbend**-

ing in her requirement for us to hand in our homework on time.

ANTONYM **cooperative** marked by willingness to cooperate; compliant

student

noun a person who takes classes or who studies something: *She has been a ballet **student** for years.*

▸ **apprentice** a person who is learning a craft or trade by working for a skilled worker: *My brother is an electrician's **apprentice**.*
▸ **learner** a person who acquires skill or knowledge: *My English instructor says that I am a fast **learner**.*
▸ **pupil** a person who is being taught in a school or by a private teacher: *Some of the **pupils** from the class have formed a study group.*
▸ **scholar** a person who has gotten a great deal of knowledge from studying: *The professor was known as a great **scholar** of microbiology.*
▸ **trainee** a person who is being trained: *The store manager showed the **trainees** how to use the cash register.*

study *verb* to apply oneself to learning something, especially by reading: *see* **learn**

stuff *verb* to put something carelessly into a space: *see* **fill**

stumble *verb* to trip and almost fall: *see* **stagger**

stunt *noun* an act that shows unusual skill or daring, often done to attract attention: *see* **action**

stupid

adjective slow to understand; mentally dull: *I am **stupid** when it comes to computers.*

▸ **dumb** foolish or stupid: *I felt **dumb** when I forgot your name.*
▸ **idiotic** showing great stupidity or foolishness: *It would be **idiotic** to wear shorts in a snowstorm.*

▸ **moronic** very stupid: *It was **moronic** to say that New York is the nation's capital.*

ANTONYM **smart** having a quick mind; bright

stupidity *noun* the quality of being pointless, worthless, or unintelligent: *see* **nonsense**

sturdy *adjective* strongly made or built: *see* **tough**

stutter *verb* to speak with many pauses and repetitions of sounds: *see* **talk**

sty *noun* a pen where pigs are kept: *see* **cage**

style *noun* a particular way of dressing: *see* **fashion**

stylish *adjective* conforming to the current style: *see* **elegant**

subdue *verb* to bring a person or group under control by physical force or persuasion: *see* **defeat**

subject *noun* a course or area of study: *see* **class**

subject *noun* something or someone that is thought about, discussed, or represented: *see* **topic**

submerge *verb* to place or plunge something into a liquid: *see* **flood**

submit *verb* to put something forward for someone's consideration or approval: *see* **suggest**

substitute

noun someone or something that takes the place of another; a replacement: *I often use honey as a **substitute** for sugar.*

▸ **alternate** a person or thing available to serve in another's place: *He was chosen as an **alternate** to go to the political convention.*
▸ **replacement** a person or thing that replaces another person or thing: *When my favorite CD became scratched, I bought a **replacement**.*
▸ **stand-in** a temporary substitute, especially an actor who takes another's place

while a scene is being set up: *He works as a* **stand-in** *for a famous actor.*

▶ **understudy** a person trained to do the work of another in case of illness or absence: *I was chosen to be an* **understudy** *for the lead actress.*

substitute

verb to put someone or something in the place of another: *The coach* **substituted** *some of the players at halftime.*

▶ **exchange** to give one thing in return for another; to trade: *My friend and I* **exchanged** *telephone numbers.*

▶ **replace** to take or fill the place of another; to provide a substitute for someone or something: *Computers have* **replaced** *typewriters in modern offices.*

▶ **swap** (informal) to trade or exchange something: *I* **swapped** *shifts with another waitress.*

▶ **switch** to replace one thing with another; to trade: *I* **switched** *places to let her sit by the fireplace.*

subtract

verb to take something away from something else: *The clerk* **subtracted** *the value of the coupons from our grocery bill.*

▶ **deduct** to take away one amount from another; to subtract: *My brother* **deducted** *five dollars from what I owed him when I washed his car.*

▶ **extract** to remove one thing from another: *Saffron is the most expensive spice in the world because it has to be* **extracted** *from the crocus flower by hand.*

▶ **remove** to move or take something from a position or place: *She* **removed** *the vase of flowers from the table.*

▶ **take away** to remove something: *The waiter* **took away** *our plates.*

ANTONYM **add** to find the sum of two or more numbers

subvert *verb* to undermine the character, morals, or allegiance of someone: *see* **undermine**

success

noun the attainment of something desired or attempted: *The fundraiser for the marching band was a big* **success.**

▶ **accomplishment** something accomplished; an achievement: *It is an* **accomplishment** *to graduate from high school.*

▶ **achievement** an outstanding accomplishment: *The invention of the wheel is still one of the greatest* **achievements** *of mankind.*

▶ **triumph** a noteworthy or spectacular success: *The opening night of the new play was a* **triumph.**

▶ **victory** the defeat of an enemy or opponent: *Joan of Arc was only 17 when she led the French army to* **victory** *at the Battle of Orleans.*

▶ **win** a victory in a contest or sport: *Our baseball team has had five* **wins** *in a row.*

successful *adjective* having obtained something desired or intended: *see* **lucky**

sudden

adjective happening quickly and without warning: *He almost fell over when the subway came to a* **sudden** *stop.*

▶ **abrupt** sudden and unexpected: *There was an* **abrupt** *change in temperature.*

▶ **immediate** taking place at once or very soon; happening with no delay: *This medicine is guaranteed to give* **immediate** *relief.*

▶ **unexpected** not expected; coming without warning: *I was delighted to receive your* **unexpected** *phone call.*

▶ **unforeseen** not known in advance; unexpected: *There were some* **unforeseen** *delays at the end of the project.*

suddenly *adverb* quickly, without warning: *see* **immediately**

suffer *verb* to endure great pain or distress: *see* **cope**

suffering

noun pain or distress, especially when endured for a long time: *There was widespread* **suffering** *when the crops failed for a second year.*

▸ **agony** intense and prolonged pain or suffering: *My brother and I went through* **agony** *when our parents divorced.*

▸ **anguish** unrelieved suffering, especially of the mind: *I was filled with* **anguish** *when my best friend was paralyzed in a car accident.*

▸ **distress** physical or mental discomfort, especially a state of anxious unrest: *His bad behavior is a constant source of* **distress** *to his parents.*

▸ **grief** great sadness; deep sorrow: *Grief is a natural response to the death of a loved one.*

▸ **misery** prolonged unhappiness due to great pain or distress: *Arthritis is a condition that causes much* **misery** *to those who suffer from it.*

▸ **torment** intense physical or mental pain: *A toothache can be a source of* **torment**.

sufficient *adjective* as much as is needed or wanted: *see* **enough**

suffocate *verb* to kill a person or living thing by depriving it of air: *see* **choke**

suggest

verb to offer something for consideration or action: *My teacher* **suggested** *a couple of report topics for me to think about.*

▸ **present** to recommend something for observation, examination, or consideration: *I* **presented** *the idea of a family reunion to my cousins.*

▸ **propose** to put something forward for consideration; to suggest: *She* **proposed** *that we order Chinese food for dinner.*

▸ **submit** to put something forward for someone's consideration or approval: *I* **submitted** *my application to the manager.*

suggestion

noun something offered for consideration or action: *I like your* **suggestion** *that we go to a movie after dinner.*

▸ **advice** an opinion about how to solve a problem or do something unfamiliar: *My sister gives me* **advice** *about dating.*

▸ **counsel** (formal) an opinion about what should be done: *I asked my teacher's* **counsel** *about which classes to take next year.*

▸ **proposal** a plan or scheme that is offered for others to consider: *My friend made a* **proposal** *that we start a reading group.*

▸ **recommendation** something that is advised: *I followed my doctor's* **recommendations** *about changing my diet.*

suit *noun* a set of matching outer garments, especially one consisting of a coat with trousers or a skirt: *see* **clothing**

suitable *adjective* right for a certain purpose or occasion: *see* **proper**

suitcase *noun* a sturdy, often rectangular, piece of luggage: *see* **bag**

suite *noun* a series of connected rooms used together: *see* **room**

sulk *verb* to be sullenly quiet or angry: *see* **pout**

sullen *adjective* showing bad humor or resentment: *see* **resentful**

sum *noun* the whole amount, quantity, or number: *see* **amount**

summit *noun* the highest point of something, especially a mountain: *see* **top**

summon *verb* to send for someone: *see* **call [2]**

sundown *noun* the time of sunset: *see* **sunset**

sunrise *noun* the time when the sun rises: *see* **morning**

sunset

noun the daily disappearance of the sun below the western horizon: *The planet Venus is sometimes visible just after* **sunset**.

▸ **dusk** the time of evening just before dark: *Bats sleep all day and become active at* **dusk**.

▸ **nightfall** the coming of darkness at the end of the day: *The air becomes cool at* **nightfall**.

▸ **sundown** the time of sunset: *We planned our hike so that we'd be back by sundown.*

▸ **twilight** the time of day when the sun is just below the horizon, but there is still a little light left in the sky: *Deer often come out to feed at twilight.*

ANTONYM **sunrise** the time when the sun rises

super *adjective* (informal) first-rate: *see* **excellent**

superb *adjective* of unusually high quality: *see* **excellent**

superintendent *noun* a person who supervises or is in charge of something: *see* **boss**

superior *adjective* higher in quality or nature than another: *see* **better**

supervise *verb* to oversee the work or performance of someone or something: *see* **manage**

supervisor *noun* a person who oversees or manages someone or something: *see* **boss**

supper *noun* the evening meal or the last meal of the day: *see* **meal**

supple *adjective* moving and bending with grace and agility: *see* **flexible**

supplies *noun* materials or provisions stored and dispensed when needed: *see* **equipment**

supply

noun an amount available for use: *The supply of paper for our copying machine is almost gone.*

▸ **fund** a sum of money or other resources set aside for a specific purpose: *I make a monthly contribution to my retirement fund.*

▸ **hoard** a supply that is hidden away: *She keeps a small hoard of chocolate in her desk drawer.*

▸ **inventory** the supply of goods on hand, as in a store or school: *The inventory of classroom supplies is getting low.*

▸ **provisions** a stock of necessary supplies, especially food: *We bought extra provisions because a big snowstorm was forecast.*

▸ **stock** a supply for future use: *We keep a stock of canned foods for emergency use.*

▸ **store** a stock or supply: *Squirrels build up a store of nuts and seeds for the winter.*

supply *verb* to make something available for use: *see* **equip**

support *verb* to bear or carry the weight of a structure or object: *see* **brace**

support *verb* to supply someone with things needed to live or survive: *see* **help**

supporter *noun* a person who promotes or favors someone or something: *see* **follower**

suppose *verb* to be inclined to think or conclude something: *see* **guess**

suppress

verb to put an end to something, as by force; to crush: *The military suppressed the riot.*

▸ **censor** to remove material from or prevent the publication of something: *The violent movie was censored before it was released.*

▸ **inhibit** to restrain or hold someone back; to prevent: *Fear of sounding stupid inhibits many students from taking part in class discussions.*

▸ **repress** to hold something down by force or effort: *I repressed my desire to say something mean.*

▸ **stifle** to keep something in or hold something back; to suppress: *I tried to stifle my laughter as I read the funny book in the library.*

supreme *adjective* greatest in power, authority, or rank: *see* **best**

sure *adjective* impossible to doubt or dispute: *see* **certain**

surely *adverb* without doubt: *see* **certainly**

surgeon *noun* a doctor who specializes in surgery: *see* **doctor**

surplus *adjective* left over after normal or actual use: *see* **extra**

surprise

verb to cause someone to feel wonder, astonishment, or amazement, as at something unexpected: *The low price of the car surprised me.*

- ▶ **amaze** to fill someone with great wonder; to astonish: *After living in the mountains all my life I was amazed by how flat the Canadian prairies are.*
- ▶ **astonish** to overwhelm someone with surprise or disbelief: *The results of the experiment astonished the researchers.*
- ▶ **astound** to greatly astonish someone, as at something previously unimaginable: *I was astounded to learn that Mt. Everest is more than five miles high.*
- ▶ **daze** to stun or confuse someone, as with a blow, shock, or surprise: *The driver of the car was dazed but unhurt after the accident.*
- ▶ **shock** to surprise and upset someone greatly: *It shocked our family when my father got laid off.*
- ▶ **startle** to fill someone with sudden alarm; to surprise someone suddenly: *It startled me when the door slammed shut.*

surrender *verb* to give something up to another: *see* **resign**

surround *verb* to shut in or enclose something on all sides: *see* **wrap**

survey *verb* to take a general or comprehensive look at something: *see* **browse**

survive *verb* to continue to live or exist through difficult circumstances: *see* **last²**

suspect *verb* to have doubts about something: *see* **doubt**

suspend *verb* to attach something from above, especially so as to hang freely in midair: *see* **hang**

suspend *verb* to stop something for a time: *see* **stop**

suspicion *noun* a feeling or belief, especially that something is wrong or bad but with little evidence to support it: *see* **intuition**

suspicious *adjective* tending to have doubts about; distrustful: *see* **jealous**

sustain *verb* to supply someone or something with necessities: *see* **feed**

swagger *verb* to walk with a bold, proud, or defiant manner: *see* **walk**

swallow *verb* to cause food or drink to pass from the mouth through the throat and into the stomach: *see* **drink**

swamp

noun a lowland area often covered with water and typically supporting trees: *Alligators live in Florida's swamps.*

- ▶ **bog** soft, undrained, water-soaked ground: *Cranberries grow well in bogs.*
- ▶ **everglade** a large area of marshland covered in places with tall grass: *Florida is famous for its everglades.*
- ▶ **marsh** low, wet land typically filled with grasses, reeds, and bushes: *The marsh on our farm serves as a bird sanctuary.*
- ▶ **wetland** a watery lowland area, such as a marsh or swamp, especially one regarded as a natural habitat of wildlife: *New legislation has been passed to protect the wetlands.*

swap *verb* (informal) to trade or exchange something: *see* **substitute**

swarm *noun* a large number of people, especially in motion: *see* **crowd**

swat *verb* to deliver a sudden, sharp blow to something: *see* **hit**

sway *verb* to swing gently back and forth from side to side: *see* **wave**

sweep *verb* to clean or gather something with a broom or brush: *see* **clean**

sweet *adjective* easy to love; gentle and kind: *see* **charming**

swell *verb* to increase in size or volume as a result of pressure from the inside: *see* **increase**

swelling *noun* a spot that has increased in size or volume as a result of internal pressure, especially through disease or injury: *see* **bump**

swift *adjective* moving or able to move very fast: *see* **fast**

swig *verb* to take large swallows of a liquid: *see* **drink**

swindle *verb* to cheat or defraud someone of money or property: *see* **cheat**

swindler *noun* a person who cheats someone out of money or property: *see* **imposter**

swing *verb* to move something back and forth from a central point: *see* **wave**

swish *noun* a hissing or rustling sound: *see* **rustle**

switch *verb* to replace one thing with another: *see* **substitute**

swoosh *noun* a rushing or swirling sound: *see* **rustle**

symbol *noun* something that stands for or represents something else: *see* **sign**

sympathy

noun a feeling of pity or sorrow for the distress of another: *We had a lot of sympathy for our friend when we found out that his dog had been killed by a car.*

- ▸ **compassion** a feeling of sharing the suffering of someone else, along with a desire to help: *Mother Teresa was known for her compassion for the sick and the poor.*
- ▸ **consideration** thoughtful concern for others: *His consideration for others is one of the reasons he is well liked.*
- ▸ **goodwill** a kindly or friendly attitude: *Her goodwill made us feel welcome in her home.*
- ▸ **kindness** kind treatment or a kind act; a favor: *I will not forget your kindness to me.*
- ▸ **pity** a feeling of sorrow or sympathy for the suffering of another: *We felt pity for the hungry children.*

symptom *noun* a sign or indication, especially of illness: *see* **sign**

syrup *noun* a thick, sweet liquid, as that made by boiling sugar and water: *see* **juice**

system *noun* an orderly way of doing something: *see* **method**

T

tab *noun* (informal)   a bill or check, especially for a meal in a restaurant: *see* **bill**

table *noun*   an orderly presentation of data, usually arranged in columns and rows: *see* **chart**

tablet *noun*   a small, often disk-shaped piece of medicine: *see* **pill**

tactful *adjective*   having the ability to speak or act without offending others: *see* **polite**

tag *noun*   a strip of paper, metal, or leather attached to something for the purpose of identifying or labeling it: *see* **label**

tail *verb* (informal)   to follow someone closely in order to watch: *see* **follow**

tailor *verb*   to alter or adapt something for a particular situation or purpose: *see* **change**

taint *verb*   to spoil something, as with disease or decay: *see* **pollute**

take *verb*   to carry, transport, or lead someone or something to another place: *see* **carry**

take away *verb*   to remove something: *see* **subtract**

take place *verb*   to happen, especially as an event: *see* **happen**

tale *noun*   a story, often an imaginary or made-up one: *see* **story**

talent *noun*   an outstanding natural ability: *see* **ability**

talk

verb   to express one's thoughts and ideas in spoken words: *I like to **talk** with my friends about what happened during the day.*

- ▸ **babble**   to talk without pausing about foolish or idle matters: *She is always **babbling** about her boyfriend.*
- ▸ **chat**   to talk in a relaxed, friendly way: *I **chatted** with the sales clerk as he rang up the sale.*

- ▸ **chatter**   to talk fast without much purpose: *The children were **chattering** back and forth as they played in the sandbox.*
- ▸ **converse** (formal)   to exchange thought or ideas with another person: *The woman and I **conversed** about the weather while we waited for the bus.*
- ▸ **gossip**   to talk and spread rumors about other people: *We **gossiped** about his behavior at the party.*
- ▸ **stutter**   to speak with many pauses and repetitions of sounds: *The first time I gave a speech, I was so nervous that I **stuttered**.*
- ▸ **visit** (informal)   to converse or chat: *My friend and I **visited** on the phone for an hour.*

talk

noun   the act of talking; a conversation: *My roommates and I had a **talk** about how to divide the housework.*

- ▸ **conversation**   an exchange of thought or ideas between two or more people: *I enjoy **conversations** with interesting people.*
- ▸ **dialogue**   a formal exchange of thoughts on a particular subject: *Our principal has called for a **dialogue** between students and faculty about the school dress code.*
- ▸ **discussion**   a serious conversation on a subject or topic: *My teacher had a **discussion** with me about going to college.*
- ▸ **interview**   a formal conversation between two people during which one person asks for facts or information from the other: *The magazine writer wrote about his **interview** with the famous athlete.*

tall

adjective   having greater than ordinary height: *The Sears Tower in Chicago is a very **tall** building.*

- ▸ **elevated**   raised or placed above a given level: *The choir stood on an **elevated** platform during the concert.*

▸ **high**   having relatively great height; a great distance above the ground: *The birds perched on the **high** branches of the tree.*

▸ **lofty**   (formal) very high or tall: *The mountain's **lofty** peak turned pink in the sunset.*

▸ **towering**   of impressive height; very tall: *The **towering** basketball players gathered around their coach.*

ANTONYM **short**   lacking in height

tame *adjective*   not afraid of people; easily handled or taught: *see* **gentle**

tamper *verb*   to interfere in a harmful manner: *see* **interfere**

tang *noun*   a sharp, strong flavor or taste: *see* **flavor**

tangible *adjective*   ▷ possible to touch ▷ able to be treated as a fact: *see* **real [2]**

tangle *noun*   a confused state or condition: *see* **mess**

tangled *adjective*   mixed together in a confused mass: *see* **messy**

tangy *adjective*   sharp and somewhat acid in taste: *see* **tasty**

tap *verb*   to strike something gently with a light blow: *see* **touch**

tardy *adjective*   arriving, coming, or happening after the event has started: *see* **late**

target *noun*   someone or something that is criticized, laughed at, or attacked: *see* **victim**

tart *adjective*   having a sharp and highly acid taste: *see* **tasty**

task *noun*   a piece of work assigned or done as part of one's duties: *see* **chore**

task *noun*   an often difficult or tedious undertaking: *see* **project**

taste *noun*   the sensation of sweet, sour, salty, or bitter flavors produced by a substance placed in the mouth: *see* **flavor**

tasteful *adjective*   having, showing, or being in keeping with good taste: *see* **elegant**

tasty

adjective   having a pleasing flavor: *I enjoyed the **tasty** meal.*

▸ **bitter**   having a sharply unpleasant taste: *He shuddered at the **bitter** taste of the medicine.*

▸ **pungent**   biting or sharp to one's sense of taste or smell: *The aged cheese had a **pungent** taste.*

▸ **savory**   highly appealing to one's sense of taste or smell: *I couldn't stop eating those **savory** appetizers.*

▸ **sour**   having a strongly acid taste: *The **sour** candy made my mouth pucker up.*

▸ **spicy**   having the flavor, smell, or quality of spice: *Those Thai peppers are too **spicy** for me.*

▸ **tangy**   sharp and somewhat acid in taste: *I like the **tangy** flavor of yogurt.*

▸ **tart**   having a sharp and highly acid taste: *Lemons are very **tart**.*

▸ **zesty**   having extra flavor or interest: *He made the soup **zesty** by adding some cayenne pepper.*

tattered *adjective*   torn into shreds; ragged: *see* **ragged**

taunt *verb*   to say mean or insulting things to someone: *see* **tease**

taut *adjective*   pulled or drawn tight: *see* **stiff**

tavern

noun   a place licensed to sell alcoholic beverages to be drunk on the premises: *In most states, you have to be 21 to enter a **tavern**.*

▸ **bar**   a place with a counter at which alcoholic drinks and sometimes food are served: *My friends and I had some drinks and sang karaoke at our favorite **bar**.*

▸ **pub**   a restaurant and bar where food and alcoholic beverages are sold and drunk: *We went to a lot of **pubs** when we were in Ireland.*

▸ **saloon**   a room with a bar where alcoholic drinks are sold and drunk: *The **saloon** had been decorated to resemble one from the Old West.*

taxicab *noun* an automobile that carries passengers for a fare: *see* **car**

teach

verb to pass on knowledge or skill to someone: *My brother is **teaching** me how to set up my own website.*

- ▶ **coach** to teach or train athletes, athletic teams, or performers: *I **coach** a girls' soccer team.*
- ▶ **drill** to give instruction in a subject by having students repeat something again and again: *My friend helped to **drill** me on information for my citizenship test.*
- ▶ **educate** to provide someone with fundamental or thorough knowledge: *Parents are responsible for **educating** their children in what is right and wrong.*
- ▶ **instruct** to teach someone in an organized way: *Our swimming coach **instructed** us in the proper form for the butterfly stroke.*
- ▶ **introduce** to provide someone with a first experience or a beginning knowledge of something: *My grandmother **introduced** me to cooking when I was a child.*
- ▶ **train** to instruct someone in the particular skills of an art or profession: *It is the responsibility of managers to **train** new employees.*
- ▶ **tutor** to give individual instruction to a student; to teach a student privately: *I **tutor** students in math after regular school hours.*

teacher

noun a person who teaches: *She plans to be an elementary school **teacher** when she graduates from college.*

- ▶ **advisor** a person who offers advice, especially officially or professionally: *I had to meet with my **advisor** before registering for classes.*
- ▶ **counselor** a person who gives counsel or guidance, as with personal problems: *I went to see the school **counselor** when my parents were getting a divorce.*
- ▶ **governess** a woman employed to teach and train the children of a household: *The*

governess helped the children with their geography lessons.

- ▶ **instructor** a person who instructs; a teacher: *He is an **instructor** at the local junior college.*
- ▶ **mentor** someone who takes a personal interest in developing another person's skills: *My boss became a **mentor** to me and taught me all about the business.*
- ▶ **professor** a teacher at a college or university: *That **professor** is so good that I am going to take another class from her.*
- ▶ **tutor** a private instructor who gives additional, special, or remedial instruction: *I am seeing a **tutor** to help me with my French classes.*

team

noun a group of people on the same side, as in a game or contest: *I am on the archery **team**.*

- ▶ **cell** the smallest unit of an organized group or movement: *The FBI located a terrorist **cell** in our city.*
- ▶ **crew** a group of people who work together at a particular task: *The work **crew** cleaned up the park.*
- ▶ **platoon** a group of people working or traveling together: *A **platoon** of reporters accompanied the official on her trip abroad.*
- ▶ **squad** a small, organized group of people who work for a common goal or cause: *The **squad** of firefighters quickly put out the fire.*
- ▶ **unit** a single group regarded as a part of a whole: *He was transferred to the manufacturing **unit** of the company.*

tear *verb* to pull something apart or into pieces by force; to rend: *see* **rip**

tease

verb to make fun of someone playfully; to try to annoy someone for amusement: *I **teased** my sister by making weird noises while she was practicing the flute.*

- ▶ **bait** to try to provoke someone with repeated insults: *It is traditional in baseball* for opposing teams to **bait** each other's pitcher.

▸ **kid** to make fun of someone in a friendly or affectionate manner: *He likes to **kid** his sister about her boyfriend.*

▸ **mock** to imitate someone, especially in a way that insults: *The rude girl **mocked** her teacher's expressions when his back was turned.*

▸ **needle** to provoke or tease someone in a persistent manner: *My friends are always **needling** me about my height.*

▸ **taunt** to say mean or insulting things to someone: *My sister **taunted** me about my bad haircut.*

technique *noun* skill or command in handling the fundamentals of an art or sport: *see* **art**

tedious *adjective* long and tiring: *see* **boring**

teenager

noun a person between the ages of 13 and 19: *I helped organize a group of local **teenagers** to volunteer at the soup kitchen.*

▸ **adolescent** a person in the period of growth and physical development that leads from childhood to adulthood: *Most of today's Olympic gymnasts are still **adolescents**.*

▸ **juvenile** a young person, especially in a legal context: ***Juveniles** under the age of 18 may not sign a legal contract.*

▸ **youth** a young person, especially a young male in late adolescence: *Our neighbor works as a counselor for troubled **youths**.*

televise *verb* to broadcast something by television: *see* **announce**

tell

verb to express something in words; to give an account of something: *Please **tell** me about yourself.*

▸ **communicate** ▷ to make something known: *Humans have developed the ability to **communicate** complex ideas through speech.* ▷ to express oneself in such a way that one is clearly understood: *Sometimes I have trouble **communicating** with my father.*

▸ **describe** to use words to tell about something: *She **described** her trip to Hawaii in vivid detail.*

▸ **inform** to tell someone about something specific: *I called my mother to **inform** her that I would be home late.*

▸ **mention** to speak about something briefly or in passing: *He **mentioned** that he would be away next weekend.*

▸ **narrate** to tell a story in speech or writing: *The class listened to the speaker **narrate** her experiences in China.*

▸ **recite** to repeat something from memory: *Children learn to **recite** the Pledge of Allegiance when they are in grade school.*

▸ **recount** (formal) to tell about something in detail; to narrate: *He **recounted** his experiences in the Peace Corps.*

▸ **relate** to tell or narrate something: *My parents like to **relate** the story of how they eloped.*

temper *noun* a person's usual state of mind or emotions: *see* **personality**

temperament *noun* the manner of thinking, behaving, or reacting that is characteristic to a specific person: *see* **personality**

temperamental *adjective* excessively sensitive, irritable, or moody: *see* **moody**

temporary *adjective* lasting, used, or enjoyed for a limited time only: *see* **short [2]**

tempt

verb to persuade or try to persuade someone to do something foolish or wrong: *My friend **tempted** me to go to a movie when I should have stayed home and studied.*

▸ **entice** to attract someone by arousing hope or desire: *He was **enticed** into the store by the display of fishing equipment.*

► **lure** to attract someone by offering something tempting: *The smell of baking bread lured customers into the bakery.*

► **seduce** to persuade someone to engage in wrongful or immoral behavior: *The desire for money sometimes seduces people into a life of crime.*

temptation *noun* a strong appeal exerted by something usually regarded as unwise or wrong: *see* **attraction**

tenant *noun* a person who pays rent to live on or use property that is owned by another person: *see* **occupant**

tendency

noun a general pattern of thinking, acting, or behaving in a certain way: *I have a tendency to stay up late on the weekends.*

► **Inclination** a tendency based on personal preference: *He has an inclination to drive fast.*

► **leaning** a usually moderate tendency; a preference: *My leaning is toward staying home tonight rather than going out.*

► **penchant** (formal) a strong inclination; a definite liking: *Our history professor has a penchant for quoting poetry during his lectures.*

► **preference** a liking of one person or thing over another: *She has a preference for movies with a happy ending.*

tender *adjective* considerate and protective: *see* **gentle**

tenderness *noun* gentle affection: *see* **love**

tense *adjective* full of anxiety or nervous tension: *see* **nervous**

tentative *adjective* not definite or positive; not fully worked out: *see* **hesitant**

tepid *adjective* moderately warm: *see* **hot**

term

noun a word that has a certain meaning, usually in a special vocabulary: *I've learned a lot of computer terms at my job.*

► **expression** a particular way of saying something: *My grandmother's favorite expression is, "Bloom where you are planted."*

► **phrase** a brief expression: *"At sixes and sevens" is a phrase that means something is all mixed up.*

► **word** a spoken sound that communicates a meaning; a written form of such a sound: *I used my thesaurus to look up a different word for "big."*

terminal *adjective* marking the end of a section or series: *see* **last**[1]

terminate *verb* to discontinue the employment of someone: *see* **dismiss**

terrible

adjective causing great fear, shock, or distress: *My brother told me the terrible news about the car accident.*

► **abominable** causing disgust or hatred; detestable: *Genocide is an abominable crime.*

► **awful** very bad or unpleasant: *It was awful when my computer crashed and I lost everything I had just written.*

► **dreadful** causing dread or alarm; terrible: *A dreadful earthquake caused great destruction in the region.*

► **horrible** causing great fear, shock, or disgust: *There was a horrible loss of life when the crowded ferry sank.*

► **horrid** causing horror; horrible: *I had a horrid feeling when I saw the car almost hit my friend.*

► **monstrous** very evil, cruel, or wrong: *Biological warfare is a monstrous act that can threaten entire populations.*

► **tragic** causing great suffering or sorrow; disastrous: *The nuclear disaster at Chernobyl was a tragic event.*

ANTONYM **wonderful** very good; excellent

terrific *adjective* very good or fine: *see* **excellent**

terrified *adjective* filled with terror: *see* **afraid**

terrify *verb* to fill someone with intense fear or terror: *see* **scare**

territory *noun* the land and waters under the authority of a single government: *see* **area**

terror *noun* an intense, overpowering fear: *see* **fear**

terse *adjective* brief and to the point; concise: *see* **blunt**

test

noun a series of questions, problems, or tasks designed to measure one's knowledge or ability: *We are having a history **test** tomorrow.*

▸ **audition** a trial performance designed to measure artistic skill: *She did very well at the **audition** and was asked to join the ballet company.*

▸ **exam** an examination: *Our teacher said the **exam** would consist of two essay questions.*

▸ **examination** a set of questions or exercises that measure one's ability, usually more thoroughly than on a test: *Our final **examination** in geology was two hours long.*

▸ **final** the last examination of an academic course: *Even if I fail my **final**, I'll still get a 'C' in the class.*

▸ **midterm** an examination given at the middle of a school term: *I studied very hard for my chemistry **midterm**.*

▸ **questionnaire** a printed form with a series of questions: *He filled out a brief **questionnaire** on his medical history.*

▸ **quiz** a short test that can be either written or oral: *We were allowed to leave class after we had finished the **quiz**.*

testy *adjective* irritable, impatient, or exasperated: *see* **irritable**

textbook *noun* a book used for the study of a subject: *see* **book**

textile *noun* woven or knit fabric: *see* **fabric**

thankful *adjective* aware and appreciative of a benefit: *see* **grateful**

thankfulness *noun* a feeling of appreciation for a benefit or favor: *see* **appreciation**

thanks *noun* an acknowledgment of a favor or gift: *see* **appreciation**

thaw *verb* to change from a solid to a liquid by gradual warming: *see* **melt**

theater

noun a building, room, or outdoor structure used for the presentation of plays, films, or other dramatic productions: *We went to see a play at the new **theater**.*

▸ **amphitheater** a round building with tiered seats around a central arena: *The Shakespeare festival was held at the outdoor amphitheater.*

▸ **arena** a large building used especially for the presentation of sports events and spectacles: *Spectators filled the **arena** for the boxing match.*

▸ **auditorium** a large room or building used for public meetings or performances: *The choir concert was held in the school **auditorium**.*

▸ **bowl** a stadium or outdoor theater shaped like a bowl: *Two college football teams play at the Cotton **Bowl** every year.*

▸ **coliseum** a large amphitheater for public sports events, entertainment, or assemblies: *We have season tickets for the hockey games at the **coliseum**.*

▸ **stadium** a large, usually open structure that is used for sports events and has tiered seating for spectators: *The rock concert was held at the football **stadium**.*

theft

noun an act or instance of stealing: *The man reported the **theft** of his car to the police.*

▸ **burglary** the crime of breaking into a building with the intention of stealing: *The store owner didn't discover the **burglary** until the next morning.*

▸ **extortion** the act of obtaining something from another by threats or force:

*The gangsters used **extortion** to control the politician.*

▸ **larceny** the crime of taking another's property without right or permission; theft: *The suspect was convicted of **larceny** for stealing computer equipment from the school.*

▸ **robbery** the act of unlawfully taking property or valuables from a person or place, especially by force: *The people who committed the bank **robbery** were wearing ski masks.*

▸ **shoplifting** the act of stealing displayed merchandise from a store: *The store has signs posted warning that **shoplifting** is against the law.*

theme *noun* the subject of a formal talk or piece of writing: *see* **topic**

theory *noun* a statement designed to explain an event or group of events: *see* **philosophy**

therapy *noun* the treatment of illness or disabilities: *see* **remedy**

therefore

adverb for that reason or cause: *My car broke down, and **therefore** I was late to work.*

▸ **as a result** consequently: *I was late to work, and **as a result** I was fired.*

▸ **consequently** as a result; therefore: *I was fired from my job, and **consequently** I filed for unemployment.*

▸ **ergo** consequently; hence: *I am living on unemployment, and **ergo** I don't have a lot of money right now.*

▸ **hence** for this reason; therefore: *I do not have a lot of money right now, and **hence** I cannot go with you to the movies.*

▸ **so** because of the reason given; consequently: *I can't afford to go with you to the movies, and **so** I will stay home and go to bed early.*

▸ **thus** therefore; consequently: *I went to bed early last night, and **thus** have plenty of energy to look for a new job today.*

thesis *noun* a dissertation advancing an original point of view: *see* **essay**

thick *adjective* tightly packed together: *see* **solid**

thief

noun a person who steals: *The **thief** escaped through the window.*

▸ **burglar** a person who breaks into a building in order to steal: *The **burglar** stole our TV and stereo.*

▸ **pickpocket** a thief who steals from someone's pockets: *A **pickpocket** stole his wallet on a crowded subway.*

▸ **robber** a person who takes property from a person or place unlawfully, usually with the threat or use of force: *The **robber** held up the convenience store at gunpoint.*

▸ **shoplifter** a person who steals merchandise from a store: *The **shoplifter** was arrested as she left the store.*

thin

adjective having little fat on the body: *My grandmother is always feeding me because she thinks I'm too **thin**.*

▸ **gaunt** very thin and bony, as from starvation or disease: *Many wild animals become **gaunt** during winter due to lack of food.*

▸ **lean** not fleshy or fat; thin: *The athlete had a **lean**, muscular body.*

▸ **skinny** very thin: *The marathon runner was **skinny**, but strong.*

▸ **slender** thin and delicate in build; gracefully slim: *Deer have long, **slender** legs.*

▸ **slim** attractively thin; slender: *The dancer had long limbs and a **slim** waist.*

ANTONYM **fat** having much or too much body fat

things *noun* personal belongings: *see* **property**

think

verb to use one's mind to form ideas and make decisions: *He had to **think** for few moments before he figured out the riddle.*

▸ **believe** to accept the truthfulness of something: *I **believe** that it is important to be kind to other people.*

▸ **brainstorm** to solve specific problems or develop new ideas by group discussion: *Our church group **brainstormed** ideas for the party.*

▸ **imagine** to form a mental picture or idea of something: *Can you **imagine** being immortal?*

▸ **meditate** to think quietly; to reflect: *She **meditated** a long time before making her decision.*

▸ **muse** to be absorbed in one's thoughts: *I **mused** on what it would be like to be able to travel through time.*

▸ **ponder** to think about something carefully and at length: *He **pondered** whether or not to get a second job.*

▸ **reason** to use one's ability to think clearly and sensibly: *I **reasoned** out the math problem step by step.*

thirsty *adjective* ▷ wanting or needing to drink. ▷ needing rain or watering: *see* **dry**

thorough *adjective* not overlooking anything: *see* **careful [1]**

thoroughly *adverb* in a very thorough way: *see* **completely**

though *conjunction* despite the fact that: *see* **but**

thought *noun* a result of thinking: *see* **idea**

thoughtful *adjective* aware of other people's needs and feelings: *see* **kind¹**

thoughtless *adjective* lacking thought or care: *see* **careless**

thread *noun* a fine, thin cord made of twisted fibers, used especially in sewing: *see* **string**

threadbare *adjective* worn so much that the surface of a fabric is gone and the threads show through: *see* **ragged**

threat *noun* an indication of possible danger or harm: *see* **danger**

threaten *verb* to give signs that something troublesome or dangerous is about to happen: *see* **alert**

threshold *noun* the piece of wood or stone put beneath a door: *see* **entrance**

thrifty

adjective practicing careful and wise management of one's money and other resources: *A **thrifty** shopper tries to buy things on sale.*

▸ **economical** making the most of one's money; not wasteful in spending: *She tries to be **economical** by buying things in bulk.*

▸ **frugal** spending only what is needed for necessities: *I have been **frugal** since I got laid off.*

▸ **penny-pinching** giving or spending money very reluctantly: *My friends say that I am **penny-pinching**, but actually I'm broke.*

ANTONYM **wasteful** spending or using more than is needed

thrill *verb* to give someone a sudden sensation of joy, fear, or excitement: *see* **please**

thrilled *adjective* filled with a sudden sensation of joy, delight, or excitement: *see* **happy**

thrilling *adjective* causing a sudden, intense sensation: *see* **exciting**

thrive

verb to be or stay in a good or healthy condition: *My father is pleased that his new business is starting to **thrive**.*

▸ **bloom** to grow or flourish; to develop quickly: *My interest in Spanish **bloomed** after being an exchange student in South America.*

▸ **flourish** to grow or develop very well; to thrive: *My vegetable garden **flourished** after I fertilized it.*

▸ **flower** to develop fully; to reach a peak of development: *Their romance **flowered** into marriage.*

▸ **grow** to increase and spread; to gain size or strength: *Trade between the two countries **grew** rapidly.*

▸ **prosper**   to be fortunate or successful; to thrive: *The town **prospered** when a new factory was built nearby.*

throng *noun*   a large group of people crowded closely together: *see* **crowd**

through *adjective*   having finished: *see* **done**

throw

verb   to send an object through the air with a fast motion of the arm: *I went out to a big field to practice **throwing** my boomerang.*

▸ **fling**   to throw something with force or violence: *I was so frustrated with my homework that I **flung** my textbook onto the floor.*

▸ **heave**   to throw something with effort or force: *It took two men to **heave** the anchor overboard.*

▸ **hurl**   to throw something with great force: *An unusual way to test whether pasta is done cooking is to **hurl** it against the wall to see if it sticks.*

▸ **pitch**   to throw an object with careful aim, as in a sport: *I **pitched** the softball to the batter.*

▸ **sling**   to hurl or fling something: *How far can you **sling** a rock?*

▸ **toss**   to throw something with a quick, easy motion: *I **tossed** my coat onto the bed.*

throw out

verb   to force someone to leave a place: *She was **thrown out** of the concert when she tried to climb on the stage.*

▸ **banish**   to force someone to leave a country or place by official decree: *Napoleon was **banished** to the Island of Elba in 1814.*

▸ **eject**   to throw or drive someone out: *The rowdy people were **ejected** from the club by two bouncers.*

▸ **evict**   to make a tenant leave by a legal process: *The tenants were **evicted** for not paying their rent.*

▸ **exile**   to force a person to leave his or her country: *The dictator **exiled** many of his enemies.*

▸ **expel**   to force someone to leave a group or organization: *The student was **expelled** from school for bringing a weapon to class.*

▸ **kick out** (slang)   to throw someone out: *She was **kicked out** of class for being rude to the teacher.*

thrust *verb*   to push someone or something with sudden force: *see* **push**

thud *noun*   a dull, heavy sound: *see* **bang**

thunder *verb*   to roar in strong emotion: *see* **shout**

thus *adverb*   therefore; consequently: *see* **therefore**

thwart *verb*   to prevent someone from accomplishing a purpose or goal: *see* **prevent**

ticket *noun*   a price tag or label attached to something being sold: *see* **label**

ticket *noun*   a legal summons given to a person accused of breaking a traffic law: *see* **penalty**

tidy *adjective*   orderly and neat: *see* **clean**

tie *verb*   to fasten or secure something with a cord or rope: *see* **join**

tilt

verb   to cause something to slope, as by raising one end: *I **tilted** the bowl to get all the cake batter out.*

▸ **lean**   to place something so that it angles away from an upright position: *She **leaned** the ladder against the wall.*

▸ **pitch**   to cause a boat to alternately dip its bow and stern: *The waves **pitched** the boat so much that I got seasick.*

▸ **slant**   to have a direction that is neither horizontal nor vertical; to slope: *The leaning Tower of Pisa **slants** 5.5 degrees.*

▸ **tip**   to move something away from a vertical or balanced position: *The wind **tipped** the sailboat so far to one side that it almost capsized.*

timber *noun*   trees or land covered with trees: *see* **wood**

time *noun*   a span of years marked by similar events and conditions, or associated with certain historical figures: *see* **age**

timid *adjective*   easily frightened: *see* **shy**

tinge *noun*   a hint of color: *see* **color**

tinker *verb*   to make minor repairs or adjustments without skill or certain knowledge: *see* **dabble**

tint *noun*   a light, pale, or delicate color: *see* **color**

tiny *adjective*   extremely small: *see* **small**

tip *noun*   a piece of useful information: *see* **clue**

tip *verb*   to move something away from a vertical or balanced position: *see* **tilt**

tire

verb   to become weak from work or effort: *She does not **tire** easily.*

- ▶ **deplete**   to gradually use up a supply of something: *Some crops **deplete** nutrients from the soil more than others.*
- ▶ **drain**   to use up all of a person's energy, attention, or emotion: *The long performance **drained** the actors.*
- ▶ **exhaust**   to use up all of a person's strength or energy: *Moving the heavy furniture **exhausted** us all.*
- ▶ **fatigue**   to tire someone out after long effort: *Working so much overtime is **fatiguing** him.*
- ▶ **wear out**   ▷ to exhaust someone completely: *We were **worn out** from playing basketball all day.* ▷ to make something unusable through long or heavy use: *Children **wear out** clothes quickly.*
- ▶ **weary**   to become physically or mentally tired: *I **wearied** of that song after hearing it so many times on the radio.*

tired

adjective   weakened from work or effort; needing rest: *The **tired** workers took a break and rested.*

- ▶ **bushed**   (informal) extremely tired: *I am **bushed** from chopping all that wood.*

- ▶ **drowsy**   half-asleep; dull with sleepiness: *If you are so **drowsy**, why don't you take a nap?*
- ▶ **exhausted**   completely tired or worn out: *The athletes were **exhausted** by the end of the Ironman Triathlon.*
- ▶ **sleepy**   ready for or needing sleep: *The mother put the **sleepy** baby to bed.*
- ▶ **weary**   physically or mentally tired: *My brother is always **weary** after he gets home from football practice.*
- ▶ **worn-out**   extremely tired; physically or mentally exhausted: *I was **worn-out** after taking the big test.*

ANTONYM **rested**   not tired; having had enough sleep

tiresome *adjective*   causing a person to be tired, bored, or annoyed: *see* **boring**

title *verb*   to name a book, painting, musical composition, or other work: *see* **call [1]**

toddler *noun*   a young child who is just learning how to walk: *see* **child**

toil *noun*   exhausting labor or effort: *see* **work**

token *noun*   something that serves as evidence or proof of something: *see* **souvenir**

tolerance *noun*   the capacity for recognizing and respecting the beliefs or practices of others: *see* **patience**

tolerant *adjective*   showing willingness to let other people hold opinions or follow practices that are different from one's own: *see* **patient**

tolerate *verb*   to put up with hardship, annoyance, or bad conditions: *see* **cope**

toll *noun*   a fixed charge for a privilege or service: *see* **price**

tome *noun*   a large or scholarly book: *see* **book**

tonic *noun*   something that restores a person's strength or energy: *see* **remedy**

too *adverb*   in addition: *see* **also**

tool

noun   a device that helps a person to do work: *A hammer is one **tool** that every carpenter has.*

▸ **device**   a piece of equipment that is made for a particular purpose: *The safety pin is one of the most practical devices ever invented.*

▸ **gadget**   a small mechanical or electronic device: *We have a gadget that automatically peels apples.*

▸ **implement**   a specially made object used in doing a task: *Pens and pencils are writing implements.*

▸ **instrument**   a tool used for a special purpose, especially one used in science, medicine, or technology: *A thermometer is an instrument for measuring temperature.*

▸ **utensil**   an instrument or container, especially one used in a kitchen: *Forks and spoons are eating utensils.*

top

noun   the highest or uppermost part, point, or surface: *There's a blinking red light at the top of the airport control tower.*

▸ **crest**   the highest part of something, especially a mountain or wave: *I climbed to the crest of the hill.*

▸ **crown**   the top part, especially of the head: *The salesman measured around the crown of my head to determine what size hat I would need.*

▸ **peak**   ▷ a tapering point that projects upwards: *The peak of my hat has a pom-pom sewn to it.* ▷ the pointed top of a mountain: *The high peaks formed a jagged line against the sky.*

▸ **ridge**   a long, narrow crest, as of high ground: *The ridge of the mountains was covered in snow.*

▸ **roof**   the top covering of something, such as a building or vehicle: *We plan to replace the roof of our house next summer.*

▸ **summit**   the highest point of something, especially a mountain: *The summit of Mount Everest is 29,035 feet above sea level.*

ANTONYM **bottom**   the lowest part of something

topic

noun   a subject treated in a speech, conversation, or piece of writing: *The weather is a common topic of conversation.*

▸ **issue**   something that is being discussed or argued about: *Health care is an issue that affects everyone.*

▸ **matter**   a subject of thought, concern, feeling, or action: *I went to the bank to take care of a financial matter.*

▸ **subject**   something or someone that is thought about, discussed, or represented: *The instructor told us to choose a research subject by the end of the week.*

▸ **theme**   the subject of a formal talk or piece of writing: *The theme of his speech was Home Safety.*

topple *verb*   to totter and fall, especially from being too heavy on top: *see* **fall**

torment *noun*   intense physical or mental pain: *see* **suffering**

tornado *noun*   a violent, whirling wind: *see* **storm**

toss *verb*   to throw something with a quick, easy motion: *see* **throw**

total *verb*   to find the sum of something: *see* **add**

total *adjective*   complete in extent or degree: *see* **all**

totally *adverb*   fully; absolutely: *see* **completely**

totter *verb*   to sway as if about to fall: *see* **stagger**

touch

verb   to feel something with a part of the body, especially the hand: *Please don't touch the cookies until they cool.*

▸ **feel**   to be or become aware of something through the sense of touch: *The doctor gently felt my neck to see if it was swollen.*

▸ **handle**   to touch, hold, or manipulate something with the hands: *I handled the crystal bowl with care.*

▸ **pat**   to stroke or tap something gently with the open hand: *We patted the horse when it came over to the fence.*

▸ **pet**   to stroke or pat a person or animal in a gentle manner: *My cat purrs when I pet her.*

▶ **rub** to move something back and forth against a surface: *I **rubbed** a cool cloth over my forehead to help myself relax.*

▶ **stroke** to gently move the hand over something: *She **stroked** the dog's ears.*

▶ **tap** to strike something gently with a light blow: *He **tapped** the nail one more time with the hammer.*

tough

adjective strong and not likely to break or tear with use: *Leather is a **tough** material.*

▶ **durable** capable of standing hard wear or long use: *We bought this truck because it is **durable**.*

▶ **hardy** strong and healthy; capable of surviving unfavorable conditions: *The **hardy** tree survived the fire.*

▶ **long-lived** functioning or living for a long time; durable: *The battery for my laptop computer is not very **long-lived**.*

▶ **rugged** very strong or durable; tough: *These **rugged** boots will last for years.*

▶ **sturdy** strongly made or built: *I bought a **sturdy** mountain bike for off-road riding.*

tour *noun* a trip during which many interesting places are visited: *see* **journey**

tour *verb* to travel from place to place, especially for pleasure: *see* **travel**

tournament *noun* a contest made up of a series of games: *see* **contest**

tow *verb* to pull something along behind by a chain, rope, or cable: *see* **pull**

tower

noun a very tall building or part of a building: *We could see for miles from the top of the castle's stone **tower**.*

▶ **belfry** a tower in which a bell or bells are hung: *A new bell was placed in the **belfry** to celebrate the year 2000.*

▶ **minaret** a tower on a mosque from which the people are called to prayer: *Minarets are often tall and slender, though on some mosques they are short and thick.*

▶ **spire** a structure, such as a steeple, that becomes narrow at the top: *The **spire** on*

the tall office building has a light to warn airplanes.

▶ **steeple** a tall tower that rises from the roof of a building, especially one on a church or courthouse: *The **steeples** of New England churches were usually the tallest structures in a town.*

▶ **turret** a small, usually round tower on a building: *Victorian-style houses often have projecting **turrets** on the upper floors.*

towering *adjective* of impressive height; very tall: *see* **tall**

town

noun a populated area that is larger than a village but smaller than a city: *My best friend lives across **town** from me.*

▶ **city** a place where many people live close to one another: *I like living in a big **city** because I enjoy going to museums and the theater.*

▶ **commune** a small, often rural community, whose members share common interests and often income and property: *My sister lives with other artists in a **commune**.*

▶ **metropolis** a large city: *Los Angeles is a **metropolis** that is spread out over many miles.*

▶ **settlement** a small community established by settlers: *We visited the historic Plimouth Plantation, an early Pilgrim **settlement**.*

▶ **village** a group of houses that make up a community smaller than a town: *My father grew up in a **village** in the Philippines.*

toxic *adjective* capable of causing injury or death, especially by chemical means: *see* **fatal**

toy *verb* to amuse oneself idly: *see* **dabble**

trace *verb* to copy something exactly by following lines seen through a sheet of transparent paper: *see* **draw**

track *verb* to follow the footprints or trail of someone or something: *see* **follow**

track *noun* a path, route, or course: *see* **path**

tract *noun* an expanse of land or water: *see* **area**

tract *noun* a leaflet or pamphlet containing a declaration, especially of a religious or political nature: *see* **booklet**

trade *noun* the business of buying and selling commodities: *see* **business [2]**

trade *noun* an occupation, especially one that requires skilled labor: *see* **job**

trade *noun* an exchange of one thing for another: *see* **sale**

trademark *noun* a name or symbol that legally identifies a product: *see* **label**

trader *noun* a person who sells or exchanges goods or commodities: *see* **merchant**

trade show *noun* a large meeting focused on the needs and developments of a certain profession: *see* **meeting**

tradition

noun an idea, custom, or belief that is handed down from generation to generation: *It is an American **tradition** to celebrate the Fourth of July with fireworks.*

- ▶ **convention** a practice or procedure widely observed in a group; a custom: *In China, it is the **convention** for brides to be married in a red dress.*
- ▶ **custom** a practice followed by people of a particular group or region: *It is the **custom** for Muslims to fast during the days of Ramadan.*
- ▶ **institution** an established custom, practice, or pattern of behavior: *The **institution** of marriage is found in various forms throughout the world.*

traditional *adjective* passed down by or in agreement with tradition: *see* **conservative**

traffic *noun* commercial activity, especially of an illegal or improper nature: *see* **business [2]**

tragedy *noun* a disastrous event involving great loss or suffering: *see* **disaster**

tragic *adjective* causing great suffering or sorrow: *see* **terrible**

trail *verb* to follow the traces or scent of someone or something: *see* **follow**

trail *noun* a path or track, especially through the woods: *see* **path**

train *verb* to instruct someone in the particular skills of an art or profession: *see* **teach**

trainee *noun* a person who is being trained: *see* **student**

training *noun* knowledge or skill gotten through instruction: *see* **experience**

trait *noun* a typical and clearly defined characteristic: *see* **quality**

tramp *noun* person who travels and works from place to place: *see* **beggar**

tranquil *adjective* free from commotion or disturbance: *see* **calm**

transmit *verb* to send something from one person or place to another: *see* **send**

transparent *adjective* allowing most or all light to pass through: *see* **clear [2]**

transpire *verb* (formal) to happen: *see* **happen**

transport *verb* to carry someone or something, especially in a vehicle: *see* **carry**

trap

verb ▷ to catch an animal or person in a trap: *We **trapped** the gopher snake in a bucket and let it go in the canyon.* ▷ to catch someone by cleverness or deception: *The prosecutor **trapped** the witness into admitting he had been lying.*

- ▶ **ambush** to attack someone from a concealed position: *The guerillas **ambushed** the supply truck.*
- ▶ **decoy** to lure another into danger by using deception: *The Indians **decoyed** the soldiers into a trap by pretending to run away.*
- ▶ **net** to catch something in a net: *The fishing fleet returned to port after **netting** its catch.*
- ▶ **snare** to trap something in a device such as a noose: *The cowboy **snared** the calf with a lasso.*

ANTONYM **release** to set someone or something free

trash *noun* objects to be thrown away, usually not including food: *see* **garbage**

travel

verb to go from one place to another, as on a trip: *He travels all over the world on business.*

- ► **cruise** to sail or travel about in an unhurried way: *We cruised to Catalina Island on our neighbor's sailboat.*
- ► **journey** to travel, especially over a great distance: *The early Polynesians journeyed vast distances across the open ocean to reach the Hawaiian Islands.*
- ► **migrate** to move regularly from one region to another, especially at a particular time of the year: *Salmon migrate upriver during spawning season.*
- ► **sightsee** to tour sights of interest: *I want to sightsee in Paris this summer.*
- ► **tour** to travel from place to place, especially for pleasure: *They toured through Holland by bicycle.*

treacherous *adjective* marked by hidden or unforeseen hazards: *see* **dangerous**

treasure *verb* to value something very highly: *see* **love**

treasured *adjective* valued highly, especially for sentimental reasons: *see* **valuable**

treat *noun* a source of special delight or pleasure: *see* **fun**

treatise *noun* a piece of formal writing that deals with a certain topic and is usually longer and more detailed than an essay: *see* **essay**

treatment *noun* the use of something to relieve or cure a disease or injury: *see* **remedy**

treaty *noun* a formal agreement between two or more countries: *see* **agreement**

trek *noun* a journey or trip, especially one involving difficulty or hardship: *see* **journey**

trek *verb* to make a slow, hard journey on foot: *see* **walk**

tremble

verb to shake from fear, cold, excitement, or anger: *I trembled in anticipation as*

they announced the winner of the chess tournament.

- ► **quake** to shake without being able to stop; to tremble: *I started to quake with cold when the rain soaked through my jacket.*
- ► **quiver** to shake with a slight vibrating motion: *The leaves quivered in the wind.*
- ► **shiver** to undergo shaking that cannot be controlled: *The skiers shivered with cold as they waited for the ski lift.*
- ► **shudder** to tremble or shiver suddenly, especially from fear: *We all shuddered as we listened to the scary ghost story.*

tremendous *adjective* extremely large in amount, extent, or degree: *see* **big**

trend *noun* a new or developing fashion or style: *see* **fashion**

trespass *noun* (formal) a violation of a moral or social law: *see* **crime**

tribe *noun* (informal) a large family: *see* **family**

trick *noun* a mischievous action: *see* **joke**

trickle *verb* to flow or fall in drops or in a thin stream: *see* **leak**

trifle *verb* to play or toy with something: *see* **dabble**

trim *noun* something added as a finishing decoration: *see* **accessory**

trim *verb* to make something neat, even, or tidy by clipping, smoothing, or pruning: *see* **cut**

trip *verb* to strike the foot against something and almost fall: *see* **fall**

trip *noun* a going from one place to another: *see* **journey**

triumph *verb* a noteworthy or spectacular success: *see* **success**

trivial *adjective* having no lasting importance or value: *see* **unimportant**

trophy *noun* a prize or memento received as a symbol of victory, especially in sports: *see* **award**

trot *verb* to run with slow, short strides: *see* **run**

trouble

noun a difficult, dangerous, or upsetting situation: *I was worried that my friend might be in **trouble** with the police.*

- ▶ **difficulty** something that causes trouble or gets in the way: *Did you experience any **difficulties** in registering for college?*
- ▶ **dilemma** a situation that requires a person to choose between options that are equally bad or unfavorable: *After the company was sold, the manager faced the **dilemma** of taking a cut in pay or losing his job.*
- ▶ **predicament** a difficult or embarrassing situation: *I was in a **predicament** when I locked the keys in the car.*
- ▶ **quandary** a condition of uncertainty or doubt: *She was in a **quandary** about whether or not she should quit her job.*

truant *adjective* absent without permission: *see* **absent**

truce *noun* a temporary stopping of fighting: *see* **peace**

truck *noun* any of various heavy motor vehicles designed for carrying or pulling loads: *see* **car**

true

adjective being in agreement with fact or reality: *The witness swore that everything she said was **true**.*

- ▶ **accurate** free from errors or mistakes: *I double-checked the form to make sure that the information I had given was **accurate**.*
- ▶ **correct** free from error; accurate: *The **correct** spelling of that word can be found in a dictionary.*
- ▶ **right** in accordance with fact, reason, or truth; correct: *I got most of the answers on the test **right**.*
- ▶ **valid** supported by facts, evidence, or reason; acceptable: *Illness is a **valid** excuse for missing work.*

ANTONYM **false** not true, real, honest, or correct

trunk *noun* a large, sturdy box in which clothes or belongings can be packed for travel or storage: *see* **container**

trust

noun firm belief in the honesty, character, truth, or strength of someone or something: *She has no **trust** in him since he used her credit cards without permission.*

- ▶ **confidence** a feeling of certainty that a person or thing will not fail, usually based on knowledge or experience: *He has **confidence** in his ability to perform the piano solo.*
- ▶ **faith** strong belief or confidence in a person or thing, even without conclusive proof: *I loaned him the money in **faith** that he would pay it back.*

trust

verb to have or place confidence in someone or something: *It is usually best to **trust** your instincts.*

- ▶ **believe in** to have faith or confidence in someone or something even without sure proof: *Our coach said that he **believed in** our team's ability to work together and win.*
- ▶ **count on** to rely on someone or something to perform as expected: *Can I **count on** you to pick me up for the meeting?*
- ▶ **depend on** to place trust in someone or something, especially for help or support: *My parents **depend on** me to start dinner before they get home from work.*
- ▶ **rely on** to have complete trust or confidence in someone or something: *My neighbor **relies on** me to feed his fish when he goes away on business.*

ANTONYM **distrust** to have no confidence in someone or something

trustworthy *adjective* able to be trusted: *see* **dependable**

truth *noun* something that is true or that accurately describes reality: *see* **fact**

truthful *adjective* telling the truth: *see* **honest**

try

verb to make an effort; to attempt: *He always **tries** to get his homework done before leaving campus.*

▸ **attempt**   to try to do something, especially something difficult: *He is **attempting** to sail around the world.*
▸ **endeavor**   to make a serious or sustained effort: *I am **endeavoring** to get on the honor roll this semester.*
▸ **strive**   to try hard to achieve something: *I am **striving** to finish this essay before it's due.*

trying *adjective*   causing strain, hardship, or distress: *see* **hard**

tub *noun*   an open, flat-bottomed, usually round container: *see* **bucket**

tube

noun   a hollow cylinder, as of glass or rubber, that is often used to carry liquids: *The patient was given a blood transfusion though a **tube** attached to her arm.*

▸ **cylinder**   a hollow or solid object that is shaped like a tube or pipe: *The poster was mailed to me in a cardboard **cylinder**.*
▸ **hose**   a long, flexible tube used for carrying fluid or air: *I coiled the garden **hose** when I was done watering the flowers in the yard.*
▸ **pipe**   a usually rigid tube that a liquid or gas can flow through: *Our water **pipes** froze last winter.*
▸ **shaft**   a long, narrow, vertical passage or opening, as one that goes into a mine: *The mine's main **shaft** was lined with timbers.*
▸ **straw**   a thin tube made of paper or plastic through which a person can drink a liquid: *I drank my soda through a **straw**.*

tug *verb*   to pull at something strongly or move something by pulling strongly: *see* **pull**

tumble *verb*   to fall suddenly: *see* **fall**

tumbler *noun*   a drinking glass having no handle or stem: *see* **glass**

tummy *noun* (informal)   the human stomach or belly: *see* **stomach**

tumult *noun*   noise and commotion: *see* **commotion**

tune *noun*   a melody, especially one that is simple and easy to remember: *see* **song**

tunnel *noun*   an underground or underwater passage: *see* **hall**

turmoil *noun*   a state of extreme confusion, emotional disturbance, or excitement: *see* **confusion**

turn *verb*   to move or cause something to move around a center: *see* **spin**

turn down *verb*   to refuse to accept something: *see* **reject**

turret *noun*   a small, usually round tower on a building: *see* **tower**

tutor *verb*   to give individual instruction to a student: *see* **teach**

tutor *noun*   a private instructor who gives additional, special, or remedial instruction: *see* **teacher**

twilight *noun*   the time of day when the sun is just below the horizon, but there is still a little light left in the sky: *see* **sunset**

twine *noun*   a strong cord or string, as of cotton or hemp: *see* **string**

twinge *noun*   ▷ a sudden but temporary physical pain ▷ a brief, sharp feeling of something unpleasant: *see* **pain**

twinkle *verb*   to shine with slight, quick flashes of light: *see* **shine**

twirl *verb*   to rotate or spin something quickly: *see* **spin**

twitch *noun*   an involuntary jerk or spasm of a muscle: *see* **cramp**

twosome *noun*   two people associated with each other: *see* **pair**

type *noun*   a group or class sharing common traits or characteristics: *see* **kind**[2]

typhoon *noun*   a tropical hurricane occurring in the western Pacific Ocean: *see* **storm**

typical *adjective*   showing the common characteristics that identify a group, kind, or class: *see* **normal**

typically *adverb*   as a usual routine: *see* **often**

tyrant

noun a ruler who exercises power in a harsh, cruel manner: *The **tyrant** was overthrown by the people.*

▸ **autocrat** a person with unlimited power or authority: *Our boss sometimes acts like an **autocrat**.*

▸ **despot** a ruler with absolute power, especially one who rules oppressively: *Nero was a cruel Roman **despot** who thought of himself as an actor and musician.*

▸ **dictator** a usually unelected ruler who has great power and often governs a country in a cruel or unfair way: *Joseph Stalin was the **dictator** of the Soviet Union from 1929 until 1953.*

▸ **overlord** a ruler having power or supremacy over other rulers: *In feudal society, kings were **overlords** to dukes and other noblemen.*

ugly

adjective not pleasing to look at: *I think that purple wallpaper is **ugly**.*

▸ **hideous** very ugly and disgusting: *Some of the insects in this book are **hideous** to look at.*

▸ **homely** not pretty or attractive: *I think bulldogs have **homely** faces.*

▸ **plain** lacking beauty or distinction: *The photograph showed a pioneer woman with a **plain** face and a weary smile.*

▸ **unattractive** not pretty or attractive: *This dull outfit makes me feel **unattractive**.*

ANTONYM **beautiful** being very pleasing to the senses or the mind

ultimately *adverb* after all is done: *see* **eventually**

umpire *noun* a person who rules on plays in sports, such as baseball: *see* **judge**

umpire *verb* to act as an impartial judge, especially in a sport: *see* **negotiate**

unable *adjective* lacking the necessary power, authority, or means to do something: *see* **helpless**

unaccompanied *adjective* being without a companion: *see* **alone**

unattractive *adjective* not pretty or attractive: *see* **ugly**

unaware *adjective* not aware: *see* **ignorant**

unbelievable *adjective* not to be believed in: *see* **incredible**

unbending *adjective* not flexible or yielding: *see* **stubborn**

unbiased *adjective* without strong feelings for or against something: *see* **fair**[1]

uncertain *adjective* not certain: *see* **hesitant**

uncivil *adjective* not using polite manners: *see* **rude**

unclear *adjective* not clearly defined: *see* **vague**

uncommon *adjective* rare or unusual: *see* **rare**

uncomplicated *adjective* not complex or involved: *see* **easy**

uncoordinated *adjective* not able to perform complicated movements or tasks: *see* **awkward**

uncounted *adjective* ▷ not counted ▷ not capable of being counted: *see* **many**

uncover *verb* to remove the cover from something: *see* **open**

uncovered *adjective* having the cover removed: *see* **naked**

undecided *adjective* not yet settled or decided: *see* **hesitant**

under

preposition in or to a lower position or place than something else: *I think there is a mouse **under** the sofa.*

▸ **below** in or to a lower place; lower than something else: *We stood on the bridge and watched the river **below** us.*

▸ **beneath** lower than something else; below: *There is a basement **beneath** our house.*

▸ **underneath** under or below: *My backpack is **underneath** my desk.*

ANTONYM **over** higher than something else

undermine

verb to weaken, injure, or impair something, often slowly or gradually: *Smoking has **undermined** his health.*

▸ **erode** to wear something away or make something gradually disappear: *The river **eroded** the canyon walls over many thousands of years.*

▸ **sabotage** to commit destructive acts in an effort to defeat an enemy or hinder a plan: *When Napoleon invaded Russia, the people* **sabotaged** *his progress by burning their own crops.*

▶ **subvert** to undermine the character, morals, or allegiance of someone: *In the 1950s, many Americans feared that Communism would* **subvert** *the democratic system.*

underneath *preposition* under or below: *see* **under**

understand

verb to have a clear idea of the nature or significance of something; to get the meaning of something: *We* **understood** *electricity better after performing the experiments in the physics lab.*

▶ **apprehend** (formal) to have consciousness of something: *They didn't fully* **apprehend** *the danger they were in until the river swept their boat away.*

▶ **comprehend** to understand something fully: *Do you* **comprehend** *the symbolism in this poem?*

▶ **grasp** to take something into the mind: *I'm not sure I* **grasp** *your idea.*

▶ **know** to have a practical understanding of something: *Do you* **know** *how to ride a horse?*

▶ **perceive** to become aware of something through the senses, especially the senses of sight or hearing: *It is easy to* **perceive** *when she is angry because she glares at everyone.*

▶ **realize** to become fully aware of something: *He was happy when he* **realized** *that she liked him.*

understanding *adjective* showing or having kind, tolerant, or sympathetic feelings: *see* **patient**

understudy *noun* a person trained to do the work of another in case of illness or absence: *see* **substitute**

undertaking *noun* something one decides or agrees to do, especially something difficult or demanding: *see* **project**

undo *verb* to reverse the result or effect of something: *see* **reverse**

undomesticated *adjective* not trained to live with or be of use to human beings: *see* **wild [1]**

undoubtedly *adverb* without any doubt or question: *see* **certainly**

unearth *verb* to bring something up out of the earth: *see* **open**

uneasiness *noun* a feeling of awkwardness or of being unsure: *see* **embarrassment**

uneasy *adjective* worried or nervous about something that might happen: *see* **nervous**

unending *adjective* never coming to an end: *see* **permanent**

uneven *adjective* not level or smooth: *see* **rough**

unexpected *adjective* not expected; coming without warning: *see* **sudden**

unfair

adjective not right, just, or evenhanded: *He felt that the referee made an* **unfair** *call.*

▶ **biased** showing a preference for or a hostile feeling against a person or thing; prejudiced: *Some people think that intelligence tests are culturally* **biased** *toward the middle and upper classes.*

▶ **one-sided** limited to one side or group; not evenhanded: *Her version of what happened is true as far as it goes, but it's* **one-sided**.

▶ **partial** favoring one person or side over another; biased: *The judge in the talent show tried not to be* **partial** *toward the contestants from his own school.*

▶ **prejudiced** biased for or against someone, especially having an irrational dislike of a particular race, religion, or group: *He is* **prejudiced** *against all religions except his own.*

▶ **unjust** not just or fair: *Your anger at him is* **unjust** *because you don't know all the facts.*

ANTONYM **fair** free of bias; just

unfasten *verb* to open something, as by disconnecting it or untying it: *see* **open**

unfasten *verb* to open, unlock, or untie something: *see* **release**

unforeseen *adjective* not known in advance: *see* **sudden**

unforgettable *adjective* not likely to be forgotten: *see* **memorable**

unfriendly *adjective* not friendly; unpleasant or hostile: *see* **mean**[1]

ungenerous *adjective* not willing to give or share: *see* **greedy**

unhappiness *noun* lack of happiness or joy: *see* **sadness**

unhappy *adjective* not happy: *see* **sad**

unhurried *adjective* without hurry; slow and relaxed: *see* **slow**

unhurt *adjective* not hurt or injured: *see* **safe**

uniform *noun* a suit of distinctive clothing worn by members of a group: *see* **clothing**

unimportant

adjective not important or significant; of little meaning or value: *He thinks clothes are* **unimportant** *compared to a person's character.*

▸ **insignificant** of little importance; minor: *The teacher said that the mistakes I made on my test were* **insignificant**.

▸ **petty** small and unimportant; not worth one's concern: *My friend doesn't let* **petty** *problems bother her.*

▸ **trivial** having no lasting importance or value: *Why are you so mad over a* **trivial** *thing like a bad haircut.*

ANTONYM **important** strongly affecting the course of events or the nature of things; significant

uninteresting *adjective* not interesting: *see* **boring**

union *noun* an organization of workers formed to protect and promote their interests: *see* **club**

unique *adjective* being the only one of its kind: *see* **rare**

unit *noun* a single group regarded as a part of a whole: *see* **team**

unite *verb* to bring two or more things together so as to form a whole: *see* **join**

united *adjective* combined into one: *see* **joint**

universal *adjective* relating to or affecting the whole world: *see* **international**

university *noun* a school of higher learning that offers advanced degrees as well as regular undergraduate degrees: *see* **school**

unjust *adjective* not just or fair: *see* **unfair**

unkempt *adjective* not neat or tidy: *see* **messy**

unkind *adjective* not kind or generous: *see* **mean**[1]

unlike *adjective* not like something else: *see* **different**

unlikely *adjective* not having a strong chance of happening: *see* **incredible**

unlimited *adjective* having no limits or bounds: *see* **infinite**

unlock *verb* to open something by undoing a lock: *see* **open**

unmannerly *adjective* having bad manners: *see* **rude**

unnecessary *adjective* not necessary; needless: *see* **useless**

unpleasant

adjective not pleasing to the mind, emotions, or senses: *I have* **unpleasant** *memories of the month I spent in the hospital.*

▸ **disagreeable** not to one's liking; unpleasant or offensive: *Skunks have a strong and* **disagreeable** *odor.*

▸ **objectionable** causing offense or disapproval: *Many people find profanity* **objectionable**.

▸ **offensive** causing anger, displeasure, or resentment: *It is* **offensive** *to hang up on someone in the middle of a conversation.*

ANTONYM **pleasant** giving pleasure; agreeable

unravel *verb* to separate the elements of a mystery or problem: *see* **solve**

unruly *adjective* difficult or impossible to discipline or control: *see* **bad [2]**

unsafe *adjective* not safe: *see* **dangerous**

unsatisfactory *adjective* not satisfactory; inadequate: *see* **bad [1]**

unskilled *adjective* lacking skill or technical training: *see* **inexperienced**

unsophisticated *adjective* inexperienced or naïve: *see* **ignorant**

unstable

adjective having a strong tendency to change; not firm: *The buildings in this area are **unstable** because of the recent earthquake.*

- ▸ **insecure** not sure or certain; doubtful: *We have an **insecure** financial situation now that my mother is out of work.*
- ▸ **precarious** dangerously lacking in security or stability: *The climber stood on a **precarious** ledge.*
- ▸ **unsteady** not steady; shaky: *The toddler walked in an **unsteady** way.*
- ▸ **volatile** tending to change suddenly and rapidly; explosive: *Her **volatile** temper makes her difficult to work with.*
- ▸ **wobbly** tending to wobble; unsteady: *This chair is **wobbly** because one leg is shorter than the others.*

unsteady *adjective* not steady; shaky: *see* **unstable**

unsure *adjective* not sure: *see* **hesitant**

untidy *adjective* not tidy and neat: *see* **messy**

untie *verb* to free an object or person from something that binds or restrains: *see* **release**

untied *adjective* having been loosened or come undone: *see* **loose**

untrue *adjective* contrary to fact: *see* **wrong**

untrustworthy *adjective* not worthy of being trusted: *see* **dishonest**

unused *adjective* never having been used: *see* **original [1]**

unusual *adjective* not usual, common, or ordinary: *see* **rare**

unwell *adjective* being in poor health: *see* **sick**

unwieldy *adjective* difficult to carry or handle because of shape or size: *see* **heavy [1]**

unwilling *adjective* not willing or inclined to do something: *see* **hesitant**

unwind *verb* to become free of anxiety, worry, or tension: *see* **relax**

unwrap *verb* to remove the wrapping from something: *see* **open**

unyielding *adjective* not bending or flexible: *see* **stiff**

up *adverb* from a lower to a higher position: *see* **above**

upheaval *noun* a sudden, violent disruption or upset: *see* **confusion**

uphold *verb* to give support to something: *see* **prove**

upright *adjective* morally respectable: *see* **moral**

uprising *noun* a popular revolt against a government or its policies: *see* **rebellion**

uproar *noun* a condition of noisy excitement and confusion: *see* **noise**

upset *adjective* full of angry or worried feelings: *see* **angry**

urge *verb* to encourage or inspire someone to take action or make an effort: *see* **encourage**

urgent

adjective needing immediate attention: *He received an **urgent** phone call that his wife had gone into labor.*

- ▸ **critical** being in a state of crisis or emergency; full of danger or risk: *The accident victim was in **critical** condition.*
- ▸ **crucial** of the utmost importance; critical: *It is **crucial** that I do well on this exam.*

> **pressing** demanding immediate attention; urgent: *She dealt with the most pressing issues first.*

use

verb to put something into service for a particular purpose: *I am learning to use a computer to pay my bills online.*

> **apply** to put something into action: *He applied the brakes in order to stop the car.*
> **employ** (formal) to make use of something: *Early computers employed vacuum tubes instead of microchips.*
> **operate** to work or run something: *I watched a video on how to operate my new sewing machine.*
> **utilize** to put something into use, especially for a practical purpose: *Automobile makers began to utilize gas engines in the 1880s.*
> **wield** to handle a weapon or tool with skill and ease: *Be careful when you wield that chopping knife.*

useful

adjective being of use or service; helpful: *I have found a dictionary to be very useful in writing papers.*

> **beneficial** producing or promoting a favorable result; helpful: *Ladybugs are considered beneficial insects because they prey on pests like aphids.*
> **convenient** ▷ suited to one's comfort or purpose: *A microwave oven is a convenient way to warm up leftovers.* ▷ close at hand; nearby: *There is a convenient bus stop across the street from our apartment.*
> **handy** readily accessible; convenient: *I like to keep a bottle of drinking water handy.*
> **helpful** providing assistance; useful: *The librarian was very helpful in finding books for my term paper.*

> **portable** carried or moved with ease: *We brought a portable radio to the beach.*
> **practical** capable of being used or put into effect; simple and useful: *A Swiss Army knife is a practical tool.*

useless

adjective being of no use; having no practical value: *A flashlight with no batteries is useless.*

> **futile** having no useful results; hopeless: *It is futile to try to get him to change his habits.*
> **hopeless** offering no hope of success: *I decided it was hopeless for me to make the basketball team.*
> **pointless** having no purpose, sense, or meaning: *It is pointless to argue over who is the better actor.*
> **unnecessary** not necessary; needless: *It is unnecessary to bring anything to the party.*

ANTONYM **useful** being of use; helpful

usher *verb* to escort people to their seats, as in a theater: *see* **escort**

usual *adjective* commonly encountered, experienced, or observed: *see* **normal**

usual *adjective* in accordance with customary or normal practice: *see* **regular**

usually *adverb* ordinarily; in the normal course of events: *see* **often**

utensil *noun* an instrument or container, especially one used in a kitchen: *see* **tool**

utilize *verb* to put something into use, especially for a practical purpose: *see* **use**

utopia *noun* an ideally perfect place, especially in its social, political, or moral aspects: *see* **paradise**

utter *verb* to produce a sound or sounds with the voice: *see* **say**

vacant *adjective*   not currently used, filled, or occupied: *see* **empty**

vacate *verb*   to go away from a place and no longer occupy it: *see* **leave**

vacation

noun   a time of rest from work, school, or other regular activities: *I am going to the Florida Everglades during my Christmas* **vacation**.

- ▸ **furlough**   a vacation or leave of absence from duty, especially one given to soldiers or sailors: *My brother has a 30-day **furlough** before he has to return to his ship.*
- ▸ **holiday**   a day on which general business activity halts in order to celebrate a particular event; a day off: *Veterans Day is a national **holiday** honoring veterans of the U.S. armed services.*
- ▸ **leisure**   free time in which one can do as one pleases: *I enjoy playing cards in my **leisure**.*
- ▸ **recess**   a short period for rest or play, as at a school: *The children ran around the playground during morning **recess**.*
- ▸ **sabbatical**   an academic leave of absence, often with pay, given every seven years: *The professor studied in the Middle East during his **sabbatical**.*

vagrant *noun*   a person with no permanent home or way of earning money: *see* **beggar**

vague

adjective   ▷ not clear or distinct: *He could only give a **vague** description of the person who tried to rob him.*   ▷ not clear in meaning or expression: *The candidate was deliberately **vague** about her position on abortion.*

- ▸ **indefinite**   not clearly defined; not precise: *Her plans for the weekend are **indefinite**.*

- ▸ **obscure**   hard to understand; not easy to see or figure out: *The book was too **obscure** for me to understand.*
- ▸ **unclear**   not clearly stated or defined; not explicit: *The directions to his house were **unclear**.*

vain *adjective*   thinking too highly of one's own appearance, qualities, or achievements: *see* **proud**

valiant *adjective*   courageous and bold in a difficult situation: *see* **brave**

valid *adjective*   supported by facts, evidence, or reason: *see* **true**

validate *verb*   to declare something to be legally true or binding: *see* **prove**

vale *noun* (formal)   a valley: *see* **valley**

valley

noun   a long, narrow area of low land between mountains or hills, often with a river running through it: *We live in a **valley** that has rich farmland.*

- ▸ **canyon**   a deep valley with steep walls on both sides that were formed by running water: *The Colorado River runs through the Grand **Canyon**.*
- ▸ **dale** (formal)   a small valley: *The **dale** was covered in wildflowers.*
- ▸ **gorge**   a deep, narrow passage, as between mountains: *The Columbia River **Gorge** is a popular place for windsurfing.*
- ▸ **ravine**   a narrow, steep-sided valley typically smaller than a gorge: *The **ravine** was overgrown with trees and shrubs.*
- ▸ **vale** (formal)   a valley: *We stood on a hill and looked out over the **vale**.*

valor *noun*   courage and boldness in combat: *see* **courage**

valuable

adjective having great importance or value, especially worth a lot of money: *My watch is not very* **valuable**.

▸ **precious** having very great value: *Gold and silver are considered* **precious** *metals*.

▸ **priceless** of great or inestimable value; beyond price: *This museum has some paintings that are* **priceless**.

▸ **prized** highly valued, esteemed, or treasured: *His stereo and his CD collection are his most* **prized** *possessions*.

▸ **treasured** valued highly, especially for sentimental reasons; cherished: *They have* **treasured** *memories of their honeymoon*.

▸ **valued** considered of great worth or importance; prized: *Good grades are highly* **valued** *in my family*.

value *verb* to believe something to be of great worth or importance: *see* **respect**

valued *adjective* considered to be of great worth or importance: *see* **valuable**

vanish *verb* to disappear without a trace: *see* **fade**

vanity *noun* too much pride in one's looks, ability, or appearance: *see* **pride**

vanquish *verb* to defeat an opponent in a conflict, contest, or competition: *see* **defeat**

vapor *noun* fine particles of matter in the air, such as mist, steam, smoke, or smog: *see* **mist**

variety *noun* a number of different kinds of things within the same group or category: *see* **assortment**

variety *noun* a group that differs in a certain way from other similar groups: *see* **kind²**

various

adjective of different kinds: *This truck comes with* **various** *features, such as air conditioning, power windows, and a CD player.*

▸ **assorted** consisting of a variety of usually related items: *He gave her a box of* **assorted** *chocolates*.

▸ **diverse** differing from others in a general group: *Our class has students from widely* **diverse** *backgrounds*.

▸ **miscellaneous** made up of different things mixed together: *This drawer has* **miscellaneous** *tools in it.*

▸ **mixed** made up of a combination of different things or kinds: *The movie attracted a* **mixed** *audience of all different ages.*

varmint *noun* an animal that is thought of as undesirable, obnoxious, or troublesome: *see* **animal**

vase *noun* an open container used for holding flowers: *see* **bottle**

vast *adjective* very great in size or amount: *see* **wide**

vault *verb* to jump or leap over something, especially with the help of one's hands or a pole: *see* **jump**

vehicle *noun* a device for transporting people or things, especially a motor vehicle: *see* **car**

vehicle *noun* a medium through which something is transmitted, expressed, or accomplished: *see* **method**

veil *verb* to conceal or disguise something behind something else: *see* **hide²**

velvety *adjective* having the soft, smooth texture of velvet: *see* **soft [1]**

vendor *noun* a person who sells something, especially on a small scale: *see* **merchant**

veneration *noun* profound respect or reverence: *see* **worship**

venomous *adjective* containing or producing poison: *see* **fatal**

vent *verb* to give forceful expression to a strong, pent-up emotion: *see* **express**

venture *noun* an undertaking that is dangerous, daring, or of uncertain outcome: *see* **adventure**

verdict *noun* the decision reached by a jury at the end of a trial: *see* **decision**

verify *verb* to prove the truth of something by presenting evidence or testimony: *see* **prove**

versus *preposition* against someone or something in a contest: *see* **against**

verve *noun* energy and enthusiasm in the expression of ideas: *see* **energy**

very

adverb to a high degree: *I would be **very** happy to come to your recital.*

- ▶ **extremely** to an exceptionally high degree; exceedingly: *She is **extremely** interested in going skiing with us this weekend.*
- ▶ **highly** to a high degree; very: *They are a **highly** compatible couple.*
- ▶ **much** to a great degree or extent; very: *We were **much** impressed by his resume.*
- ▶ **quite** to the fullest extent; completely: *I thought her story was **quite** interesting.*

vessel *noun* a hollow container or holder, such as a bowl, pitcher, or jar: *see* **bottle**

veto *verb* to prevent or reject something, especially by executive authority: *see* **forbid**

vex *verb* to irritate or annoy someone: *see* **offend**

vibrate *verb* to move back and forth very rapidly: *see* **shake**

vicinity *noun* the area near or about a place: *see* **area**

vicious *adjective* cruel and mean: *see* **fierce**

victim

noun a person or animal that is harmed, killed, or made to suffer: *Paramedics rushed the accident **victim** to the hospital.*

- ▶ **casualty** a person who is killed or injured in an accident or a battle: *There were over two hundred **casualties** in the train crash.*
- ▶ **prey** an animal hunted or caught by another for food: *The roadrunner is a bird whose **prey** includes snakes and other birds.*
- ▶ **target** someone or something that is criticized, laughed at, or attacked: *Older or weak animals are the primary **target** of wolf packs.*

victory *noun* the defeat of an enemy or opponent: *see* **success**

view

noun ▷ a way of seeing something, as from a particular position: *I had a good **view** of the stage from the second row of seats.* ▷ something seen, especially at a distance: *We paused during our hike to admire the **view** across the valley.*

- ▶ **landscape** an expanse of scenery that can be seen from one place: *The artist painted a summer **landscape** of woods and fields.*
- ▶ **panorama** a view or picture of everything that can be seen over a wide area: *From the top of the skyscraper you get a **panorama** of the city below.*
- ▶ **prospect** (formal) something presented to the eye; a scene: *The balcony in our hotel room has a pleasant **prospect** of the offshore islands.*
- ▶ **scene** a view, especially when thought of as forming a whole: *The snow-covered mountains make a beautiful **scene**.*
- ▶ **sight** something seen or worth seeing: *Our apple tree is a lovely **sight** when it is in full bloom.*
- ▶ **vista** a distant view, especially one seen through an opening: *From the window of my apartment I get a **vista** of the river.*

viewpoint *noun* a way of thinking about something: *see* **opinion**

vigilant *adjective* on the alert, especially against danger: *see* **alert**

vigor *noun* physical or mental energy or strength: *see* **energy**

vigorous *adjective* strong, energetic, and active in mind or body: *see* **healthy**

vile *adjective* hateful and disgusting: *see* **evil**

village *noun* a group of houses that make up a community smaller than a town: *see* **town**

villain

noun a wicked or very bad person: *In old Westerns, the good guys wear white and the **villains** wear black.*

▸ **cad** an unprincipled, unmannered man: *Only a **cad** would say something mean about his date's looks.*

▸ **heel** (informal) a dishonest person; a cad: *I think he's a **heel** because he asked her out but didn't tell her he was married.*

▸ **rascal** a person who is playfully mischievous; a dishonest but likeable person: *My brother is a **rascal** who likes to play tricks on me.*

▸ **rat** (informal) a hateful, sneaky person, especially one who gives out information about the wrongs of friends or associates: *He was a **rat** to tell her what we had said about her.*

▸ **rogue** a person who tricks or cheats others; a scoundrel: *That **rogue** cheated me out of my money!*

▸ **scoundrel** a wicked or dishonorable person: *The **scoundrel** was caught and punished for his crimes.*

vim *noun* liveliness and energy: *see* **energy**

violation *noun* a breaking of the legal code: *see* **crime**

violence *noun* physical force exerted for the purpose of causing damage or injury: *see* **strength**

violent *adjective* physically forceful: *see* **fierce**

virtuous *adjective* having or showing virtue, especially moral excellence: *see* **moral**

visit *verb* (informal) to converse or chat: *see* **talk**

visitor *noun* a person who stays with one as a temporary guest: *see* **guest**

vista *noun* a distant view, especially one seen through an opening: *see* **view**

visual aid *noun* an instructional aid that presents information visually: *see* **chart**

vitality *noun* physical or intellectual vigor: *see* **energy**

vivid *adjective* bright and strong; brilliant: *see* **colorful**

vocation *noun* a profession or occupation, especially one for which a person is particularly suited or qualified: *see* **job**

voice *verb* to make one's outlook or viewpoint known by speaking or writing: *see* **express**

void *adjective* containing no matter: *see* **empty**

volatile *adjective* tending to change suddenly and rapidly: *see* **unstable**

volume *noun* the amount of space something occupies or contains: *see* **amount**

volume *noun* one book in a related set or series of books: *see* **book**

voluntary *adjective* made, done, or acting of one's own free will: *see* **willing**

volunteer *verb* to offer help or a service of one's own free will: *see* **give**

vow *noun* a solemn promise or oath: *see* **promise**

voyage *noun* a long journey to a distant place, made on a ship or airplane: *see* **journey**

W

wad *noun* a small mass of soft material: *see* **chunk**

waft *verb* to move gently through air: *see* **float**

wag *verb* to move or swing something repeatedly: *see* **wave**

wage *noun* payment for work or services: *see* **income**

wager *verb* to risk an amount or possession on an uncertain outcome: *see* **gamble**

wail *verb* to make loud, long crying sounds, especially in grief or protest: *see* **cry**

wait *verb* to stay in a place in expectation of something: *see* **stay**

walk

verb to move on foot at an easy, steady pace: *I walk to school every day.*

- ▶ **amble** to walk or move at a slow, leisurely pace: *The cat ambled through the door as I held it open for him.*
- ▶ **hike** to go on a long walk for pleasure or exercise: *My friend and I like to go hiking through the woods.*
- ▶ **march** to walk with regular and measured steps, often in a group, as soldiers do: *The band marched down the street in perfect formation.*
- ▶ **stride** to walk with long steps: *The graduating seniors strode across the stage to receive their diplomas.*
- ▶ **stroll** to walk in a slow, relaxed way: *The couple strolled around the mall and looked in the store windows.*
- ▶ **strut** to walk with a pompous and self-important bearing; to swagger: *That rooster is always strutting around the chicken yard.*
- ▶ **swagger** to walk with a bold, proud, or defiant manner: *The winning team swaggered off the field.*
- ▶ **trek** to make a slow, hard journey on foot: *The soldiers trekked all day through the swamp.*

wall

noun a solid structure that forms an upright side of a building or room or divides two areas: *I painted my bedroom walls red.*

- ▶ **fence** a structure set up to prevent entry into an area or to mark it off: *Our neighbor put up a tall fence to give her more privacy.*
- ▶ **hedge** a row of shrubs or small trees that are planted closely together to form a fence or boundary: *Fields in Ireland are often divided by thick hedges instead of walls.*
- ▶ **partition** something, such as a partial wall, that divides up a room: *The large office was divided into individual workspaces by partitions.*
- ▶ **screen** a light, movable frame used to divide, hide, or protect: *The nurse put a screen around the hospital bed when the patient was being bathed.*

wander

verb to move from place to place without a special purpose or destination: *We wandered around downtown San Francisco until time for dinner.*

- ▶ **gallivant** to roam about in search of pleasure or amusement: *My sister and her friends like to gallivant on the weekends.*
- ▶ **meander** to move aimlessly and idly without a fixed direction: *I meandered through the flea market to see if anything caught my attention.*
- ▶ **ramble** to walk about casually or for pleasure: *I like to ramble through the park with my dog.*
- ▶ **range** to wander freely over a wide area: *The cattle ranged over the fields.*
- ▶ **roam** to move about freely or restlessly: *The cat roamed from room to room.*
- ▶ **rove** to roam or explore at random, especially over a wide area: *He roved the world in search of adventure.*
- ▶ **stray** to wander beyond an established limit; to become lost: *The shepherd searched for the sheep that had strayed from the flock.*

want

verb to feel a desire or need to have something: *What do you **want** for Hanukkah?*

- ▸ **covet** to wish for something that belongs to another: *I must admit that I **covet** your computer.*
- ▸ **crave** to have an intense desire for something: *She **craved** ice cream when she was pregnant.*
- ▸ **desire** to want something strongly or passionately: *He **desires** to become an architect.*
- ▸ **wish** to want something, especially something impractical or unattainable: *I **wish** we could go to a movie tonight, but I have to work late.*
- ▸ **yearn** to have a strong, often melancholy desire for someone or something: *I **yearn** to visit my homeland.*

war

noun a state of open, armed conflict between nations, states, or parties: *The United States declared **war** on Japan after the bombing of Pearl Harbor.*

- ▸ **battle** an encounter between opposing forces; armed fighting: *The news program showed scenes of the **battle**.*
- ▸ **combat** fighting, especially armed battle: *My cousin received special training in **combat** when he joined the Army.*
- ▸ **conflict** a state of open, often prolonged fighting; a battle or war: *There has been **conflict** in the Middle East for decades.*
- ▸ **skirmish** a minor battle between small forces: *There was a **skirmish** on the border.*
- ▸ **struggle** a great or difficult effort to achieve a goal: *This new drug is a breakthrough in the **struggle** against AIDS.*

wares *noun* items for sale: *see* **merchandise**

warm *adjective* showing friendliness and enthusiasm: *see* **affectionate**

warm *adjective* somewhat hot: *see* **hot**

warn *verb* to make someone aware of present or possible danger: *see* **alert**

warrant *verb* to provide good reason for something: *see* **earn**

wary *adjective* on guard against possible danger: *see* **careful [2]**

wash *verb* to clean something with soap and water: *see* **clean**

waste *noun* worthless or useless material, often left over from a process: *see* **garbage**

wasteland *noun* an empty, usually barren place where few plants or animals can live: *see* **wilderness**

watch *verb* to look at something closely for a period of time: *see* **look**

watchful *adjective* paying close attention to something: *see* **alert**

wave

verb to move something back and forth or up and down: *I **waved** my hand at my friend.*

- ▸ **flap** to move or swing sharply while fixed at one edge or corner: *The flag **flapped** noisily in the wind.*
- ▸ **sway** to swing gently back and forth or from side to side: *The tree branches **swayed** in the breeze.*
- ▸ **swing** to move something back and forth from a central point: *The little boy **swung** his lunch box as he walked to the bus stop.*
- ▸ **wag** to move or swing something repeatedly: *My dog **wags** his tail when he's happy.*

waver *verb* to be uncertain or indecisive: *see* **hesitate**

way *noun* a method, means, or technique: *see* **method**

weak

adjective lacking strength, power, or energy: *My leg was **weak** after being in a cast.*

- ▸ **feeble** woefully lacking in strength, as from old age or illness: *My grandfather is too **feeble** to take care of himself anymore.*

▸ **frail** lacking physical strength or endurance; delicate: *The old woman was frail and in ill health.*

▸ **shaky** unsteady and unsound: *He was shaky from the fever.*

▸ **sickly** tending to become sick easily; having delicate health: *Theodore Roosevelt was a sickly child, but he became stronger through exercise.*

ANTONYM **strong** having much power, energy, or strength

wealth

noun a great amount of money or valuable possessions: *One way people acquire wealth is by investing in stocks of profitable companies.*

▸ **affluence** a plentiful supply of goods or money: *America is known as a nation of affluence.*

▸ **capital** wealth that can be used to produce more wealth: *The company invested some of its capital in new machinery.*

▸ **fortune** a large amount of money or property: *The developer made a fortune in real estate while the market was high.*

▸ **riches** great wealth in the form of money, land, or valuable possessions: *The royal family of Great Britain has great riches.*

wealthy *adjective* having considerable wealth: *see* **rich**

wear out *verb* ▷ to exhaust someone completely ▷ to make something unusable through long or heavy use: *see* **tire**

weary *verb* to become physically or mentally tired: *see* **tire**

weary *adjective* physically or mentally tired: *see* **tired**

wedge *noun* a block of material, such as wood or cheese, that is wide at one end and tapers to a point: *see* **slice**

wee *adjective* (informal) very little; tiny: *see* **small**

weep *verb* to shed tears as an expression of deep emotion: *see* **cry**

weigh *verb* to think about something in great detail in order to make a decision: *see* **consider**

weight *noun* a load or burden: *see* **burden**

weighty *adjective* having great weight: *see* **heavy [1]**

weird *adjective* strikingly odd or unusual: *see* **strange**

welcome *verb* to greet someone with pleasure, hospitality, or special ceremony: *see* **greet**

welfare *noun* help, such as money, that is given to those who are in need: *see* **relief**

well

adverb in a way that is good, proper, satisfactory, or successful: *She sings very well.*

▸ **excellently** in a manner that is excellent: *My teacher said that I did excellently on the final test.*

▸ **fine** very well: *My work is going fine.*

▸ **nicely** in a good, pleasant, or agreeable way: *That blouse goes nicely with your skirt.*

▸ **satisfactorily** well enough; adequately: *The addition on our house is coming along satisfactorily.*

▸ **splendidly** very well; magnificently: *My friends said that I played splendidly at the recital.*

well-fixed *adjective* (informal) financially secure: *see* **rich**

well-heeled *adjective* having plenty of money: *see* **rich**

well-known *adjective* known to many people: *see* **famous**

well-mannered *adjective* having or showing good social behavior: *see* **polite**

well-off *adjective* having enough money to live comfortably: *see* **rich**

well-to-do *adjective* wealthy and prosperous: *see* **rich**

wet

wet

adjective being covered, moistened, or soaked with a liquid, especially water: *We got* **wet** *when it started to rain.*

▸ **damp** slightly wet; moist: *I used a* **damp** *sponge to wipe the kitchen counter.*

▸ **drenched** wet through and through: *The children played in the sprinklers until they were* **drenched**.

▸ **moist** slightly wet; damp: *I put the clothes back in the dryer because they were still* **moist**.

▸ **soaked** completely wet; drenched: *His soccer jersey was* **soaked** *with sweat by the end of the game.*

▸ **soggy** soaked or heavy with moisture: *The towel was* **soggy** *after I used it to soak up the spilled water.*

ANTONYM **dry** free from liquid or moisture; not wet or damp

wetland *noun* a watery lowland area, especially one regarded as a natural habitat: *see* **swamp**

whack *verb* to strike something with a hard blow: *see* **hit**

wharf *noun* a landing facility built along a shore where ships can load or unload: *see* **dock**

wheedle *verb* to persuade someone or get something by using flattery or deceit: *see* **persuade**

wheeze *verb* to breathe with difficulty, producing a hoarse whistling sound: *see* **breathe**

when *conjunction* at the time that: *see* **after**

whiff *noun* a brief, passing odor carried on the air: *see* **smell**

whim *noun* a sudden wish, desire, or idea: *see* **impulse**

whimper *verb* to cry with weak, broken, whining sounds: *see* **moan**

whimsy *noun* creativity that is marked by playfulness and humor: *see* **imagination**

whine *verb* to complain in a childish, annoying way: *see* **complain**

whine *verb* to make a sad, high-pitched sound as in pain or complaint: *see* **moan**

whip *verb* to beat something, such as cream, into a foam: *see* **mix**

whir *verb* to make an airy buzzing or vibrating sound: *see* **hum**

whirl *verb* to run or cause something to turn quickly: *see* **spin**

whisper

verb to speak in a very low, soft voice: *He* **whispered** *to me during the movie.*

▸ **mumble** to speak in an unclear way, as with the lips partly closed: *I can't understand what you're saying because you're* **mumbling**.

▸ **murmur** to speak in a low, quiet voice: *The mother* **murmured** *to her baby.*

▸ **mutter** to speak in a low voice while barely moving one's lips: *The students* **muttered** *in protest when the professor assigned homework over the holidays.*

whitish *adjective* somewhat white: *see* **pale**

whittle *verb* to cut small pieces or shavings from a piece of wood: *see* **carve**

whiz *verb* to move or go past at great speed: *see* **zoom**

whole *adjective* being the entire amount, extent, or duration of something: *see* **all**

wholly *adverb* entirely: *see* **completely**

wicked *adjective* morally bad: *see* **evil**

wide

adjective taking up a large amount of space from side to side: *The easy chair was too* **wide** *to fit through the door.*

▸ **broad** ▷ wide from side to side: *This highway is* **broad** *enough for four lanes of traffic.* ▷ large in size, extent, or scope: *The teacher said that my essay topic was too* **broad**.

▸ **extensive** large in quantity, area, or range: *We drove though* **extensive** *desert lands on the way to California.*

▸ **spacious** having much space; roomy: *Our new home is more* **spacious** *than our old one.*

▸ **vast** very great in size or amount; very great in area or extent: *The ship was soon lost to view on the* **vast** *ocean.*

ANTONYM **narrow** small or slender in width

widen *verb* to make something wide or wider: *see* **stretch**

widespread *adjective* existing, happening, or used in many places by many people: *see* **common**

wield *verb* to handle a weapon or tool with skill and ease: *see* **use**

wife *noun* a woman who is married: *see* **spouse**

wild

adjective [1] not grown, cared for, or controlled by people: *I like to explore places that are* **wild**.

▸ **native** originating, growing, or produced in a certain place or region: *My neighbor has a garden of plants that are* **native** *to our state.*

▸ **natural** found in or produced by nature; not artificial or man-made: *This soup is made with all* **natural** *ingredients.*

▸ **primitive** ▷ relating to forces of nature; elemental: *The expedition spent two months in the* **primitive** *jungles of the Amazon basin.* ▷ simple and crude; not sophisticated: *The shipwrecked sailors survived the winter by building* **primitive** *huts of earth and stone.*

▸ **undomesticated** not trained to live with or be of use to human beings; wild: *Lions and tigers are* **undomesticated** *animals.*

ANTONYM **tame** accustomed to living or trained to live with human beings

wild

adjective [2] having or showing no discipline or control: *Nobody can control that boy's* **wild** *behavior.*

▸ **desperate** reckless or violent because of despair: *The* **desperate** *man rushed his child to the hospital when she fell out of a tree.*

▸ **rash** said or done with too little thought; foolish: *It was* **rash** *of me to buy a new stereo before checking my budget.*

▸ **reckless** not careful or cautious: *The police officer arrested the* **reckless** *driver.*

▸ **lawless** disregarding or violating the law: *The mayor promised to rid the city of* **lawless** *street gangs.*

wilderness

noun an unsettled, uncultivated region that has been left in its natural condition: *The national parks were created to preserve areas of scenic* **wilderness** *from development.*

▸ **desert** a dry area, often covered with sand, in which few plants or animals live: *I love the open spaces of the* **desert**.

▸ **forest** a dense growth of trees covering a large area: *There are mountain lions in the* **forest** *near my home.*

▸ **jungle** a very heavy growth of tropical trees and plants: *The Mayans built great cities that were later abandoned and overgrown by* **jungle**.

▸ **wasteland** an empty, usually barren place, such as a desert, where few plants or animals can live: *The empty mine and all the area around it is now a polluted* **wasteland**.

will

noun strong purpose; determination: *Athletes must have a strong* **will** *in order to make it to the Olympics.*

▸ **ambition** a strong desire to achieve something: *My* **ambition** *is to graduate from college with a business degree.*

▸ **determination** firmness of purpose; resolve: *I admire his* **determination** *to learn another language.*

▸ **discipline** controlled behavior resulting from training of the mind, body, or character; self-control: *It takes discipline to get up every morning and go to the gym.*

▸ **drive** a strong motivation that prompts activity; aggressiveness: *He is the top salesman in the department because he has so much drive.*

▸ **initiative** the ability to begin or carry out a task or plan: *The woman who founded Mothers Against Drunk Driving had a lot of initiative.*

▸ **persistence** the quality of refusing to give up or let go: *It takes patience and persistence to train a horse to do circus tricks.*

▸ **resolve** firmness of purpose; resolution: *I am serious in my resolve to eat healthier foods.*

willfully *adverb* with stubborn insistence: *see* **deliberately**

willing

adjective acting or ready to act: *Would you be willing to go to the library with me?*

▸ **agreeable** willing to agree or say yes: *Are you agreeable to going to San Antonio for a vacation?*

▸ **cooperative** willing to help or work with others for a common purpose: *I like to work with her because she is cooperative.*

▸ **ready** feeling in the mood to do something; willing: *I'm ready to go home whenever you are.*

▸ **voluntary** made, done, or acting of one's own free will: *The teacher said that doing the extra assignment was voluntary.*

ANTONYM **unwilling** not willing; hesitant or reluctant

wilt *verb* to become limp: *see* **droop**

wily *adjective* full of plans and tricks intended to deceive others: *see* **crafty**

win *noun* a victory in a contest or sport: *see* **success**

wince

verb to squeeze the eyes and hunch the shoulders, as in pain, embarrassment, or distress: *I winced when I stubbed my toe.*

▸ **cringe** to draw back in fear: *The dog cringed when the man shouted at it.*

▸ **flinch** to shrink or jerk back suddenly, as from surprise or pain: *She flinched at the sudden burst of loud music.*

▸ **recoil** to draw back in fear or disgust: *I recoiled when I opened the refrigerator and smelled the rotten leftovers.*

wind

noun air that is in motion: *The autumn wind blew through the trees and sent the leaves sailing to the ground.*

▸ **breeze** a light, gentle wind: *There is just enough of a breeze to keep us cool.*

▸ **draft** a current of air: *He closed the window to stop the cold draft.*

▸ **gust** a sudden, strong rush of wind: *A gust of wind blew the hat off my head.*

wink *noun* a quick opening and closing of one eye, especially to indicate approval: *see* **signal**

wipe *verb* to rub something with cloth or paper in order to clean or dry it: *see* **clean**

wire *noun* a thin, flexible metal strand: *see* **rope**

wisdom

noun understanding of what is true, right, or of lasting importance: *That class introduced me to the wisdom of Eastern philosophy.*

▸ **common sense** good judgment gained from everyday experience: *Common sense tells you not to try to pat a growling dog.*

▸ **intelligence** the ability to learn, think, and understand: *It takes a lot of intelligence to run a successful business.*

wise

adjective having or showing intelligence and good judgment: *I'm not sure if it was wise to sign up for so many classes this semester.*

▶ **logical** able to reason clearly and rationally: *You need a **logical** mind to write a computer program.*

▶ **prudent** having or showing caution and good sense; sensible: *It is **prudent** to lock your car door.*

▶ **rational** having the ability to think things through: *It is hard to remain **rational** when I am angry.*

▶ **reasonable** showing good judgment or common sense: *The **reasonable** thing to do is to talk over our differences and try to reach a compromise.*

▶ **sane** having or showing good judgment; sensible: *I talk to my father when I need **sane** advice.*

▶ **sensible** showing good judgment; reasonable: *It is **sensible** to get a good night's sleep when you have a test the next day.*

wish *verb* to have or feel a desire for something: *see* **hope**

wish *verb* to want something, especially something impractical or unattainable: *see* **want**

wistful *adjective* full of wishful yearning: *see* **sad**

withdraw *verb* to move to another, usually quieter or more private place: *see* **leave**

wither *verb* to dry up or shrivel from or as if from loss of moisture: *see* **fade**

withhold *verb* to refrain from giving, granting, or permitting something: *see* **deprive**

within *preposition* inside the limits or extent of something: *see* **in**

witness *verb* to see or have personal knowledge of something: *see* **look**

witty *adjective* expressing amusing insights: *see* **funny**

wobble *verb* to move unsteadily from side to side: *see* **shake**

wobbly *adjective* tending to wobble: *see* **unstable**

wolf *verb* to eat something quickly, hungrily, or greedily: *see* **eat**

woman

noun an adult female human being: *My English teacher is a **woman**.*

▶ **female** a female person, animal, plant, or plant part: *My cat is a **female**.*

▶ **lady** a girl or woman, especially one who has polite manners: *My parents taught me that a **lady** is courteous to others.*

▶ **maiden** an unmarried girl or young woman: *That song is about a young **maiden** who follows her true love to war.*

wonder

noun something very unusual or remarkable; a marvel: *The Grand Canyon in Arizona is considered one of the **wonders** of the natural world.*

▶ **marvel** someone or something that causes surprise, astonishment, or wonder: *The Sphinx is one of the **marvels** of ancient Egypt.*

▶ **miracle** an event that seems impossible because it cannot be explained by the laws of nature: *His quick recovery from the serious illness was considered a **miracle**.*

▶ **phenomenon** a person or thing that is remarkable or outstanding: *Mozart was a musical **phenomenon** by the age of six.*

wonderful

adjective causing a feeling of amazement, admiration, or delight: *She had a **wonderful** experience on her trip to Alaska.*

▶ **extraordinary** beyond what is ordinary; very unusual: *He has an **extraordinary** memory for historical facts.*

▶ **fantastic** excellent; superb: *You look **fantastic**!*

▶ **glorious** ▷ deserving great honor, praise, and fame: *I like reading about the **glorious** civilizations of Egypt, Greece, and Rome.* ▷ having great beauty; magnificent: *We watched a **glorious** sunset of red, gold, and purple.*

▶ **marvelous** of the highest or best kind or quality: *We had a **marvelous** time on our vacation.*

▸ **remarkable** attracting notice as being unusual or extraordinary: *He made remarkable improvement in school this year.*

▸ **splendid** of great beauty or quality; excellent: *The committee did a splendid job of organizing the awards ceremony.*

ANTONYM **horrible** dreadful; very unpleasant

woo *verb* to seek someone's affection, especially with the intent of romantic involvement: *see* **romance**

wood

noun the hard material beneath the bark of trees and shrubs that makes up the trunk and branches: *The white ash tree has hard wood that is good for making baseball bats.*

▸ **board** a piece of lumber that has more length and width than thickness; a plank: *I made a bookcase out of bricks and boards.*

▸ **lumber** timber that has been sawed into boards and planks: *The construction site had large stacks of lumber.*

▸ **plank** a long board: *He put a plank across the stream to use as a bridge.*

▸ **slat** a narrow strip of metal, plastic, or wood: *I cleaned the slats on the miniblinds.*

▸ **timber** trees or land covered with trees: *The forester walked through the timber and indicated which trees were to be cut down.*

word *noun* a spoken assurance or a promise: *see* **promise**

word *noun* a spoken sound that communicates a meaning; a written form of such a sound: *see* **term**

work

noun the physical or mental effort that is required to do something; labor: *It took a lot of work to paint our whole house.*

▸ **drudgery** hard, boring, or unpleasant work: *To me, housework is pure drudgery.*

▸ **effort** the use of physical or mental energy to do something: *It takes a lot of effort to learn another language.*

▸ **exertion** the act of making a great effort to do something: *I was tired after the exertion of the aerobics class.*

▸ **labor** hard work: *It took a lot of physical labor to build the addition onto our house.*

▸ **toil** exhausting labor or effort: *The workers were weary from their toil.*

workable *adjective* capable of being put into operation: *see* **possible**

workbook *noun* a booklet containing exercises and problems that a student may do directly on the pages: *see* **book**

worker *noun* one who does manual or industrial labor: *see* **employee**

work out *verb* to engage in strenuous exercise so as to prepare for an athletic competition or to improve one's physical fitness: *see* **practice**

workshop *noun* a place where manual or light industrial work is done: *see* **factory**

world *noun* the earth and all its people: *see* **earth [1]**

worldwide *adjective* involving or extending throughout the entire world: *see* **international**

worn-out *adjective* no longer usable or in good condition: *see* **ragged**

worn-out *adjective* extremely tired: *see* **tired**

worried *adjective* uneasy or concerned about something: *see* **nervous**

worry

noun an uneasy feeling that something bad might happen: *I felt a lot of worry when my father went in for heart surgery.*

▸ **anxiety** a feeling of uneasiness and distress about something in the future: *I have a lot of anxiety about tomorrow's history test.*

▸ **care** worry or stress caused by one's responsibilities: *The woman had many financial cares trying to raise a family on a single income.*

▸ **concern** something that causes one to feel troubled or anxious: *One of the school board's main concerns is keeping students in school until they graduate.*

▸ **pressure** a burden that causes distress; strain: *My last job had too much pressure.*

▸ **strain** a severe demand on one's body, mind, or resources: *The cost of my sister's college tuition put a strain on our family budget.*

▸ **stress** physical or mental pressure: *Meditation has been proven to reduce stress.*

worship

noun religious ceremonies and prayers: *The members of the church gather several times a week for worship.*

▸ **devotion** passionate attachment to a person, cause, or deity: *She tutors children in reading out of her devotion to the cause of literacy.*

▸ **piety** religious devotion and reverence to God: *Our rabbi is a great example of piety.*

▸ **reverence** a feeling of awe and respect mixed with love: *It is appropriate to display reverence when in a house of worship.*

▸ **veneration** profound respect or reverence: *Great political leaders often inspire veneration in their followers.*

worthwhile *adjective* worth the time, effort, or cost involved: *see* **good**

wound *verb* to hurt a person or animal by cutting or breaking the body: *see* **hurt**

wrap

verb to cover something with a material such as cloth or paper: *She wrapped the birthday present in pretty paper.*

▸ **encase** to enclose something in or as if in a case: *I bought a piece of amber with an insect encased in it.*

▸ **enfold** (formal) to cover something with or as if with folds of material: *The father enfolded the sleepy baby in a blanket.*

▸ **envelop** to enclose or surround something completely with or as if with a cover-

ing: *The huge nightgown enveloped her from head to foot.*

▸ **gift-wrap** to wrap something as a gift with fancy paper, ribbon, or other trimmings: *The store clerk offered to gift-wrap my purchase.*

▸ **sheathe** to provide something with a protective covering: *The antique sword was sheathed in a jeweled scabbard.*

▸ **surround** to shut in or enclose something on all sides: *We walked into the forest until the trees completely surrounded us.*

ANTONYM **uncover** to remove a cover from something

wrap up *verb* to settle something finally or successfully: *see* **finish**

wrath *noun* (formal) violent, vengeful anger: *see* **anger**

wreck *noun* a serious or destructive collision: *see* **accident**

wreck *verb* to damage something badly or beyond repair: *see* **destroy**

wretched *adjective* very unhappy or distressed: *see* **sad**

wrinkle *noun* a small fold or crease on a normally smooth surface: *see* **fold**

write

verb to put something down in words: *I have to write an essay for my English class.*

▸ **author** to write something such as a book or play, especially for publication: *Samuel Clemens authored his books under the pen name "Mark Twain."*

▸ **autograph** to write one's signature in or on something: *The basketball player autographed my T-shirt for me.*

▸ **compose** to create a musical or literary work: *I have composed several songs to play on the guitar.*

▸ **inscribe** to write, print, carve, or engrave something: *She inscribed her name in her textbook.*

▸ **jot** to write something down quickly or in a short form: *I jotted down a list of things I needed to buy at the market.*

▸ **pen** to write or compose something with or as if with a pen: *He **penned** a letter to his girlfriend.*

▸ **scrawl** to write something quickly or in a messy way: *My boss **scrawled** his name at the end of the letter.*

▸ **scribble** to write or draw something quickly or carelessly: *My niece likes to **scribble** with her crayons.*

writer

noun one who writes, especially as an occupation: *The **writer** sent his manuscript to the publisher.*

▸ **author** the creator of an original literary work, such as a novel, poem, short story, or essay: *The children's **author** has won many awards for her books.*

▸ **journalist** one who writes for a newspaper or magazine: *Thomas Friedman is a **journalist** who writes a regular column.*

▸ **novelist** one who writes lengthy works of fiction: *Nora Roberts is a well-known romance **novelist**.*

▸ **poet** one who writes poems: *Wyslawa Zsymborska is my favorite **poet**.*

wrong

adjective not conforming with fact or truth; not correct: *You put the **wrong** Zip Code on all these letters.*

▸ **erroneous** containing error or developed from error: *Your information is wrong, which has led you to an **erroneous** conclusion.*

▸ **false** contrary to fact or truth; based on mistaken or untrue information: *He used a **false** passport to get into the country.*

▸ **incorrect** not correct: *I had three **incorrect** answers on the test.*

▸ **mistaken** wrong or incorrect in opinion, understanding, or perception; based on error: *I thought I heard someone at the door, but I was **mistaken**.*

▸ **untrue** contrary to fact; false: *The report in the newspaper was **untrue**.*

ANTONYM **right** being correct, just, moral, or true

yank *verb*   to pull something with a sudden, sharp movement: *see* **pull**

yard *noun*   a piece of ground associated with a building: *see* **park**

yarn *noun*   soft fibers twisted into long strands for use in weaving or knitting: *see* **string**

yawn *verb*   to open the mouth wide with a deep inward breath, as when sleepy or bored: *see* **breathe**

yearn *verb*   to have a strong, often melancholy desire for something or someone: *see* **want**

yell *verb*   to shout or cry out very loudly: *see* **shout**

yelp *noun*   a short, sharp bark or cry: *see* **bark**

yet *adverb*   at this time: *see* **anyway**

yet *conjunction*   nevertheless; despite this: *see* **but**

yield *verb*   to give or surrender something to another: *see* **resign**

youngster *noun*   a child or young person: *see* **child**

youth *noun*   a young person, especially a young male in late adolescence: *see* **teenager**

Z

zany *adjective*   comical in an exaggerated or ridiculous way: *see* **silly**

zeal *noun*   enthusiastic devotion to a cause ideal, or goal: *see* **enthusiasm**

zenith *noun*   the highest point or most advanced degree of something: *see* **prime**

zest *noun*   added flavor or interest: *see* **flavor**

zesty *adjective*   having extra flavor or interest: *see* **tasty**

zip *noun*   high energy or spirit: *see* **energy**

zip *verb*   to move with great speed or energy: *see* **zoom**

zone *noun*   an area or region set off from another by a special characteristic or use: *see* **area**

zoom

verb   to climb suddenly and sharply; to move rapidly: *The small plane **zoomed** into the sky after takeoff.*

▶ **dart**   to move suddenly and swiftly: *The little boy **darted** away from his mother.*

▶ **dash**   to move with sudden speed: *I **dashed** across campus when I realized I was late to my next class.*

▶ **scamper**   to run or go quickly or lightly: *The squirrel **scampered** up the telephone pole.*

▶ **whiz**   to move or go past at great speed: *The cars **whizzed** around the racetrack.*

▶ **zip**   to move with great speed or energy: *The cyclists **zipped** around the corner.*

IRREGULAR ENGLISH VERBS

Most English verbs form their past tense and past participle simply by adding *–ed*, as in the following example:

bake My mother is teaching me to *bake* bread.
  baked Yesterday I *baked* a loaf of sourdough bread.
  baked I have *baked* many different kinds of bread using my mother's recipes.

However, some English verbs do not follow this pattern but instead form their past tenses and past participles irregularly. The following list includes the most common irregular English verbs along with example sentences showing idiomatic usage of past tenses and past participles.

arise What time did you *arise* this morning?
  arose I *arose* at seven o'clock.
  arisen You should have *arisen* at six o'clock to get ready on time.

awake What time did you *awake* this morning?
  awoke I *awoke* at five o'clock, but I went back to sleep.
  awoken I was *awoken* by the sound of the garbage truck.

be I'll *be* at home this afternoon. A couple of my friends will *be* there too.
  was, were I *was* at the movies last night, but my friends *were* at a party.
  been I've *been* at home since three o'clock. My friends have *been* here with me all afternoon.

bear I can hardly *bear* the sorrow of her death.
  bore He *bore* his burden with quiet strength.
  borne My father has *borne* many responsibilities during his life.

beat I need to *beat* the rug to get the dirt out of it.
  beat Clouds of dust rose when I *beat* it.
  beaten The rug had not been *beaten* for a long time.

begin When did you *begin* your homework?
  began I *began* my homework an hour ago.
  begun If I had *begun* my homework earlier, I would be finished by now.

bend These spoons are easy to *bend*.
  bent I *bent* this one when I accidentally stepped on it.
  bent I have *bent* the spoon back into its proper shape.

bet I *bet* this horse will win the race today.
  bet I *bet* 20 dollars on that horse last week.
  bet I should have *bet* on a different horse, because that one lost.

bid It's fun to *bid* on items at an auction.
  bid She *bid* 15 dollars for a gold picture frame.

bid She would have *bid* more, but that's all the money she had with her.

bind Please help me *bind* this package.
  bound You *bound* the string around your finger.
  bound I could have *bound* the package better by myself.

bite This kind of dog does not usually *bite* people.
  bit The mail carrier said our dog *bit* her yesterday.
  bitten I think she was *bitten* by our neighbor's dog, not ours.

bleed Dry air sometimes makes my nose *bleed*.
  bled My nose *bled* a lot when we first moved into this apartment.
  bled It has not *bled* as much since we got a humidifier.

blow You will *blow* a fuse if you plug one more thing into the socket.
  blew See! You *blew* a fuse!
  blown How many fuses have you *blown* this week?

break Did you *break* this dish?
  broke Yes, I *broke* it when I dropped it in the sink.
  broken That's the third dish you have *broken* this month!

breed I used to *breed* rabbits.
  bred Last year each rabbit I *bred* had ten babies.
  bred This year I have not *bred* any rabbits.

bring He said he will *bring* potato salad to the picnic on Sunday.
  brought He *brought* potato salad to our last picnic.
  brought He has *brought* potato salad to every picnic we have ever had.

build He is going to *build* a patio deck.
  built He *built* it with leftover lumber from his last project.
  built I think he should have *built* it with brick.

buy I stopped by the bookstore to *buy* a book.
  bought I *bought* the new book by my favorite author.
  bought I have *bought* all the books that this author has written.

cast It's time to *cast* our ballots for the president of our organization.
  cast He *cast* his ballot for his friend Alicia.
  cast When all the ballots had been *cast*, Alicia was the winner.

catch My son likes to *catch* fish.
  caught He *caught* a lot of fish last week.
  caught He threw back most of the fish that he had *caught*.

choose I always *choose* yellow because it is my favorite color.
  chose I *chose* to buy a yellow car.
  chosen Would you have *chosen* a yellow car?

cling They told me to *cling* on tight when the roller coaster goes around the curve.
  clung I *clung* on with all my strength.
  clung I had *clung* on so tight that my fingers were white.

come I asked my friend to *come* to my house for dinner.
  came My friend *came* for dinner on Thursday.
  come My friend had *come* on the wrong night, so we went out for hamburgers instead.

cost The toys in this store *cost* a lot of money.
  cost They *cost* less last week when the store had a sale.
  cost I would have bought this toy today if it had still *cost* what it did last week.

creep We watched the cat *creep* toward the bird.
  crept It *crept* closer and closer to the bird.
  crept The bird flew away when the cat had *crept* too close.

cut I went to the barber to *cut* my hair.
  cut The barber *cut* my hair too short.
  cut I wish I had had my hair *cut* somewhere else.

deal It's your turn to *deal* the cards.
  dealt You *dealt* me a terrible hand.
  dealt Are you sure you have *dealt* all the cards?

dig The neighbor's dog likes to *dig*.
  dug He *dug* a hole under the fence.
  dug Look at all the holes he has *dug* in my yard!

dive My little niece asked us to watch her *dive* into the pool.
  dived (or **dove**) She *dived* (or *dove*) into the pool with a big splash.
  dived We looked as if we had *dived* into the pool, too.

do Can you *do* this arithmetic problem?
  did I *did* the problem easily.
  done I have *done* problems much harder than that.

draw My nephew likes to *draw* cars.
  drew He *drew* cars all over his school assignments.
  drawn He has *drawn* even more cars since I gave him a package of drawing paper.

dream My friend *dreams* almost every night.
  dreamed (or **dreamt**) Every day he tells me what he *dreamed* (or *dreamt*) the night before.
  dreamed (or **dreamt**) I have often *dreamed* (or *dreamt*) of the day when he would talk about something else.

drink My friend says I should *drink* more water.
  drank I *drank* five glasses of water today.
  drunk My friend says I should have *drunk* at least three more glasses.

drive They *drive* to the city every Saturday to go shopping.
  drove They *drove* 50 miles to reach the city.
  driven In one year they have *driven* more than 5,000 miles to do their Saturday shopping.

eat Would you like something to *eat*?
  ate I *ate* a big dinner just a little while ago.
  eaten I think I have *eaten* quite enough for today.

fall He heard something *fall*.
  fell A tree *fell* down right in front of his house.
  fallen It would have been worse if it had *fallen* on his car.

feed The farmer *feeds* his cows twice a day.
  fed He *fed* them this morning.
  fed He has *fed* them early this evening so he can go out with his wife.

feel She often *feels* happy.
  felt She *felt* happy today.
  felt She has *felt* happy all week.

fight I am going to *fight* this traffic ticket.
  fought I had to pay a fine even though I *fought* the ticket.
  fought If I hadn't *fought* it I would have had to pay a bigger fine.

find What did you *find* when you cleaned the basement?
  found I *found* a bag full of money.
  found I wish I had *found* real money instead of play money.

flee We watched the deer *flee* as we approached.
  fled Three does and two fawns *fled* into the woods.
  fled They had already *fled* by the time we got our cameras out.

fling She saw the little boy *fling* the rock into the lake.
  flung He *flung* it as far as he could.
  flung He was proud of how far he had *flung* the rock.

fly I saw the birds *fly* into the yard.
  flew One of the birds *flew* in the open window.
  flown It had *flown* in the window and out the door before I realized what was happening.

freeze Is it going to *freeze* tonight?
  froze It *froze* last night.
  frozen The roses would have *frozen*, but I covered them with straw.

get Would you *get* a pizza on your way home from work?
  got I *got* a pizza last night.
  gotten (or **got**) In fact, I have *gotten* (or *got*) a pizza every night this week.

give I want to *give* you something special for your birthday.

gave You *gave* me a beautiful present for my last birthday.
given I have *given* you only a small token of my love for you.

go Where shall we *go* for a vacation this year?
went Well, we *went* to the beach last year.
gone We have *gone* to the beach two years in a row.

grind Will you *grind* some coffee?
ground I *ground* some just a few minutes ago.
ground That's funny, I thought I would smell it if you had *ground* the coffee.

grow He likes to *grow* vegetables.
grew He *grew* his first vegetables when he was 12 years old.
grown He has *grown* vegetables every year since then.

hang He *hangs* his coat on a hook that is on the back of the door.
hung He *hung* up his coat but it fell off the hook.
hung He had *hung* too many things on the hook.

have Do you *have* 20 dollars that I could borrow?
had I *had* 20 dollars, but I loaned it to my brother.
had I have *had* three people ask to borrow money today.

hear Did you *hear* that noise?
heard I *heard* something strange, but I'm not sure what it is.
heard I have never *heard* anything quite like that before.

hide Did you play *hide* and seek when you were a child?
hid Yes, I always *hid* in unusual places.
hidden (or **hid**) I would have found you wherever you had *hidden* (or *hid*).

hit I hate it when another car *hits* mine in the parking lot.
hit Someone *hit* my car last week while I was grocery shopping.
hit My car had been *hit* in the same place a few months ago.

hold You have to be careful when you *hold* a baby.
held I *held* my brother's new baby on my shoulder last night.
held I had not *held* a baby for a long time before last night.

hurt I try not to *hurt* other people's feelings.
hurt I didn't realize I *hurt* your feelings with that remark.
hurt I wish I hadn't *hurt* your feelings.

keep My grandfather *keeps* his money under the mattress.
kept My grandmother turned the mattress over and found where he *kept* the money.
kept Perhaps he should have *kept* it in the bank.

kneel I have to *kneel* to clean under the bed.
knelt (or **kneeled**) I *knelt* (or *kneeled*) for half an hour before I finished cleaning.
knelt (or **kneeled**) I must have *knelt* (or *kneeled*) too long because now I can't get up.

knit She likes to *knit*.
knit (or **knitted**) She *knit* (or *knitted*) her boyfriend a sweater for his birthday.

knit (or **knitted**) She had *knit* (or *knitted*) him one before, but this one turned out better.

know Did you *know* that Mary and Richard are getting married?
knew I *knew* about that last week.
known I should have *known* that you would hear it first.

lay I usually *lay* my keys on my bureau at night.
laid This morning they weren't where I thought I *laid* them.
laid I had *laid* a handkerchief over them and couldn't see them.

lead We asked him to *lead* because he was familiar with the area.
led He *led* us over very rough ground for three hours.
led When we complained he told us that he had *led* us by the shortest route.

leap Can you *leap* across the stream?
leaped (or **leapt**) I *leaped* (or *leapt*) onto a rock in the middle of the stream.
leaped (or **leapt**) I could have *leaped* (or *leapt*) across the stream with one leap.

leave Why did you *leave* the party early?
left I *left* because I wasn't feeling well.
left It was a boring party—I wish I had *left* with you.

lend Will you *lend* me your class notes?
lent I'm sorry, I *lent* them to someone else.
lent I could have *lent* them to you yesterday.

let *Let* me go with you.
let I *let* you go with me last time.
let I shouldn't have *let* you go before, because you are too young.

lie Why don't you *lie* down and take a nap?
lay He *lay* down to rest for a little while.
lain He was so tired, he could have *lain* there all day.

light Please *light* the fire.
lighted (or **lit**) I *lighted* (or *lit*) the fire but it went out.
lighted (or **lit**) I have *lighted* (or *lit*) that fire three times!

lose Did you *lose* something?
lost I *lost* one of my contact lenses.
lost I must have *lost* it somewhere around here.

make I like to *make* things out of wood.
made I *made* a small table for my mother's birthday.
made I have *made* something for everyone in my family.

mean I didn't *mean* to step on your foot.
meant I *meant* to dance with you gracefully.
meant I had *meant* to take dancing lessons before we went dancing.

meet I have to *meet* someone for lunch.
met I never *met* this person before.
met How will you know if you have *met* the right person?

mow My mother asked me to *mow* the lawn.
mowed I *mowed* the lawn five days later.
mowed (or **mown**) I suppose I should have *mowed* (or *mown*) it sooner.

pay How much did you *pay* for that haircut?
    paid How much do you think I *paid* for it?
    paid Whatever you have *paid* for it, it was too much money.

prove What are you trying to *prove* by that silly stunt?
    proved I *proved* I can make you angry, didn't I?
    proved (or **proven**) You have *proved* (or *proven*) that before now.

put I need to *put* oil in the car.
    put I *put* oil in the car just a week ago.
    put I have *put* too much oil in this car and will take it to a mechanic.

quit I decided to *quit* my job today.
    quit I am glad you *quit* that job.
    quit You should have *quit* a long time ago.

read Would you like to *read* this book?
    read Thank you, but I *read* it last week.
    read I have *read* two other books by that author.

rid We decided to *rid* the house of all our useless junk.
    rid We *rid* the attic of junk and started on the basement.
    rid I hope we have not *rid* ourselves of anything we'll want later on.

ride Let's *ride* our bicycles today.
    rode We *rode* for ten miles.
    ridden I am so sore that I wish we hadn't *ridden* so far.

ring I like to hear the wind chimes *ring*.
    rang They *rang* all night during the big wind storm.
    rung They have never *rung* so loud as they did in that storm.

rise They like to get up early and watch the sun *rise*.
    rose It was cloudy when the sun *rose* this morning.
    risen It had *risen* high in the sky before the clouds disappeared.

run Look at that cat *run* through our yard!
    ran It *ran* so fast it hardly seemed to touch the ground.
    run It must have *run* away from our neighbors' dog.

say What did you *say*?
    said I *said* that it's time to stop working.
    said I wish you had *said* that an hour ago!

see Do you *see* those big white birds?
    saw I *saw* them yesterday
    seen Well, I have never *seen* them before.

seek I'm not sure what kind of job to *seek* next.
    sought The last job I *sought* was in the field of data processing.
    sought I should have *sought* advice from a career counselor first.

sell We want to *sell* this old washing machine.
    sold We *sold* it for 50 dollars.
    sold We probably could have *sold* it for more.

send Can you *send* me an employment application by mail?
    sent I *sent* one to you last week.
    sent If you have already *sent* one then you don't need to send another.

set Please *set* the table for dinner.
    set I *set* the table last night.
    set Then you will have *set* the table two nights in a row.

sew I like to *sew* for a hobby.
    sewed I *sewed* so many things that I started selling some of them.
    sewn (or **sewed**) You might say that I have *sewn* (or *sewed*) my way into a new business.

shake Politicians love to *shake* hands.
    shook I *shook* the President's hand at the rally.
    shaken I wonder how many hands the President has *shaken*?

shed Snakes *shed* their skin as they grow bigger.
    shed My corn snake *shed* his skin yesterday.
    shed He has *shed* his skin three times since I got him at the pet store.

shine Please *shine* your flashlight over here.
    shone (or **shined**) I *shone* (or *shined*) the flashlight where she pointed.
    shone (or **shined**) A pair of raccoons scampered away from where I had *shone* (or *shined*) the light.

shoot We go to a firing range to *shoot* guns.
    shot I *shot* at the target six times.
    shot I had *shot* the bull's-eye just one time out of six.

show Will you *show* us what you learned in dance class?
    showed The teacher *showed* me a new step today.
    shown (or **showed**) I haven't *shown* (or *showed*) anyone the new step yet because I'm still learning it.

shrink Hot water often *shrinks* wool garments.
    shrank (or **shrunk**) I *shrank* (or *shrunk*) this sweater by washing it in hot water.
    shrunk I have *shrunk* too many clothes this way.

shut Please *shut* the door.
    shut I *shut* the door when I came in.
    shut Well, you must not have *shut* it tightly.

sing I like to listen to frogs *sing*.
    sang Last night the frogs *sang* so loud we couldn't hear ourselves talk.
    sung I guess we should have just *sung* along with them.

sink Our rowboat will *sink* if we don't fix the hole in it.
    sank (or **sunk**) It *sank* (or *sunk*) almost six inches before we bailed out all the water.
    sunk It would have *sunk* to the bottom if we hadn't rowed to shore and fixed the hole.

sit I hope I get to *sit* down on the bus.
    sat I *sat* in an empty seat when I first got on.
    sat After I had *sat* for a few minutes I gave my seat to a pregnant woman.

slay The knight set out to *slay* the dragon.
    slew He *slew* it with one stroke of his sword.
    slain He had *slain* many dragons before that one.

sleep I *sleep* during the day because I work nights.
    slept I *slept* three hours and got up to go shopping.
    slept Now that I am at work I wish I had *slept* at least three hours more.

slide I watched my suitcase *slide* down the luggage chute.
  slid It *slid* into a big bin.
  slid After all the luggage had *slid* into the bin, it was taken to the airplane.

sling This looks like a good place to *sling* our hammock.
  slung We *slung* the hammock between two trees.
  slung I wish we hadn't *slung* it where there are so many mosquitoes.

slit I used my finger to *slit* open the envelope.
  slit Unfortunately, I *slit* my finger on the sharp edge of the paper.
  slit I should have *slit* the envelope with a letter opener.

sow We *sow* seeds in our garden every year.
  sowed We *sowed* 15 different kinds of vegetables and 12 kinds of flowers this year.
  sown (or **sowed**) That is the most we have *sown* (or *sowed*) in several years.

speak I like to hear her *speak*.
  spoke She *spoke* at the club meeting yesterday.
  spoken She has *spoken* at our club three times now.

speed You will have to *speed* to the hospital to get there in time.
  sped (or **speeded**) He *sped* (or *speeded*) to the hospital so that the baby wouldn't be born in the car.
  sped (or **speeded**) If he had *sped* (or *speeded*) any faster, he probably would have been stopped by the police.

spend How much did you *spend* on that computer?
  spent I *spent* less than I expected.
  spent I would have *spent* twice as much but I got a real bargain.

spin He can *spin* a basketball on the end of his finger.
  spun He *spun* the ball to show me how he did it.
  spun The ball has *spun* for a long time without falling off his finger.

spit It's not polite to *spit* in public.
  spat (or **spit**) It looks like someone *spat* (or *spit*) here on the sidewalk.
  spat (or **spit**) They should not have *spat* (or *spit*) right where people walk.

split The recipe says to *split* the chicken breast in two.
  split I *split* it with a sharp knife.
  split It looks like I have *split* in into unequal pieces.

spread Butter is hard to *spread* when it's cold from the refrigerator.
  spread I warmed the butter first and then *spread* it on my toast.
  spread I have *spread* the butter on my toast, and now I'm going to eat breakfast.

spring I watched the rabbit *spring* into the air.
  sprang (or **sprung**) It *sprang* (or *sprung*) very high.
  sprung It must have *sprung* five feet in the air before it ran away.

stand I don't want to *stand* here and wait for her any longer.
  stood I *stood* in front of this store for an hour.
  stood I have *stood* here so long that the store clerks are getting suspicious.

steal Don't leave your purse where someone might *steal* it.
  stole Someone *stole* my purse last year.
  stolen My purse was *stolen* from my car when I forgot to lock it.

stick I bought my little niece some stickers to *stick* in a book.
  stuck She *stuck* them in all the wrong places.
  stuck She had even *stuck* one on her face.

sting Bees don't usually *sting* unless they're disturbed.
  stung A bee *stung* me last summer when I stepped on it.
  stung Have you ever been *stung* by a bee?

stink What *stinks*?
  stank (or **stunk**) The toilet backed up and *stank* (or *stunk*) up the house.
  stunk It has *stunk* like that all day, but the plumber is coming to fix it.

strew The flower girl was instructed to *strew* the flowers as she walked down the aisle.
  strewed Everyone laughed when she *strewed* the flowers.
  strewn (or **strewed**) She had *strewn* (or *strewed*) flowers on the carpet, on the guests, and on the bride and groom, too.

strike Watch the batter *strike* at the ball.
  struck He *struck* at the ball and missed it.
  struck He missed the ball three times and has *struck* out.

string Let's *string* up these pretty lights.
  strung We *strung* them up outside around the patio.
  strung We have *strung* up so many lights that it looks like a carnival!

strive Our teacher wants us to *strive* to get a perfect score on the test.
  strove (or **strived**) We *strove* (or *strived*) to answer every question correctly.
  striven (or **strived**) Our teacher said he could tell that we had *striven* (or *strived*) to do our best.

swear Do you *swear* to tell the whole truth and nothing but the truth?
  swore The witness *swore* that she would tell the truth.
  sworn She was *sworn* in before giving her testimony.

sweat Our gym instructor says it is good to *sweat* during exercise.
  sweat (or **sweated**) I *sweat* (or *sweated*) a lot because I exercised so hard during class.
  sweat (or **sweated**) I have *sweat* (or *sweated*) completely through my gym clothes.

sweep I need to *sweep* the kitchen floor.
  swept I *swept* the kitchen floor.
  swept I have *swept* the kitchen floor, and now I think I'll mop it.

swell Dried beans *swell* when they absorb liquid.
  swelled The beans used to stuff this fuzzy toy rabbit got wet and *swelled* up.
  swelled (or **swollen**) The fuzzy toy rabbit has *swelled* (or *swollen*) to twice its size.

swim Would you like to *swim* at the beach today?
  swam I *swam* yesterday, but I would like to go again today.
  swum In fact, I have *swum* every day this week.

swing Watch that cowboy *swing* his rope.
  swung He *swung* it in big circles over his head.
  swung He must have *swung* it four or five times before he lassoed the calf.

take Please *take* me fishing with you.
  took He *took* me fishing with him.
  taken The fishing was so bad, I should have *taken* a book.

teach I *teach* school.
  taught I *taught* my students many things during the year.
  taught My students have *taught* me even more than I taught them this year.

tear *Tear* the paper into little pieces.
  tore We *tore* the paper into little pieces and put the pieces into a bucket of water.
  torn We had *torn* the paper to make papier-mâché for an art project.

tell What did you *tell* her?
  told I *told* her that you were secretly in love with her.
  told You should have *told* her that you were crazy!

think Who do you *think* will win the election?
  thought What, you *thought* the election wasn't until next year?
  thought You obviously have not *thought* much about politics lately.

throw Please *throw* that ball to me.
  threw She *threw* the ball to me.
  thrown I didn't catch it because she had *thrown* it too hard.

thrust Please don't *thrust* your elbow in my ribs like that.
  thrust He *thrust* his elbow in my ribs again to get my attention.
  thrust I would have *thrust* him away from me, but we were sitting in a movie theater.

wake *Wake* up! *Wake* up!
  woke (or **waked**) I *woke* (or *waked*) suddenly.
  waked (or **woken**) I would rather have *waked* (or *woken*) to soft music.

wear What are you going to *wear* today?
  wore The same clothes I *wore* yesterday.
  worn You have already *worn* those clothes three days in a row.

weave I like to watch her *weave*.
  wove (or **weaved**) I bought a blanket that she *wove* (or *weaved*).
  woven (or **weaved**) She had *woven* (or *weaved*) ancient Navajo patterns into the blanket.

weep Do you *weep* at sad movies?
  wept I *wept* at the end of the movie "Titanic."
  wept In fact, I've seen "Titanic" five times now and I have *wept* every time.

wet The art teacher told us to *wet* the paper.
  wet (or **wetted**) He carefully *wet* (or *wetted*) the watercolor paper.
  wet (or **wetted**) After he had *wet* (or *wetted*) the paper, he started to paint with watercolors.

win Do you ever *win* when you play the slot machines?
  won Once I *won* five hundred dollars.
  won I have never *won* any money at the slot machines, but I have *won* the lottery.

wind After I buy a skein of yarn I *wind* it into a ball.
  wound I bought yarn last week and *wound* it into a big ball.
  wound The kitten likes to play with yarn that I have *wound* into a ball.

wring *Wring* the water out of the sponge.
  wrung He *wrung* the water out of the sponge and wiped the counter.
  wrung After he had *wrung* out the sponge again he put it away.

write I like to *write* stories.
  wrote I *wrote* stories when I was a child.
  written Have you *written* any stories lately?

IDIOMATIC USE OF PREPOSITIONS

Picking the right preposition to use is generally a matter of idiomatic custom rather than a grammatical rule. It often happens that even words with closely related meanings, such as the verbs *acquiesce, agree,* and *concur,* will use different prepositions in otherwise similar sentences.

The following list contains common English verbs, adjectives, and nouns that regularly appear in combination with certain prepositions. The prepositions listed are the ones most often used with the words in question. Example sentences showing common idiomatic usage are included for every word and every different sense. Note that different contexts and different meanings often require a different preposition, as illustrated in the example sentences.

ability at *or* **with**
I am taking a class to improve my *ability at* public speaking.
His *ability with* numbers is amazing.

abound in *or* **with**
The coastal waters *abound in* (or *with*) fish.

access to
This door is the only *access to* the basement.
You need a password to gain *access to* the company's financial data.

accessible by *or* **to**
The islands are only *accessible by* ferry.
Public buildings are required to be *accessible to* people in wheelchairs.

accompanied by, with, *or* **on**
She was *accompanied by* her husband and children.
The lecture was *accompanied with* (or *by*) slides of South American wildlife.
The singer was *accompanied on* the piano.

account *(v.)* **for** *or* **to**
We need to *account for* the shortage in the cash register.
We will have to *account to* the manager for the cash register shortage.

acquiesce in *or* **to**
The company said it would *acquiesce in* the ruling to pay for the cleanup.
The administration finally *acquiesced to* the protesters' demands.

acquit of
The defendant was *acquitted of* all charges.

adapt for, from, *or* **to**
These textbooks can be easily *adapted for* home schooling.
This movie was *adapted from* a book by the same name.
Cactuses are well *adapted to* desert conditions.

addicted to
Sometimes I worry that I am *addicted to* chocolate.

adequate for, in, *or* **to**
The water supply is no longer *adequate for* the city's growing population.
It is important that your diet be *adequate in* protein.
She worried about having an income *adequate to* her children's needs.

adjacent to
The parking lot is *adjacent to* the stadium.

admit to, into, *or* **of**
You must be 18 years or older to be *admitted to* (or *into*) this dance club.
The problem simply does not *admit of* a solution.

advocate *(n.)* **of** *or* **for; advocate** *(v.)* **for**
They are strong *advocates of* (or *for*) animal rights.
The role of the defense attorney is to *advocate for* the defendant in a trial.

affiliate *(v.)* **with** *or* **to; affiliate** *(n.)* **of**
The local chapter of our club is *affiliated with* (or *to*) the national organization.
The hospital is an *affiliate of* the state university.

affinity for, with, *or* **between**
An elementary school teacher needs a special *affinity for* children.
My *affinity with* (or *for*) animals led me to become a veterinarian.
There is a strong *affinity between* the two friends.

afraid of *or* **for**
Most people are *afraid of* the dark.
The recent layoffs have made many people *afraid for* their jobs.

agree on, with, *or* **to**
Scientists can't seem to *agree on* which foods are good or bad for you.
Do you *agree with* the jury's guilty decision?
The workers *agreed to* the terms of the new contract.

akin to
His writing is somewhat *akin to* Ernest Hemingway's.

alien to
Lying and cheating are *alien to* his character.

ally *(v.)* **with** *or* **to; ally** *(n.)* **of**
France was *allied with* (or *to*) the American Colonies during the Revolutionary War.
The United States was an *ally of* England, France, and the Soviet Union during World War II.

aloof from
The new student kept himself *aloof from* his school-mates at first.

amused by *or* **at**
I am often *amused by* my five-year-old nephew.
I was especially *amused at* (or *by*) what he said at dinner last night.

analogy between, of, to, *or* **with**
The speaker made several *analogies between* sports and business.
She used the *analogy of* a road map to explain how her plan would work.
He described the structure of an atom by *analogy to* (or *with*) the solar system.

angry at, with, about, *or* **over**
I am *angry at* (or *with*) you for not paying your share of the rent.
My mother is angry *about* (or *over*) the amount of junk e-mail she receives.

anxious for, about, *or* **over**
I am *anxious for* summer vacation to begin.
Many people are *anxious about* (or *over*) the problems in the economy.

apprehensive of, about, *or* **for**
I'm a bit *apprehensive of* (or *about*) tomorrow's job interview.
His mother was *apprehensive for* his safety the first time he drove the car by himself.

argue about, over, for, against, *or* **with**
Many married couples *argue about* (or *over*) money.
The council member *argued for* spending more money on public education.
The conservationists *argued against* building a road through the wilderness area.
Don't *argue with* success!

aspire to, toward, *or* **after**
Many people *aspire to* (or *toward*) a better way of life.
The guru encouraged his followers to *aspire after* truth.

assent *(n., v.)* **to**
My parents gave their *assent to* my plan to go away to college next year.
Will you *assent to* the conditions of the loan?

attempt *(n.)* **at**
This is my first *attempt at* making bread.

attest to
Can you *attest to* the truth of his statement?

attuned to
Politicians try to stay *attuned to* the opinions of the voters.

augment by *or* **with**
The library's collection was recently *augmented by* several thousand volumes.
Her Social Security payments were *augmented with* income from several other sources.

averse to
I am *averse to* buying on credit.

aversion to, toward, *or* **for**
He has a strong *aversion to* (or *toward* or *for*) cigarette smoke.

basis of, for, *or* **in**
We made our decision on the *basis of* the information we had at the time.
There is no *basis for* your complaint.
Your prediction has no *basis in* reality.

bid *(v.)* **for** *or* **on**
The senator announced his *bid for* the presidency.
The buyer made a second *bid on* the antique dining table.

blame *(v.)* **for** *or* **on**
Is carbon dioxide to *blame for* global warming?
The coach *blamed* the loss *on* a weak defense.

boast *(v.)* **about** *or* **of**
She's always *boasting about* her grandchildren.
Will you stop *boasting about* (or *of*) all your accomplishments?

capacity of, for, *or* **as**
This container has a *capacity of* two gallons.
He has a wonderful *capacity for* enjoying life.
She was acting in her *capacity as* the senior member of the committee.

capable of
Experiments have shown that baboons are *capable of* abstract thought.

careless about, in, of, *or* **with**
He is *careless about* putting food back in the refrigerator.
She is somewhat *careless in* (or *about* or *of*) her appearance.
I wish you weren't so *careless with* (or *of*) other people's money.
My friend is sometimes *careless of* the consequences of his words.

caution *(v.)* **about** *or* **against**
The police officer *cautioned* the driver *about* her speed.
Experts have *cautioned against* prescribing the new drug until further tests have been done.

center *(v.)* **on, upon, around,** *or* **in**
The discussion *centered on* (or *upon*) the latest economic developments.
Her concern is *centered around* her family.
The fighting was *centered in* the mountains south of the city.

charge *(v.)* **for** *or* **with**
The company doesn't *charge for* shipping on orders over 75 dollars.
The president *charged* the ambassador *with* an important mission.
The defendant was *charged with* manslaughter.
The last scene of the movie was *charged with* suspense.

clear *(adj.)* **of; clear** *(v.)* **from** *or* **of**
Is the room *clear of* tables and chairs?
Please *clear* everything *from* your desks.
We *cleared* our desks *of* everything except pencil and paper.

coincide with
The ad campaign was timed to *coincide with* school graduation.

common to
Researchers have identified a gene that is *common to* most of those who have the disease.

comparable to *or* **with**
This set of encyclopedias is *comparable to* (or *with*) other sets in this price range.

compare with *or* **to**
How do engineers' salaries *compare with* (or *to*) those of other professionals?
Shakespeare *compared* the world *to* a stage.
My singing cannot *compare with* the more advanced students.

compatible with
Do you think science is *compatible with* religion?

complementary to
Alternative medicine is sometimes viewed as *complementary to* conventional medicine rather than opposed to it.

compliment *(n., v.)* **on**
I received a nice *compliment on* the article I wrote for the newspaper.
I want to *compliment* you *on* the wonderful meal you served.

concern *(n., v.)* **about, over, with,** *or* **for**
Environmentalists have expressed their *concern about* (or *over*) climate change.
He chose social work as a career out of a *concern for* others in society.
I helped found the program, but I've had little *concern with* the details of running it.
We are all *concerned for* (or *about*) his health.
Don't be *concerned over* (or *about*) the rumors that have been going around.
I need to be more *concerned with* the day-to-day operation of the project.

concur with *or* **in**
I *concur with* your recommendation.
We *concur in* viewing the situation as extremely serious.

conducive to
It is important for a teacher to create a classroom atmosphere that is *conducive to* learning.

confide in *or* **to**
Sometimes it helps to *confide in* a friend when you are having problems.
I don't feel I can *confide* this secret *to* anyone but you.

conform to *or* **with**
The results of the experiment did not *conform to* my expectations.
Cars and trucks must *conform with* (or *to*) US emission requirements.

consist of *or* **in**
The United States *consists of* 50 separate states.
Aristotle said, "Dignity does not *consist in* possessing honors but in deserving them."

consistent with
To "walk your talk" means to make sure that your actions are *consistent with* your words.

contemporaneous with
The antiwar protests of the 1960s were *contemporaneous with* the height of the Civil Rights movement.

contemporary *(adj.)* **with; contemporary** *(n.)* **of**
Carbon dating showed that the pottery was *contemporary with* early Incan civilization.
Walt Whitman and Frederick Douglass were *contemporaries of* Abraham Lincoln.

contempt for
I have nothing but *contempt for* cheaters.

contemptuous of
Laura's big brother was *contemptuous of* her efforts at chess until she beat him.

contend with, against, *or* **for**
The early pioneers had to *contend with* many dangers in their efforts to settle the frontier.
To *contend against* the forces of nature is as futile as throwing rocks at the sun.
The rival parties *contended for* control of the legislature.

contingent on *or* **upon**
The adoption of the new program is *contingent on* (or *upon*) the availability of funds.

contrary to
Contrary to what most people think, experienced pickpockets do not place their hands all the way into their victims' pockets.

contrast *(n.)* **between, to,** *or* **with; contrast** *(v.)* **with** *or* **to**
The teacher asked me to explain the *contrast between* fission and fusion.
The weather is cool and rainy, in *contrast to* last week's heat wave.
The green of the oasis makes a sharp *contrast with* (or *to*) the browns of the surrounding desert.
When you *contrast* this year's performance *with* (or *to*) last year's, you can see a real improvement.

convict *(v.)* **of**
She was *convicted of* shoplifting.

correspond with *or* **to**
The witness's statement did not *correspond with* (or *to*) his earlier testimony.
The pupil of the eye *corresponds to* the aperture of a camera.
We *corresponded with* each other by letter and e-mail.

culminate in *or* **with**
All their planning and effort *culminated in* a wonderful family reunion.
The show *culminated with* (or *in*) an extravagant dance number.

cure *(n.)* **for; cure** *(v.)* **of**
Many people have tried to find a *cure for* the common cold.
He is completely *cured of* his insomnia.

decide on, upon, for, *or* **against**
We have *decided on* (or *upon*) going to Japan for our vacation.
Did the judge *decide for* the defendant? No, she *decided against* him.

deficient in
Early sailors' diets were often *deficient in* vitamin C.

depend on
I *depend on* my computer for getting my work done efficiently.

deprive of
I don't want to *deprive* you *of* a chance to go to the concert.

derive from
The word "thesaurus" *derives from* a Greek word meaning "treasury."

desire *(n.)* **for**
I was born with a *desire for* travel and adventure.

despair *(v.)* **of**
She *despaired of* ever getting back the money she had loaned.

destined for
These old clothes are *destined for* the thrift shop.

deviate from
The conductor did not want the orchestra to *deviate from* the musical score.

devoid of
My friend liked this book, but I thought it was *devoid of* any interest.

differ from, on, over, as to, *or* **with**
I have many opinions that *differ from* those of my parents.
Scientists and politicians *differ on* (or *over*) the desirability of human cloning.
We have the same goal, but we *differ as to* (or *over*) how to achieve it.
I *differ with* your interpretation of the problem.

different from *or* **than**
How are black bears *different from* grizzly bears?
The neighborhood is *different than* it used to be.

differentiate between, among, *or* **from**
Some people find it hard to *differentiate between* the "b" and the "v" sound.
I am learning to *differentiate among* the various styles of jazz.
I still can't *differentiate one* SUV from another.

disappointed by, with, *or* **in**
We were *disappointed by* (or *with*) the team's poor performance.
They were *disappointed with* (or *in*) the curtains they bought from the catalog.
What makes you think I'm *disappointed in* you?

discourage from
I was *discouraged from* ordering from that company again.

disdain *(n.)* **for**
I have *disdain for* their advertising methods.

disengage from
I'm hoping to *disengage from* active politics for a while.

disgusted with, at, *or* **by**
I was *disgusted with* him for tracking so much mud into the house.
She was *disgusted at* (or *by*) the outcome of the election.
I'm *disgusted by* the mess in your room.

dislike of *or* **for**
She has a *dislike of* (or *for*) fast food restaurants.

disqualify from *or* **for**
He was *disqualified from* the race because of drug use.
She was *disqualified for* active duty because of her knee injury.

dissent *(v., n.)* **from** *or* **against**
Only one senator *dissented from* the majority vote.
A crowd gathered outside the statehouse to *dissent against* the budget cuts.
The judge indicated his *dissent from* the ruling.
The protesters marched in *dissent against* the new policy.

dissimilar to
The food here is *dissimilar to* what I'm used to eating at home.

dissociate from
My brother *dissociated* himself *from* his friends when

he realized they were using drugs.

dissuade from
He tried to *dissuade* her *from* taking a job in another part of the country.

distaste for
He had a *distaste for* the hectic pace of city life.

distinguish from, between, *or* **among**
I can't *distinguish* his handwriting *from* yours.
I have trouble *distinguishing between* prepositions and conjunctions.
Before long she could *distinguish among* the various dialects spoken on the island.

distrustful of
I am *distrustful of* salesmen who offer me something for free.

dote on
Grandparents are known for *doting on* their grandchildren.

eligible for
Full-time students are *eligible for* health care at all university facilities.

embellish with
The beautiful vest was *embellished with* beads.

emigrate from
People have *emigrated from* all over the world to the United States.

empty *(adj., v.)* **of**
The house was *empty of* furniture when we bought it.
I *emptied* the bowl *of* its contents.

enamored of *or* **with**
They are very much *enamored of* (or *with*) each other.
I became *enamored with* (or *of*) playing the guitar when I was quite young.

encroach on *or* **upon**
The weeds are starting to *encroach on* (or *upon*) our vegetable garden.

end *(v.)* **with** *or* **in**
The meal *ended with* coffee and dessert.
Their marriage *ended in* divorce.
Why do all FM radio stations *end in* (or *with*) an odd number?

entrust to *or* **with**
He *entrusted* the letter *to* his best friend.
He *entrusted* his friend *with* delivering the letter.

envious of
I can't help feeling a little *envious of* my brother's athletic skill.

essential *(adj.)* **to** *or* **for; essential** *(n.)* **of**
Vitamins are *essential to* (or *for*) good health.
Good communication skills are *essential for* succeeding at this job.
What do you believe are the *essentials of* a good life?

estrange from
He became *estranged from* his family when he joined a radical political group.

excuse *(v.)* **from** *or* **for**
Please *excuse* me *from* attending the meeting.
Can you ever *excuse* me *for* not remembering your birthday?

expect from *or* **of**
I *expect* an apology *from* you for not sending me an invitation.

We are *expecting* great things *from* (or *of*) the soccer team this year.

They have done everything that could be *expected of* them.

experience *(n.)* **in, with,** *or* **of**

I don't have any *experience in* scuba diving.

Does anyone here have any *experience with* power tools?

My friend has had first-hand *experience of* racism when she was growing up.

expert *(n., adj.)* **in, at,** *or* **with**

She is an *expert in* Chinese pottery.

I'm getting to be an *expert at* removing stains from the rug.

He is an *expert with* the video camera.

He is *expert in* (or *at*) restoring damaged paintings.

The mayor is *expert at* public relations.

She is *expert with* woodworking tools.

fascinated by *or* **with**

We were *fascinated by* the documentary about breaking the color barrier in professional sports.

I was *fascinated with* (or *by*) the idea of starting my own business.

favorable to, toward, *or* **for**

The city council appears to be *favorable toward* the current plan to build a high school in our part of town.

The lawmakers are pushing for a bill *favorable to* (or *toward*) soybean producers.

The article reported that the job market is *favorable for* university students.

fear *(n.)* **of** *or* **for; fear** *(v.)* **for**

She has a *fear of* walking alone after dark.

He insisted that the children wear life vests out of *fear for* their safety.

They *feared for* their lives as the plane went into a dive.

fond of

I am especially *fond of* ripe peaches.

fondness for

He has a *fondness for* babies and small children.

foreign to

Jealousy is *foreign to* her nature.

free *(adj., v.)* **of** *or* **from**

I try to eat only foods that are *free of* (or *from*) artificial preservatives.

The extra income left her *free from* any worries about money.

The treatment helped *free* him *of* (or *from*) his dependence on drugs.

The animal managed to *free* itself *from* the trap.

freedom of *or* **from**

Americans pride themselves on having *freedom of* speech and *freedom from* censorship.

friend of *or* **to**

He's been a *friend of* mine ever since we were little.

Maria has always been a good *friend to* me.

frightened by *or* **at**

The boy was *frightened by* the dog until he got more used to it.

She was *frightened at* (or *by*) the thought of staying by herself while her parents were gone.

grateful to *or* **for**

I am *grateful to* you for listening to me.

They were *grateful for* all their blessings.

grieve for, over, *or* **at**

She still *grieves for* her husband who died two years ago.

He *grieved over* (or *at*) his father's death.

I *grieve at* the thought of your moving away.

hinder from

Please don't *hinder* me *from* doing what I think is right.

hindrance from *or* **to**

She should be allowed to do her job without any *hindrance from* outside forces.

The heavy suitcase was a *hindrance to* me on the bus.

hint *(v.)* **at**

The review *hinted at* the outcome of the movie without giving it away.

honor *(v.)* **by, for,** *or* **with**

We are *honored by* your presence at our celebration.

She was *honored for* her academic achievements.

Will you *honor* us *with* a visit to our home?

hope *(n.)* **for** *or* **of; hope** *(v.)* **for**

I am full of *hope for* the future.

They have no *hope of* winning the championship now.

The passengers *hoped for* a break in the weather so that the airplane could take off.

identical with *or* **to**

That wallpaper is *identical to* the wallpaper in our dining room.

Their interests in these negotiations are *identical with* (or *to*) ours.

immigrate to

I'm writing the story of how my parents *immigrated to* America.

impatient at *or* **with**

We were getting *impatient at* the long delay.

I wish you weren't so *impatient with* me.

impervious to

This fabric is coated to make it *impervious to* water.

implicit in

The sanctity of life is *implicit in* the idea of human rights.

impressed by *or* **with**

They were *impressed by* the sheer grandeur of Niagara Falls.

I am *impressed with* (or *by*) the amount of work you have done on this project.

improve on *or* **upon**

It would be hard to *improve on* (or *upon*) the performance you just gave.

inaccessible to

The wildlife refuge was *inaccessible to* the public except by foot.

incentive for *or* **to**

The bonus system created an *incentive for* greater productivity.

The bill would offer an *incentive to* (or *for*) drug companies to develop medicines for rare diseases.

incidental to

Ticket holders assume all risks and danger *incidental to* viewing the sport of hockey.

incongruous with *or* **to**

Their selfish behavior is *incongruous with* (or *to*) the ideals they expressed earlier.

inconsistent with

Your actions are *inconsistent with* your words.

incorporate in *or* **into**

Text and graphics can be *incorporated into* (or *in*) your website.

independent of
Charter schools receive public money but are mostly *independent of* local school boards.

infer from
Can I *infer from* your answer that you are willing to help us?

inferior to
The teacher told me that this research paper is *inferior to* the one I turned in last semester.

infested with *or* **by**
The old house is *infested with* (or *by*) termites.

influence *(n.)* **on, upon, over,** *or* **of**
Does advertising have much *influence on* (or *upon*) consumer behavior?
I think his girlfriend has too much *influence over* (or *on*) him.
She was arrested for driving under the *influence of* alcohol.

initiate into
The new parents were soon *initiated into* the joys and concerns of caring for a young baby.

innocent of
The defendant was declared *innocent of* the charges.

inquire about, after, *or* **into**
He *inquired about* the job that was advertised in the newspaper.
It was kind of you to *inquire after* my parents.
The service representative will *inquire into* your complaint.

insight into
The TV documentary gave me an *insight into* the patterns of immigration to America.

inspire by *or* **with**
Many people are *inspired by* the athletes in the Special Olympics.
We were *inspired with* awe at the sight of the Mayan ruins.

instruct in
I am looking for someone to *instruct* me *in* how to do simple car repairs.

intention of
She's going to college with the *intention of* majoring in engineering.

intrude on, upon, *or* **into**
I try not to let work *intrude on* (or *upon*) my private life.
Steps must be taken to keep the toxic spill from *intruding into* the groundwater.

inundated with
The radio station was *inundated with* complaints after airing a controversial program.

involved in *or* **with**
The police suspected that the gang was *involved in* (or *with*) illegal drug trafficking.
The actress was rumored to be *involved with* her younger costar.
How much work is *involved in* refinishing a piece of furniture?

isolate from
The diseased animals were *isolated from* the rest of the herd.

jealous of
I'm *jealous of* my brother because he got the bigger bedroom.

justified in
You would be *justified in* complaining about the poor service you received.

lack *(n.)* **of**
The crops are suffering this year for *lack of* rain.

lacking in
Junk food is generally *lacking in* nutritional value.

laden with
These trees are always *laden with* flowers in the spring.

lament *(v.)* **for** *or* **over; lament** *(n.)* **for**
The nation *lamented for* the lives lost in the attack.
She's still *lamenting over* the money she lost in the stock market.
The poem is a *lament for* those killed in battle.

laugh *(n., v.)* **at** *or* **over**
We had a good *laugh over* (or *at*) the mistaken picture in the newspaper.
The children *laughed at* (or *over*) the tricks the clowns played on each other.
I try to *laugh at* myself to keep from being too serious.

mastery of *or* **over**
He is admired for his *mastery of* fine cooking.
The troops soon gained *mastery over* (or *of*) the region.

means of *or* **for**
We installed solar panels on the roof as a *means of* (or *for*) saving electricity.
White blood cells are part of the body's *means of* defense against disease.

meddle in *or* **with**
It isn't considered wise to *meddle in* other people's affairs.
I think someone has been *meddling with* my computer.

mindful of
It is important to be *mindful of* other people's feelings.

mistrustful of
I was *mistrustful of* his motive when he offered to loan me money.

mock at
The speaker *mocked at* the proposal her opponent put forth.

monopoly on *or* **over**
The company was accused of trying to gain a *monopoly on* (or *over*) the local distribution of natural gas.

muse on *or* **over**
I sometimes *muse on* (or *over*) how my life would be different if I hadn't gotten married.

necessary *(adj.)* **for** *or* **to**
This course teaches some of the skills that are *necessary for* success in today's workplace.
Pollution controls are *necessary for* (or *to*) the health of the environment.

necessity of *or* **for**
I don't see the *necessity of* (or *for*) buying another TV at this time.
The proper clothing and equipment are *necessities for* survival in extreme cold.

need *(n.)* **for** *or* **of**
There is an urgent *need for* qualified teachers in our schools.
We are in *need of* some extra help on this project.

negligent in *or* **of**
I was *negligent in* checking the fuel gauge of my car and I ran out of gas.

The doctor was accused of being *negligent of* his patients.

oblivious of *or* **to**
The children were so involved in their computer game that they were *oblivious of* (or *to*) everything going on around them.

occasion for *or* **of**
Their daughter's graduation from college was an *occasion for* great rejoicing.
We had a grand celebration on the *occasion of* my parents' 50th wedding anniversary.

occupied by, with, *or* **in**
The building is *occupied by* several commercial tenants.
He was completely *occupied with* plans to build a new sailboat.
She was *occupied in* her studies for the whole evening.

offend against
Many people thought that the television program *offended against* good taste.

opportunity of *or* **for**
I had the *opportunity of* spending the summer on a program in Nigeria.
There are many *opportunities for* advancement in this company.

opposite *(adj.)* **to** *or* **from; opposite** *(n.)* **of**
"Up" is *opposite to* "down" in meaning.
My house is *opposite to* (or *from*) the gas station.
Your opinion on the death penalty is the *opposite of* mine.

opt for *or* **against**
Did you *opt for* the red truck or the green one?
The Federal Reserve is expected to *opt against* raising the interest rate.

originate in *or* **with**
Human beings are now believed to have *originated in* Africa several million years ago.
Most scholars believe that writing *originated with* the Sumerians around 5,000 years ago.

overwhelmed by *or* **with**
I am *overwhelmed by* (or *with*) everything I have to get done by Monday.

parallel *(adj.)* **to** *or* **with; parallel** *(n.)* **between** *or* **with**
I parked the car *parallel to* (or *with*) the curb.
There are many obvious *parallels between* the American cowboy and the Argentine gaucho.
This case has a close *parallel with* one from several years earlier.

patient *(adj.)* **with**
Our English teach is always *patient with* us.

peculiar to
The custom of trick-or-treating is *peculiar to* the United States.

persevere in *or* **against**
The researchers *persevered in* their efforts to identify the virus.
The explorers *persevered against* all obstacles in their effort to reach the South Pole.

persist in *or* **into**
Why must you *persist in* this pointless argument?
The drought *persisted into* the late summer months.

persuaded by, of, *or* **into**
She was so angry that she could not be *persuaded by* rational arguments.

I've heard the rumors, but I'm not *persuaded of* their truth.
I was *persuaded into* going to a movie even though I had homework to do.

pertinent to
I finally found a magazine article that was *pertinent to* my research topic.

possessed by, with, *or* **of**
In the book I'm reading, a woman is *possessed by* an evil spirit.
He was *possessed by* (or *with*) a desire to take revenge on his tormenters.
The family was *possessed of* great wealth.

possibility of
There is a *possibility of* thundershowers this afternoon.

precedent *(n.)* **for** *or* **of**
The judge cited a 1950 case as the *precedent for* his ruling.
George Washington established the *precedent of* delivering a farewell address to Congress at the end of his term in office.

preclude from
Serving two terms as president *precludes* a person *from* serving a third term.

prefer to *or* **over**
I generally *prefer* live music *to* (or *over*) recordings.

preoccupied with *or* **by**
She was so *preoccupied with* her work that she forgot to pick up groceries on her way home.
He was *preoccupied by* (or *with*) thoughts of home.

preparatory to
I gathered all the information I needed *preparatory to* applying for a scholarship.

preside at *or* **over**
It was my turn to *preside at* (or *over*) the meeting.

presume on *or* **upon**
Thank you for offering me a ride home, but I don't wish to *presume on* (or *upon*) your kindness.

prevail over, against, on, *or* **upon**
The candidate was determined to *prevail over* (or *against*) her opponent in the race.
The salesperson *prevailed on* (or *upon*) me to buy the extended warranty.

proficient in *or* **at**
She is *proficient in* three languages.
The students must be *proficient at* (or *in*) using both the keyboard and the mouse.

profit *(v.)* **by** *or* **from**
Students can *profit by* learning good study habits.
We hope to *profit from* the growth in the real estate market.

prohibit from
Children under 17 are *prohibited from* seeing R-rated movies unless accompanied by an adult.

prone to
The program was aimed at children who are *prone to* violence.

provide for, against, *or* **with**
Both parents worked hard to *provide for* their children.
We *provided for* (or *against*) emergencies by having extra food, water, batteries, and candles.
Certain fruits and vegetables are considered especially helpful in *providing against* disease.

The refugees were *provided with* food, shelter, and medicine at the camp.

qualify as *or* **for**

She attended special classes in order to *qualify as* a court reporter.

Endangered species *qualify for* protection against extinction.

receptive to

Our manager is usually *receptive to* suggestions.

reconcile to or with

He was finally *reconciled to* the change in management at work.

She is determined to *reconcile with* her estranged brother.

How can your belief in astrology be *reconciled with* modern knowledge of astronomy?

repent of

I *repented of* the angry things I said to her.

respect *(n.)* **for, to,** *or* **of**

The government was eager to demonstrate its *respect for* human rights.

What options do students have with *respect to* meal service on campus?

The rookie baseball pitcher is gaining the *respect of* his teammates.

responsible for *or* **to**

I am not *responsible for* the mess in the kitchen.

You will be *responsible to* me on this project.

restrain from

I *restrained* myself *from* buying the pair of shoes I saw in the window.

revel in

The author *reveled in* all the attention his new novel was getting.

rich in

This region is *rich in* coal and other natural resources.

rob of

The other team's last-minute free throw *robbed* us *of* victory.

scared of *or* **by**

I don't like climbing ladders because I'm *scared of* heights.

I wasn't particularly *scared of* (or *by*) the monster movie.

We were *scared by* the sudden noise of the firecrackers.

similar to

The sisters are *similar to* one another in appearance.

slave *(n.)* **to** *or* **of**

He is a *slave to* the sports channel and never misses a game.

No one has ever accused me of being a *slave to* (or *of*) fashion.

subject *(adj., v.)* **to**

Wages and most ordinary income are *subject to* federal and state taxes.

The volunteers were *subjected to* a variety of tests.

suffer from

She *suffers from* hay fever.

suitable for *or* **to**

Is that movie *suitable for* young children?

We went to the local nursery to find garden plants *suitable to* our region.

superior *(adj.)* **to**

The Supreme Court is *superior to* all the courts in the land.

sympathetic to *or* **toward**

I was *sympathetic to* her situation and offered to help her.

It's hard to feel *sympathetic toward* someone who complains all the time.

sympathy for, toward, *or* **with**

I volunteer at a soup kitchen out of *sympathy for* the homeless.

I wish you would express a bit more *sympathy toward* me and my situation.

We were in complete *sympathy with* the protesters' beliefs.

tendency toward

My friend has a *tendency toward* self-indulgence.

thrill *(v.)* **to, at,** *or* **with**

He *thrilled to* the sound of the marching band.

She *thrilled at* the thought of visiting her grandparents in South America.

We *thrilled with* delight as the band came onstage.

tolerance for, toward, *or* **of**

My boss does not have a high *tolerance for* sloppy work.

He joined a group that promotes *tolerance toward* people of all races and creeds.

There will be no *tolerance of* rude behavior on this trip.

tolerant of

Our dog is very *tolerant of* little children.

treat *(v.)* **as, to,** *or* **with**

I like working here because everyone is *treated as* equals.

We *treated* him *to* lunch on his birthday.

They were taught to *treat* others *with* respect and dignity.

vary from

He rarely *varies from* his morning routine.

vie for

The children *vied for* their uncle's attentions.

void *(adj.)* **of**

Her expression was completely *void of* understanding.

vulnerable to

Without vaccination the children would be *vulnerable to* a variety of preventable diseases.

wait *(v.)* **for** *or* **on**

I'm still *waiting for* a reply to my letter.

All the clerks were *waiting on* other customers.

want *(n.)* **of;** **want** *(v.)* **for**

The plants were beginning to shrivel for *want of* water.

She doesn't *want for* choice of clothes to wear.

wanting *(adj.)* **in**

He is a good student but is *wanting in* neatness.

wary of

I am *wary of* people trying to sell things over the phone.

yearn for, after, *or* **over**

He *yearns for* the day when he can retire.

She is a philosopher who *yearns after* truth.

Every year I *yearn over* the flowers in the gardening catalogs.

zeal for *or* **in**

She joined the Peace Corps out of a *zeal for* helping others.

The government is promising greater *zeal in* tracking down tax evaders.